# EMPOWERING REVOLUTION

**The New Cold War History**

*Odd Arne Westad, editor*

This series focuses on new
interpretations of the Cold
War era made possible by
the opening of Soviet, East
European, Chinese, and
other archives. Books in the
series based on multilingual
and multiarchival research
incorporate interdisciplinary
insights and new concep-
tual frameworks that place
historical scholarship in a
broad, international context.

# EMPOWERING
# REVOLUTION

## America, Poland, and the
## End of the Cold War

### GREGORY F. DOMBER

UNIVERSITY OF NORTH CAROLINA PRESS  *Chapel Hill*

Research for this book was supported in part by a fellowship from IREX (International Research & Exchanges Board) with funds provided by the United States Department of State through the Title VIII Program. Neither of these organizations is responsible for the views expressed herein.

This book was published with the assistance of the Anniversary Endowment Fund of the University of North Carolina Press.

Complete cataloging information for this title is available from the Library of Congress.

ISBN 978-1-4696-1851-7 (cloth: alk. paper)
ISBN 978-1-4696-2981-0 (pbk.: alk. paper)
ISBN 978-1-4696-1852-4 (ebook)

Portions of chapter 2 were published earlier as "Power Politics, Human Rights, and Trans-Atlantic Relations," in Odd Arne Westad and Poul Villaume, eds., *European and Transatlantic Strategies to Overcome the East-West Division of Europe* (Copenhagen: Copenhagen University Press, 2009); used with permission from the publisher. A very early version of chapter 4 was published as "Rumblings in Eastern Europe: Western Pressure on Poland's Moves toward Democratic Transformation," in Frédéric Bozo, Marie-Pierre Rey, N. Piers Ludlow, and Leopoldo Nuti, eds., *Europe and the End of the Cold War* (Oxford: Routledge, 2008); used with permission from Frédéric Bozo. Portions of chapter 6 were published earlier as "Skepticism and Stability: Reevaluating U.S. Policy toward Poland's Democratic Transformation in 1989," *Journal of Cold War Studies* 13, no. 3 (Summer 2011): 52–82; used with permission of MIT Press.

FOR M, T, & L

# CONTENTS

# ILLUSTRATIONS

# ACKNOWLEDGMENTS

This book is the product of more than a decade of research and writing that was generously supported by a number of groups. A Tomaszkiewicz-Florio Scholarship from the Kosciuszko Foundation and a Title VIII East-Central Europe Research and Language Scholarship administered by the American Councils for International Education paid for language training essential to the final product. The Polish-American Fulbright Commission and an International Research and Exchanges (IREX) Short-Term Research Grant allowed me extended time to work in Polish archives. A George Washington University Hoffmann Dissertation Award, a Cosmos Club Foundation Young Scholars Award, a George C. Marshall/Baruch Dissertation Fellowship, a Woodrow Wilson International Center for Scholars East European Studies Program Short-Term Grant, and an American Consortium for European Union Studies (ACES) Research Seed Grant all supported short-term research trips to various repositories around the Washington, D.C., area, as well as time at the Ronald Reagan Presidential Library. A Hewlett Post-Doctoral Fellowship at Stanford University's Center for Democracy, Development, and the Rule of Law provided needed time for writing and revision, as well as proximity to the collections at the Hoover Institution.

As a first book this project also bears the marks of those scholars and educators who have shaped me thus far. Arne Offner at Lafayette College first introduced me to the joys of diplomatic history. Malcolm Byrne, Tom Blanton, Vlad Zubok, and Svetlana Savranskaya at the National Security Archive taught me how to navigate archives and government bureaucracies to cull the exciting bits from reams of documents. Christian Ostermann at the Cold War International History Project welcomed me into the circle of international historians. Hope Harrison, Jim Hershberg, and Jim Goldgeier taught me to be a better writer, a clearer thinker, and a more voracious researcher forever in search of "hot docs." The Russian and East European Institute and Bill Johnston and the Polish Studies Center at Indiana University, Bloomington, gave me a quiet space and access to their amazing resources when I needed to lock myself away to write. Larry Diamond, Mike McFaul, and Kathryn Stoner at Stanford University exposed me to different ways of examining the recent past and forced me to sharpen my conclusions. For the past few years my colleagues at the University of North Florida have provided a stimulating and welcoming environment. Numerous friends and colleagues have read portions of the manuscript or talked through all of the little problems that pop up along the way. They include Mary Sarotte, Sarah Snyder, Craig Daigle, Idesbald Goddeeris, Goshka Gnoinska, Mirceau Muntaneau, Frédéric Bozo, and Piotr Kosicki.

As a work of recent history, this book would not have been as successful without all the individuals who gave of their time to be interviewed. I am indebted to each of them. Ambassador John R. Davis Jr., however, deserves special mention as this project would not have been possible without him. He was the first and the last person I interviewed for the book, and he deserves immense credit for both his patience and insight during this extended process. Irena Lasota and Eric Chenoweth of CSS/IDEE gave amply of their time and connections. And, if Col. Casimir Lenard had not decided to keep a few extra boxes of files from the Polish American Congress's Washington Office down in his basement only to bring them up when I came around, the story of the Polish American Congress and that of other NGOs' roles might still remain hidden.

As this is an international history, this project would not have succeeded without consistent support from scholars outside the United States. First and foremost, I must thank Andrzej Paczkowski, whose untiring support and professional network opened more doors than I could have imagined when I began. His mentoring and intellectual input were essential. Paweł Sowiński, Krzysztof Persak, and Paweł Machcewicz, as well as the entire staff of Institute of Political Studies of the Polish Academy of Sciences, offered wise counsel and local expertise. Janey Curry made Warsaw a more welcoming place and provided a kind entrance into the Polish studies world. I am also indebted to the archivists at the Archive of Modern Records, the KARTA Foundation, the Archive of the Ministry of Foreign Affairs, and the Institute of National Remembrance, who responded to my broken Polish with a smile and more documents. A series of friends gave needed respite away from those archives, most notably Andy Hinnant and Ania Mueller and Esther Sternkopf and Bartek Sobieski.

Chuck Grench, Sara Cohen, Lucas Church, and Paul Betz have been a gleaming example of efficient professionalism at UNC Press. I am thankful for all their hard work. The book is much stronger because of the thoughtful suggestions and criticisms in the manuscript reviews by Christian Ostermann and Mark Kramer. I also thank Arne Westad for his guidance over the years and his work on this particular volume.

Finally, I want to acknowledge my family. My mother, father, and brother have supported me through my trips around the country and around Europe, traveling to visit with me when possible and providing just the right mix of motivation and ribbing when I showed signs of stalling. This book is dedicated to my wife, Mira, and our daughters, Tillie and Lulu. Mira and I met in Poland while I was working in the archives. Her constant support, creativity, patience, and warmth have nourished me in innumerable ways. As our lives have grown together and we started a family, they have provided the drive to complete this process and the comfort of knowing that when I go home it will be to shouts, hugs, and smiles.

# ABBREVIATIONS IN THE TEXT

|          |                                                              |
|---------:|--------------------------------------------------------------|
| AID      | United States Agency for International Development           |
| AFL-CIO  | American Federation of Labor and Congress of Industrial Organizations |
| APF      | American Political Foundation                                |
| BIB      | Bureau for International Broadcasting                         |
| CIA      | Central Intelligence Agency                                  |
| CCC      | Commodity Credit Corporation                                 |
| CMEA     | see Comecon                                                  |
| CoCom    | Coordinating Committee for Multilateral Export Controls      |
| Comecon  | Council for Mutual Economic Assistance, also CMEA            |
| CPSU     | Communist Party of the Soviet Union                          |
| CRS      | Catholic Relief Services                                     |
| CSCE     | Commission for Security and Cooperation in Europe            |
| CSS      | Committee in Support of Solidarity                           |
| DCI      | Director of Central Intelligence                             |
| DCM      | Deputy Chief of Mission                                      |
| DIA      | Defense Intelligence Agency                                  |
| DOD      | Department of Defense                                        |
| EC       | European Community                                           |
| EEC      | European Economic Community                                  |
| EUR      | Department of State Bureau for European and Soviet Affairs   |
| Ex-Im Bank | Export-Import Bank                                          |
| FCO      | Foreign and Commonwealth Office                              |
| FTUI     | Free Trade Union Institute                                   |
| FY       | fiscal year                                                  |
| G7       | Group of Seven                                               |
| GATT     | General Agreement on Tariffs and Trade                       |
| GR KK    | Grupy Roboczej Komisji Krajowej or the National Commission Working Group |
| GSP      | Generalized System of Preferences                            |
| HSWP     | Hungarian Socialist Worker's Party                           |
| ICA      | International Communications Agency                          |

ICFTU Independent Confederation of Free Trade Unions

IDEE Institute for Democracy in Eastern Europe

ILO International Labor Organization

IMF International Monetary Fund

INF intermediate nuclear forces

IPA Independent Poland Agency

KCEP Komisja Charytatywna Episkopatu Polski or Charitable Commission of the Polish Episcopate

KOR Komitet Obrony Robotników or Workers' Defense Committee

KPN Konfederacja Polski Niepodległy or Confederation for an Independent Poland

MBFR Multilateral and Balanced Force Reductions

MFN most favored nation

MHZ Ministerstwo Handel Zagranicznych or Ministry of Foreign Trade

MSW Ministerstwo Spraw Wewnętrznych or Ministry of Internal Affairs

MSZ Ministertwo Spraw Zagranicznych or Ministry of Foreign Affairs

NAC North Atlantic Council of NATO

NATO North Atlantic Treaty Organization

NED National Endowment for Democracy

NGO non-governmental organization

NOWa Niezależna Oficyjna Wydawnicza or Independent Publishing House

NSC National Security Council

NSDD National Security Decision Directive

NSPG National Security Planning Group

NSR National Security Review

NSZZ Niezależny Samorządny Związek Zawodowy "Solidarność"
Solidarność or Independent Self-Governing Trade Union Solidarity

NZS Niezależny Zrzeszenia Studentów or Independent Union of Students

OKN Oświaty, Kultura, Nauk or the Committee for Independent Education, Culture, and Science

OPIC Overseas Public Investment Corporation

OPZZ Ogólnopolskie Porozumienie Związków Zawodowych or All-Polish Trade Unions Agreement

PAC Polish American Congress
PACCF Polish American Congress Charitable Foundation
PAX Christian Social Association
PIASA Polish Institute of Arts and Sciences in America
PISM Polski Instytut Spraw Międzynarodowych or Polish Institute for
International Affairs
PNG persona non grata
PRON Patriotyczny Ruch Odrodzenia Narodowego or
Patriotic Movement of National Rebirth
PWAF Polish Workers Aid Fund
PZKS Polski Zwiśzek Katolicko-Społeczny or
Polish Catholic-Social Union
PZPR Polska Zjednoczona Partia Robotnicza or
Polish United Worker's Party
RFE/RL Radio Free Europe/Radio Liberty
SB Służba Bezpieczenstwo or Security Services
SD Stronnisctwo Demokratyczne or Democratic Party
TKK Tymczasowa Komisja Koordynacyjna or Interim Coordinating
Commission
TR Tymczasowa Rade NSZZ "Solidarność" or Temporary Council of
NSZZ Solidarność
UchS Unia Chześcijańska-Społeczna or Christian-Social Union
USIA United States Information Agency
VOA Voice of America
WiP Wolność i Pokój or Freedom and Peace
WRON Wojskowa Rada Ocalenia Narodowego or Military Council of
National Salvation
ZOMO Zmotoryzowane Odwody Milicji Obywatelskiej or Motorized
Reserves of the Citizens' Militia
ZSL Zjednoczonne Stonnictwo Ludowe or United People's Party
ZWID Zespoł Wideo or Video Association

# EMPOWERING REVOLUTION

# Introduction

On November 15, 1989, Lech Wałęsa became the third foreign, private citizen to address a joint session of the U.S. Congress, following in the footsteps of the Marquis de Lafayette and Winston Churchill. Wałęsa was not a head of state or even a government representative, but the chairman of the Independent Self-Governing Trade Union "Solidarność" (Niezależny Samorządny Związek Zawodowy "Solidarność" or NSZZ Solidarność), formed in August 1980 by striking workers on the Baltic Coast. Initially, he had not been invited to the United States to address Congress. He was in Washington, D.C., to attend the National Convention of the AFL-CIO, but in the weeks between scheduling his visit and his arrival, political developments in Eastern Europe had taken a revolutionary turn. Just six days before his address, the Berlin Wall—the most potent symbol of the division of Europe and the Cold War in that sphere—had fallen. Events in Berlin had been preceded by massive weekly opposition rallies in Leipzig, precipitated by an emigration crisis sparked by young East Germans flocking to Hungary to get to the West. The reform-minded Communist leadership in Budapest had opened its border with Austria, providing an escape hatch from the repressive East German regime. The Hungarians were also planning for multiparty elections, an unthinkable development just a year earlier.

This barrage of revolutionary events, which eventually caused the Communist regimes in Czechoslovakia and Romania to collapse as well, began in Poland. In February 1989, Poles held negotiations between the Polish United Workers' Party (Polska Zjednoczona Partia Robotnicza or PZPR) and opposition leaders, to forge a power-sharing agreement based around semifree elections completed in June. In those elections Solidarność-affiliated candidates won ninety-nine out of one hundred seats in a newly created upper house of parliament (Senat) and all the lower house (Sejm) seats open to them. In the wake of this victory, Wałęsa and his advisers staged a political coup d'état, negotiating a deal with disgruntled members of the rapidly dissolving Communist coalition, upending the PZPR's parliamentary majority, and clearing the way for an opposition-led government. On August 24, Tadeusz Mazowiecki, a longtime member of the opposition and an adviser to

Wałęsa, was charged with creating a Solidarność-led government, the first non-Communist government in Poland since 1948.

Thus, when speaking to the joint session of Congress, Wałęsa was more than just the head of NSZZ Solidarność; he was the recognized leader of the broader Solidarność movement and a spokesman for revolutionaries in Eastern Europe. In his speech, Wałęsa provided an insider's view of the dynamic political shifts rapidly accelerating throughout the region. He requested increased American economic and structural support to help his country move from a "bankrupt" centralized economy to a market-based system open to the West. He also took the opportunity to express gratitude to the United States for its role in Poland's democratic transformation. He spoke reverently about the American Declaration of Independence and the country's Constitution, directly linking the ideals expressed in those documents to the rebirth of democracy in his homeland. He also thanked the United States specifically for its support of the Polish opposition, particularly after Solidarność had come under attack and was forced underground during a period of martial law. As he said, "I'm expressing words of gratitude to the American people. It is they who supported us in the difficult days of martial law and persecution. It is they who sent us aid, they protested against violence." He continued, "Today, when I am able to freely address the whole world from this elevated spot, I would like to thank them with special warmth. It is thanks to them that the word 'Solidarity' soared across borders and reached every corner of the world. Thanks to them, the people of Solidarity were never alone."[1]

This was a joyous occasion on Capitol Hill. As Barbara Mikulski, a Polish American Congresswoman explained, "I never thought this day would come. I just didn't think it was Poland's destiny to be free."[2] The Cold War was not yet over, but the political realities of the previous half century were dissolving rapidly. For his role, Wałęsa was feted as a hero, with dinner at the White House and banquets on Capitol Hill. While Wałęsa's speech was dominated by pleas for increased American aid, his broad, almost vague words of gratitude are intriguing. Just who among the American people had supported the Solidarność movement? Why was this support important? Clearly, Wałęsa was referencing U.S. government actions, but he also mentioned non-governmental organizations like the AFL-CIO and Polish American groups. Did they provide political guidance? Moral support? What types of aid were sent? More broadly, how did American actions and policies affect the shape, timing, and outcome of Poland's revolution?

The purpose of this book is to answer those questions about American influences on Poland's democratic transformation, focused on the period from the declaration of martial law early on the morning of December 13, 1981, to the creation of the Mazowiecki government on August 24, 1989. To competently answer these questions, however, it is necessary to move beyond a simple bilateral framework.[3] From the earliest days of American-Soviet confrontation following World War II, Poland was entrenched in the bipolar competition between the superpowers, so policies pursued in Poland must be placed in the broader context of the Cold War and its end.[4] As Wałęsa's speech acknowledged, Mikhail Gorbachev, the leader of the Soviet Union, also deserves credit for the revolutionary changes.[5] With Poland just a single example of a broader transnational pattern of anti-Communist, pro-democracy revolutions sweeping the Soviet empire out of Eastern Europe, clearly broader intra-bloc trends were at work.[6] And, of course, events in Poland can be explained by the internal logic of political processes there.[7] Encompassing all these dynamics, this study seeks to complicate, historicize, and internationalize the understanding of Poland's revolutionary moment in 1989, with an analytical emphasis on gauging the effectiveness of American policy to promote democracy.

As the focal point for American policy toward Eastern Europe in the 1980s, Poland provides a rich example of the forces that brought the Cold War to its end. It allows insight into the Reagan administration's movement away from the heightened tensions of the "second Cold War" toward greater engagement with the Communist world, as well as into the internal fissures in the Reagan administration that fostered this shift. Poland is a fascinating example of how economic policies pursued during the era of détente created high levels of indebtedness among East European states that limited possibilities for internal reforms and provided a key point of Western leverage in the 1980s. This case presents ample evidence of the ways that NGOs functioned as an essential point of contact between East and West. Poland also cogently illustrates how internal demands for reform, combined with long-standing economic and political pressures from both the East and the West, proved a volatile mix that sparked revolution across the region. In its broadest goal, this book takes Poland as a case study to synthesize disparate debates on the nature of Western influence and the end of the Cold War by highlighting where Soviet reforms created space for change in Eastern Europe and rejecting claims of any direct American responsibility for the collapse of Communism. It nonetheless acknowledges that U.S. policies sustained and empowered the indigenous grassroots political movements that deserve ultimate credit for transforming Eastern Europe in 1989.

Public accounts, including newspaper articles and memoirs written shortly after the era, provide a broad narrative for understanding American policy toward Poland from 1981 to 1989.[8] In its bare-bones form, the story line unfolded as follows: In the wake of the declaration of martial law, President Ronald Reagan announced a series of economic and political sanctions, some of which were also implemented by NATO allies, to pressure the Polish government to return to the liberalizing path it had pursued prior to December 1981—specifically the PZPR's embrace of a more pluralistic society and its acceptance of independent trade unions. Throughout the decade, America maintained three basic objectives: the end of martial law, the release of all political prisoners, and the resumption of negotiations between the PZPR, representatives of the Catholic Church, and leaders from the opposition. Promoting these objectives was meant to move the country toward the end goal of national reconciliation. Sanctions were lifted or further imposed to push the PZPR to fulfill U.S. objectives. Simultaneously, the United States led a concerted effort to support Solidarność and to rebuild the opposition movement. Martial law was lifted in July 1983, all political prisoners were finally released in September 1986, and representatives from the government, church, and Solidarność sat down to negotiate Poland's future during the Round Table process from February through April 1989, fulfilling all three American objectives. Conventional wisdom in the United States accepts a more or less causal link between American policies and these important changes within Poland.[9]

Yet defining the parameters of what constitutes "American policy" during this period and deciding how best to situate that policy in broader international contexts is difficult. First, policy was aimed at two separate constituencies within Poland: the Communist government and the democratic opposition. So, American efforts really comprised two concurrent policies with overlapping concerns. In conceptualizing this structure it is more helpful to think of a triangle—with the United States, the PZPR, and Solidarność at the three corners—than to envision a bilateral relationship with Poland and the United States at opposite ends.[10] Further confusing the picture, U.S. policies occasionally focused directly on the Polish people, who fell somewhere between the two corners of Solidarność and the PZPR.

Second, it is misleading to think about a singular policy pursued by the U.S. government. Voices within the executive branch often disagreed among themselves. The State Department frequently advocated steps that the Defense Department or Central Intelligence Agency (CIA) argued vehemently against. Most of these disagreements came to a head at the White House in the National Security Council, with the president making a final decision; yet prior to these definitive decisions the individual departments often pursued policies at odds with viewpoints in other parts of the executive branch. Moreover, American representatives in Warsaw sporadically pursued independent policy lines, ones consistent with the broad outlines of policy but formulated at the embassy level rather than back in Foggy Bottom. Further complicating the image of a cohesive governmental policy, White House directives frequently required budgetary approval and so were forced to acquiesce to criticisms from Congress. Both congressional and White House decisions were often shaped by domestic American political concerns.

Third, American policy toward Poland was molded by numerous NGOs that operated on the fringes of government. Powerful constituencies like the AFL-CIO and the Polish American Congress lobbied both Capitol Hill and the White House, each advocating their own positions. Both of these groups, as well as smaller organizations like the Committee in Support of Solidarity and the Institute for Democracy in Eastern Europe, also acted independently to support Solidarność and the wider opposition movement by sending needed money and material. After 1984, the National Endowment for Democracy (NED)—a quasi-nongovernmental organization that received money from Congress but made decisions independently about recipients of democracy assistance—served as an intermediary between the government and the smaller groups shepherding aid to the opposition. American business leaders with financial commitments in Poland also advocated their own approaches. Finally, private humanitarian organizations including Catholic Relief Services (CRS), CARE, and Project HOPE played a central role in American policy by sending hundreds of millions of dollars in aid, staving off a humanitarian crisis and simultaneously improving America's image abroad.

Fourth, Americans were not the only Westerners concerned about Poland. The U.S. government frequently butted heads with leaders within the Western alliance. Confrontations were frequent within NATO, but they also spilled over into organizations like the International Monetary Fund (IMF) and multilateral institutions that coordinated lending. With Solidarność activists spread throughout the West after the declaration of martial law, American activities were swayed by Polish émigré organizations, most notably the Solidarność Coordinating Office Abroad in Brussels. The Vatican too, with a Polish pope at its head, pursued policies that both limited and amplified the actions Americans took.

Fifth, Poland was situated firmly within the Soviet sphere of influence in Eastern Europe. It was a full member of the Warsaw Pact, with explicit military commitments to its neighbors and the political ties that came with them. While trade with the West had increased during détente, Poland's primary economic partnerships remained with the Communist world, coordinated through the Council on Mutual Economic Assistance (CMEA) or Comecon. Like the other members of that group, Poland relied heavily on economic aid and subsidies from the Soviet Union. The PZPR was also obligated to coordinate its domestic and foreign policies with dictates and guidelines from the Communist Party of the Soviet Union (CPSU). With the rapid succession of Soviet leaders in the first half of the 1980s, the PZPR often had to revise or reverse its domestic policies at the Kremlin's behest. Thus commitments to the Communist world greatly limited the PZPR's options to pursue reform.

Sixth, and finally, both the PZPR and Solidarność had their own domestic concerns. Although its members were not elected, the PZPR politburo regularly acted to dissipate domestic tensions or to curry favor with the public. General Wojciech Jaruzelski (the PZPR first secretary and head of state during this period) and a group of advisers pursued gradual reform, but their efforts were often complicated by more hard-line voices in the politburo. Similarly, as an underground political movement, Solidarność was only as formidable as the constituency it could claim to represent: without popular support it would be powerless. Moreover, the Solidarność movement was not cohesive, but made up of loosely coordinated national, regional, and local structures that worked well together at points but often disagreed on both actions and policy considerations. As an important third column in the Polish domestic sphere, the Catholic Church mediated between the state and the opposition, but certainly not without their own interests. American policy was refracted through all these constituencies within the national context.

Mapping out all these influences and limitations on "American policy" produces a picture that looks more like an intricate web of overlapping silks (sometimes pulling in different directions) than a simple triangle. Yet it is only possible to get an accurate view of American policies and their effects in Poland by taking into account as many of the disparate opinions, arguments, viewpoints, goals, constituencies, and perspectives as possible. Complexity provides clarity rather than confusion. This book strives not only to describe American policy as it looked finally formed but also to explore how that policy came to be, investigating the many leaders, groups, organizations, countries, and common people who shaped it in Washington, Warsaw, and points beyond.

Methodologically, the book relies most heavily on non-American sources. Because many American records remain classified, particularly in terms of the day-to-day implementation of policy, Polish sources from the Ministry of Foreign Affairs Archive, the Archive of Modern Records (the repository for PZPR records), and the Karta Foundation (a repository of opposition materials) are utilized to provide a kind of back door into the vacillations and shifts in American foreign policy. With detailed information from Polish archives, material from memoirs, leaked papers, and unattributed statements in the public record (which are often too vague to be used conclusively on their own) can be placed in a more stable framework. Combining these insights with the rapidly increasing number of declassified pages at the Reagan and Bush presidential libraries, as well as with U.S. material released through focused Freedom of Information Act requests, it is possible to write authoritatively on American policy before the full U.S. record is open. Relying on the building blocks of Polish sources creates a much stronger foundation for analyzing when changes in Polish behavior were motivated by domestic dynamics, intra-bloc concerns, relations with the Kremlin, or international players other than the United States. This approach provides a nuanced picture of U.S. power, highlighting missed opportunities, mistakes, and victories that are obscured or distorted when viewed from a purely American perspective.

Because this work focuses extensively on NGOs, private repositories and institutional collections form the keystone for the book's findings. Access to both the publicly available collections and the unprocessed records of the AFL-CIO available through the George Meany Memorial Archives was pivotal, as was special access to the records of the Polish American Congress's Washington office. Materials from humanitarian groups, especially from Catholic Relief Services, were central to uncovering that side of the story. Finally, the openness of some of the smaller organizations involved in supporting the Polish opposition provided a necessary framework for information from non-written sources.

Finally, my research methodology has been deeply influenced by the critical oral history model pioneered by scholars associated with the Cold War International History Project and the National Security Archive. Generally, the model combines in-depth, multinational, and multilingual archival research with oral history interviews. The inspiration for this book first came during a conference (sponsored by these two groups) marking the tenth anniversary of Poland's revolution. The conference brought participants from all sides of the events to a single table, surrounded by scholars armed with binders full of recently unearthed documents—documents that I had been charged with photocopying and collating. When telling the story of a conspiratorial movement like Solidarność and the web of Polish émigrés that supported it, it is absolutely essential to include oral histories. For reasons of secrecy and security, written records were either never kept or they were destroyed. Similarly, the personality clashes, back-stories, preconceptions, and backroom conversations that informed the decisions made by all the individuals involved can be difficult to recreate from the written sources alone. Writing this book twenty to twenty-five years after the events in question has meant that significant numbers of participants remain alive, with minds sharp enough to recall their stories. Interviews fill in the gaps and provide the mortar that holds the written sources together.

The chapters that follow proceed chronologically. Chapter 1 begins with an overview of the Polish crisis from August 1980 to December 1981 and then explores the month directly following the declaration of martial law, stressing government-to-government relations. It also follows American attempts to coordinate policy with its allies, while explaining the deep rift in Polish-American relations caused by the declaration of martial law. Chapter 2 begins in January 1982 and describes the growth of humanitarian aid and early efforts by American trade unions to support Solidarność as it rebuilt as an underground organization. This chapter also traces internal American government arguments about the efficacy of sanctions, as well as the increasing role played by Congress and concerns about international propaganda. Finally, this chapter shows how policy toward Poland slowly became embroiled in disagreements within NATO over building a natural gas pipeline, causing the Reagan administration to reevaluate its path and pursue a more pragmatic approach.

Chapter 3 begins in the last months of 1982 and ends in January 1985, following the ups and (mainly) downs of Polish-American relations. Specifically, it examines how decisions to lift individual American sanctions were used to push for gradual reforms as part of what was known as the "step-by-step" policy. In one particular instance, the United States used a secret diplomatic back channel to negotiate an informal quid pro quo, exchanging sanctions for political prisoners. This chapter also explains the continuing work by humanitarian organizations, as well as the creation of the National Endowment for Democracy, which greatly increased resources available to support the opposition underground. It also explores the role of Radio Free Europe and of the Catholic Church within Poland, as the PZPR took small steps to liberalize and reform the system.

Chapter 4 backs away from purely Polish-American relations to take a broader view of the effects of Poland's international situation on changes within its borders. This includes both Soviet bloc and West European pressure, with a particular emphasis on the process by which foreign concerns about human rights abuses became linked to the internal economic situation. The chapter ends with a discussion of the international influences on the PZPR's September 1986 decision to declare a complete amnesty for political prisoners, parsing American efforts from broader Western influences. Chapter 5 returns to bilateral Polish and American concerns and follows efforts to normalize relations through a series of high-level negotiations. This chapter explains the American decision to lift all remaining economic sanctions on February 19, 1987, and details Vice President George H. W. Bush's visit to Warsaw in September 1987. It concludes with a visit by the American diplomat John Whitehead, demonstrating how much the bilateral relationship had improved since 1985.

Chapter 6 recounts the growing tension within Poland as expressed through massive strikes in the spring and summer of 1988. The chapter argues that America's long-standing position linking economic aid with Polish steps to resume negotiations empowered the opposition during the secretive Magdalenka meetings in the fall of 1988. It then examines Washington's decision to pause and redefine U.S. policy in the new Bush administration as the Round Table negotiations progressed under their own momentum. Change continued to accelerate through the spring and summer of 1989 during a series of political crises, complicating President Bush's trip to Warsaw in July. The chapter ends by discussing American elation at the creation of the Solidarność-led government and by arguing that the United States helped stabilize and slow Poland's democratic breakthrough by pursuing evolutionary, rather then revolutionary, change. The concluding chapter summarizes key findings and evaluates American influences on Poland's internal developments, providing a detailed explanation of how and under which specific circumstances the United States' limited power successfully shaped, colored, and influenced internal dynamics in the decade leading to Poland's democratic breakthrough.

With the events of 1989 twenty-five years in the past, the world we inhabit now seems less influenced by the end of the Cold War than the start of the so-called war on terror. Yet local activists around the world continue to take to the streets to transform their countries by embracing democratic principles, fighting to create more pluralistic and transparent societies. Even in the vastly different geopolitical environment of the twenty-first century, American policy toward Poland in the 1980s provides a useful, successful example of how a patient and temperate application of political and economic sanctions, a sensitivity to working alongside allies, and a strong commitment to independent, moderate voices calling for reform—empowering a segment of the indigenous opposition rather than forcing an American-led model of transformation—can change the world, promote democracy, and enhance the United States' strategic interests.

## CHAPTER ONE

# A Watershed in the Political History of Mankind

## The Reaction to Martial Law, December 1981 to January 1982

At 11:30 P.M. on Saturday night, December 12, 1981, elite units of the Polish People's Militia and the Ministry of Internal Affairs (MSW), backed by the Polish Army, took to the streets to round up and imprison the leadership of the Solidarność trade union. They cordoned off regional Solidarność headquarters, captured union leaders meeting in Gdańsk, set up roadblocks and checkpoints throughout the country, and cut all lines of communication. At 6:00 A.M. on Sunday, December 13, General Wojciech Jaruzelski addressed the nation on the radio, announcing that martial law had been imposed: "Our homeland was on the edge of a precipice . . . , we found ourselves facing a difficult test. We must show ourselves equal to this test, we must show that 'We are worthy of Poland.'"

Word from the American embassy in Warsaw about irregular military movements first reached Secretary of State Alexander Haig at 3:00 A.M. in Brussels, where he had spent the evening dining with Western diplomats in preparation for a NATO meeting. On the other side of the Atlantic, President Ronald Reagan was away from the White House at Camp David. Haig spoke with Vice President George H. W. Bush instead, and the two decided not to whisk Reagan back to Washington. The vice president reassured Haig that there was no hurry to get back, saying, "Nothing will happen in Washington for now, Al."[1] Secretary of Defense Caspar Weinberger was over the Atlantic in a plane headed to London. The National Security Council (NSC) staff lacked a permanent national security adviser. President Reagan was not briefed on the news until the next morning. In Haig's words, the Reagan administration found itself in a "surprised state" without a clear plan for how to react.[2]

The United States initially responded with caution, but anger in the White House soon produced punitive measures. A week after the declaration of martial law, the Reagan administration declared economic sanctions against Poland and extended similar punishment to the Soviet Union. Washington also actively advocated for multilateral sanctions within the NATO framework and eventually succeeded in getting a tough rhetorical response from European allies, though little immediate multilateral action. In Poland, martial law successfully eviscerated the opposition, much to the relief of the Soviets and of Poland's neighbors. Warsaw, however, had not expected a forceful Western response. The American pattern of surprise followed by anger was thus replayed within the Polish government, which responded with surprise and then anger of its own at Western sanctions. In the first month after the declaration of martial law, both sides took unexpected steps, opening a deep wound in U.S.-Polish relations that would leave lasting scars.

## The Polish Crisis

December 1981 was the final act of what was known outside of Poland as the "Polish Crisis," which began in August 1980 with workers' strikes along the Baltic coast, most notably at the Lenin Shipyards in Gdańsk. As with earlier crises in 1956, 1970, and 1976, workers were responding to food price increases.[3] Unlike during previous strikes, this time the workers demanded expressly political as well as economic accommodations in their strike announcement. They also elected as their head negotiator Lech Wałęsa, an electrician active in the free trade union movement who had been fired for political activity in 1976.[4] Joining with other strikers along the Baltic coast in an Inter-Factory Strike Committee, the Gdańsk workers laid out a list of twenty-one demands to end their occupation strike, addressing social, economic, and political concerns. Deciding against the use of force, the PZPR politburo sent negotiators to Gdańsk and Szczecin (also on the Baltic coast). With Bronisław Geremek, Andrzej Gwiazda, Bogdan Lis, and Tadeusz Mazowiecki at his side, Wałęsa successfully negotiated and signed the Gdańsk Accords with the government on August 31, 1980, allowing unprecedented political concessions, including: independent trade unions, the right to strike without reprisals, the right to "freedom of expression," pay increases, improved working conditions, Saturdays off, and Sunday Masses broadcast over loudspeakers.

The leaders of the Szczecin and Gdańsk strikes soon met with other workers' representatives, including leaders like Zbigniew Bujak from Warsaw and Władysław Frasyniuk from Wrocław, to expand into a loosely coordinated national movement. In mid-September delegates from thirty regional Inter-Factory Strike Committees from throughout the country (each had been formed as strikes spread in August) joined together to found a single, national union, the Independent Self-Governing Trade Union "Solidarność" (referred to simply as Solidarność or the English equivalent, Solidarity). A National Coordinating Commission was created to lead the union, and delegates elected Wałęsa as their chairman. The union was not rigidly hierarchical or centralized; rather it was a mechanism for organizing local factory commissions into regions and for facilitating coordination between the regions. Nonetheless, regional and local groups maintained substantial autonomy.[5] The precise relationship between the center and the periphery was left ambiguous and used to the union's advantage. The National Coordinating Commission could "issue authoritative statements of policy, saying that the union stood for this or for that, and had such and such a demand to present." Simultaneously, "regional union authorities were responsible for activities carried on in their own areas and frequently took decisions in conflict with those of central union leaders. The central union body alternately called the recalcitrant local to heel or allowed it to do as it pleased, whichever seemed best at the time."[6] During the course of the crisis the trade union grew to include nearly 9.5 million members, or more than one in four Poles. With Solidarność as an example, other segments of society joined the effort for greater pluralism and created their own organizations: the Independent Self-Governing Trade Union of Individual Farmers (Rural Solidarność) and the Independent Union of Students (Niezależny Zrzeszenia Studentów, or NZS), respectively.

Once formed, Solidarność focused on consolidating the concessions won in Gdańsk. The process alone of registering the union with the government lasted until mid-November 1980. Once registered, the union began to push for economic reforms, including work-free Saturdays. To generalize, the sixteen months prior to martial law involved a precarious tug-of-war between the people and the Communist Party to determine Poland's future. Solidarność's main demands remained consistent and included calls to cease attacks on the union, pass a law legalizing independent trade unions, hold elections to national councils, establish an independent council made of government and union officials to guide economic reforms, and provide Solidarność with media access.[7] In this confrontation, the union's main tool to pressure the government was its ability to call for regional or national work stoppages and strikes. For example, on March 27, 1981, a national, four-hour strike was called because of the government's unwillingness to recognize Rural Solidarność and following a provocation between PZPR officials and local Solidarność activists in Bydgoszcz, in which three opposition members had been severely beaten. The National Coordinating Commission called off a follow-up strike for March 31 when the PZPR agreed to register Rural Solidarność and publicly stated that those responsible for the Bydgoszcz beatings would be punished.

In addition to Solidarność, the Catholic Church worked in its long-standing role as an advocate for the people. Unlike in other Communist countries where the church had been eviscerated (as in the Soviet Union) or co-opted (as in Hungary), the Polish Catholic Church retained a strong, independent voice throughout the Communist period. During the Polish crisis, the church (led by the archbishop of Warsaw, Cardinal Stefan Wyszyński until his death on May 28, 1981, and then by his successor, Cardinal Józef Glemp) viewed itself as an intermediary between the opposition and the PZPR. During tense periods the church often publicly called for moderation and met frequently with representatives from both sides. The church's attitude toward the opposition, however, should not be confused by its willingness to work with the PZPR: "Although the Church did not encourage radical actions or demands, it was nonetheless unambiguous in its support for the union."[8]

On the other side of the equation from the forces for change, the PZPR was under constant pressure from the Kremlin and from more conservative voices within the Warsaw Pact to limit and slow reforms. Before the Gdańsk Accords were even signed, the CPSU politburo created a special commission to oversee policy toward Poland, headed by the ideology secretary, Mikhail Suslov. In accordance with the advice of the Suslov Commission and in line with the Brezhnev Doctrine, the Soviet Ministry of Defense readied three tank divisions and one motorized rifle division to be prepared to intervene in Poland at the end of August.[9] The troops were not mobilized, but after the Gdańsk Accords were signed, the Kremlin continued to signal its disapproval and nervousness by making strong recommendations to its Polish colleagues on the best methods to regain control. Regular high-level meetings of Polish and Soviet officials—including Soviet General Secretary Leonid Brezhnev, Suslov, Marshal Victor Kulikov (the commander of Warsaw Pact troops), Stanisław Kania (who replaced Eduard Gierek as PZPR first secretary on September 5, 1980), Józef Czyrek (the Polish foreign minister) and Jaruzelski (who was both minister of defense and prime minister after February 9, 1981)—took place in Warsaw, Moscow, Crimea, and even in a railroad car in Belorussia. At each meeting the Soviets emphasized the threat of counterrevolution, told the Poles that they needed to take decisive action against the opposition, and warned about grave consequences if they did not.

Pressure for decisive action also came from Poland's neighbors, particularly from East Germany and Czechoslovakia. In November 1980, the East German leader Erich Honecker warned Brezhnev that counterrevolutionary actions might lead to the "death of Socialist Poland" and called for a meeting of fraternal parties to "work out collective measures to assist the Polish friends in overcoming the crisis"—a clear reference to the Brezhnev Doctrine of fraternal socialist assistance that was used to explain military intervention in Czechoslovakia in 1968.[10] When East European first and general secretaries did meet in December 1980, the Czechoslovak leader Gustav Husák echoed Honecker's concerns about Kania's weak leadership and the "threat to our joint interests," raising the example of 1968 as an apt analogy to Poland's current state. While Hungary offered some criticism, János Kádár maintained the position that the situation should be dealt with internally.[11] Nonetheless, Czech and East German leaders continued to raise alarm bells and called for replacing the Warsaw leadership, which "pulled the wool over [their allies'] eyes," with a "reliable, combat-ready Marxist-Leninist leadership."[12]

From August 1980 until December 1981, the subtext of a possible Soviet-led military intervention dominated Polish-Soviet and intra-bloc relations. Brezhnev used the implicit threat of a Soviet-led Warsaw Pact invasion to control developments. Fears of a Soviet-led invasion peaked in December 1980 when the leaders of the Warsaw Pact met for an extraordinary session to discuss the situation in Poland, while numerous regional strikes tested the PZPR's patience with Solidarność. In February 1981, the Warsaw Pact launched preparations for joint military operations on Polish soil, bringing in Soviet military advisers. The operations, named Soyuz-81, began in March 1981 just before tensions over the Bydgoszcz incident reached a breaking point.[13] Just as in Czechoslovakia in 1968, the USSR used the Warsaw Pact's military and political coordinating capabilities to remind Poles of the realities of power in Eastern Europe and to pressure the Polish leadership to act decisively against the opposition. The Kremlin never made a final, definitive decision to intervene militarily, but the option remained a possibility. The Brezhnev Doctrine was never expressly or publicly revoked during the crisis.[14]

Under this external pressure the PZPR leadership quickly came to view a Polish-led military crackdown as one way out of the crisis. On October 22, 1980, Jaruzelski personally began preparations to update plans for instituting martial law. The CPSU politburo discussed the desirability of imposing martial law at least as early as October 29, 1980.[15] The option remained on the table throughout the months leading to December 1981, with the PZPR holding war games in February 1981 to practice implementing military rule. By September 13, 1981, final preparations for Operation X, the imposition of martial law, were in place.[16]

Across the Atlantic, Presidents Carter and then Reagan both kept a watchful eye on events. Carter visited Poland in 1977, prioritized policies to defend human rights and workers' rights' advocates in Eastern Europe, and named a Polish American academic, Zbigniew Brzeziński, as his national security adviser, so his administration was thoroughly steeped in policy toward the region. The primary American concern throughout the crisis was a Soviet-led invasion. Therefore Washington focused most of its public efforts on keeping the Polish crisis an internal process without "external interference." Washington closely watched Soviet troop movements and buildups with spy satellites, looking for any signs of an invasion. When American analysts and politicians feared that an invasion was imminent in December 1980, Carter stated publicly that the United States' relationship with the Soviet Union would be "directly and adversely affected by any Soviet use of force in Poland."[17] Just after the Bydgoszcz incident, President Reagan sent a "strongly worded" letter to Brezhnev "against any extension of the Soyuz-1980 exercises into an invasion of Poland."[18] Both administrations used a full array of diplomatic tools to notify the Soviets of the detrimental consequences of an invasion, including both public and private pronouncements explaining the punitive steps the United States would take if the Soviets intervened militarily.

As a secondary focus, the Carter and Reagan administrations offered economic carrots to the Polish regime to reward continued political liberalization.[19] During the 1970s, Poland had accepted large Western loans to prop up its economy. By the end of 1980, Polish debt to the West had risen to about $23 billion and was beginning to come due, weighing down an already weak economy experiencing major shortages. The cost of living rose 15 percent in the first six months of 1981, and in July a 20 percent cut in meat rations was announced, giving evidence of just how fragile the Polish economy had become. These weaknesses were only exacerbated by the strain of strikes and political instability. The Reagan administration understood that the "fate of Poland's challenge to Soviet hegemony and Communist orthodoxy depends largely on economic forces," so it worked with Congress to stabilize the internal economic conditions by providing concessionary sales of $60 million in grain.[20] In August 1981 the Reagan administration also agreed to delay payment of 90 percent of Poland's debt to the United States for eight years to help alleviate some of the economic strain and to reward the PZPR for its concessions to Solidarność.

While the specific policies pursued by Carter and Reagan remained consistent, shifts in the broader geopolitical context of those actions were significant, with the Polish crisis occurring in a period often referred to as the "second Cold War." Building on existing trends within the Carter administration, Reagan came into office in January 1981 taking a much harder line against the Soviet Union's expansionist policies throughout the developing world, publicly rejecting any hopes of revitalizing détente. Reagan proposed creating a more robust American nuclear and conventional military capability, increasing defense spending by 7 percent (compared to Carter's call for a 5 percent increase), reauthorizing the B-1 bomber program, and creating a six hundred–ship navy, among other steps. Rearmament was coupled with an apparent disregard for the efficacy of nuclear arms agreements to stabilize superpower relations, with the Reagan administration stifling INF (Intermediate Nuclear Forces) negotiations by tabling proposals for arms control that would be readily rejected by the Soviets.[21] All these wider moves in U.S.-Soviet relations prompted an increasingly antagonistic superpower relationship as a background to events in Poland.

The Vatican also took an active role in the Polish crisis, influencing events both within Poland's borders and beyond. As a Pole and a national hero, Pope John Paul II (the former bishop of Kraków, Karol Wojtyła) had both a personal interest in events and an immense impact on public opinion. Throughout the crisis, he spoke publicly about the need for calm and moderation, as did other Catholic officials in Poland. Reflecting the church's preference for Solidarność, behind the scenes the pope actively coordinated policy with the United States. During Carter's term, Brzeziński was in regular contact with the pope about developments in their shared homeland; under Reagan, this working relationship intensified to the point where the U.S. government was exchanging highly classified intelligence (spy satellite photos, closely held analysis, etc.) with the pope on a regular basis in return for information and analysis from the Vatican. With parishes, churches, and cathedrals in every town and city throughout an almost homogenously Catholic country, the Vatican was extremely well informed. As the national security adviser Richard Allen remarked, "An ideal intelligence agency would be set up the way the Vatican is. Its intelligence is absolutely first rate." Both during and after the crisis, Reagan's director of Central Intelligence, William Casey, and the ambassador-at-large, General Vernon Walters, traveled frequently to Rome acting as liaisons between the White House and the Vatican, sharing intelligence, and briefing the pope on American policy. The pope's delegate to Washington, Pio Laghi, and the Philadelphia bishop John Krol (a Polish American who had been close with the pope since Vatican II) functioned as the pope's representatives in Washington.[22]

In the weeks prior to December 1981, Solidarność continued to call for political and economic reforms consistent with goals articulated earlier, while Moscow persistently pushed the PZPR to take action against the opposition. In this laboratory of pressures, the NSZZ Solidarność's National Congress met from September 26 to October 7, 1981. During the meeting Wałęsa's leadership and policies were questioned openly, with delegates criticizing his autocratic style, particularly his decision in March 1981 to call off a second strike after receiving only limited concessions from the government. More generally, the congress highlighted contention within the union over Wałęsa's moderate position of consistently pursuing a compromise position of reform through cooperation with the government. "Whereas Szczecin union leader Marian Jurczyk demanded free elections to the Sejm, Andrzej Gwiazda of Gdańsk exhorted workers to take greater control in the workplace, and Bydgoszcz leader Jan Rulewski mocked and challenged the Warsaw Pact itself, Wałęsa began his election speech by urging respect for the state authorities."[23] Overruling Wałęsa's calls for moderation, the National Congress called for significant political reforms including increased self-government for workers. The congress also approved a "Message to the Working People of Eastern Europe," actively promoting the creation of free trade unions beyond Poland's borders, a move seen as a simple expression of international labor solidarity within Solidarność, but as a provocation in the Kremlin. Wałęsa was reelected as chairman with 55 percent of the vote, but he faced significant competition from Rulewski, Gwiazda, and particularly Jurczyk.[24]

Poland remained in a precarious position. Domestic tensions remained high as a confrontation between Solidarność and the PZPR appeared more and more likely. In the late fall of 1981, localized strikes and work stoppages were called almost daily with little if any coordination with Solidarność's central leadership. At the grassroots, the opposition was growing increasingly impatient with the government's lack of reform. Wałęsa and his circle of advisers were losing control of the movement.[25] In this atmosphere of frustration regional leaders from around Warsaw called for a protest rally in the capital city on December 17.

During its fourth plenum from October 16 to 18, 1981, the PZPR Central Committee took steps to respond to the shifting situation. Reacting to Solidarność's congress, the group removed Kania from his leadership position and elected Jaruzelski to a third office: first secretary. The Soviets interpreted this change as a sign that the PZPR was steeling itself to implement martial law. Jaruzelski did, in fact, begin to take concrete steps toward declaring martial law, including extending the period of military service for conscripts and dispersing military operational groups around the country. In November and early December the general also launched an anti-Solidarność propaganda campaign, accusing the union of breaking with the Gdańsk Accords and grabbing for greater political power. Pressure from the east remained steadfast in favor of martial law, with Marshal Kulikov arriving in Warsaw on December 7 to keep an eye on Jaruzelski. In the hours and days before the final decision, Jaruzelski appeared agitated and nervous, almost paralyzed in the face of Soviet pressure to act decisively against the opposition. He vacillated about taking the final steps toward military rule, but by 2:00 P.M. on December 12, the general had made the final call for Operation X to go into motion.[26] Tanks and militia were fully mobilized ten hours later, overtaking the country and rounding up the opposition.

## Mixed Signals and Missed Intelligence

Despite the White House's feeling of being caught off guard by the declaration of martial law, Jaruzelski's move was not a total surprise to the Americans. The Reagan administration had been well informed about the possibility and specifics of implementing military rule months before the final steps were taken. Since the early 1970s, a Polish Army officer named Ryszard Kukliński had been working for the CIA, sending information on the Warsaw Pact's war plans. During the Polish crisis, Colonel Kukliński was a member of the group charged with preparing for martial law. Kukliński's reports helped spark the intervention scares in December 1980 and March 1981, as well as the subsequent flurry of anti-Soviet posturing. Kukliński also sent regular intelligence on preparations for martial law, including detailed information on war games plans from February 1981 onward. In the fall of 1981 he sent numerous warnings about the imminent threat of military rule. His reporting came to an end in October 1981 after Kukliński's colleagues had become aware that high-level information was being leaked to the Americans. When the colonel saw signs that he was being trailed by internal security service personnel and believed martial law was imminent and unstoppable, he asked to be taken out of Poland.[27] On November 7, 1981, the CIA whisked Kukliński and his family away from Warsaw, granting them asylum in the United States.[28]

Armed with this intelligence, the Reagan administration was at least partially prepared for martial law.[29] Eight days after Reagan entered office, the Department of State wrote a contingency memo on U.S. responses "to the use of force by the Polish government against the Polish people," advocating a flexible approach calibrated to optimize American leverage.[30] The Reagan administration also made explicit statements to the PZPR about negative consequences if the PZPR utilized force against its own people. During the intervention scare that peaked on March 28, the White House issued a statement "to make clear to all concerned our view that any external intervention in Poland, or any measures aimed at suppressing the Polish people, would necessarily cause deep concern to all those interested in the peaceful development of Poland, and could have a grave effect on the whole course of East-West relations."[31]

There was, however ambiguity in American statements—warning primarily against external intervention and only secondarily against the Polish use of force. For example, when Deputy Prime Minister Mieczysław Jagielski visited Washington in early April 1981, Vice President Bush's briefing memorandum included a suggestion to "emphasize the consequences of the Polish suppression of workers";[32] yet in his actual conversation he did no such thing. Bush said that he was "reassured" by comments that Poles would deal with their problems peacefully, and instead he emphasized "how seriously the American people would view the imposition of an external force," adding that the "United States has no intentions in involving itself in internal Polish affairs."[33] As summarized in mid-May 1981, American policy was to "refrain from any words or actions which would complicate the resolution of Poland's problems by the Poles themselves. We have stressed that we have no intention of interfering in Poland's internal affairs and have urged the Soviets and others to show similar restraint."[34] In addition, on September 19, 1981, a week before Solidarność's National Congress, the Warsaw embassy official Howard E. Wilgis presented the head of Ministry of Foreign Affairs (MSZ) Department III, Józef Wiejacz, with a statement from Haig that read, "In the present situation we think it extremely important that Poland's leadership realize the devastating effect that repressive measures taken by them could have on United States attitudes towards Poland." This statement, however, was preceded by paragraphs condemning Soviet pressure, mentioning American sympathy toward the government, explaining that the United States did "not wish to interfere in Poland's internal affairs," and voicing American fears that instability in Poland could lead to greater instability in Europe and "unforeseen consequences"—meaning civil war and expanded conflict.[35] While the Reagan administration was concerned about martial law, its messages to Warsaw were encased in language about external interference.

These mixed messages stand in stark contrast to the clear warnings about the grave consequences of a Soviet invasion. The Reagan administration's messages about the possibility of a domestic crackdown never had the clarity of its statements about the consequences of a Soviet intervention; statements about the consequences of martial law were clothed in language focused primarily on threats of strong reactions to external influences, desires to respect Poland's sovereignty by not interfering, and warm words expressing sympathy and dangling the possibility of continued economic assistance.

This ambiguity reflected internal dynamics within the Reagan administration and a lack of unity on Poland policy before the declaration of martial law. Because the administration had assumed power in the middle of the crisis, policy took on a reactive quality. The NSC did not have time to prepare overriding guidance on policy toward Eastern Europe until well after December 1981, and the administration was often split between more ideological perspectives advocated by neoconservative members of the cabinet and more pragmatic approaches advocated by Bush and officials in the State Department. As the director of the Soviet and East European desk in the NSC, Richard Pipes, recalls, the "vice president did not agree with the president" on the proper approach.[36] Reagan's own attitude toward policy making bred divided action within the foreign policy machinery. According to Pipes, "President Reagan had many virtues, but he didn't take up his time with the details of government. . . . He gave a lot of freedom to members of his administration. They would do, as a matter of fact, what they wanted and therefore there was confusion."[37]

The PZPR also received advice from American business leaders that contradicted official U.S. government statements. Western bankers and businesses did not want a Soviet intervention because they understood it would lead to bloodshed and complete economic collapse. Military rule was also viewed negatively—lenders understood that you could not expect strong productivity if miners and workers did not want to work.[38] Rather than prescribe particular policy expectations, however, business leaders expressed their desires for stability. Following a September 1981 conference of Polish government officials and executives from private American banks, MSZ officials reported that the bankers based their decisions about economic credits solely on economic criteria, that improved rates on loans would require increased efficiency, and that ongoing strikes and political problems made efficiency impossible. In their words, "In today's situation banks cannot safely engage in Poland with new money. . . . Today the central source of uncertainty regarding the Polish economy resides in the lack of social-political stability."[39] Similarly, in a memo from September 17–19 meetings between PZPR officials and a delegation from the U.S. Commerce Department, the Americans made the point that the most important factor in improving chances for increased economic contacts was "moving toward a clear, effective program of stabilization."[40]

Adding to this mix, the U.S. government was silent about martial law as events moved toward a crescendo. After September 1981, the United States issued no explicit warnings against the use of internal force although Kukliński had been removed, an event that confirmed that the West knew about Polish plans.[41] The main issue in Polish-American relations through the late fall of 1981 was not the prospect of martial law, but considerations of increased aid. Warsaw had applied for $740 million to purchase agricultural commodities and for $200 million in emergency food aid, and the Poles were hoping for lenient terms to reschedule debts due in 1981 and 1982. In an attempt to gauge his government's chances of receiving this much-needed aid, Deputy Premier Zbigniew Madej visited Washington from December 7 to 10. While the American briefing memo for Madej's meeting with Deputy Assistant Secretary Jack Scanlan mentions the negative impact that the use of force would have on bilateral relations, it also states that the United States respected the course followed by Polish authorities and had carefully avoided "interfering in Poland's internal affairs," a policy the White House expected to continue.[42] The Polish record of the meeting reports on the later points, but it does not include any warnings about martial law, presumably because Scanlan did not mention or emphasize that talking point.[43] The Polish record of Madej's conversation with Bush does not mention martial law either, only that the vice president inquired about the "possibility of the government cooperating with the union movement to realize an economic program for exiting the crisis."[44] If the Reagan administration had been looking for a chance to signal its disapproval of plans for martial law, these meetings with Madej presented just such an opportunity. There is no evidence on either side, however, that strong or even muted warnings were made.

In part, martial law was not emphasized in these December contacts because Washington never viewed it as likely. From August 1980 to December 1981, the

White House, the Department of State, and the CIA remained myopically focused on Soviet military intervention. The top priority was always to deter a Soviet invasion.[45] It was a "strongly held conviction of both U.S. intelligence analysts and policy officials before martial law was imposed, that the Poles would not impose martial law."[46] The intelligence services also consistently reported that if internal repression was used, it would fail, lead to internal conflicts, and be followed by the introduction of Soviet forces, reverting the discussion to external intervention.[47] Moreover, American analysis concluded that Jaruzelski was a reformer, not a hard-liner. Policy makers consistently cited his standing as a patriotic Polish officer who was famous for saying that "Poles won't shoot Poles."[48] Jaruzelski and Kania were seen as "moderate in that they prefer not to use violence to restore state authority."[49] Finally, raw intelligence from Kukliński was closely guarded, so information about specific preparations for martial law did not receive a wide audience. The director of the Office of East European Affairs at the Department of State recalls that neither he "nor any of his superiors up to the secretary of state were informed" about the Kukliński reports.[50] Pipes claims that he and Haig had not seen the intelligence prior to December 13. Only the national security adviser Richard Allen (who left the White House around November 23 under the shadow of a bribery scandal), Defense Department officials, and various other intelligence analysts knew the specifics of Kukliński's reporting. Apparently, much of the administration was "ignorant that throughout the year the Polish government . . . was laying the groundwork for a military crackdown."[51]

From the American perspective, tensions between the CPSU and the PZPR, as well as between Solidarność and the PZPR, appeared to be lessening at the end of 1981. Following a rather tense summer, by September 4 Pipes was reporting to Allen that Jaruzelski and Kania "reached a modus vivendi with their Soviet patrons," trading efforts to limit the opposition from forming an official political party and minimizing party democracy for the leeway to pursue economic liberalization on the Hungarian model.[52] Although October had been a very tense month internally—with Solidarność's National Congress and a series of strikes and clashes with police—in November Jaruzelski seemed to be pursuing a conciliatory policy. On November 4, Jaruzelski, Glemp, and Wałęsa met to discuss the possibility of a Front of National Accord. Although this meeting yielded little concrete progress, the Washington intelligence community viewed the move toward negotiation and reconciliation with "cautious optimism."[53]

In the two weeks prior to martial law, Washington's main concern was not internal repression but Poland's deteriorating economic situation. According to one briefing memorandum, Poland's economic outlook was "extremely grave." More important, economic collapse offered "the best chance to restore Soviet domination."[54] The State Department was pushing a line to "consolidate" the gains made by Solidarność by furthering economic aid, arguing in part that "if the Polish experiment fails because of economic collapse, and we are seen as having failed to help, this will be seen throughout the world . . . as a failure to support a people struggling for freedom."[55] Writing again to Reagan on December 1, the secretary of state advocated maintaining the recent calm by strengthening Wałęsa's hand in negotiations by providing necessary aid to avert the possibility of further economic decline precipitating a crisis—"the sort of crisis that could demoralize and discredit the democratic forces and lead to the re-imposition of an inflexible Soviet-style Communist dictatorship."[56] With this in mind, the NSC held a meeting on December 8 to discuss $740 million in long-term agricultural aid, including $100 million in emergency aid in the form of corn and soybean meal destined for Poland's poultry industry that the Cabinet Council on Economic Affairs had already approved. Writing to Director of Central Intelligence (DCI) Casey on December 4, the director of the DCI/DDCI Executive Staff Robert Gates stated that investing foreign aid was a risky proposition, but "that our national security interests are well served by gambling $740 million (or other sums) in credits in the hope that it will allow the Polish experiment to continue and in the knowledge that the experiment's very survival will contribute to the long-term unraveling of the Soviet position in Eastern Europe."[57]

In international circles, the main conversation vis-à-vis Poland in the days prior to the imposition of military rule was also aid. At a December 10 dinner in Brussels, French, German, British, and American foreign affairs officials did not mention martial law. Rather, the quadripartite group "emphasized the necessity of continuing Western assistance to Poland in order that the Polish experiment in pluralism would continue."[58] As late as December 11, the Department of State reported to the secretary's team in Brussels that "tensions in Poland have lessened in the wake of the government's apparent decision not to submit an 'emergency measures' law . . . and the increasingly active role played by the church."[59] Twenty-four hours after this message was sent, however, tensions spiked; by December 12 they had passed a breaking point.

## Shock, Anger, and Protests

When word reached Washington late on December 12 that tanks and armored vehicles were moving around Warsaw and surrounding Solidarność headquarters, Washington officials emanated a unanimous sense of shock. As the secretary of state recalled, "the timing of [martial law] . . . came without forewarning to the United States."[60] The *New York Times* noted, "High officials here have made no secret that the repression so swiftly and stunningly imposed last Sunday morning by General Jaruzelski caught them by surprise."[61] Assistant Secretary of Defense Richard Perle went as far as to refer to "a collective failure" in intelligence gathering and assessment prior to December 12.[62]

This sense of surprise in Washington was matched only by a feeling of anger. Policy makers on all sides of the political spectrum were sincerely upset by Jaruzelski's decision, none more so than the commander in chief. Upon hearing the news, Reagan was "absolutely livid" and decided to take a stand, allegedly saying to Pipes that "something must be done. We need to hit them hard and save Solidarity."[63] Reagan's anger was equally apparent when he met with Polish American leaders on December 21. As one participant reported, "the President was awfully angry."[64]

Before the Washington policy community could decide how to react, it needed to understand just what was happening. As part of martial law, Polish troops cut off both internal and international phone communications,[65] so the American embassy in Warsaw and consulates in Kraków and Poznań could only report what they saw themselves. The United States could not readily receive information on the situation beyond these three cities. Poland was blanketed with a heavy cloud cover, so satellites and photographic intelligence were of no help. Even the Vatican, which had been such an important source of intelligence during the crisis, remained in the dark for the first few days.[66]

In this news blackout, Jaruzelski had the first word. In his remarks that began broadcasting every hour on Polish radio beginning at 6:00 A.M. on December 13, the leader of the Communist Party and the state argued that Poland was deep in crisis: "Our country is on the verge of an abyss. . . . Chaos and demoralization have reached the level of defeat. The nation has reached the border of mental endurance . . . now, not days but hours are nearing a nationwide catastrophe." This catastrophe was precipitated by the growing "aggressiveness of extremists, clearly aiming to take apart the Polish state system." In response, Jaruzelski declared martial law and created the Military Council of National Salvation (Wojskowa Rada Ocalenia Narodowego or WRON) to guide the state. The general lamented the use of force against the Polish people and declared that his intention was not a military takeover of the government. Democracy (such as it was) had not been abandoned;

WRON had been formed only "to create guarantees of reestablishing order and discipline." For this reason, "a group of people threatening the safety of the country" had been preventively interned, including "extremists in Solidarity," "members of illegal organizations," and "sharks of speculation gaining illegal profit." Jaruzelski explained that he had taken these actions with a heavy heart, knowing that this would not be an easy time for his compatriots. Invoking a long tradition of benevolence in the Polish armed forces, the general asked Poles to accept his decision to pull the country back from the precipice of instability and confrontation.[67]

In private the Polish government reiterated these points to Washington in more specific terms. Meeting with Scanlan on December 14, the Polish ambassador Romuald Spasowski referred specifically to his government's beliefs that Solidarność had been "leading the nation into civil war" and that action was taken to "avoid an internal tragedy which could have had a serious impact . . . on European security"—a clear assertion that Jaruzelski acted to preclude a Soviet military intervention. The ambassador hoped that other countries would "understand the situation" and stated that Poland remained "interested in good relations with Western countries."[68] With its initial statements the PZPR attempted to ease concern about instability, to show that it had the situation under control. In both public and private Jaruzelski argued that martial law was the lesser of two evils. The country had been on a spiral toward chaos that could only lead to civil war, or worse, to a Soviet invasion. In his messages both to the people of Poland and to the international community, Jaruzelski sought sympathy and understanding, because he and the military had acted to save Poland from consequences worse than military rule.

Soon after the first reports of martial law, however, accounts began to seep out about workers clashing with government forces. In line with existing union policy, "union militants" called for a general strike in response to the government's provocation, raising the possibility of open conflict.[69] On December 14, the *Washington Post* reported that the call for a general strike had been followed in large steel mills and mining operations, with Polish troops massing around the striking workplaces.[70] Sit-in strikes were held in "hundreds of the largest enterprises: in all the shipyards, ports, mines, iron and steel works, and in most factories in the metal and light industries."[71] Most of these strikes were broken on the night of December 14–15 by forces from the MSW backed by elite military units, who stormed the factories using explosives to break down doors and gates, and tear gas and floodlights to overcome the strikers. Strikes in mines in Silesia proved to be harder to break, with miners holding sit-in strikes in the mine shafts. This led to the bloodiest episode of martial law, when government forces stormed the mines and fired on workers, killing six immediately and mortally wounding three others.

The Western public response was swift. Poles living in America gathered privately for shots of vodka, to share news, and to worry.[72] In New York City, Eric Chenoweth, Irena Lasota, and a few members of Solidarność stranded in the United States formed the Committee in Support of Solidarity, with the intention of keeping the American public aware of events and aiding the opposition. The AFL-CIO pledged its full support to its "Polish brothers and sisters" and called "upon the governments and peoples of the free world to raise their voices in protest against the ongoing destruction of human rights in Poland."[73] Spontaneous or loosely organized protests took place almost immediately in New York. Internationally, crowds protested on the streets outside Polish embassies in Paris, Vienna, London, Brussels, Milan, Rome, Lisbon, Athens, Toronto, and Tokyo.[74] On Monday, December 14, protests in the United States expanded to the Polish embassy on 16th Street in Washington, D.C., and to the Polish consulate in Chicago. In Paris three to four thousand protesters marched in support of Solidarność, with smaller events taking place in Milan, West Berlin, Madrid, Copenhagen, Vienna, and The Hague.[75]

### First Steps

In the first seventy-two hours after the declaration of martial law, the U.S. government took a decidedly cautious public approach. Reagan did not return to the White House until Sunday morning and Haig lingered in Brussels to keep from appearing too anxious and triggering alarms in Moscow. Speaking in Brussels on December 13, Haig emphasized that the United States was deeply concerned and carefully watching the situation. Reagan took a similar tact when responding to reporters on returning from Camp David, stating, "We're monitoring the situation. Beyond that, I can't have any comment."[76] This caution was mirrored by America's NATO allies and pursued in private correspondence as well.[77] When the undersecretary of state and a former ambassador to Poland, Walter Stoessel, met with the Soviet deputy chief of mission in Washington on December 13, he emphasized his government's deep concern about Poland and "stability in the region," urged restraint, and warned against "an over-reaction or excess excitement."[78]

This muted response in part reflected the limitations of American power and its history with revolution in the region. Following American inaction in November 1956 and tacit American acceptance of the Soviet invasion of Czechoslovakia in August 1968, Poles, Americans, and the world knew that the United States would not react militarily to events in Poland. At the same time, Washington had learned from the Eisenhower administration that the United States did not want to incite violence to cause needless bloodshed. More practically, the Reagan administration did not want to give the Soviets an excuse to deploy troops. Earlier contingency planning for the Polish government's use of force against the Polish people had, in fact, noted that martial law could be "staged as a pretext for greater Soviet involvement."[79] Provocative or inflammatory comments were kept to a minimum.

The Catholic Church also emphasized caution. Speaking to a crowd of pilgrims outside his Vatican window on December 13, Pope John Paul II prayed, "Polish blood cannot be shed. . . . Everything possible must be done to peacefully build the future of the Homeland."[80] Speaking at Częstochowa (home of the Black Madonna, Poland's most important relic), Cardinal Glemp took a similar tone: "We must calmly reflect on the situation, the aim of which should be peace and the saving of lives, so that we avoid bloodshed." Later that same day, Glemp further explained, "I am going to call for reason even if it means laying oneself open to insult, and I shall ask, even if I have to go barefoot and beg on my knees: Do not begin a fight of Pole against Pole. Do not lose your heads, brother workers."[81]

In private, however, Washington's policy wheels began to take measured first steps. Meeting with Spasowski on December 14, Scanlan informed the Polish government that they had suspended consideration of the $740 million agricultural aid package, as well as the $100 million in emergency feed aid that had already been tentatively approved.[82] When the U.S. ambassador to Poland, Francis Meehan (who was in West Germany when martial law was declared), returned to Warsaw and met with Foreign Minister Czyrek on December 16, Czyrek "argued vigorously" that he could not understand the decision to suspend agricultural aid. Meehan, however, saw no change in the PZPR's position: "I do not believe my broader comments had any particular impact on Czyrek. . . . But at least he is in no doubt that [U.S.] economic assistance is not on. That kind of language he understands."[83] While the PZPR had been confronted with serious, violent opposition, there was no sign that Warsaw officials were going to change course. Defense Intelligence Agency reports echoed this analysis, reporting, "martial law has been implemented in Poland with more efficiency and less resistance than had been expected."

They concluded rather bleakly that, "having taken the gamble, Jaruzelski must pursue his present course until he wins or loses."[84]

On December 17, Reagan made his first substantive public statement, raising political pressure on the Polish leadership, but dangling an incentive as well. Stating that he viewed the situation in the "gravest of terms," the president focused his remarks on human rights, declaring the arrest and imprisonment of thousands of union leaders and intellectuals a "gross violation of the Helsinki pact."[85] Turning to the question of aid, he added: "We have always been ready to do our share to assist Poland in overcoming its economic difficulties, but only if the Polish people are permitted to resolve their own problems free of internal coercion and outside intervention." For the United States to help solve Poland's economic problems, however, martial law would have to be suspended, prisoners would need to be freed, and free trade unions would need to be restored.[86] These same frustrations and their policy implications were explained in a private meeting between Spasowski and Scanlan. Decrying the use of force and the arrest of the country's "most patriotic and devoted workers and intellectuals," Scanlan stated that "when the U.S. sees the Polish military regime move toward a genuine political accommodation by permitting a free atmosphere of negotiation by free men, we will be prepared to help economically."[87] As before the declaration of martial law, bilateral relations focused on economic aid, this time with the White House dangling continued economic opportunities to mitigate the PZPR's repressive policies.

### Sanctions

A week after the declaration of martial law, it was becoming increasingly clear that military rule would not be temporary, and the American response shifted toward more proactive steps. By this point, however, the response to martial law was not just a matter of reacting to Poland and the Poles. From the beginning of the December crisis, the Reagan administration believed that the Kremlin was complicit. Although intelligence from Kukliński was not employed to predict martial law, it was quickly exploited to confirm Soviet involvement. On December 15, Haig reported to the Western Allies that, "for some time our government has been holding very sensitive intelligence which convincingly confirms that the Soviets were intimately involved with the Polish government from the outset in the planning of this weekend's operation."[88] The White House interpreted Marshal Kulikov's visit to Warsaw on December 11 as further evidence of Soviet coordination. As the State Department explained to the Allies, Jaruzelski was a "tool of the Soviets. . . . No reasonable man can believe that this tragedy would be happening without Soviet pressure."[89] At his December 17 press conference, Reagan went public with a simple but persuasive argument: "It would be naive to think [that martial law could be declared] without the full knowledge and the support of the Soviet Union. We're not naive."[90] These sentiments were repeated in private the following day when Undersecretary Stoessel met with the Soviet ambassador Anatoly Dobrynin, to warn that the present situation "would inevitably have an adverse impact on U.S.-Soviet relations, since the influence of the Soviets in Poland was overwhelming."[91]

These internal discussions and Reagan's public comments about Soviet complicity were consistent with his long-standing opinions about the Communist system. In Reagan's worldview, Moscow treated Eastern Europe as a colonial possession, so it would be inconsistent to believe that Jaruzelski had acted on his own.[92] More important, Reagan and neoconservative members of his administration viewed martial law as a real opportunity to subvert Soviet capabilities, possibly even to change the global balance of power. Poland presented the Reagan White House with a chance to intensify its battle against communism in general. As Reagan noted in his diary, "This may be the last chance in our lifetime to see a change in the Soviet empire's colonial policy re Eastern Europe."[93] Reagan and his advisers had viewed Solidarność as an organization that could undermine communist power, and they certainly were not going to abandon their hopes now that Solidarność was under attack. Even more grandly, Reagan believed that he had been handed a historic opportunity to turn back communism, akin to Franklin Roosevelt's decision to lead America into World War II to defeat fascism. Reagan was inspired by his sense that Poland was "the last chance of a lifetime to go against this damned force."[94] He believed he had been charged with the mission of defeating communism; the declaration of martial law and the possibility of supporting Solidarność gave him the opportunity to push that mission. "The president was gung-ho, ready to go."[95]

Full NSC meetings were called for December 19, 21, 22, and 23 to discuss the possibilities for sanctions against both Poland and the USSR. The president was the most vocal proponent of tough actions. On the other side, Haig was concerned about relations with the Allies, and Commerce Secretary Malcolm Baldridge, Agriculture Secretary John Block, and Treasury Secretary Don Regan worried about the effects of economic sanctions on American businesses.[96] The main discussions, therefore, revolved around the extent of sanctions. On December 19 the NSC resolved to suspend the remaining shipment of surplus dairy products to Poland (which had been previously allocated), suspend the renewal of Export-Import Bank insurance, and activate international organizations (the U.N. Secretary General, the U.N. Human Rights Commission, and the ILO) "to weigh in on human rights questions." The NSC also opted against declaring Poland in default on its debt agreement and in favor of delaying an International Harvester license for exports to the USSR. Additional options vis-à-vis Poland under consideration at the December 21 meeting included: suspending its request to join the IMF, invoking tougher CoCom (Coordinating Committee for Multilateral Export Controls) standards, reconsidering fishing allocations in American waters, writing a presidential letter to Jaruzelski, advising private banks not to declare Poland in default, and calling for a papal visit.[97]

While disagreements about sanctions policy regarding Poland were mild, the NSC was more deeply divided about how to respond to the Soviets. In meetings chaired by Admiral John Nance, the acting assistant to the president for national security affairs, DCI Casey wanted "forceful measures," with Regan, Baldridge, and Block arguing for either massive punishment or no punishment at all (in effect arguing for no punishment, given that it was unlikely that extreme measures would be employed). Haig took a "centrist" position.[98] At the December 21 NSC meetings, these three groups were given a laundry list of eighteen possible actions to consider against the Soviets. They included: a letter to Brezhnev; recalling Ambassador Arthur Hartman from Moscow; suspending or delaying new talks on long-term grain agreements and maritime agreements; arranging high-level consultations with NATO allies, Japan, and China; suspending Aeroflot flights; halting the export of oil and gas equipment to the Soviet Union; reconsidering export licenses for American pipe-laying equipment; strengthening American and Allied agreements for CoCom restrictions; an embargo on all new contracts for exports to the USSR; and denying new official credits, credit guarantees, and credit insurance for exports to the USSR. Regarding internationally coordinated actions against the Soviets, the NSC included the possibility of calling an emergency session of NATO foreign ministers and the U.N. Security Council, postponing the resumption of Commission for Security and Cooperation in Europe (CSCE) talks in Madrid, conducting an "extensive campaign of public condemnation," postponing INF negotiations, and suspending Mutual and Balanced Force Reductions (MBFR) negotiations.[99]

The NSC met again on December 23 to continue discussing options vis-à-vis the Soviet Union and to approve a final list of sanctions against Poland. For Poland, the State Department created a comprehensive list of

President Reagan, Secretary of State Haig, and Secretary of Defense Weinberger discussing possible sanctions on Poland and the Soviet Union during an NSC meeting on December 23, 1981. Photo courtesy of the Ronald Reagan Library.

economic sanctions, ordered from "limited" to "severe." In addition to op-tions explained earlier, the list included limited steps such as suspending activities of the Joint American-Polish Trade Commission, requesting sus-pension of activities by the private Polish-U.S. Economic Council, canceling both government and private American participation in the Poznań Trade Fair, reducing the number of personnel allowed at the Polish commercial office in New York, and suspending all LOT flights. The "medium" options comprised steps to suspend technology transfer, to restrict Polish access to American ports, and to complicate business contact between the two countries by calling on American businesses to curtail their contacts and by limiting visas for Poles coming to the United States. "Strong" options included withholding fisheries and restrictively enforcing an agreement on import quotas for Polish textiles. "Severe" options included continued sus-pension of funds for agricultural aid, concerted opposition to IMF mem-bership, pushing for hard requirements on Poland's international debt and rescheduling agreements to force default, working with private banks to force default, calling for a full embargo on Polish imports, and suspending Poland's most favored nation (MFN) trading status.[100]

The final decision on Poland drew from all four levels. In a letter sent to Jaruzelski on December 23, Reagan recognized the "considerable external pressure to roll back reforms" and maintained that the United States was not questioning Poland's choice of political system or military alliances. However, he wrote, "The United States government cannot sit by and ignore the widespread violation of human rights occurring in Poland. To do so would make us party to the repression of the rights of the Polish people." He then went on to list economic sanctions taken, declaring that his government was no longer considering the request for $740 million in agricultural aid (including $100 million in emergency aid), nor would the United States deliver the remainder (about 10 percent) of $74 million in dried milk and butter that the U.S. had agreed to the previous April. The letter also threatened to take further action if repression increased or continued unchanged. The letter ended on an optimistic note stating that Washington would reconsider these sanctions once the PZPR had "taken concrete steps to end repression, freed those who have been subject to arbitrary detention, and begun a search for reconciliation and a negotiated accommodation with the true representatives of all of the social, spiritual, and political elements of Polish society."[101]

Addressing the American public in a prime-time message that same night, the president spoke about the meaning of Christmas and made public his decision to impose sanctions on Poland. Focusing again on human rights violations, the president said, "I want emphatically to state tonight that if the outrages in Poland do not cease, we cannot and will not conduct 'business as usual' with the perpetrators and those who aid and abet them." He then outlined the specific new steps taken: halting the renewal of Export-Import Bank insurance credits, suspending all LOT flights to and from the United States, suspending Poland's rights to fish in American waters, and working with NATO to "increase restrictions on technology trade." In the public formulation, the president elucidated a slightly different set of conditions necessary for reconsidering sanctions: "to free those in arbitrary detention, to lift martial law, and to restore the internationally recognized rights of the Polish people to free speech and association." The president concluded his message with symbolic flair, calling for all Americans to place a candle in their window "as a beacon of our solidarity with the Polish people. . . . Let the light of millions of candles in American homes give notice that the light of freedom is not going to be extinguished."[102]

With this pronouncement, the White House ended its period of cautious non-comments. The Reagan administration took actions it considered "severe" by suspending previously approved agricultural aid and the consideration of future aid. It also took the "strong" step of suspending fishing rights and the "medium" steps of suspending LOT flights and weakening Polish-American commercial relations by ending consideration of Export-Import credit insurance. Smaller actions regarding joint trade commissions and trade fairs did not merit announcement during prime time, but they were exercised quietly. Importantly, the White House kept its strongest options in reserve: declaring Poland in default, rescinding MFN, and blocking Poland's entrance into the IMF. Reserving these options gave the administration flexibility to take future steps if the situation worsened.

Presaging further action against the Soviet Union, Reagan's Christmas speech noted that "through its threats and pressures" the Soviet Union "deserves a major share of blame for the developments in Poland."[103] Reagan had already sent a letter to Brezhnev outlining American arguments about Soviet interference in internal Polish matters, and he invoked the Helsinki Final Act to justify American policy. Brezhnev rebuffed Reagan's arguments, completely rejecting claims of Soviet interference. The first secretary flipped Reagan's arguments, condemning the United States for interfering in sovereign affairs by declaring sanctions in response to an internal Polish decision. The CPSU leader also "resolutely" rejected calls for changes in the Communist system and claimed that American statements in support of change, both before and after the declaration of martial law, constituted American interference in Polish and Communist bloc affairs. Brezhnev further rejected Reagan's use of the Helsinki Final Act, reminding the president that it "stipulates the refraining from any interference in affairs which come under the internal competence of another state." Brezhnev concluded by insinuating that the tone of Reagan's letter was offensive and inappropriate for superpower communications, but that the Soviet Union hoped to continue conversations about the arms race and attempts to "preserve peace on earth."[104]

This response made sanctions against the Soviet Union "inevitable."[105] NSC members and State Department officials met on December 27, and on December 28 Vice President Bush chaired a meeting of a Special Situation Group to determine steps to take. The next day, Haig sent a letter to the Soviet foreign minister Gromyko that "in light of President Brezhnev's response . . . we can only conclude that thus far your government is unwilling to help bring about the process of national reconciliation." Haig then explained the list of economic sanctions that would be implemented.[106] In a statement later that day, President Reagan made these sanctions public. The list included: suspending Aeroflot service, closing the Soviet purchasing commission, suspending new and renewed export licenses for high-technology equipment and materials, postponing negotiations on long-term grain agreements, suspending U.S.-Soviet maritime agreement negotiations, calling for a review of all U.S.-Soviet exchange agreements, and expanding the list of oil and gas equipment (including pipe layers) that needed licenses for export to the USSR. Reagan concluded by saying that the United States was willing to pursue improved relations, but in a jab at policies pursued under détente, he said, "American decisions will be determined by Soviet actions."[107] With this announcement, the Reagan administration completed a second decisive unilateral policy, imposing sanctions both on Jaruzelski in Belweder Palace and on his overseers in the Kremlin.

As with sanctions imposed against Poland, the final list of actions against the Soviet Union was not as harsh as it could have been. Most notably, the White House did not suspend negotiations on INF or MBFR negotiations, and decided only to suspend those on new grain agreements (rather than imposing a grain embargo as the Carter administration had done following the invasion of Afghanistan). Reagan had lifted the grain embargo the previous April because he felt that it overly burdened American farmers. Given the recentness of the decision and Reagan's convictions, the option of reinstating the embargo was never on the table.[108] On the issue of suspending arms negotiations, pragmatists in the State Department convinced the president that stepping away from arms negotiations would severely alarm European allies, decreasing the likelihood that they would come into line with Washington's more reserved list of sanctions.[109] The president and the NSC were not such convinced unilateralists, nor angry enough to risk torpedoing the entire sanctions policy by pushing a strategy unpopular with European governments. As the Reagan administration knew, sanctions would not be effective without Allied coordination.

### Getting the Allies in Line

Even before the martial law crisis, the Department of State had coordinated with NATO members on their response to events in Poland. A full year earlier, in December 1980, the North Atlantic Council (NAC) of NATO had met to discuss how to respond to the use of force in Poland, focused on contingency plans for responding to a direct Soviet intervention. The Carter administration recognized the possibility of "Polish use of force against elements of the population" but felt that for the NAC it was "more profitable to focus our attention on the issue of what we would do in response to full-scale Soviet intervention." These contingency agreements were meant to be flexible according to the exact situation, and the agreements included incremental steps for situations that did not involve Soviet troops directly— known as "gray area" scenarios.[110] So while NATO did not have contingency plans if martial law was imposed without clear Soviet intervention, it did at least have a basic list of actions with which to begin the conversation.

When martial law was declared, Haig was already in Brussels for an annual NAC meeting. The British foreign secretary, Lord Peter Carrington, was also in Brussels, with the German foreign minister, Hans-Dietrich Genscher, and the French foreign minister, Claude Cheysson, on their way. With a distinct lack of information, there was a frenzy of activity in Brussels on December 13, but little action was taken. Haig focused instead on maintaining close contact with the Allies to "lead the alliance in these early hours." On the evening of December 13, Joseph Luns, the NATO secretary general, called a meeting of the "quad"—the foreign ministers of Britain, France, West Germany, and the United States—to facilitate coordination and exchange intelligence and analysis. After these meetings, which were more symbolic than substantive, Haig returned to Washington.[111]

In the first days after the declaration of martial law, each ally took individual public stances, ranging from tough talk to sympathetic words. President François Mitterand's government announced that France "deplores the chain of events," but Cheysson added that "the matter remained an 'internal Polish affair that must be handled by the Poles.'"[112] Lord Carrington issued a statement that the British "shall observe a policy of strict non-intervention, and we expect the same of all signatories of the Helsinki Final Act."[113] West German chancellor Helmut Schmidt, who had been meeting in Berlin with East German leader Erich Honecker when martial law was declared, took a similar tact that "all the nations that signed the Helsinki declaration on European security should adhere to its non-intervention principle." The West Germans went a step further, releasing a statement that West Germany was following events with "sympathy and concern."[114] By invoking the sovereignty clause of the Helsinki Accords, the West Europeans were signaling that the Soviets should not intervene militarily. Yet the West Europeans were simultaneously acknowledging that martial law was an internal, sovereign matter, implicitly accepting part of Jaruzelski's argument for how and why martial law was declared.[115]

European statements did not evoke the anger felt by Washington or the American belief that Poland presented an opportunity for the West to stand up against the injustice and tyranny of communism. Reagan's cabinet received the Europeans' comments with trepidation. So the State Department quickly moved to bring the NATO allies more in line with the American position.[116] This offensive began on December 15, when Haig sent a letter to Cheysson, Carrington, and Genscher arguing that American intelligence provided evidence of Soviet involvement in martial law planning, to show the Europeans "the realities of the situation . . . and about the general environment in which [they were] operating."[117] A similar letter sent the following day questioned the validity and relevance of Jaruzelski's argument that martial law was "established by Polish nationalists in order to avoid Soviet intervention." The secretary's point was to push the three allies to increase pressure "to restore the reform process" and "a genuine process of negotiation and reconciliation," and not regress to a pre-August 1980 situation.[118]

Simultaneously, the NAC was discussing possible responses, with negotiations focusing on implementing the "gray area" contingencies agreed to earlier. The State Department took an incremental view that coordination with the NAC was not meant to move the Europeans to a particular position, but to exchange information and act "as a stage-setter for possible follow-on consideration of alliance actions."[119] But the Americans faced an uphill climb; Canada, West Germany, and Norway all agreed with Jaruzelski's argument that martial law was imposed to prevent chaos. The French, British, and Italians appeared closer to American thinking, but U.S. reporting gave a clear sense that it would be difficult to push economic sanctions through the NATO framework.[120] Within Western Europe, martial law was a "divisive issue: there was no common understanding of the events or the significance of martial law."[121]

The American full-court press on NATO began in earnest following Reagan's December 17 statement. The U.S. ambassador to NATO, William Bennet Jr., focused conversation on the worsening situation and on the "clear and gross violation of the Helsinki Final Act," as well as violations of standards of diplomatic conduct. (NATO members were unanimously upset that the Poles had cut telecommunication lines for foreign embassies.) Bennet blamed both the PZPR and the CPSU. The American ambassador also asked that each national government intensify its respective statements. In coordination with the Americans, both the French and the British planned to make strong protests at an upcoming meeting of the CSCE in Madrid. Canada and West Germany remained reluctant to toughen their rhetoric.[122]

Washington also continued to press bilaterally for tough action. On December 19, Haig sent another letter to Cheysson, Carrington, and Genscher, warning that the West was "facing a critical, possibly tragic juncture." The letter warned against "further repression, disintegration, and possible Soviet intervention," and Haig urged his friends to "bring pressure to bear on Jaruzelski to make some move toward reconciliation with the Church and Solidarity" and to "take steps to make clear to the Soviets that we understand the key role they are already playing and make more credible our deterrent to their intervening." Continuing, Haig called on his colleagues to remember the "genuine historical importance" of the moment and even tried to shame them into action: "Western inaction at this time will not be forgotten by those who assess the character of our nations and our individual qualities as statesmen in the years to come."[123] A day later, Reagan followed with his own message to Mitterand, Thatcher, and Schmidt. Demonstrating his anticommunist convictions, the president called Poland a "watershed in the political history of mankind—a challenge to tyranny from within." Echoing earlier communications, Reagan pleaded, "There are measures we can take now to help prevent both further repression and Soviet intervention. These measures must be addressed to the Soviet Union as well as to the Polish regime."[124]

To work out the details for an Allied response, Undersecretary of State for Political Affairs Lawrence Eagleburger was dispatched to Europe. He met with the pope to share intelligence and to brief the Vatican on American policy. It was essential to keep the pope well informed in order to have the Vatican make statements in support of America's strong response against both Poland and the Soviet Union. Eagleburger also met with the Italian foreign minister Emilio Colombo, where the Americans found basic agreement with their policies; Italian trade unions had raised a public outcry about the treatment of Solidarność, pushing Italy toward the American position.[125] The two countries shared such similar positions that the United States wanted to bring the Italians into the quad discussions.[126]

From Rome, Eagleburger flew to Bonn, where he met with Genscher on December 21. The West German foreign minister was "not as reluctant as expected," and the two found considerable agreement on the need to use economic measures against Poland.[127] In return Eagleburger shared Reagan's and Haig's confidential belief "that General Jaruzelski just might succeed in suppressing Solidarity and convincing the Soviets that he has rolled back reform." After Eagleburger provided a litany of evidence proving Soviet involvement, Genscher conceded that political actions against the Soviets were necessary, particularly a presidential letter to Brezhnev.[128] Eagleburger's analysis of the conversation was, however, that the Americans would have to "play hell getting him [Genscher] to accept more than political moves [against the Soviets] immediately."[129] From Bonn, Eagleburger flew to Paris and London to coordinate with more like-minded allies.

A December 23 NAC meeting showed evidence of growing European consensus with U.S. positions. First the British called for action against the Poles and Soviets at the upcoming CSCE meeting in Madrid. The British also reported that the European Economic Community (EEC) had agreed to suspend shipments of beef to Poland until it could be guaranteed that the food was delivered to its intended recipients. The Danes approved stronger CoCom restrictions. Of all of the Europeans, the Italians took the hardest line, flatly stating that they would have trouble continuing their current economic relationship with Poland. The West Germans remained the key stumbling block: they argued against calling a special ministerial-level NAC meeting to discuss Poland, rejected economic measures, and opposed using the CSCE as a forum to present Western disgust.[130] Objections to a special ministerial-level NAC meeting were lifted, however, in response to increasingly negative European public opinion about martial law.[131]

The Poles also began to lobby their friends in the West. As Foreign Minister Czyrek articulated a week after imposing martial law, "The position of Western Europe is positive for us: they are not joining the American economic sanctions."[132] To maintain this advantage, the PZPR sent the Central Committee member and deputy prime minister Mieczysław Rakowski to Bonn on December 30. Rakowski spoke frankly with Genscher about the internal situation, the church's evolving role, and the possibility of a return to dialogue. Genscher explained that December 13 had been a "shock" for the Germans, but this shock was not enough to cause them to take severe action. Genscher did not "want to appear to be judging" the Poles, and near the end of the conversation he added, "We must continue a dialogue, we will do our best to help Poland."[133]

While Genscher was meeting with Rakowski, Chancellor Schmidt was inside the United States, vacationing in Florida before previously scheduled meetings with Haig and Reagan. Haig explained the weight of the situation to the president: "Given the FRG's political, economic, and military weight we need Germany almost as much as they need us, particularly on an issue such as Poland," adding, "dealing with Schmidt is difficult and frustrating. . . . On Poland, Schmidt is moving toward our position . . . and your meeting provides a good chance to bring him further along."[134] Following Reagan's meeting with Schmidt on January 5, the two made a joint statement that worked hard to show consensus between the allies. For the first time, Schmidt agreed with the president on "the responsibility of the Soviet Union," but there was no consensus on specific punitive steps against either the Soviet Union or

Poland.[135] The press correctly interpreted this weak statement as a failure to move the Federal Republic of Germany closer to the American position.[136]

The depth of the disagreement between the United States and West Germany became more apparent when Haig and Schmidt met privately on January 6. Implicitly criticizing Reagan's earlier letters and statements, Schmidt suggested "the West needed to be realistic regarding the possibilities for change in Eastern Europe." Instead of entertaining the option of sanctions, Schmidt took the opposite approach and suggested that the West offer "massive foreign assistance under the conditions normally established for developing countries." At one point tensions bubbled over when the chancellor exclaimed that he would "not be blackmailed" by unattributed threats of American troops pulling out of Germany, after which the conversation spiraled into a wide-ranging argument about the merits of détente and *Ostpolitik*, with Schmidt arguing that the West needed to accept the "fact that changing the consequences of [World War II] and Yalta could very well involve a war in Europe."[137] For the West Germans, Reagan's push for change in Eastern Europe and the American decision to use sanctions were exceedingly provocative moves that threatened European stability. So, while West Germany made a few small concessions in public, in private the two governments remained deeply divided.

Having run into this wall, the secretary of state went back to work on drafting an Allied declaration to be presented at the ministerial-level NAC session, scheduled for January 11. While Haig had been optimistic before speaking with Schmidt, after the meeting he approved a severely scaled-back version of a proposed Allied declaration on Poland. The first draft called for curtailing high-level diplomatic visits with Poland and the USSR and listed specific economic sanctions (including redirecting commodity assistance to humanitarian assistance and suspending the "issuance of licenses on high technology *and* energy equipment"). The approved second draft, however, did not refer to specific steps but instead pushed for language supportive of Washington's position, language that only committed the Allies to "do nothing to weaken the effects of" American sanctions.[138] At an NSC meeting both Cap Weinberger and the president vocally disagreed with taking a more malleable line with the Allies.[139]

Regardless, when Haig returned to Brussels on January 10, he pursued the scaled-back package on sanctions, calling only for strong statements (not specific actions) and pushing for a commitment to not interfere with an individual ally's sanctions.[140] In the final NAC communiqué issued on January 11, NATO publicly condemned martial law, deplored Soviet pressure on the

Poles, mentioned the "significance of the measures already announced by President Reagan," and pledged "not to undermine the effect of each other's measures." On the all-important issue of sanctions, the Allies did take a few significant steps. They suspended new credits to Poland, delayed consideration of rescheduling Poland's debt, and ensured that humanitarian aid would reach the people directly, not be hijacked by the PZPR. The statement, however, made no specific commitments to impose sanctions on the Soviet Union, only an agreement to further consultations.[141] Haig left Brussels on a positive note, saying, "We sought a common near-and-long-term strategy to help the Polish people, and today the alliance produced one."[142] Yet no matter how he spun it, the communiqué was at best a qualified success. Suspending new credits, delaying debt rescheduling, and ensuring that aid went directly to the Polish people all had important long-term effects, but the actions taken by NATO lacked the immediate punch that American-style economic sanctions had been designed to deliver. In the thirty days following the declaration of martial law, the American government succeeded in creating consensus in Washington about a punitive response, but this political will could not be exported to Europe.

### The View from Warsaw

For General Jaruzelski and the PZPR leadership, Reagan's policies were not a primary concern. Rather, for the first few weeks after December 13, WRON met continuously to coordinate martial law. The measures undertaken were both expansive and draconian, with tens of thousands of MSW, *milicja* (police), and Army troops involved. Martial-law restrictions included imposing a nighttime curfew, restricting freedom of movement, banning all public meetings, closing all border crossings and ports of exit, limiting bank withdrawals, introducing legal reforms including summary jurisdiction and expanding military courts, as well as suspending all secondary-school and university classes.

Around six thousand Solidarność activists were imprisoned in twenty-four interment centers. Most high-level Solidarność leaders were captured on their way to hotels in Gdańsk following a National Coordinating Commission meeting there. Wałęsa was apprehended the first night as well, and he was flown to Warsaw against his will for talks with the PZPR leadership. A few key leaders, including Fransyniuk, Bujak, and Lis, managed to evade capture and immediately went "underground," returning to their home districts to plan strike actions. These strike actions had little long-term effect. The military government successfully broke most occupation strikes with force, and, with the exception of the Wujek mines, without a major loss of life. The last major strike had ended by December 28.[143] By almost all accounts, martial law was executed "to perfection" and was successful in controlling the upper echelons of Solidarność.[144]

With the Solidarność leadership under control, the PZPR leadership's main concern became invigorating the party *aktiv* throughout the government bureaucracy. Solidarność's calls for pluralism and self-government prior to December 1981 had threatened the government by decentralizing power within the party. Party members had implemented "horizontal structures" for decision making (rather than vertical, top-down structures). Workers in the MSW had even taken steps to create a trade union.[145] Democratic centralism was threatened, and Jaruzelski desperately needed to regain a strict measure of control over the Communist Party to have any chance of reforming the economy to a point where Poland could function independently.[146]

In terms of international relations, the Polish leadership's primary concern was its main ally, and Jaruzelski's decision to declare martial law came as a great relief to Moscow. On December 13, Brezhnev called Jaruzelski to congratulate him, and he expressed "his warm feelings towards [Poland] and stated that we have effectively engaged the fight against the counterrevolution. They were difficult decisions, but appropriate ones." According to Jaruzelski, his public announcement "met with high acclaim" in Moscow.[147]

In relations with COMECON members, messages soon moved beyond congratulations; the Poles were desperately interested in increased economic aid as a reward for stabilizing the country. During their December 13 conversation, Jaruzelski personally asked Brezhnev to increase assistance. That same day the Kremlin sent out a telegram to leaders in Czechoslovakia, Hungary, East Germany, Cuba, Mongolia, Vietnam, and Laos, asking them to consider sending economic and political support.[148] The Czechs—who had been very reluctant to send aid during the crisis—sent 800 million crowns of goods, some as a gift.[149] The Hungarians acted most quickly by sending an official delegation to Warsaw on December 27–29 to discuss the Hungarian experience of rebuilding after the 1956 revolution.[150] Later, Kádár "warmly thanked the Polish leadership for having put a stop to counterrevolution and anarchy by way of relying on their own resources and thus rendering an enormous service to Poland and to the whole socialist community as well."[151] By January 14, 1982, the Kremlin had agreed to increase grain, oil, gas, and benzene shipments.[152]

Despite Soviet attempts to increase economic aid, the PZPR felt the sting of American sanctions almost immediately, specifically the suspension of

$740 million in agricultural aid and especially an emergency appropriation of $100 million. The agricultural aid (mainly in the form of corn and grain) had been earmarked to be used as feed for the Polish poultry industry—an important source of protein in a country where most ham was sold for export. As Jaruzelski proclaimed at a December 13 politburo meeting, "The issue of buying corn in the USA is very important, the production of poultry will depend on that."[153] When word reached Warsaw that Reagan had suspended this aid, the politburo became concerned about how a lack of grain would affect an already strained food situation. Five days later the Central Committee member Marian Woźniak emphasized this point, arguing that "the biggest problem is acquiring wheat and fodder outside the framework of the USA's embargo."[154] From the perspective of well-informed outsiders, the Poles' problems went well beyond just chicken feed and grain. As a Hungarian delegation reported, "The present poor condition of the national economy is a major burden. . . . To make matters worse, the USA had just affected an economic blockade, thus badly affecting the economy which had developed a cooperative dependence on the economies of the capitalist countries over the past ten years."[155]

From an American perspective, sanctions had an almost immediate positive impact. Reagan and his administration had wanted to punish Warsaw for imposing martial law. While it is unclear how much of an immediate effect suspending new credits, ending fishing rights, and blocking LOT flights to the U.S. had, the decision to suspend consideration of agricultural aid worried the Polish leadership. Moreover, the lack of feed eventually led to a large-scale slaughter of poultry when food reserves dried up, causing long-term damage to the poultry industry by reducing the number of reproducing chickens.[156] In addition, the Poles were forced to turn toward the East for greater economic aid. Because subsidies for East European purchases of oil and gas were already draining money from the Soviet economy, expanded Polish needs and increased aid from the Soviet Union fit perfectly with the desire to punish the Soviets. Moreover, by causing the Poles to draw more resources and capital out of the Soviet Union, economic sanctions against Poland fit well within the neoconservative plans to wage economic war to weaken the system from within.[157]

## Surprise and Distrust

American economic sanctions had a secondary, much less positive set of effects: sanctions caused a complete break in trust between Washington and

Warsaw. On this issue it is essential to examine expectations on both sides of the Atlantic prior to December 13, 1981. Jaruzelski believed that he had chosen the lesser of two evils, and that Western Europe and the United States would prefer military rule over further instability or a Soviet invasion. Jaruzelski's government had gauged the West Europeans correctly, particularly the West Germans. He had completely misread the Americans.

From information gained well after the events in question, it appears that the principal miscommunication between the Poles and the Americans came just a few days before the imposition of martial law, when Deputy Premier Madej met with Vice President Bush. From statements made by General Jaruzelski in 1997, it is clear that he interpreted the vice president's expressions of sympathy and his offers of economic support as a signal that the United States would accept martial law, at least grudgingly. As he has stated, "And that for me it was an unusually important signal; that the United States knew about [plans for martial law], and they knew about it from sources, not only from Ryszard Kukliński . . . but also from CIA materials, and from the American embassy in Poland, that the process [of moving toward martial law] was going on."[158] The significance of an absence of a strong warning was magnified by the Reagan administration's previous ambiguous statements, as well as American businessmen's calls for stability. Based on these patterns, Jaruzelski sincerely believed that the United States would not take a retributive stance against his middle path. As he recalled later:

> I admit, whenever I have such a rotten idea [robaczywe myśli], that
> the Americans would have deliberately liked us to go into a trance
> in advance of that coming event, which we had to bring to an end
> sooner, or later [there would be a] greater explosion, a greater
> tragedy, in connection to the coming intervention, to which we
> would become embroiled with the Soviet Union. . . . For a long time,
> I believed that. Later I corrected that idea. I am attentive. Clearly the
> Americans realistically, wisely, wanted to [keep this from happening],
> and for Poland, and to save stability in Europe, the Americans would
> recognize that [the imposition of martial law] was a lesser evil.[159]

In retrospect it is clear that Jaruzelski attempted to weigh the American reaction to martial law prior to making his final decision.[160] The Polish government expected the Americans to begrudgingly accept martial law and, presumably, to maintain long-standing relations.

Contemporaneous analysis by the MSZ shows a similar expectation. A week after the declaration of martial law and four days after Scanlan had

met with Spasowski to explain that the United States was ending consideration of further aid, *but* two days before Reagan announced economic
sanctions, the MSZ American department wrote a memo asking, "Does
the U.S. government have a considered, united policy toward Poland?" The
general conclusion was that "it is possible to state that so long as the Polish crisis does not threaten territorial agreements within Europe and does
not shift power as a result of a Soviet intervention, the Polish Problem will
not occupy a high place in the list of the United States' priorities in their
anti-Soviet politics." More generally, the information note recommended
following the same "peaceful, patient line" they had been taking. The memo
outlined the steps desired by the Reagan administration toward national
reconciliation. Economic sanctions were not mentioned as a possibility.
Rather, the memo substantiated Jaruzelski's view of martial law as the lesser
of two evils and painted the solution as a middle path between chaos and
Soviet intervention. MSZ analysts argued that the United States and the
West would accept martial law, albeit reluctantly. The working assumption
was that if the PZPR controlled the internal situation, the West would continue to offer at least modest economic support. Based on this analysis, the
MSZ was even hopeful that relations with the West could soon return to a
pre-August 1980 state.[161]

As soon as the Reagan administration responded substantively to the declaration of martial law, the PZPR leadership realized the flaws in its analysis.
As Czyrek noted on December 19, "The USA has launched an offensive in the
name of the Polish experiment. . . . The USA is pressuring other governments
including the USSR. They want to sustain [Solidarność]."[162] This break with
Polish expectations, in turn, led to an emotional response from the Poles.
American actions did not make sense to the PZPR, and Jaruzelski responded
angrily. This anger is constantly revisited and evident in subsequent relations between Polish and American officials during the 1980s (see chapters 2
and 3 especially). Even sixteen years after the decision to impose sanctions,
the general was still fuming about the hypocrisy of the Reagan administration's decision to impose sanctions based on human rights abuses. Again,
in Jachranka in 1997, Jaruzelski spoke about how the economic sanctions
hurt the common Polish people. He openly questioned why the Reagan administration had such a friendly relationship with the Romanians who had
employed de facto martial law for twenty years. He asked the same question about the decision to support Augusto Pinochet in Chile. He openly
condemned the American position of support to regimes in Saudi Arabia,
Mobutu Sese Seko's Zaire, Pakistan, Greece, and Turkey, where human rights

abuses were well documented.[163] The transcript reads as if economic sanctions were a personal affront.

In Washington, the decision to introduce martial law also exposed intense emotions. As Pipes recalls about the December 21 NSC meeting at which the White House began to compose a specific list of economic sanctions, "Real rage dominated after the declaration of martial law. . . . The president erupted. It was a fantastic meeting, because the president delivered a great, emotional speech, the temperament of which reminded [Pipes] of the Quarantine Speech by Roosevelt in 1937. 'This is a turning point . . .' [Reagan contended], 'If the Allies don't go with us, we will go it alone, if that becomes necessary.'"[164] This rage and emotion grew in part from the fact that the declaration of martial law truly had come as a surprise to many in the administration. They had been caught off guard. Moreover, the decision to impose martial law played on Reagan's feelings about the evil nature of communism. The president decided at that moment to take a stand, seeing himself like Roosevelt standing up to the Nazis. This was not a logical or rational response; it was driven by Reagan's fury in the moment.

Of course, anger is often hard to quantify, and it is certainly hard to recreate how this anger directly influenced events on the ground, but reframing this anger as an issue of trust proves insightful. According to one definition, "in its more instrumental form, trust is viewed as the expectation that specific others will reciprocate trusting behavior. In other words, people think they know what others will do, so they can adjust their level of cooperative behavior and precaution taking."[165] More specific to the case at hand, trust violations are defined as "unmet expectations concerning another's behavior, or when that person does not act consistent with one's values."[166] Feelings of anger or bitterness, as well as the state of feeling "confused" or "stunned," are often associated with the initial "hot cognitions" after trust has been broken and distrust has been created.[167]

This conceptual framework fits well the pattern of relations between Washington and Warsaw surrounding the declaration of martial law. Both Reagan's and Jaruzelski's anger came from a perception that the other side had not lived up to expectations. For Reagan, he expected the PZPR to continue to negotiate with Solidarność and not to take any drastic steps. When the Reagan administration was considering sending $740 million in agricultural aid prior to the declaration of martial law, this decision was based on the trust that the White House had of their counterparts in Warsaw. It was a fragile trust, but it was trust. Similarly, after hearing words of sympathy from Vice President Bush, Jaruzelski expected a similarly sympathetic reaction to martial law. By declaring martial law, Jaruzelski broke the trust Reagan had placed in him. By imposing economic sanctions, Reagan broke the trust Jaruzelski had placed in him.

In the first thirty days after December 13, 1981, the American government reacted emotionally, acting unilaterally to impose economic and political sanctions against both Poland and the Soviet Union. Washington also worked to impose sanctions in a multilateral forum, with only limited results. For Poland and its allies, the main issue in the first month was not Western sanctions, but efforts to manage the country's internal situation. While American economic actions did have a nearly immediate sting, their effects were also emotional. In understanding Polish-American relations from December 1981 onward, it is essential to recognize the significant emotional break that had occurred. For Reagan, Poland was personal. Bilateral relations were similarly personal for Jaruzelski, who was equally enraged. Expressions of anger and shock indicated a breakdown in trust between the two countries, or more precisely, the creation of distrust between the White House and Belweder Palace. This distrust, in turn, created an environment ripe for emotional and angry reactions. The course of the next five years in Polish-American governmental relations can, in fact, be seen as a series of attempts to both create trust between the two sides and alternately to sabotage that trust, time and time again.

CHAPTER TWO

# We Are a Card in Their Game

## American Policy Takes Shape,
## January to September 1982

On June 18, 1982, President Reagan attended a hastily convened meeting of the NSC to decide on whether to implement sanctions on American technology destined for a joint West European–Soviet natural gas pipeline.[1] Concerns about pipeline equipment first surfaced after the president's announcement of sanctions on technology sales to the Soviet Union two weeks after the declaration of martial law, and they had led to two special missions to coordinate East-West trade policy with America's allies. Reagan personally attempted to use these sanctions as leverage with Western leaders during a G7 summit in Versailles to find a compromise position and get a tougher policy on Soviet access to Western credit. As in earlier American attempts to get European concessions, the president returned "thoroughly disappointed and angry with the lack of any decisive moves by the allies on credit restrictions." After the trip, the president's anger turned into a decision. On June 18, Reagan "ruled from the bench," agreeing with advice from Caspar Weinberger, William Casey, and William Clark to apply American sanctions against oil and gas technology exports to the Soviet Union retroactively and enforce them extraterritorially. Despite warnings that this would create a substantial rift within NATO, the president felt that not taking this step would make the United States look "flabby" in the face of continued repression in Poland.[2] In response, Secretary Haig, who was not involved in the meeting and who had argued strongly to preference Allied unity over enhanced sanctions, offered a letter of resignation. The president accepted, exposing deep fractures within his cabinet.

During 1982 the Reagan administration and the foreign policy community worked to formulate a long-term strategy toward Poland, but within the White House, discussions about how to proceed broke down over disagreements between hard-liners focused on punishing Communists and more moderate voices who wanted to engage with the East by combining

48

punishments and rewards. Smaller debates about what to do in Poland became embroiled in larger concerns about how to treat the Soviet Union, leading to tense relationships and ultimately a break with America's allies. Policy toward Poland became bogged down in the national security bureaucracy as the two opposing camps vied for the upper hand.

With more difficult decisions and less centralization in policy making, intertwined initiatives—mostly outside of the White House's complete control—took shape. The administration spearheaded a global propaganda campaign against the PZPR and its Soviet comrades. Congress became increasingly involved, using budgetary oversight to join the conversation on how to enforce economic sanctions. Outside government, humanitarian organizations added a counterweight to sanctions. Trade unions and other nongovernmental groups also responded to martial law, providing substantial Western support to Solidarność, which was regrouping as an underground organization. In response, General Jaruzelski's government reacted by pushing back against American policy, maintaining a strong hold over the country and strengthening partnerships with the East. Bilateral U.S.-Polish relations hit a new low. Yet after a personnel change in the executive branch, a subtle shift occurred in the balance of forces within the administration; relations with the Allies were patched and bilateral relations with Poland were placed on a new framework that fostered a gradual approach to promoting change.

### Idealists versus Pragmatists and Carrots versus Sticks

As the Reagan administration completed its first year in office, it remained divided on the best ways to fight the Cold War, particularly in terms of economic actions. One useful way to categorize these divisions is into two opposing camps: "pragmatists" and "ideological Cold Warriors." As Raymond Garthoff explains: "The pragmatists wanted to control trade but also to use it by linkage as a carrot to gain Soviet concessions. . . . [The ideological Cold Warriors] wanted to wage economic warfare to strain the Soviet economy and polity."[3] The divide derived from a broader national discussion about the efficacy of détente. Hard-line members of the administration—people often linked to the neoconservative wing of the Republican party like U.N. Ambassador Jeanne Kirkpatrick, Secretary of Defense Caspar Weinberger, and NSC adviser on the Soviet Union and Eastern Europe Richard Pipes—advocated a new relationship with the Communist world based on a stronger America willing and able to stand up to Soviet aggression. This meant waging economic war to weaken

Warsaw Pact capabilities and to undermine Communist regimes throughout the world, isolating them from Western goods and money if need be.[4] On the other side of the issue, members of the Reagan administration more directly linked to Henry Kissinger and the Nixon White House—including Secretary of State Alexander Haig and Vice President Bush, as well as numerous career diplomats in the Department of State—tended to push for continued engagement and linkage.[5]

Although many of Reagan's statements during the election of 1980 fostered the public image of a tough-talking, saber-rattling, anti-Communist, neoconservative idealist, the policies pursued vis-à-vis Poland are evidence of a president who listened to both sides and often supported policies that embraced pragmatic solutions. In terms of the initial response to martial law, sanctions clearly fell within the realm of economic warfare. However, beginning with Reagan's December 23 announcement of sanctions, it was understood that these sticks could become carrots (sanctions were always reversible) if the PZPR took the proper steps. Reagan also left open the possibility of greater engagement by adding that if the Polish government honored human rights commitments, America would "gladly do our share to help the shattered Polish economy, just as we helped the countries of Europe after both World Wars."[6]

The possibility of large-scale incentives (the kind of help provided to Europe after World War II) to entice the PZPR to change its policies was not just a throw-away line at the end of an otherwise hard-line speech. The idea was initially proposed by H. Allen Holmes, the acting director of the Department of State European and Soviet Office (EUR), who wanted to hold a summit of the big five NATO leaders to focus world attention on recent events and to announce a "joint Marshall Plan for Poland." Holmes argued that the plan would be "premised on a process of reconciliation moving forward," put the Soviets on the defensive, and "give a positive dimension to our carrots and sticks policy."[7] Writing in late December, Ambassador Meehan explained that Jaruzelski could yet be induced to "make good on his commitment to return the country to renewal" because the general was "committed to a process of change in Polish political, economic, and social life. I would not entirely dismiss his claim that he acted on December 13 to prevent a drift to civil war, and the inference that he saw himself acting in Polish national interests, since civil war would inevitably mean foreign intervention."[8] Meehan wrote a second cable defining the kind of incentives he had in mind: "To restore either fishing or landing rights if Jaruzelski takes concrete steps toward reform and renewal." The ambassador realized that it would be difficult to manage

Polish relations in a carrot-and-stick framework, but he believed that the United States held some tasty carrots, particularly the ability to reschedule debt. He also echoed Holmes's earlier memo proposing a more dramatic policy with the "feel of classical Post-WW2 U.S. world leadership. . . . Not small carrots; great big carrots . . . to support a broad-based Western economic recovery program for Poland provided certain clear political and economic criteria were met."[9]

Meehan's ruminations on carrots also showed up in contacts with MSZ representatives. Meeting with Józef Wiejacz, the director of Department III, on December 28, Meehan referenced the reversibility of American sanctions and emphasized that Washington was "impatiently waiting" to see what the PZPR did in the new year, hinting at the possibility of rewards.[10] On December 30, Dan Howard, the embassy officer in charge of scientific, educational, and technical exchanges, took a more straightforward approach, mentioning that Meehan was advocating for both carrots and sticks. He specifically stated that if the Poles took steps to continue reform and restore individual freedoms, Washington could respond with economic help, "on the scale of the 'Marshall plan.'"[11] The State Department codified incentives in January 1982 in guidelines that included a call to "be ready swiftly to offer a carrot if any genuine step toward reconciliation is taken, but a carrot that is proportional to the step, leaving the rest of our sanctions intact."[12]

The Americans went as far as to broach the idea with the Soviets. In the first two weeks of January 1982, Paul Nitze, the president's lead negotiator at the Intermediate Nuclear Forces Treaty talks in Geneva, spoke with his Soviet counterpart, Yuli Kvitsinskii. At the second of two meetings, Nitze read from an official statement, which emphasized that the offer made on December 23 to help the shattered Polish economy if the country moved toward national reconciliation was "a serious one." Kvitsinskii rejected the proposal based on the expressed Soviet emphasis on national sovereignty, saying: "No one was in a position to prescribe to the Polish state how to order its affairs." The possibility of a U.S.-Soviet agreement on Poland appears to have gone no further.[13]

Nonetheless, the State Department continued to advance the possibility of substantial incentives. On March 10, Holmes prepared an action memo for Haig to start an interagency planning process to craft a public push for a package resembling the Marshall Plan. Holmes acknowledged that it would meet resistance both in the White House and in Congress; nonetheless, he believed that "we would be wrong not to exploit the public relations windfall which would be ours were we to come forward now with a major assistance proposal." Deputy Secretary of State Walter Stoessel returned the memo for revision, writing, "Haig has always favored the carrot. The question is, What are its econ[omic] and pol[itical] components? Before *any* interagency work is started I want a memo for the Secretary that lays out a *detailed* proposal on what EUR think the carrot would look like."[14] Two weeks later, a detailed incentives memo made its way to Haig's desk, laying out a package that included lifting sanctions and approving new credits if Jaruzelski took the three steps demanded by the West.[15] No actions were taken and no finalized policy was adopted, but the option of both smaller and larger incentives remained on the table.

While the neoconservatives were focusing on how to punish Poland and the USSR, the State Department and the embassy in Warsaw looked to restore some kind of working relationship with the PZPR, moving as far as to engage directly with the Soviets to foster a breakthrough. Haig had been in favor of incentives from the beginning, but in the president's emotional fever following December 13, members of the NSC who pushed for tough measures played into Reagan's instincts and won out in the early stages of the policy-making process. The administration was in need of a "coherent comprehensive policy on Eastern Europe" and remained conflicted on how to promote change.[16] On February 2, 1982, the NSC asked the Department of State to review Presidential Directive 21, the standing national security document on policy toward Eastern Europe.

An interagency group was created that met occasionally during March and April and focused on one central issue: whether to continue to embrace the doctrine of differentiation or to transition to a policy of nondifferentiation. Differentiation had been official policy since the mid-1960s, when President Lyndon Johnson made "bridge building" a priority.[17] As it was defined in the spring of 1982, differentiation meant "that the U.S. should . . . encourag[e] diversity [between the Soviet Union and Eastern Europe] through active political and economic policies tailored to individual countries." In particular, differentiation was meant to "encourage liberalizing tendencies in the region," "increase economic dependence of Eastern European countries on the West," "expose the region to demands for better human rights performance," "increase antagonism between Moscow and some of the East European states," and "weaken the Warsaw Pact as a unified military institution."[18] The main weapons to achieve these ends were economic: agreements for government loans, favorable trade arrangements, special technology-transfer exceptions, and concessionary sales agreements to provide aid.[19] Reagan's decision on December 8, 1981 (overturned after December 13), to reward Jaruzelski with

$740 million in feed grain for his leniency toward the Solidarność trade union reflected his government's earlier application of differentiation.

Nondifferentiation advocated the opposite approach. It called for the "[U.S. government] and its allies to minimize political and economic contacts with the region . . . [to] weaken the USSR." Under nondifferentiation, Soviet power would be undermined by "increasing strains within the [Warsaw] Pact and forcing diversion of resources away from military use," "helping to stem the flow of Western technology to the USSR," and "weakening the appeal of communism" by causing it to lose its allure by forcing a "deterioration in the quality of life [in Eastern Europe] and harsher police regimes."[20] Sanctions against both Poland and the Soviet Union fit within the nondifferentiation framework.

The process of finalizing a broad policy document on Eastern Europe remained open until the final quarter of 1982. Through late spring and summer 1982, the president and his NSC had more pressing issues than approving policy reviews on Eastern Europe in general or Poland policy in particular. On March 19, Argentine forces landed on South Georgia Island, part of the United Kingdom's possessions in the South Atlantic, provoking a crisis in the Falkland Islands. President Reagan was shot on March 30, remaining in the hospital until April 12 and only returning to the Oval Office on a limited basis beginning April 25. Internationally, trouble was also brewing in the Middle East. Israel had come under attack from internal bombings and rocket attacks from southern Lebanon. In June, the Israeli army clashed with the Palestinian Liberation Organization, as well as with Lebanese and Syrian forces. The White House was also facing massive antinuclear protests, including a June 12 march in New York City that mobilized five hundred thousand protestors calling for a nuclear "freeze." Declassified materials from NSC meetings show that strategic arms negotiations and the Falkland crisis were the main topics of concern.[21] Specific directions for the future of U.S.-Polish relations therefore remained undefined.

### Debt Repayment

Concurrent with the differentiation debate, the executive and legislative branches of the U.S. government quarreled over how to exploit Poland's debt to Western lenders. By December 1981, Poland had accrued roughly $26 billion in debt to the West. Of this, $3.15 billion in loans (14 percent) came from the United States, of which $1.3 billion was in nonguaranteed loans from private banks. The remainder of the American portion came from the U.S. government: $1.6 billion in direct credits and guarantees by the Credit Commodity Corporation (CCC), $244 million in Export-Import Bank loans, and $6 million in AID loans.[22] In April 1981, the United States and other Western governments (who conducted negotiations through an ad hoc group known as the Paris Club) agreed to reschedule 90 percent of Poland's debt for 1981, deferring repayment until 1986. The PZPR signed another agreement with private Western banks on December 4, 1981, to reschedule $2.4 billion in principal. As part of this agreement with the London Club (the ad hoc and unofficial group that negotiated agreements for private bankers), the Polish government agreed to pay $500 million in interest by the end of 1981.

When martial law was declared, neither of these agreements had been paid in full. Polish diplomats concerned about private bankers' reactions met with bank representatives on December 14, telling them that Poland was still planning to pay the full amount of their back interest by December 28.[23] The Polish finance minister, Marian Krzak, also met with representatives from the Paris Club to clarify martial law economic policy: Poland intended to maintain "normal economic relations with Western partners" and hoped to get a $350 million bridging loan from Western governments to cover a shortfall in export proceeds and the withdrawal of short-term deposits, to be able to pay the balance due to the London and Paris Clubs.[24] When Western governments refused to offer bridging loans and the Soviet Union declined to bail Poland out, it was clear that the country would not be able to make its payments. Lenders had to decide whether to declare Poland in default.

The Reagan administration understood that control over debt repayment and rescheduling offered the United States its strongest point of leverage. According to State Department calculations, even with the economy in shambles Polish exports could pay for all necessary Western imports. But in the coming year the Warsaw government did not have enough hard currency to cover its debt payments. To keep their economy afloat, the Poles needed $5.6 billion in public and private debt rescheduling and $3.8 billion in new export and agricultural credits from the West. Thus Western economic leverage after December 13 came from "continuing trade relationships; debt service relief, both public and private; and access to new credits, both public and private." This leverage, however, would be weakened if the Poles declared a unilateral moratorium on Western debt repayment, decreasing the need for hard currency. "Western economic levers [were] most effective if the Poles [attempted] to service their external hard currency debt." This meant that it was in the U.S. government's best interests for public and private American banks *not* to declare Poland in default.[25]

Not everyone, however, agreed with this assessment. More ideological members of the cabinet, particularly Weinberger and Kirkpatrick, believed that the United States should push the Polish economy toward complete collapse and declare default. If the United States declared default, private bankers could do the same, after which the private banks could attempt to seize Polish assets through court action.[26]

In Washington the initial focus of the default debate was whether to recall Poland's debts on government loans rescheduled in April 1981. As part of the April 1981 agreement, Western creditors had included a so-called Tank Clause, which allowed them to rescind the agreement under exceptional circumstances—understood as either Soviet military intervention or Polish use of force. If the Tank Clause was exercised, debt servicing became due and payable immediately. Invoking the clause would cause private banks to declare default as well. According to an interagency report, default would have "no effect on Poland's ability to borrow, since it cannot borrow now. Polish trade, however, would be hampered in the short run." The report concluded that not exercising the clause would keep pressure on the Soviets and Poles to continue to make some payments, that invoking the clause could lead to widespread budget and financial difficulties in Western Europe (particularly the solvency of West German lenders), and that refusing to participate in rescheduling Poland's debts coming due in 1982 would be a much more effective step to limit access to Western credits. The State Department and Haig were particularly concerned that a unilateral American decision for default would further damage Allied cohesion because the action would necessarily hurt European banks, which held the majority of debt. Advocates for default (represented by the Defense Department) acquiesced to the State Department's arguments in the final report, but inserted language not to invoke the Tank Clause "at the present time."[27]

On January 31, the conclusions of this debate became public when the Reagan administration announced its decision to pay $71 million to U.S. banks to cover Poland's past due payments on CCC guaranteed loans. In return, American banks agreed not to call for Poland to repay its loans in full, ending the possibility of default. The White House made clear that this was only a temporary arrangement until Warsaw could pay its debts again. But this initial payment led to a much larger commitment of up to $308 million in fiscal year 1982 and up to $613 million through the end of fiscal year 1983.[28] To cover this expenditure, the White House attached a provision to increase the CCC's borrowing authority to a spending bill for unemployment benefits, agricultural loans, and heating assistance for the poor.[29]

In a domestic atmosphere obsessed with deficit spending, this was a difficult message to swallow. Conservative commentators spoke out angrily. On February 3, the *Wall Street Journal* editorial page condemned the decision, because Washington was "slipping into tacit collaboration with martial law by making it easier for the Soviet bloc to finance repression."[30] Public uncertainty increased after it became clear that Washington's decision protected West German bankers who had made the largest loans, and therefore had the most liability if default were declared. The decision to bail out Warsaw also appeared to contradict the president's earlier commitment to no longer conduct "business-as-usual."[31]

With high public interest and a clear budgetary role, Congress stepped into the discussion. Congressional interest in Poland had been high since the declaration of martial law: Republican senators Larry Pressler and Charles Percy from the Foreign Relations Committee traveled to Poland on January 15, 1982; a number of committees held hearings; and the Congressional Research Service issued several reports.[32] Prior to early February, Congress's role was mainly advisory, but with an appropriations issue on the table, legislators could now have a direct effect. On February 8, New York Democratic senator Daniel Patrick Moynihan introduced an amendment, requiring the president to report to Congress when CCC funds were used to pay for Polish loans. He also convened hearings of the Senate Appropriations Committee (together with Republican senator Robert Kasten of Wisconsin), calling Undersecretary for Defense Policy Fred Ikle and Assistant Secretary of State for Economic and Business Affairs Robert Hormats to Capitol Hill. Facing tough criticism from Moynihan that the "United States and its allies have not found a way to apply meaningful pressure on either the military junta in Warsaw or its masters in Moscow," the State and Defense Department representatives put forth a united front despite closed-door disagreements. Ikle emphasized that the agreement to pay debt was temporary and could be reversed easily. Because Washington was dealing with "the chronic failure of the Communist economic system," Ikle argued that the president could pursue a "prudent policy." Hormats noted that the United States had already stopped the flow of new credits and delayed consideration of new rescheduling talks. He also restated internal arguments "that our officially declaring Poland in default might be used by the Polish government as an excuse to relieve itself of its obligations to make repayments. In addition, [default] would be a sanction that would be hard to reverse if the Polish situation improved."[33] These arguments did little to calm either Moynihan or Kasten; however, in the full Senate, the executive branch's arguments prevailed and Moynihan's amendment was defeated.

Nonetheless, Moynihan continued to use hearings as a forum to criticize the Reagan administration's policy. On March 16, Tom Gleason of the International Longshoremen's Association, and Tom Kahn, assistant to AFL-CIO president Lane Kirkland, expressed labor's condemnation: the AFL-CIO was "disappointed by the mild sanctions." Labor was especially critical of the moral ambiguity of bankers who willingly loaned money to Communist regimes.[34] In more detailed comments made outside of Senate hearings, Kirkland argued that "in effect, President Reagan told the Soviets to disregard his tough talk. He announced that the United States would not use the most potent economic weapon at our disposal in defense of Solidarity." He further admonished the administration for allowing bankers and giant grain companies to dictate American policy: "We believe the people ought to have something to say about how their government responds to the suppression of freedom in Poland."[35] Another voice at the hearings, the former ambassador to Poland Richard T. Davies, went as far as to say that "the Reagan administration appears to be long on threats and short on the kind of actions which are essential ingredients of leadership."[36]

Congressional interest in Poland's debt crisis also led to a House of Representatives fact-finding mission. From March 4 to 7, seven congressmen from the House Foreign Affairs, Budget, and Appropriations Committees (led by Wisconsin Democratic representative David Obey) traveled through Poland meeting with embassy, government, Solidarność, and church officials. For the Polish government this was an important trip to show American lawmakers that economic sanctions were making it difficult to move "beyond the crisis," increasing the likelihood that martial law would be prolonged.[37] The trip also allowed PZPR leaders to argue that sovereign Polish decisions would not be shaped by outside pressure. Decisions about when to end martial law, when to release Solidarność internees (particularly Lech Wałęsa), and when to resume talks with the church and society would be determined based on internal dynamics and developments.[38]

On the issue of default, the congressmen returned convinced that the president had made the correct choice. They also came back with a more positive outlook for Poland's internal development. All were impressed by how the Polish public was handling the hardships of martial law, and all were struck by Poles' optimism. The congressmen also reported back on "how difficult it is for an American president or any American administration to really have a direct and significant effect on events over there." More broadly, the congressmen believed that developments were taking on an "evolution-ary" progression. Changes and reforms were not going to occur quickly, so it was "awfully important for [the U.S. government] to try to figure out the right mix of both carrot and stick in order to affect events as best we can."[39]

In the first three months of 1982, the White House agreed on a pragmatic policy to use Poland's $26 billion international debt as diplomatic leverage rather than to declare default. The U.S. government even decided to pay the balance on loans in the face of substantial public criticism. This was a victory for pragmatists in the State Department. More generally, by broadening discussions from 1600 Pennsylvania Avenue to include voices from the legislative branch, the dynamics of decision making changed. More people and more voices were forcing themselves into the discussion on America's Poland policy.

## Propaganda Wars

With an eye toward the global Cold War, Washington looked for ways beyond sanctions to punish the Poles and particularly the Soviets, settling quickly on the possibilities for propaganda.[40] The United States was handed its first victory in this propaganda war when the Polish ambassador to the United States, Romuald Spasowski, called Deputy Assistant Secretary Jack Scanlan, seeking political asylum. Scanlan honored the request, and by the evening of December 20, Spasowski was in front of news cameras, condemn-ing the Jaruzelski government for declaring martial law and for placing so many professors and workers into prisons. Referring to the PZPR's "brutality and inhumanity," the ambassador explained that he had defected in solidar-ity with Wałęsa, explaining, "There is only one morality in the human fam-ily, the morality of people who live according to the principles of truth and justice. . . . It is this morality which shall prevail."[41] Two days later, Reagan met with Spasowski and his wife, expressing his gratitude and providing a tear-filled photo opportunity for the press corps.[42] For Reagan, "It was an emotional meeting for all of us and left me with more disgust than ever for the evil men in the Kremlin who believed they had the right to hold an entire nation in captivity."[43]

On the same day that Reagan met with Spasowski, the International Communications Agency (ICA) Advisory Board members discussed ways to condemn events in Warsaw. One member, Allen Weinstein, the executive di-rector of the *Washington Quarterly*, went so far as to say that "the U.S. needs to undertake 'ruthless politics of symbolism and moral gestures.'" Overall the group—including ICA director Charles Wick, career Foreign Service officer Len Baldyga, assistant to the president David Gergen, and the editor of *Commentary*, Norman Podhoretz—proposed thirty-three options. Among them, a single theme emerged: "To keep the media pot boiling" and to "create a great moral wave" against the human rights abuses.[44]

Ultimately, this media blitz took the form of a day to "Let Poland be Poland." By January 8, American diplomats began pressuring their European, Japanese, and Australian allies to take part in what was then called, "Light a Candle for the People of Poland" (reflecting language from the president's Christmas speech). Diplomats were asked to urge foreign leaders to videotape statements to be combined with footage of events in Poland and images of international protests against the declaration of martial law.[45] In the end, Wick spent between $350,000 and $450,000 of privately donated money to produce a ninety-minute program with statements from Reagan, Margaret Thatcher, Orson Welles, and Frank Sinatra, among others.

The results, however, were mixed. According to the State Department's analysis, "with reruns and new runs we anticipate that 50 countries and 300 million people will have seen 30 minutes or more. This is an historic high for any [U.S. government] information effort."[46] Analysis from outside the government, however, proved less rosy. A number of PBS stations declined to air the special. In Western Europe, most stations aired only thirty minutes of the program or simply showed highlights on the nightly news. The press also chided Washington for exploiting Polish suffering for obvious propaganda benefit. *Time* magazine called the international response to the program "mixed" and suggested that a star-studded television spectacular might be an "inappropriate response to military repression." The *New York Times* ran an article focusing on the international criticism sparked by the program, and the BBC declared it a "complete failure."[47]

More important than these short-term exercises, December 13 served as a catalyst for long-term changes in America's public diplomacy infrastructure. As a former broadcaster, Reagan believed in the power of radio and spoke about America's "neglected ability of communications."[48] Events in Poland galvanized bureaucratic support for international broadcasting efforts. Writing to Haig on December 30, 1981, Eagleburger pushed for action "to step up our radio broadcasting to Poland, the rest of East Europe, and the USSR."[49] Haig agreed and cosigned a memo to Reagan with Wick and Frank Shakespeare, the Bureau for International Broadcasting (BIB) chairman, arguing that the Polish crisis underlined the importance of radio broadcasting, which had been neglected during détente.[50]

This initiative reached full consensus on June 7, when Haig sent a draft National Security Decision Directive (NSDD) on international broadcasting to the Oval Office under the title, "Response to Martial Law: Modernization of Our International Radios." Reagan approved the draft on July 15 as NSDD 45. The decision directive prioritized improvement in programming and technical abilities in international broadcasting as high as "other programs deemed vital to the national security." The NSDD called for the Voice of America (VOA) and Radio Free Europe/Radio Liberty (RFE/RL) to "undertake a major, long-term program of modernization and expansion." Particular emphasis was placed on overcoming Soviet jamming, which had increased after December 13.[51]

On June 19, Reagan went public with this intensified policy on international broadcasting at a signing ceremony for Captive Nations Week. The president illustrated the impetus for his plan by mentioning a letter Solidarność leaders had sent about the "power of ideas and the effectiveness of broadcasting as their carrier." Reagan then called for rebuilding and modernizing RFE/RL and VOA. He concluded with trademark rhetorical flare: "The love of liberty, the fire of freedom burns on in Poland just as it burns on among all the peoples of the captive nations. To the leaders of Solidarity, to the people of Poland, to all those who are denied freedom, we send a message today: Your cause is not lost."[52]

Events in Poland provided a similar impetus for Congress to pass an official budgetary request for the BIB (which controlled the RFE/RL budget). For fiscal year (FY) 1983 the administration asked for a $13.2 million supplement, an increase of almost 15 percent. Wick and his deputies in RFE/RL, Jim Buckley and Ben Wattenberg, testified to Congress that Soviet actions in Poland and Afghanistan were the main reasons for the needed modernization. Supplementary materials also argued that RFE/RL required immediate funds because Soviet jamming efforts had increased "measurably . . . in the wake of turmoil in Poland."[53] The push worked. In addition to the supplement, RFE/RL received $21.3 million specifically for facility modernization and enhanced programming in 1983, as well as another increase in its annual appropriation.[54]

The Reagan administration came into office with a desire to intensify propaganda against the Communist bloc. This was an uncontroversial viewpoint, shared by ideological Cold Warriors and pragmatists. Events in Poland, however, invigorated the White House's predisposition. Martial law was the catalyst behind NSDD 45 and allowed Reagan to concretely increase funding for RFE/RL. Without martial law, the executive branch may well have pursued these policies, but the president's urgency and public arguments would have taken a very different form. More centrally, in the months following December 1981, Poland's shadow began to stretch further across Washington, affecting how, when, and why policies were debated and implemented.[55]

## Humanitarian Aid

Martial law also forced Reagan to engage with nongovernmental organizations to ensure that sanctions did not spark a humanitarian crisis. Reagan wanted sanctions to penalize the regime, not the common people. Humanitarian and charitable groups coordinating with the U.S. government had, in fact, spearheaded a food program for Poland since early 1981. In March 1981, Pope John Paul II called on Catholics to send food to Poland, where shortages and rationing were becoming facts of everyday life. Cardinal John Krol, the archbishop of Philadelphia, met with Spasowski shortly thereafter to discuss American aid. CARE, Catholic Relief Services (CRS), and Project HOPE (a group specializing in medical aid and equipment) also heeded the pope's request. The PZPR responded by signing Politburo Decision 26/81, which opened the way for Western charitable groups by promising "to deliver such gifts from overseas benefactors intended for the specific agencies." The Polish American Congress (PAC), the national organizational and lobbying group for Polish American fraternal organizations and charities, also began a drive called "Tribute to Poland."[56] By the end of July 1981, the PAC had raised more than half a million dollars, spent on food packages for adults and families with babies distributed individually and purchased through CARE, as well as on hygiene and diabetes medicines distributed through Project HOPE.[57]

Further aid came through CRS. In May Reverend Terrance J. Mulkerin, CRS's coordinator for disaster and relief services, traveled to Poland to make contacts. By the end of August, CRS was "finalizing an agreement with the U.S. Department of Agriculture to purchase at favorable prices dairy products— milk, cheese, butter—for shipment to Poland."[58] Following Father Mulkerin's second trip in September 1981 to meet with Cardinal Glemp, American embassy officials, and bureaucrats from the Ministry of Health, CRS finalized the outline for a "Family Feeding Program" to distribute just under $15 million in AID wheat flour, rice, and vegetable oil. The materials sailed to Gdańsk on vessels paid for by the Catholic Church and the Polish government. From there it was handed over to the Charitable Commission of the Polish Episcopate (Komisja Charytatywna Episkopatu Polski or KCEP), which distributed the food to each of Poland's twenty-seven Catholic dioceses. Aid was distributed at the parish level by local priests to the elderly and to "families with young children who would find it physically difficult to wait in lines or economically difficult to purchase food."[59] In a nearly homogenous Catholic society where parish priests saw most people weekly and habitually visited each family in their parish (Catholic or not) at least once a year, this dispersal program provided near complete coverage. By December 10, 1981, CRS had responded to urgent requests for aid by "shipping 16,921,128 lbs. of food valued at a total of $10,181,512.89."[60]

After December 13, need grew under the strains of military rule. Price increases were quickly approved, causing food costs to rise an average of 241 percent, and fuel and energy to rise 171 percent. All of this lowered Poles' real incomes by 32 percent in 1982.[61] Rationing, empty shelves, and long lines became a fact of life.[62] To make matters worse, the winter of 1981–82 turned harsh, particularly in the Płock area about seventy-five miles northwest of Warsaw, where devastating floods occurred after ice dams formed on the Wisła (Vistula) River. Voluntary organizations, however, responded decisively. By mid-January 1982, CRS and CARE had raised $3.7 million in cash and $1.5 million in private donations; CARE planned to send dairy products valued at $29 million in 1982, in addition to about twenty thousand food packages in February 1982 alone. In January 1982, CRS shipped about one million pounds of food and clothing every two weeks. Catholic Relief Services also purchased truck tires, truck batteries, and spare parts to service the government-owned trucks that delivered materials around the country.[63] Smaller organizations like the protestant Church World Services and Lutheran World Relief shipped blankets, quilts, clothing, and hygienic items like water purification tablets and soap.[64] As the *Christian Science Monitor* reported: "[Humanitarian aid officials] agree that as Poland's difficulties have increased, so has the generosity of contributors. Since the crackdown, says an official of the Boston bank which handles contributions to the Polish Relief Fund, 'the response has just been outstanding.'"[65]

The U.S. government's humanitarian response, however, was not as clear cut as it searched for a way to walk the line between punishing Poland's government and supporting its people. From the beginning Reagan had been adamant that the U.S. government needed to continue humanitarian aid shipments,[66] but it was unclear how this would be balanced against sanctions. The early announcement on December 14 that consideration of

$740 million in long-term agricultural aid through direct U.S. government subsidies from the CCC to the Polish government would be suspended meant that government-to-government programs were severed.[67] However, the Reagan administration agreed that private-sector humanitarian programs could continue. Specifically, $30 million of indirect Food for Peace aid already promised to CRS and CARE was maintained.[68] On December 15, Senate Foreign Relations Committee staffers contacted Father Mulkerin to talk about reprogramming the $100 million in suspended direct CCC aid (the poultry feed) into Title II aid that could be distributed privately.[69] Members of the European and economic bureaus of the Department of State also contemplated replacing the poultry feed with $100 million in indirect humanitarian aid. The final memorandum to the president proposing increased aid, however, made clear that legally the U.S. government could not simply replace the $100 million in suspended CCC credits with an equivalent amount in Title II funds: any increase in humanitarian aid required a supplemental appropriation, not just a reprogramming of preapproved funds.[70]

As the discussion moved to the White House, a final decision became embroiled in concerns about extracting political concessions from the PZPR. On January 14, Philip Johnston, the executive director of CARE, briefed State Department officials on his recent trip to Poland and presented a letter from Jaruzelski requesting $100 million worth of feed grain to be overseen by CARE. To receive this large of a package, Johnston was told that the PZPR would have to agree to two conditions: lifting martial law and releasing political prisoners.[71] When Johnston met with Walter Stoessel on February 26, CARE's executive director learned that the proposal for feed grain had been rejected. A secondary request for $60 million to help support small private farmers was also rejected.[72] Ambassador Meehan had spoken with officials in Warsaw about Johnston's proposals, but the Poles were not willing to lift martial law or release detainees to gain access to feed grain. As Holmes summarized, "we remain at square one."[73]

Catholic Relief Services simultaneously worked to increase its government-sponsored programs, with little progress. On January 8, CRS sent a "Generic Grant Proposal" to the State Department with requests for $3.5 million of food, diapers, and formula for children, and spare parts and fertilizer for farmers.[74] When Father Mulkerin attended a meeting of the Task Force on Poland in Washington, D.C., on March 9, he inquired about requests for increased Food for Peace aid and CCC help, but he left the meeting with "very negative vibes. . . . It [seemed] obvious to us that there [was] no urgent desire to approve either of the two programs . . . : in fact, a number of exquisitely bureaucratic reasons why the [Food for Peace and CCC] programs should not be approved were presented. . . . Unless high level intervention is forthcoming the final answer will be negative."[75]

While the White House stalled, CRS struggled forward. Father Mulkerin visited Poland again from April 22 to May 24 to meet with KCEP colleagues, other Western aid organizations, government officials, and American embassy staff. Mulkerin reported back that in the first quarter of 1982, KCEP had successfully distributed huge amounts of aid: 4,277,000 packages of butter, 1,134,000 packages of cheese, 1,383,750 packages of dried milk, 754,000 rations of wheat flour, 1,152,300 rations of rice, and 1,648,500 rations of vegetable oil. Yet this was still not enough: KCEP asked CRS to increase programs for infants, providing hard-to-find items like diapers, cotton shirts, rubber pants, layettes, bottles, and nipples. Catholic Relief Services responded by writing another grant proposal to provide materials for children and infants, as well as an "Emergency Program to the Płock region" for families and farmers hit by the January flood.[76]

When Father Mulkerin returned to CRS headquarters in New York at the end of May, the bureaucratic process in Washington had finally concluded. According to a draft written by an interagency group studying humanitarian aid, the decision to provide increased aid was political, not humanitarian. People were not starving, nor were they on the brink of starvation: "Despite the gloomy economic situation and outlook . . . Poland's situation is not so poor that it would meet the normal criteria for granting of [Title II food] aid." But, as the report argued, humanitarian aid offered certain political advantages: "Our assistance is widely visible in Poland, undermining regime propaganda and providing material evidence of Western support for Solidarity and the Church." These efforts "would help refute European criticism of sanctions and the view that Poland is a screen for a U.S. policy of confrontation with the Soviets. Our assistance also undermines Soviet propaganda portraying themselves as the only true friends of Polish workers."[77]

These political arguments found support within the White House. By the end of May the president had authorized $60 million in aid, targeted toward needy children, the elderly, and handicapped people. Of this, $23.7 million was marked for the rest of fiscal year 1982, with $37.5 million in the first quarter of fiscal year 1983.[78] Enough Title II assistance would go to CRS and CARE for Poland to maintain the programs' current levels through the end of December 1982, "with the understanding that the program[s] . . . would be continued through the balance of FY 1983 at a total not to exceed $40.0 million." The president also approved $5 million for Project HOPE.[79]

Six months after the declaration of martial law, nongovernmental organizations were utilizing U.S. government funds to alleviate humanitarian needs. The final program was not as large as the $100 million agricultural aid package that had been agreed to before martial law, but neither had Poland been completely cut off. Meat, protein, and luxury goods remained scarce, but the country had enough vegetables and grain to feed its population. American governmental aid combined with private donations and other Western European aid eased hardship, but the picture remained bleak. According to Mulkerin, the grain harvest in 1982 represented a significant shortfall from even the previous year, sugar beet and potato production were down, and the broiler chicken industry no longer existed because of distress slaughtering. He concluded, "The target groups we serve continue to be in need. The food supply situation has deteriorated."[80]

Representatives of CRS were disappointed at the level of U.S. government support. They saw a larger need than they were able to serve. However, the White House was successfully walking the tightrope, balancing punishing the Polish government against supporting its people. Washington ensured that the public was not in danger of starving, but no attempt was made to flood the country with new aid to fulfill all needs. Funding was appropriated for humanitarian purposes because both the public and the administration felt strongly that the Polish people should not be abandoned. The United States had rewarded Poland for its steps toward greater pluralism before the introduction of martial law; now was no time to revoke that commitment to the Polish people. Humanitarian aid after December 13 also fulfilled political goals. Officials supported continued funding to CARE, CRS, and Project HOPE because it played well in the Western press, counteracted Polish propaganda, and showed that economic sanctions were not meant to punish the Polish people but were aimed at the Polish government and its supporters in Moscow.

## The Growth of Conspiracy

As Poles acclimatized to their new, harsher reality under martial law, Solidarność rebuilt. Operations to capture Solidarność leaders and clashes between strikers and the authorities had been violent and often brutal, but they had not destroyed either Solidarność or the larger opposition movement. One of the most widespread signs of resistance was the explosion of antigovernment graffiti, with slogans like "The winter is yours but the spring will be ours," "CDN" (the Polish acronym for "to be continued"), or just simply painting the name Solidarność in its easily recognizable script.

Large numbers of people also embraced more subtle forms of protest: placing lighted candles in windows on the thirteenth of every month and taking long strolls during evening newscasts on state-sponsored television.[81]

Activists also continued to print and distribute *niezależny* (independently printed) publications: illegal flyers, pamphlets, and weeklies. Protest flyers and pamphlets popped up immediately, often printed in shops where workers first held occupation strikes. After strikes were broken, opposition activists created new (or revitalized existing) underground presses to produce huge numbers of weekly newssheets and journals. The most famous of the independent weeklies included *Z dnia na dzień* (*From Day to Day*) from Wrocław, *Observator Wielkopolski* (*Wielkopolska Observer*) from Poznań, *Biuletyn Małopolski* (*Małopolska Bulletin*) from Kraków, *Głos Wolnego Hutnika* (*Voice of the Free Steel Worker*) from Nowa Huta, and *Wola* (*Will*), *Tygodnik Wojenny* (*Wartime Weekly*), and *Tygodnik Mazowsze* (*Mazowsze Weekly*) from Warsaw. *Tygodnik Mazowsze* became the most widely produced and circulated publication, serving as the major outlet for pronouncements from the remaining Solidarność structures.[82]

Entire underground printing "houses" functioned under martial law. The most well known and important were CDN, NOWa (Niezależna Oficyjna Wydawnicza, or Official Independent Publishing House), and Krąg. Krąg had operated since 1977, NOWa was the most significant independent publisher prior to December 13, and CDN was a new creation. Both Krąg and NOWa had existing connections to the West: NOWa had signed a publishing agreement with the Polish émigré periodical *Kultura*, run by Jerzy Giedroyc in Paris, and Krąg had a similar agreement with ANEKS publishers, run by Eugeniusz Smolar in London. In the first months of 1982, each of these underground houses began producing books and independent weeklies. All three houses published *Tygodnik Mazowsze*, although NOWa was the first to do so. Krąg published *Wola*, *Kos-a* (*Committee for Social Resistance*), and *Tu Teraz* (*Here Now*), while CDN published *Wiadomości Dnia* (*News of the Day*), and *CDN-Głos Wolnego Robotnika* (*Free Worker's Voice*).[83] With these major houses and numerous individual activists throughout the country, illegal, independent, underground periodicals grew to an epidemic. According to one estimate, "during the course of 1982 at least eight hundred illegal periodicals appeared."[84] Building on information-exchange relationships with publishers begun in the 1970s, Radio Free Europe's Polish Section "devoted hour after hour" to rebroadcasting "underground essays and manifestoes of the democratic opposition," substantively increasing the reach of the presses' own distribution networks.[85]

As independent publishing grew, Solidarność's central organs reorganized. On the night of December 12, 1981, government forces captured around six thousand Solidarność activists, including most national leaders who were meeting in Gdańsk, a shattering blow to the trade union's national organization. On a local level, however, regional strike committees remained intact. A handful of well-known Solidarność leaders evaded capture and lived an underground existence, relying on friends and coconspirators to hide. Five of the most important, nationally known Solidarność leaders who eluded capture were Bogdan Lis and Bogdan Boruszewicz from Gdańsk, Władysław Frasyniuk from Wrocław, Władysław Hardek from Kraków, and Zbigniew Bujak from Warsaw.

In their new underground life, each of these leaders worked to recreate a national structure of Solidarność. In the first days after December 13, Wrocław and the surrounding region of Dolny Śląsk was able to maintain the strongest regional organization, so Frasyniuk was first to approach other regional leaders. Through his close confidante, Barbara Labuda, Frasyniuk sent messages to Hardek and Bujak about coordinating a national strike to force the government to release internees, end martial law, and push for the reemergence of Solidarność.[86] This, however, led to the first of what became innumerable disagreements over tactics. Bujak responded to Frasyniuk and Lis, arguing that the opposition should have a decentralized, informal structure that would focus on supporting internees and their families, distributing independent press, collecting and exchanging information, and developing a means to affect public opinion. Bujak's formulation would gradually create a nationwide movement based on passive resistance and civil disobedience. While Frasyniuk called for swift, large-scale retaliation, Bujak advocated a "long march" toward reform.[87]

This was a debate about both tactics and goals. A nationwide strike necessitated a more cohesive, hierarchical organization with strong ties to industrial plants and workers who would follow the lead of a central authority. The long-march approach would be much less centralized, allowing for loose coordination between autonomous groups. The more centralized leadership advocated by Frasyniuk could be infiltrated more easily by the security services, causing the whole structure to be exposed, rather than just a single cell.[88]

The debate over tactics and goals continued in February and March, a slow process given that letters could only be sent through trusted couriers. In early April 1982, Frasyniuk and Bujak exchanged correspondence, in which Frasyniuk argued that any new organization's name should reflect their "temporary" situation, until the trade union could be resurrected. He also wrote that the organizations did not have to provide specifics about their goals; people already knew what Solidarność stood for. On the issue of tactics, Bujak argued that the new body need not be the source for answers to every problem. On April 20, Bujak, Hardek, Lis, and Frasyniuk met secretly in a villa in the Żoliborz neighborhood of Warsaw to create a new national body: the Interim Coordinating Commission (Tymczasowa Komisja Koordynacyjna, or TKK).[89] The TKK's first announcement provided few details other than that the committee had been created to coordinate among their four regions and to fight for an end to martial law, a release of internees and prisoners, and the return of citizen's rights. The announcement also declared that the group was a temporary structure, until the NSZZ Solidarność trade union could be reconstituted with Lech Wałęsa at its head.

In interviews published in *Tygodnik Mazowsze*, Bujak, Frasyniuk, Hardek, and Lis expanded on their thoughts for founding the TKK. Frasyniuk and Hardek called for a strong organization that could coordinate among disparate opposition groups to prove the people's continuing power to the authorities. Both Lis and Bujak underlined the need for society and the government to negotiate, for the country to move toward a normalized relationship between the state and the people, and for the government to take steps that would allow Poland to acquire new money and new credits from the West to get Poland's economy moving again.[90]

To demonstrate the movement's continued strength, Solidarność activists and supporters took to the streets on May 1. Thousands of activists in most major cities gathered to counter-demonstrate against official rallies. May Day demonstrations were large in Solidarność's traditional strongholds in Gdańsk, Wrocław, and Kraków, but the single largest crowd of about thirty thousand appeared in front of the Old Town Castle in Warsaw to chant slogans, hear speeches, and sing national hymns. The authorities appeared caught off guard by these counterdemonstrations and most proceeded peacefully.[91] When ten thousand demonstrators appeared in Warsaw's Old Town two days later on May 3, the anniversary of the signing of Poland's first democratic constitution in 1791, riot police came out in force, dispersing the crowds with water cannons, tear gas, and truncheons. Similar incidents took place throughout the country.[92] The unrest continued on May 13, when the TKK called for a fifteen-minute nationwide strike. Again the regime reacted forcefully, firing at least eleven hundred workers and taking administrative actions against others. As the U.S. Defense Intelligence Agency concluded, these events "clearly exhibited the depth of feeling among Poles against martial law and the degree to which opposition, particularly Solidarity, could still guide the dissent of large numbers of workers and citizens. . . . [The events] were all remarkable shows of force against a regime committed to suppress such activities."[93] Yet with so many leaders still interned, the future of Solidarność remained uncertain.

## Western Support for Conspiracy

With a revitalized opposition movement, groups of émigré Poles, Solidarność activists trapped outside Poland, and sympathetic individuals from the West began to take steps to send covert aid. The highest-profile American group supporting Solidarność was the AFL-CIO. Even before events in the Lenin Shipyards in 1980, Lane Kirkland "had long been convinced that ordinary working people, and not diplomats, would bring about Communism's demise." More simply, two movements that Kirkland felt passionately about—anticommunism and free trade unionism—converged in Solidarność.[94] Shortly after the Gdańsk Accords, Kirkland announced the creation of the Polish Workers Aid Fund (PWAF)—which was given an initial donation of $25,000—to support Solidarność monetarily.[95] By November 1981, the PWAF had raised nearly $250,000 from private donations, T-shirt sales, individual union donations, and shop floor collections.[96]

For guidance on how to spend these funds, the AFL-CIO turned to Solidarność itself. Charles Kassman, an International Confederation of Free Trade Unions (ICFTU) representative, sent the first report about Solidarność's needs following a trip to Warsaw and Gdańsk from September 9 to 15, 1980. Wałęsa had heard about Kirkland's $25,000 pledge and was "skeptical of large financial contributions at the time being." As Kassman reported, "It is obvious that the AFL-CIO's gift of $25,000 has created problems for the Committee. They will probably have difficulties in explaining to the authorities what the money will be used for and that it is not proof of a conspiracy between Gdańsk and the USA. The sum has not yet been accepted." Wałęsa did, however, ask for donations of "practical" support in the form of office equipment, specifically duplicating machines, writing paper, and carbon paper.[97] AFL-CIO representatives from the A. Philip Randolph Education Fund confirmed these requests when they met with Wałęsa in late spring 1981. They are quoted as saying, "financial aid can be a delicate matter, because it could be regarded that we are financed by somebody." However, "there was general agreement that what [was] most needed [were] . . . items not purchasable in Poland, such as printing presses, cameras, mimeograph machines."[98] Funds from the AFL-CIO distributed prior to December 13, 1981, were used precisely as Wałęsa requested: for the mundane matters of office and printing supplies.[99]

After the declaration of martial law, Kirkland remained staunchly committed to Solidarność. He unequivocally condemned the imposition of martial law, blaming both the PZPR and the Soviets. Federation statements also supported robust sanctions against both countries. Further, Kirkland proclaimed that his organization would do whatever it could: "Poland's working men and women are struggling against tremendous odds to build and maintain a trade union. Their battle is ours. We shall not let them down." Again, the AFL-CIO deferred to Solidarność for guidance.[100]

In the week after December 13, the AFL-CIO also spoke with members of the Reagan administration seeking common interests. On December 15, State Department officials met with AFL-CIO Secretary Treasurer Tom Donohue, Executive Assistant to the President Ken Young, and Special Assistant for International Affairs Dale Good. After a briefing on what the administration knew, the government officials asked if there was a chance that members of the Polish government searching Solidarność offices might find "any written communications . . . which could be an embarrassment to either [AFL-CIO or Solidarność] and which could provide fuel for Polish government propaganda." Donohue assured them that everything would be "straightforward" and that there had been nothing of a "covert" nature.[101] On December 18, Reagan met with Kirkland. The president greeted him by joking, "Well, at least we have something we can agree on." Kirkland responded, however, by calling for a sharp American reaction to martial law, including tough economic sanctions and declaring default. Kirkland also mentioned that the union was looking into sending support through existing channels. "We'll use whatever resources we can," he added, "but whatever [additional] resources could be provided [by the government] would be [helpful]."[102] Meetings between AFL-CIO and government officials continued during the following few months, at which the administration coordinated policy with the union to help push both domestic and European public opinion toward accepting sanctions on Poland and the USSR.[103] Even after Reagan's sanctions announcement, however, Kirkland and his deputies called for even tougher economic and political policies.

Another essential nongovernmental group that joined the fight to protect free trade unions was the Committee in Support of Solidarity (CSS). This organization was founded in New York City on December 14, 1981, to gather information and to inform the American public, the U.S. government,

A gathering of CSS's staff and volunteers on the balcony of their office at 275 Seventh Avenue in New York City in the summer of 1982. Among those pictured are Martyna Szałańska (2nd from left), Irena Lasota (holding the top left corner of the banner), Jerzy Warman (kneeling), Jakub Karpiński (to the right of Lasota), Piotr Naimski, Chris Wilcox (center), Paweł Nasalski (5th from right), Eric Chenoweth (2nd from right), and Jan Kalinowski. Photo courtesy of Eric Chenoweth and the Committee in Support of Solidarity.

and international bodies about repression against Polish society as well as Solidarność's resistance to the Communist regime.[104] As a less public goal, the CSS was also formed for "maintaining contact with Solidarity."[105] The group's members included sympathetic Americans like Eric Chenoweth; opposition leaders stranded in the United States, including Mirosław Chojecki (head of NOWa), Piotr Naimski (a member of KOR), and later Wacek Adamczak (a member of Solidarność's National Commission) and Mirosław Dominczyk (a National Commission member and chairman of the Kielce Region); as well as émigré Poles who had been active in the democratic opposition in the 1960s and 1970s, like Irena Lasota and Jakub Karpiński. The committee was also well connected to American Polonia and to American trade unionists. Émigré writers Stanisław Barańczak and Czesław Miłosz, as well as the philosopher Leszek Kołakowski, all signed CSS's first press release. The group's executive director Chenoweth had been employed by the

Polish Workers' Task Force of the League for Industrial Democracy, where CSS had its first offices. In addition, Tom Kahn, the AFL-CIO's international affairs department director, and Arch Puddington, the director of the League for Industrial Democracy, sat on CSS's board. By January 1982, Kahn and Kirkland had agreed to take a direct stake in CSS by paying the group's Telex bills and for Chojecki to travel to Belgium.[106]

At the end of 1981, Chojecki traveled to Brussels to meet with other Solidarność activists who had been stranded in the West. A group of about thirty met in Zurich on December 19 and then in Brussels on January 8–9. Following this second meeting, Magda Wojcik, the former assistant head of the international department of Solidarność, sent a letter to international unions asking for assistance to set up Solidarność information offices. It had "been agreed that no 'Solidarity in Exile' is formed but that in every country where there are members of our Union they all should come together and work jointly in an 'Information Office of Solidarność.'"[107] As of December 22, 1981, Krzystyna Ruchniewicza had created one such group in Brussels. Sławomir Czarlewski and Seweryn Blumsztajn also started a Solidarność Co-ordinating Committee in Paris that had soon raised 8 million francs (about $1 million) from French trade unions.[108]

Following this initial decision to create national information offices, word reached activists in the West that the TKK wanted to create a central office to coordinate foreign contacts. On July 1, 1982, Lis sent a letter calling for activists to create a single office in Brussels under the leadership of Jerzy Milewski, a member of the National Commission who had political organizing experience. This decision was (and remains) controversial within the émigré community because it undermined the activities of some of the offices that had already been founded (particularly the one in Paris). Solidarność activists ultimately accepted the decision, however, because it was "justified from a political point of view as well as the necessity for arranging a central structure authorized to maintain contacts with central unions and procure funds from them for the union's underground activity."[109]

The creation of the Solidarność Coordinating Office Abroad was announced in a July 18 press release, after a meeting in Oslo "with an explicit mandate from the authorities of Solidarność in Poland." The Brussels office's main tasks were the "1) coordination of effective and wide support for the Union in Poland, 2) cooperation with trade unions and their international organizations, and 3) coordination of activities intended to inform the public about the actual conditions faced by ISTU 'Solidarność.'" Office staff included Bohdan Cywinski (ideological and political matters), Ruchniewicz (finances), Milewski (director and contact with trade unions), Chojecki (co-ordination of aid to Solidarność in Poland), Czarlewski (coordination of aid to Solidarność in Poland), and Blumsztajn (information).[110] The Solidarność Coordinating Office Abroad opened its doors in Brussels on July 29, 1982, with a branch office in Paris.[111]

On August 1, Milewski sent his first communication to Kirkland, outlin-ing the new office's role and requesting support from his brothers in inter-national trade unions. Generally, the trade union's tactics for moving toward a peaceful solution to the "socioeconomic crisis" were to "show restraint in its demands and willingness to reach a compromise with the authorities," while simultaneously "demonstrate[ing] to the authorities the strength of Solidarność . . . [by] preparing various actions and short strikes." The co-ordinating office was given responsibility "for the rapid delivery of large amounts of printing and radio equipment, as well as funds, to all parts of Poland." Milewski asked the AFL-CIO to help pay for the coordinating bu-reau's expected annual operating fee of $175,000 and to help provide part of the $800,000 needed to purchase the necessary "material and equipment (photographic, broadcasting, communications, printing, etc.)."[112] The AFL-CIO was not able to provide the entire operating budget, but it did send smaller amounts of support.[113]

Although the AFL-CIO was supportive of Solidarność's new office, the union also created its own channels to run aid overseen by CSS codirector Irena Lasota. Initially Lasota sent material to her friends and contacts in the opposition in parcels disguised as care packages. They included censored books and small amounts of cash (in American dollars) hidden in common objects. Disguising contraband remained an essential part of the task: to aid independent publishers, Lasota purchased containers of Hershey's syrup, emptied the contents, cleaned them, and refilled them with printing ink. Because there were so many care packages sent by well-meaning Americans, Lasota assumed that the government could not possible search all incoming mail, ensuring that a fair amount of support arrived at its intended destina-tions.[114] Lasota and the CSS also sent specific communications and electronic equipment needed by the opposition. The details of the operation remain sparse, but on June 18, 1982, Lasota sent receipts to the AFL-CIO for under $500, for one 14–812 audio recorder, two adapter cassette recorders, two ac-cessory tapes, and transistors from Alpine Radio and Television Corp. As agreed to previously with the AFL-CIO, the materials had already been sent to Poles who had asked Lasota for them.[115] These first steps were small but important because the AFL-CIO had established lines of communication through CSS to send materials requested by the democratic opposition. The American conspiracy to support Solidarność had begun in earnest.

West European unions were also quick to support Solidarność as it emerged in the underground. From Spain to Sweden, trade unions had been captivated by the Polish crisis, and they spearheaded the huge marches and protests that occurred throughout Europe in mid-December 1981 (see chapter 1). All condemned the imposition of martial law and worked to increase humanitarian aid, including the West German Trade Union Confederation, which sent some 972 tons of humanitarian aid in the first year and a half of martial law. Some unions made symbolic gestures, like Spaniards who unfurled three Solidarność banners during the singing of the Soviet national anthem at a 1982 World Cup match between Poland and the USSR. Many like the Italian Confederation of Workers Trade Union combined humanitarian missions with material support, like "radio components, offsets, copying machines, ink (hidden in tomato cans), and books" sent through regular couriers. As a neighbor just across the Baltic from Gdańsk, Sweden served as a key transit point for West European support to Solidarność both before December 1981 and after, with the Trade Union Confederation of Sweden having about $300,000 on hand in January 1982 to support the underground opposition, as well as a broader campaign to send food supplies in the first year. The French Democratic Labor Confederation along with other French unions proved to be Solidardanosc's most significant benefactors during martial law, providing political support by holding regular "Solidarity Days" to raise awareness, organizing summer holidays for Polish children to visit France, and raising more than $1.6 million by March 1982 to support Solidarność through the Coordinating Office and individual unions—focused particularly on printing and communication equipment, humanitarian items, and cash to help fired workers.[116] The movement to support Solidarność in the underground was a transnational phenomenon.

## Developments in the Polish Communist Party

For Jaruzelski and his colleagues, their main concern during 1982 was not what was happening externally, but rather what was transpiring within the country's borders. In early January, the general centralized power in a directorate of seven PZPR members, including himself, Minister of Internal Affairs Czesław Kiszczak, Deputy Defense Minister Florian Siwicki, Deputy Prime Minister Mieczysław Rakowski, and three Central Committee members. In politburo meetings during the first three months of 1982, the leadership focused almost exclusively on reforming the economy, and on purging and strengthening the party. To reinvigorate the Communist Party *aktiv*, the group spent significant time drafting a paper, "O co walczymy, dokąd zmierzamy" ("What we are struggling for, where we are heading").[117] Economic reforms were launched as part of a "First Stage" of economic revitalization and included "a considerable broadening of enterprise autonomy, the abolition of intermediate management units, a greater role for market mechanisms, the abolition of restrictions on the private sector in small-scale industry, and an end to the underprivileged status of private agriculture vis-à-vis cooperatives and the state farms."[118] Political reforms initiated a Patriotic Movement of National Rebirth (PRON) to take over for the Front of National Unity in an attempt to reinvigorate government structures and increase the party's popular legitimacy by creating "the appearance of a ruling coalition."[119] Although efforts to transform Polish society were the government's main focus, they were not very effective. Jaruzelski and other leaders were constantly claiming to be reforming the system, but "the techniques of government were completely identical to the old methods." The political and economic reforms introduced only reworked old ideas and rehashed failed attempts. No bold steps were actually taken, creating a pattern of "change without change."[120]

Although international affairs were considerably less important than internal improvements, the PZPR did engage with the outside world. In addition to a visit from Hungarian communists (see chapter 1), Jaruzelski and members of his inner circle traveled within the bloc to request increased economic support. Jaruzelski's first trip out of Poland after December was to Moscow on March 1–2. On the first day he spoke with Brezhnev and high-level leaders about the internal situation and the steps taken since introducing martial law. The bilateral portions of the meeting focused on "manifestations of full understanding" to show Soviet approval of Jaruzelski's decisions, questions of economic help, and proclamations about "opening a new era in the development of close relations and cooperation between our parties and nations after the difficult period triggered by the Polish crisis." Jaruzelski also proposed specific economic initiatives: long-term credits worth $1 billion, one million tons of crude oil, 250,000 tons of grain in the second quarter of 1982, making Soviet raw materials available to Polish industries, and considering the idea of building a gas pipeline to the West through Poland.[121] Lower-level Polish and Soviet officials also negotiated a general agreement for developing Poland's economy during the coming few years, focused on projects to exploit Poland's industrial potential, create tighter connections with Soviet industry, and "make Poland's economy independent from the capitalist countries."[122] When the PZPR international department produced a final report, the outcome became clear: "Strengthening and expanding Polish-Soviet economic and scientific-technical cooperation should have primary [*zapewniony*] priority."[123]

For his second trip, Jaruzelski visited Budapest. This afforded him the opportunity to hear again that imposing martial law was the right decision. The Hungarian Communist Party leader János Kádár also briefed the Poles on Hungary's internal situation: its economy, its problems with the Catholic Church, and its foreign debt. Kádár explained Hungary's decentralized economic model and entertained Jaruzelski's calls for greater bilateral economic cooperation. No specific agreements were signed, but general possibilities of increased coal shipments from Poland and long-term cooperation to produce buses were discussed. Jaruzelski made clear to Kádár that he saw Hungary as an example to be emulated. While Hungary's economic system was flawed, its mix of decentralization and private initiative offered the best working example of a successful socialist economy in Central Europe; ideas for revitalizing the Polish economy in the wake of martial law were drawn from Hungarian experiences with its New Economic Mechanism. Beyond economics, the Poles wanted to understand the Hungarians' "exit from the 1956 crisis, especially in areas like winning back society, the press, the intelligentsia, and youth trust."[124]

Other PZPR officials traveled throughout the Socialist bloc. From March 24 to 26, politburo member Marian Woźniak and directors from the PZPR foreign and economics departments visited Yugoslavia, looking for economic help (corn, truck batteries, and nickel).[125] Politburo member and Minister of Foreign Affairs Józef Czyrek made short trips to visit Erich Honeker in East Berlin and Gustav Husák in Prague on March 29 and April 4. Again, the fraternal leaders praised their Polish guests, and the allies planned to intensify economic cooperation, a demonstrable shift from the tense bilateral relations before December 1981.[126]

These trips show a clear reevaluation of Poland's foreign policy. Poland turned toward the socialist world in the aftermath of December 13. The PZPR took no initiatives to engage with the West. Rather than pressing on with previous policies and seeking to undercut American sanctions by working with sympathetic Western economies like West Germany, the PZPR reoriented the country's economy toward the East as its chosen path to recovery. According to one politburo report, "The key issue for resuscitating our economy, in most of its industries, is the intensification of production for export. . . . Cooperation with the USSR and other socialist countries has essential significance." The report also highlighted economic relations with nonaligned, developing nations. Hopes for improved trade with the West, however, were placed at a minimum. The Poles believed that their policies prior to December 1981 had led to an "irrational" situation in which they had relied too extensively on capitalist goods and technology; the time had come to reorient their economy. Economic relations with the Soviet Union and the Communist bloc were given the highest priority by strengthening commitments and coordination through Comecon.[127] Because of Poland's inability to pay its debts and Western sanctions, the possibilities of an influx of new investment from public and private sources in the West were remote and improbable. Therefore the PZPR chose to pursue limited opportunities domestically and within the Socialist bloc.

For some in Washington this was the desired response, but it also limited American options. Pipes, from the NSC, Assistant Secretary of Defense Perle, Defense Secretary Weinberger, and DCI Bill Casey had backed economic sanctions as part of their global strategy to wage economic warfare against Moscow. From their perspectives, sanctions were designed to punish Jaruzelski *and* to draw more resources from the Soviets. In this sense, sanctions succeeded. In another sense, however, economic sanctions had a detrimental effect. By pulling away from reliance on the West, Jaruzelski decreased Western leverage. Politically and especially militarily the United States had little influence. Prior to December 1981, all meaningful connections were based on trade and economic policies that had blossomed during détente. America's most effective pressure points had been to offer credits, aid, and favorable terms either on new loans or on rescheduled debt. By turning East, Jaruzelski decreased American influence. As the CIA put it, "Sanctions will tend to make Warsaw more dependent on Moscow and its CMEA partners. Jaruzelski is thus faced with the choice of presiding over a deeper and more permanent integration of the Polish economy into that of the Soviet Union or undertaking the political measures necessary for the lifting of sanctions."[128] Jaruzelski and his colleagues in the politburo took the first option. Sanctions effectively punished Poland; the country's economic condition clearly showed that. But this came at a cost to long-standing economic links with the West.

The Poles also isolated themselves politically by taking a provocative line against the United States. In meeting after meeting with American officials, representatives from the MSZ berated their American counterparts with complaints. Numerous MSZ officials objected to American statements regarding Poland's internal situation, mimicking the Soviet line on sovereignty as codified by the Helsinki Final Act. Jan Kinast from the MSZ also regularly and vociferously protested RFE broadcasts.[129] In the days after December 13 the Polish Section of RFE increased its broadcast time to run twenty-four hours a day and shifted programming away from entertainment and music to focus on news, with an estimated 17 million Poles listening at least once a month.[130] This included rebroadcasting information from underground publications, which the PZPR leadership considered tantamount to "'instructing and inspiring' an anti-government conspiracy." As protests and strikes broke out around the country in May, RFE not only reported on clashes between the opposition and the authorities but announced in advance the times and places of demonstrations, an activity the MSZ condemned as "disguised 'incitement' of Poles to disobey the communist authorities."[131]

The Poles also took steps to antagonize American diplomats, doing whatever they could to punish the United States on the ground in Warsaw, Poznań, and Kraków. Herbert Wilgis lodged formal complaints with the MSZ Department III Vice Director Stanisław Pawliszewski, protesting Polish infringements against American diplomats: only one of six telephones in the American consulate in Kraków were working and the American consul in Poznań was constantly harassed. Every time the consul in Poznań, his wife, or his child stepped out of their house, a *milicja* officer ordered them to leave the sidewalk and go home. Kinast simply replied that the lack of telephones was a problem for everyone during martial law and that everyone, including the consul, needed to obey the curfew.[132] These types of meetings were typical for the first months after martial law, evidence of diplomatic hostility on both sides.

Hostility toward the United States permeated policy making at the highest levels of Poland's leadership. Jaruzelski himself was one of the strongest critics of U.S. policy. He consistently complained that sanctions were illegitimate policies that infringed on sovereign rights. The break in trust caused by Reagan's reaction to martial law (see chapter 1) did not heal quickly. As a former information officer in the Polish Army, Jaruzelski was attuned to the threat posed by propaganda and was consistently exasperated by RFE broadcasts. More generally, Jaruzelski resented his country being used as a lightning rod in the global Cold War. As he explained to the politburo, "We are a card in their game which they want to carry on." He believed that Reagan was using martial law as a pretext to pursue bellicose policies against the Soviets and the rest of the Socialist bloc. However, he thought that the American moves were backfiring. In particular he noted Japan's and Europe's desire to trade with the Soviet Union, and the growth of anti-Americanism in Europe.[133] Like MSZ officials berating American diplomats, Jaruzelski showed no signs of acquiescing to American pressure; he was prepared to play out the "game" the Americans had begun when they declared sanctions.

In mid-May 1982, the level of hostility increased to the point of a full diplomatic standoff. On May 10, two American embassy officers, John Zerolis and Daniel Howard, were declared persona non grata (PNG) and asked to leave the country within four days. The two had been apprehended while meeting with a recently released opposition scientist and were detained by security services, in violation of their diplomatic status. In retaliation, Lawrence Eagleburger met with the chargé d'affaires at the Polish embassy in Washington, Zdisław Ludwiczak, to inform him that the Polish government's actions were "so transparent as to be beneath contempt." Eagleburger declared Andrzej Koroscik and Mariusz Wozniak of the Polish embassy persona non grata. Because their main science and technology officer (Howard) had been expelled, the Americans also severed all scientific and technology exchanges.[134]

Foggy Bottom considered the plunge in relations important enough to request a meeting between Meehan and Jaruzelski.[135] The general declined the request, but the foreign minister saw Meehan on May 24. Washington instructed Meehan to call the meeting because "bilateral relations with Poland are at a critical point" and because recent Polish actions were a "riddle" to the Americans. As Meehan explained, the future of relations depended on PZPR actions, threatening, "If the Polish side desires to completely eliminate relations we are prepared to accommodate you." The U.S. government wanted to see "a true and frank dialogue with Solidarity and the Church, lifting martial law, and freeing internees," emphasizing that for the United States to respond favorably, Jaruzelski needed to make more than just "cosmetic" reforms.

The foreign minister did not respond in a conciliatory manner. Czyrek launched into the usual line of condemning RFE broadcasts and criticizing American sanctions, which had cut Polish exports to 57 percent of their 1981 levels and had decimated American imports to 6.5 percent compared to a year earlier. Czyrek even declared: "Little substance of relations remains, because already we are out of everything." He defended martial law as a "protective umbrella for conducting reforms, which had always provided an occasion for turmoil in Poland." Czyrek summarized ongoing church-PZPR communications but rejected dialogue with Solidarność, saying, "There is no possibility of an agreement based on a return to the situation before December, nor before August 1980. . . . If such a possibility existed we would not have introduced martial law." He then returned to the issue of sanctions, saying, "You have achieved Poland's political isolation, you continue economic restrictions incorporating coal, ham, in scientific cooperation. This will not continue without effect. The effects are easy for you, but in Polish policy they have caused definitive consequences: seeking new partners, other relations, etc."[136]

Both sides ended the conversation on May 24 with platitudes hoping for better relations. The overall substance of the conversation, however, made the prospect of improvements unlikely. America's economic and political sanctions were taking a toll. In response, Jaruzelski and his advisers had retaliated, not by succumbing to the pressure, but by aggressively working to make life difficult for American diplomats. The Poles were taking what few steps they could to limit contacts. After six months of martial law, American sanctions and the Polish reaction had forced bilateral relations to a stalemate, with few prospects for recovery.

## NSDDs and Pipelines

In Allied relations, there was a spike in NATO cohesion in late winter, followed by a deepening rift between Western Europe and the United States that bottomed out in the summer of 1982. Following the ministerial-level NAC meeting in January (see chapter 1), the Allies held to their commitment not to interfere with individual country's sanctions and showed greater consistency as it became increasingly clear that NATO's three conditions for returning to the status quo ante (ending martial law, releasing all political prisoners, and resuming a national dialog) would not be met quickly. While no country took as harsh a position as the United States, all of the NAC member states except Greece took steps to limit political contacts with Poland, with some states cutting off cultural and scientific exchanges and others acting to restrict the movement of Soviet diplomats in their countries. France went as far as to limit LOT flights and suspend Poland's fishing rights. In coordination through the Paris Club, Poland's major creditors also agreed to suspend consideration of rescheduling Poland's debt from 1982. Most important, all NAC member states (and Japan) suspended consideration of new economic credits.[137]

The Allies also found common ground during a CSCE follow-up meeting in Madrid. Haig was designated to represent the United States, and the Americans lobbied NATO countries to send their foreign ministers to highlight the gravity of the Polish situation, a policy EEC states readily supported.[138] When CSCE talks resumed on February 9 (after a scheduled hiatus), Haig, Genscher, and other Western foreign ministers planned to speak out about human rights violations. In response to harsh criticism from the U.S. delegation, the Polish delegate (who was coincidentally heading the session) coordinated with the Soviet representative to use parliamentary procedures to block further speeches by French, British, Italian, and other West European representatives. This infuriated the Europeans. As a Canadian delegate explained, "The whole thing has been a fabulous stroke of luck for the West. We came here with Genscher and Haig still disagreeing on key points, and with others equivocal about where they stand. Now the Russians have made everybody so angry through their arbitrary tactics that they're all rallying behind Haig."[139] Tensions remained high, and on March 12 the meeting was suspended until November.[140] Under the aegis of the Helsinki Final Act and concern about human rights abuses, the Allies had fully coalesced to condemn abuses in Poland. Moreover, the West successfully *acted together* to suspend the Madrid meeting, despite earlier Allied—particularly West German—fears of causing rifts in East-West relations.[141]

The possibility of further coordinated actions, however, soon fell apart as the NSC continued to push the West Europeans to enhance sanctions on the USSR. In this context, the East-West issue that received the most attention from January 1982 through that fall was not Poland but the construction of a natural gas pipeline from Siberia to Western Europe.[142]

Although it had been a concern before December 1981, blocking construction of the Siberian gas pipeline was quickly linked to events in Poland. On December 27, 1981, Haig cabled American diplomats in West European capitals, referring to "the shift in Italian attitudes toward Siberian pipeline as a result of Polish crisis [which] raises potentially very significant opportunity." Haig asked American diplomats to look for similar developments in other capitals.[143] This initial optimism, however, met with a sober assessment from Ambassador Arthur Burns in Bonn. Pressure on the pipeline issue would "be counterproductive and interpreted as an U.S. attempt to use the Polish crisis to implement policies vis-à-vis the Soviets which were not accepted earlier."[144] Nonetheless, when the president announced sanctions against Moscow, he included the decision to suspend "licenses . . . for export to the Soviet Union for an expanded list of oil and gas equipment."[145]

Pipeline sanctions were a contentious issue within the White House as well, once again pitting pragmatists against idealists in the buildup to a planned mission to Europe by former Senator and Undersecretary of State for Security Assistance James Buckley, who was charged with fighting for sanctions against the Kremlin and explaining Washington's reasons for blocking the pipeline. For ideological Cold Warriors, "sanctions were targeted on oil and gas technologies because these were needed by Moscow to keep the weakening economy upright." The Defense Department pushed to halt the pipeline's construction by denying essential American technology (specifically rotors manufactured by General Electric to transport gas through the pipeline). Pragmatists in the State Department recommended dropping any hope of halting construction: they feared that blocking technology would cause a full break in Allied relations. As a compromise, the State Department recommended that Buckley use uncertainty about how Reagan would eventually rule on pipeline sanctions "to obtain other concessions from the allies in more general areas of East-West trade," namely, to restrict new loans and credit agreements with the Soviets.[146] This became the consensus position.[147] But when the NSC met on February 26, disagreements remained: Haig called for pipeline equipment to be exempt. Weinberger, who was the only voice in opposition, advocated keeping pipeline sanctions and applying them retroactively and extraterritorially, meaning that existing contracts would be affected and that neither American corporations nor their subsidiaries would be allowed to sell technology for the project.[148] Reagan backed the State Department's negotiating position but held off on a final decision until after Buckley's trip.

Buckley traveled to Bonn, Paris, London, Rome, and Brussels from March 15 to 19 with a high-level team from Defense, Commerce, and the NSC. Buckley asked that the West work more closely to limit and restrict new loans and financial credits to the Soviets, to little success. Buckley "met everywhere with failure: all the Europeans opposed our stand."[149] Despite this setback, Buckley and George Shultz, the president of Bechtel Corporation who had been recruited to discuss East-West trade issues, traveled repeatedly to Europe in April and May to negotiate restricting credits to the USSR in return for dropping the pipeline sanctions.[150] Neither found success.

Reagan then traveled to Europe June 2–11 for meetings in European capitals and a G7 summit at Versailles, with the issues of credits and pipeline sanctions unresolved. Reagan personally advocated tougher credit restrictions against the Soviets, but like Buckley and Shultz, the president returned "thoroughly disappointed and angry with the lack of any decisive moves by the allies on credit restrictions." A week later, the president's anger morphed into a decision. On June 18, at the hastily called NSC meeting described at the beginning of the chapter, Reagan decided to apply American sanctions against oil- and gas-technology exports to the Soviet Union retroactively and enforce them extraterritorially.[151]

The response to the decision was sharp. In Europe, the announcement "provoked a storm of protest." Europeans declared the decision illegal and broke completely with U.S. policy, determined to fulfill their contracts and complete the deal with the USSR. The recently elected French president Mitterrand "reportedly told one visitor that after long efforts to establish rapport with Reagan, he had concluded that there was not a single issue on which he could trust the American president."[152] Even Reagan's close collaborator Margaret Thatcher denounced the action: "It is wrong for one powerful nation" to try to prevent the fulfillment of "existing contracts that do not, in any event, fall under its jurisdiction."[153] In Washington, Haig was so upset that the decision had been made in his absence that he submitted a letter of resignation. He announced he was stepping down as secretary on June 25, and he was replaced almost immediately by Shultz, who was officially sworn in as secretary of state on July 16.

When Shultz stepped into office, his initial concern was violence in Lebanon; however, he soon started shifting American policy on the pipeline issue and sanctions in general. As a trained economist, Shultz "was skeptical of the effectiveness of sanctions, especially when applied unilaterally." He argued that sanctions were "a wasting asset . . . the longer the sanctions last, the less they mean."[154] More specifically, in August the French government forced French companies working on the pipeline to honor their agreements with Moscow. To enforce sanctions the U.S. government would have had to directly confront Paris, evidence of just how fractured U.S.–West European relations were. Sanctions meant to punish the Soviet Union were now taking a harsher toll on the Western alliance than on the Soviet bloc. In response to the breakdown "even Cap Weinberger agreed that [the United States] should engage the Europeans in working out the problems."[155] After meetings in Europe and Washington, Shultz forged a new agreement in which the West Europeans agreed to "security-minded principles" to determine economic exchanges, specifically, to refrain from any new natural gas agreements with the USSR, to enhance restrictions on technology exports through CoCom, and to harmonize export credit policies. This was not as strong as the commitment Reagan wanted, but it did repair the fissure. At the end of November, Reagan codified this new framework in NSDD 66, "East-West Relations and Poland-Related Sanctions," cancelling the Poland-inspired sanctions against the Soviet Union on oil and gas equipment.[156]

Changing personnel also directly affected the reception of the more pragmatic arguments from the State Department. Simply, Shultz was not Haig. In the months before the June 18 decision, Haig had been enmeshed in increasingly acidic arguments with Clark and Weinberger.[157] His volatile personality and his territoriality about foreign affairs bothered the president; in Reagan's own words, "[Haig] had a toughness and aggressiveness about protecting his status and turf that caused problems within the administration."[158] By mid-June Reagan was convinced that Haig was "no longer a member of the team," and, by one account, the president orchestrated the June 18 decision to provoke his resignation.[159] With personal relations so low, the messenger undoubtedly hurt the State Department's messages. In contrast, the president had handpicked Shultz to be secretary of state before announcing Haig's resignation, and he "thought Shultz's calm, professional manner [was] a refreshing contrast to Haig's excitability."[160] Reagan and Shultz quickly forged a strong working relationship. As Shultz recalled, Reagan "increasingly took his side of the issue."[161] Pragmatic voices within State now had an amicable and respected spokesman to argue against the idealists.

With Shultz occupying the sixth floor in Foggy Bottom, the White House renewed the general discussion of national security policy toward Eastern Europe. On September 2, Reagan signed NSDD 54, "United States Policy toward Eastern Europe," in which the president decisively supported the Department of State's position. Rather than accepting nondifferentiation to seek decreased economic and political contacts with nations behind the Iron Curtain, Reagan endorsed differentiation "to encourage diversity through political and economic policies tailored to individual countries." Unlike in President Johnson, Nixon, and Carter's variety, in this version "implementation will differ in that we will proceed more cautiously and with a clearer sense of our limitations, including budgetary ones." However, the goals of differentiation remained the same: to encourage liberalizing trends, further human and civil rights, reinforce the pro-Western orientation of their peoples, lessen economic and political dependence on the Soviet Union, and encourage private markets and free trade unions. Finally, differentiation was calibrated to discriminate between countries in terms of their "relative independence from the Soviet Union in the conduct of foreign policy" and "greater internal liberalization as manifested in a willingness to observe internationally recognized human rights and to pursue a degree of pluralism and decentralization, including a more market-oriented economy."[162]

The endorsement of differentiation was a de facto rejection of more ideological voices. The White House concluded that its long-term strategy was to reengage with Eastern Europe to pull it away from the Soviet Union, rather than to isolate Eastern Europe to draw resources from the Soviets. Before Haig's exit, differentiation had bureaucratic momentum as standing policy, but a shift to nondifferentiation remained a possibility. This possibility ended with NSDD 54, and it was an early sign that under Shultz's guidance Washington was reorienting relations with the Socialist bloc to return to a more pragmatic foundation.

Shultz's approach to East-West relations also colored policy toward the Soviet Union. NSC staffer Richard Pipes began drafting NSDD 75, "U.S. Relations with the Soviet Union," early in 1982, but the process only gained bureaucratic momentum after Shultz came into office.[163] This particular directive is often presented as a triumph of neoconservative policy making because of its references to undermining the Soviet system, oblique concepts of rolling back Soviet power, and arguments for changing the USSR internally.[164] The document, however, is much more restrained than these readings accept. Limiting Soviet power was by no means a new idea, and for East European policy, NSDD 75 wholly embraced the time-tested method of differentiation. Most important, this directive was based on the idea that the Soviet Union would only change slowly over "the long haul." As the document notes, "The interrelated tasks of containing and reversing Soviet expansion and promoting *evolutionary change* within the Soviet Union itself cannot be accomplished quickly," giving the range of five to ten years as a period of considerable uncertainty for the Soviets, not of upheaval. Similarly, the document ends on a restrained note, "The U.S. must demonstrate credibly that its policy is not a blue-print for open-ended, sterile confrontation with Moscow, but a serious search for a stable and constructive long-term basis for U.S.-Soviet relations."[165]

This decision directive bears the marks of both the neoconservative's ideological approach and Shultz's more pragmatic strategy, particularly on the Reagan administration's negotiating stance vis-à-vis the Soviets. First, the administration would only enter into negotiations "consistent with the principle of strict reciprocity." Moreover, dialogue would continue to "address the full range of U.S. concerns about . . . internal behavior and human rights violation." Most important, the United States would "try to create incentives (positive and negative) for the new leadership to adopt policies less detrimental to U.S. interests" and "remain ready for improved U.S-Soviet relations if the Soviet Union makes significant changes in policies of concern to it."[166]

At their core, however, both of these policy documents were fundamentally pragmatic, evidence of the State Department's and Shultz's moderating effect. Both NSDD 75 and NSDD 54 allowed for a normalized system of relations with the East Europeans and the Soviet Union, a system in which negotiations would be pursued. In contrast to earlier Republican administrations and in a nod to neoconservative inclinations, these negotiations would be based on an expectation of significant concessions by the other side. Nonetheless, diplomatic engagement and quid pro quo relationships with the Soviets and East Europeans fit well within the overall directives ultimately approved. More important, with Shultz the pragmatists had a reliable and persuasive voice in the Oval Office, one whose influence increased with time.

In the nine months from January to September 1982, Polish policy cast an expanding shadow over an array of concerns beyond martial law and sanctions. American diplomats in Warsaw and Washington tried to move policy onto a new footing that included carrots as well sticks, with some even suggesting an initiative akin to the Marshall Plan. Events in Poland gave public credibility and added urgency to requests for new funding for broadcasting behind the Iron Curtain. Poland was central in debates about international financial agreements and aid procedures. In the NSC hard liners used Poland to fight for tougher sanctions against the Soviets.

During the debate about pipeline sanctions, however, the Polish cause became obscured. The pipeline issue moved the Reagan administration's focus away from Poland qua Poland. Poland was only important in terms of how it was used to secure global goals. As Haig recalled, "The Polish crisis provided a convenient pretext for dealing with the pipeline, which had long nettled [neoconservatives'] strategic sensibilities."[167] Discussions on how to engage Poland and Eastern Europe were pushed to the background. With Poles cutting economic ties with the West and strengthening them with the East, American leverage decreased. Still angry about sanctions, the Poles pursued a provocative and antagonistic policy that caused relations to spiral downward, leading to a PNG crisis.

As the White House distanced itself from daily policy in Poland and bilateral relations worsened, all the major story lines surfaced that would dominate Polish-American relations during the following five years. Congress took a direct role in determining policy. Propaganda moved onto the front lines. Solidarność reorganized itself in the underground, proving through street demonstrations and independent publications that it had survived to fight again. An international web of conspirators lead by labor and Polish émigré organizations surfaced to support opposition. American humanitarian organizations solidified their role as well, delivering millions of dollars' worth of aid. Finally, under Shultz's guidance the White House agreed to a softer approach toward Eastern Europe, embracing engagement and the policy of differentiation.

Headlines about martial law and Poland began to fade. The White House's interest also began to wane as Shultz and the rest of the cabinet turned to focus on the Soviet Union *without* links to Poland. Poland occasionally reappeared on the front page, was the subject of an NSC decision, or popped up in a presidential speech, but it moved progressively to the background. Out of the spotlight, Poland would not spark the same ideological arguments that had motivated American decisions during 1982, freeing relations to evolve incrementally. In the first three quarters of 1982, in effect, the situation in Poland stabilized, with all the major issues and players materializing. During the following three years, however, Poland's transformation and American policy did not follow a straight trajectory; both turned and twisted as time progressed. Improvements in bilateral relations proved hard to come by.

CHAPTER THREE

# Bilateral Relations Were about as Cold as You Can Imagine

## Diplomatic Stalemate, September 1982 to January 1985

When John Davis arrived in Warsaw as chargé d'affaires *ad interim* in September 1983, he was the third in a string of chargés since Ambassador Meehan exited earlier in the year. Davis thought it would be a temporary position; he only had a six-month mandate. The working assumption was that during those six months, he and his superiors in Washington would be able to improve bilateral relations with the Polish government to allow an exchange of full ambassadors. That assumption proved incorrect. With meeting after meeting leading to dead end after dead end, both sides stubbornly refused to give ground. Following one particularly tense meeting with MSZ officials, Davis returned to the embassy and made light of the stalemate in his casual, low-key manner: "Well, it looks like I am going to have to buy another shirt."[1] His six-month mandate lasted more than six years.

Davis's experience was neither unique nor particularly noteworthy in the long series of contentious meetings that characterized bilateral relations in the mid-1980s. Lasting improvements in bilateral relations were hard to come by. Beginning in November 1982 Jaruzelski did take steps toward liberalization, but internal dynamics meant that these changes did not follow a predictable trajectory. After a period of dragging its feet, the White House ultimately codified a "step-by-step" relationship with the PZPR in which specific steps toward liberalization would be rewarded by lifting individual sanctions, but in a volatile environment this led Washington to suspend some sanctions and, in a few cases, to impose new ones. Both sides met with successes and failures, but a significant breakthrough in relations remained elusive.

Beyond the scope of government-to-government relations, humanitarian organizations continued their work, with Congress playing a central role. Legislators approved appropriations to support a second pillar of independent society—individual, private farmers—and passed legislation to provide direct payments to improve Poland's health-care infrastructure. Capitol Hill also worked with the White House to give nongovernmental organizations a new, powerful source of funding—the National Endowment for Democracy—buttressing continued efforts by the transnational network keeping Solidarność alive. In Warsaw, the American embassy took steps to independently support the opposition, creating close personal relationships with Solidarność activists increasingly living aboveground. Davis also utilized discreet channels to free high-profile internees in return for reducing specific sanctions. Despite these positive trends beneath the surface, at the beginning of 1985 Polish-American ties found themselves in yet another diplomatic crisis, showing just how little relations had progressed.

## Internal Dynamics of Change

On July 22, 1982, the Jaruzelski regime began rolling back martial law by announcing a limited amnesty for political prisoners. In all, more than twelve hundred prisoners were released, and Jaruzelski hinted that martial law might be suspended by the end of the year. Despite this gesture, advocates within Solidarność for a strong, centralized underground society were skeptical that they could reach a compromise with the government. To show their continuing strength, the TKK called for street demonstrations on August 31, the second anniversary of the signing of the Gdańsk Accords.[2] For activists like Jacek Kuroń, the demonstrations were designed to show that the people had not been intimidated and to force the authorities into direct negotiations.[3]

On August 31, large crowds gathered and clashed with *milicja*, Zmotoryzowane Odwody Milicji Obywatelskiej (Motorized Reserves of the Citizens' Militia or ZOMO), and police. According to the MSW, demonstrations occurred in sixty-six cities and involved about 118,000 people. Marchers hurled rocks, paving stones, and even Molotov cocktails at the authorities, in stark contrast to peaceful demonstrations the previous May. Jaruzelski and Minister of Internal Affairs Kiszczak were prepared, and riot police and security forces used deadly force to control the situation. Two people in Lublin and two people in Gdańsk died after government forces fired into the crowds. Despite the turnout elsewhere, demonstrations in Warsaw proved to be much smaller than organizers hoped, drawing only about 15,000 people, compared to the 50,000 to 100,000 that opposition leaders had been expecting.[4] With international attention focused on the capital, this smaller-than-expected turnout and the authorities' ability to "quash antigovernment demonstrations" with "comparative ease" led the international press to conclude that "the suspended Solidarity trade union [had failed] to devise an effective strategy for combating martial law."[5]

The PZPR leadership also interpreted the August 31 events as a victory. Although crowds were substantial, few workers took part; most demonstrators were either youth or members of the intelligentsia. To the authorities this was a sign of Solidarność's decreasing popularity with the working class, the opposition's former stronghold. The MSW also arrested almost 5,000 of the most militant oppositionists, and there were no major disruptions in production. This was not the decisive show of power that TKK leaders had planned. The American intelligence community came to similar conclusions: "The demonstrations probably did nothing to shake Jaruzelski's conviction that time is on his side and that he can eventually wear down Solidarity's will to resist."[6] As Jaruzelski put it, "Solidarność extremists performed their funeral march."[7]

This perceived victory emboldened the PZPR to go on the offensive against Solidarność. After a September 2 politburo meeting, six leading members of KOR—Jacek Kuroń, Adam Michnik, Jan Lityński, Henryk Wujec, Mirosław Chojecki, and Jan Józef Lipski—were charged with treason.[8] In addition, officials discussed officially declaring Solidarność illegal and dissolving it, with new government-sanctioned unions created in its stead.[9] On September 23 and 28 the politburo met, with some fearing that Solidarność would react with massive strikes and demonstrations, possibly crippling the country. The PZPR also consulted with the Catholic Church. On October 2, Bishop Bronisław Dąbrowski, Cardinal Glemp's main negotiator, assured the Communist leadership that the church would not have a comment on the issue.[10] Following a final politburo meeting on October 5 and a meeting between politburo member Stanisław Ciosek and Lech Wałęsa (who remained in prison) to gauge his reaction, the politburo passed the legislation onto the Sejm. The Sejm rubber-stamped it on October 8, creating a new system of trade unions and declaring Solidarność illegal. The government anxiously awaited workers' reactions, but there were no major protests or violent clashes.[11] The PZPR had won another tenuous victory.

The reaction from the United States was swift, clear, and tough. On October 9, President Reagan declared the new law for independent trade unions a "sham," announced that he was suspending Poland's most-favored-nation trade status, and threatened that he was "prepared to take further steps as a result of this further repression."[12] From the American perspective, suspending MFN was not economically important but would "have great symbolic and political significance . . . particularly to the Poles who attach great importance to the MFN."[13] Unlike sanctions in December 1981, this punitive step came as no surprise to Warsaw. On October 6, two days before the Sejm's announcement, Davis (then head of the East European department in the State Department European Bureau) met with Jan Kinast, the director of MSZ Department III, addressing rumors about the new union law. Davis clearly warned Kinast that any move against Solidarność would have very negative effects.[14] As Jaruzelski remarked to Rakowski, "It was, after all, known with [Reagan] and so it goes; onto [Foreign Minister] Olszowski where he will remain alone on the battlefield."[15]

At the same time that the PZPR acted against the clear wishes of the United States, the Polish leadership took seemingly contradictory steps by acquiescing to other Western requests. First, the PZPR pursued closer contacts with the Catholic Church. Early in 1982 Glemp and Jaruzelski exchanged letters on the possibility of Pope John Paul II visiting Poland (a possibility that was postponed for a year in July).[16] Channels remained open, and on September 30, the episcopate proposed a meeting between Glemp, Jaruzelski, and Wałęsa to move toward national reconciliation. Glemp also called for Wałęsa to be freed from internment as a sign of goodwill.[17] Jaruzelski and his advisers did not reject the possibility; instead they used Wałęsa to gain leverage. As Jaruzelski explained to Rakowski: "We will free Wałęsa, but we must get something in exchange for him from the church."[18] The PZPR leadership was concerned about possibly debilitating strikes called for by the TKK on November 10 to mark the first anniversary of the signing of Solidarność's constitution.[19] Party officials also worried about antigovernment demonstrations on November 11, a holiday celebrating the creation of independent Poland at the conclusion of World War I. The PZPR wanted the church to use its influence to ensure that calm prevailed.

Jaruzelski and Glemp met on November 8 and agreed to a loose quid pro quo. Jaruzelski dangled a papal visit and freeing Wałęsa. In response, Glemp was sympathetic toward the general's situation and openly criticized RFE and Western sanctions. Overall Jaruzelski categorized the meeting as "constructive and useful."[20] Immediately afterward the two sides announced that the pope would visit in June 1983. The Catholic Church and government together voiced "concern for the preservation and strengthening of peace, order and honest work in society."[21] In Western media the November 8 meeting was correctly viewed as "an apparent attempt to defuse protest strikes and demonstrations."[22] This cooperative strategy worked: no major strikes materialized on November 10, and street demonstrations on November 11 were small and nonviolent.

Improved relations with the church remained a central policy concern for the PZPR. As the politburo concluded, "gradual movement toward normalized relations between the nation and the church" should be a primary goal. They even hoped to elevate diplomatic relations with the Vatican to envoy and nuncio "in the face of the growing role of the Vatican in international politics, particularly European [politics]."[23] Moreover, the papal visit was a chance to influence outside perceptions: "In relation to the pope's planned visit it will be important to prevent negative internal aspects while simultaneously developing external aspects which contribute to overcoming Poland's isolation in the West."[24] Good relations with the Vatican were helpful both domestically and internationally.

This new church-government dialogue also took a more surprising turn. On November 11, evening news readers announced that Wałęsa would be released from Arłamow prison. The former leader of Solidarność returned to Gdańsk a few days later, welcomed home by a group of about fifteen hundred people. When the politburo met on November 18 to review the decision to free Wałęsa, Jaruzelski explained that it was a "suitable moment" to release him "to become a regular citizen." He continued, "Wałęsa at home, that is a difficult problem for [him]. Wałęsa cannot go into the underground. The legend of a steadfast and interned Wałęsa has been disgraced. Freeing [him] was a definite surprise for capitalist countries. It is peaceful in Gdańsk. There were not many welcomers." Kiszczak supported these views: "Without [Bronisław] Geremek and other advisers, he is an illiterate politician."[25] In the wake of poorly organized strikes and demonstrations throughout the second half of 1982, the PZPR leadership decided that a free Wałęsa did not pose a significant threat. The move also reflected the growing spirit of cooperation between the PZPR and the Catholic Church.

The PZPR politburo took a further liberalizing step at its November 18 meeting: members agreed to suspend martial law. The question of how to proceed was posed as a choice between three options: 1) lifting martial law, 2) suspending martial law, and 3) continuing martial law. Both WRON and Jaruzelski voted for the second option. Suspending martial law showed the party's strength and confidence. On the other hand, if problems with food delivery or the pope's visit led to an emergency situation, martial law could be reimposed easily without a new law from the Sejm. The politburo accepted WRON's suggestion and the discussion turned toward implementation. Comments from politburo members help illustrate the major motivation for ending martial law. There was no talk of foreign pressure or American sanctions. Instead, suspending martial law allowed the government to focus on pressing economic measures. To extricate the country from crisis, the economy had to be improved. Martial law was too large a burden to carry. Restrictions on movement and communication were obviously slowing growth. As Jaruzelski summarized, suspending martial law was "only one step toward normalization. It is very important [now] to focus on economic measures."[26] On December 12, Jaruzelski announced that martial law would be suspended by the end of the year.[27]

The Sejm followed Jaruzelski's direction, suspended martial law on December 31, and released a significant number of internees. High-level detainees, including Wałęsa's adviser Geremek and the former Solidarność spokesman Janusz Onyszkiewicz, as well as Tadeusz Mazowiecki and Andrzej Czuma, were released just before Christmas. This amnesty did not, however, include seven "radical" activists charged with crimes against the state: Andrzej Gwiazda, Seweryn Jaworski, Marian Jurczyk, Karol Modzelewski, Grzegorz Palka, Andrzej Rozpłochowski, and Jan Rulewski. Nor did it include the four KOR activists charged with treason. Władysław Frasyniuk and Piotr Bednarz, members of the TKK from Dolny Śląsk who were captured in October and November, were also denied amnesty. Finally, activists who had been arrested and charged with crimes following demonstrations in the summer and fall of 1982 were also excluded. According to the Polish Helsinki Watch Committee, "courts and misdemeanor courts passed more than 30,000 prison sentences in political cases," none of which were affected by the December 1982 amnesty.[28]

The PZPR's decisions to schedule a papal visit, release Wałęsa, and suspend martial law were all steps toward liberalization that the West had been demanding for a year. The PZPR was not, however, acquiescing to Western demands. Instead, the decision-making process was driven by domestic factors, particularly the leadership's belief that it needed the church as a partner to restart a functioning society. As the decision to outlaw Solidarność showed, the PZPR did not feel the need to enter into a dialogue with Solidarność; the union was a nuisance that was gradually loosing its influence. The Catholic Church, however, remained a critical force needed to regain public trust. Announcing a papal visit and releasing Wałęsa were moves to promote such trust. Suspending martial law was a necessity for improving the economy. All were internal concerns.

Rather than conceding to the West, Jaruzelski persistently pursued policies that intensified confrontation with the United States. With few points of leverage open to him, Jaruzelski often turned to propaganda to diminish Washington's influence. As a former propaganda officer, Jaruzelski understood the importance of information. In the first days of martial law, the Poles and the Soviets increased the jamming of RFE and VOA.[29] They also began a sustained effort to attack American radio in the government-sponsored press.[30] As early as June 1982 the politburo worked to coordinate international propaganda activities better and to move from a "defensive reaction to events" toward a more "offensive" stance.[31] In line with this plan, it pursued commentaries and interviews in the Western press to "show the hypocrisy of Reagan's policies, using meaningful examples from the U.S. (i.e., relations with striking traffic controllers . . .)."[32] From the general's perspective, the PZPR needed to turn Wałęsa's release and the suspension of martial law into a propaganda asset: "We must be on the offensive. Create a movement admonishing . . . Reagan on the Polish issue."[33]

In the wake of Reagan's decision to suspend MFN, Jaruzelski publicly attacked Washington as the "main inspirer of anti-Polish actions," derided Reagan for being "blinded by an anti-Polish obsession," and announced that the government would take steps to limit "contacts between Polish citizens and American missions and agencies." (He repeated these missives to the Political Coordinating Commission of the Warsaw Pact in January 1983, presenting himself as a committed supporter of the pact's anti-Reagan line.)[34] These public attacks presaged a politburo effort to also make anti-American policies more "concrete," beginning with a crackdown on Western journalists.[35] A BBC journalist was arrested and expelled on December 31. The Polish government revoked employment papers for Poles working with foreign press organizations. In early January 1983, Ruth Gruber, the United Press International station chief, was arrested for suspicion of crimes against the nation, specifically for accepting two cans of film sent from Gdańsk. She lost her accreditation and was expelled.[36] The American embassy took Gruber's arrest seriously and lodged official complaints with the MSZ because she was held overnight and denied access to U.S. embassy officials.[37]

The Polish security services (SB or Służba Bezpieczeństwa) also stepped up direct actions against American diplomats. The SB tailed diplomats as they moved about Warsaw and the country, noting who they met with and when. Informants within the domestic staff of some embassy officials provided vague updates to the SB on who visited the house and snippets of conversation.[38] On particular occasions, when diplomats were viewed as more deserving of monitoring or were suspected of CIA ties, the SB staged break-ins, during which listening devices were implanted in the walls and documents within the house were photographed.[39] And on occasion, the SB would purposefully make their presence known to intimidate American officials, as when John Dobrin's car was stopped, surrounded by officers, and photographed.[40]

Even more disconcerting, Polish authorities attacked the inner workings of the embassy. Polish embassy employees were threatened with arrest if they did not receive new permits from the government employment office. In some cases the workers resigned their positions.[41] When Ambassador Meehan met with Wiejacz to stress the seriousness of the situation, he added complaints about police stationed outside of the embassy when they screened popular American movies (*Coal Miner's Daughter*, for example), in an obvious attempt to intimidate guests. Meehan also explained that the United States would limit the numbers of Poles working in economic offices in New York and Washington if the Polish staff at the U.S. embassy did not receive the necessary paperwork. Wiejacz remained resolute. He explained that it was a sovereign Polish decision to decide who worked where. In response to American complaints, he objected to continuing inflammatory broadcasts on RFE and VOA, as well as to Washington's promotion of groups in the United States working to support Solidarność. As Wiejacz recorded: "The Polish side has shown patience for a long time in the face of sanctions, restrictions, and pressure against our country from the United States. I explained that if the U.S. continues actions against us, we will be forced to respond with future steps."[42]

An additional problem also surfaced in bilateral relations: Meehan was stepping down as ambassador. Because Ambassador Spasowski had not been replaced, neither country would have full diplomatic representation. At his farewell meeting, Meehan expressed concern that Washington's choice to replace him, John Scanlan, had not yet received agrément (a diplomatic procedure in which the host country gives legal approval for a candidate to be appointed ambassador). The State Department believed this to be a standard, formal procedure that should be taken without political significance. Moreover, Meehan warned that if it was not resolved soon, a solution would "become considerably more difficult and evolve into a serious problem between both nations."[43] When Meehan left Warsaw on February 11, 1983, the MSZ continued to balk at granting agrément to Scanlan, leaving the Americans without ambassadorial representation.

With Meehan gone, Herbert Wilgis took over as chargé d'affaires *ad interim*. Through the rest of the winter and the spring of 1983 relations continued to limp forward with neither side taking steps to improve the situation. Most of Wilgis's meetings involved responding to complaints about RFE and VOA broadcasts, which the Poles considered an infringement on sovereignty. Wilgis consistently clarified that VOA was a U.S. government agency, but that RFE operated independently, so the government could not be held responsible for its content. Wilgis also consistently invoked the Helsinki Final Act, which guaranteed the free distribution of information and news across borders. The Poles categorically rejected these arguments as often as Wilgis made them.[44]

Moreover, the Polish government took bolder steps to impede American informational activities. On April 27, Kinast announced that they would be closing down the American Library.[45] The library was attached to the embassy and provided Poles with access to Western periodicals and books, as well as with the occasional movie. *Milicja* officers regularly harassed and intimidated Polish citizens trying to enter. The MSZ argued that by providing access to materials, like *Problems in Communism* and Western publications on Solidarność, the library was interfering in internal Polish matters. The MSZ also directly connected the decision to close the library with "aggressive propaganda" from RFE and VOA. The Americans considered actions impeding the library's work to be violations of consular agreements; the embassy kept the library open despite MSZ orders.[46]

From the fall of 1982 to the spring of 1983, Polish-American relations continued a public spiral downward. The PZPR's campaign to combat American propaganda deserves most of the blame. Moves to expel American journalists, harass embassy staff, limit American representation in Warsaw, and impede activities within the embassy were all attempts to go on the offensive against Washington. The two sides were deadlocked over who would make the first move toward normalizing relations. By acting tough in response to U.S. sanctions, Jaruzelski did little to change American attitudes; however, it was a sign of the PZPR's determination to remain resolute in the face of American pressure.

## Changing Attitudes in Washington

Despite confrontation on the ground and in the airwaves, diplomats moved slowly behind the scenes to put U.S.-Polish relations on a different footing. By May 1982, Dale Herspring in the Department of State had drafted a more codified carrot-and-stick approach to bilateral relations, a step-by-step approach lifting sanctions in return for small moves by the PZPR.[47] With hopes increasing that Jaruzelski might be announcing bold steps on July 22, the White House leaked word that it was looking to change relations, with the *New York Times* reporting that "President Reagan [was] searching for ways to ease economic sanctions against Poland."[48] This public sentiment was followed by a private overture. In September 1982, Ambassador Meehan met with the new minister of foreign affairs Stefan Olszowski to discuss bilateral relations, taking a less confrontational stance.[49] After some polite chat, including mentioning McDonald's interest in buying Polish potatoes, Meehan stated that the U.S. government had noted "with importance" Jaruzelski's actions to free detainees over the summer, but was waiting to see what happened next. Olszowski proposed "the possibility of taking even small steps, which could lead in the direction of improved Polish-American relations."[50] When Meehan met with Polish officials a few days later, they suggested a number of areas for possible agreement, including airlines, fishing quotas, scientific-technical cooperation, returning Poland's representative in Washington to the level of ambassador, increasing safety for Polish diplomatic posts, and streamlining visa procedures for diplomats and embassy workers.[51] Meehan "expressed satisfaction" with the possibility of exchanging opinions and reviewing concrete matters within the purview of bilateral relations.[52]

The topic of small steps was not broached again until December. A week before the anniversary of the declaration of martial law, a Polish diplomat in Moscow informally invited the Americans to respond to the "small steps" framework, suggesting that "the United States . . . might consider 'suspending' one or more of the sanctions now in effect against Poland as a signal of its willingness eventually to lift sanctions if and when more progress is achieved."[53] When Meehan met with a MSZ representative three days later, he reiterated Reagan's general policy to return to the status quo ante and provide economic help if the PZPR ended martial law, released political prisoners, and began a dialogue with the Catholic Church and "freely formed trade unions."[54] However, he came with no specific suggestions for small steps that could be taken immediately. The lack of movement between September and December was clearly frustrating to the MSZ representative, who explained, "We can live without the USA."[55]

By the end of 1982, the PZPR's contradictory moves—taking expressly provocative and aggressive steps against the U.S. embassy while improving relations with the church, releasing Wałęsa and other internees, and suspending martial law—meant that the Reagan administration saw little reason to rescind sanctions. Analysts from the CIA concluded that the moves taken by the PZPR were primarily tactical, with the planned papal visit announced to improve relations with the church and Wałęsa's release taken "to remove a symbol of defiance and potential rallying point for domestic protests." These tactical moves had been paired with important steps to continue to "quash the underground press, arrest fugitive leaders, and generally prevent underground organizational work." As they concluded, "Warsaw seems in no good mood to make conciliatory gestures to the U.S."[56] Jan Nowak-Jezioranski (an NSC consultant well connected to American and European Polonia), Jerzy Milewski (the official representative of Solidarność in the West), and Richard Pipes all advocated maintaining sanctions with no concessions.[57] Even Secretary Shultz, who headed the department most pushing for some action to rescind sanctions, concluded that "it would be extremely difficult to proceed with any positive steps to remove sanctions if the Poles were simultaneously seeking to dismantle our bilateral relations."[58] Decisions about how to proceed came to a standstill.

In the winter of 1983 alliance politics broke the political logjam. The Paris Club had agreed in January 1982 to block consideration of debt rescheduling, and the U.S. government continued to pay interest on government loans, in line with the decision not to declare Poland in default. In July 1982, however, the British, West Germans, French, and Canadians raised the issue of debt rescheduling talks at the NAC, making the very practical point that not holding rescheduling talks meant that Poland received a 100 percent rescheduling, as they were being forced to repay nothing.[59] Two months later, the Italians joined the others to call for rescheduling talks because "an unconditional postponement of this debt could not be allowed to continue."[60] In November 1982, private lenders agreed to reschedule 1981 debts through the London Club, increasing incentives for West European governments to do the same in the Paris Club. By January, creditor nations—the United Kingdom and several "neutrals," including Switzerland—made "their doubts about the appropriateness of delaying a Polish rescheduling" clear.[61] In early March, the European Community publically called for debt rescheduling without linkage to human rights conditions. The policy-planning mechanisms in Washington, however, had ground to a halt because of divisions within the State Department, which had failed to produce a proposed policy document in early January. NSC staffer Paula Dobriansky worried that if the White House continued with an ad hoc approach or did not make a decision, the West Europeans might "break ranks" and reschedule debt independently. Therefore she advocated that the administration "signal our pragmatism, good faith, and forestall any dissensions." Specifically, Dobriansky called for a private démarche to Poland in coordination with Allies, "offering tangible quid pro quos to the Poles in exchange for serious concessions on their part."[62]

The NSC's increased pressure and a forthcoming meeting of the Paris Club on April 11 led to a National Security Policy Group (NSPG) meeting with the president on April 8. In the buildup to the meeting, the Department of State and NSC agreed on the efficacy of linking debt rescheduling to a successful papal visit, another general amnesty, and the cessation of worker harassment. The NSC, however, wanted to include American support to Poland's application for IMF membership as an incentive and reiterate, through a high-level emissary, the necessity of both economic reform and the restoration of workers' rights to form unions if bilateral improvements were to improve.[63] On the State Department's side, Shultz wanted to allow selected LOT flights to New York if conditions were met. He also proposed a direct démarche to the Soviets through his ongoing contacts with Soviet ambassador Dobrynin.[64] When President Reagan sat in on the NSPG meeting, he was given four options: 1) offer large-scale economic incentives to return to a pre–martial law situation (the Marshall Plan option); 2) NSC's preferred option of debt rescheduling and IMF membership combined with a private démarche to push for long-term improvements in economic and labor policies; 3) the State Department's preference for debt rescheduling and LOT flights; and 4) to do nothing.[65] At the meeting, Weinberger advocated doing nothing and Don Regan of the Treasury expressed skepticism that the United States could fully control Poland's IMF membership. The president saw linking individual sanctions to specific political and human rights changes as "an opportunity to benefit the Polish people and keep our allies unified," but he refrained from making a definitive decision. Instead he called for further policy coordination combining aspects of points 2 and 3.[66] In terms of the upcoming Paris Club meeting, Reagan asked that American representatives clarify that Washington was "seriously considering" debt rescheduling and would report to the Allies as soon as a decision was made.[67]

An interagency process then began, culminating with the final policy for next steps on Poland approved by President Reagan on May 6. The policy was conceptualized as a series of four steps based on the PZPR meeting specific human rights and political concessions. If the pope's visit was successful and peaceful, and the majority of political prisoners were released, the United States would allow for Paris Club talks to begin on rescheduling debts from 1981. Washington would take the additional bilateral step of informing the

President Reagan discussing "next steps" on Poland during the April 8 NSPG meeting, with (clockwise from left) Secretary of State George Shultz, Counselor to the President Ed Meese, Chief of Staff James Baker, Secretary of Commerce Malcolm Baldridge, Secretary of Defense Casper Weinberger, and Chief of Staff Donald Regan. Photo courtesy of the Ronald Reagan Library.

Poles of possibly allowing a fishing allocation in U.S. waters. As step 2, if the PZPR stopped harassing Wałęsa and other workers and began pursuing economic reforms that allowed for workers' councils and strengthened private agriculture, the United States would then proceed with opening talks on rescheduling Poland's debts from 1982. If human rights and political conditions continued to improve, step 3 (rescheduling of the 1983 debt) would begin. In step 4, the U.S. government would pursue economic normalization with Poland (MFN, IMF membership, new credits, etc.) if the PZPR restored workers' rights to form free labor unions. Steps 1 to 3 were seen as short term, and step 4 was a long-term goal. The policy was designed as a step-by-step approach in which subsequent steps would not be taken until early benchmarks were met. It was also meant to be flexible (allowing for steps to be altered as the situation changed) and included a tank clause to unilaterally or multilaterally end the process if events warranted.[68] When Reagan approved the policy, he rejected NSC desires to have a special emissary approach the Poles. Briefing the Poles on the policy, with specific references to the quid pro quo on step 1 and general guidelines on any further moves on sanctions, would be conducted through the usual State Department channels.[69]

When the new policy was presented to the NAC in mid-May, the Europeans reacted negatively and strongly, slightly altering the path forward. The French, West Germans, and British all questioned the "desirability and feasibility of closely linking rescheduling to specific human rights/political conditions."[70] To help change European perspectives, Dobriansky and Deputy Assistant Secretary Mark Palmer traveled to Brussels, briefing the allies on the proposed approach at an NAC meeting on May 19. By this point, even one of the last holdouts on debt rescheduling (Denmark) was calling for talks to resume because of the steps taken toward normalization and the upcoming papal visit.[71] The Europeans were also very concerned about "express linkage" between political events like the papal visit and economic decisions like rescheduling,[72] because an American or Western démarche to Poland explicitly linking debt rescheduling to a papal visit and the release of prisoners would be rejected by the Poles. Moreover, this kind of move could be used by the Soviets (who were exceedingly wary of a papal visit) against the reformers in the PZPR. Ultimately the British agreed with American policy, but the West Germans and the French were reluctant to approach the Poles directly.[73] To maintain Allied unity, the United States did not contact the Poles to explain the new step-by-step policy in the buildup to the papal visit. Washington now took a wait-and-see approach.

The importance of this extended policy-review process from December 1982 to May 1983 should not be overlooked. From President Reagan's December 1981 speech first announcing sanctions, it had been clear that the punishments were retractable if the PZPR took steps to liberalize, including ending martial law, releasing political prisoners, and restarting a dialogue with the people's representatives. A clear policy of explaining how individual steps toward liberalization would be linked with specific sanctions, however, had not been formulated. That specific framework now existed, and it was American policy to convert the sticks into carrots to promote transformation. For some, like Davis, who was still in Foggy Bottom in spring 1983, eventually this policy "would result [in] greater freedom of press, greater freedom of information, and eventually freedom of representation and elections. You would get a different regime."[74] For other more cynical diplomats, "The idea was to figure out a way that [the Poles] could start crawling out of their hole."[75] Regardless, the U.S. government and its representatives in Warsaw now had a well-defined framework to trade sanctions for concessions on a clear quid pro quo basis, a new policy more in line with the small-steps framework proposed by the Poles.

## Small Steps in Warsaw

While the White House waited to see what came of the papal visit, the Polish government prepared for John Paul II's arrival. A papal visit came with some risks. The pope's visit in 1979 was accepted as one of the catalysts for Solidarność, and the PZPR wanted to make sure it did not make the same mistakes again. As Jaruzelski explained: "The pope's visit is the last chance to reanimate [Solidarność]."[76] Cognizant of PZPR fears and the political sensitivity of the visit, the pope made his trip seem as innocuous as possible. As two of the pope's advisers explained, the chief themes of the visit were "dialogue and understanding" and "peace, détente, and disarmament."[77] When the PZPR sent Mirosław Ikonowicz to meet with Father Stanisław Dziwsz at the Vatican in April, Dziwsz assured him that the visit would be "beneficial for everyone" and had been planned "because we are all Poles and we are working for the sake of the country."[78] Not all the pope's plans for his visit sat easily with the Polish Communists, however. In early April the Vatican signaled that the pope wanted to meet Wałęsa and his family.[79] The pope and Glemp also privately and publicly pressured the PZPR to declare an amnesty before John Paul's arrival,[80] but the PZPR gave no indications of acquiescing to either request. When Glemp confronted Jaruzelski about an amnesty, the general replied: "That is out of the question . . . [but] the visit may speed up the process."[81]

In late 1982 and early 1983, the PZPR also received signals from Moscow that a rapprochement with the church and a papal visit could go ahead. Brezhnev had been very skeptical of the role of the Catholic Church in Poland, but in the wake of Brezhnev's death in November 1982, the new general secretary, Yuri Andropov, showed greater flexibility. After returning from a trip to Moscow a month after Brezhnev's death, Jaruzelski informed Rakowski that he "had a friendly conversation with Andropov" and, as a result, had seen a change in East German and Czech attitudes toward internal developments. All three nations (which had advocated taking harsh steps to control the situation during the 1980–81 period) were showing increased sympathy for Poland's plight, giving Jaruzelski more room to maneuver.[82] Rakowski confirmed this view of Andropov with Hungarian diplomats who told him, "Andropov is a remarkable person and, in turn, we should not be afraid of a courageous realization of our own concepts of socialism."[83]

Andropov also acted on his words. When Józef Czyrek, the Central Committee member in charge of relations with the Soviet bloc, traveled to Moscow in March 1983, he gained approval for the PZPR's policy of improving relations with the church.[84] Just after the papal pilgrimage, the top PZPR leadership traveled to Moscow for an unexpected Warsaw Pact meeting to talk over American moves to place short-range missiles in Western Europe, providing Jaruzelski a chance to meet with Andropov personally.[85] Consistent with his earlier statements, Andropov "fully understood" the PZPR's decisions to allow the pilgrimage. Consequently, at least one PZPR politburo member saw Andropov as "a person who sees the necessity of reform and change."[86] During Andropov's tenure, pressure from the Soviet bloc decreased, and Poland was allowed to follow the path it chose toward national reconciliation. As Rakowski put it, the reformist wing in the PZPR felt as if they had a partner in Moscow, "a person who understood Poland's specificity."[87]

As the pope's visit drew near, the opposition flexed its muscles. On April 9-11, Wałęsa took the bold step of meeting with the TKK to plan for the pope's arrival.[88] Opposition activists also made preparations for annual street demonstrations on May 1 and 3, and Wałęsa held a press conference with Western news agencies calling for Poles to participate—statements that received heavy play on RFE.[89] With Wałęsa's endorsement, the May 1 and 3 demonstrations brought nearly one hundred thousand protesters to the streets in twenty cities. Warsaw remained quiet, but forty thousand protestors clashed with police in Gdańsk.[90] Wałęsa claimed victory, but politburo members saw it as a much less decisive matter; as Rakowski concluded in his diary: "It would have been better if there were no demonstrations, but that was simply impossible. What are the lessons of the demonstrations? Only one: one should patiently record the event and remember that [progress] takes time, time, and more time."[91]

Less than a month before his visit, the PZPR was still unsure of how the pope would interact with the opposition. As one report noted, "[The church's role] will be positive, if it is in the interests of Poland, for the visit to confirm the advancing process of stabilization. It is not certain that the church will be at the same cooperative point in the elimination of accents which could constitute support for the opposition (for example meeting with Wałęsa)."[92] In the weeks leading up to the pope's arrival, the Vatican dropped calls for an amnesty, but it continued to request a meeting with Wałęsa. Jaruzelski remained steadfast in his responses, even contemplating arresting Wałęsa to ensure that a meeting did not take place.

When the pope arrived on June 16, nerves were taut.[93] On his first morning, the pope met with Jaruzelski for a private conversation at Belweder Palace. Then over the course of the next seven days, the pope appeared in front of crowds (often numbering more than a million) in Warsaw, Gdańsk, Katowice, Częstochowa, and Kraków. His homilies and addresses touched on wide-ranging topics including Polish history, human and civic rights, national sovereignty, freedom, and creating national reconciliation through trust. The political implications of his words could not be overlooked, however, particularly after John Paul publicly reprimanded Jaruzelski after their first meeting. Everywhere he went the pope was greeted with chants for Wałęsa, Solidarność banners, and fingers held in a "V," a common Solidarność symbol.[94] This was "the first moment since December 13 that Solidarność could demonstrate its presence without the threat of drastic repression— with flags, banners, cheers, peacefully displayed before and after the papal masses."[95] The pope also had two unexpected meetings: a second private meeting with Jaruzelski during which the general acquiesced to requests to meet with Wałęsa as a "private citizen," and a private meeting with Lech Wałęsa and his family on the pope's final day in Kraków.[96]

## Small Rewards from Washington

With the pope's visit over, the conversation in Washington restarted about how best to respond. On the last day of the pope's trip, Reagan addressed a gathering of Polish Americans in Chicago, saying, "I urge the Polish authorities to translate the restraint they showed during the papal visit into willingness to move toward reconciliation rather than confrontation with the Polish people."[97] The same day, Democratic congressmen including Clement Zablocki of New York, Dan Rostenkowski of Illinois, Lee Hamilton of Indiana, and Dante Fascell of Florida wrote a letter to the president, arguing that the release of Wałęsa and the papal visit deserved "some reciprocal action," possibly restoring LOT flights, extending fishing rights, reopening MFN, and supporting initiatives to expand Poland's private sector.[98] Former national security adviser Zbigniew Brzeziński joined the chorus, calling to unilaterally return fishing rights.[99] Following a meeting between the president and Cardinal John Krol of Philadelphia (who had accompanied the pope on his trip), unnamed "officials acknowledged there have been discussions within the administration about whether the United States should make a good-will gesture, such as lifting the sanctions against Polish fishing in American waters."[100] The Department of State viewed the pope's visit as a very positive accomplishment, and on July 7 Undersecretary Eagleburger met with Ludwiczak in Washington to inform him that the U.S. government was officially considering restarting debt negotiations through the Paris Club and lifting restrictions on fishing rights in American waters if liberalization continued and if a substantial number of political prisoners received amnesty.[101] Consistent with the NSPG policy written two months earlier, the Americans had now explained step 1 of their new step-by-step policy.

As had been rumored, Jaruzelski announced to the Sejm that martial law would be repealed at midnight on July 21 and that most political prisoners would soon be released. On the surface these actions fulfilled two of Washington's three criteria for lifting sanctions, but as the president explained, "We're going to go by deeds, not words."[102] When Eagleburger met with Ludwiczak again on July 27, he made clear that the extent to which sanctions would be lifted was still under consideration and depended on freeing "the majority of political prisoners" with "the resurgence [powstanie] of free trade unions especially critical for full normalization of mutual relations."[103] The situation on the ground, however, changed very little. The law repealing martial law included provisions making it easier for the PZPR to impose a new "state of emergency" (rather than a state of "military rule"); the law also made many of the extraordinary powers invoked under martial law part of the government's permanent powers, greatly reducing citizens' and activists' rights. The amnesty was also substantially limited: people with sentences less than three years were released and longer sentences were cut in half, but about sixty of the most well-known and influential opposition members, including eleven KOR and Solidarność activists charged with crimes against the state, remained in prison. According to a U.S. Department of Labor report, "the workers' rights problem has either seen no progress or become worse."[104]

Because of continued Allied pressure the White House did act on its offer to allow debt negotiations. As the Washington Post reported, "most Western European governments opposed continued suspension of negotiations since they were being required to keep up the high interest payments on the guaranteed credits to private institutions."[105] In private discussions the Europeans made it clear that if the United States did not go along with debt-rescheduling talks, they were "prepared to move on their own."[106] At a Paris Club meeting on July 29, the United States "agreed 'in principle' to participate in debt rescheduling. [They] made it clear, however, that [U.S.] participation [would] be dependent on the release by Polish authorities of the 'vast majority' of political prisoners."[107]

Despite these incremental U.S. moves, bilateral relations remained tense. When Senator Christopher Dodd led a trip to Poland from August 8 to 10, he was allowed to visit Wałęsa in Gdańsk; yet he also received the usual barrage of criticisms: sanctions were hurting the Polish people, American policy infringed on Polish sovereignty, aggressive American propaganda went too far, and Solidarność was the main cause of economic problems.[108] When a later delegation led by Congressman Clarence Long met with Jaruzelski on August 17, the atmosphere became nasty. Jaruzelski delivered a diatribe blaming the United States for the horrible state of bilateral relations—"the worst it had been since the beginning of the Cold War." Long became so fed up with the general's windy explanations that he interrupted Jaruzelski to say that he had to go to the bathroom. When the parties returned they clashed again, and Long asked Jaruzelski to get to the point.[109] America's small move to allow debt rescheduling did not prompt a comparable shift on the Polish side. In both meetings Jaruzelski simply restated harsh criticisms of American policy, choosing to disregard the opportunity to pursue continued improvements.

Bilateral relations also suffered setbacks because of the Korean Airlines Flight 007 crisis. Following the downing of a civilian Korean airliner on the night of September 1, American diplomats posted a transcript of U.N. Representative Jeanne Kirkpatrick's confrontation with the Soviet representative in a display case outside the embassy. The Poles viewed this as a deeply provocative act, repeatedly requesting meetings with American officials to complain about this "brutal" form of propaganda.[110] In response the Americans once again delayed full consideration of debt rescheduling and fishing rights.[111] When Davis arrived in Warsaw as the new chargé d'affaires *ad interim* in mid-September, he was confronted by this spike in animosity.[112] Davis's first meeting with Kinast was spent clarifying the American announcement deferring the decision to lift sanctions.[113]

A month after the Korean Airlines disaster, the Americans were once again ready to move. In a further attempt to maintain Allied unity on loans, which was near a breaking point after the issue was postponed in light of the tragedy in Korea, both the State Department and the NSC recommended that the president approve step 1 of the step-by-step process.[114] On October 28, Eagleburger met with Ludwiczak to discuss next steps, which Davis reiterated in Warsaw two days later: the United States agreed to start assigning temporary fishing quotas to Poland beginning in 1984, which became renewable the following year. Polish companies would also be allowed to begin "joint ventures" with American fishing companies as soon as December. Future quotas, however, would depend on how the eleven KOR and

Solidarność activists were treated during their trial for crimes against the state. The administration also dropped all remaining restrictions on full negotiations with the Paris Club.[115] White House spokesman Larry Speakes announced the decision on November 2, publicly taking the United States' first small step.[116]

The Polish response was clear. On November 3, MSZ Vice Minister Wiejacz called Davis to say that the Polish government was "very profoundly disappointed."[117] He also delivered an official note summarizing, over eight pages, Poland's view of bilateral relations. Echoing language from Jaruzelski's meeting with Long, this diplomatic note chastised Washington and charged that sanctions were "unfriendly and unlawful actions" that infringed on Polish sovereignty. Further, the "Polish government rejects such pressures." The note threatened that if all sanctions were not lifted "the further deterioration of relations may become inevitable." The note concluded by specifically suggesting that ending objections to Poland's membership in the IMF could lead to real improvements.[118]

Thus, in November 1983, the Poles rejected American overtures to improve bilateral relations. The steps allowing Poland to begin new negotiations with the Paris Club and to regain fishing quotas proved too small. Instead of seeing these actions as positive movement toward normalization, the Polish government snubbed the Americans. More important, the Polish Communists placed *American* actions at the center of any hopes to improve relations. The MSZ's overriding opinion was "that it is not about what we are up to—the USA must leave behind its destructive approach and take up more significant steps."[119] The Poles had decided that Washington needed to flinch first for relations to improve.

### Expanding Government Support for Solidarność

With few prospects for improved relations with the PZPR, Davis turned toward the other part of the equation: relations with the opposition. He and his wife Helen had been stationed in Warsaw in the 1960s and 1970s when he served as an economics officer, so shortly after arriving, the Davises decided to host a party for their old friends. They invited about 120 people to the ambassador's residence, mainly journalists, artists, economists, film directors, and academics. On the night of the party, however, around two hundred people showed up, including some Solidarność leaders who had been released from jail. A number of unexpected guests explained that they had just assumed that they were supposed to receive invitations. As Davis

A snapshot from one of the Davises' salons at the American ambassador's residence in Warsaw, with (left to right) Jacek Kuroń, Adam Michnik, Helen Davis, Joanna Onyszkiewicz, and Janusz Onyszkiewicz. Photo courtesy of John R. Davis Jr.

explains, "A lot of the [guests] without invitations [were] saying that *they* [the authorities] stole our invitation."[120]

After this success, the Davises began hosting informal receptions at their residence once or twice a month. Usually John would get a recent American movie to show, and his wife and staff would cook a large batch of beef burgundy, lasagna, or stroganoff. Formal written invitations were never issued nor were phones used; Helen would simply issue verbal invites to her friends at literary gathering spots like Czytelnik or at church groups, telling those present to pass the invitation on to others. Anywhere between thirty to fifty people would come for dinner and a movie, providing the Davises a regular chance to see old friends and make new acquaintances. With a few exceptions, Helen and John's contacts were either Solidarność members or sympathizers. As John recalls, their old friends "started bringing their Solidarity friends and made sure we got to know them socially as well as politically. By '84–'85 we were having, every week or ten days, we'd have most of the leadership of Solidarity over that was out of jail. Then as people would come out of jail we would add them to the mix."[121] So, in addition to cultural figures like the film director Andrzej Wajda and the poet Julia Hartwig, well-known Solidarność members like Geremek, Onyszkiewicz, Frasyniuk, Henryk Wujec, and Bogdan Lis soon joined the gatherings.[122] Adam Michnik and Zbigniew Bujak became regular attendees later.[123]

From all accounts these parties were more social than political. Only a select few embassy officers—the deputy chief of mission, political officers, and other ranking members—would be invited; junior members were kept out of the loop.[124] As Helen Davis describes it, she inadvertently created a "salon" in Warsaw: "I had a very sort of carpe diem approach to the whole posting. I decided that since [John] was not an ambassador . . . I didn't have to be ambassadorial. I didn't have to be elegant. I could meet as many people as possible in the shortest time possible . . . so I started having dinner two or three times a month."[125] These meetings were not formal gatherings with an agenda or speeches but social gatherings with Poles sitting at tables of eight to ten with, perhaps, an embassy officer assigned to each table.[126] Politics was not the focus of these gatherings, but the subject did come up. For opposition activists these dinners became a place to discuss their situation openly. As Geremek remembers:

> John Davis tried to give a very personal touch to these meetings. They weren't political meetings with reports, but a dinner, sometimes in the garden, sometimes in his residence, friendly dinners. During these dinners we had the opportunity to discuss, among us, in his presence, among us to discuss the situation, to discuss what can be done, what we have to do and also to present some projects and programs. John Davis had the—how to say this—the tact to be a distant witness of it and not a participant, [not a] political partner in these discussions.[127]

As Onyszkiewicz has explained, "There was a sense of security and a sense of luxury. We could simply exchange views on the situation, but also find out more or less what John Davis's opinion was" of domestic events or U.S. policy.[128] So, as relations with the Polish government were floundering, John and Helen Davis were getting to know Solidarność leaders, gaining their trust, and strengthening relations.

The CIA also took steps to improve the support network for the democratic opposition. The declaration of martial law had caught the agency off guard, and it was not as prepared as the AFL-CIO to begin funneling support to Solidarność immediately. According to Robert Gates, the deputy director for intelligence at CIA in 1982, DCI Casey felt "that Lane Kirkland and his AFL-CIO were doing a 'first-rate' job in Poland helping Solidarity—better, he thought, than CIA could do. Indeed, Casey was worried that if CIA got involved, we might 'screw it up.'"[129] Reservations aside, the CIA did pursue a covert policy. Rather than taking the usual step of issuing a covert action finding, the president and his national security adviser Clark informally gave Casey the authority to run the operation as he saw fit. Reportedly, Casey's plan had four foci: provide money, provide advanced communications equipment for leaders to connect within the country, offer training to Solidarność members in using the equipment, and share intelligence.[130] Of these functions the most substantial were efforts to send money. From operations headquartered in the Frankfurt CIA station, "Casey constructed a web of international financial institutions. The money trail was constantly shifting to avoid detection," with Western businesspeople and corporations knowingly and unknowingly funneling money.[131] Although Casey initiated the covert plan in the spring of 1982 and had some early success coordinating with Israeli intelligence to run fifteen radio transmitters through a supply line from Sweden to northern Poland, his financial web did not start operating until the end of that year. The exact amounts of these funds and the channels that were utilized remain unclear (money is relatively easy to smuggle compared to printing presses or containers of ink), but most accounts agree that the CIA successfully sent around $2 million a year, which translated to about $10 million over the life of the program.[132]

The funding operation's complex web was not only instituted to maintain secrecy from the Polish government but to obscure the money's source from opposition activists themselves. There were no direct links between the CIA and Solidarność; instead, support was sent through third parties and intermediaries in Western Europe to maintain deniability. According to Gates, "The union did not know in specific terms what, if anything, it was getting from CIA."[133] Davis took this a step further. He "insisted that the CIA, at least the CIA in the embassy, stay away from [Solidarność]. 'I don't want to be introduced to anybody from Solidarity,' [Davis] said, 'who turns out to be talking to one of you guys.'" The reasoning behind Davis's position was quite simple: "The one thing I was afraid of was that the Solidarity leadership would get pinned as foreign agents. That was the danger. . . . I did not want the Polish government to be able to say or prove that, 'Here is, you know, Geremek, talking to a CIA agent. These people are not true Poles; they are acting as agents of the United States.' That's what I did not want."[134]

From the beginning of his posting, Davis understood that the United States needed to walk a fine line between displaying support for Solidarność and pursuing formal ties that could be used by the Polish government to question the movement's patriotism or legitimacy. Holding private gatherings at his home, rather than meetings at the embassy, added a layer of deniability for Solidarność members. The gatherings were social, not political; they were personal, not professional. Also, by basing connections with Solidarność leaders on personal relations, Davis added to opposition leaders' security. As one of Davis's officers recalls, "Solidarity contacts were handled in Davis's back pocket . . . because [of] the dangers for these people for contacts with Americans. . . . No one would accuse Davis of being a CIA agent, when some of us [lower-level officers] might have been accused."[135] There was never any doubt within the Polish government that the CIA and the embassy were supporting the opposition, but American policy—particularly policy pursued by Davis—was subtle, restricted, and discreet enough to make it difficult to legitimately tar Solidarność as part of some kind of American-led conspiracy.

Beyond Warsaw and Washington, the U.S. government also increased support to Solidarność via RFE headquarters in Munich. Given the particularities of RFE's charter that policy guidance was provided by officials in Washington but daily content was shaped by the individual language services, the director of the Polish service, Zdzisław Najder, had the greatest influence on RFE's content and policies. Najder was a Solidarność collaborator who assumed the director's position in March 1982 on the recommendation of the former director Jan Nowak-Jezioranski. More than any other role, RFE's Polish Section aided the opposition by broadcasting its messages back into Poland, acting as a kind of bullhorn for the movement. Specifically, Najder used his "wide network of contacts among the opposition within and outside Poland . . . to acquire inside information."[136] These contacts included connections with long-standing émigré activists like Jerzy Giedroyc in Paris, and close contacts with activists in the underground, including Zbigniew Bujak.[137] As independent publishing houses printed more and more samizdat, Najder's office received copies and broadcast portions, even translating the information and broadcasting it on other language services to the rest of the Soviet bloc.[138] According to one study, "the circulation of one *samizdat* rose from a maximum of eighty thousand when distributed on paper to many millions when transmitted by radio."[139] Broadcasts by RFE that spread calls for strikes and demonstrations by providing specific instructions such as where and when protesters should meet continued to exasperate PZPR leaders.[140] Najder also received shipments of microfilmed documents smuggled through, among others, a contact named Jerzy Łojek in Paris. The microfilm images included Solidarność proclamations and internal decisions, as well as PZPR materials documenting policies against the movement.[141] Unlike underground literature, these internal Solidarność and government documents were not read on the air, but were used to inform and enrich editorials and commentaries.

Najder and his colleagues also conspired to send material support to the opposition. Najder received one note from the end of 1983 that reads, "June 27 I got the SONY TC-D5 M tape recorder, together with the instruments." The sender then asked for more recording equipment including microphones, microcassettes, tape recorders, batteries, and a mixer.[142] Najder also received a similar note from two men in Lublin requesting three microcomputers, diskettes, a converter, a hard drive, and a printer.[143] Monthly financial records from the Polish service note "Confidential Payments" from the "Outside Consultation" budget, with which Najder appears to have been using RFE funds to pay for materials that were later sent into Poland. Records from RFE also contain numerous references to payments made to "freelancers" who were also important members of the Solidarność support network, including Irena Lasota, Seweryn Blumsztajn, and Jerzy Milewski. There is no specific use listed for the funds, but RFE money was making its way into opposition activists' hands, either to pay for information they had smuggled out, reports they had filed with RFE, or material they were sending back in.[144]

For his efforts, Najder was despised and lauded. The PZPR tried him in a Polish court and sentenced him to death in absentia in March 1983. In August 1984, the PZPR spokesman Jerzy Urban even went as far as to state that "if you would close . . . Radio Free Europe, the underground would completely cease to exist.[145] As Wałęsa summarized from the other side, RFE was more than just a radio station. "Presenting works that were 'on the red censorship list,' it was our ministry of culture. Exposing absurd economic policies, it was our ministry of economics. Reacting to events promptly and pertinently, but above all, truthfully, it was our ministry of information."[146] Urban's condemnation and Wałęsa's accolades should be taken with a grain of salt; nonetheless the RFE played an important role relaying information back to a wider Polish audience and providing tangential support to the opposition.

## Nongovernmental Organizations Plod Steadily Along

As RFE, the CIA, and the American embassy strengthened their support for the opposition, nongovernmental groups including the AFL-CIO and CSS expanded on earlier successes. In November 1982, the director of the AFL-CIO's Polish Workers Aid Fund and the head of the International Affairs

Department in Washington, Tom Kahn, signed off on paying Lasota just over $3,000 for two shipments of shortwave radio receivers, tape recorders, two-way radios, and a number of antennas.[147] The money was provided in accordance with their "agreement . . . to reimburse [CSS] for limited shipments of items to Poland" and drawn from the remaining PWAF money.[148] In 1983, Lasota's and CSS's efforts intensified. In March 1983, Lasota sent a Polish "internal passport" to Kahn and asked him to duplicate it for her as soon as possible. The request was filled on March 29, suggesting that the AFL-CIO was forging Polish government documents.[149] Five months later, Lasota sent her largest invoice to date, requesting $5,410 for "printing and recording" equipment bought in France with Piotr Naimski.[150]

By August 1983, however, it appears that money from the PWAF was getting tight. Sensing that financial realities were changing, Lasota wrote, "I hope you do not find [the sum] outrageous. From what we know it is already in Poland. It is being used to 'promote democracy in the world,' right?"[151] Kahn sent a note giving credence to Lasota's concerns: "Since the fund from which this check is drawn is limited, we will need to consult in advance before any additional funds can be committed."[152] From AFL-CIO records it appears that Kahn did not pay for any further deliveries to Poland with Polish Worker's Aid funds until July 1985, when he requested about $500 for radios, electrical equipment, and round trip tickets to London.[153] Shortly after this final reimbursement, Kahn transferred control of the operation to Adrian Karatnycky, a Ukrainian American who ran it for the remainder of the decade.

While Lasota concentrated her efforts on sending material and monetary support, her codirector Eric Chenoweth ran the informational work for CSS. The group, with an annual budget between $55,000 and $95,000, received most of its funding from grants from Smith Richardson, the Rockefeller Brothers Foundation, the John M. Olin Foundation, and later from George Soros, as well as consistent money from the AFL-CIO and individual unions for specific expenses.[154] These funds primarily supported the publication of a monthly periodical, *Reports*, which translated and published the most interesting and relevant articles taken from the underground press, as well as news about which activists had been released and who had been arrested. It reached a circulation of about eight hundred in 1984, including academics, members of Congress, government officials, and concerned citizens.[155] Beginning in 1984, CSS also maintained an archive of the underground publications it received.

To publicize human rights abuses, the CSS regularly produced special reports, one in late 1982, one just after the amnesty declaration in 1983, and one in August 1984. Working closely with the Polish Helsinki Committee, Chenoweth maintained a list of political prisoners, including addresses for their families so that they could be sent aid packages. In 1984, CSS translated and published the Polish Helsinki Committee's report, *1984 Violations of Human Rights in Poland*, which detailed suspicious deaths, instances of torture, legal abuses, and changes in Polish law that legalized infringements on basic human rights.[156]

Armed with information, CSS maintained public awareness of conditions in Poland. They sent speakers around the country to college campuses and community groups. Chenoweth and others, including the former Solidarność National Commission member Wacław Adamczyk, wrote editorials and articles that appeared in the *New York Times*, the *Wall Street Journal*, and the *Times of London*. Lasota regularly provided articles for Polish-language newspapers in the United States, particularly *Nowy Dziennik* from New York City. Chenoweth and Lasota wrote letters to Shultz, Reagan, Clark, and Dobriansky, consistently advocating a tough stance on sanctions against the PZPR.[157] Together with their patrons in the AFL-CIO, CSS members also lobbied Congress. In one of its biggest successes, CSS held a press conference in March 1983 to expose the use of military penal camps to repress Solidarność activists.[158] Overall, CSS operated as an informal information office for Solidarność and the wider Polish opposition.

## The National Endowment for Democracy

In 1984 the AFL-CIO, CSS, and other NGOs found a new partner in Washington to promote democracy and support Solidarność's underground activities. During his European trip in June 1982 to meet with the G7 at Versailles, Reagan gave a well-received speech to the British parliament on promoting democracy and peace. Specifically invoking the situation in Poland, Reagan called on the free nations of the world to stand strong against "refined instruments of repression," to fight for "the gradual growth of freedom and democratic ideals" by fostering "the infrastructure of democracy—the system of a free press, unions, political parties, universities—which allows people to choose their own way, to develop their own culture, to reconcile their own differences through peaceful means."[159] This call to action sparked two parallel policy initiatives: one within the administration and one led by the American Political Foundation, an organization created in 1979 "to encourage international non-governmental bipartisan political exchanges between American political activists and their counterparts in Europe and elsewhere."[160]

Within the administration, Reagan's speech led to a cabinet-level meeting on August 3, 1982, and eventually spawned NSDD 77, "Management of Public Diplomacy Relative to National Security," signed on January 14, 1983.[161] This decision directive called for the creation of an International Information Committee to promote democracy through "aid, training and organizational support for foreign governments and private groups to encourage the growth of democratic political institutions and practices." Its goals necessitated close coordination with foreign policy decisions, but the committee would also collaborate with private initiatives run by labor, business, university, philanthropy, political parties, and press groups engaged in parallel efforts.[162] The administration requested $65 million for this "Project Democracy" as part of its fiscal year 1984–85 budget request.[163]

Working concurrently with the government process, the American Political Foundation proposed a study to understand how the United States could improve its infrastructure for supporting democracy abroad.[164] After gathering a powerhouse of Washington insiders for their board of directors—the Republican and Democratic parties' national chairmen, the vice-chairman of RFE, current and former NSC staff members, Democratic politicians Dante Fascell and Christopher Dodd, the vice president of the U.S. Chamber of Commerce, and Lane Kirkland—the foundation received a $400,000 grant from AID to survey past and present private-sector democracy-promotion programs and to compose recommendations on how to improve the capacities of political parties, the labor movement, and business.[165]

While they completed the study, the administration's budget request for Project Democracy came under intense criticism from Capitol Hill. In particular, members of the House Foreign Affairs Committee Subcommittee on International Operations expressed concerned that any money appropriated would support existing programs, throwing new money at tired solutions. Congress was also troubled that Project Democracy might only be used to promote the Reagan administration's particular political and ideological policies abroad. Finally, committee members were concerned that if funds were used evenhandedly—including in friendly or allied countries with a history of antidemocratic actions like Chile, South Korea, or the Philippines—this could create conflicts of interest.[166]

As controversy swirled, the American Political Foundation completed an interim report with its own specific recommendations.[167] Leaders from the group, including Kirkland, presented their conclusions to the congressional subcommittee hearings in April 1983, and proposed starting a nongovernmental, private-sector organization called the National Endowment for

Democracy (NED). The endowment would have a bipartisan board of directors and would be responsible for dispersing congressional funds through grants to individual programs meant to promote democracy. It would not run democracy promotion programs; rather, it would receive money from Congress and pass grants on to other parties. In addition, the foundation recommended the creation of four sister institutions: the National Democratic Institute for International Affairs (run by the Democratic Party), the National Republican Institute for International Affairs (run by the Republican Party), the Center for International Private Enterprise (run by the U.S. Chamber of Commerce), and the Free Trade Union Institute (FTUI, an existing organization run by the AFL-CIO). These four organizations would receive funding from NED and would be responsible for overseeing or running programs meant to promote democracy.[168]

The Subcommittee on International Operations (chaired by American Political Foundation board member Fascell) determined that NED provided a better mechanism than Project Democracy. By creating a private-sector grant-giving organization, NED solved the conflict-of-interest problems: the U.S. government appropriated the money to NED, but it did not decide where the money went. Therefore the executive branch could not be held directly accountable for how the money was used. Second, because NED funds would go to institutions run by the two main political parties, business, and labor, congressional money would not promote only the executive branch's priorities. This approach also had the explicit support of the White House, creating a perfect political storm.[169] On November 22, 1983, President Reagan signed the fiscal year 1984–85 appropriations bill into law, granting $31.3 million to the National Endowment for Democracy.

With NED funded, CSS and other organizations requested support for ongoing and new programs. In April 1984, CSS composed a grant to fund a new East European Democracy Project, which had three goals: 1) to coordinate the distribution of financial and material assistance (printing equipment, ink and stencils, and recording equipment) to the underground free trade unions, independent underground publishing houses, and independent movements for education; 2) to publish and distribute Polish writings banned in Poland, works by other East European dissidents, and general works on democracy and democratic systems; and 3) to translate Solidarność proclamations and statements into other East European languages (particularly Czech) to spread Solidarność's ideas.[170] In September 1984, CSS wrote a second grant proposal directly to FTUI, one focused on sending new printing equipment to independent publishing houses like CDN and

NOWa, providing material aid to writers working in Poland, and translating more Western books into Polish.[171] The East European Democracy Project received a grant of $91,825 from NED for fiscal year 1984 to support independent publishing in Poland and to translate materials about Solidarność into Czech, Russian, and Ukranian.[172] Two other smaller grants for Poland-related activities were approved by NED: one to the International Freedom to Publish Committee to help support the publication of *Zeszyty Literackie* (a Paris-based publication that provided an outlet for writers working within Poland), as well as one to the Polish Institute of Arts and Sciences in America (PIASA) "to provide [food, medicine, and other support] to Polish political prisoners and to assist in maintaining independent cultural, educational, and scholarly activities in Poland."[173]

The Free Trade Union Institute, which had become nearly defunct for lack of money in 1983, also received NED grants for activities in Poland.[174] Of the $11 million the institute received in fiscal year 1984, the majority went to administrative costs, Asia programs, and projects in Latin America. Just over $500,000 supported European projects aimed at "assistance to a series of research, cultural, and intellectual organizations promoting democratic values, and assisting unions in totalitarian countries. These organizations [were] located in Paris, London, and Brussels and assist union rights efforts throughout Western Europe, Soviet Union, and Poland." Although records are sketchy, FTUI likely provided between $200,000 and $300,000 to Solidarność, through the Coordinating Office Abroad in Brussels.[175]

For fiscal year 1985, the total level of NED grants for Poland increased, and it was administered through different groups. Grants to FTUI and money for CSS programs were combined into one appropriation of $540,000, designated for CSS to continue its translations and publication activities, to "support individual Polish exiles in Europe," and to provide for the Coordinating Office's activities. As before, a small sum was given to *Zeszyty Literackie*, this time administered by the Aurora Foundation. Freedom House, a human rights group in New York, received a modest amount to support the Committee for Independent Culture, which ran flying universities and underground cultural activities (see chapter 4). The Aurora Foundation also received money to assist the work of the Polish Legal Defense Fund, a human rights group that worked with dissidents in and out of jail.[176]

In the big picture, NED gave a much-needed infusion of money. As Kahn's August 1983 note to Lasota made clear, the PWAF was drying up. By the end of 1983, CSS was writing to Zbigniew Brzeziński, a member of its board of supervisors, to ask for letters of recommendation for funding applications because it was "becoming more and more difficult to raise sufficient funds."[177] Until the beginning of 1984, direct American support to the Polish underground was quite modest and depended almost exclusively on the AFL-CIO and private donations. The Solidarność Coordinating Office Abroad survived its first years not because of American money but because of fund-raising among European unions, particularly a donation of about $1 million from French unions.[178] Jerzy Milewski and his colleagues were then looking for new funding sources, equivalent to "1 tank" or about $1 million per year.[179] The National Endowment for Democracy began to fill that gap. In terms of resources for American-based projects, Lasota and her colleagues likely doubled their resources. By creating a separate Poland project, the CSS ensured that the money would go to supporting the opposition directly, rather than having funds also go into producing the committee's publications. With a new source of money, other groups like PIASA also got into the game, increasing not only the total sum of money but also the contacts and routes needed to provide support.

## Humanitarian Efforts Press On

From the end of 1982 through 1985, charitable and humanitarian efforts run by American groups hit a new peak. Frozen turkey, rice, oil, milk, cheese, flour, and used clothing continued to form the brunt of American aid, with Catholic Relief Services running the largest program. The group oversaw nearly weekly shipments to Gdańsk on freighters from New York, Wilmington, Baltimore, Charleston, Jacksonville, New Orleans, Galveston, and Houston.[180] According to Polish government records, between 1981 and 1985 CRS was responsible for 266 thousand tons of aid worth $188 million.[181] Once in Gdańsk, the aid was trucked to centers run by KCEP, which oversaw its distribution to needy families throughout twenty-seven dioceses.[182] Additional humanitarian support came from PACCF: 701 tons in 1982; 1,384 tons in 1983; 706 tons in 1984; and 842 tons in 1985.[183] Project HOPE and CARE also continued their work, with CARE providing 120 thousand tons of aid worth $60 million and Project HOPE sending one thousand tons of medical equipment worth $23 million.[184] In total between 1981 and 1985, American humanitarian aid sent through nongovernmental organizations totaled 402 thousand tons worth $362 million.[185]

Based on the success of their relationship with American charitable groups, the Catholic Church attempted to intensify cooperation and create a new fund for Polish farmers. Unlike in other countries in the Soviet bloc, three-quarters of Poland's farmland remained in individual, private farmers' hands. Moreover, 80 percent of the country's food came from private farmers. On September 14, 1982, Cardinal Glemp sent a letter to Jaruzelski proposing the creation of a church-run foundation "using material help from abroad [the West] for the sake of overcoming the deep crisis and softening the effects of economic sanctions."[186] Throughout 1982, the Reagan administration had quietly pursued the possibility of starting an initiative to foster individual farming, even going as far as to contact the Rockefeller Brothers Foundation, but it scrapped the idea as a government-sponsored concept in November 1982 because it might be viewed as providing support to the Polish regime.[187] Nonetheless, when Cardinal Krol returned from the pope's 1983 visit to Poland, he spoke with Reagan about starting a private fund to develop agriculture and reported to Polish officials that the president showed "significant interest" in the idea.[188] In April 1984, the Sejm passed a law allowing autonomous, private foundations, opening the way for the church to create the agricultural fund.

The Poles followed this advance by sending church representatives to request money for a pilot program. Father Aloyszy Orszulik and Professor Andrzej Stelmachowski (members of the organizing committee for the agricultural fund) were sent to lobby both in Western Europe and in North America during June and July 1984. While in Washington, they met with Assistant Secretary of State Edward Derwinski; Deputy Secretary of Agriculture Richard Lyng; new National Security Adviser Robert McFarlane, and Dobriansky;[189] and with members of the House and Senate Committees on Foreign Relations. Outside of government, the Polish emissaries spoke with AFL-CIO president Kirkland, with John Rockefeller of the Rockefeller Brothers Foundation, with Cardinal Krol, and with Brzeziński.

Although Stelmachowski and Orszulik were not government representatives per se, the American reaction was, nonetheless, tempered by ongoing conflicts in bilateral relations. Money for the agricultural fund was treated as part of the step-by-step process, not as a separate issue. Also, the trip gave policy makers a chance to meet with Polish representatives when exchanges were at a minimum. Stelmachowski and Orszulik's meeting with McFarlane and Dobriansky was only scheduled to be ten minutes, but it lasted more than an hour. As Davis recognized, the church project had the possibility of creating "a rival center of economic power outside of government control;"[190] therefore the NSC was very supportive but careful to say that the program had to be fully independent of the state. It could not be seen as supporting the regime directly.[191] In reporting to the MSZ, the agriculture fund representatives emphasized "that their conversations play[ed] an important role in actions on matters of lifting the U.S. government's restrictions."[192]

The trip was also a success for the agricultural program. The Polish delegation received pledges for $28 million to provide training, modern machinery, and fertilizer to private farmers. The U.S. Congress pledged $10 million, with an additional $3 million from the American Catholic Church and $1 million from the Canadian Catholic Church. The European Community, who the Poles met with in Bonn, pledged a comparable amount. On August 17, 1984, Reagan gave his public support to the measure.[193] A month later the Senate Committee on Foreign Relations approved the appropriations. As the program was devised, foreign money would be given directly to the church agricultural foundation, which would purchase farm machinery, fertilizer, and machinery in the West. They would then sell the equipment at reduced prices to farmers for zlotys, with the proceeds going to pay for administrative expenses and social projects in rural areas.[194] Both measures were meant to bring needed money and equipment to less-developed provinces and alleviate food shortages.

Beyond the agricultural fund, Congress took independent steps to increase other types of humanitarian aid. Fascell and forty-six other representatives cosponsored legislation (H.R. 4835) to appropriate funds to construct the Clement Zablocki Memorial Outpatient Facility at the American Children's Hospital in Kraków. Zablocki was a Polish American congressman from Milwaukee who chaired the Foreign Relations Committee for seven years before his death in December 1983; he had been instrumental in the original legislation to build the children's hospital. Fascell's legislation freed excess zlotys held by the U.S. government to construct the new hospital wing, and it appropriated an additional $10 million to furnish the wing, provide needed medical equipment, and purchase necessary medical supplies. The bill was approved by Congress in June 1984.

Humanitarian efforts did not suffer the same fate as bilateral relations between 1982 and 1985. The Polish people still needed Western help. Catholic Relief Services, the Polish American Congress Charitable Foundation, CARE, and Project HOPE continued to send massive amounts of food, clothing, and medical supplies, with American aid accounting for at least half of the entire sum of foreign aid sent to Poland between 1981 and 1985. Beginning in 1984, Congress also directly involved itself by pledging money for Polish farmers and millions more to build and furnish a wing of a children's hospital. These humanitarian agreements and the tacit or explicit cooperation they required between Americans and Poles were not just tangential notes.

These agreements and the political will they required were among the few bright spots in U.S.-Polish relations in the mid-1980s and allowed both sides to continue to talk and work together, no matter how bad government-to-government relations got. As with the internal situation, the Catholic Church played an essential role in enabling this channel for dialogue.

## Sanctions and Domestic Politics

Reagan's announcement in November 1983 that his administration was considering allowing Polish ships to fish in American waters and that he supported debt rescheduling negotiations at the Paris Club reinvigorated the debate about how to proceed, both in the United States and in Poland. In an October 26, 1983, letter to the president, Kirkland pressured the White House to maintain sanctions. Joined by CSS, the AFL-CIO considered any move to relax sanctions "profoundly misguided and unwarranted. To return to business as usual would put the blessings of the United States on continued repression in Poland . . . [only encouraging] the hardliners in Warsaw and Moscow."[195] On the other side of the debate, PAC president Al Mazewski understood that repression continued, but he supported debt rescheduling and lifting the embargo on fishing rights "to break the impasse in the U.S.-Polish relations and to signal our good will to offer assistance."[196] Both sides sincerely believed they were arguing for the best interests of the Polish people; Kirkland and the CSS specifically invoked Solidarność positions to argue that sanctions should not be withdrawn.

Two other sources added pressure to lift sanctions further. First, John Paul II expressed "his hope and wish that the economic and commercial sanctions against Poland be lifted in the near future."[197] In private, the United States got the same position from the Vatican's unofficial foreign minister, Archbishop Achille Silvestrini. As the U.S. embassy in Rome reported: "The message that it is time to lift sanctions is unmistakable."[198] In addition, 1984 was an election year, and the White House showed signs of thinking about domestic ramifications: Faith Whittlesey, the assistant to the president for public liaison, pushed the NSC to make more favorable advances toward Mazewski, the "recognized leader of most Poles in the U.S." and the president of an organization "that has been very helpful in getting the president's message out to the eight million Polish Americans."[199]

The Solidarność underground's position was also evolving. When Solidarność leaders initially heard about American sanctions during internment, most responded with joy, feeling that they had a powerful advocate in their fight against the PZPR.[200] Once in public, it was tricky to balance sanctions' negative effects on Polish peoples' lives with the positive pressure the sanctions put on the PZPR. In his analysis, TKK member Zbigniew Bujak weighed sanctions against the aid Poland would have received from the West, as well as how it might have been used to ameliorate material and food shortages. He supported sanctions, saying, "Here there is not the slightest doubt as to the answer. Only an insignificant part of the aid would have been put to this use."[201] By the end of the first year of martial law, however, the opposition's position had grown more sophisticated: American sanctions were only symbolically important. On the one hand, sanctions provided a propaganda tool for the Jaruzelski government to blame Reagan for the country's problems. On the other hand, lifting sanctions would not really change anything because the government actually needed new Western credits to revive the economy. In the opposition's eyes, sanctions were not the cause of economic hardship; they were just a symbol showing American disapproval of the PZPR and American support for Solidarność. [202]

In the face of constant anti-sanctions propaganda in 1983, the opposition's position shifted further, culminating in a press conference by Wałęsa in December calling for the end of sanctions. As Jerzy Milewski explained in private correspondence, the PZPR was constantly claiming that American sanctions made it necessary to raise prices on food and basic goods. By the end of 1983, these claims had gained some traction within society, and "therefore the leadership of NSZZ Solidarność decided that, for the good of the trade union, it would be better to appeal for the withdrawal of the economic sanctions before the beginning of next year."[203] Solidarność had not changed its opinions about the relative importance of economic sanctions versus new credits, but supporting sanctions had become too politically expensive.

Wałęsa's call to lift sanctions had a direct effect on American decision making. Secretary Shultz explained that "it is important that we move now to reinforce Wałęsa's decision. . . . A failure on our part to respond to his appeal could undermine his credibility within Poland and the international community." The NSC concurred: "It is important to be responsive to Wałęsa's appeal as it would enhance his credibility and bolster his standing in Poland." So, on January 16, 1984, the president approved a revision of the existing step-by-step policy, ending the embargo on Polish rights to American fisheries, granting Poland a fishing quota for 1984, and allowing LOT to fly eighty-eight charter flights between the United States and Poland. Wałęsa had specifically mentioned these sanctions in his appeal to Washington.[204]

The State Department's request for a special emissary to send the message was denied once again, and the decision was made public on January 19, 1984.[205] A second set of sanctions had now been lifted.

## An Attempt at Quiet Diplomacy

While the White House and Solidarność were revising their public positions on sanctions, John Davis continued to use the step-by-step framework to improve the situation in Warsaw. Rather than engaging in a debate through the MSZ, Davis conducted new negotiations through a confidential emissary, Adam Schaff. Schaff was a Warsaw University professor and Communist Party intellectual who had served as a Central Committee member in the 1960s and was best known for his attempts to create a "humanistic" Marxism. He was purged from the party in the late 1960s, but eventually regained favor among the reform wing associated with Jaruzelski. In the early 1980s, he was deeply opposed to Solidarność and even suggested that Jaruzelski deserved the Nobel Peace Prize.[206] Schaff also served as an unofficial PZPR emissary in July 1983, when he met privately with the pope.[207] Building on this prior role, Schaff approached Davis to talk "on behalf of Poland's highest authorities" beginning around New Year's 1984, and the two brokered a deal "that the Polish government would be prepared to release the eleven prominent Solidarity leaders and KOR activists who are awaiting trial, if the U.S. would further ease some of its sanctions."[208] The eleven prisoners include four activists linked to KOR (Kuroń, Michnik, Romaszewski, and Wujec) and seven activists linked to Solidarność (Andrzej Gwiazda, Seweryn Jaworski, Marian Jurczyk, Karol Modzielewski, Grzegorz Palka, Andrzej Rozpłochowski, and Jan Rulewski), all of whom had become causes célèbres with a very public "Petition against the Warsaw Trials," which received thirty-three hundred signatures. On February 16, Reagan signed off on the deal and instructed Davis to agree to lift two sanctions—to restore regularly scheduled LOT flights and to release Marie Skłodowska-Curie Foundation funds for joint scientific exchanges—if the Poles released the eleven opposition members. In addition, the U.S. government would "consider sending an ambassador to Warsaw to engage in a high-level dialogue to review the state of our bilateral relations."[209]

General Jaruzelski's initial response was less than satisfactory. The American proposal was unacceptable primarily because it "did not address the important point of major sanctions" and did not respond to Jaruzelski's request to meet with a high-level emissary to discuss bilateral issues. Schaff also reported that the American position effectively pushed the Poles closer to the

Soviets, and that his dialogue with Davis should be considered "terminated or at least postponed." Schaff did, however, mention that he would be in Vienna at the end of the month and that a meeting could be arranged there.[210] A few weeks later, the PZPR kept dialogue open, but requested that Reagan appeal publicly for the eleven prisoners and offer them asylum in the United States if they were exiled. The State Department recommended the White House take this step for humanitarian purposes, but the NSC rejected the idea of a public statement given how unpalatable forced exile was within the Polish underground. At the end of March, Reagan agreed to send Undersecretary Eagleburger to Vienna to meet with Schaff, continued to push for the prisoners' freedom privately, and decided to accept the prisoners if they chose exile. However, he rejected a public statement on the matter.[211]

Eagleburger and Schaff met in Vienna at the end of March, but the outcome was similarly disappointing. Eagleburger presented a "non-paper," outlining moves the Poles would have to take to see all sanctions lifted, presumably in line with the step-by-step policy from the previous May.[212] After consultations with Warsaw, Schaff came back, rejected Eagleburger's proposals, and stated that the PZPR's publically acknowledged line calling for all American sanctions to be lifted remained in place. Jaruzelski also rejected a call for an exchange of ambassadors, and Schaff explained that the channel for dialogue had been suspended. In response, the State Department adopted "a wait and see attitude" on whether the PZPR might follow through with releasing the high-level prisoners, despite the lack of agreement.[213] The NSC considered the informal negotiations over, and discussions of how to proceed paused.[214]

The sputtering process of Schaff's informal dialogue with Davis and then Eagleburger reflected a muddled process within the PZPR about exactly what to do with the eleven high-profile activists still in prison. The church had consistently called for their release, and on January 5, Jaruzelski met with Glemp to talk about the issue.[215] By the end of January, politburo members were beginning to see a trial as a losing proposition. Rakowski wrote in his journal: "The trial against the KOR members and the seven from Solidarność is a necessary evil. After what kind of shit is it necessary? Certainly not lucky. Politically the trial will be groundless. There will be sentences and then what? For half a year we will lose points, the entire West will have screamed, and we will not profit at all."[216] On February 10, the PZPR politburo met to discuss its options. Although that day was dominated by the death of Soviet secretary general Juri Andropov, the MSW offered three possible paths: 1) to hold a trial that would only incur greater resistance from the West and the church; 2) to declare an amnesty as was favored by the church; or 3) to "begin a trial process of both groups and discontinue them on the basis of a planned amnesty on the 40th Anniversary of the Polish People's Republic," which would have the same advantages as declaring an amnesty in relations with the church.[217] As a compromise, the third option afforded the best solution. As the NSC noted, "Polish authorities appear already to be inclined to release the eleven prisoners as they feel that putting them on trial would only serve to embarrass the government. Even Professor Schaff asserted that 'Poland was desperately anxious to solve the prisoner problem and was aware of its delicacy.'"[218] The PZPR was looking for a way to release the prisoners because of pressure from the church and the West. So while accepting the inevitable, Jaruzelski and his advisers were trying to take advantage of the release by linking the move with weakened sanctions.

As spring turned into summer, the PZPR continued to struggle with how best to handle the eleven. The government offered the dissidents amnesty if they agreed to leave the country (a deal brokered by U.N. Secretary General Javier Pérez du Cuéllar). They also offered amnesty if the defendants agreed to refrain from political activity for a period of time. In both cases, the dissidents refused.[219] Kiszczak also negotiated with Glemp and Dąbrowski, who pressured the government time and again to release the prisoners. After a tense spring—during which students held demonstrations across the country to keep crucifixes in classrooms, Solidarność ran a campaign calling for Poles to boycott parliamentary elections, and the usual street demonstrations occurred on May 1 and May 3—the PZPR stuck with the original plan and directed General Kiszczak to "continue negotiations [with the church] in accordance with the plan that had been put forward."[220] As part of implementing the plan Kiszczak spoke with local party officials to convince this group, who were often more hard line than leaders in Warsaw, of the soundness of releasing the prisoners.

In the meantime, the PZPR took two public steps that seemed to contradict the deal the United States had brokered with Schaff. On June 12 the PZPR announced that the four KOR leaders in the group of eleven would head to trial in one month.[221] Second, amid conflicting rumors that an amnesty was both forthcoming and that hard-line members of the government were attempting to block the amnesty, Schaff was expelled from the Communist Party "for publishing 'politically harmful' articles . . . [and for] conduct 'incompatible with his party membership.'"[222] Publicly there was no mention of his role in negotiations with Davis, but Schaff's removal raised concerns about the viability of the deal he had brokered.

After a few shaky months, the Poles and the Americans ultimately fulfilled their respective ends of the agreement from February. The trial of the KOR members began on July 13 as planned, but was suspended on July 19 before the first witness testified. Then on July 22, the fortieth anniversary of the founding of Communist Poland, the Sejm ratified an amnesty declaration that promised to free all political prisoners except those charged with a few specific crimes. In addition to more than 650 political prisoners, 35,000 inmates who had been imprisoned on minor crimes related to demonstrations were also released. Members of the underground organizations and independent presses were also offered amnesty if they turned themselves in.[223] Most important, Kuroń, Michnik, Gwiazda, Wujec, Romaszewski, and the other members of the eleven were set free. Władysław Frasyniuk and Józef Pinior were also released. Only Bogdan Lis, a member of the TKK, and Piotr Mierzewski, who had been with Lis in early June when they were captured, remained in prison on charges of treason. Two weeks after the amnesty, White House spokesman Larry Speakes announced that "in accordance with his step-by-step approach," the president had decided to drop two sanctions: LOT would now be allowed to return to regularly scheduled flights and full scientific and technical exchanges were again permitted. Both sides had now kept up their respective ends of the Schaff-Davis deal. Further, the president offered to back the "reactivation of Poland's application for membership in the International Monetary Fund" if the amnesty proved to be complete and reasonable (meaning that the activists were not quickly rearrested).[224]

Through the end of 1984, the issue of Poland's IMF membership dominated discussions in Washington and bilateral talks.[225] By the end of August, a decision on whether to view the Polish amnesty as "complete and reasonable" led to an NSC meeting. Secretary Weinberger voiced the strongest concerns that while 630 political prisoners had been freed, 22 remained in prison. In addition, those freed could be rearrested for political activity, and it was unclear just how long those released would remain free. The NSC did recognize, however, that allowing Poland to restart its IMF membership application did not guarantee Polish membership; rather, the process would require painful economic changes within the country. Given that once Washington lifted its veto on Polish IMF membership the country could not rescind it, the NSC decided not to consider the amnesty complete at that time.[226] Under pressure from European allies and members of the Polish American community to revoke the veto on IMF membership, the State Department recommended that they clarify their position with the Poles.[227]

With NSC support, U.S. policy changed to allow the IMF membership process to begin if Lis and Mierzewski were released (the two-high ranking Solidarność officials still in jail).[228] On October 20, Davis approached Kinast with a second offer to trade sanctions for political prisoners. Undersecretary of State Michael Armacost made a simultaneous offer to Ludwiczak in Washington. As Davis made clear, "The USA wants to start the procedure for Poland to join the IMF," but it was concerned about twenty-two people who fell under the amnesty but remained in prison. As Davis explained, the United States had announced to the IMF board that they were willing to drop restrictions on Poland's membership, but only if the amnesty was "full and reasonable." Yet "the administration [could not] accept in good measure that the amnesty is 'full and reasonable' so long as Lis and Mierzewski find themselves in prison."[229]

The second sanctions-for-prisoners deal was also a success. On December 8, both Lis and Mierzewski were released. Less than a week later, unnamed Treasury officials quietly confirmed that the United States had dropped its veto against Poland's IMF membership, making no specific mention of the deal for opposition activists.[230] There was no presidential statement on the issue. In reporting the news to the pope, however, the NSC made the decision's parameters clear: "In response to Poland's implementation of the July 1984 amnesty (in particular the release of Bogdan Lis and Piotr Mierzewski), we withdrew our objection to Poland's membership application in the IMF."[231] As part of the step-by-step policy another sanction had been dropped in return for the release of Solidarność leaders.

### Dis-agrément

Despite both sides holding up their respective ends on bargains for political prisoners negotiated through special channels, the official bilateral relationship remained thoroughly frigid in 1984. Even after Reagan announced that he was dropping sanctions following the July amnesty, the Poles staunchly defended their hard-line approach. On August 16, Davis was presented another eight-page government note nearly identical to the November 1983 missive. The note criticized the American actions as "still far from meeting actual needs both in terms of the damages inflicted against Poland and its people, as well as in terms of the requirements for normalization of mutual relations." Reagan's move was too little, too late. The PZPR could "see a positive element" in it, but normalizing relations still depended on the United States "relinquishing the policies of interference in [Poland's] internal affairs, including oppressive propaganda, a return to normal terms of trade, economic and financial cooperation, to equitable cooperation in all areas as well as taking measures designed to make good on the losses caused by the policies of restrictions."[232]

Possibilities for bilateral improvements in the fall of 1984 were further hampered by tragic internal developments. On October 30 a pro-Solidarność priest, Father Jerzy Popiełuszko, was found murdered. Popiełuszko, who was frequently criticized by the government for his support for the opposition, was kidnapped by members of the Polish security services on October 19 and then beaten to death. In the face of pressure from the Catholic Church and a massive public outcry (two hundred thousand mourners attended his funeral and Solidarność called for strikes in his honor), the PZPR investigated the crimes and took the unprecedented step of bringing three internal security service officers to trial on murder charges. Unlike in the Korean airliner crisis, the Reagan administration only released a statement that America shared "the grief of the Polish people at the news of the tragic death" and called for those responsible to be brought to justice.[233] The NSC viewed the murder as an attempt by hard-liners to destabilize the fragile normalization then under way, an attempt to "embarrass Jaruzelski and Kiszczak, inflame the church and Solidarity [to] provoke a new round of unrest, and block any prospects for intensified dialogue."[234] The British shared this opinion, adding that the general's response to "tragedy could have the effect of strengthening Jaruzelski's position against hardline opponents in the Party."[235] Responding harshly to the murder would have only increased the possibility of a clash and strengthened those within the Polish government seeking to discredit Jaruzelski's slow reform program.

In the wake of the Popiełuszko crisis, the PZPR continued to follow the same line against Washington, leading to another diplomatic crisis. On December 14, Davis told Kinast that the embassy would be making an official request for agrément to appoint John Scanlan ambassador. Armacost made the same announcement to Ludwiczak in Washington. The White House had first made its intentions to appoint Scanlan known in November 1982 and had continued to raise the issue intermittently during the following two years. Each time the Americans raised the possibility of exchanging ambassadors, the Poles did not respond. On December 17, Kinast explained to Davis that the Polish government did not consider allowing Poland to enter the IMF a sufficient change to "justify the exchange of ambassadors." Instead, Kinast suggested the appointment of a special envoy from Washington to discuss the entirety of U.S.-Polish relations, a position he had advocated originally in Washington in February 1983. In response, Davis made clear that his earlier proposal "was not the object of an auction."[236]

On December 19, the Americans forced the Poles' hand. That day Davis delivered an official note requesting written agrément from the Polish People's Republic to appoint Scanlan ambassador. With the note came an oral ultimatum: "Should there be no response within thirty days, we will have to draw our own conclusions. We would then have no choice but to establish relations at the chargé level for the foreseeable future." Davis continued, "If this occurs, then as Under Secretary Armacost told Mr. Ludwiczak on December 14, it will be a long time before there will be an American ambassador in Warsaw or a high-level discussion of the type Deputy Foreign Minister Kinast suggested."[237] In fact, according to the May 1983 decision, which inaugurated the step-by-step policy, Reagan specifically did not want to appoint a special emissary. The president repeatedly decided that all negotiations would go through traditional diplomatic contacts.[238] Davis met again with Kinast after Christmas to reiterate his earlier statements and to make clear that the embassy "did not reject . . . the idea of a dialogue at a high level, but they consider[ed] the accreditation of a USA ambassador the completion of the first step."[239]

Ambassador Davis did not hear back from the MSZ until after the New Year, when he was called to meet with MSZ Director of Department III, Juliusz Biały. Rather than talk about Scanlan, Biały delivered a "sharp protest" against a program broadcast earlier in January on RFE, which included a mock speech by Adolph Hitler insinuating comparisons between Jaruzelski and Hitler and between the PZPR and the Nazis.[240] Davis met with Biały again six days later to make an extended presentation on the intricacies of RFE's relationship with the U.S. government and to disavow the broadcast.[241] Davis's presentation fell on deaf ears. On January 17, Kinast met with Davis again, to officially reject the ultimatum regarding Scanlan "or any ultimatum pertaining to relations between Poland and the United States of America." Kinast also explained that "the present request for agrément is of a character and form which preclude any possibility for the Polish side of ever taking it into consideration."[242] Two weeks later Davis declared the request for agrément null and void, and added: "With regard to the Polish proposal for special talks, our view is that existing diplomatic channels should be used to discuss legitimate bilateral issues."[243] Shortly thereafter, Davis returned to Washington for consultations.

The PZPR's rejection of agrément was not just a knee-jerk response to the RFE broadcast in early January, even though this clearly hit a nerve at the PZPR's highest level. The Poles had blocked an exchange of ambassadors for more than two years. In meeting after meeting and confrontation after confrontation the MSZ did its best to rebuff American pressure. Polish diplomats consistently invoked the tough language of their November 1983 and August 1984 notes, which outlined the concessions they expected *from the Americans* before they could return to normal bilateral relations. Scanlan's fate was an important symbol of this stance. As Colonel Wiesław Gornicki, Jaruzelski's aide and close personal adviser, wrote in an internal memo, "Agrément for Scanlan is one of the effective instruments of pressure in our hands."[244] Rather than some kind of emotional response to an RFE broadcast, the PZPR's decision—to deny Scanlan the necessary approval to be the next ambassador—was symptomatic of the PZPR's policy to remain resolute in the face of American pressure.

While reminiscing at a conference in 1999 about his time in Warsaw, John Davis spoke about the step-by-step process, saying, "Some of our friends in Solidarność will be surprised, when one day documents are released on this, that their exits from prison were in exchange for restoring landing rights to LOT in Chicago or for the right for Poland to fish in waters off Alaska."[245] Now that some of the documents have emerged, they bear out Davis's statement: prisoners-for-sanctions exchanges constituted a high point for the Reagan administration's policy toward Poland. These negotiations were also a real highlight of Davis's first few years in Warsaw. As he describes the experience: "I wound up going into the foreign office, I would always find myself starting with the thing about the Helsinki Final Act because that gave me the right to intervene on human rights, since they were fellow signatories. Then we would get into trying to get Michnik . . . or Lis or whoever it was out of the pokey." Next he would "always ask for everybody [in prison]. But then they would wind up giving two or three and I would give them a little bit of something in recognition, to encourage them to go on. Of course the trick was not to be put in a position where they would keep rearresting people so they could get more concessions to let them out. We never paid twice for the same guy."[246] From the American perspective, this is how the process worked, and it clearly succeeded. Adam Michnik, Jacek Kuroń, Jan Lityński, Henryk Wujec, Andrzej Gwiazda, Seweryn Jaworski, Marian Jurczyk, Karol Modzelewski, Grzegorz Palka, Andrzej Rozpłochowski, Jan Rulewski, Piotr Mierzewski, and Bogdan Lis—all important members of the opposition—owed their freedom at the end of 1984, in part, to Davis's diplomatic efforts.

Taking into account Polish documents, however, the extent of the American victory is less clear. Political prisoners were also released because of evolving risk calculations. Kiszczak argued before Wałęsa's release that Solidarność's former leader was not a threat as a private citizen. Jaruzelski felt similarly about the amnesty in 1984: "The amnesty was addressed to society and not to the opposition; this circle which they are concentrating on leaving prison is, nevertheless, minute; the opposition is strengthened by the exit to freedom of these Solidarność activists, but their base has decreased; . . . the opposition has a program to fight against us, but they don't have a positive action program."[247] The PZPR did not fear the opposition as much as they had in December 1981, primarily because they believed the opposition was losing its relevance to the people and its influence with workers.

These revised calculations played directly into Davis's negotiations. Before Davis and Schaff agreed to a framework for releasing the eleven prisoners, the politburo had already decided that a trial would be politically risky and that it was in the government's best interest to release those jailed. As regards Lis, Jaruzelski "confided in" Rakowski on August 23 "that he [had] taken a decision about freeing Lis and his companion. This way the entire problem of political prisoners will go away."[248] This was two months before Davis offered a deal for Lis. Given the specifics of chronology, it becomes clearer that American proposals did not directly provoke the decisions to release political prisoners. Nonetheless, Davis's offers to lift sanctions certainly helped nudge the politburo toward releasing important activists by counteracting the sting of having another opposition member out on the street.[249] American policy buttressed reformist trends, but it was not essential in freeing political prisoners.

A causal link between America's step-by-step policy and the PZPR's small moves toward liberalization is further weakened when looking beyond the specific issue of political prisoners to include the entire scope of bilateral relations. When Poland first proposed the small-steps framework in November 1982, and then sent Kinast to meet with officials in Washington in February 1983, the White House was in the midst of forging consensus on the "next-steps" framework. When the Reagan administration finally approved the approach in May 1983 and began lifting sanctions the following fall, the PZPR made it clear with its official government note that the Americans were doing too little, too late. The Poles stonewalled the Americans on improving bilateral relations with the hope that America would acquiesce to Warsaw's demands and drop all their sanctions.

It is difficult to pinpoint the source of Poland's resolve to resist American pressure. Here, however, it seems helpful to look back to the beginning of the crisis, and at the deep sense of anger and distrust that American sanctions originally provoked (see chapter 1). The disgust did not fade after 1982. It comes across in Jaruzelski's tirade to Congressman Long in the summer of 1983. The basic outline of this argument resurfaced in the Polish government's November 1983 and August 1984 notes. Time did not lessen the sense of betrayal. Instead, the Reagan administration's reluctance to drop significant sanctions after martial law was lifted pushed the PZPR toward further confrontation. Anger and distrust dominated and continually subverted bilateral relations.

Poland's diplomatic protests against American pressure might appear as a case of, "thou dost protest too much." But the Poles backed their protests with policy meant to use every point of leverage they had to force the Americans to accept the Communist regime's legitimacy and repeal sanctions. Polish security services harassed members of the Western press. They harassed Poles who worked at the American embassy as well as American diplomats. The PZPR tried to shut down the American library. Time and time again, the MSZ called American diplomats into the ministry to complain strenuously about RFE broadcasts. When the American government requested agrément to post a new ambassador in Warsaw, the MSZ rejected the deal outright rather than give in to American pressure, despite the possibility that accepting Scanlan could have improved relations. At every possible turn the Polish government did what it could to sour the bilateral relationship until the other side blinked.

Unfortunately for the PZPR, its actions had little meaningful leverage against the Americans and did nothing to change attitudes in the White House. As Christopher Hill remembers: "The leadership in Washington . . . made it very clear to the Poles that ultimately *we don't care*. If they want to take the relationship down to zero, we are happy to take it down to zero. It's up to them. The purpose of such a line, which seems such a brutally hard line, is to make it clear to the regime that they need us more than we need them."[250] In retrospect, bilateral relations remained stalled from 1982 to 1985 because neither side was fully committed to making improvements. With the exception of deals to free political prisoners, government-to-government relations at the beginning of 1985 were as bad as they had been at the end of 1982, and future improvements were nowhere to be seen. When Davis returned to Washington for consultations in 1985, he was "disappointed. It looked like a long hard slog. At that point it looked hopeless."[251] Both sides had defined what they expected to happen to improve relations, but neither side was willing to take those steps.

And yet during this diplomatic stalemate, Jaruzelski and his politburo moved to normalize the situation in Poland: Wałęsa was freed, martial law was suspended and then lifted, the pope made a pilgrimage, and the Sejm passed annual amnesties for political prisoners. More than any other players, reformers in the PZPR and leaders of the Catholic Church produced these changes. The Catholic Church saw itself as an intermediary between the people and the government and sought to ameliorate suffering on the ground. The church did not always get exactly what it wanted, but it did succeed in getting important concessions. In return, the PZPR found a partner.[252] The PZPR relied on the church to shape popular opinion and to keep the masses from revolting. The Communists also increasingly relied on the Catholic Church (particularly the pope and the Vatican) to improve Poland's international image and exert pressure on the West to end sanctions. In terms of U.S. policy, this strategy found success; the pope's personal contacts with Reagan were integral to the president's decisions to drop sanctions.

This second point leads to another source of pressure on the Communist government: Western economic sanctions and restrictions on credits. References to Western pressure are common in documents, and there is no doubt that by 1984 economic sanctions were taking a toll. By the PZPR's own calculations, Western imports dropped from $6.233 billion in 1981 to $4.317 billion in 1983. Because of restrictions on loans and credits, the Poles had to pay cash for these goods. In 1981 the government spent $1.313 billion in cash for imports, compared to $3.752 billion in 1983. Together this meant that the Polish government was paying 286 percent more in 1983 for 34 percent less in imported goods.[253] In a country that suffered from shortages of consumer and technological goods even in the best of times, this decrease proved acutely painful.

While the PZPR leadership publicly blamed the United States for sanctions and economic troubles, West European nations, Canada, and Japan had also imposed restrictions. The United States was not the only culprit or cause of Poland's problems. References to the "West" in internal PZPR documents were not synonymous with references to the United States. During the following few years, as internal economic and political trends continued to work against the PZPR, this economic pressure intensified, highlighting the importance of European policies in Poland's transformation. In addition, American humanitarian aid and support to Solidarność—that continued and, in some cases, increased between 1982 and 1985—would begin to bear fruit. Under ever-increasing pressure and in a changing international setting, the Polish government neared an important turning point in 1986.

CHAPTER FOUR

# A Circle of Mistakes

## International Pressures, Domestic Response,
## January 1985 to September 1986

On September 19, 1986, Jacek Kuroń held a private gathering in his apartment in the Żoliborz neighborhood of Warsaw to mark the tenth anniversary of the founding of KOR. That organization was still outlawed, as was
its progeny Solidarność, and leaders of both groups had been in and out of
prison for the previous five years. But this was not a somber gathering. The
activists were celebrating a new victory: a complete amnesty for all political prisoners. The amnesty included well-known recidivists Adam Michnik,
Bogdan Lis, and Władzsław Frasyniuk. Zbigniew Bujak, who had managed
to evade capture longer than any other high-level Solidarność leader, joined
the gathering not as a fugitive but as a free man. This was a night to meet
with old friends, share stories, and drink. As Michnik explained to a journalist, he had promised "that he would not start drinking until nine" but
was already "drunk with happiness." Kuroń summed up the joyous mood,
embracing Bujak and exclaiming, "There has never been a gathering like
this, never!"[1]

This was also a joyous occasion for the Americans who had made the
treatment of activists and political prisoners a focal point of their demands.
Unlike the decisions to release specific prisoners in 1984, however, the 1986
amnesty had more than one foreign parent. In the year prior to the complete amnesty, bilateral Polish-American relations remained weak, near
broken, and the PZPR's decision to release all remaining political prisoners
was not a response to American actions. Rather, the PZPR was reacting to
long-standing economic concerns and the shifting input of two other international interests: the Soviet Union and Western Europe. As domestic
problems clashed with concerns about foreign affairs, the PZPR ultimately
chose to succumb to these foreign pressures, leading the country in a new
direction.

## Frozen Relations

In the first half of 1985, bilateral relations between Washington and Warsaw dissolved, undermining the small improvements won in the preceding two years. First, despite Ambassador Davis's successful efforts to free democratic activists in 1984, in the first half of 1985, the PZPR continued harassing and incarcerating high-profile members of the opposition. On February 13, Michnik, Lis, and Frasyniuk were arrested in Gdańsk while trying to meet with TKK members; they eventually received jail terms ranging from two and a half to three and a half years. Andrzej Gwiazda was arrested in February and landed in jail for two months. Kuroń and Seweryn Jaworski were arrested and sentenced to two months in jail for participating in annual May 1 demonstrations in Warsaw. When U.S. embassy staff raised the issue of recent political incarcerations, Polish diplomats responded by dismissing the report as "morally duplicitous, politically harmful, and legally groundless."[2]

Second, the MSZ torpedoed relations with American diplomats yet again, precipitating two persona non grata crises. In February, Defense Attaché Fred Myer and his wife were arrested for photographing military installations in Warsaw and detained for six hours without communication. In addition, Mrs. Myer was forced to undress and "perform demeaning physical exercises." After being released, both were required to leave the country within forty-eight hours. In response, the Polish defense attaché in Washington, Zygmunt Szymański, was forced out of the United States.[3] A second PNG crisis erupted in May when William Harding, the first secretary in Warsaw, and David Hopper, the consul in Kraków, were detained and declared persona non grata after observing and participating in May 1 demonstrations in Nowa Huta, a Stalinist-era, working-class district outside of Kraków. In response, four Polish diplomats including the second secretary at the embassy and three members of the consular staff in Chicago were all forced to leave the United States.[4]

With the Americans happy to let relations fall away and the Poles unwilling to change unless Washington dropped its remaining sanctions, relations moved toward zero. Davis was back in Washington for consultations for the first few months of the year, and there was little political desire for improvements even after he returned. In mid-March contacts with Polish diplomats in the United States were limited to the office-director level.[5] Throughout 1985 the policy process for refining the step-by-step process slowed to a crawl.[6] Without any significant revisions in policy, bilateral relations remained chilly and continued on the same well-worn path.

## Economics

For the PZPR politburo, U.S.-Polish relations remained a sideshow because economic normalization retained center stage. As Rakowski put it informally, "three-quarters of Poland's political problems would disappear if Polish living standards of 1979 could be restored. . . . For anyone governing Poland the primary problems were economic. All others were secondary."[7] Oversimplifying, the economy suffered from high inflation (roughly rates between 10 and 20 percent per year), decreasing productivity, lack of consumer goods, market disequilibrium within the system, deficits in foreign trade, substantial debt-repayment problems, and inefficiencies in the management system. These problems were common across Eastern Europe, but they proved more acute in the Polish case because of recurrent political crises. According to a study by the Planning Commission of the Council of Ministries, national production dropped 6 percent in 1980 and then 12.1 percent in 1981, which, although influenced by other factors, was "fundamentally caused by strikes."[8] Martial law was declared in part to control against impending economic collapse (see chapter 1).

Implementing martial law had important ramifications for economic reforms already in the works—the so-called First Stage reforms. These economic reforms, which had been devised in the relatively reformist period between August 1980 and December 1981, centered on the "Three S's" campaign: self-reliance and self-financing for enterprises and self-management by workers. The program was designed to improve efficiency by creating managerial and worker incentives, decentralizing investment money at the enterprise level, and cutting the number of bureaucratic ministries that oversaw industry and trade.[9] Implementing these reforms during martial law had advantages. The government "returned discipline to the economy," "militarized a number of the industries most important for the economy," and "gave rise to conditions facilitating the launch of implementations of economic reforms as well as reforms in retail prices."[10] Price reforms were a key part of the agenda, with price increases implemented in January and February 1982 for both consumer goods and enterprises. In 1982, real incomes dropped by 17.3 percent, vastly decreasing the percentage of the budget spent on price subsidies. Budget deficits dropped from 14.8 percent of GDP in 1981 to 1.8 percent in 1983.[11]

Militarizing the state, however, was not enough, and reforms were undercut by contradictory actions taken by the government. The self-management of workers was suspended on December 31, 1981. Taxes were levied on individual enterprises' profits, greatly decreasing incentives at that level. With the militarization of the state, direct planning was again instituted, effecting about 60 percent of industrial production, and industrial ministries were maintained that were supposed to be liquidated under the initial plans. Self-reliance and self-financing fell by the wayside in most sectors of the economy. Overall, "the flurry of reform legislation introduced between 1981 and 1983 was unable to prevent the resurrection of the old system."[12] As a retrospective report stated, "With certainty, martial law did not dissolve all of the problems."[13]

The PZPR also pursued reforms in international trade. To alleviate some of the pressures of Western sanctions, Warsaw's first response was to turn to its neighbors behind the Iron Curtain, with PZPR officials traveling to Moscow, Budapest, Prague, Berlin, Sarajevo, and Bucharest seeking economic support and suggestions for reforms (see chapter 2). Continuing this policy, Jaruzelski took the extraordinary step of writing personal letters in November 1982 to his fellow heads of Communist Parties (Leonid Brezhnev, Erich Honeker, Todor Zhivkov, Gustáv Husák, János Kádár, and Nicolai Ceauşescu), explaining the progress made under martial law, blaming Poland's economic problems on policies pursued by the capitalist West, and suggesting specific aid packages that each country could send.[14] Concurrently, the PZPR strengthened ties with the Socialist bloc through the Council for Mutual Economic Assistance (CMEA), meeting with member states in Moscow in February and April 1983 to increase output by more closely coordinating each country's national economic plans.[15]

This strategy to invigorate the economy through reforms and with support from allies did not produce significant results. Although Jaruzelski did receive increased aid from CMEA countries, particularly the Soviet Union,[16] growth continued to lag through the end of 1982. The economic picture remained bleak, with national production income, consumption, and imports all showing decreases, even compared to the dismal numbers from 1981. Moreover, through the end of 1982, all major economic indicators gathered by the government showed losses between 10 percent and 33 percent when compared to numbers from 1978.[17] The GDP was about 80 percent of what it had been in 1978.[18] Poland's economy was also burdened by huge debts to the West. In the government's view, the "fundamental" cause of economic decline was "high debt and its servicing." Making matters worse, "In 1984 and 1985 [the government] will not be able to draw any new credits to import commodities. Nevertheless, the level of our debt will continue to increase incrementally."[19]

At the center of these international economic concerns was the need to increase resources available for industry, the driving force that could grow the economy. To be able to produce more, industry needed to be able to buy raw materials, parts, semifinished goods, and technology—often from the West. A number of projects begun during the era of easy Western credit in the 1970s were not complete and so still needed materials from the outside. For example, the British had supported building a modern PVC plant in Włocławek that still needed £4 million in investment. The British also had a joint Polish-Massey-Ferguson tractor factory in Ursus that still required £120 million to be completed. Funds for both had been suspended in December 1981.[20] Even those projects from the era of détente that had been completed still relied on the West for parts and semifinished goods. By 1982, government investment in industry was down 50 percent from 1978. To make up the difference, the Polish economy would have to export more to strengthen government cash reserves. As the foreign trade section of the National Social-Economic Plan for 1983–85 made clear, "Poland cannot count on a firm increase in trade sales with [the Soviet Union and Warsaw Pact countries]."[21] Increased revenues would have to come from somewhere else.

The possibility of increased exports or new funding from the West was bleak. As one report from 1983 concluded, the United States had suspended MFN, Poland would "not be able to attain any transactions credits," and a recession in the West had increased protectionism.[22] While Western governments had agreed to debt-rescheduling talks to reduce Poland's repayment burden, Western Europeans remained unified against making new credits available. Beyond political concerns, there were no good reasons for private entities to invest in the Polish economy. Old investments had not been particularly profitable. The London Club of private lenders had begun the process of rescheduling debt as well, but private business's experience with Poland—as a creditor that could not meet its debts—meant that new opportunities would not arise. Beyond the issue of public support for Solidarność and the public relations costs of working with a disliked regime, British companies, for example, "had been burned quite badly" when the loans from the 1970s became due, so "disenchantment was really quite strong."[23] Similarly, investments remained far too risky for American businesses and bankers without loan guarantees through the Export-Import Bank or other government bodies.[24] The heady days of détente when Western cash flowed freely were gone now that Poland had proven that it could not repay those loans in a timely manner. The Polish economy was stuck between a need for increased exports and an inability to attain the outside investment necessary to fund those increases.

The fundamental points of this conundrum were obvious to economists beyond party circles. Solidarność advisers had argued about a cycle of economic problems since the beginning of martial law. Opposition economists also understood the necessity of increasing foreign trade and the relationship between economic growth and foreign credits. An article from March 1982 in *Tygodnik Mazowsze* argued that "today there is a kind of circle of mistakes. It is not possible to create products for export because we cannot import parts, raw materials, and goods from the West. It is not possible to import more, because there is a lack of foreign currency from exports."[25]

From the beginning of the crisis, opposition critics argued that the Communist Party's economic reforms would never be enough to get the country back on its feet. In early 1982, Bujak emphasized a common refrain: without a working economy there was little possibility to normalize the domestic situation.[26] One article on the government's reform program was simply titled "The Same Mistakes."[27] Another commentator bluntly wrote, "The authorities' economic activities are inconsequential and chaotic."[28] Parts of the opposition argued that the only exit from economic crisis was to seek new Western money. Put quite simply in one analysis, "the economic situation will deteriorate without Western credits."[29] For Solidarność new credits were the key economic issue. Of course, to get these credits the opposition knew that the PZPR would have to acquiesce to Western political demands and negotiate with Solidarność or other opposition groups. So as long as the West maintained its link between new credits and national dialogue, Solidarność had a strong economic argument in its favor.

The quick secession of leaders in the Kremlin also complicated the PZPR's path toward economic liberalization. Under the leadership of Juri Andropov, the Soviets had acquiesced to Jaruzelski's policy of improving relations with the church and allowing a papal visit for the sake of normalizing domestic relationships, a step that Brezhnev had criticized before his death in November 1982. When Konstantin Chernenko assumed the general secretary position following Andropov's death in February 1984, Jaruzelski and others expected Polish-Soviet relations to remain on this positive course. Jaruzelski reported back to Warsaw during Andropov's funeral that "[The Soviet leadership] are realists. They know that the one direction, which we represent, has a chance to be favorable for socialist results."[30]

Contrary to these expectations, Chernenko pursued a much more controlling and conservative line. When Jaruzelski met face to face with him in May 1984, Chernenko lectured his guest on the best path forward. This included calls for "future actions to strengthen the leading role of the PZPR in the nation and in society." Specifically, the general secretary called for the PZPR to "eradicate the roots of antisocialist elements, liquidate soil for enemy activities, restrict church interference in political life, affirm the decisive influence of Marxism-Leninism in society, liquidate decentralization [wielosektorowości] in the national economy, move rural areas toward the path to socialism, and pay off Western debts burdening the Polish economy."[31] The restriction on "decentralization" in the economy was particularly important, because it limited the scope of economic restructuring and called into question the First Stage's "Three S's" campaign. In addition, Warsaw had been experimenting with independent "Polonia" firms—small-scale manufacturing firms that were allowed to receive funding from Poles living abroad—which worked outside the centrally planned economy to improve productivity.[32] With a prohibition on decentralization, the future of these reforms was unclear.

More generally, using phrases couched in ideological meanings (i.e., "leading role of the party"), Chernenko harkened back to the relationship with Brezhnev. Like Brezhnev, he advocated stronger steps against the opposition and the church, with a heavy reliance on ideological doctrine and much less room for Poland's "specificity." Second, Chernenko was lecturing the Poles on what policies they should implement. Andropov was much more willing to speak with Jaruzelski about their problems, and then following coordination, support the policies the Poles chose. With Chernenko's rise to the head of the party, Warsaw was under demanding scrutiny from Moscow once again.

Overall, the Polish government's range of options to remove itself from the crisis was considerably restricted from the East. In December 1981, Jaruzelski proved that he was willing (if reluctant) to do as he was told when the Kremlin made demands. It would have been inconsistent for him to defy the Soviet Union to promote internal political or economic reforms in the face of pressure from Chernenko. Moreover, as ineffective as increased deliveries from the Soviet Union and the Socialist bloc were in rebuilding the Polish economy, Warsaw could not risk provoking another economic or political crisis with its socialist neighbors. With little room to maneuver, the Poles had to look elsewhere to solve their economic problems.

## Subverting Sanctions

In July 1983 officials from the Ministry of Foreign Affairs, the Ministry of Finance, the Central Committee Economics Department, and the Central

Committee Foreign Department met to analyze and evaluate Western sanctions. According to their own computations, sanctions and restrictions had cost the PZPR between $8 and $11 billion from 1981 to 1983. More important, Polish officials understood that to extricate themselves from the crisis, they needed access to new long-term development credits from Western countries agreed to at preferential interest rates.[33] To get these new credits without acquiescing to Western demands, the only other path open to the PZPR was to weaken and undercut the sanctions regime.

Poland's first attempts to undermine Western sanctions and get access to new credits came in a familiar package: propaganda. In July 1983, the PZPR Central Committee Department of the Press, Radio, and Television outlined its campaign for domestic propaganda to illustrate the economic effects of American and Western sanctions and to blame them for Poles' suffering.[34] The following month, the Council of Ministers supplied a twelve-point action program to counteract American sanctions. Steps included studying the sanctions' legal basis, making more vociferous arguments against sanctions in international forums like the International Labor Organization and the United Nations, raising the issue of Poland's lost MFN status within the General Agreement on Tariffs and Trade (GATT), and emphasizing to Paris Club members how sanctions negatively effected the country's ability to repay loans.[35] At a September 1983 politburo meeting, the PZPR decided to publish a white book of public and private American diplomatic documents, substantiating Polish arguments that U.S. actions during the 1980–81 crisis and the subsequent sanctions were an illegal intervention into sovereign Polish affairs.[36] The government also formed a committee for coordinating relations with Paris Club members to improve its chances of securing preferable debt-rescheduling agreements.[37] Finally at the end of September, Henryk Jabłoński, the chairman of the Council of State, traveled to New York for the thirty-eighth annual opening session of the United Nations to break the PZPR's political isolation in international organizations.[38]

These propaganda efforts partially succeeded. In domestic Polish opinion, the PZPR demonized American actions enough to cause Lech Wałęsa to make public statements in December 1983 asking the United States to lift sanctions. As Wałęsa explained to Lane Kirkland in a private letter, "the sanctions were being blamed for all of Poland's difficulties and the economic crisis by the authorities [. . . ]. My statement supporting the lifting of sanctions undercut this argument. As the authorities were initiating a vast propaganda campaign against me, I could not postpone my statements any longer."[39] Similarly, the

Polish decision to allow a papal visit in 1983 was taken, in part, in hopes that "the pope's universally recognized authority could possibly take a stance on economic sanctions applied to our nation by the American administration and some governments of Western Europe."[40] Wałęsa's public call and the pope's position on sanctions directly influenced Reagan's decision to allow fishing rights and LOT charter flights. The Polish American Congress cited similar reasons for supporting decreased sanctions (see chapter 3). Finally, efforts to get Paris Club members to break from Washington and for other nations to support Poland's bid for IMF membership clearly improved Poland's position; Washington lifted both of these sanctions in part because of Allied pressure and concerns about breaking ranks.

While public propaganda increased pressure to lift sanctions, major restrictions remained in place on trade and new credits. With only limited success getting comparatively minor sanctions lifted, the PZPR reevaluated the issue of Western economic policy. In June 1984 the embassy in Washington provided a full report on the inner workings of American trade restrictions, particularly on high-tech items. In July 1984, MSZ Department III prepared an analysis of NATO attitudes toward East-West trade and recommended improving economic relations with Western nations not part of NATO, as well as with smaller and medium-sized nations within NATO. The report also recommended "to support Western circles interested in maintaining East-West trade" and "to continue favoring private business entities in our economic relations with capitalist countries."[41] Near the end of the 1984, the Economics Department and MSZ Department III held a short conference on American policy toward the CMEA, focused particularly on Washington's actions in response to other East European countries' attempts to gain MFN status and IMF membership.[42] Through the end of 1984, however, these new studies did little to change PZPR policy.

### Reengaging with the West

In the second half of 1984 signs of a slow move out of political isolation emerged as West European states broke with the U.S. government to pursue political contacts, accepting the permanence of the Jaruzelski regime. In early summer 1984, the British began arguing that the PZPR had "substantially fulfilled" two of the NAC's three requirements to rescind sanctions: martial law was lifted and political prisoners were released. "The third condition, the resumption of a dialogue between the parties concerned, was unlikely to be met as things stood at present." So the British proposed "a policy of gradual expansion of contacts" that would "take account of developments inside the country but not to be too dependent on them." The West Germans concurred: "By intensifying contacts with Poland, the West should maintain the Polish government's interest in an improvement of relations" and "points of view of Western policy should be more strongly emphasized."[43] Following the July 1984 amnesty, the Italians joined this position because "by intensifying the dialogue with Polish authorities we could exert further pressure on them in order to safeguard human rights and particularly the rights of the trade unions."[44] For the French, "the year 1984, it was hoped, would offer the prospect of an increased margin of maneuver . . . in East-West relations."[45] On October 22, Greek prime minister Andreas G. Papandreou became the first European head of state to visit Poland since the declaration of martial law, and high-level British, West German, and Italian officials made plans to travel to Warsaw in the following months.

These visits, however, did not mean that relations were normalized. For the British the purpose of engagement was "not to show favor or suggest that all is back to normal but to conduct a 'critical dialogue,'" a policy pursued when Malcolm Rifkind, the minister of state at the Foreign and Commonwealth Office, traveled to Poland. From November 3–7, Rifkind met with a number of ministers to discuss bilateral, especially economic relations, and he clarified that the United Kingdom no longer placed political restrictions on issuing new credits. Now, the "UK would look entirely at economic criteria" initially focused on successfully rescheduling debts through the Paris Club.[46] He also had a frank discussion of Poland's political and international situation with Czyrek and Rakowski.[47] Importantly, Rifkind paired these meetings with contacts with the opposition, meeting for two hours at the U.K. ambassador's residence with Geremek, Onyszkiewicz, Mazowiecki, and Krzysztof Śliwiński (a journalist and the former director of international contacts for Solidarność in Mazowsze). In his conversation, Rifkind listened to the opposition's analysis of the situation, including Onyszkiewicz's view that ministerial visits "were to be welcomed provided the Western governments in question took into account the interests of the Polish people, and do not restrict contacts to the establishment."[48] Rifkind also took the symbolically provocative step of laying a wreath at the grave of Father Jerzy Popiełuszko, a very public gesture meant to show strident support for Solidarność. After the trip, the Foreign and Commonwealth Office emphasized to other EC members that they needed to pursue contacts with the PZPR "on their own terms," meaning that the EC needed "to resist Polish Government attempts to persuade Western visitors to avoid contact with opinion representatives of Solidarity and other opposition."[49] Reengagement with the Poles had begun, but not on the PZPR's terms.

Building on these positive signs, in 1985 the PZPR promoted a policy of engaging the capitalist world. A yearly report, "Vital Foreign Policy Tasks for the PRL for 1985," recognized that difficulties and tensions would continue to exist with the West and that "the process of normalization in our relations with the USA will be long and difficult." Nonetheless, the MSZ prioritized "activities with the goal of finally ending Western policies of political isolation against Poland, for example, a path for developing higher-level official contacts particularly with Western Europe."[50] Regarding economic matters, the MSZ remained focused on new financial credits by "expanding economic relations, above all financial-credit [relations], the gauge of which will be negotiations regarding refinancing debt, the negotiation process for Poland's entry into the IMF and World Bank, as well as eliminating discriminatory and protectionist barriers against Polish exports."[51] The MSZ also refined its targets in the West: "It is essential to intensify activities with the goal of reorienting economic coordination on small matters and the policies of less confrontational partners. This process should not be run through the behest of trade enterprises with the large capitalist states (the USA, West Germany), but through dynamic enterprises with smaller nations."[52]

In the twelve months that followed, Jaruzelski's Poland met its goal of subverting political isolation, even with larger states. On March 6, 1985, the West German foreign minister Hans-Dietrich Genscher made an unofficial visit to Warsaw, hoping to lay a foundation for a later official visit. No major policy initiatives were produced in his meetings with Jaruzelski and Foreign Minister Stefan Olszowski, but the conversations were important because the statements made "could be used in favor of their arguments for normalizing relations with Western nations," and they "confirmed [Poland's] preparedness in creating constructive relations with [West Germany] and the realism in policies from Bonn."[53] Steps to normalize relations with Germany continued during Chernenko's funeral, when Jaruzelski met briefly with Chancellor Helmut Kohl. Again, no agreements were signed, but both sides expressed hopes for improved relations.[54]

While in Moscow for Chernenko's funeral, Jaruzelski spoke with other Western leaders as well. He thanked U.N. Secretary General Javier Pérez du Cuéllar for his work on the Polish issue in the United Nations. The general also invited Italian president Alessandro Pertini to visit Warsaw, building on an earlier visit to Italy by Jabłoński to commemorate the fortieth anniversary of the Battle of Monte Cassino.[55] Jaruzelski also met with President Mauno Koivisto of Finland.[56]

Visits to Warsaw by various Western representatives followed through spring and into the summer of 1985. West German minister of economics Martin Bangemann traveled to Warsaw to find "common efforts" to make "visible" improvements in economic relations. Jaruzelski spoke broadly about the need for a return to détente and German realpolitik in East-West relations, and he specifically asked that Poland be able to receive new credits before paying off its old debts.[57] A few weeks later British foreign minister Geoffrey Howe made an official visit, announcing British agreement to fulfill investment promises for the Włocłowek project signed prior to December 1981. However, Howe made clear that to receive significant new credits, Poland needed to rebuild its creditworthiness first.[58] Howe also visited Popiełuszko's grave, and the British placed more emphasis on internal political developments than the Germans by inquiring about the well-being of opposition figures who had been rearrested and meeting with others, including Wałęsa. From this, the MSZ concluded that Poland would still have to struggle to remake relationships with NATO countries. Nevertheless, the PZPR considered the British meeting an "important step in normalizing relations."[59]

In May and June, the PZPR continued its streak of contacts with the West. Italian prime minister Bettino Craxi came to Warsaw on May 28. The Italians expressed interest in increasing exports and imports. Craxi responded positively to the possibility of modernizing Fiat 126 production facilities, which had originally been built in the 1970s.[60] As had Howe, the Italians met with opposition members and voiced concern about ongoing trials, explaining that internal Polish events affected popular opinion in Italy, which in turn influenced possibilities for economic exchanges, debt relief, and new investment.[61] Next, Japanese foreign minister Shintaro Abe visited (only the second visit by a Japanese foreign minister in the history of bilateral contacts) to normalize and improve economic ties. The Japanese voiced support for Poland's proposals to reschedule debt in the Paris Club and for the country's membership in the IMF. No economic agreements were signed, but the two sides moved ahead with possible agreements on cultural and scientific-technical exchanges, with the Poles intrigued by exchanges to improve industrial capacity and modernize their production process.[62]

As the fall approached, General Jaruzelski turned his attention to another important meeting: the fortieth opening session of the United Nations

General Assembly. Although his visit drew large public demonstrations supported by PAC and the AFL-CIO, he did meet with the U.N. secretary general, the president of Brazil (Poland's largest Latin American trading partner), King Hussein of Jordan, Spanish prime minister Felipe González, new Soviet foreign minister Eduard Shevardnadze, Genscher, and Italian foreign minister Guilio Andreotti. As an after-report summarized, these bilateral meetings were further evidence "of the preparedness of our partners to normalize and expand the extent of relations." Moreover, Jaruzelski's appearance at the General Assembly allowed him to present his view of Polish events on an international stage. While in New York, Jaruzelski also gave interviews to American media outlets, a rare chance to speak directly to the American public.[63]

Jaruzelski's successes, however, did not extend to Polish-American relations. Prior to the general's arrival in New York, Reagan had announced that neither he nor any members of his administration would meet with Jaruzelski.[64] Jaruzelski did meet privately with three well-connected Americans— John Rockefeller, Zbigniew Brzeziński, and John Whitehead of the Council on Foreign Relations—to discuss the Rockefeller Foundation and the Rockefeller Brothers Foundation's efforts to fund the church's agriculture fund. Rockefeller received a series of talking points from National Security Adviser Bud McFarlane, laying out the White House's perspective on political elements in U.S.-Polish relations. The talking points made clear that Washington was "deeply troubled" by developments and saw them "as a reversal of favorable trends in 1984." The administration had adopted "the view that the amnesty of 1984 was a kind of trick, in that, once the U.S. responded favorably to the amnesty, the arrests resumed and many of the amnestied individuals [were] again in jail."[65] When the subject of Polish-American relations arose in a private luncheon, Rockefeller responded to Jaruzelski by referencing some of these talking points. Brzeziński and Whitehead also "succinctly and candidly" rebutted the general's statements blaming Poland's economic hardships and the poor state of relations on America. Whitehead attributed economic problems to internal "misgovernment," and Brzeziński protested against the idea that decisions about Poland were directly linked to relations with the Soviet Union. For Brzeziński, "it was simply not true that Poland was a pawn in the East-West debate."[66] Even though no official contacts with administration officials took place, the White House found a quiet way to have its voice heard.

Jaruzelski followed the New York meetings with a trip to Paris, where he met with French president Mitterand. This was the general's first visit to a Western capital since the declaration of martial law, and Mitterand was intensely criticized for receiving him.[67] Again, the meeting gave Jaruzelski an opportunity to explain the internal situation and blame the United States for problems. For his part, Mitterand placed the spotlight on progress with the church agricultural fund and on the possibility of increased economic cooperation. Mitterand wanted "to emphasize, that [he was] ready for action toward improvement in the situation," mentioning new deals to reschedule debt after which financial credits might again be available. Mitterand was also considering short-term loans. All were positive developments for Poland.[68]

Jaruzelski's encounter with Mitterand in December 1985 made for a noteworthy cap to a year of important progress. Even though Jaruzelski was asked to enter the Élysée Palace through the back door—ostensibly for security reasons—he was nonetheless directly meeting major Western leaders. After five years of political isolation and trips only within the Socialist bloc, Jaruzelski was negotiating face to face with West European politicians. The Poles could now make their case against sanctions directly. Reagan's administration continued to block high-level political contacts throughout 1985, but Jaruzelski and his comrades held direct discussions with leading officials from the big four (France, Britain, West Germany, and Italy). These meetings were both symbolically and politically significant.

More central to Poland's internal crisis, these improved political contacts advanced economic relationships. In meetings with West Europeans, the Polish government received assurances that each country backed Poland's IMF membership application, an important step toward gaining new credits. Each Western representative also expressed willingness to increase economic cooperation. Japan and Italy went as far as signing specific economic exchanges and improvements, adding promises of modernized equipment and technology. Finally, increased political will for dialogue led to a final agreement to reschedule Poland's debt to governmental lenders. After two years of negotiations (which began after Washington dropped restrictions), the Paris Club announced on July 15, 1985, that it had agreed to reschedule $12 billion in debts owed from 1982 to 1984.[69] This was a hard-won victory, but it did not include any access to the new credits the Poles had wanted as part of a deal.[70] In November, Polish representatives signed a further agreement rescheduling $1.37 billion that had come due in 1985. For the first time since December 1981, "Poland will now in theory be without unrescheduled arrears on its official debt to its major western government creditors."[71]

At the end of 1985, the MSZ provided a very optimistic view of Poland's new political and economic position. A year-end review stated, "We brought about significant progress in the process of normalizing relations with developed capitalist nations. The results gained were quantitatively and qualitatively much greater than those during 1982–1984."[72] The report noted progress made to break out of NATO-imposed isolation, particularly with Italy, France, and most importantly and unexpectedly, West Germany. In terms of relations with the United States, the MSZ concluded, "there remains an impasse."[73] In a report, "Vital Tasks for Poland's Foreign Policy in 1986," the MSZ emphasized that in the second half of the decade "Polish foreign policy will be more active and less defensive than it was during the first half," stressing that to improve Poland's place in the international environment, the MSZ needed to "cultivate political, economic, and cultural-scientific relations with capitalist nations (particularly Western Europe)"; to improve financial and credit relations; to continue to reschedule debt; and to gain access to new money.[74] After years of economic and political isolation, the PZPR was now seeing concrete improvements with Western Europe.

## Changes in the East

The PZPR also had high hopes for Poland's future because of Mikhail Gorbachev's March 1985 selection to replace Chernenko as general secretary. On hearing the news, Rakowski noted Gorbachev's youth and referred to him as "a true revolutionary cadre."[75] When Gorbachev traveled to Warsaw for a meeting of Warsaw Pact leaders a month after taking office, he gave subtle signs of his new approach to relations with the bloc. Gorbachev stated that it was necessary in discussing relations within the Socialist bloc "to speak openly, bringing up different viewpoints and working out claims, preventing stratification." While still emphasizing the shared nature of class interests, he referred to each country's own social, economic, and political histories, acknowledging national specificity. Gorbachev even stated that "every fraternal party alone determines its policies and is responsible for them to their own nation."[76] Following a private meeting, Jaruzelski reported that Gorbachev was very interested in Poland's development and agreed with the PZPR's approach toward the church. Gorbachev reported that the Soviet Union was seeking greater cooperation with Western Europe too.[77]

At the end of 1985, Poland's new foreign minister, Marian Orzechowski, traveled to Moscow and confirmed the new Soviet attitudes. Unlike in meetings with Chernenko or Brezhnev, in which the Soviets dictated policy, Shevardnadze and politburo member Nicolai Ryzhkov refrained from ideologically coded reprimands and did not lecture. They simply mentioned that they were "content" with Poland's progress and that the country was "on the proper path." As Orzechowski summarized, "During conversations one thought was affirmed: that Polish-Russian relations, after a period of constraints in many fields during 1980–82, are currently growing dynamically and have entered a new working and elastic form of cooperation at every level."[78] More like his mentor Andropov than his predecessor Chernenko, Gorbachev was showing flexibility with Eastern Europe.

Gorbachev's first year as general secretary was important for refining his overall approach to both the Soviet bloc and the West. In terms of the Soviet bloc, Gorbachev was distancing himself from the Brezhnev Doctrine and a heavy-handed leadership style. Relations with this area would be "based on equality and respect for national sovereignty and independence, as well as mutually advantageous cooperation in all spheres."[79] In describing this new style to bureaucrats in the Soviet Ministry of Foreign Affairs, Gorbachev explained, "Our friends should feel that they are walking alongside us, rather than being towed behind. . . . We should show modesty, respect for the experience of others and for their striving to find resolutions to problems on their own."[80] At the center of these new fraternal relations was the need to overcome problems of economic coordination.[81] This, in turn, reflected a deeper truth: at the core of Gorbachev's reform projects, both domestic (perestroika followed by glasnost) and international (new thinking), was a desire to improve the living conditions of his own citizens, to get the system working and providing for his people—a drive he shared with Jaruzelski.[82]

Gorbachev's views on relations with Western Europe and the United States were also shifting. With three key practical foci—"peaceful coexistence had to be cooperative, true security had to be mutual, and the USSR and the United States had to promote the concept of 'reasonable sufficiency' in their strategic thinking"—new thinking first focused on remaking the superpower relationship, particularly on finding points of possible agreement and limiting nuclear arsenals. Although Western Europe was less central to his initial policies, Gorbachev spoke about a "common European home" even before becoming general secretary.[83] At a more basic level, Gorbachev and his group of reformist advisors had all been influenced by Western ideas and displayed an affinity for bringing the Soviet government and the Soviet state more in line with Western ideals.[84] Practically, this meant that

Gorbachev sought to engage with West Europeans more than his recent predecessors.

This shifting view of East-West relations could be seen in economic as well as political relations. In mid-1985 Polish and Soviet CMEA representatives wrote to the EEC with "a proposal to establish relations between CMEA and the Community through the adoption of a general EEC-CMEA statement at a high-level meeting," a process that had been stalled since 1980.[85] In October the European Community Parliament adopted a resolution to establish "normal relations" between the community and CMEA members, although agreements would be driven by bilateral relations between the EEC and individual countries, rather than by a blanket agreement between the EEC and the CMEA.[86] In May 1986 the CMEA agreed to this framework. The organization was willing "to establish official relations with the Community and also that, alongside the establishment of such relations, various member countries of the CMEA were in principle willing to set their relations with the Community on a bilateral basis."[87] Poland quickly sent a letter of interest to engage in bilateral talks, and the EEC held exploratory negotiations with Poland on July 14–15, 1986.[88] Gorbachev's grand vision of European relations had practical effects on Poland's ability to pursue economic improvements with the West.

Gorbachev and Jaruzelski were also forging a close relationship based on their shared vision of reform. In a personal letter from September 1985, Gorbachev reassured Jaruzelski about his decision to allow Genscher's visit and wrote that his "Polish friends made a completely valid judgment."[89] In a show of support for Polish policies, Gorbachev had Jaruzelski speak first at the Warsaw Pact Political-Consultative Council meeting in Sofia.[90] The close relationship between the two Communist leaders went public in June 1986, when Gorbachev visited Warsaw during the PZPR's Tenth Party Congress, lending the Soviet Union's praise and his personal gravitas to the economic and political reforms Jaruzelski announced there. According to Gorbachev's chief foreign policy aide, Anatoly Chernyaev, "[Gorbachev] became friends with Jaruzelski. It was not just a personal bond, but an emotional and political bond to establish truly fraternal relations with Poland and with the Polish people."[91]

Gorbachev's rise to power also shifted the PZPR's analysis of its geopolitical environment. Since the declaration of American sanctions, Jaruzelski had complained that Poland was treated like a "pawn" in the game between the superpowers. From Warsaw's perspective Poland suffered the most relative to the other socialist countries during the first half

Mikhail Gorbachev and Wojciech Jaruzelski at the PZPR's 10th Party Congress in June 1986. Photo courtesy of the Polish Press Agency/Jan Morek.

of the 1980s "as an object and instrument of the West's confrontational policies."[92] Following logically from this argument, Warsaw believed that declining Soviet-American tensions would make Washington more malleable in bilateral relations with Poland. Washington would be less prone to punish Warsaw to get at Moscow. Thus the PZPR closely tracked—and was regularly briefed on—Gorbachev's policy toward the United States.[93] In an impromptu meeting of Warsaw Pact leaders in Prague in late November 1985, Gorbachev reported optimistically on the outcome of the Geneva summit, the first superpower summit in seven years. Being clear that "the most difficult and most important [steps] are still ahead," Gorbachev nonetheless noted that "Geneva was an important step in the proper direction. . . . There were certain positive achievements, opening up some new possibilities." Given this review, Orzechowski concluded that "the results of the Geneva summit have been persuasive that it is the appropriate moment for a review of the current state of Polish-American relations and for considering our behavior toward the USA, in response to the present requirements and possibilities."[94]

For Jaruzelski and the leadership in Warsaw, Gorbachev's rise to the general secretary's chair opened up new possibilities. First, Gorbachev took a much less intrusive and controlling view of internal developments, so the Poles had a freer hand domestically. Second, Gorbachev and Jaruzelski developed a personal relationship based on a shared sense of reform, boosting PZPR confidence that it could take bolder steps both domestically and internationally. Finally, Gorbachev pursued a much more cooperative line with the Europeans and a less confrontational line with the United States. With tension decreasing between the superpowers, Jaruzelski believed that the United States would be more amenable to pursuing normalized relations.

## Economics and Politics Collide

Despite improvements in Poland's international situation in 1985, the country's domestic economic forecast remained bleak. There were some improvements: industrial production increased 6.4 percent in the third quarter of 1985, more than a similar period the year before and more than the Central Yearly Plan had expected; the production of apartments and homes increased 2.4 percent from the year before; and the government continued to provide foodstuffs at a rate higher than planned.[95] But not everything was looking up. Debt was fully rescheduled but it had not been forgiven; Warsaw still needed to repay loans, just over a longer period of time. More important, economic inefficiencies, broken machinery, antiquated processes, and an unmotivated workforce continued to hinder economic output. In the all-important area of foreign trade, in the first nine months of 1985 exports to capitalist countries were down 2.4 percent from the previous year and imports had only increased 9.6 percent, attaining 73 percent of the level desired by the economic plans.[96] Strong inflationary pressures also surfaced in 1985. There was now a "significant threat to the money-market balance [that reflects] an intensification of inflationary payment pressures in comparison to 1983–84."[97] Even when government figures showed modest growth, these numbers did not factor in rising inflation, further evidence of just how weak the Polish economy truly was. In turn, this economic instability was directly linked to the possibility of social instability. The extended economic crisis "threatened at any moment to erupt in social unrest whose impact would be all the greater in that it would be channeled by underground Solidarity organizations."[98]

In response to the continuing economic crisis, the PZPR politburo spent significant time preparing a new round of economic reforms. In December 1985 the PZPR held its Twenty-Second Central Committee Plenum, focusing almost exclusively on preparing for the "Drugi Etap" (Second Stage) reforms, which were announced six months later at the PZPR's Tenth Party Congress from June 29 to July 3, 1986. The economic sections of the Drugi Etap attempted to invigorate the economy by allowing for greater individual control in markets. The reforms were modeled on Hungary's successful economic plans that allowed for new types of small businesses—"nonagricultural cooperatives of fewer than one hundred members; business work partnerships, in which no more than thirty persons created a business as a second job; and enterprise business work partnerships, or partnerships among employees of an enterprise that contracted its services back to the enterprise during off-hours"—as well as liberal joint-venture regulations.[99] The Drugi Etap embraced some timid moves to introduce market forces, but most foreign and opposition economists recognized that these minor changes would not do much to improve the situation. As an economics officer from the U.S. embassy recalls, "We were convinced that the people who were trying to run [the reforms] were sincere in trying to come up with economic plans that would make them another Hungary, [but] I don't remember anyone saying they got any kind of traction at all."[100]

The buildup to the Drugi Etap was significant, however, because it reflected an important shift in the government's thinking: the PZPR now embraced Solidarność's long-standing argument about the necessity of increasing exports through foreign investment. The MSZ's proposed goals for 1986 emphasized the need to attain new money from the West.[101] Preparations for changes to Poland's economic system led to a joint project to analyze how other socialist countries (particularly Hungary, Yugoslavia, Romania, and Bulgaria) had structured their foreign investment system and how they had attracted that investment.[102] Legal revisions were also devised to increase opportunities for foreign investment through so-called cooperative enterprises,[103] with the express purpose of enlivening "the Polish economy with the goal of increasing its export possibilities." As the proposal recognized, "With a lack of medium-term foreign payments, as well as the insignificant possibilities of obtaining investment credits in the next few years, cooperative enterprises may constitute a change to nourish the slowed investment process, and also for the fundamental development of, above all, a pro-export production field."[104]

The Drugi Etap also embraced political change. One major reform replaced the Patriotic Movement for National Rebirth (PRON), which had been formed in 1982 and had never produced results. A new Consultative Council was proposed as "a body that was to advise the chairman of the

Council of State," a post held by General Jaruzelski since November 1985.[105] This new organ was meant to "put forward propositions and cooperative proposals on all matters in order to increase normalization in social-political life in the country, as well as to deepen national reconciliation."[106] The council included members of the Catholic intelligentsia and the opposition to work in conjunction with the government and add their support and credibility to government policies. Solidarność viewed the council as an attempt to co-opt the opposition into accepting government reforms.[107] In the eyes of U.S. embassy observers, "reality on the ground [was] not as frozen as it [looked] . . . in Washington."[108] While the political steps were cautious, this was an attempt at genuine reform.

The PZPR's new economic outlook and plans soon collided with political pressures from outside its borders. Simultaneous with the buildup to the Tenth Party Congress, the PZPR was considering a new amnesty for political prisoners. Jaruzelski alluded to it as early as during his trip to the United Nations in September 1985. With talk of an amnesty in the air, the American deputy chief of mission in Warsaw, David Swartz, met with Bogumił Sujka, a member of the PZPR's International Department, in November 1985 to discuss the plight of rearrested political prisoners. During the conversation, Swartz stated that the United States was looking for an "encouraging gesture" to move relations forward again.[109] When Dennis Ortblad, the State Department's Poland Desk officer, traveled to Warsaw a month later in December 1985, he also emphasized freeing political prisoners, but noted that the Poles should not wait for a "dramatic gesture" from the Americans. Instead Ortblad hoped that the two sides could return to a negotiating pattern based on small steps.[110]

Even sending an unofficial emissary did nothing to restart meaningful bilateral conversations. In March 1986, the former ambassador to Poland and former deputy assistant secretary Walter Stoessel traveled to Warsaw to meet with Jaruzelski, Orzechowski, Cardinal Glemp, and Wałęsa to "probe Polish intentions," discuss internal developments and political prisoners again, show America's commitment to the step-by-step framework, and offer an "enhanced political dialogue."[111] On Stoessel's return, the NSC was disappointed with the mission because Stoessel "went there to tell the Poles what *they* had to do to get improved relations. The Poles gave him nothing and now he is back with a list of things *we* have to do—while the Poles are sitting back waiting for 'signals.'"[112]

When Juliusz Biały, a member of MSZ Department III, visited Washington in June 1986, neither side looked any closer to making progress. As Stoessel told Biały, both Shultz and Reagan were reluctant to make the first move. Because activists freed in 1984 had been rearrested, the Americans "did not want to be tricked again."[113] The State Department recognized that relations were stalemated and that America's European allies were pushing to accept the Jaruzelski regime's permanence, but they believed that "the short-term prospect for movement on national reconciliation is not great." Therefore, the United States' "bedrock principle should be that on the fundamental issues of credit, MFN, and high-level visits, we do not measure progress using Jaruzelski's yardstick—better bilateral relations—but ours—national reconciliation."[114] Although Washington continued to press Warsaw on political prisoners and national reconciliation, in the first half of 1986, neither the United States nor Poland were willing to overcome the impasse.

Against this backdrop, in June 1986 Jaruzelski announced plans for a new amnesty. Around three hundred political prisoners were then in jail, many of whom had been rearrested in the months after the July 1984 amnesty.[115] The initial summer 1986 announcement suggested "clemency would not extend to repeat offenders" or to "well-known activists."[116] Jaruzelski clarified an exceptions policy to the amnesty in a rare press conference following the party congress: "We shall not give up the possibility to preserve peace in Poland—and anything that might disturb this peace will not be embraced. . . . It wouldn't be logical as we open a new chapter to take steps in releasing prisoners that might get in the way of our progress."[117] Political prisoners would be dealt with on a case-by-case basis. Under these conditions, well-known recidivists like Michnik, Lis, and Frasyniuk had little chance for freedom. Another important name on the list of those unlikely to be released was Zbigniew Bujak, who had been caught at the end of May after living underground for more than five years and serving as a member of the TKK since its formation.[118] The amnesty law was passed by the Sejm on July 17 and was implemented on July 24. Initial releases included no surprises.

In response, the Catholic Church, Western Europe, and the United States rallied to pressure the PZPR to release all remaining political prisoners. Glemp called for prisoners to be freed during negotiations regarding the formation of the Consultative Council.[119] On July 9, U.S. DCM Swartz met with the head of the American section of the Polish Institute for International Affairs, Longin Pastusiak, and told him that that Washington "might abolish the embargo on credits for Poland" if the PZPR released Bujak, a message that was relayed to Jaruzelski and the politburo.[120] Italian president Pertini and his foreign minister Craxi publicly linked the possibility of a visit by Jaruzelski to the release of prisoners. This linkage not only jeopardized bilateral relations with Italy but put into question Jaruzelski's possible trip to the Vatican.

The strongest action came from the European Community. On July 30, 1986, the British ambassador presented a démarche from the EEC's twelve members to Deputy Foreign Minister Tadeusz Olechowski that expressed concern over Poland's internal situation, stating that "they see no fundamental overall improvement in the spheres of national reconciliation or human rights." Referencing the amnesty, the démarche stated, "The law's limitations, exemptions, conditions and discretionary provisions are disappointing. . . . If major figures are not released the law's favorable impact will be much reduced."[121] As Ambassador Brian L. Barder clarified, "[nothing] less than the release of all political prisoners, and no new arrests on political grounds, could be regarded as a significant step forward."[122] While the EEC considered this formal statement similar to one presented in January, Olechowski was "'astonished' at what the Polish government [was] bound to regard as interference in internal affairs . . . whether or not intentional. They would also have to regard it as a warning and a form of pressure; he would almost say blackmail."[123] Olechowski even questioned if references to the EEC's "economic importance" and to the possibility of a public disclosure of the démarche were implied threats. Barder denied they were, but Olechowski nonetheless inquired, "Were the Twelve saying that the development of their economic relations with Poland depended on what [the EEC] would regard as a satisfactory response to [its] concerns over Poland's internal policies?"[124]

These combined pressures soon showed effects. On July 31, Wałęsa's adviser Lis was released. Then, on August 7, the government announced that it was recommending to the Polish courts that Michnik be released; he was freed on August 11.

References to international pressure also surfaced in the PZPR's internal decisions. On August 6, the PZPR finalized a report, "Concerning the Implications of Our Internal Situation for Relations with Western Europe." The report stated, "the exclusion from the amnesty of the most active members of the opposition" would "have an unfavorable impact on our potential to conduct an active and effective policy toward Western Europe." This included expected problems with scheduling upcoming bilateral meetings with Italy, France, and Great Britain, as well as multilateral political contacts through the CSCE, which was about to begin a scheduled follow-up meeting in Vienna. Regarding economic consequences, if the PZPR kept the activists in prison, "the meaning of that element will grow as a condition complicating Poland's payment situation and [will create] increasing difficulties in the evolution of a deadline for financial obligations to Western nations. . . . Poland's international position in economic and payment matters may succumb to later weaknesses."[125] Keeping political prisoners in jail threatened economic recovery.

Concurrent with the writing of this report, the back channel with Washington was revived. On August 5, Adam Schaff called on Davis to start a new dialogue. Acting as a confidential emissary for Jaruzelski and a close group of advisers, Schaff explained that his actions were not known by the broader politburo or even the MSZ. For their part, the Poles were planning to fulfill long-standing American requirements for improved relations: implementing a full amnesty, creating a Committee of National Understanding including church and government officials, creating a national advisory committee made up of voices from "various fields and various political opinions" outside of the government, experimenting with "greater independence for trade unions," and exchanging ambassadors. In return the Poles wanted restored MFN and eligibility for credits, "normal treatment" for access to nonmilitary technology, and for the Americans to "not hinder" their economic revival coordinated with IMF cooperation. In Davis's estimation, the moves described would "amount to toleration of a legal opposition for the first time in a Communist state"; he therefore recommended that the back channel be approved.[126] Despite the request, no immediate actions were taken back in Washington.

When the politburo met on September 9 to consider the possibility of extending the amnesty, domestic and international elements clearly overlapped to force a final decision. As with earlier amnesties, the Communists emphasized that it would improve the government's domestic position: freeing all the remaining political prisoners "will show our strength and will [to create] social understanding, enlisting and neutralizing those social groups which are still undecided, lost, expectant." The amnesty was also a chance to show the government's "will and consistency" in building societal understanding, as well as future normalization. In terms of relations with the Catholic Church, the decision would "benefit from the possibility of increasing activities limiting nonreligious activity of some priests, as well as persuading the church to support the realization of [solutions to] social problems."[127]

In contrast to earlier amnesty decisions, however, international considerations were at the forefront of arguments in favor of freeing political prisoners. Here it is worthwhile to quote at length:

> The improvement of relations between the two superpowers,
> which has emerged in the last few months, has brought a significant
> increase in activity in the East-West dialogue. This has caused a
> certain reevaluation in the Western campaign against socialist
> nations. This has [also] significantly increased the quantity of
> economic and political visits of a high level, [and led to] contracts and
> agreements being concluded.
>
> This has not included Poland. The West applied tactics against our
> country, which made progress in normalizing relations within Poland
> dependent on assessments of the development of our [internal]
> situation, taking advantage of all convenient pretexts for the sake of
> justifying their restrictions policy.
>
> One of the Western nations' publicly presented criteria for assessing
> the internal situation in Poland is the matter of political prisoners.
>
> Not embracing the [amnesty law] as part of a frontal action against
> the opposition and the judicial process will provide an opportunity
> to malign the good name of Poland, to continue restrictions, and to
> slow the development of economic and political relations. On the
> other hand, embracing the law will permit us to develop actions in
> international policies, which should bring improvements on a great
> many levels and will be fruitful with positive results for the country.

Or as the paper put it more succinctly in the first bullet point in favor of
extending the amnesty, "It will result in progress in the stabilization of socioeconomic life, in the acceptance of ventures by national authorities, and
in significantly decreasing the threat of interference by hostile powers in the
internal situation of the nation."[128] Western pressure was working.

Taking into account all these benefits, the PZPR extended the amnesty to
include all political prisoners. The MSZ met with foreign diplomats during
the following few days to explain the decision and made it public on September 11. By September 15, 1986, Bujak, Frasyniuk, and all other remaining political prisoners had been released.[129] Western political and economic
pressure had successfully forced Jaruzelski's government to pardon all of
the members of Poland's democratic opposition. Bujak and his coconspirators could now walk the streets of Warsaw and meet openly at friends'
apartments.

A scene from the gathering at Jacek Kuroń's apartment on September 19, 1986.
Photo courtesy of Erazm Ciołek.

This amnesty proved to be the last. Unlike after previous releases, political activists were not quickly rearrested or later convicted of new crimes
against the state. September 1986 proved a watershed event, the final departure point for the democratic revolution of 1989.[130] As one of the most insightful Polish historians working on the period has concluded, "One could
thus say that the fundamental part of the struggle between the opposition
and the communists, who enjoyed a monopoly [on] power, was waged in a
period from [1977] . . . to the events of September 1986, which inaugurated
a negotiated transformation of Poland into a democratic country."[131] This
was the beginning of a new era in Poland's development, but it was not
exactly an end either. As Wałęsa said at the time, "It is a step in the right
direction. . . . A second step must still be fulfilled, a step must be taken in
the direction of pluralism."[132]

The amnesty decision provides strong evidence of how international concerns, refracted through the lens of the country's domestic economic crisis,
affected Poland's internal transformation. Threats of continuing Western
sanctions and Western pressure successfully pushed the PZPR to free all its
remaining political prisoners, because the PZPR understood that the country would never extricate itself from the economic crisis if sanctions continued. Without access to transcripts from the politburo meeting at which the
PZPR accepted a full amnesty, it is difficult to draw definitive conclusions

about the exact mixture of international concerns that provoked the decisions. But when placing the decision within the international context of 1986, it is clear that the most important international actors were the Soviet Union, Western Europe, and the United States, in that order.

First, Gorbachev's rise to power inaugurated a new era of permissiveness and reform in relations with Poland. At the Twenty-Seventh CPSU Party Congress in February and March 1986, Gorbachev had unveiled his new policies of *perestroika* (transformation) and *uskorenia* (acceleration). It was still unclear if Gorbachev's words were just words or if they would lead to meaningful changes in the Soviet Union's behaviors; nevertheless, the PZPR closely watched and analyzed Gorbachev's steps for signs of how they could affect Poland. More important, by joining Jaruzelski at the Tenth Party Congress and giving his stamp of approval to the Drugi Etap, Gorbachev was, at least, acquiescing to and, at best, fully supporting the PZPR's decision to enhance the role of the opposition (the Consultative Council) in government efforts to normalize domestic affairs. Brezhnev, Chernenko, and Andropov had never been this permissive. Expanding the amnesty therefore constituted an extension of policies that Jaruzelski understood Gorbachev and his Moscow comrades had or would approve.

In terms of influences from outside the bloc, Western pressure convinced the PZPR to free the last remaining political prisoners. By early 1986, the PZPR had concluded that it could not rebuild the Polish economy without new Western investment and possibly new Western credits. To access Western money the PZPR acquiesced to political demands that the West had been making since January 1982 for the release of political prisoners. The trickier point of interpretation comes when determining what exactly the PZPR meant by "West" and "Western." Were the Poles referring to the United States, Western Europe, or both?[133]

First, evidence of direct American influence is weak. A record of the conversation between Swartz and Patusiak was sent to the PZPR Central Committee Foreign Department and to Jaruzelski, but it was not included in materials prepared for any politburo meeting. Only the document on Western Europe, specifically mentioning the European Community démarche of July 30, was presented to the full politburo when it made its decision to pursue a total amnesty. In a July 28 meeting between Swarz and Sujka, neither side mentioned any pending deal.[134] In addition, the Schaff proposals were not acted on quickly. When the head of the State Department's East European Department, Martin Wenick, met with MSZ officials in Warsaw on August 18, the subject did not come up in any specific terms either, with the MSZ concluding that there were "absolutely no" new moves being taken by the United States. The Poles assumed that any response to the amnesty would only come after it was completed, when Washington could confirm that people were not simply being rearrested.[135] An official invitation for Schaff to visit Washington to continue the renewed dialogue was not approved until September 30, more than ten days after the final political prisoner was released. Based on the chronology it appears that Jaruzelski and his advisers had already agreed on a full amnesty and then sent Schaff to the American embassy to see what concessions this move might get them in return.

Most telling, however, was the long-term trend in U.S.-Polish contacts: relations with the United States had hardly improved since the declaration of martial law. If anything, 1985 and early 1986 were worse than the comparatively warm period of bilateral relations in 1983 and 1984. In 1986, Poland and the United States remained in a stalemate, with each side waiting for the other to take a significant step. As the MSZ noted in its annual review of 1986, there was little hope for any improvement in relations. Trust between the two was still broken. In Washington, policy makers continued to feel "tricked" by earlier deals to release political prisoners, only to see them rounded up and jailed again. On the Polish side, the PZPR was consistently angered by Washington's track record of only begrudgingly offering small incentives for steps toward liberalization as part of the "step-by-step" policy. The Poles had gone as far as rejecting the entire step-by-step or small-steps framework at the end of 1984. Despite whatever deals Jaruzelski might have been pursuing through private channels, official Polish policy was to wait for the United States to lift all remaining sanctions before responding. Finally, the MSZ had spent the previous years refusing to acquiesce to American pressure. Given that context, it is highly unlikely that an overture from Swartz and the possibility of a renewed dialogue through Schaff could have caused such a drastic reversal.

The more plausible source of Western pressure was Europe. Throughout 1985 and into 1986 Poland made real gains in relations with West Europeans. It had broken the political blockade and had begun to see some much-needed economic rewards. At the beginning of 1986, the PZPR was hopeful that political gains would lead to improved economic relations both bilaterally and with the EEC as a group. That optimism about future progress was reflected in an annual prognosis for foreign relations prepared early in 1986, which noted "an interlocking reflexivity between the internal situation and foreign affairs." Compared to the previous two years, "the expected improvement of the international climate in Europe would offer more favorable external conditions for the sake of improving the internal situation in Poland; that is, accelerating the process of overcoming the effects of the social-economic crisis and deepening socialist democracy." There had been no such improvement in either political or economic relations with the United States. When PZPR documents refer to a "reevaluation in the Western campaign against socialist nations" and increases in "the quantity of economic and political visits of a high level [that led to] contracts and agreements being concluded," the PZPR was clearly referring to the countries of Western Europe.[136] As the PZPR was plainly and painfully aware, Washington had not reevaluated its relationship with Poland; France, Italy, West Germany, and (to a lesser extent) Great Britain had.

Second, in 1986 the PZPR had begun to accept West European links between economic improvements and human rights. As noted in the MSZ's prognosis for foreign relations in 1986, "The central criterion for the credibility of Poland in the international arena remains the state of the internal situation and the national economy." Therefore "more active and effective activity by Poland in 1986 will be possible under the conditions which follow further progress in stabilizing the internal situation and developing the country's economy."[137] The United States might have been the loudest voice on human rights, but the MSZ was well aware of the importance Western Europe placed on Poland's internal development and liberalization. Margaret Thatcher, in particular, "felt very strongly . . . that martial law was not an internal affair of a sovereign country that could be coped with in the way [the British] had coped with previous crackdowns within the Soviet bloc. Something bigger and more important had happened in 1981." Throughout the 1980s under her government, the British position toward the PRL was that much tougher.[138] Records from Foreign Minister Howe's visit in 1985 reflected this viewpoint. Italy and France engaged in similar conversations, verifying West Europeans' central concerns about political prisoners. Human rights were a European concern. Whereas the PZPR had consistently rejected Washington's attempts to link restrictions to internal developments as an infringement on sovereignty, the MSZ was willing to accept the "reflexivity" in relations with the West Europeans. The British-led EEC démarche on July 30 placed the link between the internal situation and foreign affairs front and center.

Finally, in 1986 the Poles had something to lose with the West Europeans. The perceived EEC threat—to halt improvements in relations if all political prisoners were not released—would have meant a return to the political and economic isolation of early 1984, if not of 1982. Years of hard-won progress in relations with Western Europe would have been lost. The same was not true of Polish-American relations: even if the PZPR was driven by American offers articulated by Swartz and pursued by Schaff, these conversations only presented a prospect of future improvements, the *hope* of better relations. As the Poles knew well from previous experience, the United States held very tightly to its restrictions and sanctions. Trust had not been restored between the two sides to make this kind of offer carry significant enough weight to provoke a reversal in policy. In the case of Western Europe, however, the PZPR had been given a concrete and enforceable ultimatum: release all prisoners or return to political and economic isolation.

Both the United States and Western Europe put pressure on Poland in 1986. Undoubtedly an offer of new American credits would have been enticing to a government looking to increase foreign investment. Yet given that American offers do not appear in the politburo records while references to European threats do, it seems clear that Europe played the key role in this decision. After five years of bad blood there were few incentives for the Poles to believe Swartz's offer or that the reinvigoration of a back channel could somehow sway Washington's opinions and significantly transform Reagan's policies. Poland had a lot more to lose if relations with the Europeans turned sour.

Even though the United States was not most responsible for the PZPR's policy redirection in 1986, the amnesty was still tangentially a success for American foreign policy. The United States had led the drive to impose Western sanctions in the first place in December 1981 and January 1982. The American belief (shared by the internal Polish opposition) that economic sanctions and restrictions would force the Communist government to change its policies was correct. The need for foreign currency was a fundamental weakness and vulnerability in the Polish economy, exacerbated by Western restrictions of new credits and political contacts. A need to redress this investment problem led the Polish government to accept foreign intervention on matters of human rights and political prisoners. Yet if West Europeans had not begun to drop political and especially economic sanctions in 1985, the West would not have had as much leverage in 1986. Because of Western European involvement, Poland had much more to lose with a merely partial amnesty. A close reading of the September 9 politburo meeting makes clear that these European concerns were at the forefront of PZPR decision making. The amnesty of 1986 was more of an Allied triumph than a purely American one.

With this Allied victory, the PZPR took a second significant step toward fulfilling Western demands to lift economic sanctions (martial law had been lifted and all political prisoners had been released). In terms of Polish-American relations, however, contacts and trust remained strained. However, with this second demand met, not only had Poland's internal situation been transformed but so had relations with the United States.

CHAPTER FIVE

# Very Good and Getting Better

## Reengagement and Reinforcement, September 1986 to February 1988

On January 28, 1987, Deputy Secretary of State John Whitehead's plane landed on the tarmac at Okęcie Airport. He was arriving as an "authoritative" member of the Reagan administration, the highest-level visitor since 1981. Whitehead traveled to Warsaw to meet with leaders from three key constituencies, including Jaruzelski, Glemp, and Wałęsa. When he stepped off the plane, Whitehead was greeted by Jan Kinast who told him that Wałęsa would be unable to travel to Warsaw for a meeting because he had already taken all of his vacation days from his electrician's job at the Gdańsk shipyards. Whitehead was surprised and upset. In the spur of the moment, he took a gamble: if Wałęsa could not come to him, then Whitehead would fly to Gdańsk instead of meeting with Jaruzelski. By the time the deputy secretary arrived at his hotel room, the government had reversed its position and told Whitehead that Kinast had been misunderstood. Wałęsa would be in Warsaw as scheduled.[1]

After the complete amnesty in September 1986, the United States followed a cautious policy to reengage with the Polish government. Over a series of high-level meetings and negotiations, culminating in Vice President George Bush's visit in September 1987, Washington moved methodically to lift all remaining sanctions and then normalize economic and political relations. By Whitehead's second visit in January 1988, bilateral relations had experienced nearly eighteen months of improvement and trust building. During this same period, however, the United States did not neglect the opposition. Congress, NGOs, and NED took ever bolder moves to ensure that American money to Solidarność increased as the opposition played an ever greater role in public life. American humanitarian aid decreased, but events in these years showed how aid policy amplified American soft power, with positive results. Overall, the period from September 1986 to February 1988 was remarkably cordial compared to the previous five years, with bilateral relations turning toward a new direction and with long-term policies to support the opposition bearing fruit.

## To Vienna

The White House reacted guardedly to PZPR statements in September 1986 that the amnesty would apply to all political prisoners. On September 12, White House spokesman Larry Speakes explained cautiously, "We hope that this is a genuine and complete amnesty. . . . We will be monitoring the release closely to see that the government of Poland keeps its commitments." The State Department spoke in equally restrained terms, restating the administration's long-standing position, "If the Polish government takes meaningful liberalizing measures, we are prepared to take equally significant and concrete steps of our own."[2] In private Assistant Secretary of State Rozanne Ridgway told Ludwiczak that they were pleased but were waiting to see how the amnesty was implemented and how it affected dialogue within Poland.[3] In a further sign of prudence, Shultz did not meet with Foreign Minister Orzechowski during the Forty-First Opening Session of the U.N. General Assembly.[4] In Warsaw, the MSZ regarded the American response as "very qualified [bardzo powściągliwa]."[5]

Public voices, especially from Capitol Hill, pressured the White House to drop all remaining sanctions. Even before all the political prisoners were freed, thirty-three members of Congress from both political parties led by the Democratic Representative Bill Lipinski from Chicago sent a letter to the president calling for an end to sanctions.[6] Democratic Representatives Steven Solarz (who had just returned from a trip to Poland) and Dante Fascell, along with Republican congressman Frank Murkowski, held a widely covered press conference calling for the United States to "move quickly" to reinstate MFN and government guaranteed credits because "a failure to respond positively to Warsaw's initiative would forfeit our best chance of exerting influence on the course of events."[7] Similarly, the PAC National Board of Directors resolved that, if all political prisoners were released, sanctions should be lifted and a "more flexible position in regard to guaranteed bank credits" be pursued.[8] Nowak and PAC president Mazewski joined Solarz's press conference and linked lifting sanctions with maintaining leverage. In Nowak's words, "If [the Polish leadership's] hopes do not materialize, there is a likelihood of retrogression. . . . [A] carrot offered by the U.S. can help the opposition more than maintaining sanctions."[9]

Voices from the Catholic Church also supported ending sanctions. Glemp and John Paul II had consistently called for sanctions to be lifted since 1983. During a visit to the United States in September 1985, Glemp was unequivocal, calling sanctions "unjust toward the Polish nation," adding that "the rupture of economic and scientific collaboration is of great damage to the Polish people."[10] In early October 1986, Archbishop John Krol added his weight, writing a letter to the president about his recent trip to Poland in which he noted that "the greatest majority of Poles would appreciate the lifting of sanctions, and, hopefully, the Polish government would be encouraged in its efforts."[11] The message from Congress, PAC, and Cardinal Krol was clear: sanctions had lost their usefulness, maintaining them would do more harm than good.

The most important voice did not come from the United States; it came from within Poland. On September 22, Wałęsa wrote a letter to Reagan appealing for him to lift all remaining sanctions. Wałęsa was troubled by Poland's economic situation: "Our society's conditions of life and health are continuously getting worse. The specter of catastrophe is rising before us, a catastrophe which could threaten the physical existence of our people and its identity." Wałęsa appealed for Reagan to "take into consideration actions which would contribute to the betterment of Polish societal situation and eliminate the economic sanctions which are still in force against Poland. Please understand our desire to avoid anything which deepens our country's isolation from the Western world, with whom we are joined by ties of culture and moral values."[12] On October 10, Wałęsa followed this private message with a public appeal published in the Catholic weekly *Tygodnik Powszechny*, signed by him and a group of his advisers. He called for abolishing all remaining economic sanctions and for restoring scientific, cultural, and personal exchanges with America and the West.[13]

As public pressure grew, policy wheels began to spin. Davis was brought back to Washington, and initial discussion focused on whether to invite Schaff to the capital, an action that was approved by the NSC on September 25.[14] With Schaff's visit approved for the week of October 20 or 27, Schultz called a meeting of his top aides, "debating whether to complete the normalization process by dropping the last of several sanctions."[15] On October 6, the State Department recommended taking a number of significant steps, including lifting its "no-exceptions" policy on technology and equipment exports (returning to a case-by-case approach), sending an American delegation to the Poznań International Trade Fair, restarting official bilateral contacts through the Polish-American Joint Trade Commission, responding positively to Polish calls to reopen refinancing negotiations on Paris Club debt, expanding high-level contacts between the governments, and opening talks on renewing agreements on scientific and technical exchanges. State also suggested high-level parliamentary visits to the United States and welcomed the exchange of ambassadors "at the proper time."[16] These lower-priority issues had not been a central part of public debates about sanctions, but they were important symbols of a desire to rebuild a working relationship. The exchange of ambassadors and high-level visits had been particularly contentious during the previous two years. On the sanctions issues most noted in the public pressure, the memo stated, "provided that the Polish Government maintains a human rights climate that promotes progress toward genuine national reconciliation, we are prepared to discuss early next year: 1) lifting the suspension of MFN, and 2) removing the ban on official credits and credit guarantees."[17]

Although the State Department had significantly revised U.S. policy, the NSC response did not materialize quickly. It took two weeks after the State Department memo had been finalized for Dobriansky to draft and get approval for the NSC response, which basically agreed to the Department of State's position, with the added detail of emphasizing that the United States would not hinder Poland's requests for IMF membership.[18] Presidential authorization for the new policy toward Jaruzleski's government was given on October 27. The final policy remained very close to Foggy Bottom's initial recommendations, with the NSC version emphasizing a more specific definition of what "genuine" national reconciliation would include.[19] By this point Schaff's visit had been pushed back to November.

The relatively slow NSC response to important changes in the political situation on the ground in Poland was indicative of the issue's status in the White House and of continuing controversy on how best to deal with Jaruzelski. Shultz's and the White House's main focus remained Gorbachev and the Soviet Union, particularly the Reykjavik summit on October 11–12. As Deputy Assistant Secretary Tom Simons recalls, "Poland was not a front burner issue. . . . The policy toward Poland was really subsidiary to policy toward the Soviet Union."[20] In addition, the idea of rewarding Jaruzelski remained controversial. As Schultz recalls, "My effort to encourage change in Eastern Europe was actively opposed by many on the NSC staff, in the CIA, and in the Defense Department—people who believed that we should shun all 'evil empire' leaders and avoid visits to them that would 'enhance their credibility.'"[21] Debate within the Reagan administration fit earlier patterns: some within the NSC and Defense Department took a more ideological view and blocked moves toward gradual normalization. Within the Department of State, opposition came from Dick Solomon and Nelson Ledsky on the Policy Planning Staff, and from within the department's Counselor's Office, a group that even called themselves the "three ravens" for their opposition to the general direction in the State Department. The Treasury Department added its weight in favor of maintaining sanctions.[22] These divisions explain why there were no significant policy reviews in 1985 or 1986; they also posed a significant barrier to changing policy quickly in the fall of 1986. Finally, all parties were concerned that the PZPR would renege on its amnesty agreement and rearrest Solidarność leaders as they had done in 1984 and 1985.

Tipping the balance in favor of normalization, voices calling for sanctions to be lifted had a new advocate. In April 1985, Shultz replaced Deputy Secretary of State Kenneth Dam with John Whitehead, a former chairman of Goldman Sachs. Whitehead was brought in to be Shultz's "partner" at the State Department (not his deputy)—to run the department while the secretary was away on his regular diplomatic trips. After a year in office, Whitehead began looking for an area in which to specialize and chose Eastern Europe. Shultz, who felt he had neglected Eastern Europe, readily agreed to the project.[23] Whitehead also came in with a pragmatist's approach, seeing it as his job to weaken East European ties with the USSR and to foster them with the United States, often openly speaking of these countries' natural position as European nations rather Soviet satellites.[24] Shultz has compared this long-term approach to gardening, planting a seed and waiting for it to grow to maturity.[25] As he has explained, "Small steps that accumulate could wind up being a big step, even if it seemed to be taking place at any one moment. Work with small steps would be a promising and reasonable shift on our part . . . John took on this assignment with enthusiasm and flair." Whitehead also brought a fresh perspective; during one meeting, he asked, "I know I'm still learning this business, but could you tell me why we can talk to Gorbachev, but can't talk to Jaruzelski?"[26] His openness to traveling and meeting with East European leaders concerned more hard-line members of the cabinet and White House, who saw him as a "softee" who might give away too much.[27]

For those working underneath him, Whitehead gave new weight to Eastern European policy. He was a "champion on the seventh floor who [gave] us the kind of consistent policy focus that you need to get anything."[28] Whitehead also had a direct connection to Reagan, always meeting with the president to brief him personally on his trips. As Whitehead recalls, "I felt I had a bond with Reagan that I didn't have with some of his staff," meaning that he could act as a direct advocate for a pragmatic approach without having other members of the White House staff misrepresent his ideas or disregard them before his reports reached the Oval Office.[29] Finally, Whitehead showed a real affinity toward Wałęsa and Solidarność. He believed in Solidarność's intrinsic value, filling his office with Solidarność memorabilia, including a banner with the Solidarność slogan "Gdy niemożliwe, stało się możliwe" (When impossible, became possible).[30] When the Iran-Contra scandal broke in November 1986, pulling the White House and Shultz with it, Whitehead remained to oversee relations with Eastern Europe.

With steadfast leadership on the East European issue, the State Department took a bolder line, forging ahead and engaging with Polish diplomats even though the Schaff visit had been pushed back. The first outlines of the new American policy on sanctions came to the PZPR in a letter from the former Polish ambassador to the United Nations, Ryszard Frelek, in which he described his meetings with Simons, Davis, and Wenick, all of whom supported "a gradual normalization of relations with Poland through the resumption of political dialogue." Moreover, the Americans were willing to reinstate MFN, allow renewed scientific-technical cooperation, and end sanctions on Export-Import Bank credits, in a step-by-step process that would be outlined when Davis returned to Warsaw.[31] On October 30 Davis met with politburo member Czyrek, proposing a bilateral meeting during the opening session of an upcoming CSCE summit in Vienna. Although Shultz and Orzechowski would be in Vienna, the Americans did not want a high-profile meeting. Davis did not divulge any expectations, but he made clear that attitudes in Washington were changing.[32] Moreover, discussion about the path forward had moved from the secretive Schaff back channel into more traditional contacts with the MSZ.[33]

Both sides arrived in Vienna and met on November 6. The American delegation was led by Ridgway and included Simons, Davis, Wenick, and Dobriansky. The Polish team was led by Kinast and included Biały and Ryszard Krystosik, the vice director of Department III. The Americans explained that they understood each country had its own national interests, and that the meeting's purpose was to find "common interests" to be acted on. The American delegation also presented a "calendar for a return to dialogue" (also referred to as a "work plan"), which set forth steps toward normalized relations, including visits and exchanges. The highest-priority visits were a parliamentary trip to Washington, a trip by Czyrek to the United States, and a visit to Warsaw by an "authoritative" member of the Reagan administration who could speak for the White House. Other steps included a new treaty on scientific-technical cooperation, efforts to confront international terrorism, American participation in the Poznań International Trade Fair, American support for Poland's IMF membership, and a "generally positive" attitude toward Polish matters in the Paris Club.[34] Surprisingly after five years of strained relations, both sides agreed to these prescribed steps with little negotiation.

Of course, Polish representatives and American negotiators did not agree on everything. In response to Ridgway's comments emphasizing human rights and the need for Poland to engage in a dialogue with "'important parts' of society," Kinast explained that the "Solidarność chapter [of Polish history] had come to an end." There would not be a return to the situation before December 1981, but nor would there be a return to the period before August 1980. Kinast also protested American support to "antisocialist" forces, particularly through RFE and VOA, clarifying that propaganda and continued support for Solidarność would affect normalization. As in previous disagreements, he emphasized Poland's sovereignty: "The process of national reconciliation will be run on the basis of our own Polish script."[35]

Second, the Poles disagreed about the timing for dropping sanctions. Kinast wanted sanctions lifted as the first move, but Ridgway explained that sanctions would only be dropped at the end of a preliminary "transitional period" meant "to demonstrate to the leadership from both sides that achieving improved relations is possible." Emphasizing why rewards remained tentative, the Americans explained that the caution "results from what happened in Poland in 1984. Then 'you and we, alike, made a decision.' But later 'the amnesty turned out to be a funeral.' Many people drew the conclusion that 'Poland was not operating under a sense of good will.'" She concluded, "This will not stop [the United States], however, from taking leading steps to a 'renewed beginning of dialogue,' with the goal of progress in mutual relations."[36] So, in deference to previous experience, the Americans kept sanctions in place until both sides could foster trust.

Although the meeting between Kinast and Ridgway went mostly unnoticed in the media, it represented an important turning point in Polish-American relations.[37] Differences and arguments persisted, but the two sides now had a road map of clear steps to rebuild trust and move toward normalization. However, this was not a true negotiation between equals; rather, Ridgway prescribed how events would progress, laying out specific steps for both sides to take. The Americans were pleased that a complete amnesty had been declared, but the specter of earlier short-lived amnesties still loomed.

For relations to progress, the Poles had to follow the series of steps dictated by the United States.[38]

## Through the Transitional Period

With a new road map, the Polish negotiating team returned to Warsaw. On November 21, Kinast met with Davis to accept the American framework. The two spoke about plans for Simons's December visit to Warsaw, as well as a Czyrek's visit to Washington in early 1987. Davis also clarified that Whitehead would be the "authoritative" administration official sent to Warsaw in 1987. The conversation was not particularly notable for what was said, but rather for what was not said. Compared to the contentious meetings between Davis and Kinast in years past, the tenor of this meeting was cheery. There was no major disagreement. Neither side found reason to accuse the other of any insidious deed. No one stonewalled. Instead, Kinast and Davis found themselves in the unusual position of sharing opinions in a professional, pleasant manner. As Kinast summed up, "The conversation proceeded in a good atmosphere. J. Davis was obviously pleased with the presentation of our position."[39] Both sides had taken a perceptibly new approach based more on cooperation than confrontation. The new approach was confirmed by a cordial meeting between Ludwiczak and Simons on November 25.[40]

To maintain momentum, Simons traveled to Warsaw on a "familiarization visit" from December 1 to 5, his first visit since being named deputy assistant secretary. He met with the minister of finance, B. Samojlik, and the undersecretary of state in the Ministry of Foreign Trade, J. Kaczurba, to discuss economic issues, specifically American participation in the Poznań International Trade Fair and further work on a new scientific-technical cooperation treaty. In conversations about the IMF and the Paris Club, Simons emphasized that an "automatic improvement in that field is not possible," to keep Polish expectations low.[41] In his meeting with Kinast, the two reported on progress made in the "work plan," with Simons stressing that moves toward national reconciliation and human rights would determine the pace of improvement. Kinast rejected this linkage, but he nonetheless briefed Simons on internal developments, particularly on the Consultative Council and a recent national conference of the Ogólnopolskie Porozumienie Związków Zawodowych (OPZZ, or All-Polish Trade Unions Agreement), a nominally independent trade union structure that the PZPR hoped to use to provide at least the appearance of greater worker self-management.[42]

Simon's visit with Czyrek, however, showed that old tensions remained. Czyrek accused Simons of pursuing improved relations at a "slowed-down" pace. Czyrek also defended the 1984 amnesty and subsequent events, which "stemmed exclusively from domestic considerations. . . . If a mistake was made in 1984 it was that the time was not yet ripe for an amnesty." Finally Czyrek launched into an extended speech outlining Poland's "raison d'être," which included the usual historical references to experiences since World War II with complaints that "the U.S. intends merely to use Poland against the Soviet Union" and that sanctions only harmed ordinary people. In response, Simons kept his cool and emphasized that these old arguments would carry little weight, adding "the view of U.S. motivations vis-à-vis Poland, as just presented, is simply wrong. . . . As far as the U.S. is concerned, if the Polish authorities see a U.S. policy of fighting to the last Pole as the current greatest danger to Poland, Poland is as safe as if it were in the womb of the mother of God."[43]

Fortunately, Simons's visit did not conclude this brusquely. On the deputy assistant secretary's last day, Foreign Minister Orzechowski refocused conversation on the working plan: "'As realists' . . . the Polish government believes that the program proposed at Vienna and subsequently agreed to should be realized quickly, thereby bringing positive elements to the bilateral relationship." Orzechowski also presented a reserved version of Polish hopes for the future. They had "no illusions about the nature of U.S. interests towards the East. . . . Bilateral relations cannot be as they were in the 1970s . . . but real progress is possible, based on building an infrastructure of economic and cultural relations." As Simons responded, "The dialogue . . . should be based on realism and candor. The [work plan] . . . is not a maximum but a minimum program."[44]

While staying in an embassy guest house in Belgrade following his Warsaw visit, Simons drafted a memo advocating next moves, sent to Whitehead and then Shultz.[45] The memo presented "the first strong recommendation of lifting sanctions and the reasons why." Above all else, Simons pushed to respond to the final amnesty from September "to maintain our credibility with the Jaruzelski regime." In Simons's argument, "Our response to the final amnesty of September should be as we promised, the lifting of the sanctions." Armed with this memo, Shultz and Whitehead then got approval from the White House for the "game plan" of lifting the final sanctions.[46] Preparations for Whitehead's visit were made without NSC coordination; the State Department was completely in the lead now.[47]

As a final decision neared and Whitehead prepared to travel to Poland, political pressures for and against sanctions continued to swirl in Washington.

A few weeks before the trip, Mazewski and Nowak had met with Whitehead to say that PAC continued to support lifting sanctions despite concerns that political prisoners could be rearrested.[48] On the other side, the AFL-CIO's Adrian Karatnycky met with Assistant Secretary of State for Human Rights Richard Schifter on January 23 and learned that Whitehead was "sympathetic" to lifting sanctions. In the days preceding his departure, Kirkland scheduled a meeting to lobby the deputy secretary to keep sanctions, upholding the AFL-CIO's long-standing position against easing pressure on the Jaruzelski regime.[49]

## Whitehead in Warsaw

The "transitional period" concluded when Whitehead went to Poland at the end of January 1987. Warsaw was his first stop before heading to Bulgaria and Czechoslovakia with an entourage including Simons, Dobriansky, and Wenick. In Warsaw he met first with Orzechowski, during which the foreign minister went to great lengths to explain steps taken in regards to human rights (political prisoners and new unions) and national reconciliation (the Consultative Council, in particular). The Poles also showed interest in further cultural exchanges through the U.S. Information Agency, as well as greater government coordination on international terrorism and narcotics trafficking.[50] The next day, January 30, Whitehead met with Prime Minister Zbigniew Messner to address human rights again, but they also delved into economic matters, especially desires for outside investment. As Messner explained, "Only Poland can solve its [foreign debt problem], but the only way for Poland to do so is for Poland to increase exports, and this will require new credits for modernization." He went to great lengths to explain the economic reform efforts and price revisions undertaken, indirectly confirming the central role of economic concerns in PZPR decision making.[51]

On his final day, Whitehead met with Jaruzelski for nearly three hours. Once again, the deputy secretary stressed human rights. But in a shift from earlier policy, he did not emphasize the Helsinki Final Act or other treaty obligations. Instead, Whitehouse took a much simpler approach: "I told them that they have a sovereign right to resist interference in their internal affairs. But I also said that we . . . have a sovereign right to choose our friends, and that one of the criteria we use to make that choice is where a country stands in its willingness to give its citizens the basic human freedoms we value."[52] Whitehouse was not chastising Jaruzelski. His approach treated Jaruzelski more as an equal and gave him the choice of how to run his government. As

Simons recalls, Whitehead argued "if you don't want to deal with the United States, you don't have to. . . . But if you do want to deal with the United States this is the kind of country we are, these are the kinds of things we want. [It's] up to you. . . . It was friendly. It was not an ultimatum, but it was firm."[53]

Jaruzelski responded positively and refrained from the tirades he had produced for Congressman Long and subsequent visitors when human rights were raised.[54] Yet Jaruzelski also upheld his convictions. He defended the decision to declare martial law, chastised the United States for sanctions, and condemned the American tradition of treating Poland like a "pawn" in the superpower struggle. Jaruzelski also laid out four points where he saw room for Washington to make improvements. First, he emphasized the importance of maintaining the Potsdam Agreements, which set Europe's borders. Second, he explained that the "massive propaganda campaign" needed to end. Third, he rejected American support for "anti-national and destructive" groups and made clear that "there will not be an agreement with extremists." Finally, he based further improvements in relations on lifting all remaining sanctions.[55]

Jaruzelski also displayed some new flexibility. He downplayed the importance of ideological confrontation, saying that Coca-Cola had been "a symbol of evil, imperialism. But that thinking was left behind thirty years ago. We drink Coke, but I don't overestimate its taste value." He also said that he was open to some amount of pluralism. In Jaruzelski's words, "We are sympathetic toward democracy. We are not afraid of a 'constructive' opposition." He rejected Solidarność as "generals without an army," but he did talk frankly about national reconciliation. He also emphasized efforts to create trade union pluralism through the OPZZ. Finally, Jaruzelski spoke openly about Poland's massive debt problem and its sincere desire to repay the West.[56]

Jaruzelski also personally opened up to Whitehead, providing insight into his sense of betrayal following the application of sanctions in 1981 and 1982. Jaruzelski understood that the United States was pursuing a "formula to untie the knot of relations with Poland 'without losing face.'" He recognized that this was "important for a superpower, and we will do our best to get you out." Explaining the Polish position, he added, "But we also 'have face,' we have our dignity. If someone has face and money, if they lose face, they still have money. We do not have money. We only have face. We cannot and we do not want to lose it. Dignity has tremendous importance for us. We did not give it up at that time, when we experienced our dramatic difficulty. Therefore it is necessary to seek a proper solution."[57] Jaruzelski maintained

Lech Wałęsa and John Whitehead shaking hands, with John Davis in the background, on the steps of the ambassador's residence in Warsaw during Whitehead's visit in February 1987. Photo courtesy of John R. Davis Jr.

his opposition to sanctions, but he pursued a more honest conversation. He was willing to move beyond old grudges to create a more "natural" relationship. Whitehead saw himself doing the same. The governments were now indulging in a sincere dialogue, with both sides listening and responding.

Meeting Jaruzelski was not the most notable part of Whitehead's trip to Warsaw; he also had dinner with Wałęsa at the Davis residence. As with other gatherings, the dinner was not meant to be an official meeting. This was a chance for Whitehead to hear privately and directly from Wałęsa (not through advisers or intermediaries in Brussels) about what the U.S. government should do on Solidarność's behalf.[58] During dinner Wałęsa argued that there was a need for compromise, to "pass smoothly through the current phase." He also spoke about Solidarność's forthcoming economic plan and his hopes that bilateral relations would improve to increase American leverage so it could move the PZPR "in a desirable direction."

Finally, Wałęsa and his advisers clarified that Solidarność "supported the lifting of the remaining American economic sanctions. . . . The time had come for a new approach." Solidarność also explained that they wanted the sanctions lifted "in such a way that manifests the United States' continued support for Solidarity and concern for the human rights situation." The opposition did not want a return to the easy loans of the 1970s. Instead, "a new way needed to be found to use economic means to achieve Solidarity's political goal of the democratization of public life."[59] To make his point clear, Wałęsa handed Whitehead an aide-memoir requesting that all remaining sanctions be dropped immediately—including reinstating MFN and ending prohibitions on guaranteed loan credits. As for future steps, new credits should "depend on the realization of economic reform and the democratization of public life. . . . Each step on the road to democratizing public life in Poland should be answered by concrete activities in the area of economic aid."[60]

Whitehead left optimistic about the future. As he told the NAC, "I have become convinced that there are some opportunities [in Eastern Europe] for the West. I think we should be alert to every chance to influence these countries when and where we can. . . . I am convinced that the potential for change is large in the area and that the situation in these countries in relation to the Soviet Union is not hopeless."[61] Whitehead also saw Jaruzelski as a possible partner; Jaruzelski reaffirmed "that the degree of freedom that had been granted would not be rolled back." Most important, Whitehead had gotten "to hear it face to face [that Wałęsa wanted sanctions dropped]. That was what was important. [Whitehead] could then go back to Washington and say, 'I talked to Lech Wałęsa, he said . . .'"[62]

On Whitehead's return, the State Department began planning for reinstating MFN and opening up future credits (both Export-Import Bank guarantees and agricultural credits), presenting the decision as a fait accompli. The State Department met with Reagan on February 11, and the NSC followed up the next day. The NSC wanted to implement a full interagency process to coordinate lifting sanctions (slowing down the process) and voiced concerns that MFN would need to be reviewable to maintain leverage, a shift to which Whitehead quickly agreed.[63] There was, however, no extended interagency process. Wałęsa's personal note and Whitehead's new trust in Jaruzelski trumped any remaining arguments for maintaining sanctions. As a presidential message sent to all NATO capitals on February 14 said, this decision had the blessing of the representatives of the Polish people: "Both Lech Wałęsa and Cardinal Glemp told us that they feel the time is right to lift the remaining U.S. economic sanctions." As Wałęsa also requested, Reagan made his support of Solidarność very clear: "Our support for Solidarity's goals is unabated. We will monitor the progress of dialogue between the government and the people of Poland to ensure that our policy remains responsive to continued movement toward genuine national reconciliation."[64] The decision became public on February 19, 1987, in a presidential announcement lifting all remaining sanctions, most notably on MFN and CCC credits. Continuing his long-standing rhetorical flare, Reagan closed the statement saying, "Our relations with Poland can only develop in ways that encourage genuine progress toward national reconciliation in that country. We will be steady. We will be committed. The flame that burns in the hearts of the Polish people, a flame represented by the candles we lit in 1981, that flame of justice and liberty will never be extinguished."[65] U.S.-Polish relations moved into a new era, one no longer dominated by sanctions but by the real possibility of improved economic, political, and cultural ties. The step-by-step framework remained in place, but the Reagan administration only had new carrots left. The old sticks were gone.

## Transitions in the Opposition

For Solidarność, the months following the final amnesty of September 1986 were also a transitional period. With political dissidents free, Solidarność faced a choice about what to do with the structures that had led the underground opposition for nearly five years. On September 29, 1986, fifteen of Solidarność's most important leaders including Wałęsa, Geremek, Mazowiecki, Lis, Bujak, and Michnik met at Saint Bridgette Church in Gdańsk to discuss the future. Following this meeting, Wałęsa announced in *Tygodnik Mazowsze* that a new Temporary Council of NSZZ "Solidarność" (Tymczasowa Rade NSZZ "Solidarność," or TR) had been founded to demonstrate Solidarność's "preparedness to take a step on the road to dialogue and understanding" with the government.[66] The TR was meant to operate aboveground, but the opposition decided to keep most of its underground operations secret. So while the TR could play a more public role, the operational activities (printing newsletters, smuggling money and material, and distributing money and publications) remained secretive. By the end of 1986, there were two levels within the opposition: the public face of Solidarność including leading advisers and intellectuals (mainly in Warsaw and Gdańsk), and the activists involved in more direct oppositional activities who were aware of operational details.[67]

While this new public face of Solidarność showed that the opposition was regrouping, the movement did not command the same power it had during the 1980–81 period. Jaruzelski's original decision to allow a complete amnesty in part grew out of Solidarność's declining stature. By the fall of 1986, the PZPR no longer felt as threatened. In this analysis, the government placed particular significance in the fact that more than 75 percent of Poles had voted in elections for the Sejm at the end of 1985, despite the opposition's call for a boycott. In January 1986, the MSW Analytic Group concluded that at the end of 1985 there were 350 illegal groups and structures, mostly surrounding Warsaw, Wrocław, Gdańsk, Kraków, and Łódź, totaling around one hundred thousand people involved at any level in the opposition, or between 5 percent and 7 percent of the population. By May 1986, the MSW believed that the number of opposition groups and structures had dropped to 316, a decrease of 11 percent. When Bujak was arrested, the MSW reported that the "position of the TKK in the underground had been ruined." Furthermore, the preceding years had seen the growth of a new ecological and pacifist opposition movement, Wolność i Pokój (WiP, or Freedom and Peace). To the MSW this demonstrated Solidarność's weakened position. By September 1986, the PZPR believed that Solidarność was weak enough to co-opt into working with the government through groups like the Consultative Council.[68]

In the days immediately preceding the final amnesty and in the months that followed, the MSW further demonstrated that they maintained strict control, regardless of the release of political prisoners. As Bujak was about to be released, members of the security services held "some 3,000 'exposing talks' with people suspected of participating in clandestine opposition activity. . . . Many were pressed to give police written statements promising not to break the law in the future."[69] No one was actually arrested, but in a move meant to intimidate, the security services showed that they knew who was involved in underground activities. Then, on November 29, 1986, the security services intercepted a massive shipment being smuggled by the Coordinating Office in Brussels through Sweden. According to documentation from Milewski, the seizure was worth $141,209 and included twelve offset printing machines, fifty-eight duplicating machines, twenty faxes, twenty scanners, forty thousand stencils, more than four tons of printer's ink, eight computers, sixteen printers, four radio transmitters, sixty-five hundred books, and various electronic parts and supplies.[70] In addition, the security services began fining people found with independent publications and seizing cars used by the underground, making life more financially risky for opposition activists.[71] Even though Solidarność's political leaders were now operating aboveground and it appeared that Jaruzelski would no longer be placing them in jail, the government felt in control and maintained significant power over the opposition.

## The Embassy and the Opposition

Few elements in the U.S. government, however, questioned the necessity of supporting Solidarność's central organs, particularly Wałęsa and his circle of advisers. Whether or not American policy makers and Foreign Service officers believed that the democratic opposition would eventually triumph, the American government remained loyal. As Simons recalls, "No one thought that Solidarity was going to overthrow Communism in Poland . . . because as you say, [the government] have the guns, they have the ideology, they have the backing. But that does not mean you do not support Solidarity, especially in the Reagan administration. You have a strong ideological commitment to support Solidarity."[72] In Warsaw this support included a wide network of contacts run through all levels of the embassy to stay informed about opposition activities and needs in the post-amnesty atmosphere. Shortly after coming to Warsaw in June 1986 as vice consul, Cameron Munter was assigned as a liaison to opposition activists including Henryk Wujec and his wife, Ryszard Pusz, and Bogdan Lis. In the case of Wujec, who lived in Warsaw, Munter was contacted about once a month and arranged to meet at a café or other public location near the embassy. In their meetings Wujec shared information about what was going on within the opposition, news of any difficulties they were having, reactions to ongoing events, and views about the mood within the opposition. In the case of Pusz, Munter exchanged more procedural information including who had been questioned by the security services and who had been beaten. Sometimes Pusz would hand Munter "grubby pieces of paper" that he would pass on to his superiors.[73]

Similarly, when Lis traveled to Warsaw from Gdańsk, he occasionally stood on the street outside of the consular section in line with Poles applying for visas. Once inside, Munter took Lis into a back room, where the two exchanged reports, news, and any other messages. As Munter saw it, he was a "message relayer," never making policy pronouncements, but simply gathering information from his opposition contacts and sending it on to officers in the political section, including Davis and the political counsel David Pozorski.[74]

Embassy officials were also charged with maintaining contacts with other members of society colluding with the opposition. Primarily, this meant meeting with clergy, with whom the embassy consistently fostered close relations. Davis maintained personal contacts with church leaders like Cardinal Glemp and Father Bronisław Dembowski (who headed the Primate's Committee on Assistance to Prisoners). He also maintained dialogue with some active dissident priests like Cardinal Franciszek Marcharski and Father Tadeusz Gocłowski.[75] During her assignment in Warsaw from 1986 to 1988, political officer Marilyn Wyatt was assigned to liaise with a group of female activists and the wives of opposition leaders who met at Saint Anne's church in Warsaw's Old Town. Wyatt attended weekly meetings to learn who had been brought in for questioning, who was being harassed by the authorities, and other pertinent information.[76] Finally, whenever embassy officials traveled outside of Warsaw, they made sure to meet with the parish priests to hear their views on local developments and the general mood of the country.

Information gathering was a major focus of the day, because this basic job was greatly hampered by government censorship and misinformation. Reliable data on the economy, government reforms, or the opposition simply was not available. For the embassy, "what was hard was figuring out what was really going on. You couldn't do it from newspapers; you couldn't do it from statistics."[77] Thus diplomats had to talk to as many people as they could. This included exchanging information with other embassies—particularly the British, Australian, Swedish, and French—that were in step with America's outlook. Generally there was camaraderie between all Western diplomats who lived under the same travails of daily life in Warsaw, and suffered from the same lack of information. The information web also included contacts with academics and Western journalists, as well as chance encounters on the street.[78] As Munter recalls, one of his weekly routines was spending Friday afternoon at the Marine bar in the U.S. embassy, followed by burgers and fries at the Eagle Club to exchange information with whomever was there.[79] Armed with this information, the embassy could more accurately report the opposition's progress or shifts in government policy, providing the kind of analysis that aided the opposition by keeping policy makers in Washington well informed.

In certain cases American diplomats went beyond information gathering. Specifically, Munter stepped outside of his role as a "message relayer" and helped with the opposition's operational activities. On a few occasions, he drove to the outskirts of Warsaw to a prearranged location. There unnamed activists loaded his car with new copies of samizdat. The activists took the precautionary step of realigning the headlights on his car, so that it would not be obvious that his car was carrying a heavy load. He drove back to Warsaw, usually into the working-class district of Praga on the east side of the

Wisła River, and dropped the literature at an agreed-on location, such as a dumpster. The materials were then picked up by other opposition members responsible for distribution. Other lower-level embassy staffers were also involved in these kinds of jobs. As Munter explained, he was never expressly directed by his superiors to take part, but he felt that it was an unspoken piece of his role as a lower-level member of the staff to get involved in the "dirtier" aspects of supporting the opposition. By not discussing his efforts with his superiors, Munter knew that he could be dismissed as a "rogue element" if he was ever caught, thereby insulating Davis and the embassy from political fallout.[80]

As all these informational and operational contacts intensified, John and Helen Davis continued to host regular events at their residence, including increasingly frequent congressional visitors. In the first three years of the Davises' time in Warsaw, only one congressional delegation visited. In contrast, from August 1986 to August 1987, seven "codels" came, in addition to the visits by Simons and Whitehead.[81] These included two visits led by Solarz in September 1986 and August 1987; a visit to Kraków led by Fascell, a mission headed by Republican Pennsylvania senator Arlen Specter, and a trip headed by Democratic Georgia senator Sam Nunn and Republican Virginia senator John Warner, all in April 1987; a visit by Ted Kennedy in May 1987; and a parliamentary exchange led by Democratic Illinois congressman Dan Rostenkowski in June 1987.[82] Zbigniew Brzeziński also visited in May 1987, for what he called "perhaps the most valuable trip that I have had to Poland since World War II."[83] He visited graves and a family home in Przemyśl, met with Orzechowski and Czyrek, and had a lunch in Kraków with opposition academics including Andrzej Stelmachowski. He also had "a most memorable dinner with the top Solidarity leadership of Warsaw," including Bujak, Geremek, Onyszkiewicz, Michnik, Kuroń, Andrzej Wajda, Andrzej Celinski, and Klemens Szianowski. There was "a great deal of emotion in the air. But also substantive discussion." Brzeziński also went to Gdańsk to meet with Lis and Wałęsa, whom he considered "the most outstanding [opposition figure]. He is not only charismatic and has good common sense, but I was impressed by how well, intelligently, and logically he reasons."[84]

With each visit, the American embassy held both "official" meetings with government and party officials and "unofficial" contacts comprising meetings with clergy and opposition leaders. While church officials had offices, the embassy arranged meetings with opposition figures as dinners and receptions at the ambassador's residence, an extension of Helen Davis's continuing salons. The residence became a second, informal pillar for American policy, reflecting the dual tracks of relations: government-to-government and government-to-opposition. As Davis recalls, from 1986 on "we would go through the routine of having a dinner for the government officials to meet them. . . . Then the next night we would have a dinner for all the Solidarity leaders and some Church people, so [the American guests] would meet both sides. And well, we kept this up until it got to be a regular routine to the point where there was always a big party going on at our place with all of the rebels.[85]" As with Whitehead's visit in January 1987, invitees for the congressional visits included a regular group of Warsaw intellectuals and opposition figures: Michnik, Kuroń, Geremek, Onyszkiewicz, Wielowiejski, and Mazowiecki. Bujak was also a regular attendee, as was Frasyniuk when he could travel from Wrocław. As for Wałęsa and Lis, they "would come down for dinners . . . from Gdańsk, but of course it was less easy for them to make that trip. It was a long trip to come. They only usually came down for the big time visitors."[86]

For the members of Congress, these opposition dinners gave them a chance to hear another perspective on life in Poland. As with the salons, this was an opportunity for the Americans to hear how the U.S. government could help the democratic opposition, not to advise the opposition on tactics or strategies. Mirroring comments from cables about Whitehead's visit as a chance "to listen, to learn, and to explain,"[87] Kennedy stated that he was there on a "mission to listen, to learn and to do what we can."[88] Conversely, this was an important chance for Solidarność leaders to have their voices heard. As Geremek elucidated, "The purpose was to explain the Polish situation. We had the feeling that the information given in such a direct way, in a personal way, had a different importance, could touch American political leaders, members of the Congress." More important, these visitors proved to be very receptive to the opposition's point of view. Again, Geremek explained:

> We never had the impression of being given lessons of what to do
> or of [intentions] to impose a kind of political leadership. I think
> that probably we wouldn't accept it. But even on the American
> side I couldn't observe such a will. It was very [much a] partnership
> relationship. Sometimes what we had to accept from the American
> side was an interpretation of the international scene which
> concerned American-Russian, American-Soviet relations, the place of
> China . . . , but never a kind of political leadership imposed on us. . . .
>     I even had the feeling that sometimes we are more asked by
> American partners to give *our* impressions, *our* judgments on the

Soviet Union for instance or on what we want to do inside an oppressive system, inside the totalitarian regime. How do we see the possibility of action? So, it was behind *us* the experience of ten million people. In the trade union, the experience of five hundred days of freedom in which we played a political role. I would think that I liked this attitude of respect, admiration, and friendship, without the teacher's attitude or even leader's, effective leadership attitude.[89]

For American visitors this was also a chance to meet with heroes. White-head wanted to meet with Wałęsa because he "admired him deeply"[90] and "was very moved . . . to be with him."[91] As the reporting cable stated, "Mr. Whitehead began the conversation by telling Wałęsa how honored he was to have the op-portunity to meet him. Wałęsa is a famous man in America because people in the United States admire his courageous defense of his convictions."[92] In Ken-nedy's case, the purpose of his trip was to honor Father Popiełuszko, Bujak, and Michnik who had received the Robert F. Kennedy Human Rights Award in absentia in November 1986. During a meeting with Bujak and Michnik at the residence, he "praised them for 'speaking truth to power.'"[93] At a mass held at the Stanisław Kostka Church, he equated the loss of John Kennedy and Robert Kennedy with the loss of Father Popiełuszko.[94] As Jane Fonda and her husband, SDS (Students for a Democratic Society) founder Tom Hayden, put it during their visit in the spring of 1987, "We are here in order to express sup-port for Solidarność."[95] For American celebrities and politicians alike, Wałęsa and his colleagues were well-known symbols of the fight against authoritarian oppression, so Americans traveled to see them for the honor of meeting these Polish martyrs.[96]

For Solidarność leaders, these meetings also had symbolic significance to their home audience, because the PZPR consistently delegitimized the Solidarność leadership. Wałęsa had been relegated to the position of "pri-vate citizen," rather than the leader of a broader movement. As the Brit-ish noted, "The apparent determination of the authorities not to deal with Solidarity or Wałęsa remains. . . . The Government's alternative aim is to attempt to promote those organizations such as PRON and the new official trade unions as vehicles of communication with public opinion."[97] So when famous Americans met with opposition leaders, the independent press like *Tygodnik Mazowsze* gave Whitehead, Brzeziński, Kennedy, and Fonda and Hayden front-page articles. Visits were an opportunity to counteract years of government publications belittling Solidarność's relevance by showing that well-known outsiders continued to support the movement's leadership.[98]

By meeting with high-level American officials, Solidarność showed that it remained an important force, one that the PZPR would have to deal with eventually.

This symbolic importance became overtly political during Whitehead's visit. One of the participants, Onyszkiewicz, wrote an article for the independent press giving a detailed account of the meeting. His report included the news that Whitehead had threatened to cancel his meeting with Jaruzelski if he could not meet with Wałęsa. He also reported that Whitehead began the meeting by "expressing complete support and sympathy, which the USA feels for Wałęsa and the entirety of Solidarność." Onyszkiewicz also clarified that Washington had not yet made a final decision about lifting sanctions: the Americans were waiting to hear Wałęsa's opinion before acting. As Onyszkiewicz summarized, "Visiting Western politicians' conversations with Solidarność or opposition representatives happen already as a normal thing; never, however, has this led to a meeting 'at the highest levels,' i.e., Wałęsa." He continued, "Whitehead's visit may become an important step in forcing the authorities to acknowledge the de facto pluralism manifesting itself in independent organizations and social and political groups."[99] By arranging to meet Wałęsa, Whitehead had placed the chairman of Solidarność on the same plane as Jaruzelski. The PZPR also took note of these meetings, writing in August 1987 that "the process of upgrading the opposition leaders as 'trustworthy and legally elected representatives of society' is continuing (e.g., many recent invitations for Wałęsa to foreign events, contacts by western officials with the opposition leadership). The purpose of these measures is quite clearly the recreation of the opposition leadership elite."[100] Visits by Western politicians and celebrities, therefore, were important to the opposition because these events "enhanced the public perception of the union as an opposition force."[101]

In the two years after Jaruzelski announced that there would be a final political amnesty, the American embassy's support for the opposition blossomed. Salons continued, information coordination flourished, and an undetermined number of embassy officers participated in underground operations. More important, the embassy and the ambassador's residence became a central means for Solidarność to present its positions to American leaders through direct conversations, not just interviews granted to foreign journalists. The Poles could explain their views on shifting political fortunes. For the Americans this was an opportunity to meet with heroes. The meetings also gave specific opposition leaders greater visibility and legitimacy, even within Poland. No one less than Jaruzelski acknowledged the centrality of the American embassy's support for Solidarność's continued strength (albeit in a statement meant to minimize its relevance), saying that Solidarność was "just a group of people that Davis always invites over for dinner, while my wife and I eat alone on the other side of the street."[102]

## Congress and Solidarność

Concurrent with frequent visits to Poland, Congress actively sought to shift Polish-American relations in step with the administration's new policies. A Congressional Research Service report from March 1987 commissioned by Indiana Democratic congressman Lee Hamilton, "Poland's Renewal and U.S. Options," rejected a continued policy of disengagement as well as the "uncritical preference" policy most typified by the easy loan agreements of the 1970s. Instead, the report called for "conditional reengagement," which supported rewarding Poland when it took steps toward fulfilling specific criteria: creating a dialogue between the government and society, sustaining the release of political prisoners, restructuring the economy based on "efficiency criteria," reforming the economy to include market forces, or pursuing an export strategy to enhance the prospects for Polish debt repayment. The report also noted that the United States could use organizations like the IMF and the World Bank to ensure that Poland made hard economic choices to recalibrate its economic engine and help improve the standard of living.[103]

Some members of Congress also supported the democratic opposition more directly. The Republican representative Jack Kemp (from a heavily Polish American district in Buffalo, New York) submitted Joint Resolution 263 requesting $1 million in support for Solidarność.[104] Liberal Democratic representative Morris Udall of Arizona supported the resolution, adding "The brave members of the Solidarity movement deserve our encouragement and our messages of support. More than just that, they deserve concrete assistance . . . to continue their just struggle for basic human rights."[105] On May 1, the Senate Appropriation's Committee backed the recommendation that $1 million be provided to Solidarność in fiscal year 1987 "through assistance channels which have been used in the past to provide assistance to Solidarity."[106] Although the appropriation was criticized by some as nonemergency spending during a period of high deficits, the money was appropriated immediately.[107]

Congressional support did not end there. In July Kennedy, joined by colleagues including Joseph Biden, Carl Levin, Barbara Mikulski, and Jesse Helms, submitted the American Aid to Poland Act of 1987. This appropriated

$1 million for bilateral scientific and technology projects, extended the avail-
ability of $10 million for private Polish farmers (originally appropriated for
the Church Agricultural Fund) through the end of fiscal year 1989, donated
eight thousand metric tons of agricultural surplus to humanitarian organizations, provided $2 million in medical supplies and hospital equipment for
both fiscal years 1988 and 1989, freed up Polish currency held by the U.S.
government for use by private and public charitable organizations in fiscal
years 1988 and 1989, and created a joint Polish-American commission based
at the embassy in Warsaw to determine how these Polish funds should be
utilized. Finally, Kennedy's act appropriated funds directly to Solidarność by
earmarking "no less than $1 million" to be sent to Solidarność in both fiscal
years 1988 and 1989, a clause that Senator Helms insisted on.[108]

With more funding came concerns about how exactly the money would
be sent to Solidarność. As recently as October 1986, the TKK had asked that
aid "be given openly and without political or organizational conditions attached."[109] Until 1987, all U.S. government funds for Solidarność had gone
through the NED to the AFL-CIO's Free Trade Union Institute and finally to
the Brussels Coordinating Office, allowing Solidarność leaders to claim that
they only accepted money from fellow unionists. At the end of October 1986,
however, Jerzy Milewski made a direct appeal through the Senate Committee on Appropriations for funds that could come through the usual channels
*or* direct allocation by Congress.[110] On Capitol Hill, conservative members of
Congress, including Helms and Republican senator Steven Symms of Idaho,
were happy to accept a direct congressional role, a move the AFL-CIO interpreted as an attempt to undermine its position as Solidarność's main bene-
factor. The AFL-CIO, in turn, lobbied to ensure that the preexisting funding
pattern was not changed.[111]

As confusion swirled among various pro-Solidarność groups, Wałęsa
stepped in to provide guidance. He wrote to Congress expressing "gratitude
for the decision" to provide funds, but explained that they would use the million dollars "for a Solidarity social fund." As Wałęsa clarified to Kirkland in
private correspondence, they would gladly accept the money, but, "the whole
affair attracted a lot of publicity that makes the situation rather embarrass-
ing for our union. We claim all the time that we accept assistance from the
fraternal trade unions, from movements and social institutions which are
ready in manner to support the struggle of Polish trade unions for the right
to exist. The independence of our movement is one of the main [facets] of
our philosophy. Using a subsidy coming from the American state, for organizational needs of our union, would be in contradiction with this principle."

If the union accepted the money directly from Congress it would bolster arguments that Solidarity was "an alien interest."[112] Congress accepted Wałęsa's wishes, and the $1 million allocated for fiscal year 1987 went through NED to the humanitarian group International Rescue Committee to buy three ambulances and fund Solidarność-run medical clinics.[113]

As with the decision to drop economic sanctions half a year earlier, Wałęsa's word was final in policy-making circles. In both cases the U.S. government acquiesced to the desires of the man who had come to symbolize the Polish opposition. Equally as important, Wałęsa's gesture, decided in coordination with his advisers, demonstrated the movement's independence from the United States. Even faced with the temptation of $1 million (more than double the Coordinating Office's budget for 1986), the opposition believed that it was more important to maintain its patriotic purity than publicly accept money so closely associated with a foreign power. Of course, Poland very much needed the money, so Solidarność created a social fund. Once the public spotlight was off the congressional appropriations, the yearly subsidies of $1 million for fiscal years 1988 and 1989 made their way through NED to the Brussels office via FTUI. The movement's emphasis on its independence was tempered by realism.[114]

## NED, NGOs, and the Opposition

Regardless of the opposition's decision to reject directly appropriated congressional funds for political activities, Solidarność and other groups accepted large "subsidies" to continue their work in the underground, which was increasingly becoming institutionalized into a kind of second society. The largest single source for American support following the 1986 amnesty remained NED. In fiscal year 1986, NED money increased once again, totaling $934,763—up from $606,000 in 1985. Of this sum, roughly one-third was dedicated to the direct support through FTUI of Solidarność's Coordinating Office and publication efforts by CSS.[115] In fiscal year 1987 funding increased again, growing to nearly $2 million, with $920,750 from NED and an additional $1 million provided by Congress for the Solidarność Social Fund. In the established pattern, FTUI received the lion's share: $451,000.[116] The rest of the money for both years went to a number of smaller organizations focused on supporting opposition needs consistent with Solidarność's goals. To oversee the process of distributing congressional funding, NED implemented a structured, bureaucratic system to apply for support and then report how monies were being spent.[117] Each year the grantee organizations prepared proposals, signed grant agreements, provided quarterly expense reports showing that funds were being dispersed, and produced year-end reports giving at least a rough outline of how funds were utilized. These grantee organizations did not work directly with the opposition, however. They simply functioned as intermediaries who passed money to organizations working in Western Europe, Scandinavia, and the United States, taking a small fee for administrative costs. The smaller, second-tier recipient groups in New York, Paris, London, and Lund, Sweden, actually ran the programs to support the opposition. So, in each case, money from NED went through a number of hands before it reached people who were actually part of the democratic opposition in Poland.

A close reading of the paper trail created by these bureaucratic layers demonstrates American priorities, as well as the evolving nature of the opposition movement itself.[118] First, from 1984 to 1988 NED funds fell into three categories: humanitarian support to political prisoners and activists, payments to publishers and advocacy groups working in the West, and money and material sent to aid opposition groups working inside the country. In terms of humanitarian support this included $90,000 per year administered through PIASA and then the PACCF. Consistent with the PACCF's long-standing efforts, the purpose of this program was to ship food, clothes, and medicine purchased in the West via the offices of KCEP; however, as the grant application explained, "This is not a charitable project but based purely on political considerations. It is a means to provide a kind of insurance to activists in the independent movement against the risk of arrest, imprisonment, or the loss of a job." Therefore, humanitarian shipments included cash sent to offset the fines, loss of employment, and property confiscations with which the government favored to punish political activists after the 1986 amnesty.[119] Similarly, NED provided resources to the Polish Legal Defense Fund to subsidize the cost of defending activists. Also in this category, POLCUL—a charitable organization founded by Jerzy Boniecki, a wealthy Polish Australian industrialist—awarded $500 cash prizes to independent publishers, human rights activists, academics, poets, writers, journalists, and actors who were judged to have made important contributions to the opposition. These awards counteracted the harassment and fines to which activists were subjected.[120]

The second major focus for grants—support to publishers working in the West—can be divided further into two subpriorities: materials published for distribution in the West and materials published to be smuggled back into Poland. Groups like CSS in New York and the Information Centre for Polish

Affairs in London, which published the Uncensored Poland News Bulletin fortnightly, as well as the Polish Helsinki Watch, focused on providing news to the Western public and governments about human rights abuses and the internal political situation, often archiving and translating articles from the underground press.[121] On the other side, the management of *Zeszyty Literackie* outside Paris, ANEKS publishers in London, PIASA in New York, and the Independent Poland Agency (IPA) in Lund, Sweden, produced works in Polish. Issues of *Zeszyty Literackie* were produced in miniature to aid the smuggling process, and the IPA regularly produced microfilms of *Kultura* and *Zeszyty Historyczny* (*Historical Notebooks*) which were produced in Paris, so that underground presses in Poland could reproduce them domestically. Each of these publications from the West presented a forum for Polish intellectuals to reach a wider audience, while simultaneously allowing émigrés to engage in a dialogue with the internal opposition.[122]

The third and largest priority for NED projects were grants dedicated to activists working within Poland, which can be divided into three subpriorities. The jewel of this program was support through FTUI, which provided roughly two-thirds of the Solidarność Coordinating Office Abroad's yearly budget.[123] The Coordinating Office represented Solidarność at the International Confederation of Free Trade Unions and oversaw major operations to support the union's activities by sending cash, printing equipment, and communications equipment to trade union representatives. According to a budget provided by Jerzy Milewski for 1987, 10 percent of the Coordinating Office's budget went to humanitarian support for activists, 15 percent funded the national leadership, 15 percent was divided by Solidarność's regional structures, 25 percent was spent on purchasing equipment abroad (categories for printing equipment, spare parts, printing materials, communications equipment, computer equipment, and "other" are listed), 15 percent was earmarked for the Brussels office, 10 percent was given to independent organizations not associated with Solidarność, and 10 percent was given to independent presses and publishing houses not associated with the union.[124] Through FTUI and Solidarność's Brussels office, American money was thus dispersed mainly to union structures for their daily work of organizing, supporting those who could not work, and publishing independent news and reports.

In addition to supporting Solidarność structures, NED also granted more than $100,000 a year to support a second pillar of opposition activity: independent publishing houses. From 1986 onward Lasota and IDEE were placed in charge of these funds. As with her earlier work with the AFL-CIO and

CSS, Lasota's funds purchased printing equipment, spare parts, supplies, and computer equipment needed to sustain the independent presses that had flourished since the declaration of martial law (see chapter 2). Based in Paris with her husband, Jakub Karpiński, Lasota worked primarily with a consortium of publishers formed in 1985 called the Independent Publishers Foundation, which included CDN, NOWa, and Krąg. While printing equipment and replacement parts were still needed in the second half of the 1980s, the consortium's biggest problems involved gathering money, a problem that Lasota alleviated with NED funds sent in $500 to $1,500 increments, primarily by couriers traveling back and forth from Western Europe.[125] Funds provided to IPA were also used to provide printing operations with money and equipment. Finally, Mirosław Dominczyk was employed directly by Adrian Karatnycky at the AFL-CIO in a program named "Project Coleslaw" to provide another avenue of support to independent publishers and regional workers' groups that the AFL-CIO thought were not being properly funded by the Brussels office.[126]

The third pillar of opposition grants focused on programs to support educational, cultural, and scientific activities that were neglected, criminalized, or censored by the state, often referred to as "independent culture." Education, Culture, Science (Oświaty, Kultury, Nauk, or OKN)—represented in the West by the philosopher, Oxford professor, and longtime émigré activist Leszek Kołakowski and by Jan Piotr Lasota (a Polish physicist and the brother of Irena Lasota who took care of most of the day-to-day work from Paris)—received $100,000 per year from NED between 1986 and 1989. OKN was actually an umbrella group for three separate organizations, each with a different focus: the Independent Education Group (Zespoł Oświaty Niezależny), the Independent Culture Committee (Komitet Kultury Niezależny), and the Social Committee for Science (Społeczny Komitet Nauki). Each group published its own weeklies like *Tu Teraz*, as well as hard-to-find or illegal academic books and textbooks, including titles such as Kołakowski's *Communism as a Cultural Formation*, a translation of Max Weber's *Politics as a Profession and a Vocation*, and George Orwell's *1984*.[127]

More central to its mission, OKN provided scholarships to students, academics, and artists to pursue work not funded by the state. Scholarships went to students who were expelled for political reasons or who were preparing research, for example, on martial law or Polish-Jewish relations in World War II—subjects that would not have been open to students pursuing university degrees. Academics—particularly those working in the sociology, history, literature, philosophy, and economics fields, which were highly effected by political indoctrination—also received support. Money also funded youth programs and the well-known "Flying Universities": lectures and intellectual gatherings that took place secretly in private apartments or churches to teach censored subjects. For artists, money was provided to produce plays and theater events, to hold music performances, to run literary contests, and to sponsor art exhibits (more than forty in 1987 involving more than one hundred artists). The committees also supported libraries and archives that collected and lent censored literature, as well as projects for recording oral histories about the preceding few years. The committees prided themselves on ensuring that these cultural, educational, and scientific activities were supported throughout Poland, not just in Warsaw and Gdańsk.[128]

As an offshoot of these cultural and artistic activities, beginning in 1986 NED supplied money to produce and distribute video productions. The Video Association or ZWID (Zespoł Wideo) was also based in Paris and administered by Agnieszka Holland (and later by Seweryn Blumsztajn and Mirosław Chojecki).[129] The program funded new films produced in Poland and sent censored films available only in the West. These videos were viewed in small private groups known as "Flying Home Cinemas." As many as half a million Poles already owned videocassette players, so the main expenses for the program were purchasing clean videocassettes and buying film and video recording and editing equipment to be used by the underground. Both of these commodities could be bought legally in Poland, so NED cash was smuggled to be used within the country. Videos produced in Poland included recordings of independent theater productions, popular lecture series from the Flying Universities, interviews with underground leaders, coverage of special events like the papal pilgrimage, and documentaries on recent events. Films sent into Poland included banned versions of Agnieszka Holland's films, Andrzej Wajda's films *Man of Marble* and *Man of Iron*, and documentary films on martial law and the state of the opposition movement, created by a Polish émigré group in Paris called Video-Kontakt.[130]

As this review of the American funders' priorities shows, the opposition movement had become diverse and extensive by the second half of the 1980s. The democratic opposition was much more than just free trade unionists or the political activists linked with KOR and Solidarność. The opposition included high school teachers, students, clergy, intellectuals, academics, scientists, workers, professors, and artists of all kinds, not to mention those who participated in "independent" life by coming to exhibitions and theatrical performances or by sitting in a friend's living room to watch a documentary on Father Jerzy Popiełuszko. From a practical standpoint, Solidarność remained the most important priority for American politicians and NED, but the endowment did support a wider variety of activities. This included giving money to a broad section of underground publishers who were not necessarily linked with Solidarność and who even criticized the American government.[131]

Moreover, American money supported a huge network of artistic, educational, and cultural activities that did not have an expressly political purpose. In the early 1980s the political opposition led by Bujak, Lis, Frasyniuk, Kuroń, Michnik, and others made the decision to pursue a decentralized vision of opposition. By the second half of the 1980s this vision had grown into a mature, institutionalized movement, which operated within an entire second society living in opposition to the government authorities. As Timothy Garton Ash wrote at the time, "intellectual and cultural life is emancipated from the would-be-totalitarian ideological control of the Party to a degree unthinkable anywhere else in the Soviet bloc," with Poles acting "*as if* [they] live in a free country." Through the creation of the independent structures of the opposition, the dissident minority became a dissident majority.[132]

Reports by NED also illustrate a second important fact about the opposition: it was almost purely Polish. The money came from America, but once NED funds were dispersed through the grantee organizations to their final subgrantee destinations, the money was in Polish hands. All the operations that NED funded were run by Polish émigrés living in the West, who then sent money and material to their homeland. Whether it was Jerzy Milewski in Brussels; Józef Lebenbaum in Lund; Agnieszka Holland, Jerzy Giedroyc, Seweryn Blumsztajn, Mirek Chojecki, or Jan Lasota in Paris; Eugeniusz Smolar in London; or Irena Lasota in New York—all the players who oversaw the actual operations to send support to Poland were Poles.

This separation between the source of money and the way the Poles spent it was perhaps most apparent in the accounting practices of the final grantee organizations. The Coordinating Office, humanitarian aid groups, and publishing houses in Western Europe—groups that worked and functioned completely in the West before smuggling finished products—could provide regular lists of exactly how American money was spent and be held accountable. But for groups like OKN, ZWID, or IDEE that smuggled cash, activists could not provide details on how the money made its way into Poland or give a full account of how it was used once it arrived. As Jan Lasota explained to Myra Lenard, the head of PAC's Washington office: "I cannot supply you with the names of the universities and organizations which are assisted by [OKN]. They are underground institutions, and they are illegal according to communist law. I do not have that kind of information, because just passing such information it would endanger my colleagues. Please note that when [OKN] is helping some 'official organizations' as for example theaters, the information is supersecret since those institutions could face closing up."[133] Operational information was compartmentalized and only given to people who truly needed to know. Keeping exact financial records, receipts, lists of contacts, or written records of any kind could jeopardize the safety of those working for the opposition if the documents were found by the security services. When these kind of records were kept, they were not reproduced in the yearly reports for fear that operational information might be compromised.[134]

In addition, the systems for getting equipment and funds from the West to Poland were determined by the individual activists, each with his or her own preferred style. Dominczyk relied on professional smugglers to get printing or communications equipment to Solidarność groups working in Silesia and other areas in the south of the country. Chojecki, who led the Coordinating Office for the first half of the 1980s, oversaw numerous shipments of larger items like printing presses. Chojecki preferred to dismantle these items, disguise them, and send them with the help of sympathetic truck drivers working for humanitarian aid groups in Western Europe. The individual parts would be picked up by opposition activists and reassembled. In addition to printing supplies, Chojecki successfully sent radios and even an early personal computer to aid in editing samizdat.[135] Different groups also enlisted individual Poles sympathetic to the opposition. As Jan Lasota explained, these travelers could be given small pieces of equipment (radios, communications equipment, or video-recording gear) to take back. As long as the amount of equipment was small enough, they could "plausibly claim they bought [it] themselves."[136]

After 1986, the primary focus for smuggling support to the opposition was money, not equipment. The system utilized appeared to be an inherited, rather than American-inspired skill. First, smuggling dollars hidden in common objects or a few valuable consumer goods was a proud tradition for Polish travelers dating back to the 1950s.[137] Poles traveling to the West had grown accustomed to stopping at Polish bookstores in Paris, London, or Rome and picking up recent illegal literature or samizdat produced in the West to bring back home. Second, most of the reports back to the PACCF on grant activity refer to "trusted couriers" as the preferred method for sending money to the opposition. All the contact people in the West had been active in the Polish opposition before emigrating, so they were already acquainted with some of the persons they would meet to trade news and to exchange money with. If the two participants had not been acquainted personally, a simple password would be exchanged to ensure no mistakes. To safeguard against any possible confiscation becoming too damaging, each courier was asked to return with only a relatively small amount of money, usually about $500.[138]

In the first years after the declaration of martial law, travel to the West was restricted, with the government allowing few people access to their passports. One of the key couriers in this early period was Andrzej Paczkowski, a Polish academic who had lost his good standing with the government because of his involvement with the democratic opposition. Paczkowski, however, was also an avid mountaineer who happened to be the president of the Polish Alpinist Association. His passport was therefore held by the Ministry of Sport, a more lenient authority when it came to requesting travel for official association functions. Paczkowski was allowed to travel frequently to the West, meeting with Irena Lasota and others at prearranged cafés and public places.[139] When a trusted Pole could not be located, the opposition sometimes worked with sympathetic foreigners. This included many of the truck drivers delivering humanitarian aid, sympathetic journalists, or Western academics—anyone who could travel freely.[140] In one instance, an American political scientist, Jane Curry, was given a disassembled computer prior to a planned trip to Warsaw, and told to drop the parts off at a specific church in the city. Curry smuggled the computer equipment in her children's luggage and successfully dropped it off as planned.[141] Once travel restrictions were relaxed after martial law was lifted in 1983, it became much easier to find willing couriers to run money. In 1988, 1.6 million Poles were allowed to travel to the West, a record for the communist period.[142] This change in travel restrictions happily corresponded with increased amounts of American aid becoming available.

To provide a loose mechanism for accountability, the Polish opposition provided receipts of a kind to their Western donors by communicating through the underground press. Independent publications included a small thank-you section, which listed nondescript names and amounts to acknowledge donations. In the case of significant deliveries of money from the West, the underground press used codenames to acknowledge that American funds had made it to their intended destinations. For ZWID, the code in *Tygodnik Mazowsze* was "Zebra dz. Wackowi."[143] For OKN, the code for money from PACCF was "Gebroch," with "bullion" serving as the name for the independent councils. Shipments received from IPA were acknowledged in the weekly *Solidarność Walcząca*. The specific amounts of money and aid received were also in code. As Jan Lasota explained, "Smaller amounts of foreign currency are sometimes acknowledged with the name of the currency. . . . In principle [*Tygodnik Mazowsze*] is trying not to state the name of the currency and amounts of funds which are coming regularly."[144] These small notes in the underground press were then passed to patrons in the West as confirmation that money was reaching its destination.[145]

This system was based on a deep sense of trust between the Polish activists and their American patrons. Officials from NED did visit their grantees in Western Europe to check in and ask questions, but overall NED was at the mercy of the groups operating routes into Poland. As Myra Lenard explained to NED in an annual report: "Although we have experienced a few anxieties from our sub-grantees, attributed to the complexity of the reporting system, we now realize that the 'network' works. For all practical purposes we are reconciled with the fact that more detailed information, especially from Poland, is perhaps unreasonable because of security considerations." Because of the government's continued ability to round up activists at will, "many individuals are reluctant to submit great details of their operation."[146] Over time, NED and its final grantees accepted the limitations of what could be disclosed and what needed to be left unsaid.

Together with the overwhelming Polishness of the Western structures that supported the opposition, this trust-based system provides further evidence of how little operational control Americans actually had over how funds made their way into Poland or how they were spent. Washington completely relied on the opposition itself to report truthfully what was being bought, further evidence of the democratic movement's independence. Independence was an integral part of the relationship between NED and the movements it supported. The endowment understood that it was not in the business of telling democracy activists how to do their job; rather, NED was funded to respond when admirable movements and workable ideas surfaced. As NED's president Carl Gershman explained to Congress, the group sought to be responsive to democracy activists' needs: "The endowment does not seek to fashion solutions to problems in far off countries, or to impose programs developed in the U.S. on foreign democratic groups, but rather to respond to their initiatives and requests for assistance. . . . The endowment's approach is to encourage the indigenous democratic groups to define their needs and set forth their priorities and goals."[147] For NED, control over the process came from selecting programs and choosing whom to trust. Once NED funds were allocated and sent, there were few mechanisms to oversee how it was actually delivered or utilized. Operational decisions were left in the hands of Poles, either in Western Europe or within Poland. But, as the NED grant administrator Yale Richmond simply commented after a visit to Paris in late 1986, NED grants "appear to be in very good hands."[148]

In the wake of the final political amnesty of 1986, NED and American NGOs remained focused on keeping money flowing to the opposition movement, with more than three times the amount of funds available in 1987 than in 1985. While activists did not have to worry about long jail sentences any longer, they were still vulnerable to harassment and punishment through fines and confiscations. Thus, as diplomatic relations between the Polish and American governments warmed, the second line of American policy—American financial support to Solidarność and other opposition groups—grew stronger, verifying where American loyalties and hopes for the future lay: with the democratic opposition.

## The Fruits of Humanitarian Aid

As government-to-government relations normalized and American financial support for the opposition movement increased, American humanitarian assistance programs began to reap rewards from their long-standing policies. By the end of 1986, the Polish economy was not supplying all the consumer goods and commodities needed, but by no means were living conditions as bleak as during the first years of martial law. Even according to opposition figures, by 1984 the consumption of bread, vegetables and vegetable products, fish, and eggs had returned to 1980 levels, although meat consumption remained at 83 percent.[149] Despite government-mandated price increases, real wages increased roughly two percent per year from 1983 to 1986.[150] In addition, Poland had a thriving black market, based in dollars, supplementing the domestic market with much-needed consumer goods.

Humanitarian needs had decreased significantly, but they had not disappeared. In 1986, the KCEP distributed 19,775 tons of humanitarian aid, compared to 180,000 tons in 1982. This decrease was similar among all humanitarian groups.[151] American aid distributed through NGOs like CRS thus continued to flow, but at much lower levels than during the first years after martial law. Also, by 1986 the focus of the aid changed from fulfilling basic food needs to prioritizing medical shipments and donations of clothing. For example, in fiscal year 1986, of the $16,560,463 in aid from PACCF, 73 percent were medical supplies and 19 percent clothing and shoes.[152]

The cumulative amount of humanitarian aid did not go unnoticed by the Polish people. Public voices thanking the United States for the aid included

Polish church officials who worked with Americans. During Glemp's visit to the United States in September 1985, he specifically visited CRS's offices in New York to offer his "warmest thanks for the work done for the benefit of [his] countrymen." When the head of the KCEP, Bishop Czesław Domin, made a follow-up trip to meet with American donors in June 1986, he presented CRS with a Medal of Gratitude and described "prayers and masses offered to God for the donors." Domin also wrote of his "high esteem and prayerful gratitude" for all the work CRS had done with its "great material importance but also enormous spiritual value."[153] The bishop of Kraków thanked the PAC for its shipments of milk, writing, "We thank you! Your kindness and generosity move us deeply, because we are aware that ultimately all men have their own problems, and despite of this the people of the United States willingly hurry to send help where that help is needed."[154] Father Bronisław Dąbrowski from the Primate's Charitable-Social Committee wrote, "We thank you from the bottom of our hearts for the generous gift. . . . We are truly moved by such effective remembrance of our wards. Your help has not only a material significance for us, but also a spiritual [moralny] one. It is proof of the solidarity of people of good will that are always eager to provide help for those who are in need."[155]

Messages also came directly from people who received the aid, giving a full sense of the gifts' significance. As a local priest wrote, even a simple shipment of used clothes was meaningful: "Both young people and the old were very pleased. And those rather fat were satisfied. Clothes are very expensive and all these people can't afford to buy them. Pensions and salaries are very low. Four brides were dressed in these white Californian dresses. They were all very happy! We pray for God's bless for all of you and may the Good Lord keep you all in his loving care at work and in your life."[156]

Moreover, these gifts clearly took on a symbolic as well as a practical meaning. Like the church leaders, recipients wrote about the gifts' spiritual (moralny or duchowo) importance, frequently referring to a sense of no longer being alone in their struggle. As one explained: "I thank you very, very much for this—not only for the contents in your good things, but above all for the awareness that somewhere far away someone thinks about us and wants to help us."[157] As a former political prisoner put it, "Whoever remembers us [reminds us] that we are not alone, gives us strength and stimulates us in our future work."[158] Or as another recipient wrote, after being released from thirteen months in prison and receiving gifts from a stranger, "Even the smallest impulse of support for the desires and ideas for which I lost my freedom reminded me of the correctness of what I do and fills me with hope for the future."[159] American aid was reminding Poles that they were not alone and that their hardships were not forgotten.

More generally, these handwritten thank-you notes represent the sincere closeness Poles felt with the Americans who sent aid packages. In their notes, Poles included stories about their family and their children. They included pictures as well, often of events like christenings. They sent Christmas cards with warm words and "heartfelt" [serdeczny] thanks. Many notes also included their own symbolic gesture: Christmas Eve wafers (opłatki). These wafers are traditionally shared among family members and close friends, with each member breaking off a bit of wafer before offering good wishes for the coming year. While the cards, pictures, and wafers did not make for grand gestures, they were important indicators of the emotional response American aid produced. The gestures made were traditionally shared only with friends and family members, so by sending these notes to unknown people, the recipients demonstrated the close ties American charity evoked. As a young seminarian from Lublin explained in a letter to CRS, humanitarian aid was a "unifier of people in distant lands."[160]

When the U.S. government made the final decision to support humanitarian projects in Poland in May 1982 (see chapter 2), it did so for political reasons: "Our assistance is widely visible in Poland, undermining regime propaganda and providing material evidence of Western support for Solidarity and the Church."[161] Whether it was large shipments of rice, gallons of cooking oil, blocks of surplus yellow American cheese, or sacks of flour sent by the American government or tubes of tooth paste, cans of coffee, candy, a new dress, or soap sent directly by American NGOs, the message received by the Polish people was the same: you are not alone, you are not forgotten, you are not suffering unnoticed. In turn these gifts provided moral support and instilled hope. American aid served as proof that sanctions and U.S. policies were not intended to hurt the Polish people. In addition, humanitarian aid strengthened old bonds and created new ones between the Polish and American peoples when the Polish government sought to sow discord. After more than five years of humanitarian projects, both large and small, these heartfelt letters provided evidence that the American strategy was successful at maintaining and strengthening America's symbolic position in Poland.

## Toward Normalization in Bilateral Relations

In the days following Reagan's February 1987 announcement about dropping all remaining American sanctions, Washington and Warsaw found themselves on new footing, no longer arguing over economic sticks but negotiating about carrots and new agreements. In the first months, both sides followed the working plan agreed to in Vienna. Józef Czyrek visited Washington, New York, Philadelphia, and Chicago from March 2 to 11, meeting with government officials, members of Congress, businesspeople, public leaders, and U.N. officials. Czyrek's most important meetings included a short March 4 meeting with Vice President Bush, and then meetings with Ridgway, Whitehead, Shultz, Secretary of Commerce Malcolm Baldridge, and Secretary of the Treasury James Baker all on March 10—the highest-level meetings for a Polish official since 1981. Czyrek presented a friendly tone but persistently pushed to accelerate improvements in economic relations. His top priority was assurances that lifting sanctions would have practical as well as political significance. Specifically, Crzyrek hoped for new Export-Import Bank credits, access to American technology, new CCC credits, increased opportunities for joint ventures, American support for IMF and World Bank membership, and a positive influence on discussions to reschedule Paris Club debt. To support his calls for improved economic opportunities, Czyrek emphasized internal developments toward "socialist pluralism," particularly the new robust role of government-sanctioned trade unions, the powers of the Consultative Council, and the creation of a new government ombudsman to monitor human rights standards. He noted the presence of large numbers of former Solidarność members within these organizations. In terms of diplomatic relations, Czyrek announced to Shultz that Poland was now prepared to provide agrément for the next ambassador in hopes that Washington would reciprocate.[162]

In the face of Czyrek's enthusiasm, the Americans presented a much more reserved vision for the future. Shultz agreed with the call to return to full diplomatic relations; however, the Americans again emphasized that further improvements in economic relations would be based on tangible improvements in human rights and on steps toward national reconciliation. Washington also stressed that there would be no major influx of new credits or economic aid. Economic decisions would be based on practical improvements in Poland's creditworthiness. Moreover, decisions about any new joint ventures would be made by individual companies, not the U.S. government. From the American side, reengagement was meant to be gradual. The U.S. delegates' task was "to cool off exaggerated Polish expectations and to put in place a realistic framework for the next phase in our relationship." Further, "To head off the [government of Poland from] dwelling on U.S. economic aid, we will need to make clear to Czyrek: 1) we foresee continuing our cautious, step-by-step approach; 2) solutions to Poland's economic problems will be found in Warsaw, not in Washington; 3) Western financial ties with Poland must be based on sound commercial and financial criteria."[163] In American eyes, Poland had not earned a clean slate, and the Department of State made it clear that relations, economic or otherwise, would not return to the pre-December 1981 status quo ante.

Following Czyrek's visit, the two sides negotiated in a number of lower-level forums. In late February a Polish delegation traveled to Washington to discuss restarting an agreement on scientific exchanges through the Marie Curie-Skłodowska Foundation. An American delegation reciprocated with a visit to Warsaw in June.[164] The main concern was not the agreement itself, but the need to find funding to support it. Senator Kennedy solved this problem in July when he included $1 million for scientific exchanges in his American Aid to Poland Act of 1987. Minister of Environmental Protection and Natural Resources Stefan Jarzębski followed this success with a trip to Washington in September to sign a cooperative agreement with the Environmental Protection Agency.[165] At the end of May the Georgetown University Law Center hosted a conference to discuss the role of joint ventures in East-West trade.[166] On June 11–12, the Polish-U.S. Economic Council—a group organized by the U.S. Chamber of Commerce to promote American businesses meeting with Polish officials—held their Seventh Plenary Session in Poznań. Two days later the Commerce Department sponsored exhibition space for American businesses at the Poznań International Trade Convention, the first American exhibition in five years.[167]

In a step not outlined in the Vienna working plan, Washington and Warsaw also moved toward a new agreement on the contentious issue of propaganda. Shortly after the 1986 amnesty, Rakowski had suggested to Jaruzelski to revise information and propaganda policies, "which were no longer capable of convincingly representing the authorities' points of view on important political achievements."[168] In bilateral relations, this reevaluation led to a new understanding on USIA activities and a visit to Warsaw by the assistant director of the European Bureau at USIA to talk about starting new cultural and information exchanges.[169] A little more than two months later, the USIA and the PZPR agreed to begin formal negotiations to strengthen information, educational, and cultural exchanges, opening new funding sources. The MSZ interpreted this as a very positive step because Washington had avoided addressing the issue of USIA exchanges since the Poles proposed them in Vienna.[170]

Over the course of 1987, significant progress was also made regarding ambassadors. On April 7, Davis met with MSZ officers to read an official statement that the United States "happily welcomed" the offer of agrément, but that the process of choosing an American ambassador could take a few months.[171] The United States did not announce their choice for ambassador until September 21, when Swartz met with Biały to name John Davis. The same day, Ludwiczak met with State Department officials to announce that they had chosen Jan Kinast to fill the position in Washington. The following day, Davis accepted Kinast; however, Washington wanted to wait to officially announce the decision during Bush's visit, commencing just four days later.

Vice President Bush's visit, from September 26 to 29, marked a new symbolic peak in relations: Bush became the highest-ranking American visitor since President Jimmy Carter's trip ten years earlier. From the initial announcement that Bush was including Warsaw among his stops in European capitals, American journalists questioned the visit's diplomatic importance: the vice president was accused of scheduling publicity opportunities before he officially announced his candidacy for the presidency at the end of September.[172] To the media, Bush was wearing two hats: one as a statesman sent to address the evolving Polish-American relationship, and one as presidential candidate looking to improve his international portfolio. Bush's decision to hire a camera crew to shoot campaign footage only added to public suspicions.[173] State Department members also worried privately about the trip's domestic political focus. Some "found [the trip] a distasteful prospect . . . because it was politically motivated. . . . The Bush trip germinated as a campaign trip. It was scheduled in order to get to Poland and meet publicly with Lech Wałęsa, and to get a picture with Lech Wałęsa before the deadline as a candidate."[174]

For Bush, the trip did provide images of him as a statesman. He met privately with all three major groups: Jaruzelski, Glemp, and Wałęsa. He participated in the obligatory visitor's activities: placing a wreath at a memorial to the Warsaw Uprising, inspecting a private farm, viewing the Royal Castle in Warsaw, touring a television factory, and visiting the Holocaust Memorial and extermination camp at Auschwitz-Birkenau. In a new element for foreign visitors, the vice president addressed the Polish people directly and uncensored on Polish television, taking advantage of the opportunity by mentioning Wałęsa by name, a rare occurrence on Polish airwaves.

Bush's most important public appearance, however, occurred when he laid a wreath at the grave of Father Popiełuszko on Monday morning, September 28. For his ride to Stanisław Kostka Church, Bush was unexpectedly joined by Wałęsa.[175] When the two exited the limousine, they were greeted by the visit's largest crowds. After laying a wreath and placing a Solidarność

Vice President George Bush and Lech Wałęsa addressing a crowd at the Stanisław Kostka Church during his 1987 visit. Photo courtesy of the George Bush Presidential Library and Museum.

banner, the vice president and Wałęsa were whisked up to a balcony, where they addressed the crowd over a microphone that had been placed there the night before. The leaders spoke over chants of "Solidarity! Lech Wałęsa! Long live Bush! Long live Reagan!" The vice president joined the crowd by raising his fingers in the traditional Solidarność "V" for victory.[176] The next day Bush continued his European tour to Bonn.

While most contemporaneous accounts emphasized the political imagery of Bush's visit over its substance, the trip did have meaningful effects on American policy.[177] First, Bush's appearance in public with Wałęsa and a private reception for opposition figures at the ambassador's residence reiterated that the highest levels of the U.S. government fully backed the Solidarność movement. As Adam Michnik recalls, "Bush clearly signaled support for the democratic opposition. Reagan's declarations were always sharp, but the vice president's trip here, to Warsaw, and his meeting with the people were something else, courageous and meaningful symbolic gestures. It was a turning point, unusually significant for later events."[178] In terms of bilateral relations, the two governments signed the new agreement on scientific-technical cooperation and officially announced that Davis and Kinast would fill the long-open ambassador spots. It was also widely reported that in his talks with Jaruzelski, Bush agreed to use American leverage in the Paris Club to favorably reschedule more debt that had become due from 1985 to 1987. This was slightly different from the previous American policy, which had stated that Washington would no longer block these agreements. Poland signed a new agreement to reschedule $8.5 billion in debt with the Paris Club in December.[179]

Importantly, the vice president also laid out a vision of when and how Polish-American relations could improve. Bush and Jaruzelski held face-to-face talks during two days, with both sides engaging in a frank but cordial exchange. The tone of the meeting was much closer to that of Jaruzelski's talk with Whitehead in 1987 than that of his exchanges with Americans earlier in the 1980s. The two talked openly about arms control, economic reform, the state of human rights, Poland's subordinate position to the Soviet Union, debt to the Paris Club, and Poland's relationship with the IMF, Paris Club, and World Bank—a point Jaruzelski emphasized multiple times, focusing on Poland's need for new technology and new Western credits to increase their exports and salvage their economy. Bush responded positively to all of Jaruzelski's comments, but he maintained the same realistic and cautious approach the State Department had been advocating.

Bush did, however, provide a vision of the way forward. The vice president consistently argued that American policy was driven by the many millions of Polish Americans. Bush wanted to see more "institutionalized pluralism," specifically meaning "reform the electoral system to make it possible to present 'independent opinions,' reform the trade union law, and make it possible to register independent trade unions." These kinds of steps would greatly improve the PZPR's image in the United States and give Congress greater impetus to act. Refining Whitehead's negotiating stance, Bush said, "Free elections and free trade unions, that is your concern, but the more Americans are able to identify themselves with your solutions [rozwiązaniami] the more they will be able to help."[180] During the second day of talks, Bush made a similar point: if the PZPR allowed trade union pluralism, "it would make it easier for the administration to make a commitment."[181] For Bush this was positive thinking. For the Poles, of course, these were huge steps to take, and while they believed relations had entered a new stage, they concluded that Bush showed the "greatest restraint in reference to the possibility of gaining American credits."[182] The importance of Bush's vision should not be overemphasized; nonetheless, Bush committed himself to provide help—presumably in the form of economic incentives and credits—if the PZPR took concrete steps to increase pluralism and democracy.[183]

During the next few months, relations remained on a positive trajectory. Following Bush's visit, Davis presented a new list of areas for improvement in bilateral relations, including coordination against international terrorism and narcotics trafficking, increased youth exchanges, new propaganda and information agreements, pushing agreements with the IMF forward, and increased economic and financial exchanges.[184] Relations were now on such firmer ground that even after the Department of State accused the Polish military attaché in Washington of acquiring American technology improperly and asked for his removal, both sides remained calm. Events did not spiral into another PNG crisis.[185] At the end of 1987, the PZPR politburo also decided to allow Western visitors to meet with opposition officials, ending the possibility of a replay of Whitehead's first trip to Warsaw.[186] When Whitehead made a mostly ceremonial return visit to Warsaw from January 30 to February 3, 1988, a year after his first visit, the MSZ considered bilateral relations "very good and getting better."[187]

Following the Polish decision to pursue a complete political amnesty in the second half of 1986, Polish-American relations entered a new period of cordial coordination. Beginning with Ridgway's meeting with Kinast in Vienna and followed shortly afterward by Simons's and then Whitehead's visits, the U.S. government lifted all remaining sanctions. In the year following Whitehead's first visit, the two sides repaired some of the damage done to bilateral relations in the years after the declaration of martial law: diplomatic representation returned to the level of ambassador; scientific-cultural exchanges started anew; mechanisms for small-scale economic exchanges and relations were revived; the United States agreed to support Poland's propositions for economic assistance and restructuring through the IMF, World Bank, and Paris Club; and the PZPR and USIA decreased tensions in the propaganda wars. In many regards Poland's position was looking up.

But not all problems had been solved. While U.S.-Polish relations had been patched, they had not been repaired to the level before December 1981. As American diplomats made clear, economic relations would not return to the détente-era model, or even to the relationship shared during the original Polish crisis. The United States had signed no new agreements to provide direct agricultural or economic aid, as they had during 1980 and 1981. Nor had the United States signed any agreements to offer new credits to purchase technology, raw materials, and make investments that the Polish economy dearly needed. American companies would only embark on new joint ventures if they decided that these were good investments; the U.S. government had no pending plans to subsidize joint ventures with cheap, government-backed loans. While American support for the PZPR's bids to the IMF and

World Bank held out the possibility of future aid, Poland had to make painful and substantial economic reforms before international money could flow. Moreover, as Bush made clear in his September 1987 visit, the PZPR would have to pursue expansive political liberalization for the United States to open the floodgates of support.

Bilateral relations warmed from 1986 to 1988, but by no means had the United States returned to the era of détente. In line with the Reagan administration's longtime critiques, economic relations were now based on realistic economic calculations about returns on investments. The new agreements penned during 1987 showed the very limited ways in which the American government was willing to get involved in the economies of Eastern Europe. On the other side of the issue, congressional and executive-branch funding priorities proved where American hopes for the future remained: with the opposition. The lack of a significant influx of Western aid meant that the Polish economy continued to struggle under the weight of a disintegrating infrastructure, weak exports, and huge international debt. While Washington engaged more with Warsaw, Americans remained exceedingly loyal to the opposition, increasing expenditures on their behalf. Under the dual pressures of gradual economic collapse and a resilient opposition, Polish workers once again rose up in anger, returning the impetus for political change to the domestic sphere and setting the stage for the final act of Poland's transformation.

## CHAPTER SIX

# Volatility in Poland's Continuing Drama

## Solidarność's Final Victory, February 1988 to September 1989

On July 4, 1989, John and Helen Davis hosted the annual Independence Day celebration at the ambassador's residence. As Davis reported, that year's celebration "generated much more than the usual cocktail conversation." A month earlier, the democratic opposition had won a landslide election victory, taking nearly all the spots open to them in semifree elections that were part of a power-sharing agreement negotiated during the Round Table talks earlier in the year. The hot topics of conversation on July 4 were if Jaruzelski would run for the newly created office of president and whether Solidarność would seek a larger coalition in the new Sejm and Senat to create its own government. As guests nibbled and sipped, Warsaw's new political elite from both the opposition and the PZPR chatted about the future, creating a "surreal tone of the party, with lifelong enemies cordially congratulating each other on all sides." Symbolizing Poland's new political reality, Bronisław Geremek "walked arm-in-arm with Politburo member Józef Czyrek," and the PZPR's minister for youth, Aleksander Kwaśniewski, "sat under the trees with former prisoner Adam Michnik making jokes and deals." As one guest exclaimed, "This was no party; this was history."[1]

In February 1988, very few, if any, political analysts had predicted that in little more than a year, Solidarność activists would hold seats in the Polish parliament and be chatting cordially with their former jailors. In the spring and summer of 1988, however, Polish workers took events into their own hands, staging strikes that were reminiscent of August 1980 and that brought Poland to the edge of a precipice once again. Faced with immense popular discontent, the PZPR chose to engage directly with Solidarność, first secretly and then publicly in the Round Table negotiations. With domestic Polish events driving change, American diplomats dutifully reported back to Washington and reveled at the positive changes. After President George H. W. Bush was inaugurated in January, he spent the first months of 1989 reviewing existing foreign policy and then responded cautiously and prudently to events in Eastern Europe. As spring turned into summer, domestic Polish events moved rapidly, causing the American embassy to question if change was progressing too quickly. When Bush came to Warsaw in July 1989, he promoted stability and slowed the pace of change to maintain as much of the negotiated agreement as possible—a policy also followed by Davis and his deputies in Warsaw. In August, however, Solidarność took another political gamble—further accelerating the pace of transformation—and created a Solidarność-led coalition government, the first elected non-Communist government in Eastern Europe since the end of World War II. The American government could only sit back and marvel at Solidarność's political cunning.

## Tensions and Strikes

Despite advances in Poland's international position made from 1985 to 1987, none of these improvements led to a significant influx of economic aid. The country's economic future remained bleak. As a group of World Bank economists reported to the PZPR in the summer of 1987, Poland's two main economic problems continued to be debt and the country's negative balance of payments. To improve the situation, the bank highly recommended that the PZPR make the economy more pro-export and that it work to normalize prices.[2] Poland was still in the same catch-22 of needing new Western credits to build a pro-export economy to be able to repay its debts, but the country's ability to gain these new credits was greatly hampered by its inability to pay its debts in a complete and timely manner. Meeting with East German leader Erich Honecker in late 1987, Jaruzelski lamented that, while Western sanctions had been lifted, the change meant only about $20 million more per year. In Jaruzelski's words, "This doesn't deserve comment. That's nothing." Regarding the possibility for new credits, he complained, "in practice the [Western] blockade is continuing."[3]

Jaruzelski and the PZPR leadership were also increasingly concerned about domestic instability, fearing that continued economic stagnation could flare into a national crisis on the scale of 1980 or worse. Noting that the mood of dissatisfaction was strongest among workers, a PZPR report from August 1987 warned that "general anxiety is rising due to the prolonged economic crisis. An opinion is spreading that the economy instead of improving is getting worse. As a result there arises an ever greater dissonance between the so-called official optimism of the authorities ('after all it's better') and the feeling of society. . . . Social dissatisfaction is growing because of the cost of living." The same report noted that improvements in foreign policy and U.S.-Polish relations had little, or even a negative, impact on public perceptions: "For the 'average' citizen, foreign policy is something remote, without an effect on the domestic situation of the country and the standard of living of the society, and, what is worse—an impression [has been fostered] that the authorities are concentrating their efforts on building an 'external' image, neglecting the basic questions of citizens' daily lives."[4]

Outside observers were aware of these tensions as well. After hearing about "the younger generation sliding into apathy" and "a historically aging and increasingly irrelevant elite," Zbigniew Brzeziński concluded that society was "highly polarized." He continued, "There is a growing sense of frustration, which one can feel in talking to the drivers and the common people. Everybody mentions the possibility of explosion, both from the workers and the much younger people."[5] In February 1988, Brzeziński wrote to Jerzy Giedroyc that "if it was not for the economic deterioration, one could be quite hopeful about the situation. However, I fear that the combination of political and economic deterioration could create a revolutionary situation."[6] Societal anxieties about the economy, price increases, and the lack of progress in domestic PZPR policies were reaching a crescendo.

In line with the PZPR's efforts to restructure the economy through the "second stage" of reform and to better balance the economy's expenditures with its income, the government announced price increases on February 1, 1988. The price of foodstuffs, cigarettes, and alcohol increased about 40 percent, the price of gasoline rose almost 60 percent, and the price of some consumer goods augmented more than 200 percent. These price increases were coupled with rising wages, but Polish workers did not remain complacent. On April 22, five thousand workers at the Stałowa Wola steel mill southeast of Warsaw held a protest rally calling for further pay increases and greater freedom for unions. Three days later, municipal workers in Bydgoszcz held wildcat strikes, crippling the city's public transportation system. The strike ended quickly when local Communist Party leaders agreed to significant wage raises. After hearing about Bydgoszcz, four thousand workers at the Lenin Steelworks in Nowa Huta (outside Kraków) went on strike as well. The steelworkers called for wage increases but also added a political dimension, demanding that workers who had been fired for connections to Solidarność be reinstated. Three days later, workers in Stałowa Wola followed through on threats and began their strike, pushing the limits of tolerance by demanding Solidarność's reinstatement. Workers in Stalowa Wola ended their strike after receiving a significant pay raise. But on Monday, May 2, workers in the Lenin Shipyards in Gdańsk declared a strike in solidarity with the Lenin Steelworks.[7]

In response to these disturbances, the PZPR utilized tactics from its well-tested playbook. At 2 A.M. on May 5, riot police stormed the gates of the Lenin Steelworks, beating, arresting, and carrying away protestors.[8] The next night, ZOMO troops amassed outside the Lenin Shipyards, shining bright lights and beating their truncheons against police trucks as they marched toward the shipyard entrance, a show of force meant to intimidate.[9] With Wałęsa inside, government troops never stormed the gates; instead, the PZPR sent Minister of Internal Affairs Kiszczak and Władysław Sila-Nowicki, an opposition lawyer and member of the Consultative Council, to negotiate. Outside the walls of striking industries, the MSW and police harassed Solidarność leaders in a well-organized display of power: about twenty-five leaders including Bujak and Kuroń were detained. The Solidarność spokesman Janusz Onyszkiewicz was even briefly jailed for providing information to foreign journalists. The Gdańsk strikes concluded on May 10 with workers peacefully exiting the shipyards, leaving their goals unmet despite Wałęsa's efforts to motivate them.[10] With the strikes over, the PZPR appeared to have triumphed. For the party leadership, "It looked as though they were no longer in imminent danger, the strike wave would not be repeated any time soon, and the prestige of Wałęsa and Solidarity had suffered a serious blow."[11]

The United States also responded to events in established patterns. After Polish forces stormed the Lenin Steelworks, Whitehead announced publicly, "We have to condemn the violence, imprisonments, the beatings that are reported to be taking place." While sanctions were not under discussion, he explained that prior to the strikes Washington had considered taking positive steps to help Poland's debt problem through the IMF, World Bank, and Paris Club, as well as discussing allowing commercial bank loans and even direct government aid. As Whitehead emphasized, "All of those things are now in jeopardy."[12] Outside of government, in mid-June Jerzy Milewski turned to Lane Kirkland and FTUI, requesting to "speed up" the first $250,000 quarterly payment to the Coordinating Office in Brussels and to "arrange for the prompt transfer" of a second quarterly installment "to cover urgent obligations . . . regarding victims of economic repression directed at striking workers and other persons."[13] In addition, American diplomats in Warsaw found themselves under obvious and often intrusive surveillance in the spring and summer of 1988, with plainclothes and uniformed police keeping a close watch, both reminiscent of life under martial law.[14]

Although the PZPR's public posturing looked similar to previous tactics, in private the politburo had revised its approach. Meeting on April 29 under the shadow of spreading strikes, the PZPR Central Committee Secretariat discussed the possibility of beginning conversations with members of Wałęsa's inner circle, predicated on an end to strikes. This initiative built on a recent call by Bronisław Geremek to foster government-opposition talks by creating an "anti-crisis pact" to work through economic problems.[15] On May 3, the Central Committee members Józef Czyrek and Stanisław Ciosek met with the Solidarność adviser Andrzej Wielowieyski to relay these discussions to the opposition, which signaled its affirmative response by sending negotiators to both Gdańsk and Nowa Huta to diffuse tensions.[16] Following the conclusion of strikes, however, the politburo remained deadlocked about legalizing Solidarność and allowing trade union pluralism, the union's main precondition for negotiations. In particular, the head of the OPZZ, Alfred Miodowicz, staunchly argued against recognizing Solidarność because it would undermine the government-sponsored union.[17]

After the strikes were broken, progress toward negotiations continued quietly. Ciosek spoke with the director of the Catholic Church's press bureau, Father Alojszy Orszulik, mentioning that the politburo was considering creating a second house of parliament (the Senat) and allowing opposition figures to run for seats in the Sejm. As Orszulik recorded, "Ciosek stated that political pluralism in Poland is necessary."[18] Then, in a June 14 article in the Communist Party daily, *Trybunu Ludu*, the PZPR spokesman Jerzy Urban raised the possibility of a "round table" for negotiations involving a broad range of existing representatives, clearly alluding to Solidarność's participation.[19] Thus, following the first wave of strikes in 1988, the PZPR was considering negotiations with the opposition to increase political pluralism. The politburo, however, remained divided over allowing fully independent trade unions and legalizing Solidarność.

During this critical period, Gorbachev made a scheduled visit to Warsaw from July 11 to 16 for a meeting of the Warsaw Pact Political Coordinating Committee. Gorbachev met with the PZPR politburo twice and in private with Jaruzelski twice. Attention focused on discussions about "blank spots" (*biały plamy*) in Polish history (the Katyn Massacre, the Molotov-Ribbentrop Pact, Poles deported to Siberia, etc.), which the two countries had been discussing during the past year. Yet the private meetings also gave the two leaders time to discuss ongoing internal changes in both countries, including Gorbachev's recent call to create a more representative, elected parliament, the Soviet Congress of People's Deputies. In terms of Poland, the PZPR summary of this meeting reported the "USSR fully supports the program of reform."[20] Another summary noted that the USSR viewed Poland "as an innovative territory for democratic and social reform, with experiences which the USSR leadership would surely make use of in the process of perestroika," a clear sign of approval consistent with Gorbachev's position since at least 1986.[21] More important, Gorbachev's support "greatly weakened, even dissolved" arguments by hard-line politburo members who wanted to curb change.[22]

Foreign Minister Tadeusz Olechowski's late July visit to Washington provided the United States with a similar chance to explain its position on internal developments. The MSZ knew these meetings were an important chance to explain PZPR actions during the spring strikes; describe "the deepening democratization of political life, national reconciliation, as well as implanting economic reforms"; and seek concrete economic and financial-credit cooperation.[23] From July 25 to 29, he met with members of Congress, American media, IMF representatives, American journalists, and members of the Reagan administration including Shultz, Whitehead, Wick, and Bush. The message from the White House was clear: the United States was once again taking a "wait-and-see" approach but viewed internal developments as essential concerns for determining improvements in relations. Specifically, Shultz and Whitehead mentioned the need for trade union pluralism and "finding a place for Solidarność and Wałęsa." To make these hard choices easier, the Americans dangled the possibility of strong support in the IMF and for restructuring loans. The Americans even hinted at the possibility of allowing OPIC credits, involving American capital directly, and expanding cooperation between small industries. Olechowski's report was optimistic about future improvements, pointing to a visit by Whitehead in October as the next chance to explore American economic support.[24]

As political discussions swirled around Warsaw, the country was hit with a second wave of strikes. On August 15, the evening shift at the July Manifesto coal mine near Jastrzębie in southern Poland went on strike, calling for pay increases and reinstating Solidarność. The following day, workers at the Morcinek mine (also near Jarstrzębie) declared an occupation strike, as did workers at Poland's second-largest port, in Szczecin. Within a week's time, the number of occupied mines grew to ten, workers were occupying the Lenin Shipyards, portions of the Lenin Steelworks were under worker control, and numerous other small industries throughout the country were striking. This second wave of strikes was particularly dangerous for the Communist Party. First, coal was Poland's main export and a significant source of foreign currency. Second, many of the striking workers were in their teens and twenties with only vague memories of the 1980 strikes, proving that a new generation of workers had been radicalized.[25]

Under increased pressure, the politburo met again to discuss initiating talks with Wałęsa. As one study of PZPR policy in 1988 summarizes, "In the situation when the summer strikes were obviously stronger than the strikes in the spring, and Jaruzelski—despite being in charge of preparations—had not decided to introduce an exceptional state [stan wyjątkowy], initiating a dialogue with moderate opposition appeared to be the optimal solution. 'It is a bold path, but it is the path forward,' he declared to the gathered members of the Politburo, adding simultaneously that 'tomorrow the situation will be worse.'"[26] Disagreements about the best way forward (particularly on the issue of legalizing Solidarność) continued in the politburo; nonetheless, contacts with the opposition—most notably between Czyrek and Stelmachowski, the chairman of the Catholic Intelligentsia Club in Warsaw—intensified. Then on August 26, Kiszczak announced on television that he would be willing to talk with "representatives from diverse social and workers' groups" about the possibility of forming a "round table," thrusting the concept of negotiations into the public eye.[27] The politburo met again on August 28 to discuss opening direct, public negotiations with the opposition. This time the members put off a definitive decision on trade union pluralism by treating the issue of legalizing Solidarność as a bargaining chip in negotiations with Wałęsa and his inner circle.[28]

On August 31, 1988, the eighth anniversary of the Gdańsk Accords, Kiszczak met with Wałęsa, with Ciosek and Bishop Jerzy Dąbrowski as observers. Kiszczak invited Wałęsa to further talks, but stated that all strikes would have to end as a precondition for beginning preparations for a possible round-table agreement. Kiszczak mentioned the possibility of elections to the Sejm, the creation of a Senat, as well as a place for a constructive opposition in the political system. He glossed over the issue of independent unions. Wałęsa responded that trade union pluralism was central to discussions of political pluralism.[29] Wałęsa also took the "tremendous risk" of agreeing to end strikes without a full agreement to begin negotiations directly afterward. He then set out about the country urging strikers to return to work.[30] By September 4, all major strikes had ended, clearing the way for negotiations between the opposition and the government.

Throughout these crucial developments in the summer of 1988, the U.S. embassy took a patient approach. As Davis recalls, "We didn't get regularly briefed about [contacts between the opposition and the PZPR]. You could see the results, which we applauded. And the fact of the meeting [between Kiszczak and Wałęsa] was just fascinating, to put it mildly. It was clear that things were going in the right direction." More important, in line with Davis's long-standing position to stay outside of internal decisions, the embassy did not try to advise the opposition on tactics or negotiating strategies. Davis "didn't try to tell Wałęsa how to play it. . . . These guys, all the leaders of Solidarity by this time were pretty experienced at negotiating and dealing with the government. They were getting experienced in a hurry. They knew what they wanted. And in broad outlines what they wanted looked good to us. We figured that they had to make the calls."[31] In Washington, policy mimicked Davis's line: "Solidarity really owned themselves. No, we weren't giving guidance to Solidarity. Our main thing was to tell the regime to talk to them."[32] Internal dynamics, based on Polish developments and Polish thinking, drove the process for direct negotiations.

That is not to say that international concerns did not have an effect. Most important, Gorbachev's views aided reformers' arguments in the PZPR politburo. Secondarily, imposing martial law would most certainly have caused a rupture with the West. As Whitehead explained in a letter to Olechowski pressuring the PZPR to pursue enhanced national reconciliation, "the use of force would alienate many Polish citizens, and in all likelihood, the Western governments, institutions, and private sector representatives whose support is critical to economic recovery."[33] More subtly, the PZPR directly linked calculations about access to Western economic aid with the decision to begin talks with Wałęsa. As the leadership explained to Central Committee and secretariat members, "Talks and preparatory activities for the 'round table' allow us to gain political initiative and deprive our political adversary and the West of the argument that we don't want to talk, that the dialogue is being simulated and understanding is a facade." In terms of including Wałęsa in these talks, the PZPR leadership argued, "Wałęsa is being used in the West's political game toward Poland; he has gained a certain international prestige (a Nobel Prize, honoris causa doctorates, talks with politicians arriving to Poland). Thus undertaking talks with him is depriving the West an essential argument in its propaganda war."[34] Domestic considerations and fears about strikes and instability forced Jaruzelski and his comrades to the negotiating table. Pressure from the West, including American hints at future economic gains, added weight to arguments in favor of negotiations with Wałęsa and his circle. Again, Western pressure did not cause these changes, but Western policies and offers did make them more palatable.

## Magdalenka and Beyond

In the weeks after Wałęsa's initial meeting with Kiszczak, the opposition and the government continued talking, leading directly to closed-session meetings at a villa owned by the MSW in the town of Magdalenka, just outside Warsaw. The government team was lead by Kiszczak and Ciosek, and it included representatives from the OPZZ. Wałęsa and Stelmachowski led the opposition team, which also included Frasyniuk and Mazowiecki. The two sides agreed to discuss what the round-table negotiations could look like and the purview of its powers. Unfortunately, the talks quickly stumbled. In his opening remarks Kiszczak alluded to the PZPR's main reason for negotiations: economic reform. The round table "could take a stance and eventually correct the economic model, which should ensure that reforms are effectively realized, achieve economic equilibrium, and dissolve the debt issue. The economic reform program's success, through assuring equal chances and workloads to all forms of ownership, depends upon the degree of its comprehension and *social acceptance*."[35] The government wanted opposition support to take the painful and necessary steps needed to get the economy working again. Wałęsa agreed that it was "necessary to save the country from collapse" and that Solidarność would certainly help with this. However, he made his political demands clear: "For us the key question is a clear position on the question of union pluralism and the legalization of Solidarność. That was strike postulate number one."[36] Solidarność wanted political pluralism and the legalization of Solidarność; the government wanted a coordinated economic program.

Again and again during the following few hours, government negotiators raised the need to repair the economy. In response the opposition always agreed that solving economic problems was essential to moving the country forward, but they remained resolute that political reforms needed to precede these economic solutions. Without legalizing Solidarność, there would be no Round Table. After one meeting, the two sides found themselves at an impasse. Both gave positive public statements (even giving an October date for beginning the Round Table negotiations) and agreed to keep lines of communication open, but Solidarność remained steadfast about legalizing the union before the Round Table could commence.[37]

In the midst of these historic meetings, Onyszkiewicz was unexpect-edly given a passport to visit his wife's relatives in Great Britain, affording the Solidarność spokesman a chance to travel to the United States. The American leg of his trip was frantically planned in secret with Davis, and on Wednesday, September 7, Onyszkiewicz met with Reagan to brief him on recent developments. Reagan was on his way out of office, so Onyszkiewicz focused on the short-term issue of maintaining pressure on Jaruzelski to deal with Solidarność. Onyszkiewicz also met with Bush and the Democratic presidential nominee Michael Dukakis, where he added discussions about Poland's need for large-scale economic support—throwing out the round and improvised number $10 billion—if the government accepted the legal-ization of Solidarność.[38] When he spoke at congressional hearings at the end of his visit, he again emphasized the importance of legalizing Solidarność as a starting point for negotiations. He also spoke authoritatively about the need to create new associations and institutions to strengthen political plu-ralism. But Solidarność was not considering becoming a political party. In terms of Western support during the period of reforms, he said simply, "Ob-viously it would be of great importance to have an additional cushion for this period of hardships in the form of some aid, economic aid." Onyszkiewicz also argued that Jaruzelski remained undecided and cautious: "Let's hope at this critical moment that General Jaruzelski will realize that he cannot sit any longer on the fence. He must jump. Let's hope he will jump on the right side."[39] For Solidarność, it was not clear which way Jaruzelski would go, toward reform or toward repression. Yet the image presented was of a leader open to influence.

A few weeks after Onyszkiewicz's testimony, Whitehead made his third trip to Warsaw, from October 12 to 14.[40] In part, Whitehead was reviewing progress in bilateral relations and meeting with both government and op-position figures. More centrally, he traveled to Warsaw to talk about new initiatives. In his meeting with Olechowski, Whitehead explained that it was time for a new approach to bilateral relations, saying, "step-by-step passed the test and it is necessary currently to elevate relations to a new level."[41] In his conversation with Jaruzelski, Whitehead gave the impression that the United States "wants to help. They abstained from a reaction to the strikes, and even supported the authorities. . . . [He wants] to speed up the pace of growth in Polish-U.S. relations. The U.S. is ready to moderately economically support progress in reforms, not only in the long term but in the short term as well."[42] Of course, these offers had strings attached. Whitehead explained, "At this time he does not see it possible for Poland to gain financial help from abroad, because in his opinion Poland could not take advantage of it. He recognized that events like last May have a place leading to that understanding. The United States does not want to intervene. Conversely, we want to help. They will [help], if they are convinced about improvements."[43] The Americans were not talking about punishing the Poles if they stepped out of line. Nor were they talking about small steps. Rather, Whitehead spoke about concrete rewards, both now and later, if the PZPR negotiated directly with the opposition.

The American representative even spelled out what American help could look like. The list of possible moves (from easiest to most difficult) included appropriating $700,000 for scientific-technical cooperation in fiscal year 1989; providing CCC credits for agricultural purchases (dependent on a rescheduling agreement with the Paris Club); creating a charitable foundation to spend American funds in zlotys (which had been earned through agricultural sales since the 1950s); extending OPIC guarantees for investments (with congressional approval); extending Export-Import Bank credits (with congressional approval); moving Poland up the eligibility list for CCC credits; making available tax relief given to developing countries to help increase exports to the United States; providing direct American financial and economic aid; supporting Poland's programs in the IMF, World Bank, and Paris Club with America's "specific influence"; and further developing bilateral trade with the possibility of joint ventures.[44] In an uncharacteristic move, Whitehead showed Jaruzelski what he could expect if he followed the path of reform to its conclusion.

In addition to American pressure, Great Britain also prodded Jaruzelski. From November 2 to 4, Margaret Thatcher met government and opposition officials in both Warsaw and Gdańsk. Thatcher did not come bearing specific economic packages, but she did advocate continuing negotiations with Solidarność and enhanced political pluralism. Thatcher explained to Jaruzelski that the best system of government is the one that lets people choose for themselves and that the PZPR had to include Solidarność in any agreement because "they were the only opposition." More pointedly, Thatcher specifically referred to the need to legalize Solidarność. As the final MSZ report summarized, discussions with Thatcher were "difficult on account of her well-known anti-communism," but she left "with the conviction that the Polish authorities are decidedly continuing the process of democratization in the country and introducing deep economic reforms."[45]

During the last three months of 1988, the pace of negotiations between Solidarność and the PZPR lagged. The Magdalenka talks were disbanded.

Early statements that Round Table discussions would start in October were quickly placed on hold when Solidarność stubbornly demanded that the union be legalized and the PZPR refused to take the step. (By that point a huge round table had actually been custom made and assembled.) In other disheartening news, on October 29 Rakowski decided to begin liquidating the Lenin Shipyards, the birthplace and stronghold of Solidarność, under the pretense that they were unprofitable and outdated. The government spokesman Jerzy Urban announced Rakowski's call for negotiations just before making the decision public, a move Wałęsa considered a "contemptible act of political manipulation," further hindering talks.[46]

Against this backdrop, British and American actions come into focus as unsubtle attempts to prod the PZPR to accept Solidarność as a negotiating partner. For the Americans the offer's form was particularly noteworthy. Washington was proposing to move beyond the step-by-step framework, meaning that improvements in bilateral relations could accelerate and grow. Washington had long resisted offering substantial economic aid, and had only included vague language for improved economic relations. Whitehead's October offer was quantitatively and qualitatively different. To support Solidarność's push for legalization and Round Table negotiations, the United States was dangling a large, well-formed carrot, hoping that Jaruzelski would fully embrace political pluralism. Extrapolating from Onyszkiewicz's analogy, the White House was trying to coax Jaruzelski off the fence onto the right side.

The end of 1988 did include one high note. On November 30, Wałęsa debated the head of the OPZZ, Alfred Miodowicz, on Polish television. The event was designed to highlight arguments about trade union pluralism, but Wałęsa used the opportunity to defend Solidarność's entire platform. In the end, the PZPR had mistakenly given Wałęsa a chance to make his case for reform, both political and economic, in front of the entire nation. Miodowicz was trounced, with Wałęsa and Solidarność emerging as the clear winners. As Davis recalls, some Solidarność leaders were worried about Wałęsa holding his own against Miodowicz, but Davis felt "in no uncertain terms that all Wałęsa had to do was show up at the studio. This was an opportunity for national exposure again, which everyone had been waiting for, and it wouldn't matter two hoots what he said. He would be instantly the winner, because he represented the views of a great majority of the population."[47] The debate also had wider political significance. With his performance on television, Wałęsa "shattered to dust years of propaganda attempting to present him as dependent [on advisers], primitive, heading toward anarchy. That day, Solidarność returned to public life, pulling with it the attention and hopes of millions of Poles." Shortly thereafter, government polls showed that 73 percent of the population favored legalizing Solidarność.[48]

## To the Round Table

On December 20–21, 1988, and January 16–17, 1989, the PZPR held its Tenth Party Plenum. The first half of the plenum was devoted to party leadership changes. Ciosek and Kazimierz Cypryniak, as well as Marian Stępien, were moved from the secretariat to the politburo. Leszek Miller and Zygmunt Czarzasty became secretariat members. Jaruzelski also promoted some of his informal advisers, including Janusz Reykowski (who was a party first secretary from Wrocław). All of these actions removed conservatives from the politburo and replaced them with reformers for the planned talks. These moves "confirmed that Jaruzelski had then already taken the decision about legalizing Solidarność, and intently needed able negotiators who would be able to sell concessions at the Round Table for the highest possible price."[49]

The PZPR began discussions about legalization during the December meeting of the Tenth Plenum, but quickly postponed a decision until the second session. When the plenum reconvened, the PZPR leadership remained divided. Jaruzelski successfully passed resolutions calling for Solidarność to be legalized, but members of the *nomenklatura* and the OPZZ argued heatedly to block it.[50] A number of voices in the leadership remained adamant that these resolutions were forced on them and vocalized their disagreement.

To quell the conservative backlash, Jaruzelski asked for a vote of confidence in a Central Committee meeting called during the plenum. As he declared, "There were clear signals that the *aktiv* does not trust the leadership and that we are creating a dangerous crisis situation. Thus there is no other solution. Either the [Central Committee] members will put full trust in the present leadership, or this leadership will resign, and if such vote of confidence is given, then we have the right to demand the implementation of the adopted resolutions."[51] If the plenum voted against, Jaruzelski, Rakowski, Kiszczak, and Minister of Defense Florian Siwicki would all step down. When the vote was put to the full plenum, 32 of 178 Central Committee members voted against and 14 abstained. Jaruzelski and his fellow reformers remained in power and won the debate to legalize Solidarność, clearing the final hurdle for the Round Table negotiations.

In the domestic context, this vote was a sign of the deep fractures within the PZPR, suggesting that Jaruzelski did not have "complete control over the situation."[52] American observers viewed Jaruzelski's move in a much different light. Brent Scowcroft, Bush's designated national security adviser, referred to the vote of confidence as "an extraordinary turn of events," leading him to believe that "Poland was most likely to take the lead toward liberalization."[53] Davis remained less grand: "It was a very encouraging bit of news, that they had laid it on the line in favor of negotiating."[54] Jaruzelski did not have complete American trust yet, but Washington took note of fresh signs of his reformist leanings.[55] More important, as the Department of State informed the White House, "The Polish regime has finally acknowledged that Solidarity is a necessary factor for Poland's recovery and has tacitly committed itself to achieving some working understanding with the democratic opposition."[56]

With new consensus, the two sides prepared for the Round Table. On January 27, the Communist Party and the opposition sat down once again at Magdalenka to discuss the broad framework, specifically the issues of legalizing Solidarność before elections, the scope of elections, and the division of seats at the Round Table. Solidarność also agreed not to provoke strikes during negotiations.[57] The Round Table negotiations finally began on February 6, in the great hall of Namiestnikowski Palace (now the Presidential Palace) in Warsaw. Plenary sessions included fifty-six delegates: twenty from the opposition (including six explicitly representing the Solidarność trade union), six from the OPZZ, fourteen from the government coalition, fourteen "independent persons of high standing," and two representatives from the Catholic Church. To facilitate negotiations, three main working groups were formed: economic and social policy, political reforms, and trade union pluralism. There were also numerous smaller working groups: agriculture, mining, legal and court reforms, associations, territorial administration, youth, mass communications, science, education and technical training, health, and ecology. In total, 452 representatives took part in the negotiations, which lasted until April 5.

During these eight weeks, apprehension remained high. On ten different occasions, when agreement could not be reached at the Round Table, small groups of opposition and government representatives (often including Wałęsa and Kiszczak) met in Magdalenka to break the logjams, earning it a reputation as a backroom for secret deals. Even on the last day of the Round Table, when all details had been ironed out, Miodowicz managed to bring some high drama to the closing ceremonies. At the last minute he raised an objection to the speaking order for representatives at the closing ceremonies, causing a three-hour break in the live telecast. A compromise was worked out, and the live broadcast resumed. At 10:10 P.M. on April 5, five hours after the ceremony had begun, Kiszczak and Wałęsa signed a statement committing each side to the Round Table Agreements.[58]

The most important sections of the agreement stipulated the steps for political transformation. First, a new one-hundred-seat Senat was created as an upper house of parliament and was given veto power over all Sejm legislation. This veto, however, could be overturned by a two-thirds Sejm vote. All seats in the new Senat were open to opposition candidates in free elections. In another compromise, semifree elections would be held to the new Sejm, with 65 percent of seats reserved for PZPR and Communist coalition candidates.[59] Only 35 percent of seats (161 in total) would be open to opposition candidates. Part of the 65 percent reserved for the PZPR was to consist of a "National List" of candidates, mainly well-known party leaders, who would run unopposed and only needed 50 percent of the vote to take office. In return for creating a new upper house of parliament, the opposition agreed to create a new, powerful office of the president (modeled on the French presidency) that would maintain control over the armed forces and national security. As part of the compromise, Jaruzelski was agreed to as the only "serious candidate" for the new office and "was to be guarantor that further changes in the political system would be of an evolutionary nature."[60] Elections were set for June 4, with a second round for all unresolved elections (in which no candidate received more than 50 percent of the vote) set for June 18. The opposition was also permitted to start its own newspapers and received access to state television to broadcast its own programs.[61]

The opposition and the government now had a specific power-sharing agreement mapping out the future. As Davis reported, "On the political side, the Round Table Agreement meets nearly all of Solidarity's most recent demands."[62] The importance of this development was not missed in Washington, where it "was clear that the Round Table Agreement, if fully implemented, was the beginning of the end of Communist rule in Poland."[63] From here on, the question was not whether Poland would change, but how much and how quickly.

### Washington Responds

During the first four months of 1989, Davis's staff—including DCM Daryl Johnson, political officer Terry Snell and his deputy John Boris, and economics officer Paul Wackerbarth and his deputy Jack Spilsbury—provided articulate reporting and insightful analysis to keep Washington exceedingly well informed.[64] Prior to February 6, the embassy reported on the PZPR plenum, changing PZPR attitudes and approaches, Solidarność's preparations, and backroom deals to ensure the initiation of the Round Table. Once the negotiations began, the embassy briefed Washington daily on progress in each of the subgroups, and occasionally sent cables highlighting important developments. Beyond the Round Table, the embassy reported on strikes and protests that flared up as groups of workers and students expressed their displeasure at being left out of the Round Table process. Davis and his staff also regularly updated Foggy Bottom about behind-the-scenes efforts at Magdalenka. These cables reflected the strong connections Davis had cultivated with the opposition during his years hosting salons, as well as his regular contacts with PZPR officials. The accuracy of the reports remains striking.

The embassy, however, received little guidance in response. This quiet period in the State Department was, in part, caused by the change of power in Washington. Vice President Bush had won the presidential election, and on January 20, 1989, he was sworn in as the forty-first president of the United States. As with any transition, a certain pause could be expected. It was amplified in this case, however, by a purposeful and decisive break made by the new administration. Although Bush had served closely under Reagan for the previous eight years, the transition from Reagan to Bush was not fluid. As the director for European affairs in the NSC, Robert Hutchings, recalls, Bush cleared out all the Reagan officials from the NSC: "An entirely new team came in. . . . There was no such thing as a 'Reagan-Bush' foreign policy. Before 1989 there was Reagan; afterwards there was Bush."[65] The turnover in the State Department was not as severe (Simons and Ridgway remained in office during the transition); yet the key point man on Eastern Europe, Whitehead, stepped down the day Bush was inaugurated, replaced by Lawrence Eagleburger. Compared to earlier changes in American policy, Hutchings retrospectively concluded that "the foreign policy shift under the Bush administration in 1989 was as stark in substance (though not in style or rhetoric) as the change from Carter to Reagan."[66]

Bush also decided to put his mark on foreign policy by overseeing an extensive policy review. In part, this decision reflected deep uncertainty about Gorbachev's sincerity as a reformer, driven by the first secretary's bold public relations push, including a December 7, 1988, speech to the United Nations announcing the end of the Cold War and a unilateral reduction in the size of the Soviet armed forces.[67] National Security Adviser Scowcroft "was skeptical of Gorbachev's motives and skeptical of his prospects. . . . He was attempting to kill us with kindness, rather than bluster."[68] Bush's first impression of Gorbachev was that he would "package the Soviet line for Western consumption much more effectively than any . . . of his predecessors."[69] Bush, Scowcroft, and the new secretary of state, James Baker, all worried that Gorbachev's words were only a tactic to gain the upper hand in the public relations war to define the superpower confrontation. They were all skeptical that Gorbachev's statements would translate into concrete policy changes.[70] This included skepticism about Gorbachev's "new thinking" toward Eastern Europe. As with other policies from the 1980s, this perception was partially based on ideas about the failures of the past. As Scowcroft has summarized, "We had in an earlier period mistaken a twist in the road for a basic change in direction and I was determined that we should err on the side of prudence."[71]

With equal parts skepticism and caution the Bush administration undertook a series of National Security Reviews (NSR), with the three most important focused on relations with the Soviet Union, relations with Eastern Europe, and relations with Western Europe. These reviews were initiated to give the new leadership team a chance to influence thinking within the bureaucracy. As Bush explained, "I wanted the key foreign policy players to know that I was going to involve myself in many of the details of defense, international trade, and foreign policies."[72] For the national security adviser, the reviews "would take time to complete, but we wanted quickly to put our own stamp on policy. . . . We needed this opportunity to determine what direction we wanted to take, rather than simply accepting what we had inherited."[73] The "Comprehensive Review of U.S.-East European Relations" (NSR 4) was signed on February 15, 1989, beginning the review process more than a week after the Round Table had already begun.[74]

In the interagency process that occurred through February and March, the main question for Eastern European policy was how and when to respond to liberalization. Beyond negotiations in Poland, the Hungarian Socialist Workers' Party (HSWP) was also moving toward a more pluralistic society. Hungary already had the most diverse economy in the region with significant worker autonomy and various market mechanisms built into the so-called second economy. Even with these reforms the standard of living was dropping and reformers in the party like Imre Poszgay and Resző Nyers called for "political reform as the precondition to the solution of economic problems."[75] An increasingly vibrant urban opposition movement called for a more representative parliament, a nationalist opposition located in the countryside organized around the issue of the rights of Hungarian minorities in other countries, and a vibrant environmental movement coalesced to protest government plans to dam the Danube. By mid-1988 János Kádár, the head of the HSWP since 1956, was pushed out of the leadership and reformers moved to liberalize laws on freedom of association. By the end of 1988 three proto-opposition parties were forming—the populist Hungarian Democratic Forum, the urbanist Alliance for Free Democrats, and the Alliance of Young Democrats, a replacement for communist youth organizations—all of which became legal bodies after the parliament passed a law in January 1989 allowing for independent political parties. Talk of a round table for Hungary was in the air by the spring, with the possibility of free parliamentary elections by 1990. The party also began to respond to popular opinion by reevaluating its past, officially recognizing March 15 as a national holiday (a traditional day for celebrating the Hungarian Revolution of 1848) and allowing one hundred thousand people to march through Budapest between important sites linked with both the 1848 revolution and the 1956 revolution. By May 2, 1989, the HSWP was dismantling the barbed wire on its border with Austria, both to keep from paying for costly upgrades to border security and to illustrate Hungary's desire for greater openness with the West.

In responding to the variety of changes occurring in Eastern Europe, the Bush administration accepted the differentiation framework it had inherited from Reagan, but its limitations became quickly apparent. With its focus on communist states' efforts to distance themselves from the Soviet Union through foreign policy, differentiation meant that the dictatorship in Romania was treated more favorably than reformers in Poland. (Learning from Soviet invasions in Hungary in 1956 and Czechoslovakia in 1968, Solidarność had always focused on domestic concerns in its demands, never seeking to question close relations with the Soviet Union or Poland's participation in the Warsaw Pact, so Poland remained securely in line with Soviet foreign policy throughout the 1980s.)[76] With liberalizing trends accelerating in both Poland and Hungary, Washington policy makers decided to rewrite the differentiation formula to favor political liberalization more heavily.[77]

While most members of the administration were convinced of the need to revise differentiation, policy makers were deeply divided about how to reward states for liberalizing. In interagency meetings, Simons represented the Department of State with Dennis Ross, the director of the State Department's Policy Planning Staff. Robert Blackwill and Condoleezza Rice from the NSC staff attended, as well as representatives from the CIA, the Treasury, and the Department of Commerce. The State Department and the NSC argued that political liberalization should be rewarded economically. The CIA representative—who Simons considered "just kind of an original Reaganaut who thought it was wrong for the United States to give concessions to commies, especially those guys who had done 1981"—argued against economic rewards, because "even if the Round Table came to a successful conclusion, it would not basically change the structure of power." The CIA believed that these changes did not deserve economic rewards because even successful Round Table Agreements would leave the PZPR in control of the power ministries and leave the bureaucracy in place.[78] This argument was easily overridden. The Treasury, however, pushed an equally conservative view on economic rewards, arguing that Poland had not made the necessary systemic changes—the country had not restructured its economy or created possibilities for the greater realization of market forces—to make economic aid meaningful. In this view, any attempt to pump in economic aid would be ineffective and wasteful.[79]

To overcome these disagreements, Simons retrieved records from Bush's vice presidential trip to Warsaw in 1987. Together with the Poland Desk officer, Dan Fried, Simons "fished out the record and the memcon of the vice president's meeting with Jaruzelski in September of 1987, in which he said that if you continue liberalization there will be economic benefit." These memoranda of conversation were used to show what the president wanted. The CIA retorted that these references were "just a snippet from a memcon," but the NSC supported the State Department's position.[80] The interagency report recommended limited economic awards for political liberalization.

In the midst of these preparations for NSR 4, a public controversy erupted over balancing Poland policy with broader concerns about U.S.-Soviet relations. In December 1988, the former secretary of state Henry Kissinger approached the incoming Bush administration with an offer to serve as a back channel to the Soviet Union.[81] As a proposal for possible discussion, Kissinger suggested that he could cut a deal with the Soviet Union over Eastern Europe: if the Soviets agreed to cut troops and allow East European countries to continue liberalizing without threats of Soviet intrusion, the United States would agree to not exploit the situation in a way that undermined Soviet power or its regional concerns. Simons and Ridgway "hated the idea," with Simons asking, "Why buy what history is giving you for free?" Despite internal disagreement, in early January Kissinger was dispatched to inquire with Gorbachev and his advisers about the possibility.[82] The proposal became public on March 28, in a *New York Times* article in which Baker said the idea was "worthy of consideration because it is a novel approach."[83] The article caused a minor furor internationally and domestically over the possibility of accepting spheres of influence.[84] In response, the administration quickly distanced itself, with Deputy National Security Adviser Robert Gates declaring, "I am not enthusiastic about that approach."[85]

With this public outcry behind them and the interagency report prepared, Bush called a full meeting of the NSC to discuss Poland and the NSR on April 4. The main question on the table then "was whether the U.S. should offer economic incentives to support political liberalization absent any significant move toward economic reform." The Treasury and Department of Commerce were against economic incentives, continuing to say that they would be wasted. On the other side, NSC and State Department officials argued "that a political opening would have to precede economic reform and that carefully conditioned U.S. assistance could facilitate first political, then economic reform."[86] Consistent with his earlier statements, the president (along with Baker) favored providing economic rewards for political liberalization. As Bush recalls, "Although the economic conditions in Eastern Europe were so bad that the usefulness of aid might be limited, we had to try. I directed that I wanted to see aid proposals."[87]

A day later, the PZPR and the opposition signed the Round Table Agreements, and in response the president planned to outline his new approaches to foreign policy in a series of commencement speeches. Given the pace of developments, the NSC decided to schedule a speech on East European policy first, and started to decide just what economic rewards to include. Davis began the discussion nearly a month before the Round Table concluded. As Davis recognized, "This can be the breakthrough we have been working to achieve for forty years and more, and its success or failure may well affect the future course of events not only in Eastern Europe but in the Soviet Union." He recommended a coordinated response with other Western creditor nations to ensure that economic success followed political liberalization, because, "without a return to visible economic growth and greater Western engagement in Polish affairs, no agreement will capture the support and positive engagement of the bulk of the Polish population." In particular, Davis recommended a massive debt relief program through the Paris Club, which would roll over all of Poland's nearly $38 billion in government debts. Creditors would then receive a proportion of Poland's export revenues (about 15 percent), which the Western governments would recycle into government credit guarantees to support Polish purchases of Western goods. This would both reduce the debt burden and open an opportunity to receive desperately needed Western technology and goods. Davis also recommended further policy changes, including pushing for a standard IMF loan, accelerating consideration of a World Bank loan for export-oriented investment, extending OPIC coverage, planning a presidential visit, and bringing both Wałęsa and Rakowski to the United States. Other smaller, more immediate recommendations included increasing cultural and educational exchanges and promoting debt for equity swaps by private American investors.[88] Overall, Davis advocated a bold initiative to reward both the opposition and the government and to ensure that the political transformation led to the economic improvements demanded by the public.

The response from Washington was much more restrained. Speaking on April 17 in Hamtramck, a Polish American enclave within Detroit, Bush outlined his approach to Eastern Europe in general, and to Poland in particular. Most broadly, the president proclaimed his support for reform movements by asking rhetorically, "How can there be stability and security in Europe and the world as long as nations and peoples are denied the right to determine their own future, a right explicitly promised by agreements among the victorious powers at the end of World War II?" Alluding to the shift in differentiation, Bush explained, "First, there can be no progress without significant political and economic liberalization. And second, help from the West will come in concert with liberalization." Finally, Bush outlined the economic steps his administration was advocating vis-á-vis Poland: for Congress to provide access to the Generalized System of Preferences (GSP, which lowers tariff rates on certain imports to the United States), for Congress to open access to OPIC credits, to seek new debt repayment schedules in the Paris Club, to continue American support for Polish initiatives in the IMF, to promote greater private-sector initiatives, to encourage greater business and nonprofit efforts to create debt-for-equity swaps, and to support "imaginative" training, education, and cultural exchanges.[89]

In a separate meeting in Washington, Ridgway and Fried spoke with Kinast. Ridgway clarified that the moves were "conditional." The main economic incentives announced by the president would only proceed if Solidarność was finally given legal status, a move that was officially taken in a Polish court on April 17 between the time of Ridgway's meeting with Kinast and the president's speech early that afternoon.[90] The moves were also "based on the premise that the agreed reforms will be implemented and not reversed; that commitments will be met; and that disputes will be worked out fairly." Referring to private-sector initiatives, Ridgway stated that the United States "invited Poland to begin negotiations of a private business-to-business agreement." Kinast welcomed the moves as "an important step in bilateral relations."[91] The Bush administration had taken its first tentative steps to reward the PZPR and the opposition for their moves toward political transformation.[92]

## Disappointment

Even before the initiatives were announced, Washington knew that its economic response paled in comparison to the historic changes occurring in Warsaw. As Scowcroft explained, "budgets were extremely tight everywhere, and the huge federal deficit cast a pall over any additional spending." As Bush admitted, "the long shopping list of incentives for reform laid out in the speech made embarrassingly obvious our lack of resources to provide real rewards for Eastern Europe. . . . Any serious observer would see that the response was not really enough to address the magnitude of the problem."[93] In the embassy, Davis was "very disappointed." He wanted a "major reinforcement to what we perceived as a huge change in Eastern Europe. It was something we had tried to achieve for forty years and here it is and now we can't respond to it? That's unbelievable."[94] From inside the bureaucracy, Simons saw the speech as an important victory to change precedent, because it created an "agreement in principle" that would later expand into much greater sums as policy matured.[95]

This bureaucratic victory, however, created little excitement within the PZPR. In November 1988, the MSZ had greeted news of Bush's election as a positive sign, because of the new president's pragmatic nature compared to Reagan's more ideological character, particularly Bush's "more practical and calmer" approach to human rights. With Bush in office the MSZ assumed that relations would improve smoothly.[96] In a March 2 meeting with the American philanthropist David Rockefeller, Jaruzelski spent most of his time explaining the necessity of Western economic aid, even theorizing that if leading reformers like Poland and Hungary did not receive ample economic help, they might conclude that democratization was "not the optimal path." Poland was specifically looking for increased joint ventures to spur exports and gain access to Western technology.[97] When Olechowski met with Baker for the first time during CSCE meetings in Vienna on March 5, the Polish foreign minister openly called for the two nations to move beyond "step-by-step" to a policy of "'extended steps' and more development of comprehensive bilateral cooperation." This included Olechowski accepting the nine economic steps outlined by Whitehead, with particular emphasis on new Export-Import Bank credits and greater economic cooperation through joint ventures.[98] When Czyrek met with Deputy Assistant Secretary

Eagleburger on May 16, he "stressed the need for a more rapid and less conditional Western economic support."[99] Overall, the PZPR surmised that the bilateral aspects of the package announced at Hamtramck would have "little economic importance."[100]

For the opposition, the economic packages announced in Detroit paled in comparison to expectations. The concept of a substantial American economic response, on the "scale of a Marshall Plan for Poland," had become doctrine by the end of the 1980s. The hopes for large-scale economic aid were based in part on early statements made by President Reagan when unveiling his sanctions policy. In his December 23, 1981, speech, Reagan had stated that in return for honoring human rights commitments, "we in America will gladly do our share to help the shattered Polish economy, just as we helped the countries of Europe after both World Wars."[101] In Poland, the idea of such a plan first appeared in the independent press during the initial months of martial law. In an article published on March 16, 1982, *Tygodnik Mazowsze* argued that Poland needed economic help from the West "on the scale of a Marshall Plan."[102] Three months later an opposition economist argued, "In general, the debt problem of our country is rather hopeless. An exit from the crisis is not guaranteed even with additional large credits on the scale of a Marshall Plan."[103] Three years later, *Tygodnik Mazowsze* published portions of an RFE broadcast about a meeting on October 21, 1985, between Reagan and Jerzy Milewski, which included references to possible economic aid: "Milewski again turned to the president for preparations for an economic assistance plan. Such a 'mini-Marshall Plan for Poland' could be realized after the return of democratic rights and after carrying out deep economic reforms."[104] Finally, in a review of American policy, published shortly before Bush's 1987 visit, the concept appeared again. This time opposition journalists argued that "what was needed was a bold political vision model, [like the one] which appeared after the end of the war and took the form of the Marshall Plan."[105]

For Solidarność activists, references to a Marshall Plan had clear propaganda advantages. By linking democratic reforms to large-scale economic packages from the West, the opposition reinforced its own domestic political power: the economy could only be successfully reformed with massive aid from the West, but only negotiations with Solidarność could lead to large-scale Western economic support. These statements should not, however, be dismissed as merely propagandistic. Opposition leaders truthfully believed that a massive economic aid plan would be enacted if they took the prerequisite steps. In his trip to the United States, Onyszkiewicz had first improvised the very large and very round number of $10 billion in aid.[106] On December 4, 1988, the Solidarność Coordinating Office called for activists and economists to prepare a "Solidarność Economic Plan for Poland." The announcement specifically resurrected the idea of a "mini-Marshall Plan for Poland." It continued, "we do not know if such a plan is possible in general. We don't know what the proportion of these previously mentioned [ideas] were between real possibility and a propaganda code word." However, the office wanted to know if "such a plan could come to existence as something greater than slogans."[107]

Viewing Bush's plans against this background clarifies the opposition's frustration and disappointment. While Solidarność activists did not chastise their American friends, they did consistently endorse calls for more substantial aid. On April 26, Paula Dobriansky, now the deputy assistant secretary of state for human rights and humanitarian affairs, traveled with Davis to meet Wałęsa in Gdańsk. As the reporting cable summarized, "Wałęsa emphasized the importance of an appropriate Western response to the reforms now being attempted in Poland. It was in the West's own self-interest to assist this goal; this opportunity should not be missed." As he explained, "Poland offered more favorable prospects for reform than any other country in the region. The 'necktie' of indebtedness, however, hampered these chances."[108] Wałęsa was too polite to criticize the Hamtramck gestures as "inappropriate," but that was certainly the underlying message.

When Kuroń visited Washington on May 1, he reiterated the same point. Joined by PAC adviser Jan Nowak-Jezioranski, Kuroń "described a 'wise and just' scenario in which outside economic support for Poland would serve to open the road for development of private Polish capital. However, the West appeared to be holding back with economic support until Poland had achieved stability, yet stability required an influx of capital. This vicious circle frustrated Lech Wałęsa and Solidarity." Further, by not pursuing the large-scale economic package envisioned by the opposition, the United States increased chances that the domestic situation would spiral into chaos. In summary, Kuroń asked that Washington "take a radical step in support of Poland." In response, Simons "stressed that the U.S. had no ready answers. Poles on both sides tended to mythologize American resources and largess."[109] Despite opposition pleas, the Bush administration remained reluctant to pursue any revolutionary gestures.

With the White House maintaining a guarded approach, Solidarność activists turned to their benefactors in the NED for smaller-scale support. On April 1, Seweryn Blumsztajn, who headed a Solidarność office in Paris and who was responsible for NED grants to the independent video associa-tion ZWID, wrote to the president of NED, Carl Gershman, asking for a new grant. Blumsztajn explained that as part of the soon-to-be-signed Round Table Agreements, the opposition would be allowed to publish its own daily newspaper, and they "have solely the authorities' promise that [the PZPR] would provide for the supply of paper and printing facilities." To assure pub-lication, Blumsztajn requested support for what eventually became *Gazeta Wyborcza* (*Election Gazette*).[110] Two months later, he wrote a more specific request for equipment including two photocopiers, computers, and large amounts of paper.[111] *Gazeta Wyborcza* eventually received $30,000 in sup-port from NED, sent through the PACCF.[112]

When Geremek traveled to Washington at the end of May, he experienced a microcosm of this frustration with the U.S. government and success with NGOs. He met with Eagleburger and Simons on May 19 and called on the United States to take a "dramatic gesture . . . for psychological and political as well as material reasons." Specifically, he asked the United States to lead an international coalition including West Europeans and Japan to provide aid to the Poles and Hungarians (a kind of multinational Marshall Plan), which the administration was already discussing.[113] Geremek left the Depart-ment of State without any definite agreements. He did, however, stop off at the AFL-CIO to meet Kirkland. There Geremek received a suitcase full of $100,000 in cash for the ongoing election campaign, provided by the AFL-CIO and PAC.[114]

Rumors of a possible Western Marshall Plan for Poland persisted and re-surfaced as late at June. As the embassy reported, the $10 billion sum was still being talked about: "Most of the stories' permeations contend that two Western governments—presumably the U.S. and Britain—have offered this huge sum in financial aid to both the opposition and the Polish government on the condition that Solidarity be given the presidency and the prime min-ister's job." More troubling, "many well-connected and [opposition] activ-ists" as well as "some in the regime leadership itself" believed the rumors.[115] When Wałęsa met with French president Mitterand in June 1989, even he referenced a $10 billion aid program.

As spring became summer, the Bush administration's plans were showing much more consistency with PZPR economic goals than with the opposi-tion's hopes. Since the early 1980s, the authorities had focused on remedy-ing deep structural problems in the economy, particularly strains caused by massive debt to the West. For Polish diplomats, the most important steps to ensuring economic recovery were attaining new credits from the IMF and new loans from the World Bank to foster a more pro-export economy that could earn foreign currency and repay those debts. They also consistently requested help rescheduling debt at favorable terms through the Paris Club, lowering trade barriers by including Poland in the GSP, opening Polish investments to OPIC guarantees, and providing investment support from the Export-Import Bank.[116] After March 1989, the PZPR also showed interest in taking part in the newly announced Brady Plan, which was designed by the U.S. Treasury Department with Latin American countries in mind to provide American support in the form of bonds for restructuring debts. In stark contrast to pleas from Solidarność, PZPR representatives emphasized that their goal was to promote positive economic cooperation with the United States, not to seek large new credits.[117] Bush's announcements providing American support to new initiatives by the IMF, World Bank, and Paris Club, as well as his pressure on Congress to allow Polish access to the GSP and OPIC, therefore, fulfilled the PZPR's long-term goals. The opposition was left wanting for much more.

## Elections and Concerns

In the days after signing the Round Table Agreements, Solidarność's main worry was not gaining Western economic support, but rather preparing for parliamentary elections. As the opposition regularly stated, it was difficult to run 261 candidates (100 in the Senate and 161 in the Sejm, totaling all seats open to the opposition) for national election given only six weeks and starting without an existing party structure. To organize and coordinate its campaign, the opposition relied on the newly created Citizen's Committee. Its first task was to create a list of candidates and procure the necessary 780,000 signatures (3,000 per candidate) to register them by a May 10 deadline.[118] Under the auspices of the National Citizen's Committee, local committees were created and charged with nominating potential candidates. These local nominations moved through regional Citizen's Committee structures and were whittled down until they reached the national body, which made the final decision.[119] Through this process the opposition created a mix of local and national figures running on each regional ticket. For example, Onyszkiewicz, a longtime resident of Warsaw who was nationally known, ran in the southeastern town of Przemyśl, where his wife had some family.[120] In Ostrołęka in northeast Poland, the opposition ticket included Józef Gutowski, a lifelong resident and sheep farmer who was also a longtime member of Rural Solidarność.[121]

The other early concern for the campaign was money. Henryk Wujec, the national coordinator for the Citizen's Committee, expected the entire national campaign to cost $250,000. The committee had raised only $30,000 by the end of April. To make up the shortfall, candidates and campaign staff began selling "bricks" (paper certificates) of various denominations that people could take as souvenirs. In a nod to Western-style campaigning, the opposition also sold Solidarność bumper stickers. In addition, opposition spokespeople left open the possibility of accepting money from labor and fraternal organizations, but Solidarność remained "reluctant to consider positively the idea of direct foreign government appropriations for Solidarity activists."[122] Wałęsa also appealed for campaign funds directly from the Polish government.

Once the list of candidates for national office was settled on April 23 and officially registered on May 10, the candidates moved into a flurry of activity. They created local election offices, held rallies, hosted speeches, handed out bumper stickers, plastered areas with campaign literature and candidate posters, and made use of sound trucks. For a May 3 election event in Kraków, candidates led a march complete with brass band from the cathedral on Wawel Hill down to the nearby Old Town Square, where they gave speeches to a crowd of about five thousand. Candidates focused on the details of voting to educate what many considered a politically "ignorant" society that was only used to the non-competitive elections the PZPR had run for the past forty years. Specifically, opposition candidates taught people how to vote for opposition candidates and told them how to cross off the names of government candidates on the National List, to force these candidates to take part in the second round of elections on June 18.[123] Throughout the process the opposition received extensive support from the Catholic Church, with local priests opening parish meeting halls and churches for rallies. Some priests went further. As one cable reported, "Priests inform their congregations of the necessity of signing the petitions of Solidarity candidates and of voting for them in June."[124] Although he declined to run for office to "retain his authority as someone above the fray," Wałęsa aided the campaign by posing for pictures with all 260 candidates to be used in campaign literature, as well as by speaking at rallies.[125]

Throughout the campaign process, the opposition remained very cautious, nearly pessimistic, about its chances of an election victory. As Geremek told reporters a week after signing the Round Table Agreements, "We have no structures, little money, and scant access to the mass media,"[126] in contrast to PZPR bodies, which were well organized and well funded. When

Wałęsa met with American representatives on April 26, he emphasized that there were already fractures appearing in the opposition, stating, "We could lose."[127] Kuroń gave an equally reserved picture of the opposition's election chances on his May visit to Washington. He expected a majority, but less than 60 percent of the Senat seats because Solidarność support in conservative rural districts was sparse. As for the Sejm, Kuroń foresaw winning 20 to 25 percent of the lower house. Generally, Kuroń noted, "the electorate would vote for personalities rather than for parties: only about 10 percent would automatically vote for the Solidarity candidate and only 2 percent for the party candidate." Moreover, with the PZPR looking for vulnerabilities and tailoring its lists to specific races, the Communists "could emerge from the elections in reasonably good shape."[128] Continued public apathy about the political process added to the democratic opposition's reservations. As the *Washington Post* reported, "As Poland's politicians conduct a frantic, fractious campaign . . . , the challenge of winning votes has been matched by that of convincing average Poles that the exercise of partial democracy is worthwhile."[129] Newspaper accounts from the week before the election either emphasized political apathy or predicted only a modest opposition victory.[130] Even on the day of the election, Michnik and Kuroń were unsure of how it would turn out; they "did not know. No one knew."[131]

From the beginning of the election campaign, however, Davis's embassy took a much different view. They did know. Only two weeks after the Round Table concluded, Davis presented his predictions: "The elections in June are, for the regime, an unpredictable danger and, for the opposition, an enormous opportunity. The authorities, having staked a great deal, are hoping for some modest success, but they are more likely to meet total defeat and great embarrassment. The party, despite its touted superior organization, is vastly disliked and nearly incapable of persuading an electorate through traditional campaign techniques, with which it has had no experience. . . . It is difficult to see how the party's core will be able to elect many—or any—candidates to the Senate. Apparently seeing the possible outcome in a different way, the regime may have committed the sin of many crumbling power elites in seriously underestimating the strength and depth of its opposition." This optimism was based in part on activists working at "breakneck speed" with "real enthusiasm," showing that their "ability to organize and overcome doubts could make the opposition formidable competitors."[132] An enthusiasm gap was clear to other observers as well. During a May visit, Brzeziński noted that Solidarność's "campaign seems to be well organized and full of dynamism. . . . The [National Citizen's

Committee headquarters] was throbbing with life, young people, bearded students, energetic young girls, all exuding an enormous degree of hope and cheerfulness." On the other hand, the PZPR headquarters was staffed by "two biologically retarded types," sitting at desks with pamphlets.[133]

By the middle of May, the opposition's lead was even clearer to the embassy. As they reported: "Early nominations . . . allowed Solidarity to dominate the scene before official candidates were announced."[134] Two days before the first round of elections, the embassy provided an overview of the "one-sided campaign in which Solidarity has emerged as a genuine and capable party." Davis concluded that the opposition would "win a nearly total" victory, with the government coalition wining only two or three Senat seats and the opposition winning all of its possible Sejm seats.[135]

Davis and his team took it as a matter of faith (and prescient analysis) that Solidarność would win an overwhelming victory. The opposition's ability to run an organized and focused election campaign only reinforced the diplomats' predisposition. In a political climate in which Solidarność activists shied away from claiming that they could win substantial gains, Davis and his team saw beyond their anxieties, providing the White House and the Department of State with a nearly flawless analysis of the political situation on the eve of the elections. Davis's cables are even more striking given that no one else was predicting a landslide for Solidarność.[136]

However, Davis's predictions of a near total Solidarność victory were not cause for unrestrained joy; complete victory produced new uncertainties. First, a one-sided victory threatened the election of prominent government officials and Round Table participants, who were running unopposed as part of the PZPR's National List. To be elected, these candidates needed only 50 percent of the eligible vote, but many opposition candidates had been instructing voters to cross out the entire list. If these candidates did not receive the necessary votes in the June 4 round, there were no provisions for including them in the second round of voting on June 18, meaning that the seats could go unfilled. If they were unfilled, the opposition could win 38 percent of the Sejm seats, giving them power to block the two-thirds vote needed for the Sejm to veto legislation from the opposition-heavy Senat.

This new power dynamic would weaken Solidarność's position for two reasons. First, power sharing had advantages for the opposition. As Davis reported, "While the regime needs Solidarity, so, at present, does Solidarity need the regime; it does not want to be the government, saddled with more responsibility than authority."[137] Second, an overwhelming victory for Solidarność in the Sejm and Senat elections affected political calculations beyond the National List. Here, American concerns boiled down to worries about how a defeated PZPR would react, with the possibility of a hard-liner revolt leading to catastrophic outcomes. As the embassy explained, "Total victory or something close to it . . . will threaten a sharp defensive reaction from the regime. The position of the leading party reformers would be endangered. Sharper, and even possibly military responses cannot be entirely ruled out."[138] When backed against a wall in 1981, the party had responded by declaring martial law. While this possibility was less likely in 1989, the American embassy did fear a conservative backlash if Solidarność's victory was overwhelming.

When election returns began to be calculated on June 5, the outcome was clear: Solidarność had triumphed in a landslide. From early accounts it appeared that all opposition candidates for the Sejm would win and that all "but a handful" of opposition candidates to the Senat had won in the first round. Their victory was assured in the run-off elections on June 18. In terms of government candidates, early reports suggested that none of them had earned the necessary 50 percent of the vote, so they would be forced to compete in the June 18 elections, in which they needed a plurality to win. In addition, all but two names on the National List had been rejected.[139] While the opposition leadership restrained its celebration, the embassy reported that "gentle words and celebration can do little to disguise the threats and anxieties that the election results evoke." Moreover, with the rejection of the National List, the government coalition was now only guaranteed 263 seats in the combined legislature (called the National Assembly), giving it only a two-seat majority over the opposition's 261 seats.[140]

The government coalition was also rapidly dissolving, further weakening the PZPR's position. Two days after the first round of elections, the U.S. embassy informed Washington that the opposition "quietly claims to have at least ten prospective Peasant's Party (ZSL) deputies in its pockets. The glue that has held the ruling coalition together—the permanence and inevitability of PZPR rule—has been eliminated." With these defections, the opposition's majority was guaranteed in the National Assembly, and even a majority in the Sejm was becoming a possibility. Under these new circumstances, the embassy predicted that Jaruzelski's election to the presidency would be in question. To become president, Jaruzelski needed at least the tacit support of opposition parliamentarians. As Davis concluded, all of these new possibilities and concerns highlighted the "future volatility in Poland's continuing drama."[141]

Rather than solidifying the agreements reached during the Round Table negotiations, the June 4 election amplified concern over Poland's political future. The issue of how to elect prominent, reform-minded PZPR leaders, who had been rejected as part of the National List, remained open. In the new political environment, even Jaruzelski's election as president was up in the air. More important, tension in Warsaw remained high as both opposition leaders and American diplomats worried about a conservative reaction from hard-line members of the Communist Party, a possibility made all the more real by images from Beijing of Chinese tanks attacking democracy activists in Tiananmen Square on June 4. Halfway through 1989, Poland's future remained unclear despite gains from the Round Table and the opposition's election victory.

## A Presidential Crisis . . .

As concerns about political developments swirled, bilateral U.S.-Polish relations progressed. Most important, in a May 2 letter to Jaruzelski, Bush accepted an invitation to visit. The president's letter noted, "Poland has taken a step in the direction of freedom and democracy, a step that contributes to building the sort of Europe I and my country seek." While he argued that further development depended on continued internal economic and political reforms, Bush hinted at increased American backing, writing, "the successful negotiation of the round-table accords and subsequent formal registration of Solidarity has made it possible for Poland's friends to support a process of genuine reform and recovery."[142] While the MSZ expressed concerns over what Jaruzelski's official standing would be when the American president arrived (it was unclear if he would be officially elected president by that time),[143] Jaruzelski sent an official response on May 11, welcoming Bush for the following July.[144] This trip held some negative possibilities for the PZPR because it would allow Washington to "unambiguously exhibit backing for the opposition." Nonetheless, the MSZ also saw opportunity. The visit would "open a new era in the development of dialogue on the highest level," precipitating positive international, bilateral, and internal effects.[145]

The presidential trip refocused attention on America's response to Poland's transformation. To push the Bush administration's policy, the House Committee on Foreign Affairs held a session on June 7 to discuss a new bill, H.R. 2550, which created legislation to approve GSP and OPIC credits, as requested in the Hamtramck speech. The bill also appropriated $1.5 million in fiscal year 1990 and $1.56 million in fiscal year 1991 for scientific and technological exchanges, $2 million for both 1990 and 1991 for hospital equipment and medical supplies, and $1 million for 1990 and 1991 "for unconditional support of democratic institutions and activities." Representative Stephen Solarz also advocated strong language to call for a presidential task force to coordinate with allies in Western Europe and Japan to offer "major assistance to [the Poles] in getting the economy on its feet."[146]

While Washington discussed Bush's upcoming trip, the opposition and the PZPR coalition initiated a compromise on the national list. On June 6 the government proposed a new vote to be held during the second round of elections, previously scheduled to allow run-off elections.[147] On June 8 a select group of opposition and PZPR leaders met as part of the Coordinating Commission—a group similar to that which met at Magdalenka and was formed to deal with controversies and problems that occurred in implementing the Round Table Agreements. The two sides accepted the Communists' suggestion to allow seats left empty by the defeat of the National List to be reopened to coalition candidates in elections on June 18.[148] However, in another surprise, the high-profile PZPR reformers who were on the original National List decided not to run again. When Davis asked Czyrek (one of the candidates who had been crossed off on June 4) why, he said, "No, that would be too humiliating."[149] Other PZPR candidates would run for the seats instead. While this solved the problem of empty spots in the Sejm, the decision worried the Americans because it weakened the new government, replacing respected reformers with "warm bodies, but . . . not the people most needed."[150]

Unity within the Communist coalition was also rapidly disappearing. In particular, the Peasant Party leader Mikołaj Kozakiewicz was becoming increasingly independent. As he described to embassy officials: "The ZSL would be loyal to the PZPR only when it served the ZSL's interests and the PZPR's agenda."[151] In the wake of the June 18 elections, these self-destructive trends gained strength, with party leaders openly talking about the party splitting in two, into hard-liners and reformers.[152] Not only were important reformers from the PZPR too humiliated to run for election but their coalition was on the verge of breaking up.

Dissolving loyalty within the Communist coalition meant that Jaruzelski's election as president was now in question. As opposition members explained, "as many as forty or fifty" coalition parliamentarians would refuse to vote for Jaruzelski as president "to punish him for the Party's electoral humiliation." Given Solidarność's near majority, this meant that opposition politicians would have to vote for Jaruzelski to put him into office. Many opposition activists had made campaign promises against voting for Jaruzelski as president, but most also felt that making Jaruzelski president was an implicit part of the Round Table Agreements. Voting against Jaruzelski threatened the existing political arrangement, further destabilizing the situation. As the embassy reported, "most Solidarity leaders are convinced that Jaruzelski must be elected if the country is to avoid civil war."[153]

Faced with intense "hand wringing" by his friends in the opposition, Davis took an extraordinary step. Instead of remaining in his usual role of listening to political discussions and decisions, the American ambassador interjected himself to advise Solidarność on tactics, suggesting a way to elect Jaruzelski without voting for him. As a June 23 cable records: "I had dinner last night with some leading Solidarity legislators, who had better remain nameless, and jotted down for them a few numbers on the back of an embassy matchbook. I also reviewed for them an arcane Western political practice known as head counting." Davis explained to his Solidarność friends that a large number of opposition legislators could be absent from the vote for president and there would still be a quorum. Under these circumstances, even with defections from the government coalition, Jaruzelski would have enough votes to gain a majority. "Solidarity deputies and senators could then safely abstain."[154] In a historical anomaly, the American ambassador advised democratic activists on how to elect a Communist president, the same president who less than ten years earlier had been responsible for jailing, harassing, and beating them.

In the weeks leading up to Bush's arrival in Warsaw, the crisis surrounding Jaruzelski's election worsened. The embassy received reports that Jaruzelski was not willing "to creep into the presidency with a few votes" and was unsure whether he would even run for office.[155] Intensifying pressure on the Americans, Czyrek called in DCM Johnson to address the rumors he had heard that the United States was supporting "extreme opposition positions" and that Washington was opposed to Jaruzelski's election as president.[156] On June 30, during a PZPR plenum, Jaruzelski announced that he would not run for president and nominated Kiszczak instead, although discussion on a final decision continued.[157] In this extremely fluid situation, Solidarność was also positioning itself to make a grab for more power, with a July 3 cable reporting that "although he mildly denies such intentions now, Geremek does admit that Solidarity has been offered the chance to form a government from its own resources."[158] Later that day, the new editor of *Gazeta Wyborcza*, Adam Michnik, made these machinations public by publishing a front-page editorial proposing to revise the power-sharing agreement: in return for accepting a PZPR president, the opposition should be given the opportunity to elect the prime minister and create its own government.[159]

On the eve of President Bush's trip, Poland was deep into a presidential crisis. As Davis forewarned, "There have probably been few occasions when an American president has arrived for an official visit in a more fluid and fast-moving political situation than the present one."[160] The key question remained, just what would the Bush administration do with this opportunity?

### . . . and a Presidential Visit

On the evening of Friday, June 9, Air Force One landed at Warsaw's military airport, where Bush and his entourage—including Baker, Scowcroft, and White House Chief of Staff John Sununu—were greeted by Jaruzelski and Wielowieyski. Otherwise the airport was empty, but as the president's motorcade drove through town—on a route announced in RFE and VOA broadcasts—he was greeted by thousands of Varsovians lining the streets, sometimes two and three deep.[161] On his first morning, Bush went to two wreath-laying ceremonies with his wife, Barbara, and then alone to a private meeting with Jaruzelski. The Bushs had lunch at the ambassador's residence, where a mix of opposition and government officials—similar to the July 4 party, but smaller—met the president and exchanged toasts, including a toast by Jaruzelski who said, "I have lived perhaps fifty or eighty meters away from here for sixteen years . . . and it is for the first time that I have come to this building and this residence. . . . I think . . . it is also a sign of the times."[162] That afternoon Bush gave a major policy speech to the National Assembly, and he spent the evening at a state dinner hosted by Jaruzelski.

The next day Bush flew to Gdańsk. He first met with local church officials and then ate a "private" lunch in Wałęsa's home. That afternoon he gave a short speech at the Solidarity Workers' Monument (commemorating workers killed in strikes during 1970) at the gates of the Lenin Shipyards. From there he finished his tour by laying a wreath with Jaruzelski at Westerplatte, the site of the beginning of World War II. From Gdańsk he continued on his European tour to Budapest and Paris.[163] Overall the public response to the visit was more reserved than during Bush's 1987 trip. As one senior adviser summarized, "The President got a warm reception, an admiring one, but not a very intense or exuberant one."[164]

For these three days, the White House pursued a two-tiered goal. Primarily U.S. officials wanted to convey "our approval and support of progress on reform and [give] new weight to [the president's] theme of ending the division of Europe on Western democratic terms. . . . [The] visit will demonstrate our support for change in tangible ways that do not threaten the

Soviet Union." To show support, Bush offered some modest new aid and investment. In addition to the GSP and OPIC measures announced in Hamtramck, the United States and Poland signed new agreements to expand tourism and to exchange cultural centers. In terms of new measures, Bush proposed an Energy Cooperation Initiative to bring scientists to the United States to talk about nuclear and clean-coal technology, a business and economic agreement to enhance the legal foundation for American business investment, a housing privatization and development program to promote home ownership and increase the housing stock, and three environmental initiatives for the Kraków area to provide $10 million to retrofit a coal-fired plant with clean-coal technology, $1 million for air-quality monitoring, and $4 million to improve water quality and availability. In terms of debt repayment, Bush signed two bilateral agreements rescheduling Poland's debt to the United States for 1985 and 1987. The president also pledged to support "an early and generous rescheduling of Polish debt" within the larger Paris Club, deferring about $5 billion in total. The administration also promised to encourage the approval of "two economically viable project loans . . . totaling $325 million" through the World Bank. The most significant new unilateral initiative launched, however, was a $100 million "Polish-American Enterprise Fund" that would provide money for private-sector development, privatizing state firms, increasing technical assistance and training programs, funding export projects, and encouraging joint ventures between private Polish and American investors.[165]

These new initiatives were limited, and the administration worked to keep expectations of an economic bailout low. Throughout the spring, the president remained concerned that Western grants would be wasted unless meaningful economic restructuring and government-sponsored austerity were fully implemented. Just two weeks before heading to Warsaw, Bush had told German chancellor Helmut Kohl that it was "important to act carefully and to avoid pouring money down a rat hole."[166] As Baker reported to Bush, "your objective is to support the democratic political reforms under way, while bringing the government and Solidarity to understand that the U.S. and Western economic support can be effective only if the Poles implement necessary economic reforms."[167] In particular, Baker was concerned about Solidarity's expectations of a large Western response, hopes the president's trip was meant to temper.[168] These sentiments were also consistent with agencies in Washington that continued to fear that economic aid would only lead to new wastefulness. As Sununu put it rather colloquially while visiting as a member of the delegation, he did not want to pump in too much aid because the Poles would act just like "children in a candy store" and not know when to stop.[169]

The most important effect of Bush's visit to Warsaw and Gdańsk was not these announcements on economic policy; rather, the president directly affected the presidential crisis. When Bush and Jaruzelski met privately on June 10, the two engaged in an open discussion of bilateral relations, the international situation, and Poland's ongoing transformation. Bush said that he "would do nothing to complicate the difficult and delicate job that Poland and Jaruzelski face," explaining that he wanted to help without interfering in internal affairs. Jaruzelski did not push the United States for more direct economic aid, but only referred to the goal of obtaining IMF help and increasing joint ventures. (This was in stark contrast with Bush's later meeting with Wałęsa, during which the opposition leader once again brought up the issue of a $10 billion package, an idea that Bush told Jaruzelski was "unrealistic.") Bush and Jaruzelski also spoke candidly about the opposition's reticence to accept financial austerity, specifically the need to get "labor to cooperate with economic reforms"—a point Bush promised to raise with Wałęsa.[170] Bush and Jaruzelski seemed to find common ground on austerity measures and economic reforms, more common ground than was found with the opposition on the same issues.[171] Bush left concerned that "labor demands will make it difficult to implement reforms."[172]

Bush also promoted Jaruzelski's candidacy for president. As Bush recalls, Jaruzelski "opened his heart and asked me what role I thought he should now play. He told me of his reluctance to run for president and his desire to avoid a political tug-of-war that Poland didn't need. . . . I felt Jaruzelski's experience was the best hope for a smooth transition."[173] The Polish record of the conversation does not mention Jaruzelski "opening up his heart," but it does record Bush's supportive words. Bush made clear that he did not want to pursue "super rhetoric" that would be well received in the West but would hamper Poland's transformation. He also spoke highly of Jaruzelski, saying, "The personal position and popularity of General Jaruzelski in the United States has never been as high as it is right now," an opinion the president seconded in his later conversation with Rakowski. In that meeting, the prime minister expressed his "satisfaction that the president had such a high opinion of General Jaruzelski." Rakowski also clarified that Jaruzelski still might run for president.[174]

To illustrate his endorsement of Jaruzelski, Bush publicly supported the general in his comments and mannerisms. Before traveling to Eastern Europe, Bush had looked for support from his allies to bolster Jaruzelski's

President George Bush and Wojciech Jaruzelski attending a lunch at the ambassador's residence during Bush's July 1989 visit. Photo courtesy of the George Bush Presidential Library and Museum.

position, expressing a sensitivity to Jaruzelski's image "as a symbol of repression" and even remarking to Thatcher that the general "should change his glasses."[175] Bush was aware of the importance of image for public relations, and in pictures and television shots during his visit, Bush's body language looked more at ease in his meetings with Jaruzelski than in his lunch with Wałęsa. Beyond the power of images, "Bush repeatedly, and also publicly, expressed esteem for the initiators of change, of which he considered the front of the line to be General Jaruzelski as well as the present political management." Moreover, both Bush and Baker "strongly and repeatedly emphasized that transformation should proceed in an evolutionary manner, and that it is not a goal of American policy to decide about direction."[176] These were not-so-subtle signs that the United States wanted Jaruzelski to remain in a position of power, promoting slow progress toward democracy as laid out by the Round Table Agreements. The president and his entourage never publicly called for Jaruzelski to be named president, but they gave strong signals that Washington supported such a move.

Jaruzelski also received backing from Gorbachev. During a Warsaw Pact meeting in Bucharest on July 7–8, the Soviet leader showed support for his reformist colleague and called for all members of the Warsaw Pact to continue on the path of "rebuilding, reform, and refining different aspects of

President George Bush and Wojciech Jaruzelski walking to the ceremony at Westerplatte in Gdańsk during Bush's July 1989 visit. Photo courtesy of the George Bush Presidential Library and Museum.

the socialist system."[177] Reflecting their close relationship, Gorbachev was "interested in having his Polish ally assume the president's office."[178] Soviet pronouncements almost certainly affected Jaruzelski's thinking. Bush also had a direct effect. As Rakowski recorded at the time: "After the Bush visit, during which at every occasion he spoke about the contributions of [Jaruzelski], Wojciech's efforts [*akcje*] greatly increased."[179]

Shortly after Bush's visit, Jaruzelski renewed his efforts for the presidency, and he met with various constituencies to lobby for their support. By July 14, Jaruzelski had already met with representatives from the smaller coalition parties and had received a declaration of support from the ZSL Party Plenum.[180] On July 17 Jaruzelski met with opposition parliamentarians and "declared that he was prepared to discuss anything for as long as it would take." He answered numerous questions about the decision to introduce martial law, as well as both current and past policies and personal history. The meeting was, in effect, an attempt to "reveal the general as a reasonable and moderate man, rather than the imagined monster he had become for so many."[181] On July 19, the National Assembly voted to declare Jaruzelski president. Because of expected defections from the PZPR and its coalition parties, Solidarność representatives were forced to manipulate the vote. A lookout for the group monitored votes from an upper balcony using binoculars, and delegates were moved in and out of the room to create the necessary quorum. A number of opposition politicians also abstained from voting, and some even invalidated their votes when it became clear that their negative vote would tip the scales against Jaruzelski.[182] In a scene that looked very similar to a formula Davis had scribbled on the back of a matchbook, General Jaruzelski became President Jaruzelski by the smallest of margins, ending the presidential crisis.

## Search for a Multilateral Response

While the unilateral economic aid package announced during Bush's visit was reserved, the American government did coordinate a larger Western response. This included American support for West European aid programs. As Hutchings explained, "Our view from the beginning was that the West Europeans should assume the principle financial assistance burden.... Beyond these lofty considerations was the more prosaic fact that we were unwilling to come up with significant U.S. financial assistance."[183] Bush consistently preferred to activate multilateral frameworks rather than unilateral ones in response to changes in Eastern Europe, utilizing existing institutional frameworks rather than improvising new arrangements.[184]

The effort to create this coordinated response began in April through NATO. At an NAC meeting on April 13, Simons presented a report on America's evolving policy toward Eastern Europe and Poland and called on the other member nations "to use prospects for increasing economic ties, where feasible and politically appropriate, as incentives for steps toward meaningful economic reform, which to be effective would have to be accompanied by political reform and greater practical respect for human rights."[185] Most member nations agreed with Simons's presentation and steps by Washington (as announced at Hamtramck); however, the United Kingdom, Canada, and Belgium "sounded cautious notes" and pushed for a "go slow" approach.[186] As political events progressed, Washington kept a close eye on discussions within NATO countries about appropriate responses, but received few signs that their allies were pursuing policy initiatives more substantial than debt rescheduling.[187]

As the G7 summit (held in Paris from July 14 to 16) approached, this meeting became the obvious point to reinvigorate the Western response. Yet even at this high level, with Bush advocating a strong position, no major aid or investment projects were launched, and no new amounts of money were pledged. The G7 simply "welcomed the process of reform underway in

Poland and Hungary," announced that they were "in favor of an early conclusion of negotiations between the IMF and Poland," and announced that they were "ready to support in the Paris Club the rescheduling of Polish debt expeditiously and in a flexible and forthcoming manner."[188] The IMF sent a study team to Poland in August, and the Paris Club called for meetings on Polish debt in September or October. As Hutchings later lamented, "the paucity of the U.S. assistance package weakened the symbolic effect we hoped to achieve . . . and set the wrong example for our G7 partners."[189] Because Washington had not led by example and taken bold economic initiatives prior to July 1989, it was very difficult to push their European allies and Japan to take on large-scale burdens.

The most important step taken by the G7 was to call on the Commission of the European Communities to take the necessary initiatives to help Poland and Hungary, with a particular emphasis on food aid. International assistance and investment now ran through the European Community (EC). The EC jumped into its new role, meeting a few times in July to analyze needs. On August 1, the EC announced plans to send 200,000 tons of wheat, 100,000 tons of barley, and 10,000 tons of beef beginning September 1.[190] The EC also quickly signed a counterpart fund agreement to use sales of the food aid to reinvest in the Polish economy, and an agreement to lift quantitative restrictions on imports of industrial goods.[191] None of this amounted to a Marshall Plan for Poland, but in conjunction with Paris Club and IMF negotiations, Poland was finally beginning to see a strong Western response— centered in Western Europe rather than in the United States.

### "Your President, Our Prime Minister"

While a small portion of the government focused on new agreements with Western Europe, the major political question yet to be answered in Warsaw was who would form a government? The idea of an opposition government was already being publicly discussed following Michnik's editorial of July 3, "Your President, Our Prime Minister." A day after Jaruzelski's election as president, Michnik and Kuroń made a second plea to the opposition delegates to push for a Solidarność-led government. Kuroń's drive was, in part, informed by changes in the Soviet Union and by the need to preempt the possibility of a domestic social crisis, which would in turn imperil changes in the Soviet Union.[192] The new push was also influenced by changing power dynamics within the Communist coalition. As Stelmachowski, the head of the opposition's newly formed leadership body in the Senat, informed the

American embassy: "The idea of a Solidarity government had been 'greatly strengthened' by the election of Jaruzelski, because the election revealed that the so-called ruling coalition was a thing of the past." In particular, the opposition saw a "strong movement" in the ZSL and a weaker one in the Democratic Party (Stronnisctwo Demokratyczne, or SD) to formally break with the PZPR.[193]

The PZPR, however, had not given up on forming a government. Specifically, it hoped to lead a "grand coalition" including its coalition partners and some Solidarność politicians holding ministerial positions. On July 25, Wałęsa met with Jaruzelski to talk about possibilities for forming a government, both a coalition government and a Solidarność government. Following the meeting, however, Wałęsa rejected the idea of Solidarność joining a grand coalition, and opted instead to create a Solidarność "shadow government" to prepare for "solutions that sooner or later will become unavoidable."[194] Jaruzelski also stuck to his convictions and, in his constitutional role as president, nominated Kiszczak as prime minister on July 31.[195] On August 2, Kisczak managed to hold together his rapidly dissolving coalition and was elected prime minister and given the duty of forming a government.[196]

As Kiszczak worked to form a government, public concern over the country's future hit a new high. On August 1, the (still) PZPR-led government with Rakowski as prime minister implemented an earlier decision to introduce market pricing, "opening the door to a rapid increase in inflation and giving rise to numerous outbursts of protest and the threat of a general strike."[197] Workers in a number of factories, railway men, and transportation employees went on strike to call for higher wages to offset the price increases.[198] In this tense social atmosphere, Solidarność did not acquiesce to calls to create a grand coalition. Instead, Wałęsa and others spoke publicly about forming their own government, stymieing Kiszczak's efforts to form a PZPR-led one. Wałęsa also quietly instructed Solidarność activists Lech and Jarosław Kaczyński to begin secret negotiations with the ZSL and SD about a Solidarność-led coalition.[199]

In this tense atmosphere, Kiszczak sought the counsel of the U.S. government, meeting with Davis on August 11. Kiszczak focused his comments on dire predictions if Solidarność formed its own government, noting that one hundred senior military and interior ministry officials were meeting regularly to discuss the future. He also emphasized the threat of social conflict erupting on the streets as strike actions intensified, as well as growing signs that the Czechoslovak, East German, and Soviet communist leaders were "very concerned with the course of events." Kiszczak ended his comments to Davis by explaining that "the opinion in Poland is widespread, almost universal, that the opposition receives its principle support and financing and its orders from the West." Kiszczak was attempting to convince the embassy to use its influence to restrain the opposition and pressure it to stick to the letter of the Round Table Agreements, which had presumed a PZPR-led government. Bush had been helpful in getting Jaruzelski elected; now Kiszczak was looking for American support for himself.

Davis, however, rebuffed the overture. He explained cordially but clearly that "no one in the U.S. government was advising the opposition on its tactics, or as far as [he] was aware, had known in advance of the latest position Wałęsa had adopted." The U.S. government "regarded the composition of the new government as a purely internal matter to be determined among Poles." In contrast with the presidential crisis, the Americans decided not to support Kiszczak as they had supported Jaruzelski. As Davis reported back to Washington, a U.S. effort "to restrain the opposition's thrust for power . . . is probably beyond our capacity now even if we chose to try."[200] Three days later Kiszczak officially stepped down as prime minister, leaving the door open for Solidarność to establish its own government.

As the opposition solidified the Solidarność-ZSL-SD coalition, a major issue of public and private concern became determining whether the Soviet Union and Gorbachev would acquiesce to such a move. Kiszczak's warnings of concerned parties in the Warsaw Pact represented genuine fears within the government and the opposition. Jaruzelski himself "was prepared to accept [a Solidarność-led government] only if communists were also included in the government. This would result in a grand coalition . . . , except that the center of gravity would be quite different—the core of the government would be formed not by the PZPR but by Solidarity."[201] Moreover, there were strong indications coming from Moscow that the Kremlin would allow Solidarność to form a government. On July 3 the editors of *Gazeta Wyborcza* asked Vadim Zagladin, Gorbachev's foreign policy adviser, about the issue and received the following answer: "Decisions on that matter are an internal concern of our friends. We will maintain relations with every group [*wybranym*] in the Polish government."[202] On July 11, Roman Malinowski, the leader of the ZSL, spoke with the Soviet ambassador to Poland, Vladimir Brovikov, about a Solidarność-ZSL-SD coalition and did not receive any warnings against the idea.[203] On August 16, Davis received analysis from the U.S. embassy in Moscow that the Soviets would acquiesce to a Solidarność-led government: "What the Soviets most want to promote in Poland is stability and what they most want to avoid is an anti-Soviet outburst of emotion.

If Solidarity can deliver on these issues, the Soviets under Gorbachev will adapt, albeit perhaps with reluctance, to the new order."[204] Soviet opinions on the matter were sealed on August 22, when Gorbachev called Rakowski (who became the head of the PZPR after Jaruzelski assumed the presidency) to convince him to accept the new situation.[205] The exact Soviet and Warsaw Pact reaction could not be fully fleshed out, but by the third week of August, all remaining obstacles to an opposition-led government had been cleared.

On August 24, the Sejm voted to elect Wałęsa's choice, Tadeusz Mazowiecki, as the next prime minister. In total, 378 parliamentarians voted in favor, 4 against, and 41 abstained—meaning that parliamentarians from the PZPR, SD, and ZSL voted in favor. Three weeks later the Sejm overwhelmingly accepted Mazowiecki's choice of government ministers. The final composition of the government reflected a desire to create a ruling coalition with Solidarność at the core, but it included PZPR members in the power ministries. Twelve of twenty-four cabinet members were linked with the opposition, one minister had no party affiliation, four each belonged to the PZPR and ZSL, and three were given to the SD. Each major party received a spot as deputy prime minister. In a nod to Solidarność's long-held conviction not to question Poland's membership in the Warsaw Pact and in a clear attempt to calm hard-line voices in the security services, Kiszczak maintained his position as minister of internal affairs and General Siwicki remained minister of defense.[206] The opposition was prudent enough not to attempt a clean sweep. Nonetheless, Mazowiecki now sat at the head of a democratically elected and representative government.

For the Americans this was cause to celebrate. For more than forty years, U.S. policy had been aimed at returning democracy to Eastern Europe. While repressive and unrepresentative regimes still existed in nearly all other countries behind the Iron Curtain (Hungary was the exception), Poles had broken through a threshold. This was a truly historic event, for which the Americans could claim some credit. As Bush wrote to Davis and his staff, "At this historic moment in the history of the postwar period, I wish to offer you my gratitude for the job that you and your staff have done as our diplomatic representatives to Poland."[207] The euphoria of the moment, however, was perhaps better summed up by a more tongue-in-cheek message from Davis's colleagues in Foggy Bottom: "Department notes with satisfaction the essential fulfillment of the political tasks in your letter of instructions. Your next task is to promote and ensure the realization of economic prosperity in Poland, to include stable growth, full employment, low inflation, high productivity, and a Mercedes (or equivalent) in every garage."[208]

During the preceding eight years, policy makers in Washington and the embassy in Warsaw had helped shape Poland's transformation from a repressive totalitarian regime, which could only control its population by declaring martial law, into a fledgling democracy complete with competing political blocks. Economic reform, restructuring, and prosperity now offered their own list of daunting challenges, but Poland had produced a democratic breakthrough. This ushered in a new era in the country's history and the history of Eastern Europe. The Cold War was not yet over, but the old paradigms were crumbling.

In February 1988, no one predicted that within twenty months Solidarność members would be elected to the parliament, let alone that they would have supplanted the PZPR and formed their own ruling coalition. Poland's political transformation had stagnated from 1982 through 1986 and then moved forward only slowly through the spring of 1988. From 1988 onward transformation progressively accelerated, hastened by strikes rooted in Poland's persistent economic crisis. Once PZPR and Solidarność leaders started negotiating directly in the fall of 1988, a certain amount of liberalization became inevitable. Moreover, once openings for political transformation appeared, constantly shifting internal dynamics allowed Solidarność to make bolder and bolder reaches for power. At the heart of this rapid transformation lay, as Davis predicted in April 1989, a miscalculation by the regime: "the sin of many crumbling power elites [of] seriously underestimating the strength and depth of the opposition."[209] Conversely, Wałęsa and Solidarność showed considerable popular legitimacy, analytical prowess, and creativity to navigate successfully the changing political waters and constantly make decisions to come out on top.[210]

In terms of American policy, the issue of U.S. influence on this particular period of Poland's transformation is intriguing.[211] Bush himself has categorized his administration as a "responsible catalyst," pushing for change while not rocking the boat.[212] According to Secretary of State Baker, "Our push for democratization in Eastern Europe . . . was more pronounced. There we wanted to be more aggressive in assisting reformers."[213] Robert Gates claims Bush "helped grease the skids on which the Communists were slid from power."[214] More recently, Philip Zelikow has argued that "in the spring of 1989 the U.S. government became highly proactive, in its approach and its planning, especially to roll back Soviet rule in Eastern Europe," characterizing American goals as "radical."[215]

These analyses by Bush administration officials misrepresent American policy. Rather than prompting or pursuing revolution, the Bush administration exhibited a proclivity for promoting slow, stable, evolutionary change. The primary focus for American diplomats was to ensure stability and guard against a conservative backlash, taking steps to slow the pace of change when the democratic revolution was nearing a crescendo. The Bush administration did not want to stop the surge of democracy, but it did work to control the speed of change. Ultimately, the United States did play a notable role in the revolutions of 1989. But the Bush administration was not a catalyst, a substance that initiates or accelerates a reaction, rather it was an inhibitor, a substance that decreases the rate of a reaction, purposefully slowing down the transformation for the sake of stability.

Economically, this caution was grounded in a fear of deficit spending and beliefs that economic change could be best implemented by promoting the private sector, not providing a massive economic aid package as liberal Democratic presidents had done after World War II. It would have been completely inconsistent for a Republican president—who had worked with Ronald Reagan for eight years to drastically cut the size of the U.S. government and infuse the economy with more market forces—to then propose a massive government program to bail out a centralized economy. Bush's proclivity for exercising and maintaining American leadership in multilateral organizations also explains the limited economic steps taken. Finally, the White House chose an economic aid package that was more consistent with PZPR goals than with the opposition's hopes, formulating a reserved response that undercut the opposition's popular support by not fulfilling rumors of a large-scale, bilateral aid package.

Politically, Bush and his foreign policy team were afraid that forceful involvement in Eastern Europe or rapid changes there could provoke a hardline response from within the Communist system. In a sign of its distrust of Gorbachev, Washington was particularly afraid of provoking the Soviet Union. From the beginning of 1989, "the question was not whether revolutionary upheaval was coming, but whether it would lead to catastrophe or liberation, and the answer hinged on Soviet attitudes."[216] In the case of Poland, by July "the velocity and unpredictability of the Polish transformation was making Bush uneasy."[217] White House attitudes were clearly influenced by failures of American policy in 1953, 1956, 1968, and 1981 to protect revolutionaries once they overstepped the boundaries imposed by Communist authorities. The White House "wanted to facilitate further democratic change without inadvertently provoking a backlash. Another failed revolution could have set the clock back a decade in Eastern Europe and derailed Soviet reform."[218] Bush believed that "we should support freedom and democracy, but we had to do so in a way that would not make us appear to be gloating over Gorbachev's political problems.... Hot rhetoric would needlessly antagonize the militant elements within the Soviet Union and the Warsaw Pact."[219] So, instead of pushing for radical or quicker change, the Bush administration moved warily. Washington helped shape Poland's negotiated transformation by choosing to speak in restrained tones rather than with fiery rhetoric. The Bush administration kept Poles' economic hopes in check and aided and advised moderate voices in Solidarność to back a Jaruzelski presidency as the best guarantor of continued evolutionary change.[220]

The White House wanted the Round Table process to move forward and for change to continue, but at an evolutionary rather than a revolutionary pace. In acting prudently, the Bush administration did not prolong the Communist system or the Cold War. Bold moves by the opposition in August 1989 ensured that change would be radical. Regardless of the holdovers from the PZPR in the new structures, Mazowiecki's government was fundamentally democratic and different from what had preceded it. What the Bush administration did do was promote policies to change the system incrementally, a vision in line with what it was hearing from Wałęsa and his circle of advisers. Poland had already moved further than anyone had predicted at the start of 1989, and the Bush administration did not want to endanger that progress. So it pursued a nonthreatening policy and could then sit back and watch. As Scowcroft recalls, "We followed closely but quietly, we could accomplish more by saying less."[221] The White House "did not know how much change Gorbachev would allow . . . , and [Bush] saw the Eastern Europeans themselves would try to push matters as far as they could."[222]

# Conclusion
## Empowering Revolution

We did not envision ourselves as moving into a country
and overthrowing the government on behalf of the people.
No, this thing had to be internal people themselves. . . .
We could just try to be helpful.—**RONALD REAGAN**

The creation of the Solidarność-led Mazowiecki government in September 1989 fulfilled a forty-year-old goal of restoring democracy to Poland.[1] An independent, non-Communist government had taken power for the first time since World War II. The Polish opposition's victory was not a clean sweep—Jaruzelski remained in the new office of president and PZPR members continued to hold the Ministry of Defense and the Ministry of the Interior—but this new government was quantitatively and qualitatively more representative and more democratic than it had been since the creation of the People's Republic of Poland. Building on years of underground activity and tough compromises before and during the Round Table process, the opposition led by Wałęsa had won a landslide victory in semifree elections in June 1989. This victory, in turn, provided opposition activists an opportunity to forge a parliamentary majority by separating two smaller Communist coalition parties from their longtime, subordinate relationship with the PZPR. With that brilliant political move, Wałęsa and his coconsiprators brought true political power to the opposition, leading the country into new territory. The symbols and military realities of the Cold War had yet to be reorganized, but Eastern Europe's political landscape had been permanently transformed. With the formation of the Mazowiecki government, Poland experienced a democratic breakthrough—a pivotal moment or set of events that qualitatively transform a regime from non-democracy to at least minimal electoral democracy. Taking a long view of the revolution of 1989, this book is an attempt to understand, qualify, and explain the American role in that monumental transformation.

Viewing American actions through Polish eyes—of both the government and the opposition—and combining those sources with evidence from non-governmental actors as well as newly available sources from U.S. government repositories provides a complex picture of both the triumphs and defeats sustained by American foreign policy. A close inspection provides very few examples of direct, causal links between American policies and shifts in Poland. Generally, Washington had little control over or impact on moves made on the ground in Warsaw. Of course this does not mean that the United States played no role whatsoever. Instead, taking a final accounting of American policy is a matter of teasing out the specific, limited instances and forms in which American power affected Poland's development over the course of the the 1980s.

## The Question of American Leadership

One pillar of Washington's policies attempted to change PZPR actions through economic and political sanctions. This included decisions announced on December 23, 1981, following the declaration of martial law (restrictions on fishing rights, suspension of all LOT flights, the discontinuance of credits for government loans, increased trade restrictions on high-technology items, and the suspension of agricultural aid), as well as sanctions imposed over the course of 1982 (exercising veto power over IMF membership, suspending MFN trade status, allowing scientific exchange agreements to lapse, and blocking agreements to reschedule Poland's loans through the Paris Club). With the sanctions came a list of political demands: an end to martial law, the release of all political prisoners, and the resumption of a dialogue with the "true representatives" of the Polish people (although the exact formulation of this third demand shifted over time, it generally referred to the Catholic Church and representatives from the opposition, i.e., Wałęsa and Solidarność).

In the first three years after the declaration of martial law, these sanctions and political demands had little effect. In response to the Reagan administration's policies, Jaruzelski and his government strengthened political and economic ties with the Soviet bloc, decreasing American leverage. The PZPR also did all it could to stymie and restrict political relations, constantly berating American representatives in Warsaw for interfering in internal affairs, as well as harassing and limiting the American embassy's activities in Warsaw. As the most public signs of discord, efforts to limit Polish-American relations at all costs led to three crises in which diplomatic personnel were declared persona non grata: in May 1982 and again in February and May 1985. In addition, utilizing one of its few levers for reverse pressure, the MSZ refused to grant agrément to Jack Scanlan, leaving both countries without ambassadors after Romuald Spasowski defected in December 1981 and Francis Meehan left his post in February 1983. The PZPR's final rejection of Scanlan in January 1985 came after more than two years of American lobbying and despite clear statements that refusal to accept Scanlan would damage what little dialogue remained. In the years following the declaration of martial law, the PZPR knowingly and willingly did everything in its power to undermine bilateral U.S.-Polish ties.

The intensity and longevity of these attempts to sabotage relations with the United States was not necessarily a rational response. It would have been inconceivable for the United States to give in to Poland's minimal attempts at reverse pressure. As the Americans repeatedly made clear, if the Poles wanted to "take relations to zero," Washington was more than happy to oblige. The United States did not need Poland as much as Poland needed the United States and the West, and the Americans knew it. In looking for ways to comprehend PZPR actions, it is more revealing to view them as an emotional response to American sanctions. Jaruzelski and the PZPR did not expect Reagan to impose strong sanctions after December 12, 1981, creating a deep sense of distrust. The emotional response to this break in trust, expressed as anger, comes out most clearly in Jaruzelski's interactions with American congressmen and diplomats. This anger also surfaced in repeated confrontations over RFE and VOA broadcasts, particularly anything that questioned the general's patriotism. The PZPR exhibited its distrust of Washington by taking irrational steps to sabotage relations and to harm the United States by any diplomatic means possible. In response, Washington externalized its own distrust of Jaruzelski and the PZPR—especially after the 1984 sanctions-for-activists deal was reneged. Because of this break in trust Washington pursued a reserved, cautious, wait-and-see approach well into the second half of the decade, even after the PZPR took significant moves toward political and economic liberalization.

Against the backdrop of this emotional response and the corresponding decline in U.S.-Polish relations, the PZPR's limited steps to liberalize before 1985 come into focus as reactions to domestic, rather than Western or American policies. Wałęsa was released in November 1982 following a series of meetings between Archbishop Glemp and Jaruzelski, evidence of the church's preeminence in this period. A very limited contingent of comparatively unthreatening political prisoners was released in December 1982 at the same time that the PZPR took the symbolic step of suspending martial law to focus on economic problems. The decision to allow Pope John Paul II's pilgrimage in June 1983 was only taken after lengthy negotiations with the Vatican confirming that the pope would moderate his political messages, acting as an intermediary between the people and the government—a role that the Catholic Church had played since the beginning of the Polish crisis. Finally, the decision to lift martial law and declare a limited amnesty for political prisoners on July 22, 1983, was made after legal changes institutionalized many of the government's new powers and in order to normalize the economy, which was severely burdened by martial law restrictions. For this period of a little more than three years, from December 1981 to early 1985, scant concrete evidence has surfaced to indicate connections between American pressure politics and Polish moves toward political and economic liberalization. Rather, the PZPR used every piece of leverage it had against the United States to undercut its influence and pursued liberalization in spite of American policies.

Notwithstanding the strained political relationship between the PZPR and the Reagan administration, the White House did have limited success in leveraging economic sanctions for the release of a specific group of political prisoners. After the "step-by-step" approach was officially codified, Davis and Eagleburger negotiated with Adam Schaff for the release of eleven high-profile political prisoners in return for removing sanctions. Four of the eleven political prisoners were set to go on trial in the summer of 1984, but all eleven were released after only one day of one trial as part of another larger political amnesty announced on July 22, 1984. In an informal quid pro quo, the United States lifted some sanctions. After the PZPR's concerted campaign to reintern political prisoners in 1985, however, Polish-American relations reverted to their contentious foundation.

Because of the bipolar framework of international politics during the 1980s, however, it is important to note the truncated realm of possibilities for change that American or Western policy *could* even provoke. As Secretary of State Shultz explained (referring to failed American policy in the 1950s), "We wanted to be sure we didn't do what was done during the Dulles period, where they incited this rebellion in Hungary and then didn't do anything about it and the Soviets cracked down. You don't want to lead people to do things that go beyond what you are willing to support. Because we are not going to have a World War III nuclear exchange take place."[2] More centrally, given the military, political, and economic realities in Eastern Europe, the PZPR was beholden first and foremost to the Soviet Union and the Warsaw

Pact. Whether one believes that the USSR was willing to send troops into Poland if Jaruzelski's martial law plans failed or whether one believes that the Soviets had disavowed the Brezhnev Doctrine by 1981, it is undeniable that Jaruzelski was driven to declare martial law because of pressure emanating from the Kremlin. Pressure to conform to Soviet dictates persisted under Brezhnev's leadership. After Brezhnev's death, Jaruzelski found a much more willing partner for reform in Yurii Andropov. As a reflection of Andropov's relative leniency, the PZPR pursued improved relations with the Catholic Church and allowed the pope to make a pilgrimage, a decision that had been constantly deferred while Brezhnev was alive. Andropov was not willing to revolutionize Poland's political landscape or to allow the PZPR to loosen one-party control, but he more heartily embraced the individuality of each socialist country's development. This gave Jaruzelski increased room to maneuver on internal matters.

With Andropov's death in February 1984, however, General Secretary Konstantin Chernenko pursued a much more controlling line. Using phrases couched in ideology, Chernenko advocated enhanced action to limit the power of the opposition and the church, with a heavy reliance on ideological doctrine and with much less space for Poland's "specificity." Chernenko also lectured the Poles on what policies they should implement. Andropov was much more willing to speak with Jaruzelski about their problems, and then following close coordination, to allow the Poles to make some individual choices. During Chernenko's time as CPSU head, Warsaw found itself under demanding scrutiny from Moscow.

Following Gorbachev's rise to the general secretary's seat in 1985, all this shifted once again. As early as April 1985, Gorbachev gave subtle signs of his new approach to relations with the bloc. While continuing to emphasize the shared nature of class interests, he openly recognized each Soviet bloc country's distinct social, economic, and political histories. Gorbachev went as far as stating, "Every brotherly party alone determines its policies and is responsible for them to their own nation."[3] In the years following these initial statements, Gorbachev's fresh perspective blossomed into what became known as "new thinking." New thinking reimagined the relationship between the Kremlin and its client states in Eastern Europe to allow each of them to make their own domestic political decisions, with little interference from the Soviets. Nowhere was this truer than in Poland, where Gorbachev and Jaruzelski fostered a close professional relationship. Gorbachev supported Jaruzelski's "second stage" plan for economic liberalization launched at the PZPR's Tenth Party Congress in June 1986. These reforms came on the heels of Gorbachev's own policies of perestroika and glasnost. Through 1987, 1988, and 1989 this trusting and permissive relationship strengthened, with Jaruzelski striking out on his own with increasingly radical moves and checking in with Moscow only to receive blessings to proceed. Poland even became a kind of laboratory for Gorbachev to see how liberalization played out. In this way, Gorbachev's doctrine of new thinking did not push Poland toward transformation, but it allowed Poles to follow their own course.

With this interpretation of Warsaw's relationship with Moscow in mind, a clear pattern emerges: the PZPR's vacillations between repression and liberalization mirrored changes in the Soviet leadership more closely than shifts in American or Western policies. The PZPR politburo made final decisions to lift and then suspend martial law only after Brezhnev died. In a striking coincidence, two days after Brezhnev's death, Wałęsa was released from prison. This general liberalizing trend continued through the middle of 1984, when Chernenko took over and began pressuring Jaruzelski and his colleagues to slow the pace of change. The 1984 Schaff negotiations may have ended abruptly and without any major breakthrough because the Soviets got wind of them and called a halt to the process.[4] Economic and political reform began anew only once Gorbachev came to power and Jaruzelski earned the room he needed to maneuver. Through the end of 1989, PZPR leaders kept Gorbachev in the loop and coordinated their reform and liberalization efforts.

In an interesting corollary, Soviet and American efforts to improve superpower relations following Gorbachev's assumption of power positively affected PZPR decision making. Specifically, the success of the Geneva summit in decreasing East-West tensions drove the PZPR's decision to pursue improved economic and political relations with Western Europe. The emergence of a new period of relaxed superpower relations did not dictate moves within Poland, but it did lessen the international restrictions felt by the PZPR. The Polish state became less of a pawn in the superpower game. As with the Soviet-Polish relationship, the improved superpower environment exemplified by regular dialogue and intensified arms negotiations provided Jaruzelski with more autonomy. With Gorbachev pursuing a more flexible and cordial relationship with Western Europe and the United States, Jaruzelski and the MSZ could move more freely in their own relations with the West.

The PZPR's increasing room to maneuver following Gorbachev's ascension to power had the side effect of enhancing the West's ability to affect change within Poland. As the Department of State and others within the

Reagan administration recognized from the beginning of martial law, America's and the West's greatest point of leverage remained Poland's staggering debt—$26 billion in December 1981, which grew to $38 billion by 1989—and the country's need for an influx of Western currency. As the PZPR sought to improve Poland's economy through internal reforms and increased cooperation with the Soviets and their Eastern European comrades in the CMEA in the first half of the decade, Jaruzelski and his circle gradually accepted that they could not end stagnation without Western help. By 1986, the PZPR leadership understood that they could not begin paying down their immense foreign debt and be able to reinvigorate their economy without increasing foreign exports to gain much-needed Western currency; yet to increase foreign exports, the Poles needed new Western credits to buy essential technology and raw materials.

To extricate themselves from this macroeconomic catch-22, the PZPR pursued improved ties with Japan and Western Europe, most notably with Italy, West Germany, France, and the United Kingdom. This initiative included numerous lower-level visits by West European officials and culminated in Jaruzelski's meeting with French president Mitterrand in December 1985. The PZPR's hopes for economic gains soon became entwined with domestic political concerns. In early 1986, the Communist Party began to hint that it was considering a new amnesty for political prisoners, many of whom had been reinterned following the partial amnesties of 1983 and 1984. The United States did pursue low-level contacts to explore the option of lifting sanctions, but the crucial move to pressure the PZPR to free prisoners was an EEC démarche (led by Great Britain) that was perceived as a threat to summarily end all the political and economic deals under consideration by Western Europe if the expected amnesty was not complete and full. In effect, Poland would lose all the gains it had made in the previous eighteen months, returning to square one in its push to gain new Western credits. In the face of this Western front, the PZPR acquiesced. Six weeks after the July 1986 amnesty was announced, the PZPR released all remaining political prisoners.

Even though the precipitating factor was Polish interest in improved economic relations with West Europe, the amnesty was nonetheless a victory for long-term U.S. policy. From December 1981 onward, the United States was a driving force behind Western sanctions. The Reagan administration understood that sanctions could not be unilateral and showed notable sensitivity to European concerns. For the sake of Allied unity, the White House took the politically unpopular step in early 1982 to pay Polish debt to keep the country from being declared in default. Similarly, after a controversy broke out over American sanctions on the Siberian natural gas pipeline, the Reagan administration relented and allowed European companies to utilize American technology. Reagan took both of these steps despite strong arguments to the contrary by neoconservative members of his cabinet, providing examples of the president's pragmatic side. This pragmatism and a commitment to maintain Allied unity became more pronounced after George Shultz was sworn in as secretary of state.

Returning to the specifics of the Polish case, fostering Allied unity successfully limited access to new Western credits, as did Poland's lack of creditworthiness. This general but most substantive restriction pushed the PZPR to accept American and West European demands regarding changes in human rights policies and its treatment of the political opposition. In August and September 1986, West European (and American) economic sanctions succeeded in bending the PZPR to Western pressure. From this point forward, the PZPR accepted the opposition as a part of life, and opposition leaders were never again incarcerated for extended periods. In turn, the re-emergence of aboveground opposition structures reinvigorated Solidarność and allowed the opposition to seek greater accommodations with the PZPR, eventually leading to the Round Table Agreements in April 1989. This was much more of a multilateral Allied victory than a unilateral American triumph.

The conservative flavor of American policy in 1989 is also worth noting, because it was one of the few points at which the United States was directly successful at influencing PZPR policy. First, limited American economic incentives and rewards proposed by the Bush administration adhered much more closely to the PZPR's expectations than to the opposition's hopes for a massive Western economic bailout. Second, President Bush legitimized and popularized Jaruzelski as a key piece of the democratic transformation, not only pushing Jaruzelski to run for president but also publicly signaling the West's and America's comfort with him as a leader. Finally, the U.S. embassy assisted opposition parliamentarians in devising a tactic to vote Jaruzelski into the presidency with as little political liability as possible. Therefore American policy successfully maintained Jaruzelski's position in the new government when the facade of Communist dominance was rapidly crumbling.

Overall, although the step-by-step policy won a few small victories including the release of a handful of prominent political prisoners and Bush helped convince Jaruzelski to run for president, the causal relationship between American government policies and changes within Poland proves to be weak. The minor role played by the United States' political and economic policies becomes even more apparent when compared with the overarching role played by the Soviet Union. In terms of ranking the importance of various factors, developments in the PZPR were most closely tied to domestic concerns, followed then by Soviet policies, with American and Western influences falling to third place.

## Moral Leadership

Some accounts of the end of the Cold War include arguments regarding the Reagan administration's international moral leadership. In *Cold War*, John Lewis Gaddis focuses his last two chapters on three "actors" in the 1980s (Reagan, Gorbachev, and Pope John Paul II) and writes passionately about the rebirth of hope in the final decade of the Cold War. He argues implicitly that Reagan led this final transition to hope by returning to a kind of moral leadership that provoked others to act and react.[5] In the case of Poland, however, it is not only incorrect but offensive to say that the American president somehow led this moral wave. First and foremost, the events in Gdańsk in August 1980—the creation of Solidarność and the appearance of Wałęsa on the world stage—predated Reagan's rise to international prominence. Moreover, events on the Baltic coast had nothing to do with the state of political life in the United States: Solidarność was an essentially spontaneous creation in which thousands and then millions of Polish workers decided to act out against decades of political repression and economic oppression. The roots of Solidarność are found in indigenous institutions like the Workers' Defense Committee (KOR) and a history of strikes and riots, particularly events on the Baltic coast in 1970, not in any foreign pronouncement.

In addition, the Polish opposition already had their moral leader: Pope John Paul II. Solidarność viewed the country's Catholic Church and the Vatican as partners and guides in relations with the PZPR. Sitting at the top of this hierarchy was the former cardinal from Kraków, Karol Wojtyła. The massive shows of public emotion during his pilgrimages in 1979, 1983, and 1987 attest to the pope's role of providing moral guidance. Wałęsa signed the Gdańsk Accords using a novelty pen with a picture of Pope John Paul II in it, not Ronald Reagan. Chronologically and causally, the concept of Reagan's moral leadership falls short in the Polish case.

In the period after December 1981, when Reagan played a predominant role on the world stage, Poland did not look to the United States for heroes; the situation was, in fact, reversed. Americans looked to Solidarność and the wider opposition movement for its heroes. The Nobel Committee's decision to award the Peace Prize to Wałęsa in 1984 was just the most obvious example of this trend. In public statement after public statement, American leaders throughout the 1980s revered Poland's suffering leaders and workers. The Reagan administration's heavy-handed but well-meaning "Let Poland be Poland" public relations campaign made this clear: its purpose was not to provide American leadership, but to keep the media pot boiling, to express the outrage felt in the White House, and to harness a great moral wave, all in the name of keeping international focus on abuses in Poland.[6]

Moreover, American visitors making pilgrimages to Warsaw and Gdańsk viewed opposition leaders as heroes and martyrs. As Whitehead explained in 1987, he wanted to meet with Wałęsa because he "admired him deeply."[7] As the reporting cable stated, "Mr. Whitehead began the conversation by telling Wałęsa how honored he was to have the opportunity to meet him. Wałęsa is a famous man in America because people in the United States admire his courageous defense of his convictions."[8] Similarly, Ted Kennedy came to Poland to award the Robert F. Kennedy Human Rights prize to Bujak, Michnik, and Father Jerzy Popiełuszko (posthumously). As Tom Simons put it, "When John Davis threw one of his famous dinners, everybody was happy to be at it. [The opposition was] happy to eat well and drink well. We were happy to be with heroes."[9]

More important, this reverence for the Polish opposition meant that American officials looked to Solidarność for guidance on how to respond to the PZPR. John and Helen Davis became well known for holding informal monthly, salon-like gatherings at their residence. The list of invitees included writers, artists, academics, journalists, and opposition members— once they were out of jail. The purpose of these get-togethers was not to explain to the opposition what they should do, but rather to give the opposition an opportunity to meet and discuss among themselves, in the presence of Davis and his staff. The Americans listened to conversations but did not proactively shape them. Similarly, salons that included visiting congressmen and senators (particularly after 1986) were not arranged to give Americans the chance to expound on what Poles should do, but for Americans to gain insight so that they better understood Solidarność leaders' perspectives on internal dynamics. These long-standing informal relationships provided Davis and the embassy with insight into the undercurrents of Poland's transformation, as illustrated most strikingly in his prescient reporting in the buildup to the June 1989 elections. As Brzeziński noted after one of his visits, "The U.S. ambassador and his wife seem remarkably well tuned-in."[10]

For evidence of Solidarność's influence in Washington, one need look no further than policy pronouncements by the White House. The White House's decision in December 1983 to grant fishing rights was preceded directly by Wałęsa's announcement that he favored weakening sanctions. Both the AFL-CIO and the White House lobbied Congress to increase funding for NED in 1984 and 1985, invoking the names of Wałęsa and Solidarność. Most important, Whitehead traveled to Warsaw just before the final decision to lift sanctions, to confirm that Wałęsa wanted the United States to take this action. Wałęsa's clear statements that the time had come for sanctions to end provided the final push the Reagan administration needed. As Reagan wrote in his diary on February 19, 1987, "I signed a measure lifting Polish sanctions in answer to pleas by pope & Lech Wałęsa."[11] An even stronger example of Wałęsa's political clout surfaced a few months later when Congress acquiesced to Wałęsa's requests and directed $1 million in aid to the Solidarność Social Fund, rather than make a direct payment to the union itself. Both the White House and Congress consistently conferred with and deferred to Solidarność leaders when implementing policy.

All the records reviewed document only one clear example of the American government concretely influencing the Polish opposition to make a political move it was hesitant to take on its own: Davis's dinner meeting with four unnamed opposition figures on June 22, 1989, to talk about strategies for electing Jaruzelski president. When Jaruzelski was voted in as president, opposition officials admitted to rigging the vote in a manner similar to the one Davis had suggested. It is important to note that Davis did not convince the Solidarity leaders to vote for Jaruzelski; they had made this decision before approaching him. But the ambassador succeeded in instructing a group of foreign politicians on how to achieve the election of an unpopular president and former enemy with minimal political liability. That Davis purposefully did not mention the names of the involved figures in a secret Department of State cable further demonstrates how extremely rare and sensitive a situation this was. Davis knew he was overstepping his usual boundaries.

The unique qualities of this cable should not be overlooked. Solidarność, the American embassy, and American politicians were closely linked. Though they trusted one another, the overwhelming body of evidence shows that the U.S. embassy and the U.S. government spent no time or effort trying to instruct Solidarność. As Davis has consistently and adamantly explained, "I did not make any effort to be directive to Solidarity. They had invented Solidarity. It was spontaneous. It was a Polish invention. It was brilliant. I would be happy to talk to them about what they planned to do, but it was not up to me to tell them how to conduct their business."[12]

In terms of American leadership and the opposition, the direction of influence was frequently reversed from the one commonly assumed in triumphalist accounts. American leaders looked to Poland for their heroes, not the other way around. In terms of political decisions, Washington sought guidance from Wałęsa and his colleagues on how U.S. policies could help the opposition. Only under the rarest circumstances did American politicians or diplomats provide—and opposition leaders accept—advice on how to act or react. Over the entire course of the 1980s, the democratic opposition remained politically autonomous and lived up to its name: the *Independent Self-Governing* Trade Union Solidarność.

## Morale Boosters

Governmental and nongovernmental organizations also pursued a list of policies meant to interact with the Polish public directly. Again, these policies indirectly influenced the political transformation.

First of all, Washington amplified the opposition's voice by broadcasting its messages through Radio Free Europe. The RFE Polish Section kept in close contact with the opposition and often received reports and information from it. Armed with this material, RFE provided credible information about what was happening within the country, counteracting the barrage of misinformation in the government-sponsored press. Broadcasts by RFE also spread opposition calls for strikes and demonstrations, providing specific instructions such as where and when protesters should meet, a service the Polish communists found particularly inflammatory. RFE delivered information from underground activists to a much wider audience than could be reached through printed material alone.

Similarly, broadcasts of statements by American leaders in support of Solidarność and the wider opposition acted as a morale booster. They were confirmation that Poles had support from the West and the United States. It is important to note, however, that hearing Cap Weinberger call Jaruzelski a Soviet general in a Polish uniform or learning that Reagan considered the Soviet Union an "evil empire" hardly came as revelations to Poles. Rather, statements of this character confirmed what many Poles already believed. American broadcasts were well received, not because they opened Poles' eyes to the evils of the Jaruzelski regime and the Communist system, but because they showed that Poles were not alone. Poles had a strong ally who felt the way they did.

American humanitarian support to Poland also brought comfort. Even before the declaration of martial law, organizations like Catholic Relief Services, CARE, Project HOPE, and PACCF sent aid. Following the declaration of martial law aid increased, a policy supported by the Reagan administration. Between 1981 and 1985 privately donated and government-sponsored humanitarian aid sent through nongovernmental organizations totaled 402 thousand tons worth $362 million (trumping the amounts of aid sent directly to the opposition).

In terms of internal developments, American humanitarian aid complemented the Reagan administration's political and economic policies. First, while political relations between the opposition and the PZPR were tense and occasionally led to marches, localized riots, and small strikes, conflicts between the government and the people never flared into large-scale or nationwide violence. Jaruzelski's fears of a civil war, as stated on the morning of December 13, never came to fruition. People often had to wait in long lines for the simplest of foodstuffs, keeping the political pot simmering, but humanitarian needs never rose to a breaking point. By precluding a humanitarian crisis that could have led to widespread violence and a possible deployment of Soviet troops, American humanitarian aid decreased tensions so that political change could develop incrementally through reform, negotiation, and elections rather than through violent upheaval. Certainly other indigenous factors—mediation by the Catholic Church; legacies of violence from revolts in 1956, 1970, and 1976; and the opposition's militant commitment to nonviolence—similarly influenced domestic patterns of change. Nonetheless, humanitarian aid augmented the domestic tendencies for controlled, stable change, supporting nonviolent reform and revolution.

Second, by funneling aid through the KCEP, American NGOs simultaneously buttressed the Catholic Church's independence and undercut the PZPR's legitimacy. When Poles needed help they turned to the church, not to the government. The KCEP's humanitarian efforts showed that the church remained powerful in the face of increasing government militarization, and that it had Poles' best interests in mind. The Catholic Church had played a strong, independent role since the nineteenth century when the country was partitioned between the Russian, Austro-Hungarian, and Prussian empires, so the importance of cooperation with American aid groups should not be overemphasized. However, by sending aid through channels not controlled by the PZPR, American NGOs amplified preexisting local trends. In an authoritarian, one-party state the church's independence inherently undermined the government's claim to legitimacy.[13]

The PZPR's inability to provide basic foods and consumer goods also highlighted its incompetence.

Third, humanitarian aid maintained America's positive image. Numerous Polish church officials who worked with the Americans to deliver aid responded with public displays of gratitude. More important, thank-you messages came directly from recipients. Gifts as simple as used clothing, diapers, baby food, surplus orange cheese, toothpaste, and shoes took on a symbolic as well as practical meaning. Aid recipients wrote about the gifts' spiritual (usually *moralny* or *duchowo*) importance. When the writers went into detail, they frequently referred to a sense of no longer feeling alone. Poles even showed their thankfulness in handwritten cards that often included personal touches like family pictures and Christmas Eve wafers, further evidence of the closeness aid recipients felt with their American benefactors. American humanitarian aid reminded them that their hardships were not forgotten.

This sense of gratitude boosted American soft power (its attractive force) and ameliorated some of the negative effects of the Reagan administration's use of hard power (economic and political sanctions).[14] From the U.S. government's standpoint, aid was provided for political more than humanitarian reasons. Humanitarian aid alleviated suffering, but it also counteracted propaganda that American actions were harming the Polish people. Humanitarian aid provided evidence of Western support for Solidarność, the church, and the Polish people. Humanitarian aid sent through NGOs provided an avenue to prove that economic sanctions were focused on those in power, not on the common worker or farmer who had supported Solidarność. Each time a sack of rice with an American flag printed on it, a box of surplus cheese, or a tube of toothpaste arrived from across the Atlantic, it reminded Poles that the American people had not forgotten them, maintaining and strengthening the positive image of America and Americans.

America's surplus of soft power—perhaps best exemplified by the raucous reception given to Vice President Bush on his 1987 visit, with crowds chanting, "Long live Bush! Long live Reagan!"—is all the more striking when considering what happened to other sources of soft power. In the wake of the declaration of martial law, the usual conduits for soft power were blocked. As part of its sanctions regime the Reagan administration suspended cultural programs, cancelled academic meetings and exchanges, and ended American participation in trade shows. The PZPR responded in kind, further hindering soft power by strengthening the jamming of RFE broadcasts, expelling journalists, blockading the American library at the U.S. embassy, and greatly limiting American diplomats' interactions with the public. Many of these restrictions were only lifted after the September 1986 amnesty. Humanitarian aid was one of the few ways Poles could come into contact with anything American.

In this way, NGOs acted as a kind of intermediary between soft and hard power. Private organizations enabled the Reagan administration to pursue a two-track policy of punishing the PZPR while supporting the common Pole. Direct government-to-government aid was not politically palatable after Jaruzelski had declared martial law. Private humanitarian groups provided an alternate path to extend support, so aid was not a direct mechanism of the U.S. government. One of the key outcomes of this tactic was to promote a positive image of America: from 1981 to 1986, aid filtered through Polish society and reemerged on the other side in the form of maintained and even increased soft power. American humanitarian aid provided through NGOs constituted an important point of exchange between Americans and Poles, underpinning American political efforts to delegitimize the Jaruzelski government without neglecting the Polish public. NGOs provided an essential tool for tweaking the Reagan administration's policies, strengthening America's position, and bridging the gap between hard and soft power.

## Money Matters

Beyond the issue of political influence on the Polish opposition, there is of course the question of the effectiveness of sending large amounts of direct monetary and material aid to Solidarność and the broader democratic opposition. Led by the AFL-CIO, American support began making its way to Solidarność before the declaration of martial law, and it continued as the opposition rebuilt. The CIA soon got into the act as well. After the creation of the congressionally funded National Endowment for Democracy in 1983, resources increased manyfold, providing needed money not only to the underground Solidarność organizations but to other important bastions of the opposition. From 1984 to 1989, the NED provided just under $10 million to support the democratic opposition (Appendix 1), through various grantee organizations.

Regarding the issue of American leadership, while these sums were significant and did shape the course of events, they did not provide a mechanism for the United States to exercise particular influence on decision making within the opposition. Because of the way the money was allocated and distributed, Americans could not directly exercise control on its use. First, the money was allocated by Congress to NED, with only general priorities;

NED money was then funneled further down the line to sub-grantees like FTUI and the Polish American Congress. The sub-grantee organizations listed in NED annual reports, however, did not work directly with the opposition. These organizations functioned as another set of intermediaries who passed money to organizations working in Western Europe, Scandinavia, and the United States. The smaller, third-tier recipient groups (IDEE, the Solidarność Coordinating Office, etc.) in New York, Paris, London, Brussels, and Lund, Sweden, actually ran the programs to support the Polish opposition. So, in each case, money from NED went through numerous hands before it reached opposition activists.

Based on reports from the sub-grantee organizations, an important truth becomes apparent about the groups who directly sent money into Poland: they were all run by Poles. The money came from America, but once NED funds were dispersed through the grantee organizations to its final sub-grantee destination, the money was in Polish hands. All the operations that NED funded were run by Polish émigrés living in the West. America acted as a financier, but few if any Americans were directly involved in determining the support's specific use. When, why, and how American money was spent was determined by Poles.

This system was based on a deep sense of trust between the Polish activists and their American patrons. Given the operational realities of running an underground opposition movement, Solidarność officials could not provide annual reports or complete accounting statements on how American money was spent, a reality that caused some early tensions. Opposition members did try to provide a loose accounting of money and material received in Poland by printing receipt notices in independent publications then sent to the West, but this arrangement relied on the honesty of the opposition; NED was at the mercy of the groups operating the smuggling routes. Over time, the two simply learned to trust one another, accepting the limitations of what could be disclosed and what would be left unreported or unrecorded.

Taken together—the overwhelming Polishness of the Western networks that supported the democratic opposition and the trust-based system American supporters relied on in sending money—the structures for getting American aid to the opposition provide convincing evidence of how little operational control Americans actually retained over the ways that funds and material made it into Poland and how it was utilized there. Washington completely relied on the opposition to report truthfully what was being bought in Poland, verifying the democratic movement's vibrant independence. Policy makers in the United States clearly understood and accepted this arrangement. Independence was an integral part of the relationship between the AFL-CIO, NED, and the movements they supported. The endowment understood that it was not in the business of telling democracy activists how to do their job. It had been created to respond when admirable movements and workable ideas surfaced, not to instigate them. For its part, the AFL-CIO operated on long-standing traditions of brotherly support to fellow unions. Further, while the Polish opposition understood that, in general, this money came from the United States, it maintained its operational independence because there was no real mechanism for converting American money into direct influence on decision making.

Although Washington never tried to direct Solidarność, American support to the opposition did have consequences. Simply put, American money mattered to what Solidarność activists were able to accomplish. As the long-time opposition activist, publisher, and editor Konstanty Gebert bluntly put it when asked about the importance of the West: "Money. We could not have done it on our own."[15] As Eugeniusz Smolar (a founder of ANEKS) explained, American money "strengthened our activity because it was always a hand-to-mouth operation. We never had enough money."[16] The opposition had domestic sources of funding (existing bank accounts, union dues, donations, sales of samizdat), and it was also supported by West European organizations and trade unions.[17] These sources of funding were preeminent in the first three years after the declaration of martial law. After the creation of NED, however, the United States became the single largest contributor. Because of the covert nature of support and the lack of written records in many cases, it is difficult to estimate the relative size of the American contribution. Based on an analysis of American funding to the Solidarność Coordinating Office in Brussels, the $300,000 to $350,000 annual allocation from NED through FTUI accounted for between half and two-thirds of the money available to Solidarność from the West. Based on this benchmark, it is safe to assume that American funds to the opposition more broadly accounted for at least half of the outside money flowing into the country. When the annual allocation through NED was supplemented by special $1 million appropriations in 1987, 1988, and 1989, the predominance of American money grew.

This money empowered the opposition. It augmented and eased its daily work. Monetary and material support allowed the opposition to do more of what it was already doing. Radios allowed Solidarność activists to communicate more quickly than through written channels. Smuggled computers eased editing and layout work. More ink and more printing presses allowed underground publishers to produce more samizdat. More money allowed for scholarships for independent artists to produce more politically sensitive or subversive theatrical productions.

Yet the ability to magnify, augment, or boost a domestic trend does not mean that American money was a necessary and sufficient cause of political transformation. For example, in the spring of 1989, when the Solidarność adviser Bronisław Geremek visited Washington, the AFL-CIO provided him with $100,000 to fund the ongoing election campaign. It is doubtful, however, that boosting opposition election activities was essential to Solidarność's victory. Solidarność candidates won all but one seat open to them. Nearly all Communist candidates failed to receive the necessary percentage of votes to secure seats in the first round of voting. Most telling, voters took time to individually cross names off the National List to ensure that these high-profile Communist officials would not remain in government. Given the opportunity to choose their leaders, Polish citizens overwhelmingly voted *against* the Communist system. As Davis surmised at the time, "The party, despite its touted superior organization, is vastly disliked and nearly incapable of persuading an electorate through traditional campaign techniques, with which it has had no experience."[18] While many voters were motivated to go to the polls to vote *for* Solidarność, the elections in June 1989 were essentially a referendum *against* forty years of Communist rule. No amount of money could have changed the outcome. The domestic sources of the vote in June 1989 vastly outweighed the influence of an influx of Western cash.

In a separate crucial stage of Poland's democratic breakthrough, however, American money appears to have played a pivotal role. On May 3, 1988, between the spring and summer strikes, Solidarność issued a communiqué committing to "discharge financial assistance" for up to six months to workers who had lost their jobs following that spring's strikes and to cover workers' financial losses "as a result of repressions." By the end of the month, the Coordinating Office had already forwarded all the money at their disposal. So, in early June Jerzy Milewski wrote to FTUI to request that they "speed up the transfer of the first quarterly installment of $250,000" and "to arrange for the prompt transfer of the second $250,000 quarterly installment." In addition to paying workers already hurt by government repression, the money was meant to support "emergency funds to cover future events which are expected, but not specifically predictable."[19] In total FTUI forwarded $500,000 dollars to help affected workers.

When Kiszczak met with Wałęsa on August 31, 1988, the PZPR agreed to open negotiations with the opposition (what became the Magdalenka talks) on the condition that all miners, shipyard workers, and other strikers returned to work. Accepting this stipulation was a gamble by Wałęsa; the process of ending the strikes was easier said than done. After meeting with Kiszczak, Wałęsa traveled to the Lenin Shipyards in Gdańsk—the birthplace of NSZZ Solidarność and the epicenter of Wałęsa's political legitimacy—where workers "whistled, booed and raised charges of cowardice." From their perspective he had received no definite concessions from the government, only a vague agreement to continue negotiations toward trade union pluralism.[20] Neither the demand for pay increases nor that for legalizing Solidarność had been met. As one young worker who had taken part in the spring strikes lamented, "We walked out in May with empty hands. We're going to walk out again with nothing to show for it."[21] Even the Lenin Shipyards' strike committee chairman, a longtime Wałęsa supporter, was quoted as saying, "After 11 days of strikes we have advanced so little. . . . It is a bitter decision." The Gdańsk strikers only acquiesced to Wałęsa's request to end the strike after "nightlong debates and a narrow vote."[22]

At the July Manifesto Mine in Silesia, workers were so reticent to end their strike that they demanded Wałęsa personally visit. The chairman of NSZZ Solidarność was greeted by cheers, but he soon met "some very sharp moments and a sharp exchange, even swearing at first." Again "charges of betrayal" surfaced. As in Gdańsk, the final decision to end the strike came down to a contentious and close vote. As one Polish commentator opined, "Wałęsa thought he could stride right in and the miners would follow him. . . . But he got a good lesson. It took him eight hours to convince them."[23]

Certainly Wałęsa's clout, charisma, and ability to seize the political moment went a long way to convincing both young and old workers to go back to work with only promises that the government would begin negotiations to legalize Solidarność. But it is important to remember that strikers' demands were economic as well as political. They had demanded recognition of the union *and* pay increases. At the July Manifesto Mine, the demand that Solidarność be recognized had actually been scratched off the list before a Solidarność activist, who was charged with delivering the demands to Warsaw, "snuck it back in, and the strikers eventually got used to the idea."[24] Moreover, the centrality of economic matters in the April and May strikes clearly showed how essential these issues were to workers. As one shipyard worker related, "We found it hard to understand [Wałęsa's] reasoning. . . . He was talking about the state of the economy, but our economic situation was also very difficult."[25] In addition, one of the most contentious issues between workers and management were demands "for assurances of personal safety and job security"; workers were afraid of reprisals and economic repression if they ended their occupation strikes without a clearly enunciated deal.[26] Solidarność had recently received half a million dollars from the U.S. government (a sum greater than the usual annual NED allocation) to lessen the sting of lost wages and to soothe fears of economic retribution. Because of American support, Solidarność could economically support striking workers to guarantee that they received at least some pay.

In the case of striking workers in the summer of 1988, Wałęsa only narrowly succeeded in getting them to return to work. In a situation in which the vote to cease strikes was contentious, workers' economic motivations certainly played an important, perhaps pivotal role. Because Congress had already allocated $1 million for fiscal year 1988 to Solidarność (in addition to the usual NED allotment), money was available, and FTUI could respond quickly to Milewski's and Solidarność's requests for support. So American money provided Wałęsa and Solidarność with the means to offer some economic security to workers, easing their concerns and sense of uncertainty. Without international support Solidarność would not have had this safeguard. Wałęsa's pleas to end the strike for just the *possibility* of open negotiations with the PZPR might well not have been heeded. If the strikes had not ended, the deal struck with Kiszczak would have fallen apart, and it is doubtful that the Magdalenka meetings would have taken place and the Round Table negotiations would have begun the following April.[27]

American money and material support also played a second important role in shaping Poland's democratic breakthrough: it influenced dynamics *within the opposition movement* by privileging moderate voices, who called for a negotiated settlement with the authorities, over more radical voices with different visions of the future. The vast majority of American money and political support went to Solidarność-affiliated leaders linked with the center-left or social democratic strain of the broader movement. These were leaders closely affiliated with Wałęsa, the national underground committees (the TKK) that existed between 1981 and 1986, and the KOR tradition within the opposition, including people like Adam Michnik, Jacek Kuroń, Bronisław Geremek, Andrzej Wielowieyski, Bogdan Lis, Władysław Frasyniuk, Tadeusz Mazowiecki, Zbigniew Bujak, Henryk Wujec, Zbigniew Romaszewski, and Janusz Onyszkiewicz.

To understand the importance of American money for the internal dynamics, it is necessary to take a step back to highlight the heterogeneity of the anti-Communist opposition. As the Department of State noted in 1987, "Numerous dissident groups have emerged to compete with Solidarity's

Wałęsa for setting the opposition agenda."[28] Important new movements had come to prominence in the mid- and late-1980s, appealing mainly to a new generation of activists and providing an alternate means to protest against the state, most notably, Freedom and Peace (Wolność i Pokój, or WiP) and Orange Alternative (Pomarancza Alternatywa). WiP was founded in early 1985 as a pacifist movement that promoted nuclear disarmament and questioned the state's legitimacy by championing young men who exercised their right to refuse compulsory military service. It was a militantly pluralistic group that was unconcerned with creating a hierarchical organization and instead preferred to focus on promoting strategies for change, drawing its participants (primarily university and lyceum students) from a variety of backgrounds—conservative Catholics and anarchists, for example, found common cause in promoting the right to refuse military service. After the Chernobyl accident in 1986, the group shifted toward ecological causes, including blocking the opening of a nuclear reactor in the north of the country and protesting for clean water. With their successes, they took headlines away from the previous generation of oppositionists and became "the most important new opposition movement in Eastern Europe since the birth of Solidarność."[29] More generally, WiP differentiated itself from the political program of Solidarność moderates by focusing on changing specific policies pursued by the PZPR, not on restructuring the political system.

Orange Alternative was formed in late 1981 just prior to the declaration of martial law, but it did not become prominent until the second half of the 1980s, first in Wrocław and then nationally. It was not an obviously political group, but rather a social movement founded on what one of its leaders, Waldemar Fydrych, called "socialist surrealism." The group gained notoriety by spray-painting small elves—an absurdist gesture—over spots where the police had covered up overtly political graffiti, like "Solidarność Lives." They also staged elaborate and chaotic "happenings," bringing together masses of people to indirectly ridicule the system. Orange Alternative happenings included a bus tour in which students dressed in theatrical costumes, visited the Wrocław zoo to demand freedom for the bears, threw flowers to the police stationed in front of Solidarność activist Władysław Frasyniuk's house, waved red banners and sang communist songs, all the while displaying a placard (in the very distinct Solidarność script, clearly poking fun at the more established opposition) reading, "Solidity Will Win." On Children's Day 1987, Orange Alternative held an event in central Wrocław with just under a thousand high school and college students dressed in red as elves, singing children's songs, distributing candy, and dancing. When the police detained and disbursed people, the mayhem continued with joyous elves singing and throwing candy from police van windows. The police and state powers looked ridiculous on the evening news breaking up a parade of elves. There was no specific political message behind these happenings, although they were clearly antiestablishment and anti–Communist Party. Nor did Orange Alternative ever articulate a political program, but the group did influence how younger workers protested in the spring and summer of 1988. Importantly, it created a free space for a new generation of protesters, "symbolizing a kind of surreal immunity from repression through foolishness."[30] This, however, was not the serious political work of longtime Solidarność activists.

In a second category, there were more politically focused, nationalist opposition groups that consistently pursued more radically anti-Communist positions than Solidarność, including Fighting Solidarity (Solidarność Walcząca) and the Confederation for an Independent Poland (Konfederacja Polski Niepodległy or KPN). The confederation was formed in 1979 and called for change both domestically and in Poland's relations with the Soviet Union. Contrary to groups like KOR and later Solidarność, KPN's goal was not to reform the Communist system; it wanted to overthrow the system completely, to return to the interwar political situation when Poland had been politically independent. In its structure and rhetoric, KPN invoked the legacy of Poland's Home Army, the underground structure that had fought against both German and Soviet domination during World War II.[31] Fighting Solidarity, led by Kornel Morawiecki, was founded in the first year after the declaration of martial law, and like KPN it pushed for the complete overthrow of the existing system, promoting national sovereignty and independence. It was a secretive underground organization with a very tightly knit group of operatives that published and distributed samizdat and attempted to infiltrate the security services. Fighting Solidarity was popular with younger workers and often took the lead in clashes with the ZOMO that broke out around Solidarność marches staged during and after martial law.[32] The heads of both KPN and Fighting Solidarity were also members and leaders of local Solidarność branches. Although neither group had the same mass following as Solidarność, they both remained relevant to the political conversation with a highly motivated core of operatives.

There was also significant variation and frequent discord within the official organs of Solidarność itself. While NSZZ Solidarność had centralized leadership structures, the union consistently allowed for regional independence. Based on ideals of workers' solidarity, the national bodies were viewed as groups for coordinating policy rather than dictating it. The movement's national leadership had always been ambiguous about the exact relationship between the center and the periphery. Even when Wałęsa was at the height of his centralized control of the union movement in early 1981 when he was elected union president at the First Solidarity Congress, there were contentious debates that threatened to pull the movement apart. The centralized or national union structures more or less lost control of the regions in the weeks before December 1981 (see chapter 1).

After the declaration of martial law, there was an intense debate at the national level about whether to create a centralized or decentralized structure to run the underground opposition, evidence of continued disagreements on the proper role of the group as specifically a trade union concerned with workers' rights or a more general social and political movement. This renewed debate reflected the persistent ambiguity of the relationship between the center and the regions. During its underground period, even Solidarność's national body's name, the TKK or Interim Coordinating Commission, gave voice to its ad hoc nature and its limited control over regional and local structures. On the local level, the underground union structure fractured. As a single example, in the Łódź region there were at least eleven important underground committees invoking the legacy of Solidarność, some representing even smaller groups like Free Solidarity (Wolna Solidarność), Conspiracy Action (Akcja Konspiracyna), and Always Solidarity (Zawsze Solidarni).[33] Particularly after the declaration of martial law, Solidarność was not a cohesive organization. As one commentator has summarized, "By late 1986, what used to be Solidarity was now a disparate collection of political oppositionists loosely held together by the authority of Wałęsa."[34] The Department of State noted in 1987, "Dissident activity [is] hampered by internal division. . . . Solidarity leaders [are] split over issue of new programs and regional differences in tactics."[35]

Not only was the structure of Solidarność convoluted and fractured, there were also direct challenges to Wałęsa's leadership. Most notably, the National Commission Working Group (Grupy Roboczej Komisji Krajowej, or GR KK) was formed in March 1987 and included longtime, national Solidarność figures Andrzej Gwiazda, Jan Rulewski, and Seweryn Jaworski, Łódź leader Andrzej Słowik, and Marian Jurczyk from Szczecin—all of whom had been instrumental in Solidarnosc's creation in August 1980. They questioned Wałęsa's continued primacy, calling for more democratic means to elect the movement's leaders, particularly because it could operate nominally in the open following the 1986 amnesty. The group also questioned Solidarność's shift toward an overtly political agenda.[36] Anna Walentynowicz—Wałęsa's close collaborator and a primary organizer of the 1980 shipyard strikes—was also highly critical of Wałęsa for his leadership style and the "so-called Solidarity experts" for turning away from Solidarność's mission of social justice and protecting workers to embrace politics. She was particulary critical of the decision to "appease" the Communist regime by keeping Jaruzelski as president.[37] To these critics, Solidarność was "rooted in an 'anti-political' ideology of societal democratization," so Wałęsa's embrace of a dialogue with the government—his neocorporatist approach of seeking accommodation through shared political power with the Communist regime—was seen as a refutation of the union and the movement's core ideals.[38] Eventually, Jaworski, Gwiazda, and Stanisław Kocjan created a new union structure called Solidarność 80 that strove to return the union to its original ideals and purpose.

The most significant threat from within to Wałęsa's leadership and the moderates' vision for transforming Polish society arose surrounding the Round Table negotiations. In February 1989 students in Kraków took to the streets to demand the official registration of NZS (the Independent Student Union), upsetting the relative calm surrounding the negotiations. Solidarność groups in Wrocław then began calling for a boycott of nonconfrontational elections—meaning elections in which only a limited number of seats were open to competition from the opposition. The GR KK openly questioned Wałęsa's heavy hand by criticizing the way Solidarność delegates were selected for the Round Table talks. The GR KK called for a more transparent and democratic process to recreate the union structures now that it was about to be officially registered. Then, in March, these groups formed an Anti-System Opposition Congress (Kongres Opozycji Antyustrojowej) together with representatives from WiP, Fighting Solidarity, and KPN, among others. Fighting Solidarity simply did not trust the communists enough to make a deal with them. KPN questioned the right of Solidarność members to represent the entire opposition movement. Together the Anti-System Opposition Congress called for completely free elections, rejecting the premise that the Communist system could be reformed. Instead, they advocated for a completely free process to create an entirely new political system.[39] They rejected the Round Table's power-sharing format.

These voices constituted a real threat to the political tradeoffs Wałęsa and his circle of advisers were championing. They were not just a radical fringe. As Onyszkiewicz stated while reflecting on the threats to the Round Table, and referring to leaders like Jurczyk, Morawiecki, and Słowik, "We had a strong opposition within Solidarity and we were rather worried that Solidarity would break down or break up."[40] More important, there were signs that significant portions of the public were questioning the political process championed by the moderates within Solidarność. As discussed above, workers in Silesia and in his hometown of Gdańsk did not easily accept Wałęsa's calls to end strikes in August 1988. During the June 1989 elections, there were also subtle signs that the Round Table Agreements lacked uniform popular support. Most notably, 37 percent of the population chose to stay home on June 4, many of them young voters. The U.S. embassy interpreted this as a demonstration that over one-third of the population "had no faith in the reform process and no confidence that the election would improve their situation." In addition, despite Wałęsa's consistent and very public calls to vote "yes" for the National List candidates (including a televised appeal on June 3), voters joyously rejected these PZPR reformers. To the U.S. embassy, these two factors were evidence of the "radicalization of the electorate."[41] Then in early August 1989, after the government had announced price increases, strikes popped up around the country. These strikes called into question the new Solidarność parliamentarians' ability to control workers any better than the PZPR. Public support for the moderate vision of transformation through democratic reform, therefore, was not unchallenged or automatic.[42]

To the West, Wałęsa, Solidarność, and opposition were synonymous. The U.S. embassy never questioned Wałęsa's status as the head of the union and the leader of the broader movement. The AFL-CIO consistently turned to Wałęsa and his surrogates as the voice of authority for what the democratic opposition needed and wanted. For Reagan personally and for his administration more broadly, Wałęsa's voice held sway above all others. Consistent with this view, the U.S. government looked to those moderate intellectuals closely linked to Wałęsa for advice on how to tweak American policy. One need look no further than the list of usual attendees at the ambassador's residence (Geremek, Onyszkiewicz, Wujec, Wielowieyski, Frasyniuk) to get a sense of which activists invoking the name of Solidarność and legacy of August 1980 were seen as most legitimate. This was a specific subset of the opposition movement—intellectuals from the seasoned generation of oppositionists with a social-democratic perspective who generally lived in Gdańsk or Warsaw.[43] The overall movement was significantly more fractured than the West's image of it, with substantial and vocal portions of the opposition advocating very different paths to change. Similarly, Wałęsa's political sway with Polish workers and the public was not as unquestionable as was presumed by those outside the country. Paths to transformation other than the rather moderate course—a power-sharing agreement—championed by Wałęsa and his core of advisers were possible.

Returning to the issue of American influence, it is important to note that the vast majority of American money and materiel was funneled to moderates aligned with Wałęsa. More than 60 percent of all NED funding was sent through the Solidarność Coordinating Office Abroad, which took its direction from Wałęsa and the TKK. This included the four largest single allocations—$1 million payments in 1987, 1988, and two in 1989—that went directly to the Coordinating Office or the Solidarność Social Fund. Moreover, the Polish émigrés that made up the core of the American-funded support network working in the West—like Eugeniusz and Aleksandr Smolar, Jan Piotr and Irena Lasota, or Jerzy Giedroyc and the groups associated with his Dom Literackiej—all had close ties with the social democratic wing of the opposition. These ties were often formed through personal connections with Warsaw intellectuals who later created KOR, specifically during the Warsaw student movement of March 1968.[44] This meant that the majority of American money went to groups directly affiliated with or at least sympathetic to moderates. Groups like WiP or Orange Alternative were more or less ignored by American funders, while groups like KPN and Fighting Solidarność were passed over, despite the fact that they had significant support within the Polish American community.[45] This funding priority was controversial at the time and remains exceedingly divisive among participants of the broader opposition when they meet to discuss the past.[46]

By sending aid through Solidarność channels controlled by moderates, the United States gave Wałęsa and his colleagues the power of the purse. As Mirosław Chojecki recognized, he had power within the Western network of activists working to smuggle material back into Poland because he had access to money. Without the money he would not have had the same kind of influence.[47] Within Poland those groups with American support had greater and more consistent access to money. Therefore the goods necessary to run a thriving underground were more available to them. Well-funded groups have more time to work at the business of opposition, because they do not have to focus on fundraising. As Helena Łuczywo, the editor of *Tygodnik Mazowsze*, explained, because they could count on a regular influx of about $1,000 per month from Paris, they could pay their editors the equivalent of a full-time salary to free up time from other work. Their paper, a mouthpiece for the TKK and Warsaw intellectuals, could be published with greater regularity than other independent newspapers and magazines. Western support gave them "the basic comfort you get when you have a regular amount of money every month."[48] Activists with links to Solidarność moderates also had all the tools they needed: they received computers that made editing easier, they had more money to pay for paper on the black market. *Tygodnik Mazowsze* maintained stores of paper, ink, and spare parts (for printing presses) that their publishers across the country could draw on as needed.[49] Conversely, very active regional structures outside of Warsaw and Gdańsk, particularly in southern Poland (places like Nowa Huta, the mines in Silesia, and workers in Wrocław), were often neglected. Just as the United States broadly amplified the opposition's ability to act, write, and communicate, American money similarly empowered moderate groups within the opposition to do more than their radical rivals. Easier access to large amounts of American money maintained and strengthened the moderates' position within the wider opposition.

American political support to moderates in Solidarność had a parallel effect, giving the moderates greater visibility and gravitas than other circles. U.S. and Western statements singling out Wałęsa for praise or relaying his statements back to the Polish people over VOA or RFE amplified his voice internally. Geremek and Onyszkiewicz regularly had the chance to brief the American ambassador and visiting congressmen; Andrzej Słowik did not. When Thatcher visited Poland she met with Wałęsa, not Morawiecki. When Whitehead landed in Warsaw, he threatened not to sit down with Jaruzelski because his meeting with Wałęsa had been cancelled; the conflict did not arise over a scuttled meeting with Gwiazda. When Bush traveled to the Baltic coast for an intimate lunch, it was with Wałęsa, not Jurczyk. In their underground publications Solidarność publicized Wałęsa's and other leaders' meetings with American celebrities and politicians to provide evidence to the Polish public of their position as international leaders, counteracting government propaganda campaigns focused on marginalizing them. Other groups could not claim such international gravitas. As Onyszkiewicz has observed about the tense days of 1989 and his concerns about the breakup of Solidarność, "Without the very strong recognition, the very high profile given to Wałęsa, to Geremek, to others, the risk would [have been] greater."[50]

As with the earlier discussion of American political influence on PZPR policy, the point here is not to claim that the United States played the most important role in shaping the opposition. The West did not create Wałęsa or Kuroń or Mazowiecki, and it did not make them national figures. Wałęsa and his core of moderate advisers had essential sources of domestic legitimacy. This was part of the reason that the Americans and other Western nations chose to support them. But on the margins, knowing precisely who received

American money and support is important information for understanding why events transpired as they did in 1988 and 1989. American political and monetary support buttressed and empowered this subset of the opposition vis-à-vis other active groups in the fight to transform Poland. Consistent and focused American support to Solidarność moderates ensured that when the PZPR sought negotiations, moderates had dominant positions on the negotiating team. When critics within the opposition threatened to derail or undermine the political transformation while it was still unfolding, international support and international prestige helped guarantee that Wałęsa and his advisers maintained the public credibility and movement unity necessary to shepherd through controversial or politically painful decisions.

It is difficult to imagine counterfactual circumstances under which another opposition leader would have been able to overtake Wałęsa as the symbolic head of the opposition. That is not the point. Rather, this observation is meant to explain why events transpired as they did. Specifically, American support to Wałęsa and the moderate advisers around him helps explain why their rather limited vision for political transformation remained dominant. As Timothy Garton Ash commented at the time, the process unfolding in Poland was not a revolution in the traditional sense of a violent upending of a political system, but a "refolution"—a hybrid of the words "reform" and "revolution." This term was meant to convey the "desperately slow, painful process of negotiated political transformation" that ultimately transpired.[51]

The path to change in 1989 could have been very different—more violent, more radical, more sweeping. Later events in Czechoslovakia, East Germany, and Romania provide examples of Eastern European Communist regimes collapsing in very different ways. American support for opposition leaders who were committed to a self-limiting form of revolution played a supporting role in moving Poland toward a structured power-sharing agreement. By empowering moderates within the broader anti-Communist opposition, the Reagan and Bush administrations helped ensure a relatively orderly, nonviolent, negotiated transformation culminating in democratic breakthrough.

The collapse of communism looked different across Eastern Europe. In Budapest, reformers in the Hungarian Socialist Workers' Party shepherded the country through a round-table process to foster competitive elections and economic liberalization. In Berlin, Communist functionaries misspoke and unleashed a torrent of popular emotion that the state apparatus no longer chose to suppress. In Prague, Václav Havel was launched from jail to the president's office in the Royal Palace in a matter of weeks as the Communist government collapsed under the weight of massive public protests. In Bucharest, the military deposed and swiftly executed Nicolai Ceauşescu, creating a new state out of the institutions of the old. At their core, each of these transfers of power were precipitated by massive expressions of discontent with the existing system: overflowing crowds that attended the reburial of Imre Nagy in June, weekly prayer-for-peace rallies in Leipzig that grew from a few hundred participants to tens of thousands in October, general strikes and nonviolent demonstrations that saw tens of thousands of Czechs and Slovaks marching through Wenceslas Square in November, and Romanian protesters demonstrating against the removal of a Calvinist priest in the provinces, then spreading their calls for change until riots broke out in the capital in December. In Poland, people showed their discontent during the strikes of 1988 and at the ballot box in June 1989.

Understanding the precise mixture of international and domestic pressures that led to Poland's democratic breakthrough in 1989 highlights the importance of moving outside of the superpower framework for understanding the end of the Cold War. The revolutions of 1989 cannot be simplified as the story of the United States triumphing over the Soviet Union. Similarly, it is not just about Gorbachev restructuring the Communist system, only to be unable to control the forces that he unleashed within the Socialist bloc. There are important transnational connections between opposition groups, but these do not fully explain what happened either. The Polish case study shows that the end of the Cold War in Europe is much more complex. Politicians and strategists in Washington and Moscow may have been focused on the superpower confrontation, but the collapse of the Soviet empire in East Central Europe came about because local individuals (activists, intellectuals, politicians, workers, and common people) acted independently to seek individual solutions to unique problems. For its part, the United States meaningfully shaped events at the margins, where indigenous problems and international policies met. International factors accentuated some indigenous trends and mitigated others, alternately hampering or accelerating the pace of domestic developments.

In understanding America's role in bringing democracy to Poland and ending the Cold War, it is important to highlight the limitations of American power, rather than crow about its successes. Domestic factors were the primary drivers of change. The impact of American policy was circumscribed by the pace and extent of change allowed by the Soviet Union. Without liberalization in Gorbachev's Moscow, it is doubtful that Jaruzelski would have taken the steps he did. In the case of American political and economic sanctions against the Jaruzelski regime, American policies pushed the Polish government to accept the indigenous political opposition as rightful partners to the political process. These policies, however, only worked in coordination with America's allies.

In terms of American policy vis-à-vis the opposition movement, the nature of American support shows that American policy makers in the White House, on Capitol Hill, and at the American embassy in Warsaw did not unduly influence the situation. Neither Reagan nor any other American played a leadership role. The opposition did not come to power by following dictates from Americans. Instead, the United States played a much humbler role, with NGOs providing money and support to the opposition to use as it saw fit. The specific paths and targets of American aid did influence internal discussions of how best to reform the Polish system. Segments of the opposition came to depend on American aid, but that support was provided according to the opposition's own needs and wants. Ultimately, Wałęsa and the wider opposition movement triumphed not because of outside influences, but because of their own agency, dynamism, and domestic support. The triumph of American policy in the 1980s was empowering a subset of the indigenous Polish opposition that deserves credit for overthrowing the Communist system.

# APPENDIX

### National Endowment for Democracy Funds Granted
### for Work inside Poland, 1984–1989

| Fiscal Year | Grant Recipient | Purpose | Amount |
|---|---|---|---|
| 1984 | AFL-CIO Free Trade Union Institute | To support the Solidarność trade union through the Coordinating Office in Brussels | ±$300,000 |
| 1984 | Committee in Support of Solidarity/Institute for Democracy in Eastern Europe | To provide financial assistance to the democratic opposition, distribute books and pamphlets already in publication, and publish and distribute a book of documents that tell the story of Solidarity in Czech, Hungarian, Russian, and Ukrainian | $91,250 |
| 1984 | Polish Institute for Arts and Sciences in America | To provide assistance to political prisoners, and to assist in maintaining independent cultural, educational, and scholarly activities | $90,000 |
| 1984 | International Freedom to Publish Committee of the Association of American Publishers | To support the publication and distribution of *Zeszyty Literackie* | $6,000 |
| **Total 1984** | | | **±$487,250** |
| 1985 | AFL-CIO Free Trade Union Institute | To support the Committee for the Support of Solidarity for the translation and publication of documents on workers and human rights. Support was also provided for individual Polish exiles in Europe and for the Coordinating Office of Solidarność Abroad to collect detailed information on the state of the Solidarność trade union and to enable Solidarność to communicate with its members inside Poland. | $540,000 |
| 1985 | Aurora Foundation | To assist the work of the Polish Legal Defense Fund | $50,000 |
| 1985 | Freedom House | To assist the Committee for Independent Culture (OKN) | $10,000 |

| | | | |
|---|---|---|---|
| 1985 | Aurora Foundation | To publish one issue of *Zeszyty Literackie* | $6,000 |
| **Total 1985** | | | **$606,000** |
| 1986 | AFL-CIO Free Trade Union Institute | To support the Solidarność union through the Coordinating Office in Brussels and to the Committee in Support of Solidarity to translate and publish material on worker and human rights-related issues from the Solidarity press. | $304,163 |
| 1986 | Polish American Congress Charitable Foundation | To provide material assistance to political prisoners and their families ($90,000), support for the activities of OKN ($100,000), support for the Polish Helsinki Watch Committee ($5,000), support for independent video productions ($50,000), purchase of a minivan to distribute humanitarian assistance to political prisoners and their families (8,000), and administrative costs ($10,000) | $263,000 |
| 1986 | Freedom House | To assist four journals distributed through Eastern Europe: *ANEKS Quarterly, Uncensored Poland News Bulletin, Internal Contradictions in the USSR,* and various publications of the Independent Polish Agency ($96,400); to provide additional assistance to the Independent Polish Agency to collect Western press and make it available in Poland ($30,800) | $127,200 |
| 1986 | Institute for Democracy in Eastern Europe | To support the activities of the Consortium of Independent Publishers, independent publications, and self-education and human rights groups | $123,000 |
| 1986 | Aurora Foundation | To assist the work of the Polish Legal Defense Fund (±$70,000) and for the publication of four issues of *Zeszyty Literackie* (±$20,000) | $92,400 |
| 1986 | Polish Institute of Arts and Sciences in America | To publish in Polish three books on the development of democracy in Poland | $25,000 |
| **Total 1986** | | | **$934,763** |
| 1987 | International Rescue Committee | To purchase medical supplies and medicine for the Solidarność Social Fund | $1,000,000† |

| | | | |
|---|---|---|---|
| 1987 | AFL-CIO Free Trade Union Institute | To assist Solidarność through the Coordinating Office in Brussels, and to allow the Committee in Support of Solidarity to translate and publish material on worker and human rights-related issues from the underground Solidarność press | $412,750 |
| 1987 | Polish American Congress Charitable Foundation | For assistance to political activists and their families ($90,000), support for OKN ($100,000), the Polish Helsinki Watch ($10,000), POLCUL ($15,000), the Independent Video Movement ($50,000), and *Zeszyty Literackie* ($20,000), and administrative costs ($10,000) | $295,000 |
| 1987 | Institute for Democracy in Eastern Europe | For assistance to the Consortium of Independent Publishers and support to independent publishing and human rights | $116,000 |
| 1987 | Freedom House | For support to ANEKS in London and the *Uncensored Poland News Bulletin* | $55,000 |
| 1987 | Solidarity Endowment/Polish American Congress Charitable Foundation | To support the Independent Polish Agency ($39,000) and for administrative costs ($3,000) | $42,000 |
| **Total 1987** | | | **$1,920,750** |
| 1988 | AFL-CIO Free Trade Union Institute | To administer funds appropriated by the U.S. Congress to provide assistance to the independent Polish trade union Solidarność for disseminating information, sustaining union activists, and maintaining its administrative infrastructure | $1,000,000† |
| 1988 | AFL-CIO Free Trade Union Institute | To assist Solidarność through the Coordinating Office in Brussels, and to support the Institute for Democracy in Eastern Europe to translate and publish material on worker and human rights–related issues from the underground Solidarność press | $375,000 |
| 1988 | Polish American Congress Charitable Foundation | To provide assistance to political activists and their families ($90,000), for OKN ($100,000), the Polish Helsinki Watch ($10,000), POLCUL ($15,000), *Zeszyty Literackie* ($24,000), publication of *Death in the Forest* ($10,000), a traveling Polish exhibit ($4,000), and administrative costs | $263,000 |

| | | | |
|---|---|---|---|
| 1988 | Institute for Democracy in Eastern Europe | To support a broad range of independent publications in Czechoslovakia, Hungary, and Poland, through the Fund for Independent Publishing ($195,000 in total funds were allocated for all of Eastern Europe. This approximation is based on previous IDEE programs in Poland.) | ±$120,000 |
| 1988 | Polish American Congress Charitable Foundation | To assist the Independent Poland Agency in supporting independent democratic groups, particularly the independent press | $42,000 |
| 1988 | Freedom House | To enable the London-based Information Centre for Polish Affairs to publish *Uncensored Poland News Bulletin* | $27,500 |
| **Total 1988** | | | **$±1,827,500** |
| 1989 | AFL-CIO Free Trade Union Institute | To provide assistance to Solidarność in disseminating information, sustaining union activists, and maintaining its administrative infrastructure | $1,000,000† |
| 1989 | International Rescue Committee | To assist Solidarność in maintaining a social fund established to provide medical assistance and related services to workers and their families. Funds are used to purchase medical supplies and equipment, to support the SOS Coordination Pologne (a Paris-based committee that provides health treatment for Poles), and to establish health-care and social services for children of members of Solidarność. | $1,000,000† |
| 1989 | AFL-CIO Free Trade Union Institute | To support the independent trade union movement through the Brussels-based Coordinating Office of Solidarność Abroad to disseminate information in the West on trade union rights in Poland and to assist union activities inside Poland. Support is also provided for the New York–based Institute for Democracy in Eastern Europe to translate and publish materials on worker and human rights–related issues inside Poland and other East European countries. In addition, assistance is given to others engaged in support work for Solidarność publications in Poland. | $435,000 |

| 1989 | Polish American Congress Charitable Foundation | To administer seven projects designed to support the democratic movement: OKN ($90,000), Polish Helsinki Watch Committee ($25,000), the POLCUL Foundation ($25,000), *Zeszyty Literackie* ($24,000), independent video productions ($40,000), the *Uncensored Poland News Bulletin* ($25,000), and the Independent Poland Agency ($39,000) with administrative fees ($10,000) | $263,000 |
| --- | --- | --- | --- |
| 1989 | Institute for Democracy in Eastern Europe | To continue its activities in support of democracy in Eastern Europe through assistance to independent publishing houses and self-education and human rights groups. The grant provides the Consortium for Independent Publishing with funds for equipment, supplies, and personnel. | $177,000 |
| 1989 | Columbia University | To sponsor the Study Group on Polish Reform, a series of conferences with six leading economists from the United States, Great Britain, Canada, Switzerland, and Poland, recommending a plan for Poland's economic reconstruction | $108,868§ |
| 1989 | National Democratic Institute for International Affairs | To sponsor an international conference on "The Role of Parliaments in Developing National Economic Policy," providing Polish parliamentarians an opportunity to learn the means used by legislatures in other countries to consider economic issues and develop national economic policy. Participants included sixty-five Polish parliamentarians and eleven Western European parliamentarians from across the political spectrum, as well as a five-member U.S. congressional delegation led by Walter Mondale and Howard Baker. | $82,678 |
| 1989 | Center for International Private Enterprise | To develop a program of assistance to the Kraków Industrial Society | $42,500§ |
| 1989 | Polish American Congress Charitable Foundation | To support the Foundation in Support of Local Democracy to create democratic government institutions at a local level, cultivate informed participation in political life, and distribute instructional materials and working papers on local affairs | $42,500§ |

| | | | |
|---|---|---|---|
| 1989 | AFL-CIO Free Trade Union Institute | To fund independent video production through the Gdańsk Video Center | $30,000§ |
| 1989 | Institute for Democracy in Eastern Europe | To assist the Association for Free Speech, which was formed by the Consortium of Independent Publishers, to facilitate the expansion of independent publishing | $30,000§ |
| 1989 | Polish American Congress Charitable Foundation | To support the publication of *Gazeta Wyborcza* | $30,000§ |
| 1989 | AFL-CIO Free Trade Union Institute | To sponsor a three-year teacher-training program in conjunction with Teachers' Solidarity, which will allow the social studies curriculum to be systematically revised to reflect the principles and practices of democracy | $24,000 |
| 1989 | National Republican Institute for International Affairs | To provide a grant to the Kraków Chapter of Freedom and Peace (WiP) for the translation and publication of works by modern conservative intellectuals and the eventual production of a quarterly journal of opinion | $20,000 |
| 1989 | Center for International Private Enterprise | To develop a program of assistance to the Kraków Industrial Society, one of the founders of Economic Action, the Warsaw-based umbrella organization representing Poland's emerging industries | $19,275 |

| | |
|---|---|
| **Total 1989** | **$3,304,821** |
| **Total 1984–1989** | **$9,081,084** |

† was directly appropriated by Congress, not part of the NED's annual budget.
± is an approximation.
§ was funded by a grant from U.S. Agency for International Development, not part of the NED's annual budget.
This appendix is based primarily on NED Annual Reports available in the National Endowment for Democracy Headquarters Library.

# NOTES

## Abbreviations in Notes

AAN  Archiwum Akt Nowych or Archive of Modern Records
AFL-CIO  AFL-CIO unprocessed records, access granted with the permission of the AFL-CIO's Secretary-Treasurer's office
CBOS  Centrum Badanii Opinia Spóleczny or Center for Public Opinion Research
CRS  Catholic Relief Services Archive
CSS  Committee in Support of Solidarity office files
FCO  United Kingdom Foreign and Commonwealth Office
GBPL  George H. W. Bush Presidential Library
GMMA  George Meany Memorial Archives
Hoover  Hoover Institution Archives
IPN  Instytut Pamięci Narodowej or Institute of National Remembrance
ISPPAN  Instytut Studiów Politycznych Polski Akademii Nauk or Institute of Political Studies of the Polish Academy of Sciences
KARTA  Karta Archives
KM  Kolekcja Miedzeszyn or Miedzeszyn conference collection
MSZ  Polish Ministry of Foreign Affairs Archive
NED  National Endowment for Democracy headquarters library
NSA  National Security Archive
PAC  Polish American Congress Washington office files
PPUS  *Public Papers of the President of the United States*, available online at http://www.presidency.ucsb.edu
RRPL  Ronald Reagan Presidential Library

NOTE: Other specialized abbreviations specific to the collections being referenced are used throughout the notes without explanation. They will be clear to people working in those archives.

## Introduction

1. "Address by the Honorable Lech Wałęsa, Chairman, Solidarność," *Congressional Record*, vol. 136, no. 60, 101st Cong. 1st Sess., H8632-H8635; quoted at H8634.

2. Neil Lewis, "Clamor in the East: Gratitude and a Request," *New York Times* (Sept. 16, 1989), A1.

3. The classic study on U.S.-Polish relations is Wandycz's *The United States and Poland*, which ends before the rise of Solidarność. On U.S. policy toward Poland, see Davis, "Some Reflections on 1989" and "Postwar Relations."

4. There are two books focused particularly on Poland's position in the Cold War during the 1980s: Rachwald, *In Search of Poland*, and Rensenbrink, *Poland Challenges a Divided World*. These books were written without significant access to declassified material. For the best short essay on this topic, see Paczkowski, "Playground of the Superpowers."

There is also a significant amount of scholarship on the Polish crisis of 1980–81 and its international context, most notably in Kramer, *Soviet Deliberations during the Polish Crisis*; MacEachin, *U.S. Intelligence and Confrontation in Poland*; Mastny, *Soviet Non-Invasion of Poland*; Ouimet, *The Rise and Fall of the Brezhnev Doctrine*; Paczkowski and Werblan, "On the Decision to Introduce Martial Law"; and Paczkowski and Byrne, *From Solidarity to Martial Law*.

Foundational books on the international context of American policy at the end of the Cold War include, in particular, Garthoff, *Détente and Confrontation* and *Great Transition*; and Beschloss and Talbott, *At the Highest Levels*. For a more recent analysis, see Mann, *Rebellion of Ronald Reagan*. Sarotte's book, *1989*, is the best regarding American policy during the revolutions of 1989 and the Bush administration's policy regarding German unification. While each of these books refers and relates to events in Poland, that country remains a secondary topic to the superpower confrontation.

5. For studies that focus on Gorbachev's thinking and the Soviet role in the revolutions of 1989, see in particular Kramer, "The Collapse of East European Communism," parts 1–3; Brown, *Gorbachev Factor*; Levesque, *Enigma of 1989*; and Zubok, "Gorbachev and the End of the Cold War," in Wohlforth, *Cold War Endgame*.

6. For the twentieth anniversary of the revolutions of 1989, a number of narrative accounts were published chronicling events and drawing connections between them. See in particular Meyer, *The Year That Changed the World*; Pleshakov, *There Is No Freedom without Bread*; and Sebestyen, *Revolution 1989*. Garton Ash's *Magic Lantern* and *Uses of Adversity* remain useful classics. Works by political scientists, like Gati's *The Bloc That Failed* and Stokes's *The Walls Came Tumbling Down*, provide insights into the regional story of 1989. Kotkin and Gross, *Uncivil Society*, is the best recent synthesis of the dynamics of these revolutions. Kenney's contribution on the transnational nature of the revolutions of 1989 is the best work of its kind. See Kenney and Horn, *Transnational Moments of Change*. There are also a number of recent works focused on the creation of transnational human rights networks throughout the Soviet Union and Eastern Europe. See in particular Snyder, *Human Rights Activism*, and Thomas, *The Helsinki Effect*.

7. The best single-volume English-language analysis of Poland's internal transformation remains Paczkowski, *Spring*. Other particularly useful English-language sources on the dynamics of change during the 1980s include Castle, *Triggering Communism's Collapse*; Kenney, *Carnival of Revolution*; and Ost, *Politics of Anti-Politics*. The best Polish-language surveys are Dudek, *Reglamentowana rewolucja*; Garlicki, *Karuzela*; and Skórzyński, *Rewolucja Okrągłego Stołu*. For broad studies of the opposition underground, see Friszke, *Solidarność Podziemna*; and Łopiński, Moskit, and Wilk, *Konspira*.

8. On the American side, Zbigniew Brzeziński, Alexander Haig, George Shultz, John Whitehead, Lane Kirkland, Richard Pipes, Robert Gates, George H. W. Bush, and Brent Scowcroft have all written memoirs that contain useful references to Poland policy. On the Polish side, Wojciech Jaruzelski, Mieczysław Rakowski, as well as an ever-growing list of opposition politicians including Wałęsa, Kuroń, Michnik, and Geremek, have all written useful memoirs. Gorbachev's writings as well as works by Anatoly Chernyaev are enlightening on Soviet policy.

9. "Triumphalist" accounts of the end of the Cold War—scholarship that emphasizes American agency in beating the Soviet Union to conclude the Cold War—often highlight the

Reagan administration's policy toward Poland as an offshoot of the Reagan Doctrine to support freedom fighters, and as part of his overall goal to undermine Soviet and Communist power around the world. The most forthright scholar of this triumphalist view is Schweizer. See his books, *Reagan's War* and *Victory*. This strain of scholarship has also been championed by public historians. In his best-selling book, *Cold War*, Gaddis argues that "promoting democracy became the most visible way that the Americans and their West European allies could differentiate themselves" from their Communist opponents, and was therefore a central and effective part of policy that lead to the Cold War ending with the United States emerging as the only remaining superpower (225). One need only look at the laudatory coverage (both in America and abroad) of Ronald Reagan following his death in 2004 to get a sense of how pervasive this view has become. As an example, the cover of the international edition of the *Economist* featured a picture of Reagan with the simple title, "Ronald Reagan: The Man Who Beat Communism" (June 10, 2004). While antitriumphalist accounts highlighting the limitations of U.S. power in the revolutions of 1989 are widespread, triumphalism maintains its legitimacy in both public and policy circles. As Mel Leffler has argued, the triumphalist misperception that American leadership somehow catalyzed the revolutions of 1989 has influenced later foreign policy decision making. See his "Dreams of Freedom, Temptations of Power," in Engel, *The Fall of the Berlin Wall*.

 10. Within the text, the term "bilateral relations" refers to U.S. governmental policy toward the PZPR.


## Chapter 1

 1. As quoted in Haig, *Caveat*, 248.

 2. In his memoirs, the NSC staff member Richard Pipes writes about a lack of knowledge of intelligence on martial law. See *Vixi*, 169–70. For the quote from Haig, see *Caveat*, 248. Richard V. Allen had left the White House staff Washington and would not be replaced by William Clark until January 5, 1982.

 3. On the links to earlier revolts see, Curry and Fajfer, *Poland's Permanent Revolution*.

 4. On the roots of Solidarność and the strikes of 1980, see in particular Bernhard, *Origins of Democratization*; Staniszkis, *Poland's Self-Limiting Revolution*; and Zuzowski, *Political Dissent and Opposition*.

 5. Paczkowski, *Spring*, 412–13.

 6. David Ost, *Solidarity and the Politics of Anti-politics*, 106–7. The name of the National Coordinating Commission, or Krajowa Komisja Porozumiewawcza, later changed, as did the regional structures.

 7. Paczkowski, *Spring*, 442.

 8. For an analysis on the role of the church see sections seven and eight of Dudek and Gryz, *Komuniści I Kościół w Polsce*. For documents on state-church relations, see *Tajne dokumenty: Państwo-Kościół 1980–1989*; as well as numerous works by Raina in the bibliography. For the quote see Paczkowski, *Spring*, 420.

 9. See "CPSU CC Politburo Commission Order to Enhance Readiness of Military Units for Possible Use in Poland, August 28, 1980," in Paczkowski and Byrne, *From Solidarity to Martial Law*, 64–65.

 10. Kramer, "The Warsaw Pact and the Polish Crisis of 1980–81," 124.

11. "Stenographic Minutes of the Meeting of Leading Representatives of the Warsaw Pact Countries," 118.

12. "Memorandum regarding the meeting between Comrade Leonid Ilyish Brezhnev, Eric Honecker, and Gustav Husák," 129; and "Transcript of the Meeting Between Comrade L.I. Brezhnev and Comrade E. Honecker," 133. For a full exploration of East German policy toward Poland during the Polish crisis, see Kubina and Wilke, *"Hart und kompromisslos."*

13. For an overview of these events, see the introductory essay as well as specific Polish, Soviet, and Warsaw Pact documents from December 1980 and March 1981 in Paczkowski and Byrne, *From Solidarity to Martial Law.*

14. The question of whether the Soviet Union was planning to invade Poland during the crisis has been the focus of many of the studies. See particularly Kramer, *Soviet Deliberations during the Polish Crisis*; Mastny, *Soviet Non-invasion of Poland*; Ouimet, *Rise and Fall of the Brezhnev Doctrine*; Domber, "The Rise and Fall of the Brezhnev Doctrine"; Paczkowski and Werblan, "'On the Decision to Introduce Martial Law'"; Loth, "Moscow, Prague, and Warsaw"; and *Wejdą nie Wejdą.*

15. See Paczkowski and Byrne, *From Solidarity to Martial Law*, 123–28.

16. "Protocol No. 002/81 of a Meeting of the Homeland Defense Committee," dated September 13, 1981, ibid., 350–56.

17. "Situation in Poland Statement by the President," dated December 3, 1980, in *PPUS* (1980).

18. Paczkowski and Byrne, *From Solidarity to Martial Law*, xxxvi.

19. For an excellent overview of the Carter administration's policy toward Poland during this period, see Vaughan, "Beyond Benign Neglect."

20. For the quote, see NSC Briefing Memorandum, "Economic Aid to Poland," dated July 6, 1981, RRPL, Executive Secretariat NSPG, Box 1, NSPG 0019 July 14, 1981. For the decision on corn sales, see Memorandum for the President from Richard V. Allen, "NSPG Meeting, 9:30–10:00, Wednesday, July 22, 1981," RRPL, Executive Secretariat NSPG, Box 1, NSPG 0020 July 22, 1981 (1 of 2).

21. For an overview of the increase in superpower tensions, see Garthoff, *Great Transition*, 7–53; and Gaddis, *Russia, the Soviet Union, and the United States*, 295–320. For West European views of this trend in American policy, see Sjursen, *United States, Western Europe, and the Polish Crisis*, 32–36.

22. For the best exploration of the Reagan administration's relationship with Pope John Paul II, see Bernstein and Politi, *His Holiness*; particularly on the Polish crisis, 260–88, 280–82; Allen quoted at 270.

23. Ost, *Poliics of Anti-politics*, 134.

24. For the transcripts of the congress, see Sanford, *Solidarity Congress.*

25. Ost, *Politics of Anti-poliics*, 114.

26. On General Jaruzelski's state of mind prior to implementing martial law, see his *Stan wojenny. Dlaczego*, esp. 1–10 and 377–405; Jaruzelski, "Commentary"; Kramer, "Jaruzelski, the Soviet Union, and the Imposition of Martial Law"; Kramer, "Anoshkin Notebook"; and Kramer, *Kukliński Files*, 13–14.

27. Kukliński first gave details of his work in an interview from 1987, reprinted as "The Suppression of Solidarity," in Kostrzewa, *Between East and West*, 72–98. For his state of mind before asking to be removed, see 92–94.

28. For comprehensive information on Kukliński's life and reporting on martial law, see Weiser, *Secret Life.*

29. In December 2008, the CIA published a CD with eighty-one newly declassified documents from its Kukliński files, a small portion of the material Kukliński wrote for the CIA. See, Kramer, *Kukliński Files*, esp. 36–40.

30. Department of State Memo, "U.S. Policy Response to Use of Force by the Polish Government against the Polish People," dated January 28, 1981, NSA, Soviet Flashpoints Originals, Box 4. Robert Gates has written that he authored a brief on January 23, 1981, on the possibility "that the Poles would enforce coercive measures themselves as a way to keep the Soviets out." See Gates, *From the Shadows*, 228.

31. "Statement by the Press Secretary on the Situation in Poland, March 26, 1981," *PPUS* (1981). In Warsaw, this and other statements warning against the use of force against the Polish people were consistently monitored by the Polish Ministry of Foreign Affairs from late winter 1981 onward. See a number of reports from Department III to high-level PZPR officials, including the minister of foreign affairs, in "Stosunki Bilateralne PRL-USA" [Bilateral U.S.-PRL Relations], MSZ, 49/84, W-1, Dep III (1981), AP 22-1-81; and "Stanowisko USA Wobec Sytuacji w Polsce" [U.S. Position on the Situation in Poland], MSZ, 49/84, W-1, Dep III (1981), AP 22-1-81.

32. Memorandum from Alexander Haig to the Vice President, "Your Meeting with First Deputy Prime Minister Jagielski," dated April 1, 1981, RRPL, Dobriansky Files, Box 3, Poland Memorandum 1981–1983 [February–May 1981].

33. Memorandum of Conversation, "Summary of the Vice President's Meeting with First Deputy Prime Minister Jagielski," dated April 2, 1981, RRPL, Dobriansky Files, Box 3, Poland Memorandum 1981–1983 [February–May 1981].

34. Memorandum from Richard Allen to the First Lady, "Your Tea with Madame Jablonska," dated May 12, 1981, RRPL, Dobriansky Files, Box 1 [90577], Chron Files [Chron 05/12/1981–05/14/1981].

35. Notatka Informacyjna z rozmowy z charge d affairs HE Wilgisem z 19 bm [Information Note from the Conversation with H. E. Wilgis on the 19th of this month], dated September 19, 1981, MSZ, 49/84, W-1, Dep III (1981), AP 22-1-81/B. Unless otherwise noted, all translations of Polish documents and sources are by the author.

36. *Wejdą nie wejdą*, 290.

37. Ibid., 308.

38. Author's interview with Lee Kjelleran, November 20, 2007, New York.

39. Sprawozdanie z pobytu służbowego w Stanach Zjednoczonych AP w dniach od 14 do 19 wreśnia [Report from an Official Trip to the United States from 14 to 19 September], MSZ, 49/84, W-1, Dep III (1981), AP 22-1-81.

40. "Komisja Mieszana D/S Handlu X Sesja" [Tenth Session of the Joint Commission of the Department of Trade], Wizyta Wicepremiere Jagielskiego w USA [Visit by Vice Premier Jagielski to the U.S.A.], Wyzyta Wicepremiera Z Sladeja w USA [Visit by Vice Premier Z Sladej to the U.S.A.], "Memo from A. Karas, September 25, 1981," both in MSZ, 49/84, W-2, Dep III (1981), AP 23-8-81. "Effective program of stabilization" is underlined in the Polish original.

41. The KGB learned that the plans for martial law had been leaked and informed the Poles, who began a search for the source of the leak. See Kramer, *Kukliński Files*, 1.

42. Briefing Memorandum from H. Allen Holmes to Amb Stoessel, "Your Meeting with Polish Deputy Prime Minister Zbigniew Madej, December 7," NSA, Soviet Flashpoints Originals, Box 3.

43. Notatka Informacyjna z rozmowy z Johnem Scanlanem, Zastępcą Asystenta Sekretarza Stanu d/s Europy Wschodniej w Departmencie Stanu w dniu 9 bm [Information Note from the

Conversation with John Scanlen, Deputy Assistant Secretary of State for Eastern Europe in the Department of State on the 9th of this month], MSZ, 49/84, W-2, Dep III (1981), AP 23-8-81. General Jaruzelski has mentioned that there were cables from Madej that dealt with the meeting in more detail. These "szyfrograms," if they exist, have not been declassified.

44. Notatka Informacyjna [Information Note re Madej trip to Washington, sent to Czyrek on December 17, 1981], MSZ, 49/81, W-2, Dep III (1981), AP 23-08-81.

45. Memorandum from Richard Allen to the Vice President, "Your Meeting with Polish First Deputy Prime Minister Mieczysław Jagielski," dated April 2, 1981, RRPL, Dobriansky Files, Box 3, Poland Memorandum 1981–1983 [February–May 1981]. See the analysis of defense reactions to a Soviet intervention based on meetings on March 31 and April 7, 1981, in Memorandum from Robert Blackwill to Distribution, "IG Meeting on Politico-Military Responses to Soviet Military Intervention in Poland," dated December 13, 1981, RRPL, Pipes Files, Box 3, NSC Meetings: Senior Intergovernmental Group December 18, 1981 [Poland].

46. MacEachin, *U.S. Intelligence and the Polish Crisis*, 195.

47. Memorandum from Richard Allen, "National Security Council Meeting, February 11, 1981," RRPL, Dobriansky Files, Box 3, Poland Memorandum 1981–1983 [Feburary–May 1981].

48. For an example of American analysis on Jaruzelski, see "Memorandum from Lawrence Eagleburger to Secretary of State, 'General Wojciech Jaruzelski,' December 16, 1981," in Paczkowski and Byrne, *From Solidarity to Martial Law*, 478–79. This analysis of Jaruzelski was shared by the British well into the mid-1980s. See Briefing Memorandum, "Visit of Mr. Rifkind to Poland, 3–7 November 1984: Biography General Wojciech Jaruzelski," undated from FCO files released to the author through FOI. Roman Laba has shown that Jaruzelski's statement, "Poles will not shoot Poles," may be apocryphal.

49. Memorandum from Allen to the Vice President, "Your Meeting with Polish First Deputy Prime Minister Mieczysław Jagielski," dated April 2, 1981.

50. Davis, "Postwar Relations," 207.

51. Pipes, *Vixi*, 169–70, quoted 170. Claims that few people in the administration saw the intelligence are questioned by Kramer (*Kukliński Files*, 36–40).

52. Memorandum from Richard Pipes to Richard Allen, "Update on Poland," dated September 4, 1981, RRPL, Dobriansky Files, Box 3, Poland Memorandum 1981–1983 [July–December 1981]. For the increasing concern in June 1981, see Dobriansky's files in the same folder, Poland Memoranda 1981–1983 [June 1981].

53. As quoted in MacEachin, *U.S. Intelligence and the Polish Crisis*, 169.

54. Memorandum for the Cabinet Council on Economic Affairs from Roger B. Porter, dated November 27, 1981, NSA, Soviet Flashpoints Originals, Box 1.

55. Memorandum from Alexander M. Haig to the President, "The United States and Poland," dated November 12, 1981, RRPL, Pipes Files, Box 12, Chron 12/00/1981–12/06/1981.

56. See, "Memorandum from Alexander Haig to President Reagan, 'U.S. Assistance Program to Poland,' December 1, 1981," in Paczkowski and Byrne, *From Solidarity to Martial Law*, 409–11.

57. Memorandum from Robert M. Gates to the Director of Central Intelligence, "Assistance to Poland: Tuesday's NSC Meeting," dated December 4, 1981, NSA, Soviet Flashpoints Originals, Box 1. This sentiment was reiterated by the CIA in Memorandum, "Poland," dated December 10, 1981, NSA, Soviet Flashpoints Originals, Box 1.

58. Cable from SecState to Amembassy Bonn, "Quadripartite Dinner Highlights, December 10, 1981," dated December 11, 1981, NSA, Soviet Flashpoints Originals, Box 2.

59. Cable from Secstate Washington to Amembassy Brussels for Eagleburger/Price, dated December 11, 1982, NSA, Soviet Flashpoints Originals, Box 2.

60. Haig, *Caveat*, 248.

61. Hedrick Smith, "U.S. Stick and Carrot," *New York Times* (Dec. 18, 1981), A17.

62. Drew Middleton, "Soviet Action inside Poland Being Studied: Military Analysis" *New York Times* (Dec. 21, 1981), A19.

63. Schweizer, *Reagan's War*, 165–66.

64. Bernard Gwertzman, "The President Weighs Steps on Poland," *New York Times* (Dec. 22, 1981), A1. There were also rumors that sections of the State Department and Defense Department were relieved that the crisis had been abated without a Soviet intervention. Without access to complete records from Foggy Bottom and the Pentagon these rumors cannot be substantiated with any specificity.

65. Paczkowski, *Spring*, 450.

66. Bernstein and Politi, *His Holiness*, 340–41.

67. For a nearly complete translation of Jaruzelski's remarks, see "Text of Polish Martial Law Declaration," *United Press International* (Dec. 13, 1981). All quotes in the previous paragraph are from this text.

68. Cable from Secstate to Amembassy Warsaw, "Polish Government Statement on Situation in Poland; U.S. Suspension of Aid to Warsaw," dated December 15, 1981, NSA, Soviet Flashpoints Originals, Box 2.

69. Associated Press, Dateline Warsaw, Poland (Dec. 13, 1981, PM cycle).

70. "Some Polish Workers Defying Martial Law: Polish Workers Reported Striking Against New Rule," *Washington Post* (Dec. 15, 1981), A1.

71. Paczkowski, *Spring*, 451.

72. Wedel, *Private Poland*, 1.

73. "Press Release, Monday, December 14, 1981," GMMA, AFL-CIO Press Releases 1981 (December), Box 47, Folder 47/6.

74. "West Rallies Behind Solidarity," *United Press International* (Dec. 13, 1981).

75. Loren Jenkins, "Western Europeans Demonstrate against Crackdown in Poland," *Washington Post* (Dec. 14, 1981), A19.

76. John Goshko and Don Oberdorfer, "Wałęsa Is Summoned to Warsaw: U.S. Expresses 'Serious Concern' to Poland and Russia," *Washington Post* (Dec. 14, 1981), A1.

77. Leonard Downy Jr., "NATO Allies, Reacting Cautiously, Consult on Polish Crackdown," *Washington Post* (Dec. 14, 1981), A12.

78. Cable from Secstate to U.S. Delegation Secretary, "Under Secretary Stoessel's meeting with Bessmertnykh, December 13," dated December 13, 1981, NSA, Soviet Flashpoints Originals, Box 1.

79. Department of State Memo, "U.S. Policy Response to Use of Force by the Polish Government against the Polish People," dated January 28, 1981. It is interesting to note that a similar awareness of history shaped American signaling to the Soviets during 1980–81. National Security Adviser Zbigniew Brzeziński was keenly aware of American policy toward Hungary in 1956 and toward Czechoslovakia in 1968. He did not want to "stir up the pot" to incense the Soviets. Nor did he want to repeat the mistake of remaining quiet on the possibility of Soviet intervention for fear of promoting that outcome. "Special Coordinating Committee, Summary of Conclusions, 'Meeting on Poland,' with attachments, September 23, 1980," in Paczkowski and Byrne, *From Solidarity to Martial Law*, 87–90.

80. "Speech by Pope John Paul II Concerning Martial Law, December 13, 1981," in Paczkowski and Byrne, *From Solidarity to Martial Law*, 475.

81. As quoted in Paczkowski, *Spring*, 451.

82. Cable from Secstate to Amembassy Warsaw, "Polish Government Statement on Situation in Poland; US Suspension of Aid to Warsaw," dated December 15, 1981, NSA, Soviet Flashpoints Originals, Box 2.

83. Cable from Amembassy Warsaw to Secstate, "Meeting with Czyrek," dated December 17, 1981, NSA, Soviet Flashpoints Originals, Box 4.

84. Defense Intelligence Report, "Poland: Martial Law—Five Days After," dated December 17, 1981, NSA, Soviet Flashpoints, Box 26, December 1–22, 1981.

85. For an explanation of Reagan's embrace of the Helsinki Final Act and the CSCE process, see Snyder, *Human Rights Activism*, 135–46.

86. For a full record of President Reagan's remarks, see "President's New Conference, December 17, 1981," *PPUS* (1981).

87. Cable from Secstate to Amembassy Warsaw, "Polish Ambassador on Situation in Poland," dated December 18, 1981, NSA, Soviet Flashpoints Originals, Box 2.

88. Cable from Secstate to Amembassy Bonn, London, and Paris, "Message from the Secretary," dated December 15, 1981, NSA, Soviet Flashpoints Originals, Box 1.

89. Cable from Secstate to Amembassy Paris, London, and Bonn, "Messages for Cheysson, Carrington and Genscher from the Secretary," December 19, 1981, NSA, Soviet Flashpoints Originals, Box 2.

90. "President's New Conference, December 17, 1981," *PPUS* (1981).

91. Cable from Secstate to Amembassy Moscow and Warsaw, "Poland: Discussion with Ambassador Dobrynin December 18," dated December 22, 1981, NSA, Soviet Flashpoints Originals, Box 1.

92. For an excellent study of Reagan's long-standing views on communism and his struggle against it, see Schweizer, *Reagan's War*.

93. As quoted in Schweizer, *Reagan's War*, 166. For the full entry, dated December 21, see Reagan, *Reagan Diaries*, 57.

94. Pipes, *Vixi*, 171.

95. As quoted in Schweizer, *Reagan's War*, 165.

96. Pipes, *Vixi*, 171.

97. Memorandum for James Nance, "Discussion Paper for NSC Meeting," dated December 21, 1981, NSA, Soviet Flashpoints, Box 26, December 1–22, 1981. Almost all of these provisions are drawn from the January 1981 contingency plans for martial law. See note 30.

98. Pipes, *Vixi*, 171.

99. Memorandum for James Nance, "Discussion Paper for NSC Meeting," dated December 21, 1981.

100. Briefing Paper, "Possible Economic Sanctions against Poland," revised December 23, 1981, NSA, Soviet Flashpoints, Box 27, December 23–25, 1981.

101. Letter from Ronald Reagan to General Wojciech Jaruzelski, dated December 23, 1981, MSZ, 30/85, W-1, Dep III (1982), AP 22-2-82.

102. "Address to the Nation about Christmas and the Situation in Poland, December 23, 1981," in *PPUS* (1981).

103. Ibid.

104. A translation of the Russian version of Brezhnev's letter to Reagan can be found as "Hotline Communication from Leonid Brezhnev to Ronald Reagan Regarding Martial Law in Poland, December 25, 1981," in Paczkowski and Byrne, *From Solidarity to Martial Law*, 496-98. The quotes in this paragraph are taken from Cable from Secstate to Amembassy Moscow and Warsaw, "Brezhnev—Reagan Letter," dated December 26, 1981, NSA, Soviet Flashpoints Originals, Box 1.

105. Pipes, *Vixi*, 173.

106. Cable from Secstate to Amembassy Moscow, "Letter from Secretary Haig to Foreign Minister Gromyko," dated December 29, 1981, NSA, Soviet Flashpoints Originals, Box 2.

107. "Statement on U.S. Measures Taken against the Soviet Union Concerning Its Involvement in Poland, December 29, 1981," in *PPUS* (1981).

108. For a discussion of the decision to lift the embargo, see Garthoff, *Great Transition*, 45-46.

109. Cable from SecState to Amembassys Bonn, Paris, and London, "Poland: Message for the Foreign Minister," dated December 29, 1981, NSA, Soviet Flashpoints Originals, Box 1. As Haig explained, "We have taken no decisions that would affect the INF negotiations. The president recognizes the special character of these negotiations, and we do not intend to alter our stance under present conditions." This decision is also indicative of Reagan's emphasis on the special importance of arms reductions, even early in this first term.

110. Cable from Secstate to USMission NATO, "Guidance on Poland Contingencies," dated December 4, 1980, NSA, Soviet Flashpoints Originals, Box 1.

111. For Haig's account of these first hours see, *Caveat*, 247-51, quoted at 249. In Warsaw, the envoys from NATO countries also met to swap intelligence and analysis. Cable from Amembassy Warsaw to Secstate, "NATO Ambassadors' Report," dated December 15, 1981, NSA, Soviet Flashpoints, Box 26, December 1-22, 1981.

112. Maureen Johnson, "Deep Concern in the West, Protests at Polish Embassies," *Associated Press* (Dec. 13, 1981).

113. Mark S. Smith, "International News," *Associated Press* (Dec. 14, 1981).

114. "International," *United Press International* (Dec. 14, 1981).

115. See discussion of December 14 meeting with Ambassador Spasowski above.

116. For a more recent criticism of the European allies' reaction that reflects thinking at the time see, Schweizer, *Victory*. For a broader discussion of West European statements and transatlantic tensions, see Sjursen, *The United States, Western Europe, and the Polish Crisis*, esp. 63-89.

117. Cable from Secstate to Amembassy Bonn, London, and Paris, "Message from the Secretary," dated December 15, 1981.

118. Action Memorandum from Lawrence Eagleburger to the Secretary, "Consultations with the Allies on Poland," dated December 18, 1981, from Byrne, Machcewicz, and Ostermann, *Poland 1980-1982*.

119. Cable from Secstate to USMission NATO, "Poland: Dec 16 NAC on 'Gray Area' Scenarios," NSA, Soviet Flashpoints Originals, Box 1.

120. Ibid.

121. Sjursen, *The United States, Western Europe, and the Polish Crisis*, 63.

122. Cable from USMission NATO to Secstate, "Poland: NAC Discussion on Allied Public Posture," dated December 19, 1981, NSA, Flashpoints Originals, Box 1.

123. Cable from Secstate to Amembassy Paris, London, and Bonn, "Message for Cheysson, Carrington, and Genscher from the Secretary," dated December 19, 1981, NSA, Soviet Flashpoints Originals, Box 2.

124. Cable from Secstate to Amembassies Paris, London, and Bonn, "Message for Mitterand, Thatcher, and Schmidt from the President," dated December 20, 1981, NSA, Soviet Flashpoints Originals, Box 2.

125. Michael Getler, "U.S. Seeks European Support for Moves Directed at Soviet Union," *Washington Post* (Dec. 22, 1981), A12. On December 30, Reagan personally followed through with this push to keep papal support for sanctions by sending a letter requesting that the pope use his influence to "stress these truths to the leaders of the West." Cable from SecState to Amembassy Rome, "Presidential Letter to the Pope on Poland," dated December 30, 1981, RRPL, Executive Secretariat, NSC: Head of State File: Records 1981–1989, Box 41, The Vatican: Pope John Paul II Cables [1 of 2].

126. No declassified record of Eagleburger's meeting with the pope or Colombo exists. For the American attitude on bringing the Italians into the quad, see Cable from Amembassy Brussels to Secstate, "Eagleburger-Genscher Meeting on Poland, December 21," dated December 22, 1981, NSA Soviet Flashpoints Originals, Box 4.

127. Cable from Amembassy Brussels to Secstate, "My Meeting with Genscher," dated December 21, 1981, NSA, Soviet Flashpoints Originals, Box 1.

128. Cable from Amembassy Brussels to Secstate, "Eagleburger-Genscher Meeting on Poland, December 21."

129. Cable from Amembassy Brussels to Secstate, "My Meeting with Genscher," dated December 21, 1981.

130. See Cable from Secstate info to Amembassy Tokyo, "(U) Poland: NAC Discussion December 23," dated December 30, 1981; and Cable from Secstate info to Amembassy Tokyo, "Poland: December 23 NAC Consultations," dated December 30, 1981; both in NSA, Soviet Flashpoints Originals, Box 4.

131. The ministerial-level meeting was agreed to at a December 30 meeting of the NAC. For American efforts to influence European public opinion, see Memo from Alexander Haig to the President, "Influencing European Attitudes on Poland," dated December 26, 1981, in Byrne, Machcewicz, and Ostermann, *Poland 1980–1982*. For direct lobbying efforts see Cable from Sesctate to EC Collective, "Secretary's December 28 Luncheon Meeting with EC-10 Ambassadors in Washington," dated December 30, 1981, NSA, Soviet Flashpoints Originals, Box 4.

132. "Protocol No. 16 of PUWP CC Politburo Meeting, December 19, 1981," in Paczkowski and Byrne, *From Solidarity to Martial Law*, 482–95; quote on 483.

133. For Rakowski's account of the meeting and quoted comments, see his published diaries, *Dzienniki polityczne 1981–1983*, 151–52.

134. Memorandum from Alexander M. Haig to the President, "Visit of Helmut Schmidt, Chancellor of the Federal Republic of Germany, January 5, 1982," dated December 31, 1981, NSA, Soviet Flashpoints, Box 27, December 1981. See also Haig's memo after meeting with Schmidt: Memorandum from Alexander M. Haig to the President, "Your Meeting with Chancellor Schmidt," dated January 5, 1982, NSA, Soviet Flashpoints, Box 27, January 1982.

135. "Joint Statement Following a Meeting with Chancellor Helmut Schmidt of the Federal Republic of Germany, January 5, 1982," *PPUS* (1982).

136. See, for example, Reginald Dale, "Reagan Demands 'Tangible' Allied Moves on Poland," *Financial Times* (Jan. 6, 1982), A1; as well as Don Oberdorfer, "Haig Silent on Future Sanctions," *Washington Post* (Jan. 7, 1982), A1.

137. Memorandum of Conversation, "Secretary Haig's Breakfast Meeting with FRG Chancellor Schmidt," dated January 6, 1982, NSA, Soviet Flashpoints, Box 27, January 1982.

138. For Haig's appraisal of the possibility for actions before his meeting with Schmidt, see Action Memorandum from Lawrence Eagleburger to the Secretary, "Memorandum for the President on Poland, and Next Steps with the Allies," dated January 4, 1982, NSA, Soviet Flashpoints, Box 27, January 1982. For the initial text of the proposed NATO declaration, see Action Memorandum from H. Allen Holmes to the Secretary, "The Alliance Declaration on Poland," dated January 5, 1982, published in Byrne, Machciewicz, and Ostermann, *Poland 1980-1982*. For the approved text, see Action Memorandum from H. Allen Holmes to the Secretary, "Revised NATO Ministerial Declaration," dated January 6, 1982, NSA, Soviet Flashpoints, Box 27, January 1982.

139. Pipes, *Vixi*, 177.

140. Complete American records of the January 10-12 NAC have not been declassified. These statements are made based on the briefing materials and contingency plans created for Haig's trip. Those records can be found in NSA, Soviet Flashpoints, Box 27, January 1982.

141. For the full text of the January 11 NAC Ministerial Communiqué, see the NATO website (http://www.nato.intdocu/comm/49-95/c820111a.htm).

142. James Reston, "Haig's Verbal Success," *New York Times* (Jan. 12, 1982), A23.

143. Paczkowski and Byrne, *From Solidarity to Martial Law*, 514.

144. Ibid., 32.

145. See Paczkowski, *Spring*, 420.

146. For a discussion of the spread of pluralism within the party, see Paczkowski and Byrne, *From Solidarity to Martial Law*, 12-13. For a representative discussion of Jaruzelski's desire to reform the party following the imposition of martial law, see "Protocol No. 16 of PUWP CC Politburo Meeting, December 19, 1981," ibid., 482-95.

147. "Protocol No. 19 of PUWP CC Politburo Meeting, December 13, 1981," ibid., 461-72; quote on 468.

148. "Extract from Protocol No. 40 from CPSU CC Politburo Meeting, December 13, 1981," ibid., 473-74.

149. Tuma, "The Czechoslovak Communist Regime," 62.

150. For the Hungarian view of these meetings, see, "Hungarian Report to HSWP CC Politburo on Hungarian Delegation's Talks with Wojciech Jaruzelski, December 30, 1981," in Paczkowski and Byrne, *From Solidarity to Martial Law*, 499-503.

151. Tischler, "The Hungarian Party Leadership," 79.

152. "Transcript of CPSU CC Politburo Meeting, January 14, 1981," in Paczkowski and Byrne, *From Solidarity to Martial Law*, 504-7.

153. "Protocol No. 19 of PUWP CC Politburo Meeting, December 13, 1981," ibid., 461-72; quote on 470.

154. "Protocol No. 16 of PUWP CC Politburo Meeting, December 19, 1981," ibid., 482-95; quote on 483.

155. "Hungarian Report to HSWP CC Politburo on Hungarian Delegation's Talks with Wojciech Jaruzelski, December 30, 1981," ibid., 499-503; quote on 501-2.

156. Author's interview with Zbigniew Karcz, July 8, 2004. Karcz was the director of the international department of the Ministry of Finance from 1976 to 1987.

157. For a full discussion of the neoconservative plans to wage economic war against the Soviet Union, see Schweizer, *Victory*.

158. *Wejdą nie wejdą*, 283.

159. Ibid., 283-84.

160. In *Wejdą nie wejdą*, the issue of Jaruzelski's expectations following the Madej meeting took center stage, with the general commenting on the Reagan administration's inability to send him even a private letter to dissuade him from introducing martial law. The clear question that arises from this discussion, and which James Hershberg asked at the conference, was, would the general not have declared martial law if the Americans had clearly signaled that they would take a very strong, punitive stance in reaction? Jaruzelski did not respond directly to that question. This remains, however, a fascinating possibility. For discussion of this issue, see *Wejdą nie wejdą*, 282–83 and 324–26.

161. Notatka Informacyjna Obecne Stanowisko USA wobec Polski [Information Note on the Present Position of the USA Regarding Poland], dated December 21, 1981, MSZ, 49/84, W-1, Dep III (1981), AP 22-1-81/B.

162. "Protocol No. 16 of PUWP CC Politburo Meeting, December 19, 1981," in Paczkowski and Byrne, *From Solidarity to Martial Law*, 482–95; quote on 483.

163. *Wejdą nie wejdą*, 314.

164. Ibid., 223.

165. Tyler and Kramer, "Whither Trust," 12.

166. Bies and Tripp, "Beyond Distrust," 248.

167. Ibid., 254.

## Chapter 2

1. The quote in the chapter title is from General Wojciech Jaruzelski from an excerpt from the transcript of a May 25, 1982, PZPR Central Committee Meeting, AAN, KC PZPR, V/174, 507.

2. Pipes, *Vixi*, 178–83.

3. Garthoff, *Great Transition*, 45.

4. For the most complete retelling of neoconservatives' efforts to wage economic war against the Soviet Union, see Schweizer, *Victory*. Schweizer had excellent access to many members of Reagan's administration and is clearly sympathetic to neoconservative voices from that period. This sympathy makes his book an excellent source for understanding what the neoconservatives (Reagan included) believed and what they *thought* they were accomplishing. His lack of objectivity, however, often leads Schweizer to overstate the effects of these policies or to gloss over details that provide alternative explanations for the collapse of the Soviet system.

5. For a study of the continuing influence of Nixon and other pragmatists on U.S.-Soviet policy in the Reagan administration, see Mann, *Rebellion of Ronald Reagan*.

6. "Address to the Nation about Christmas and the Situation in Poland, December 23, 1981," *PPUS* (1981).

7. Memorandum from H. Allen Holmes to the Secretary, "Poland—Additional Bold Move for NSC," dated December 22, 1981, in Byrne, Machciewicz, and Ostermann, *Poland 1980–1982*.

8. Cable from Amembassy Warsaw to SecState, "Polish Situation: U.S. Policy," dated December 26, 1981, NSA, Soviet Flashpoints, Box 26, December 26–29, 1981.

9. Cable from Amembassy Warsaw to Secstate, "Polish Situation: U.S. Policy," dated December 27, 1981, NSA, Soviet Flashpoints, Box 26, December 26–29, 1981.

10. Notatka Informacyjna z rozmowy z Ambassadorem USA F. Meehan'em w dn. 28.xii.81 (część ogólno-polityczna) [Information Note from the Conversation with U.S. Amb. F. Meehan on 28.12.81 (general-political section)], MSZ, 30/85, W-2, Dep III (1982), AP 22-1-82/A.

11. Notatka z rozmowy z przedstawicielem Ambassady USA w Warszawie p. Howardem w dniu 30.xii.1981r [Note from the Conversation with U.S. Embassy Officer in Warsaw Mr. Howard on 30.12.1981], MSZ, 30/85, W-2, Dep III (1982), AP 22-1-82/A. The origin of this document remains unclear. According to a cover note, it was created outside the MSZ and sent to the American department on December 31, 1981.

12. Memorandum, "Poland—The Next Thirty Days," dated January 8, 1982, in Byrne, Machciewicz, and Ostermann, *Poland 1980-1982*.

13. Cable from USMission Geneva to Secstate, "(S) U.S. Statement on Poland," dated January 12, 1982, NSA, Soviet Flashpoints Originals, Box 1. No materials in Polish sources have surfaced to show that the Soviets raised the American démarche on a joint economic package with the PZPR. Nitze's cable mentions that Kvitsinskii spoke from notes at their second meeting; therefore, it is safe to presume that Kvistinskii briefed his superiors about the first meeting.

14. Action Memo from H. Allen Holmes to the Secretary, "Poland: Incentives as a Means of Obtaining Our Objectives," dated March 10, 1982, in Byrne, Machciewicz, and Ostermann, *Poland 1980-1982*.

15. Action Memorandum from John D. Scanlan to the Secretary, "Poland—An Incentives Package," dated March 25, 1982, NSA, Soviet Flashpoints, Box 27, March 1982.

16. Memo for William Clark from Paula Dobriansky, "U.S.-East European Relations: Implications of the Polish Crisis," dated January 22, 1982, RRPL, Dobriansky Files, Box 3, Poland Memoranda 1981-1983 [January 1982].

17. For an overview of American policy toward Eastern Europe during the 1970s, see Garthoff, *Detente and Confrontation*, esp. 549-55. For information on Johnson's policies, see Miller, *Foreign Relations of the United States, 1964-1968*, vol. 17, *Eastern Europe*, particularly document 15, "National Security Action Memorandum No. 352/1, Bridge Building," dated July 8, 1966.

18. "U.S. Policy toward Eastern Europe," attached to Memorandum from Hugh Simon to John Davis, "U.S. Policy toward Eastern Europe: HA Changes," dated April 22, 1982, NSA, Soviet Flashpoints, Box 27, April-June 1982.

19. Presidential Directive 21 (signed in 1977) had pursued differentiation, and National Security Adviser Zbigniew Brzeziński implemented a vigorous differentiation policy toward Poland prior to and during the Polish crisis. See Vaughan, "Beyond Benign Neglect."

20. "U.S. Policy toward Eastern Europe."

21. For an excised list of NSC meetings and brief topics, see http://www.reagan.utexas.edu/resource/findaid/nsexmeet.htm.

22. For this breakdown of Poland's debt, see "Fact Sheet on Poland's Debt," published as part of Senate Appropriations Committee, *Polish Debt Crisis*, 18-19.

23. Information Memorandum from Robert Hormats to the Secretary, "Actions taken in response to your calls from Brussels on Polish Economic Assistance," dated December 14, 1981, NSA, Soviet Flashpoints Originals, Box 3.

24. Cable from Secstate to Amembassy Vienna, "Finance Minister of Debt Service and Emergency Measures," dated December 24, 1981, NSA, Soviet Flashpoints, Box 26, December 23–25, 1981. This request is further evidence of Poles' expectations of a conciliatory Western policy following the declaration of martial law.

25. Action Memorandum from Robert Hormats and Lawrence Eagleburger to the Secretary, "Western Economic Leverage on Poland and Secure Phone Call to Regan," dated December 17, 1981, NSA, Soviet Flashpoints, Box 26, December 1-22, 1981.

26. Dan Morgan and Robert Kaiser, "Group of Aides Sought Tougher Stand on Poland," *Washington Post* (Jan. 15, 1982), A1.

27. "Report on the Working Group on the Implications of Invoking the Exceptional Circumstances Clause of the 1981 Polish Official Debt Rescheduling Agreement," dated January 20, 1982, NSA, Soviet Flashpoints, Box 27, January 1982.

28. Dan Morgan, "U.S. Tells Its Banks Some Polish Debt Will Be Paid," *Washington Post* (Feb. 2, 1982), A11.

29. Margot Hornblower, "Congress Approves $7.4 Billion for Aid," *Washington Post* (Feb. 11, 1982), A17.

30. "Congress's Choice on Poland," *Wall Street Journal* (Feb. 3, 1982): 24.

31. Reporting on this topic is too wide to include all references, but for a representative, if mild, sample see Leslie Gelb, "Reprieve on Polish Debt," *New York Times* (Feb. 3, 1982), A1; and Paul Lewis, "Role of the Western Banks in Poland's Debt Crisis," *New York Times* (Feb. 3, 1982), A10.

32. For the Poles' version of Pressler's and Percy's visit, see MSZ, 30/85, W-1, Dep III (1982), AP 220-1-82. The Congressional Research Service issued *Martial Law in Poland* on January 6 and *Polish Crisis* on January 9.

33. U.S. Senate Appropriations Committee, *Polish Debt Crisis*; Moynihan quoted on 50, Ikle on 7, and Hormats on 40.

34. The AFL-CIO was consistently critical of Reagan's policies, calling for much stronger economic sanctions than those that were imposed. On December 28, 1981, Kahn stated that the U.S. government should call in the balance of Polish debt, refuse to extend further credits to either Poland, the Soviet Union, or Eastern Europe; halt all grain shipments to the Soviet Union; suspend export licenses for the Siberian pipeline; restrict technology transfers; recall American delegates to the CSCE meetings in Madrid and arms talks in Geneva; publish satellite photos of detention camps in Poland; and beef up American radio broadcasts. "Statement by Tom Kahn to the Congressional Committee on Security and Cooperation in Europe," dated December 28, 1981, GMMA, Information Department, CIO, AFL-CIO Press Releases, 1937–1995, Box 47, 47/6.

35. "AFL-CIO Press Release, February 4, 1982," dated February 4, 1982, GMMA, Information Department, CIO, AFL-CIO Press Releases, 1937–1995, box 48, 48/3.

36. U.S. Senate Appropriations Committee, *Polish Debt Crisis*, 176; Kahn quote is from 163.

37. Pilna Notatka [Urgent Note], dated March 1, 1982, MSZ, 30/85, W-1, Dep III (1982), AP 220-2-82.

38. For the Polish government's reporting on Obey's trip, see Notatka Informacyjna o wizycia grupy członków Izby Reprezententów Kongresu Stanów Zjednoczonych Ameryki [Information Note about a Visit by a Group from the United States House of Representatives], dated March 11, 1982, MSZ, 30/85, W-1, Dep III (1982), AP 220-2-82.

39. Quotes taken from Obey's comments on the McNeil/Lehrer Report, "Congressmen Laud Spirit of the Polish People," dated Wednesday, March 10, 1982. For the report given directly to Reagan, see, Action Memorandum from Richard Pipes to William Clark, "Congressional Delegation's Report on Trip to Poland," dated March 17, 1982, RRPL, Dobriansky Files, Box 3, Poland Memoranda 1981–1983 [February–April 1982]. See also House Committee on the Budget, *The United States and Poland*; and Memorandum from John Davis to Allen Holmes, "Poland After Five Years," dated March 16, 1982, NSA, Soviet Flashpoints, Box 27, March 1982.

40. As early as December 19, Haig approved increasing propaganda efforts. Action Memorandum from Richard Burt to the Secretary, "Poland: Current U.S. Geopolitical Options," dated December 19, 1981, in Byrne, Machciewicz, and Ostermann, *Poland 1980–1982*.

41. For Spasowski's comments, see "Transcripts of the Statement made by the Polish Envoy on His Resignation," *New York Times* (Dec. 21, 1981), A17. A few days after Spasowski's speech, Polish ambassador to Japan, Józef Rurarz, and his wife defected as well. For a general account of Spasowski's experience, see his *Liberation of One*.

42. Memorandum for Mr. James W. Nance, "President Reagan's Meeting with Ambassador Spasowski," dated December 21, 1981, in Byrne, Machciewicz, and Ostermann, *Poland 1980–1982*.

43. Reagan, *An American Life*, 303.

44. Memorandum of meeting, "U.S. Response to Polish Crisis," dated December 22, 1981, NSA, Soviet Flashpoints, Box 26, December 1–22, 1981.

45. Cable from SecState to All NATO Capitals, "Poland," dated January 8, 1982, NSA, Soviet Flashpoints Originals, Box 3.

46. Information Memorandum from Lawrence Eagleburger to the Secretary, "Poland Solidarity Day—Net Assessment," dated February 3, 1982, in Byrne, Machciewicz, and Ostermann, *Poland 1980–1982*.

47. "Better to Let Poland Be?" *Time Magazine* (Feb. 8, 1982); Reuters, "TV Program on Poland is Criticized by Many," *New York Times* (Feb. 2, 1982), A8; and "'Let Poland Be Poland': 'Complete Failure' of US TV Programme," *Summary of BBC World Broadcasts* (Feb. 2, 1982).

48. For quote, see Skinner, Anderson, and Anderson, *Reagan in His Own Hand*, 128. For a discussion of Reagan's views on the role of international broadcasting, see Schweizer, *Reagan's War*, 191–99.

49. Action Memorandum from Lawrence Eagleburger to the Secretary, "Response to the Polish Crisis: Radio Broadcasting," dated December 30, 1981, NSA, Soviet Flashpoints, Box 26, December 30–31, 1982.

50. Memorandum for the President from Alexander Haig, Frank Shakespeare, and Charles Wick, "Response to the Polish Crisis: Radio Broadcasting," dated January 5, 1982, NSA, Soviet Flashpoints, Box 27, January 1982.

51. Action memorandum from Richard Burt and Mark Palmer to Secretary Haig, "Response to Polish Martial Law: Modernization of our International Radios," with attachments, dated June 7, 1982, NSA, Soviet Flashpoints, Box 27, April–June 1982. For the final version of NSDD 45, "United States International Broadcasting," dated July 15, 1982, see the National Archives and Records Administration's Archival Records Collection (ARC) online.

52. "Remarks on Signing the Captive Nations Proclamation, July 19, 1982," *PPUS* (1982).

53. Senate Foreign Relations Committee, *BIB Supplemental Authorization Act, Fiscal Year 1983*.

54. Nelson, *War of the Black Heavens*, 173.

55. For a further example, see the discussion of Reagan's speech to the British Parliament in June 1982 and the creation of the National Endowment for Democracy in chapter 3.

56. This early information on food efforts to Poland is compiled from sources in the CRS Archives; CRS, EURMENA XVII-C, Box 4, Poland Correspondence 1970–1986, 1981 Poland Food Aid.

57. Letter from PAC President Aloysius Mazewski to Members of the Board, dated July 31, 1981, CRS, EURMENA XVII-C, Box 4, Poland Correspondence 1970–1986, 1981 Poland Food Aid.

58. Letter from Edwin Broderick to Most Reverend Albert Abramowicz, dated August 21, 1981, CRS, EURMENA XVII-C, Box 4, Poland Correspondence 1970–1986, 1981 Poland Food Aid. Food from AID generally came from resources provided as part of the Food for Peace program. Food for Peace, or Title II of Public Law 480, allowed the U.S. government to provide food aid to be distributed by private voluntary organizations (PVOs) when humanitarian need existed. The U.S. government also supported food aid in humanitarian cases by allowing PVOs to purchase food at concessionary prices through the CCC.

59. Memorandum, "Poland Operational Plan Coverage Outline," dated October 16, 1981, CRS, EURMENA, XVII-C, Box 4, Poland Correspondence 1970–1986, 1981 Poland Gen.

60. Letter from CRS Director of Operations Jean J. Chenard to Russel Stover Candy Company, dated December 10, 1981, CRS, EURMENA, XVII-C, Box 4, Poland Correspondence 1970–1986, 1981 Poland Gen.

61. Paczkowski, *Spring*, 476.

62. For a full accounting of the PZPR's predictions for food production in 1982, see Wnioski z aktualnej sytuacji w skupie produktów rolnych i prognoza do staw żywca, zboża i mleka [Findings on the Current Situation in Purchase of Agricultural Products and the Prognosis for Livestock, Grain, and Milk], dated March 1982, AAN, KC PZPR, V/173, 214–225.

63. Letter from Robert Charlebois to Janet Turner, dated January 5, 1982, CRS, EURMENA Program Correspondence Box 11, 1982 Poland: PL-IE-002 Spare parts for Trucks: Tires and Accumulators.

64. For a laundry list of assistance sent in January 1982, see "Emergency in Poland Operations Report #2, January 14, 1982," CRS, EURMENA, Program Correspondence Box 11, 1982 Poland: Agreement/Operational Plan & Relate (Bi-Lingual).

65. Rushworth Kidder, "US Helping Hand Extends to Poles," *Christian Science Monitor* (Dec. 31, 1981), 14.

66. Haig, *Caveat*, 250.

67. For a further discussion of this move as it relates to economic sanctions, see chapter 1.

68. Memorandum from Richard Pipes to James Nance, "Polish Contingency Plans," dated December 18, 1981, RRPL, Pipes Files, Box 12, Chron File 12/16/1981–12/23/1981.

69. Memo from Father Mulkerin to File, dated December 15, 1981, EURMENA XVII-C, Box 4, Poland Correspondence 1970–1986, 1981 Poland Gen.

70. Memorandum from Alexander Haig to the President, "Humanitarian Aid for Poland and the Kirkland Proposal," dated January 7, 1982, with attachment, NSA, Soviet Flashpoints, Box 27, January 1982.

71. Memorandum for William Clark, "General Jaruzelski's Request for Humanitarian Assistance (Feed Grain for Poultry)," dated January 16, 1982, NSA, Soviet Flashpoints, Box 27, January 1982.

72. Johnston made a second trip to Poland from February 15 to 23 to meet with Polish government officials about the possibility of starting a program for individual, private Polish farmers. For Polish records related to this trip, see Notatka [Note re Meetings with CARE officials], dated February 17, 1982; and Notatka o wyniku rozmów przedstawicieli organizacji CARE oraz Ministerstwa Rolnictwa i Gospodarki Żywnościowej [Note about results of a conversation with officers from CARE and the Ministry of Agriculture and Food Economics], dated March 4, 1982, both in MSZ, 30/85, W-3, Dep III (1982), AP 39-4-82.

73. Briefing Memorandum from H. Allen Holmes to the Deputy Secretary, "Your Meeting with Mr. Philip Johnston, Executive Director of Care, February 26, 10:00 A.M.," dated February

26, 1982, NSA, Soviet Flashpoints, Box 27, February 13–29. For the Polish version of Meehan's meeting with Vice Premier Ozdowski and Jan Kinast on January 19, when he placed political conditions on the extension of CCC credits, see Notatka [Note from January 19 of Vice Premier Ozdowski request of U.S. Ambassador to Poland Francis Meehan], dated January 20, 1982, MSZ, 30/85, W-3, Dep III (1982), AP 39-4-82.

74. See proposal in CRS, EURMENA, Program Correspondence Box 11, Poland 1981–1983.

75. Memo from Bishop Broderick to Anthony Foddai, "Poland," dated March 24, 1982, CRS, EURMENA, XVII-C, Box 4, Poland Correspondence 1970–1986, 1981 Poland Gen. An interagency group on Poland met to discuss humanitarian aid and other issues on March 25, 1982. For a snapshot of how the bureaucracy was moving on humanitarian aid, see Information Memorandum from Allen Holmes to Lawrence Eagleberger, "March 23 Interagency Group Meeting on Poland," dated March 26, 1982, NSA, Soviet Flashpoints, Box 27, March 1982. From January 7 to February 24, Father Mulkerin surveyed the situation to determine Poland's post-December 13 needs. For his report, see Report, "Overview of CRS Program in Poland," dated March 4, 1982, CRS, EURMENA, Program Correspondence Box 11, Poland 1981–1983.

76. For an account of Mulkerin's April to May trip, see "Overview of the CRS Program in Poland," undated, CRS, EURMENA, Program Correspondence, Box 11, Poland 1981–1983. For specifics on the emergency program for Płock, see Interoffice Memorandum from Father Mulkerin to Oscar, undated, CRS, EURMENA, Program Correspondence, Box 11, Poland 1981–1983. Both are attached to an Interoffice Memorandum, "6/10/82 Meeting on Poland," dated June 10, 1982, CRS, EURMENA, Program Correspondence, Box 11, Poland 1981–1983.

77. See Confidential Memorandum, "Draft Decision Memo on Options for Humanitarian Assistance to Poland," dated May 12, 1982, NSA, Soviet Flashpoints, Box 27, April–June 1982.

78. *Wall Street Journal* (May 28, 1982). For CRS's view, see Memorandum from Oscar Ratti to Father Charlebois, "CRS Program in Poland," dated May 28, 1982, CRS, EURMENA, Program Correspondence, Box 11, Poland 1981–1983.

79. Letter from W. Antoinette Ford to Bishop John Broderick, dated June 28, 1982, CRS, EURMENA, Program Correspondence, Box 11, 1982 Poland: Agreement/Operational Plan & Relate (Bi-Lingual).

80. Report to File, "Overview of the CRS Program in Poland," undated, CRS, EURMENA, Program Correspondence, Box 11, Poland 1981–1983.

81. Paczkowski, *Spring*, 455.

82. Ibid., 458.

83. For a full exploration of these publishing houses' roots and their creation, see Paweł Sowiński, "Siła wolnego słowa—Nowa, Krąg, CDN (1982–1989)," in Friszke, *Solidarność Podziemna*, 637–65, esp. 637–42.

84. Paczkowski, *Spring*, 458. The Polish government estimated that 850 separate underground titles were produced in 1982; see "Formy, Metody, i Treści Oddziaływania Nielegalnej Propagandy na Świadomość Społeczną" [Forms, Methods, and Contents of Various Illegal Propaganda in the Social Consciousness], dated November 1986, Hoover, Poland, Sluzba Bezpieczenstwa Department III, Box 6, 6/1. The most complete collection of these underground publications can be found at the KARTA archives in Warsaw. They have more than three thousand independent periodicals in their collection, alongside nearly five thousand censored books and brochures. For a full listing, see Iwaszkiewicz, *Archiwum Opozycji*.

85. Puddington, *Broadcasting Freedom*, 268.

86. This position of waging an open confrontation with the authorities was later most eloquently argued by Jacek Kuroń. Kuroń, a founder of the Workers' Defense Committee (KOR) in 1976, was one of the most influential advisers to Solidarność but was still interned in January 1982.

87. Victor Kulerski, a long-standing opposition activist, is generally credited with creating the formulation of the "long march."

88. Friszke, "Tymczasowa Komisja Koordynacyjna NSZZ 'Solidarność' (1982–1987)," in his *Solidarność Podziemna*, 17–182, specifically at 21.

89. For an account of the meeting and an analysis of the events that led to this creation, from which this summary is taken, see Friszke, "Tymczasowa Komisja Koordynacyjna," 17–27. For an English source on this early period of Solidarność, see Łopiński, Moskit, and Wilk, *Konspira*.

90. *Tygodnik Mazowsze* (April 28, 1982), 1–2, KARTA, Archiwum Opozycji.

91. John Darnton, "Thirty Thousand Poles Defy Army in Warsaw in May Day March," *New York Times* (May 2, 1982), A1.

92. John Darnton, "Polish Protesters Clash with Police in Several Cities," *New York Times* (May 4, 1982), A1.

93. Defense Intelligence Agency Intelligence Appraisal, "Poland: Situation After Six Months of Martial Law," dated June 23, 1982, NSA, Soviet Flashpoints, Box 27, April–June 1982, 5.

94. Puddington, *Lane Kirkland*, 163.

95. See "Statement by the AFL-CIO Executive Council on Strikes in Poland," dated August 20, 1980, GMMA, Information Department, AFL-CIO Press Releases 1980, Box 45, 45/2; and "Statement on the Polish Workers Aid Fund," dated September 4, 1980, GMMA, Information Department, AFL-CIO Press Releases 1980, Box 45, 45/3.

96. The AFL-CIO Secretary-Treasurer kept immaculate records on donations to the PWAF from November 1980 through the end of 1981. Most of the individual donations are less than $20, with larger donations from individual unions up to $10,000. For donation information see AFL-CIO, International Affairs Department Files, Inactive Records, "After Nov. 24 PWAF [Polish Workers Aid Fund]" and "Letters of Contribution from Individuals to the AFL-CIO Polish Workers Aid Fund, 1981."

97. "Report to the ICFTU on visits to Warschau and Gdańsk, 15/9–18/9/1980," undated, AFL-CIO, International Affairs Department, Inactive Records, "Wałęsa, Lech."

98. "A. Phillip Randolph Education Fund, Report to AFL-CIO President Lane Kirkland on: Poland and the American Labor Movement," ca. May 1981, AFL-CIO, Kirkland Presidential Files, Inactive Records, "Polish Workers Strike and Fund." Bayard Rustin, Charles Bloomstein, and Adrian Karatnycky took the trip.

99. As the second Polish Workers Aid Fund Update reported, "The AFL-CIO Polish Workers Aid Fund has supplied typewriters, both electric and manual, duplicating machines, office supplies and small appliances, and in a larger outlay of funds, a small bus-like vehicle which is now in regular use by Solidarity"; quoted from "Update #2," AFL-CIO, International Affairs Department, Unprocessed records, "Update #2." Notably, the AFL-CIO provided fax machines (a highly advanced piece of office machinery at this point in time) that later became an important means of smuggling out information. The single largest donation on record from the PWAF was sent to ICFTU President Jan Vanderveken, who utilized the money to purchase and send Solidarność a new offset printing plant; see Letter from J. Vandervenken to Lane Kirkland, dated August 20, 1981, AFL-CIO, International Department Files, unprocessed records, "Letters of Contribution

from Individuals to the AFL-CIO Polish Workers Aid Fund, 1981 (Box 2)." A total of $152,000 was spent on office supplies and material for Solidarność prior to December 13. See "Note to Editors," dated June 14, 1982, GMMA, AFL-CIO, Information Department, AFL-CIO Press Releases 1937–1995, Box 49, 49/2.

100. AFL-CIO Press Release, dated December 14, 1981, GMMA, AFL-CIO, Information Department, AFL-CIO Press Releases 1937–1995, Box 47, 47/2.

101. Cable from SecState to Amembassy Warsaw, "Department Briefing for AFL-CIO Executive Staff," dated December 16, 1981, NSA, Soviet Flashpoints Originals, Box 1. Concern about the provocative nature of AFL-CIO support to Solidarność was long standing. Carter's Secretary of State Edmund Muskie pressured Kirkland not to send aid (see Puddington, *Lane Kirkland*, 168–69), a pattern continued in the Reagan administration; see Briefing Memorandum from H. Allen Holmes to the Secretary, "Your February 10 Meeting with Lane Kirkland: Poland," dated February 9, 1981, NSA, Soviet Flashpoints Originals, Box 4.

102. For Kirkland's recollections, see "An Interview with Lane Kirkland," conducted for the Labor Diplomacy Oral History Project by John F. Shea and Don R. Krienzle (November 13, 1996), 20 (copy available at the GMMA library). According to Puddington, the meeting took place on December 15 (*Lane Kirkland*, 174), but documents place the meeting on December 18. For Reagan's briefing materials, see Memorandum from James W. Nance to the President, "Your Meeting with Lane Kirkland," dated December 17, 1981, RRPL, Dobriansky Files, Box 3, Poland Memoranda 1981–1983 [July–December 1981].

103. Puddington, *Lane Kirkland*, 174–75. See also Briefing Memorandum from H. Allen Holmes to the Secretary, "Your Meeting in Chicago with Lane Kirkland, AFL-CIO," dated January 29, 1982, NSA, Soviet Flashpoints, Box 27, January 1982.

104. "Annual Report, Committee in Support of Solidarity, 1983," CSS, Administrative Files, "CSS Annual Reports 1983–1986."

105. Memo from Tom Kahn to Tom Donahue, "Committee in Support of Solidarity," dated June 8, 1982, AFL-CIO, Unprocessed Records, "Committee in Support of Solidarity."

106. Ibid. See also Memo from Kahn to Tom Donohue, dated April 1, 1982; and Note from Tom Kahn to William Collins, in AFL-CIO, Unprocessed Records, "Committee in Support of Solidarity."

107. The original call for support came in a letter from Magda Wojcik to Lane Kirkland dated January 18, 1982. For this letter and the letter from Magda Wojcik to Tom Kahn, dated January 18, 1982, see AFL-CIO, International Affairs Department Files, unprocessed records, "Wojcik, Magda."

108. Friszke, "Tymczasowa Komisja Koordynacyjna," 62–63.

109. For an explanation of the creation of the body, see ibid., 60–63; quote from 63.

110. Solidarity International Press Release, dated July 18, 1982, AFL-CIO, International Affairs Department Files, unprocessed records, "Solidarność 1982 #2."

111. For in-depth information and a taste of the controversy, see Goddeeris, "Lobbying Allies."

112. Letter from Jerzy Milewski to Lane Kirkland, dated August 1, 1982, AFL-CIO, International Affairs Department Files, Inactive Records, "Milewski, Jerzy."

113. In October 1982, Kirkland authorized a payment of $20,000 to support Solidarność, sent to Jakub Swiecicki, a liaison officer for the Coordinating Office who worked in Sweden. Memo from Tom Kahn to Tom Donohue dated October 26, 1982, AFL-CIO, unprocessed records, "Solidarność 1982#1."

114. Author's interview with Irena Lasota, June 19, 2007.

115. For this note and the receipts see AFL-CIO, International Affairs Department Files, Inactive Records, "Committee in Support of Solidarity."

116. The overview in this paragraph comes from Goddeeris, *Solidarity with Solidarity*, esp. 36–38, 65, 85, 176–79, and 203–9.

117. For one politburo conversation on this paper, see the records for Protocol 23 of the February 6, 1982 in AAN, Mikr. 2998, KC PZPR Syg. 1829, 220–228.

118. Paczkowski, *Spring*, 475.

119. Ibid., 470. In Poland, a few parties including the ZSL and SD had been allowed to continue to exist alongside the PZPR. These parties existed in the Sejm but rarely acted with any autonomy.

120. Ibid., 470, 465. For a fuller explanation of this phenomenon of change without change, see *Spring*, 465–77.

121. Pilna Notatka z wizyty w Moskwie Delegacji Partyjno-Państwowej z I Sekretarzem KC PZPR, Prezesem Rady Ministrów tow. Wojciechem Jaruzelskim, w dniach 1–2 marca 1982 r. [Urgent Note from the Visit to Moscow by the Party-Government with First Secretary of the PZPR Central Committee, Head of the Council of Ministers Wojciech Jaruzelski from 1 to 2 March 1982], dated March 5, 1982, AAN, KC PZPR, V/172, 555–61; quotes from 556 and 560.

122. Podstawowe Problemy Współpracy Gospodarczej Między PRL i ZSRR oraz Pomocy Radzieckiej dla Polski [Basic Problems of Economic Cooperation between the PRL and USSR as well as Soviet Help for Poland], dated March 1982, AAN, KC PZPR, V/172, 562–66; quote from 562.

123. Programowe założenia Umocnienia i Rozwoju stosunków Polski z ZSRR [Program Assumptions for Strengthening and the Development of Polish-USSR Relations], dated April 27, 1982, AAN, KC PZPR, V/174, 32–51; quote from 50.

124. For the report on Jaruzelski's visit to Hungary, see Notatka Informacyjna z przebiegu wizyty delegacji partyjn-państwowej PRL w Budapescie w dniu 21 kwietnia 1982 r [Information Note from the proceedings of the visit of the PRL Party-National delegation in Budapest on 21 April 1982], dated April 23, 1982, AAN, KC PZPR, V/173, 719–730; quote from 729.

125. See Sprawozdanie z pobytu delegacji KC PZPR w Jugosławii (24–26.iii.1982 r) [Report from the Trip by a PZPR Central Committee Delegation to Yugoslavia (24–26.3.1983)], dated March 27, 1982, AAN, KC PZPR, V/173, 250–63.

126. See Czyrek's comments on his trip to East Berlin in AAN, PZPR KC, V/173, 199–201.

127. See excerpts on foreign trade in Referat Biura Politycznego KC PZPR na VIII Plenum KC [PZPR Central Committee Politburo Report for the 8th Central Committee Plenum], dated March 13, 1982, AAN, KC PZPR, V/173, 553–56; quote from 553. This report also called for circumventing sanctions by attaining needed imports from the West through secret arrangements with other Socialist countries.

128. Special National Intelligence Estimate, "Poland's Prospects over the Next 12 to 18 Months," dated March 25, 1982, in Byrne, Machciewicz, and Ostermann, *Poland 1980–1982*.

129. For an example of these complaints, see Notatka Informacyjna [Information Note from the 20th of this month for a conversation with U.S. Ambassador Francis Meehan], MSZ, 30/85, W-2, Dep III (1982), AP 22-1-82/A.

130. John Tagliabue, "Poland Censors Old Annoyer: Radio Free Europe," *New York Time* (May 11, 1982), A2.

131. Michael Dobbs, "Poles' Radio Dial Is Battleground of Fierce East-West Struggle," *Washington Post* (May 27, 1982), A30.

132. Notatka Informacyjna z rozmowy Tow. St. Pawliszewskiego, wicedyrektorz Departamentu III z radcą-ministrem Ambasady USA w Warszawie H.E. Wilgis'em [Information Note from St. Pawliszewski's, vice director of Department III, conversation with DCM of the U.S. Embassy in Warsaw, H. E. Wilgis], dated February 25, 1982, MSZ, 30/85, W-2, Dep III (1982), AP 22-1-82/A.

133. Excerpt from the transcript of a May 25, 1982, PZPR Central Committee Meeting, AAN, KC PZPR, V/174, 506–9; quote from 507.

134. Cable from Secstate to Amembassy Warsaw, "Official Informal No. 56," dated May 13, 1982, NSA, Soviet Flashpoints Originals, Box 1. For MSZ materials on the incident, see the folder "Wydalenie z USA Pracowników Ambasady PRL w Waszyngtonie" [Expulsion from the U.S. of PRL Embassy Staff in Washington], MSZ, 30/85, W-2, Dep III (1982), AP 35-6-82.

135. For details of the meeting between the American embassy officer Vought and Pawliszewski on May 21, during which the American asked for the meeting, see Notatka Informacyjna [Information Note], dated May 22, 1982, MSZ, 49/86, W-1, Dep III (1983), AP 10-1-83.

136. For the Polish stenogram from the May 24 meeting between Czyrek and Meehan, see Rozmowa Ambasadora F. J. Meehan'a z Ministerem J. Czyrkim w dniu 24 maja 1982 r. [Conversation of Ambassador F. J. Meehan with Minister J. Czyrek on 24 May 1982], MSZ, 30/85, W-2, Dep III (1982), AP 22-1-82.

137. "ISD/290(Final). International Staff Document. Report by Acting Chairman to the members of the Political Committee, on the compendium of measures taken or contemplated by the Allies concerning Poland and the USSR," dated March 1, 1982, available online (http://www.nato.int/cps/en/natolive/81368.htm).

138. Cable from SecState to USMission NATO, "CSCE: Guidance for January 27 NAC," dated January 27, 1982, NSA, Soviet Flashpoints Originals, Box 4.

139. John Goshko, "East-West Parley Suspended After Poland Assailed," *Washington Post* (Feb. 10, 1982), A1.

140. *Bulletin of the European Communities* 15, no. 3 (1982): 62.

141. For a fuller explanation of this episode, see Domber, "Power Politics, Human Rights, and Trans-Atlantic Relations." For a discussion of the Madrid meeting, see Snyder, *Human Rights Activism*, 150–57.

142. Plans for the more than three thousand–mile Siberian pipeline project emerged from Europe's energy fears following the oil crises of the 1970s. Negotiations began in 1979, and the deal to create the pipeline was announced by Helmut Schmidt on a state visit to Moscow in July 1980. It was designed to run from Siberia through the Soviet Union and Czechoslovakia to West Germany. For a full explanation, see chapters 2 and 3 in Blinken, *Ally vs. Ally*.

143. Cable from Secstate to Amembassies Bonn, Paris, The Hague, and Brussels, "The Polish Crisis and the Siberian Gas Pipeline," dated December 27, 1981, NSA, Soviet Flashpoints Originals, Box 1.

144. Cable from Amembassy Bonn to Secstate, "The Polish Crisis and the Siberian Pipeline," dated December 28, 1981, NSA, Soviet Flashpoints Originals, Box 1.

145. "Statement on U.S. measures taken against the Soviet Union Concerning its Involvement in Poland," December 29, 1981, *PPUS* (1981).

146. Blinken, *Ally vs. Ally*, 11.

147. Action Memorandum from Robert Hormats to the Secretary, "Terms of Reference for the Mission to Europe on Sanctions vis-à-vis the Soviet Union," dated February 20, 1982; and Memorandum from Paul Bremer, "Small Group Meeting on the Proposed Buckley Mission to Europe, February 24, 1982," dated February 26, 1982, both in NSA, Soviet Flashpoints, Box 27, February 13–29, 1982.

148. Pipes, *Vixi*, 178.

149. Ibid.

150. Blinken, *Ally vs. Ally*, 100–101.

151. Pipes, *Vixi*, 178–83.

152. See Sjursen, *The United States, Western Europe, and the Polish Crisis*, 76–82, quote from 80.

153. Blinken, *Ally vs. Ally*, 105.

154. Shultz, *Turmoil and Triumph*, 137, 138.

155. Ibid., 138.

156. NSDD 66, "East-West Relations and Poland-Related Sanctions," dated November 29, 1982, RRPL, Matlock Files, Series II USSR Subject Files, Box 29, NSDDs [32, 54, 75, 130, 133].

157. According to Pipes, Haig also made the inexcusable mistake of offending Nancy Reagan while at Versailles. See Pipes, *Vixi*, 182.

158. Reagan, *American Life*, 254–56, 271, 360–62; quote from 271.

159. Cannon, *President Reagan*, 169.

160. Ibid., 170–71; quoted in fn.

161. For Shultz's take, see *Turmoil*, 135–45; quote from 140.

162. A copy of NSDD 54, dated September 2, 1982, can be located RRPL, Matlock Files, Series II USSR Subject Files, Box 29, NSDDs [32, 54, 75, 130, 133].

163. NSDD 75, "U.S. Relations with the Soviet Union," dated January 17, 1983, available online at www.fas.org/irp/offdocs/nsdd/nsdd-75.pdf.

164. Schweizer, *Victory*, esp. xv–xvi, and 130–32.

165. NSDD 75, quote from 8, 6, and 9; emphasis added.

166. For similar arguments, see Matlock, *Reagan and Gorbachev*, esp. 52–54; and Mann, *Rebellion of Ronald Reagan*, esp. 30–33.

167. Haig, *Caveat*, 252.


## Chapter 3

1. Davis, as quoted by Ambassador Christopher Hill, who was second economics officer in Warsaw from June 1983 to July 1985. Author's interview with Hill, May 12, 2004.

2. For the announcements calling for strikes on August 31, see *Tygodnik Mazowsze* (July 28, 1982 and August 18, 1982), both in KARTA, Archiwum Opozycji.

3. For an explanation of Kuroń's standpoint on strikes, see Paczkowski, *Spring*, 459. For a retelling of the discussions within the TKK before the demonstrations, see Friszke, "Tymczasowa Komisja Koordynacyjna NSZZ 'Solidarność' (1982–1987)," in *Solidarność Podziemna 1981–1989*, 28–36.

4. Ibid., 36–37.

5. Michael Dobbs, "Solidarity Lacks Effective Strategy in Combating Martial Law," *Washington Post* (Sept. 2, 1982), A16.

6. Special National Intelligence Estimate (SNIE 12.6–82), "Poland's Prospects over the Next 12 to 18 Months," dated September 1, 1982, NSA, Soviet Flashpoints, Box 28, July-September 1982.

7. Rakowski, *Dzienniki polityczne 1981–1983*, 333-34.

8. Kuroń, Michnik, Lityński, and Wujec were already interned; Chojecki and Lipski (who were living in Paris and London) were charged in absentia.

9. Krzysztof Bobinski, "Compromise Hint on Creation of New Polish Trade Unions," *Financial Times* (Sept. 13, 1982), A18; and Michael Dobbs, "Polish Press Floats Idea of Final Solidarity Ban," *Washington Post* (Sept. 23, 1982), A34.

10. Rakowski, *Dzienniki polityczne 1981–1983*, 356.

11. For Rakowski's account of this period, see ibid., 339-70.

12. "Radio Address to the Nation on Solidarity and United States Relations with Poland, October 9, 1982," *PPUS* (1982). Shortly after the president's announcement, the Department of State concluded that it could not count on Congress to pass a new law, so the executive branch utilized a provision in the GATT treaty with Poland to suspend MFN. On October 27, Reagan signed Presidential Proclamation 4991, officially suspending MFN status. On the internal dynamics of the decision, see Action Memorandum from Richard McCormack, Davis Robinson, and Richard Burt to Mr. Wallis, "Implementation of the Decision to Suspend MFN Treatment for Poland," dated October 15, 1982; Cable from Secstate to Amembassy Warsaw, "Consultation with Polish Charge on Suspension of Poland's MFN Status," dated October 23, 1982; Action Memorandum from Powell Moore to Under Secretary Eagleburger, "Congressional Telephone Calls on Polish MFN," dated October 25, 1982; and Cable from Secstate to USMission NATO, "Suspension of Poland's Most-Favored-Nation Status," dated October 27, 1982, all found in NSA, Soviet Flashpoints, Box 28, October–December 1982.

13. Cable from Lawrence Eagleburger to Secretary Shultz, "Impact of U.S. Suspension of MFN on Tariff Treatment for Poland," dated October 9, 1982, NSA, Soviet Flashpoints, Box 28, October–December 1982.

14. Notatka Informacyjna z rozmowy z John'em Davis'em w dniu 6.x.1982 r [Information Note from a conversation with John Davis on 6.10.1982], dated October 6, 1982, MSZ, 30/85, W-2, Dep III (1982), AP 22-1-82.

15. Rakowski, *Dzienniki polityczne 1981–1983*, 365.

16. For the text of Glemp's letter and a discussion of Jaruzelski's response, see records for the June 29, 1982, politburo meeting in AAN, Mikr. 3002, Sygn. 1833, 1–16.

17. September 30 marked the first anniversary of the first meeting between Wałęsa, Glemp, and Jaruzelski.

18. Rakowski, *Dzienniki polityczne 1981–1983*, 362.

19. Opposition leadership had also been calling for workers to boycott the new government-sanctioned trade unions. For the general strike announcements, see the front pages of *Tygodnik Mazowsze* (Oct. 20, 1982 and Oct. 27, 1982), both in KARTA, Archiwum Opozycji.

20. Rakowski, *Dzienniki polityczne 1981–1983*, 400.

21. For quotes of the announcement, see Krzysztof Bobinski, "Jaruzelski Agrees to June for Pope's Visit," *Financial Times* (Nov. 9, 1982), A3.

22. For the quote, see Michael Dobbs, "Poland Sets Date for Pope's Visit," *Washington Post* (Nov. 9, 1982), A1. For more analytical coverage, see Eric Bourne, "Polish Regime, Church Try to Defuse Tensions," *Christian Science Monitor* (Nov. 10, 1982), 1; and John Kifner, "For Poland's Church a New Relationship with the State," *New York Times* (Nov. 14, 1982), D3.

23. Report, "Wytyczne Polityki Wyznaniowej" [Guidelines for Vatican Policies], dated February 4, 1983, AAN, KC PZPR, V/191, 11–16; quotes from 11 and 15.

24. Węzłowe Zadania Polityki Zagranicznej PRL w 1983 r [Objectives for PRL Foreign Policy in 1983], dated ca. January 1983, AAN, KC PZPR, V/190, 8–27; quotes from 8 and 17.

25. Protokoł nr. 56 z posiedzenia Biura Politycznego KC PZPR w dniu 18.xi.1982 [Protocol no. 56 from minutes of the PZPR CC Politburo on 18.11.1982], dated November 18, 1982, AAN, KC PZPR, V/182, 217–52; quotes from 227 and 230. For information on the letter sent from Wałęsa to Jaruzelski, see Michael Dobbs, "Poland Said It Will Free Lech Wałęsa, Union Leader Sent Conciliatory Letter to Gen. Jaruzelski," *Washington Post* (Nov. 12, 1982), A1.

26. Protokoł nr. 56, 246.

27. For a translation of some of the general's speech, see, "Excerpts from the Speech by the Polish Leader," *New York Times* (Dec. 13, 1982), A9.

28. Polish Helsinki Watch Committee, *Poland under Martial Law*, 322.

29. According to scientific research and RFE surveys of émigrés and refugees, the jamming effectively weakened RFE's signal from 46 percent in 1981 to 24 percent in 1984, but listenership in western Poland hovered consistently around 66 percent during the same period. See Report, "Impact of Jamming on the Reception of RFE/RL Programs," dated August 1984, Hoover, RFE/RL, Corporate Records, 380, Engineering—Jamming 1978–1987; and Report, "Audience and Opinion Research/East European Area," ca. 1987, Hoover, RFE/RL, Corporate Records, 420, 420.4. According to the second report, VOA had a listernership in the mid-40 percent range during the same period, while only about 25 percent of Poles regularly listened to the BBC. According to other opinions, RFE listernership was closer to a quarter of the Polish population; see Paczkowski, *Spring*, 484. The discrepancy may be due to the RFE's own survey being focused on western Poland, where the signal would have been stronger.

30. For a selection of these articles mostly from the 1980s, see Grabowska, *PRL atakuje Radio "Wolna Europa."*

31. Report, "Kierunki propagandy PRL na zagranicę w warunkach polityki Zachodu zmierzającej do izolacji politycznej i blokady ekonomicznej Polski oraz prowadzonej prezeń wojny pzychologicznej przeciwko naszemu krajowi" [Direction of Foreign PRL Propaganda under Western Political Conditions of Poland's Political Isolation and Economic Blockade, As Well As Referring to the Psychological War against Our Country], dated June 24, 1982, AAN, KC PZPR, XI/308, 291–95; quote from 294.

32. For the text of this politburo decision, see AAN, BP PZPR, Mikr. 3005, Sygn. 1836, 279. In August 1981, Reagan fired thirteen thousand members of the Professional Air Traffic Controllers Organization three days after they walked off their jobs. Jaruzelski believed this to be inconsistent with Reagan's pro-trade union statements.

33. Ibid., 247–48.

34. For quotes see, John Kifner, "Poland's Leader, in Bitter Speech, Threatens to Restrict Ties to U.S.," *New York Times* (Dec. 4, 1982), A7. For Jaruzelski's speech to the January 4 Warsaw Pact meeting, see Przemówienie Przewodniczącego delegacji polskiej na posiedzeniu Doradczego Komitetu Politycznego Układu Warszawskiego I Sekretarza KC PZPR, prezesa Rady Ministrów, gen. armii Wojciecha Jaruzelskiego, wygłoszone w Pradze, 4 stycznia 1983 r [Address by the head of the Polish Delegation to the Political Consultative Committee of the Warsaw Pact, First Secretary of the PZPR Central Committee, chairman of the Council of Ministers general Wojciech Jaruzelski, delivered in Prague, 4 January 1983], AAN, KC PZPR, V/189, 8–17.

35. These decisions were taken at the politburo meeting of November 23, 1982. See AAN, PZPR BP, Mikr. 3012, Sygn 1843.

36. The film delivery was widely viewed in Western papers as a government-sponsored trap. For press coverage on the Gruber case, see Bradley Graham, "U.S. Reporter in Warsaw Held by Polish Police," *Washington Post* (Jan. 12, 1983), A20; Graham, "Poland to Expel UPI Reporter Held Overnight," *Washington Post* (Jan. 13, 1983), A1; "To Suppress Solidarity, Poland Cracks Down on Western Press," *Christian Science Monitor* (Jan. 14, 1983), 6; and "Poland vs. Press," *Christian Science Monitor* (Jan. 17, 1983), 24.

37. Notatka Informacyjna [Information Note about meeting with H.E. Wilgis], dated January 13, 1983; and Pilna Notatka z rozmowy z Ambassadorem USA F. Meehan w dniu 13.I.1983 [Urgent Note from a conversation with U.S. Ambassador F. Meehan on 13.I.1983], dated January 14, 1983, both in MSZ, 48/86, W-1, Dep III (1983), AP 22-1-83.

38. For an overview of SB policies against the Americans in this period, see a master's thesis prepared within the Academy of Internal Affairs, "Działalność Wzdiadowcza Porwadzona z pozycji Rezydentury Uplasowanej w Ambasadzie USA w Warszawie," dated June, 7, 1983, IPN BU 01521/2238. For representative files on the diplomats David Swartz, Patrick Flood, Hugh Hamilton, Herbert Wilgis, Mark Ramee, and John Vought, see IPN BU 0248/115, IPN BU 0222/1136, IPN BU 0222/1201, IPN BU 0222/28, IPN BU 0222/71, and IPN BU 0222/1208, respectively.

39. For the reports on break-ins into Wilgis's home, see IPN BU 0222/28, 94–95 and 108. For reports on the break-ins into John Dobrin's house, see IPN BU 0222/70, 170–76 and 260–61. Both men were political secretaries. The transcripts of any recordings that might have been made have been destroyed.

40. Dobrin was suspected of being the CIA resident in Warsaw and had the most extensive file reviewed. He was stopped and photographed on February 7, 1984, in retribution for the FBI harassing the Polish intelligence resident in Washington a month earlier. For the report, see "Notatka Służbowa," dated February 8, 1984, IPN BU 0222/70, 279–80.

41. Notatka Informacyjna, dated January 13, 1983.

42. Pilna Notatka z rozmowy z Ambassadorem USA F. Meehan w dniu 13.I.1983, dated January 14, 1983.

43. Pilna Notatka z wizyty pożegnalnej Ambasadora USA F. Meehana w dniu 9 Lutego br. [Urgent Note from the final visit by U.S. Ambassador F. Meehan on 9 February], dated February 11, 1983, MSZ, 48/86, W-1, Dep III (1983), AP 10-1-83. This note was sent to Jaruzelski, Olszowski, and Czyrek among others.

44. For one such conversation between Meehan and the MSZ, see Notatka Informacyjna [Information Note re meeting between Wilgis and Kinast re American Propaganda], dated April 27, 1983, MSZ, 48/86, W-2, Dep III (1983), AP 53-3-83. Usually Jaruzelski did not receive information notes on MSZ meetings, yet in reviewing the Department III files, a pattern emerges in which the general received information on meetings devoted to complaints about RFE broadcasts. This pattern applied particularly to MSZ complaints about RFE broadcasts that specifically mention Jaruzelski. For two examples, see Notatka dot. złożenia protestu w sprawie RWE i Głosu Ameryki [Note regarding notice of protest in the matter of RFE and Voice of America], dated August 20, 1982, MSZ, 30/85, W-3, Dep III (1982), AP 53-2-82; and Notatka Informacyjna z rozmowy z Chargé d'Affaires a.i. USA—Johnem Davisem w dniu 22.xii.1983 [Information Note from a conversation with U.S. chargé d'affaires a.i. John Davis on 22.12.1983], dated December 22, 1983, MSZ, 48/86, W-2, Dep III (1983), AP 53-3-83.

45. Notatka Informacyjna, dated April 27, 1983.

46. Although the Poles announced the closing of the library on February 27, mentioned in ibid., a longer conversation on the issue took place on May 3. The quotes are taken from this later meeting. See Pilna Notatka z rozmowy z Chargé d'Affaires a.i. Stanów Zjednoczonych Ameryki H. E. Wilgis'em w dniu 3 maja 1983 r. [Urgent Note from a conversation with U.S. chargé d'affaires a.i. H. E. Wilgis on 3 May 1984], dated May 4, 1983, MSZ, 48/86, W-1, Dep III (1983), AP 10-2-83.

47. Draft Memorandum, "Western Policy toward Poland," dated May 6, 1982, RRPL, Dobriansky Files, Box 3, Poland Memoranda 1981–1983 [May–September 1982].

48. Leslie Gelb, "Reagan Is Seeking Ways to Moderate Poland Sanctions," *New York Times* (July 9, 1982), A1. For American hopes, see Memo from Pipes to Clark, "Martial Law in Poland," dated July 9, 1982, and Memo from Dobriansky to Clark, "Pre-July 22 Polish Developments," dated July 19, 1982, both in RRPL, Paula Dobriansky Files, Box 3, Poland Memoranda 1981–1983 [May–September 1982].

49. Olszowski replaced Czyrek as minister of foreign affairs in July 1982. Czyrek remained in charge of relations with the Socialist world in the politburo.

50. Pilna Notatka z rozmowy z Ambassadorem USA w Warszawie F.J. Meehan'em w dniu 11 wrzesien 1982 r. [Urgent Note from a conversation with U.S. Ambasador in Warsaw, F. J. Meehan on 11 September 1982], MSZ, 30/85, W-2, Dep III (1982), AP 22-1-82. Unlike most other MSZ documents, the report on Olszowski's meeting with Meehan was sent to the highest level of the leadership, including Jaruzelski, Rakowski, Kinast, and Czyrek. Meehan requested the meeting with Olszowski on August 31, and an overview of U.S.-Polish relations was prepared for Olszowski prior to the meeting. See Notatka w sprawie prośby Ambasadora USA Francis J. Meehan'a o przyjęcie przez Towarzysza Ministra S. Olszowskiego [Note regarding the request by U.S. Ambassador Francis J. Meehan to meet with Comrade Minister S. Olszowski], MSZ, 48/86, W-1, Dep III (1983), AP 10-1-83. After this meeting, Meehan met once with Wiejacz, and during this meeting small steps were mentioned, but not discussed. Wiejacz did write that Meehan "presented a more elastic stand than in previous conversations." See Notatka Informacyjna z rozmowy z Ambasadorem USA w Warszawie Meehan'em w dniu 16 wrzesien 1982 r [Information Note from a conversation with U.S. Ambassador in Warsaw on 16 September 1982], MSZ, 30/85, W-2, Dep III (1982), AP 22-1-82.

51. After Spasowski defected, Zbigniew Ludwiczak was left as the head of the embassy at the level of chargé d'affaires. Regarding security for diplomatic posts, the Polish consulates in Chicago and New York had been vandalized and were regular sites for protests.

52. Pilna Notatka z rozmowy z Ambasadorem USA F. Meehanem w dn. 24.ix.br. [Urgent Note from a conversation with U.S. Ambassador F. Meehan on 24.9], MSZ, 30/85, W-2, Dep III (1982), AP 22-1-82. Meehan was scheduled to return to Washington for consultations in early November.

53. Cable from Amembassy Moscow to Secstate, "Polish, Soviet Signals on How U.S. Should Respond to Martial Law Suspension," dated December 8, 1982, NSA, Soviet Flashpoints Originals, Box 1.

54. This formulation of the three steps needed before sanctions could be lifted is noteworthy because it did not specifically refer to Solidarność. The president mentioned these in a speech on December 10, 1982, for Human Rights Day. See "Remarks on Signing the Human Rights Day and Day of Prayer for Poland Proclamations," December 10, 1982, *PPUS* (1982).

55. Pilna Notatka z rozmowy z Ambasadorem USA F. Meehan w dniu 11 bm [Urgent Note from a conversation with U.S. Ambassador R. Meehan on the eleventh of this month], dated December 11, 1982, MSZ, 30/85, W-2, Dep III (1982), AP 22-1-82. As with other important "urgent notes," this one was sent to Jaruzelski, Czyrek, Kiszczak, and Olszowski, as well as other politburo members and MSZ staff. Deputy Secretary of State Mark Palmer met with Ludwiczak in Washington a few days earlier to deliver a similar message.

56. Directorate of Intelligence, "Poland: Near Term Assessment," dated January 3, 1983, RRPL, Dobriansky Files, Box 3, Poland Memoranda 1981–1983 [January–February 1983].

57. Memo from Richard Pipes to William Clark, "Poland," dated December 15, 1982, RRPL, Dobriansky Files, Box 3, Poland Memoranda 1981–1983 [November–December 1982], underlined in the original. For information regarding Nowak's meeting, see Memo from Walter Raymond to William Clark, "Poland," dated January 4, 1982; for Dobriansky's meeting with Milewski, see handwritten notes regarding a meeting with Nowak and Milewski, dated January 6, 1983, both in RRPL, Dobriansky Files, Box 3, Poland Memoranda 1981–1983 [January–February 1983].

58. Memo from George Shultz to the President, "Poland: Responding to the Suspension of Martial Law," dated December 22, 1982, RRPL, Dobriansky Files, Box 3, Poland Memoranda 1981–1983 [November–December 1982].

59. "C-R(82)41. Council meeting on 28 July 1982. Item II on Poland," dated August 19, 1982, available online (http://www.nato.int/cps/en/natolive/81366.htm).

60. "C-R(82)46. Council meeting on 13 September 1982. Item II on Poland," dated October 11, 1982, available online (http://www.nato.int/cps/en/natolive/81366.htm).

61. Memorandum from David Pickford, "Senior Interdepartmental Group on International Economic Policy (SIG-IEP)" with attachments, dated January 10, 1983, RRPL, Executive Secretary NSC, National Security Decision Directives, Box 91286, NSDD 66 [4 of 5].

62. Memorandum for William Clark from Paula Dobriansky, "U.S. Policy toward Poland: NSC Strategy," dated March 3, 1983, RRPL, Paula Dobriansky Files, Box 3, Poland Memoranda 1981–1983 [March 1983].

63. Memorandum from William Clark to George Shultz, "Poland: Next Steps," undated, RRPL, Dobriansky Files, Box 3, Poland Memoranda 1981–1983 [April 1983].

64. Memorandum from George Shultz to the President, "Poland: Next Steps," dated March 28, 1983, Dobriansky Files, Box 3, Poland Memoranda 1981–1983 [April 1983]

65. Memorandum from William Clark to the President, "NSPG Meeting on Poland in the Situation Room," ca. April 8, 1983, Dobriansky Files, Box 3, Poland Memoranda 1981–1983 [April 1983].

66. Maintaining the status quo and a Marshall Plan approach were rejected. Handwritten notes of April 8 NSPG meeting on Poland, dated April 8, 1983, Dobriansky Files, Box 3, Poland Memoranda 1981–1983 [April 1983].

67. Memo from Paula Dobriansky and Roger Robinson to William Clark, dated April 8, 1983, Dobriansky Files, Box 3, Poland Memoranda 1981–1983 [April 1983].

68. Memo "Next Steps on Poland," attached to Memo from William Clark to the President, "Poland: Next Steps," dated May 5, 1983, Dobriansky Files, Box 3, Poland Memoranda 1981–1983 [May 1–12, 1983].

69. Note from Bud McFarlane to Paula Dobriansky, dated May 7, 1983, Dobriansky Files, Box 3, Poland Memoranda 1981–1983 [May 1–12, 1983].

70. Memo to William Clark from Paula Dobriansky, "Poland: Next Steps Update," dated May 13, 1983, RRPL, Dobriansky Files, Box 3, Poland Memoranda 1981–1983 [May 13–31, 1983].

71. "C-R(83)24. Council meeting on 19 May 1983. Item 1 on Poland," dated June 24, 1983, available online (http://www.nato.int/cps/en/natolive/81366.htm). See also "USNATO-POL-OUT-NS-83-93. United States Delegation. Talking points used by US Deputy Assistant Secretary of State Mark Palmer at the North Atlantic Council, on a US review of the situation in Poland," dated May 19, 1983, available online (http://www.nato.int/cps/en/natolive/81379.htm).

72. C-R(83)26 PART II. Council meeting on 30 May 1983. Item II on Poland," dated July 6, 1983, available online (http://www.nato.int/cps/en/natolive/81366.htm).

73. Memo to William Clark from Paula Dobriansky, "Poland Update," dated May 27, 1983, RRPL, Dobriansky Files, Box 3, Poland Memoranda 1981–1983 [May 13–31, 1983].

74. Author's interview with Davis, November 23, 1999.

75. Author's interview with Hill, May 12, 2004.

76. Rakowski, *Dzienniki polityczne*, 525.

77. For Rakowski's retelling and reactions to this interview, see ibid., 460.

78. Untitled report [regarding Ikonowicz's visit to the Vatican], dated April 1983, AAN, XIA/1417; Korespondencja z cztokami BP i Sekretarzami KC PZPR, 1983, [Correspondence with members of the Politburo and Secretariat of the PZPR Central Committee, 1983], 1–15.

79. Rakowski, *Dzienniki polityczne 1981–1983*, 511.

80. John Kifner, "Free Prisoners, Pope Asks Poland," *New York Times* (April 30, 1983), A4.

81. Rakowski, *Dzienniki polityczne 1981–1983*, 494.

82. Ibid., 443.

83. Ibid., 487.

84. Notatka w dniach 16–17.03.1983 przebywała w Moskwie z roboczą wizytą delegacja Komitetu Centralnego PZPR, której przewodniczył czl. BP sekretarz KC—Józef Czyrek [Note from 16–17.3.1983 working visit in Moscow by a PZPR Central Committee delegation, lead by Polituro Secretary Józef Czyrek], dated March 18, 1983, AAN, KC PZPR, V/193, 155–61.

85. For the report on the meeting of the Warsaw Pact leaders on June 28, see Notatka Informacyjna o spotkania przedstawicieli państw Układu Warszawskiego w Moskwie 28 czerwca 1983 r [Information Note about a meeting of representatives of the Warsaw Pact in Moscow 28 June 1983], dated June 29, 1983, AAN, KC PZPR, V/201, 36–44.

86. Rakowski, *Dzienniki polityczne 1981–1983*, 575.

87. Ibid., 620. From the Polish record it is difficult to fully evaluate how far Andropov was willing to allow East European governments to pursue reform. As Garthoff argues, Andropov still required ideological coordination and conformity within the Socialist bloc. Andropov did, however, allow a fair amount of economic reform. See Garthoff, *Great Transition*, 564. In the case of Poland, this demand for ideological conformity can be seen in May and June 1983, when a small crisis in relations broke out when the Polish periodical *Polityka* published an article that was severely criticized in the Russian periodical *Nowy Czas*. Also, the references to Andropov's views on change refer to his flexibility in allowing reforms within the Communist system, not some predisposition to allow for political liberalization. Andropov certainly did not want to see the PZPR give up any power to the opposition; Andropov was not Gorbachev.

88. *Tygodnik Mazowsze* (April 14, 1983), 1, in KARTA, Archiwum Opozycji. For a further discussion, see Friszke, "Tymczasowa Komisja Koordynacyjna," 58–59.

89. On preparations for the May events, see *Tygodnik Mazowsze* (April 21, 1983), 1, in KARTA, Archiwum Opozycji. For other articles on the upcoming papal visit and planned demonstrations on May 1 and May 3, see *Tydgonik Mazowsze* beginning on March 3, 1983. For Wałęsa's news

conference, see John Kifner, "Wałęsa Comments on May 1 Protests," *New York Times* (April 21, 1983), A12.

90. Memo, "Political Developments in Poland," dated June 15, 1983, RRPL, Dobriansky Files, Box 3, Poland Memoranda 1981–1983 [June–August 1983].

91. Rakowski, *Dzienniki polityczne 1981–1983*, 520. For a full discussion in the politburo on the demonstrations, see records from the politburo meeting on May 4, 1983, in AAN, KC PZPR, V/197.

92. Report on the internal situation, Wydzial Informacyjna KC PZPR, dated May 23, 1983, AAN, KC PZPR, V/198, 207–21; quote from 217.

93. During the visit, both private sources and public accounts make constant note of Jaruzelski's nervousness. See Rakowski's entries for June 17 through 23, *Dzienniki polityczne 1981–1983*, 561–68.

94. The pope's visit was widely covered in the American press. For some representative articles, see Bradley Graham, "Pope Greets Poland as Land That 'Suffers Anew,'" *Washington Post* (June 17, 1983), A1; Michael Dobbs, "'Solidarity Will Be Reborn—But Inside Us': Poles Hope for a Revival of Unity," *Washington Post* (June 17, 1983), A25; Dobbs, " Pope's Chief Theme Is Polish History," *Washington Post* (June 18, 1983), A16; John Kifner, "Angry Chants and 'V' Signs fill Warsaw," *New York Times* (June 18, 1983), A1; Kifner, "Pope Hails the 'Solidarity' of Poles and Gets a Tumultuous Ovation," *New York Times* (June 19, 1983), A1; Kifner, "Misjudgment by Warsaw," *New York Times* (June 20, 1983). A1; and Bradley Graham, "Pope Issues Appeal to Poles for Accord Based on Trust," *Washington Post* (June 22, 1983), A1.

95. Friszke, "Tymczasowa Komisja Koordynacyjna," 76.

96. Rakowski, *Dzienniki polityczne 1981–1983*, 565.

97. "Remarks to Polish Americans in Chicago, Illinois, June 23, 1983," *PPUS* (1983).

98. A copy of the letter is located in MSZ, 49/86, w-1, Dep III (1983), AP 22-1-83, "Stanowisko USA wobec Zawieszenia i Zniesienia Stanu Wojennego w Polsce od 23.xii.1983 do 31.xii.1983 r" [U.S. Position regarding Suspending and Lifting Martial Law in Poland from 23.11.1983 to 31.12.1983].

99. Michael Gertler, "Brzeziński, West Berlin Mayor Urge Quick U.S. Nod to Poland," *Washington Post* (June 16, 1983), A21.

100. Lou Cannon, "U.S. Links Lifting of Sanctions to Poles' Intent to Lift Martial Law," *Washington Post* (June 28, 1983), A6.

101. For the State Department's analysis of the papal visit, see Memo to William Clark from Charles Hill, "Poland," dated June 25, 1983, RRPL, Dobriansky Files, Poland Memoranda 1981–1983 [June–August 1983]. The specific date of the meeting, July 7, and the general outlines of the information are confirmed in files from the MSZ; see MSZ, 48/86, W-1, Dep III (1983), AP 22-1-83, "Stosunki Bilateralny PRL-USA" [Bilateral PRL-U.S. Relations]; see in particular the account in "Ocena polityki USA wobec Polski. Wnioski. Program działania" [Assessment of U.S. policies regarding Poland: Conclusions: Action Program], dated Ocotber 17, 1983, 5.

102. As quoted in Graham, "Warsaw Abolishes Martial Law: Amnesty Decreed; New Rules Limit Dissident Activities," *Washington Post* (July 22, 1983), A1. See also Kifner, "Poland Says It Lifts Martial Law: Curbs Now Put into Law," *New York Times* (July 22, 1983), A1.

103. "Ocena polityki USA wobec Polski. Wnioski. Program działania," 5.

104. Memo to William Clark from Paula Dobriansky, "Poland: Department of Labor Analysis," with attachements, dated August 6, 1983, RRPL, Dobriansky Files, Poland Memoranda 1981–1983 [June–August 1983].

105. Dobbs, "U.S. Takes Step to Resume Talks on Polish Debt," *Washington Post* (July 30, 1983), A1.

106. Briefing Memorandum, "Western Policy towards Poland," dated August 10, 1983, NSA, End of the Cold War, Box 1, September 6–9, 1983: Shultz's Trip to Madrid.

107. Ibid.

108. Notatka Informacyjna z pobytu w Polsce senatora amerykańskiego Christophera Dodd'a w dniach 8–10 sierpnia br. [Information Note from the visit in Poland by American Senator Christopher Dodd from 8–10 August], dated August 11, 1983, MSZ, 48/86, W-1, Dep III (1983), AP 220-4-83.

109. For a summary of Long's visit, see Notatka Informacyjna z pobytu grupy członków Izby Reprezentantów Kongresu USA z Kongresmanem Clarence D. Long'iem w Polsce w dniu 17.08.83 r. [Information Note from the visit of a group from the U.S. House of Representatives with Con-gressman D. Long to Poland on 17.8.1983], dated August 22, 1983, MSZ, 48/86, W-1, Dep III (1983), AP 220-6-83. For a full transcript of the meeting with Jaruzelski, see Zapis z rozmowy Towar-zysza Premiera Gen. W. Jaruzelskiego z grupą kongresmenów amerykańskich w dn. 17.viii.1983 r [Transcript from Comrade Premier General W. Jaruzelski's conversation with a group of Ameri-can congressmen on 17.8.1983], dated August 17, 1983, AAN, KC PZPR, V/203, 200–228, esp. 211 and 218.

110. Author's interview with Hill. See also, Notatka Informacyjna, dated September 9, 1983, MSZ, 48/86, W-2, Dep III (1983), AP 53-3-83.

111. This is the text of a Department of State announcement, found in English in MSZ, 48/86, W-1, Dep III (1983), AP 22-1-83.

112. Davis replaced Hugh Hamilton, who had replaced Herbert Wilgis as chargé d'affaires at the end of August 1983. Wilgis's final meeting with the MSZ took place on August 23, 1983; see Notatka Informacyjna z wizyty pożegnalnej chargé d'affaires USA H. Wilgis w dniu 23 sierpnia 1983 r [Information note from the final visit by U.S. chargé d'affaires H. Wilgis on 23 August 1983], MSZ, 48/86, W-1, Dep III (1983), AP 10-2-83. Following Davis's arrival, Hamilton remained at the embassy as DCM.

113. Pilna Notatka z rozmowy z chargé d'affaires USA, Johnem Davis'em [Urgent Note from a conversation with chargé d'affaires John Davis], dated September 17, 1983, MSZ, 48/86, W-1, Dep III (1983), AP 22-1-83.

114. Memorandum from the Secretary of State to the President, "Poland: Next Steps," dated October 13, 1983, and Memorandum for the President from Robert McFarlane, "Poland: Next Steps," dated October 20, 1983, in RRPL, Dobriansky Files, Box 3, Poland Memoranda 1981–1983 [September–October 1983].

115. Notatka Informacynja z rozmowy z Chargé d'Affaires a.i. USA—Johnem Davisem w dniu 31.x.1983 [Information Note from a conversation with U.S. Chargé d'affaires John Davis on 31.10.1983], dated October 31, 1983, MSZ, 48/86, W-2, Dep III (1983), AP 36-1-83 and AP 22-1-83. This information note was sent to politburo members including Jaruzelski, Czyrek, and Olszowski.

116. A copy of this statement can be found in RRPL, Dobriansky Files, Box 3, Poland Memo-randa 1981–1983 [November 1983].

117. Notatka Informacyjna z przekazania Chargé d'Affaires a.i. USA J. Davis'owi noty Rządu PRL do Rządu USA w sprawie polityki USA wobec Polski [Information Note transferring to U.S. chargé d'affaires J. Davis a PRL government note to the U.S. government in the matter of

U.S. policy regarding Poland], dated November 4, 1983, MSZ, 48/86, W-1, Dep III (1983), AP 22-1-83/B. This information note was sent to all members of the politburo.

118. Unofficial Translation of November 3, 1983, PRL Government Note [in English], dated November 3, 1983, MSZ, 48/86, W-1, Dep III (1983), AP 22-1-83/B.

119. Zapis ze spotkanie tow. Z. Ludwiczak Chargé d'Affaires a.i. PRL w Waszyngtonie z kierownictwem Departmentu III i pracownikami Zespołu Ameryki Północnej Departmentu III—w dniu 19.09.1983 r. [Transcript of meeting with PRL chargé d'affaires a.i. to the U.S. Z. Ludwiczak and the staff of the North American Group of Department III, on 19.09.1983], dated September 19, 1983, MSZ, 48/86, W-1, Dep III (1983), AP 23-3-83.

120. Author's interview with Davis, November 23, 1999. Written records or recordings were not made of these parties, so no specific archival documentation is currently available. However, information gathered during conversations from these gatherings did regularly appear in the cable traffic back and forth with Washington.

121. Ibid.

122. Author's interview with Bronisław Geremek, July 26, 2006.

123. Davis, "Postwar Relations," 212.

124. Author's interview with Hill.

125. Conference proceedings from "Communism's Negotiated Collapse: The Polish Round Table Talks of 1989, Ten Years Later," held at the University of Michigan, April 7–10, 1999 (available online at www.umich.edu/~iinet/PolishRoundTable/frame.html); quoted from the morning session of April 8.

126. Author's interview with Cameron Munter, June 11, 2004. Munter was a consular officer and then economics officer in Warsaw 1986–1988.

127. Author's interview with Geremek.

128. Author's interview with Janusz Onyszkiewicz, Warsaw, July 8, 2010.

129. Gates, *From the Shadows*, 237.

130. Schweizer, *Victory*, 75.

131. Ibid., 76.

132. The $10 million figure comes from Paczkowski, "Playground of the Superpowers," 385. According to Schweizer the CIA funneled about $2 million a year from 1983 to 1989. Schweizer's and Gates's accounts of the events do not line up as to the timing of the beginning of the financial operation. Schweizer believes they began in early 1982, but Gates writes that they did not get rolling until the end of 1982. Given Gates's access to classified material and the specificity of the dates he cites, I am inclined to believe his account over Schweizer's, although it is credible that Casey began planning for the support operation in early 1982. See Gates, *From the Shadows*, 237–38 and Schweizer, *Victory*, 76–77. Without access to CIA files, this amount is impossible to verify. It is surprising, however, that the total amount Gates claims to have been sent is equivalent to the money provided by the NED. Given that Poland would have been awash with dollars if it had received $20 million in funds, I believe this might be a case of double counting, meaning that Gates is probably including the NED amounts in his $10 million figure. In this case, the CIA money becomes much less significant.

133. Gates, *From the Shadows*, 237.

134. Author's interview with Davis, November 23, 1999.

135. Author's interview with Hill.

136. Puddington, *Broadcasting Freedom*, 270.

137. There are a series of letters between Najder and Giedroyc from 1982 to 1984 in Najder's private papers, as well as a letter from Bujak, dated April 23, 1986, in Hoover, Zdzisław Najder Files, Box 3.

138. Urban, *Radio Free Europe*, 124.

139. Jacques Semelin, "Communication et résistence: Les radios occidentales comme vecteur d'ouverture a l'est" (Paris: Reseaux no. 53, CNET, June 1992), 9–24, as summarized in Nelson, *War of the Black Heavens*, 160.

140. Pilna Notatka z rozmowy z charge d'Affaires USA w Warszawie John'em Davis'em w dniu 18 kwetnia 1984 r. [Urgent Note from a conversation with U.S. charge d'affaires a.i. John Davis on 18 April 1984], dated April 23, 1984, MSZ, 59/86, W-8, Dep III (1984), AP 53-5-8.

141. Najder's papers at the Hoover Institution Archives include an impressive amount of correspondence between Wojtech and Olek, two pseudonyms. From other correspondence it appears that Olek was J.Ł., likely Jerzy Łojek who lived in Paris and regularly corresponded with Najder. It is unclear who his contact in Poland was. Najder's files include a collection of Solidarność and government documents, a few examples of samizdat, and at least one example of the smuggled microfilm. See Hoover, Zdzisław Najder Files, Box 10, [Unlabeled].

142. Hoover, Zdzisław Najder Files, Box 10, [Unlabeled].

143. Hoover, Zdzisław Najder Files, Box 5, Scripts. There is no hard evidence to suggest that Najder took steps to purchase these materials himself and send them into Poland, but he was at least tangentially involved in the web of Western activists.

144. For examples of these kinds of payments, see Hoover Institution, RFE/RL, Broadcast Records, Blue Box 3, Operations Summary 1986, January–December. The RFE/RL collection contains dozens of these monthly Operation Summary reports. Given the RFE's history, it seems probable that these funds had a connection to Casey's CIA operation.

145. Nelson, *War of the Black Heavens*, 158.

146. Message to the Polish Section, RFE, May 3, 1992, BIB 1993 annual report, 5, RFE/RL, as quoted ibid., 160.

147. Handwritten note from Irena Lasota to Tom [Kahn], dated November 2, 1982; and handwritten note with attachments from Irena Lasota to Tom Kahn, dated November 21, 1982, AFL-CIO, International Affairs Department, Inactive Records, "Committee in Support of Solidarity." From Lasota's notes it is unclear just how these radios and electronic materials made their way into Poland, but they were presumably used to allow better communication between underground leaders or to aid Radio Solidarność, a clandestine radio station operated by Zbigniew Romaszewki that sporadically broadcast short informational bulletins, primarily in the Warsaw area.

148. Memo from Tom Kahn to Tom Donahue, dated November 5, 1982, and AFL-CIO, International Affairs Department Files, Inactive Records, "Committee in Support of Solidarity."

149. Internal passports were documents needed by Polish citizens to travel domestically. Again it is unclear who the passport was for, if it was for Lasota herself or her collaborators. From the exchange of notes it does appear that the AFL-CIO was forging Polish government documents to help members of the underground move about the country. See handwritten note from Irena Lasota to Tom [Kahn], dated ca. March 1983; and Telephone message to Tom Kahn from E, dated March 29, 1983, both in AFL-CIO, International Affairs Department, Inactive Records, "Committee in Support of Solidarity." Lasota has confirmed that they received copies of the internal passport, but could not remember if they were ever used. Author's interview with Lasota, June 19, 2007.

150. Note from Irena Lasota to Tom Kahn, dated August 8, 1983; and note from Tom Kahn to Tom Donohue, dated August 17, 1983, AFL-CIO, International Affairs Department, Inactive Records, "Committee in Support of Solidarity."

151. Note from Irena Lasota to Tom Kahn, dated August 8, 1983.

152. Letter from Tom Kahn to Irena Lasota, dated August 22, 1983, AFL-CIO, International Affairs Department, Inactive Records, "Committee in Support of Solidarity."

153. Memorandum from Tom Kahn to William Collins, dated July 8, 1985, with attached letter and receipts from Eric Chenoweth, dated July 1, 1985, AFL-CIO, International Affairs Department, Inactive Files, "Committee in Support of Solidarity."

154. In 1982 Chenoweth had an operating budget of $84,500, supported mostly by a grant from the Smith Richardson Foundation and a smaller amount from the Rockefeller Brothers. In 1983, CSS's operating budget dropped to just under $55,000, donated primarily by the AFL-CIO and other individual unions, as well as a grant from the John M. Olin Foundation. In 1982 and 1983, CSS also received consistent payments from the AFL-CIO to reimburse them for Telex bills and travel to meetings in Washington, as well as Solidarność-related events around the country and in Europe. Expenditures for 1984 grew to just over $95,000, with more than half from the Free Trade Union Institute and the rest from the Olin Foundation and the AFL-CIO. According to internal records, each year the majority of these funds went to pay salaries, rent, duplication fees, and to purchase the necessary office equipment, most notably photocopiers. For information on 1982 financial records, see CSS Records, CSS: Fundraising (Budget, income) 1982. For financial information on 1983, see letter from Eric Chenoweth to Ms. E. Tischer (IRS) with attachments, dated February 17, 1985, CSS, CSS: Corporate Records, U.S. Corporation Co. For 1984 reports, see Financial Report January–December 1984, in the same file. On Soros's contribution, see Kaufman, *Soros*, 185.

155. The Indiana University Herman B. Wells Library has a full run of the CSS *Reports*.

156. Polish Helsinki Watch Committee, *1984 Violations of Human Rights*. The information about CSS activities in 1983 and 1984 in this section is culled from annual reports from 1983 and 1984–85, located in CSS, CSS: Annual Reports 1983–1986.

157. For letters to government officials, see blue-marked folder and "Correspondence/Let Sanct," both located in the CSS records.

158. From Tom Kahn's records, it appears that the AFL-CIO generally reimbursed the CSS for trips to Washington to pursue lobbying activities there.

159. "Address to Members of the British Parliament, June 8, 1982," *PPUS* (1982).

160. Joel M. Woldman, "The National Endowment for Democracy," *Congressional Research Service Brief*, September 3, 1985, 3, located in NSA, National Endowment for Democracy Collection, Box 2, "Duplicates."

161. Ibid.

162. NSDD 77, "Management of Public Diplomacy Relative to National Security," dated January 14, 1983, available online through the NARA's ARC system (www.archives.gov/research/arc/).

163. "Current Policy No. 456: Project Democracy," February 23, 1983 (Washington, D.C.: Department of State, 1983), 2–3; located at NSA, National Endowment for Democracy Collection, Box 2, "GAO Reports."

164. The APF kept the White House well informed of its progress and potential suggestions. Memorandum for William P. Clark from Walter Raymond, "American Political Foundation

Study," dated September 29,1982, RRPL, Assistant to the President for National Security Affairs Records, OA 85, Project Democracy [1].

165. APF Report, "The Democracy Program: A Brief Introduction," dated January 1983, NSA, National Endowment for Democracy Collection, Box 2, "NED General."

166. House Committee on Foreign Relations, *Authorizing Appropriations for Fiscal Years 1984–1985*, esp. comments by Representatives Fascell and Kastmeyer on 123 and 128.

167. American Political Foundation Democracy Program Report, "The Commitment to Democracy: A Bi-partisan Approach," dated April 18, 1983, on file at the NED Headquarters Library, Washington, D.C.

168. For testimony to Congress summarizing the APF report, see House Committee on Foreign Relations, *Authorizing Appropriations for Fiscal Years 1984–1985*, 881–83.

169. Letter from William Clark to William E. Brock, dated March 14, 1983, included as an appendix to "The Commitment to Democracy: A Bi-partisan Approach."

170. Proposal to the National Endowment for Democracy submitted by the Committee in Support of Solidarity, dated April 10, 1984, AFL-CIO, International Affairs Department, Inactive Records, "Committee in Support of Solidarity."

171. Proposal to the Free Trade Union Institute, AFL-CIO, submitted by the Committee in Support of Solidarity, dated September 20, 1984, AFL-CIO, International Affairs Department, Inactive Records, "Committee in Support of Solidarity."

172. See Annual Report 1984–1985, undated, CSS, CSS: Annual Reports 1983–1986 and Total Budget January-December 1985, undated, CSS, CSS: Corporate Records, U.S. Corporation Co.

173. Report, National Endowment for Democracy Fiscal Year 1984 Grants Awarded, dated ca. October 1984, RRPL, Walter Raymond Files, OA91068, NED 1984–1985 [12 of 14]. A chart with specific dollar amounts is attached as an appendix.

174. Author's interview with Eugenia Kemble, January 18, 2008.

175. Andrzej Friszke estimates that the AFL-CIO provided $200,000 per year to the Coordinating Office in 1983 and 1984. In 1985 and 1986 he estimates that they received $300,000 ("Tymczasowa Komisja Koordynacyjna," 133). This figure is roughly confirmed in Carl Gershman's testimony for 1987 appropriations for NED, which set the level of funds going through FTUI to Solidarność in 1986 at $304,163, and as Gershman laments in his testimony, funding levels from NED had remained stagnant. See "National Endowment for Democracy Regional Listing of Approved Programs in FY 1986," in House Committee on Appropriations, *Departments of Commerce, Justice, and State, the Judiciary and Related Agency Appropriations for 1987*, 498.

176. For a report on NED's fiscal year 1985 expenditures, see *Departments of Commerce, Justice, and State, the Judiciary and Related Agency Appropriations for 1987*, 485–86. In fiscal year 1985, NED had its congressional appropriations slashed. The $18.5 million that was given for the program came from a fund designated for salaries. In fiscal year 1986, congressional funding for NED was reinstated, but it was more than $1 million less due to budgetary constraints.

177. Letter from Lasota and Chenoweth to Brzeziński, dated December 29, 1983, Library of Congress, Zbigniew Brzeziński Papers, Box II: 197, Committee in Support of Solidarity 1983–1984.

178. For specific information on union support in Europe, see chapter 2 and Goddeeris, *Solidarity with Solidarity*.

179. For Milewski's conversation with Dobriansky on the issue of funding, see handwritten notes of meeting with Jan Nowak and Jerzy Milewski, RRPL, Dobriansky Files, Box 3, Poland Memoranda 1981–1983 [January–February 1983].

180. Report, "Shipments to Poland as of May 5, 1983," dated May 5, 1983, CRS, EURMENA, Program Correspondence Box 11, "1983 Poland: Shipping Reports."

181. W nawiązaniu do ustaleń telefonicznych z Tow. V-dyrektorem Pawliszewskim podajemy informację nt. dostaw humanitarnych z USA w latach 1981–85 [In reference to the telephone arrangements with Com. Vice-director Pawliszewski sending information about humanitarian shipments from the U.S. from 1981 to 1985], dated October 24, 1985, MSZ, 2/89, W-8, Dep III (1985), AP 39-2-85.

182. For information on KCEP, see Kreihs, *Dobro ukryte*, esp. 59–90. According to Polish government documents, the KCEP distributed more than 530 thousand tons of aid from 1981 to 1985, so the CRS contribution amounted to about half of the final amount. The other aid KCEP distributed came primarily from Western Europe, especially West Germany and France.

183. Kreihs, *Dobro ukryte*, 69.

184. W nawiązaniu do ustaleń telefonicznych z Tow. V-dyrektorem Pawliszewskim podajemy informację nt. dostaw humanitarnych z USA w latach 1981–85, dated October 24, 1985.

185. Ibid.

186. List od Primasa Glempa do Wojciecha Jaruzelskiego [Letter from Glemp to Wojciech Jaruzelski], MSZ, 42/92, W-5, Dep III (1988), AP 54-0-88. For the MSZ Department III's early opinions on an agricultural fund, see Opinia dla Towarzysza gen. armii Wojciecha Jaruzelskiego—Prezesa Rady Ministrów dotycząca propozycji Prymasa Polski udzielenia pomocy zagranicznej na rzecz polskiego rolnictwa [Opinion for Com Gen. Wojciech Jaruzelski, Chairman of the Council of Ministers, regarding the proposition by the Primate of Poland to accept foreign help for Polish agriculture], dated ca. September 1982; and Stanowisko MSZ w sprawie propozycji Prymasa Polski udzielenia pomocy zagranicznej na rzecz polskiego rolnictwa [MSZ position on the matter of the Primate of Poland's proposition to accept foreign aid for Polish agriculture], dated September 24, 1982, both in MSZ, 42/92, W-5, Dep III (1988), AP 54-0-88.

187. Meeting Minutes, "NSC Meeting Regarding the Polish Debt, the Private Sector Initiative for Poland, and the Latin American Debt," dated September 30, 1982, RRPL, Dobriansky Files, Poland Memoranda 1981–1983 [November–December 1982].

188. Szyfrogram Nr. 621/III from New York, dated July 14, 1983, MSZ, 42/92, W-5, Dep III (1988), AP 54-0-88.

189. Robert McFarlane replaced William Clark as national security adviser in October 1983.

190. Cable from Amembassy Warsaw to NSC, "Meetings on Polish Church Plan," dated June 16, 1984, RRPL, Dobriansky Files, Box 3, Poland Memoranda 1984–1985 [April–July 1984].

191. Memo for Robert McFarlane from Paula Dobriansky, "Your Meeting with Father Aloyzy Orszulik," dated June 28, 1984, Dobriansky Files, Box 3, Poland Memoranda 1984–1985 [April–July 1984].

192. Pilna Notatka z rozmowy w dniu 20.7. br. z prof. A. Stelmachowskim i prof. W. Trzeciakowskim na temat ich rozmów w Europie Zachodniej, USA i Kanadzie w sprawie funduszów dla kościelnej Fundacji [Urgent note from a conversation on 20.7 with Prof. A. Stelmachowski and Prof. W. Trzeciakowski regarding their conversations in Western Europe, U.S., and Canada on the matter of funds for the Church Foundation], dated July 23, 1984, MSZ, 42/92, W-5, Dep III (1988), AP 54-0-88; quote from 5.

193. "Remarks at a White House Luncheon Marking the 40th Anniversary of the Warsaw Uprising, August 17, 1984," *PPUS* (1984).

194. Senate Committee on Foreign Relations, *Agricultural Activities in Poland*, 98–108. Although Western funds were raised for a pilot version of the Church Agricultural Fund, the fund never came into existence. Ultimately the PZPR blocked the creation of the independent, church-run foundation. For a full explanation of the problems the fund faced, see Siwek, *Fundacja rolniczej*.

195. Letter from Lane Kirland to the President, dated October 26, 1983, RRPL, Dobriansky Files, Box 3, Poland Memoranda 1981–1983 [November 1983]. For CSS's opinion, see Letter from Irena Lasota and Eric Chenoweth to Secretary George Shutlz, dated November 23, 1983, CSS, [blue-labeled folder].

196. Mailgram from Alojsius Mazewski to the President of the United States, dated October 21, 1983, RRPL, Dobriansky Files, Box 3, Poland Memoranda 1981–1983 [November 1983].

197. Cable from Amembassy Rome to Secstate, dated December 30, 1983, RRPL, Dobriansky Files, Box 3, Poland Memoranda 1984–1985 [January 1984].

198. Cable from Amembassy Rome to Secstate, "Vatican Views on Wałęsa's Sanctions Statement," dated September 23, RRPL, Dobriansky Files, Box 3, Poland Memoranda 1984–1985 [January 1984].

199. Handwritten note from Faith Whittelsey to Bud McFarlane with attachments, dated February 23, 1984, RRPL, Dobriansky Files, Box 3, Poland Memoranda 1984–1985 [February 27-18, 1984].

200. Author's interview with Onyszkiewicz.

201. Interview with Bujak in *Tygodnik Mazowsze* (Feburary 11, 1982), in KARTA, Archiwum Opozycji.

202. Kassandra (Jacek Kołobinski), "W zamydlonych oczach Zachodu" [In the Soapy Eyes of the West], *Tygodnich Mazowsze* (December 16, 1982), 4, in KARTA, Archiwum Opozycji.

203. Telex Message from Jerzy Milewski to Lane Kirkland, dated December 6, 1983, AFL-CIO, Lane Kirkland Presidential Files, Inactive Records, "Wałęsa on Sanctions." Wałęsa also took the time to write a personal letter to Kirkland explaining that he did not mean to cause any friction with the AFL-CIO's earlier position. Letter from Lech Wałęsa to Lane Kirkland, dated January 28, 1984, AFL-CIO International Affairs Department Files, Inactive Records, "Committee in Support of Solidarity."

204. For the quick back-and-forth on this issue, see Memorandum for the President from Secretary of State, "Poland: Next Steps," dated January 11, 1984; Memo for the Secretary of State, "Poland: Next Steps," dated January 16, 1984; and Memorandum for the President from Robert McFarlane, "Poland: Next Steps," dated January 16, 1984, all in RRPL, Dobriansky Files, Poland Memoranda 1984–1985, Box 3 [January 1984].

205. John Goshko, "Reagan Eases Polish Sanctions after Appeal from Wałęsa," *Washington Post* (Jan. 20, 1984), A16. This announcement confirmed fishing quotas that had been mentioned earlier in the year, meaning that the administration had dropped any restrictions on quotas based on how political prisoners were treated. The announcement on airline communications did not allow for LOT to maintain regularly scheduled flights, only eighty-eight chartered flights.

206. See Davies, *God's Playground*, 551–53; and Paczkowski, *Spring*, 298.

207. Rakowski, *Dzienniki polityczne 1981–1983*, 289, 337.

208. Memorandum from Paula Dobriansky to Robert McFarlane, "Poland: Response to Unofficial Emissary Schaff," dated February 9, 1984, RRPL, NSC, European and Soviet Affairs Directorate, Box 91186, Vatican. In Polish documents the group is often just referred to as "the eleven."

209. Memorandum from Robert McFarlane to the President, "Poland: Response to Unofficial Emissary Schaff," dated February 16, 1984, RRPL, NSC, European and Soviet Affairs Directorate, Box 91186, Vatican.

210. Cable from Amembassy Warsaw to Secstate, "Response from Jaruzelski," dated March 2, 1984, RRPL, Dobriansky Files, Poland Memoranda 1984–1985 [March 1984].

211. Memorandum for the President from Robert McFarlane [with Reagan's handwritten comments], "Poland: Response to Jaruzelski," dated March 26, 1984; and Memorandum for George Shultz from Robert McFarlane, "Poland: Response to Jaruzelski," dated March 28, 1984, RRPL, Dobriansky Files, Box 3, Poland Memoranda 1984–1985 [March 1984].

212. For Schaff's account, see his *Notatki Kłopotnika*, 123–27.

213. Memorandum for Robert McFarlane from Charles Hill, "Polish Response on U.S.-Polish Dialogue," dated April 24, 1984, RRPL, Dobriansky Files, Box 3, Poland Memoranda 1984–1985 [April–July 1984].

214. Memorandum for Robert McFarlane from Paula Dobriansky, "Polish Response on U.S.-Polish Dialogue," dated May 1, 1984, RRPL, Dobriansky Files, Box 3, Poland Memoranda 1984–1985 [April–July 1984].

215. Rakowski, *Dzienniki polityczne 1984–1986*, 12.

216. Ibid., 18.

217. Koncepcje polityczno-prawne zakończenia postępowań karnych przeciwko członkom kierwonictwa anytpaństwowego związke pn. "KSS-KOR" i ekstremistycznym działaczom b. "Solidarności" [Politico-legal conceptualization for ending the criminal proceedings against leaders of the anti-State group KSS-KOR and Solidarnosc extremists], dated ca. Febryary 1, 1984, AAN, KC PZPR, V/219, 228–39; quote from 234.

218. "Poland: Response to Unofficial Emissary Schaff," dated February 16, 1984.

219. For information on the U.N. secretary general's visit to Poland in February, see Notatka Informacyjna z oficjalnej wizyty w Polsce Sekretarza Generalnego ONZ, Javiera Pereza de Cuellara [Information Note from the official visit to Poland of U.N. Secretary General Javier Pérez du Cuéllar], dated Feburary 24,1984, AAN, KC PZPR, V/221, 206–212. Michnik and other KOR dissidents had routinely been given the option of emigrating from Poland to secure their release, beginning in 1982. Each time, however, he and his colleagues rejected the offers. For Michnik's reactions to these offers, see his pronouncements, "Why You Are Not Emigrating . . ." and "A Letter to General Kiszczak," translated by Maya Latynski in *Letters from Prison*.

220. Decision #2, Protocół 115 for PZPR Politburo Meeting May 2, 1984, AAN, KC PZPR, Mikr. 3054, Sygn. 1885, 31.

221. Michael Kaufman, "Trial Date Is Set for 4 Solidarity Advisors," *New York Times* (June 13, 1984), A3.

222. Christopher Bobinski, "Most of Poland's Political Prisoners Likely to Be Freed," *Financial Times* (June 15, 1984), A3; and "Hardliners Force Delay in Polish Amnesty," *Financial Times* (July 12, 1984), A2. For the quote, see "Poland Expels Marxist Scholar," *Globe and Mail* (Toronto) (June 29, 1984).

223. Bradley Graham, "Poles Declare Amnesty for Political Prisoners," *Washington Post* (July 22, 1984), A1.

224. Statement by Principal Deputy Press Secretary Speakes on United States Sanctions Against Poland, August 3, 1984," *PPUS* (1984). The presidential decision was made on August 2, 1984. See memo from Dobriansky to McFarlane, "Poland: Response to Amnesty" with attachment, RRPL, Dobriansky Files, Box 3, Poland Memoranda 1984–1985 [August 1984].

225. Poland signed the original treaty to create the IMF and was making final preparations for membership in 1980 and 1981. Officials from the IMF visited Warsaw to observe progress just prior to the declaration of martial law.

226. NSC Meeting Minutes, "IMF Membership for Poland," dated August 28, 1984, RRPL, Dobriansky Files, Box 3, Poland Memoranda 1984–1985 [August 1984].

227. Bobinski, "General Jaruzelski Takes a Calculated Gamble," *Financial Times* (July 24, 1984), A14. Charlotte Saikowski, "US May Ease Up on Warsaw to Avoid Gain by Hard-Liners," *Christian Science Monitor* (Dec. 13, 1984), A3.

228. Memorandum for the President from Robert McFarlane, "Poland: IMF Membership," dated October 12, 1984, RRPL, Dobriansky Files, Box 3, Poland Memoranda 1984–1985 [September–November 1984].

229. Notatka Informacyjna z rozmowy w dniu 20 października 1984 r. z Chargé d'Affaires a.i. Ambasady USA J. Davis'em [Information Note from the conversation on 20 October 1984 with U.S. embassy chargé d'affaires J. Davis], dated October 20, 1984, MSZ, 59/86, W-5, Dep III (1984), AP 22-1-84/A.

230. Clyde Farnsworth, "U.S. Said to Drop Its Bar to Poland in Monetary Fund," *New York Times* (Dec. 15, 1984), A1.

231. Memo from Robert McFarlane to Tyrus Cobb, "Your Meeting with the Pope," dated January 8, 1985, RRPL, Tyrus Cobb Files, OA 90901, The Vatican-1985 (1 of 2).

232. Unofficial Translation of the position of the PRL regarding the announcement by the authorities of the USA of their readiness to lift some restrictions, dated August 16, 1984, MSZ, 35/90, W-4, Dep III (1987), AP 223-1-87. For a record of Davis's meeting when he received this note, see Notatka Informacyjna z przekazania Chargé d'affaires a.i. USA J. Davis'owi Stanowisko Rządu PRL w sprawie zapowiedzi władz USA gotowości zniesienia niektórych restrykcji [Information Note from presentation of U.S. chargé d'affaires J. Davis on the PRL position on the matter of a response to the U.S. to lifting no restrictions], dated August 17, 1984, MSZ, 35/90, W-4, Dep III (1987), AP 223-1-87.

233. "Statement on the Death of Father Jerzy Popiełuszko of Poland, October 31, 1984," *PPUS* (1984).

234. Memo from Paula Dobriansky to Robert McFarlane, "Implications of Popiełuszko Murder," dated November 21, 1984, RRPL, Dobriansky Files, Box 3, Poland Memoranda 1984–1985 [September–November 1984].

235. Brief Memo, "Visit by the PUS to Bonn: 18–19 November," dated November 16, 1984, FCO, FOI materials released to the author.

236. The information on this episode is culled from informal notes and brief records in MSZ, 2/89, W-6, Dep III (1985), AP 10-5-85. The quotes come from a handwritten chronology in those files.

237. Letter from John Davis to Stefan Olszowski with attached note, dated December 19, 1984, MSZ, 2/89, W-6, Dep III (1985), AP 10-5-85. The decision to announce an ultimatum was made in Washington without consultations with Davis. Author's interview with Davis, April 27, 2007.

238. Handwritten note on White House stationary from John [Poindexter] to Judge [Clark], dated May 6, 1983, and Memo from Bud McFarlane to Paula Dobriansky, dated May 7, 1983, both in RRPL, Dobriansky Files, Box 3, Poland Memoranda 1981–1983 [May 1–12, 1983].

239. See footnote 236.

240. Pilna Notatka z rozmowy z J. Davis'em, chargé d'affaires a.i. USA w Warszawie w dniu 10 bm. [Urgent Note from a conversation with J. Davis, U.S. chargé d'affaires a.i. in Warsaw, on the tenth of this month], dated January 11, 1985, MSZ, 2/89, W-8, Dep III (1985), AP 53-5-85. This urgent note was sent to politburo members including Jaruzelski.

241. Notatka Informacyjna z rozmowy w dniu 16 stycznia 1985 r. z chargé d'affaires a.i. USA [Information Note from a conversation on 16 January 1985 with the U.S. chargé d'affaires], dated January 18, 1985, MSZ, 2/89, W-8, Dep III (1985), AP 53-5-85.

242. Notatka dla Towarzysza Min. J. Kinast [Note for Comrade Minister J. Kinast], with attachment, ca. January 17, 1985, MSZ, 2/89, W-6, Dep III (1985), AP 10-5-85.

243. See note 236.

244. Report, dated February 1, 1984, MSZ, 59/86, W-5, Dep III (1984), AP 22-1-84.

245. Paczkowki, *Polska 1986–1989*, 267.

246. Interview with Davis, November 23, 1999.

247. Rakowski, *Dzienniki polityczne 1984–1986*, 113.

248. Ibid., 119.

249. Within this framework it is possible to view Polish moves as attempts to use prisoners as points of leverage against the Americans. The historical record shows that the PZPR decided to use Wałęsa's release to get concessions from the Catholic Church. Jaruzelski and his colleagues may have viewed other prisoners in a similar way. Deals with the Americans were only finalized after the politburo had decided to release the prisoners, so it is consistent to view negotiations linking sanctions to prisoner releases as a means for Poland to gain some relief. The full extent of this conclusion is only tentative and deserves further research.

250. Interview with Hill; emphasis in the original.

251. Interview with Davis, April 27, 2007.

252. The term "partner" is not meant to insinuate that the church's loyalties lay anywhere other than with the Polish people. Unlike its relationship with the United States, however, the PZPR's relationship with the church entailed open negotiations, with both sides making concessions. Recent revelations about parish priests and church officials working as informants to the security services, however, have muddied the clarity of the church's role as intermediary.

253. The figures in this section come from information in a document prepared by the International Department of the Ministry of Finance, dated March 15, 1984: Notatka w sprawie oceny skutków restrykcjii zostosowanych przez kraje zachodnie wobec Polski w sferze stosunków finansowo-kredytowych [Note concerning the assessment of the effects of the restrictions imposed by the Western countries against Poland in the financial-credit sphere], attached to Notatka Informacyjna [Information Note], dated April 26, 1984, MSZ, 14/89, W-3, Dep III (1986), AP 223-2-86.

## Chapter 4

1. The quotes and story are taken from Michael Kaufman, "A Rousing Polish Party Celebrates an Amnesty," *New York Times* (Sept. 21, 1986), A16.

2. Notatka Informacyjna z rozmowy z chargé d'Affaires a.i. USA w Warszawie, David'em Swartz'em w dniu 19 lutego 1985 r. w sprawie raportu Departmentu Stanu dotyczącego przestrzegania praw człowieka w poszczególnych państwach w 1984 r. [Information Note from a conversation with U.S. chargé d'affaires David Swartz on 19 February 1985, concering the Department of

State's report on Human Rights abuses in 1984], dated February 20, 1985, MSZ, 2/89, W-6, Dep III (1985), AP 22-1-85/A.

3. For information on the Myer affair, see MSZ, 2/89, W-8, Dep III (1985), AP 35-6-85. Quoted material on the specifics of the treatement of the Myers is from a Pilna Notatka [urgent note] from a February 22 meeting between David Swartz and a Polish diplomat named Zych, located in these files. According to some of the records, Reagan was personally upset by reports about the Myers. For the security services file on Myer, see IPN BU 01034/950. According to these files, he and his wife did not immediately explain that they were American diplomats.

4. For information on the Hopper/Harwood affair, see MSZ, 2/89, W-8, Dep III (1985), AP 35-8-85. See also, IPN BU 01034/928.

5. Memo from Robert Kimmit, "US Government Contacts with Polish Officials," dated March 11, 1985, RRPL, Dobriansky Files, Box 3, Poland Memoranda 1984–1985 [January–April 1985].

6. In December 1984 there was a push to design a broad contingency plan to respond to Polish events, but the State Department delayed finishing its review until mid-June 1985 because of internal disagreements on how to utilize the IMF issue. See Memo for John Poindexter from Paula Dobriansky, "Poland Backsliding Paper," dated May 23, 1985, and Memo from Richard Burt and Elinor Constable to the Secretary, "U.S. reaction to Polish Events," ca. June 15, 1985, both in RRPL, Dobriansky Files, Box 3, Poland Memoranda 1984–1985 [May–June 1985]. In late 1984 and early 1985, the Department of State was also preoccupied with reevaluating relations with the USSR in light of Shultz's January 1985 meeting with Gromyko. After Chernenko died, focus on Soviet policy became much more pressing. Author's interview with George Shultz, Stanford University, February 19, 2008.

7. "Record of the Meeting Between the Minister of State at the Foreign and Commonwealth Office, Mr. Malcolm Rifkind, and Deputy Prime Minister Rakowski, at the Council of Ministers Building, 09.00 HRs, 7 November 1984," undated, FCO, FOI materials released to the author.

8. Informacja o skutkach gospodarczych wywołanych restrykcjami wprowadzonymi przez państwo zachodnie przeciwko Polsce [Information about the effectives of economic sanctions imposed by Western nations against Poland], dated June 9, 1983, AAN, KC PZPR, V/203, 11–30.

9. Slay, The Polish Economy, 54–55.

10. Informacja o skutkach gospodarczych wywołanych restrykcjami.

11. Wernik, The Polish Economy in the Eighties, 12–13.

12. Slay, The Polish Economy, 60. See 55–65 for an excellent summary of why the attempted reforms failed.

13. Informacja o skutkach gospodarczych wywołanych restrykcjami, quote from 13–14.

14. The letter to Brezhnev is dated October 30, and the rest are dated November 3, 1982. Each of the letters starts out similarly, but includes specific requests for aid tailored to each country. All letters are signed by Jaruzelski and are located in AAN, KC PZPR, XlA/1394, 3–30.

15. Informacja o spotkaniu konsultacyjnym Sekretarzy Komitetów Centralnym oraz Stałych Przedstawicieli krajów członkowskich RWPG w sprawie przygotowań do narady gospodarczej na najwyższym szczeblu [Information about the consultative meetings of the Secretaries of Central Committees as well as standing chairmen from member nations of Comecon on the matter of preparations for economic consultations at the highest level], dated March 30, 1983, AAN, KC PZPR, V/197, 249–53.

16. Informacja dotycząca odpowiedzi Sekretarza Generalnego KPZR i Sekretarzy Partii krajów socjalistycznych na propozycje zawarte w listach I Sekretarza KC PZPR Gen. armii Wojciecha Jaruzelskiego (przekazanych do ZSRR 30 października i do pięców krajach socjalistycznych w listopadzie 1982) [Information to date on responses from the secretary general of the CPSU and the party secretaries from socialist countries on proposals from letters by First Secretary of the PZPR Central Committee Gen. Wojciech Jaruzelski (sent to the USSR on 30 October and to the five socialist countries in November 1982)], dated February 7, 1983, AAN, KC PZPR, V/191, 189–92.

17. Informacja o skutkach gospodarczych wywołanych restrykcjami, 13.

18. Wernik, *The Polish Economy in the Eighties*, 13.

19. Ibid.

20. Briefing Memorandum, "Visit of Mr. Rifkind to Poland, 3–7 November 1984: Bilateral Relations: Commercial, Essential Facts," dated October 26, 1984, FCO, FOI material released to the author.

21. [Handel Zagraniczny Sekcja] Narodowy Plan-Społeczno-Gospodarczy Na Lata 1983–1985: Podstawowe Uwarunkowania Rozwoju i Założenia Polityki Społeczno-Gospodarczej Na Lata 1983–1985 [(International Trade Section) of the National Social-Economic Plan for 1983–1985: Basic Conditions for Development and Assumptions for Socioeconomic Policies for 1983–1985], dated March 1, 1983, AAN, KC PZPR, V/191, 365–370; quote on 365.

22. Ibid., 368.

23. Author's interview with Tim Simmins, July 9, 2004. Simmins was an economics officer in the British embassy from 1985 to 1988.

24. Author's interview with Lee Kjelleran, November 21, 2007.

25. "Perspektywa Marozmu" [Perspective of a moron], *Tygodnik Mazowsze* (March 31, 1982), 1, in KARTA, Archiwum Opozycji.

26. "Zmusić władze to porozumienia" [Twisting the Authorities' Arm for Understanding], *Tygodnik Mazowsze* (April 28, 1982), 2, in KARTA, Archiwum Opozycji.

27. "To same błędy" [The Same Mistakes], *Tygodnik Mazowsze* (June 19, 1982), 2, in KARTA, Archiwum Opozycji.

28. "Porozumienie a gospodarka" [Understanding and the Economy], *Tygodnik Mazowsze* (June 30, 1982), 2, in KARTA, Archiwum Opozycji.

29. "Uwagi o kompromisie" [Beware of Compromise], *Tygodnik Mazowsze* 18 (June 16, 1982), 1, KARTA, Archiwum Opozycji.

30. Rakowski, *Dzienniki polityczne 1984–1986*, 32.

31. Notatka Informacyjna z wizyty w ZSRR tow. W. Jaruzelskiego w dniach 4 i 5 maja 1984 r. [Information Note from the visit to the USSR of com. W. Jaruzelski on May 4 and 5, 1984], dated May 8, 1984, AAN, KC PZPR, V/228, 63–78; quote from 69.

32. Slay, *The Polish Economy*, 64.

33. Informacyja o skutkach gospodarczych wywołanych restrykcjami wprowadzonymi przez państwa zachodnie przeciwko Polsce i Straty z tytułu wprowadzenia, przeciwko Polsce, restrykcji przez państwa zachodnie [Information about the economic effects of restrictions imposed by Western nations against Poland and losses caused by the imposition, against Poland, of restrictions by the West], dated July 16, 1983, MSZ, 35/90, W-4, Dep III (1987), AP 223-1-87.

34. Program kampanii informacyjno-propagandowej na temat skutków społecznych i ekonomicznych zachodnich sankcji gospodarczych wobec Polski [Information-propaganda

campaign on the social and economic effects of Western economic sanctions against Poland], dated July 28, 1983, AAN, KC PZPR, V/202, 379–82.

35. Program działań zmierzających do zapewnienia podstaw dla dochodzenia roszczeń z tytułu strat poczynionych w polskiej gospodarce—w wyniku zastosowania restrykcji przez państwu zachodnie [Action program aiming for assurance bases for investigating claims with the title system of losses in the Polish economy—in effect caused by Western nations' restrictions], dated August 16, 1983, AAN, KC PZPR, V/203, 8–10.

36. For documents on the decision to publish the white book, see records for the politburo meeting on September 2, 1983, in AAN, KC PZPR, Mikr. 3029, Sygn 1860, 263. The white book was compiled by the Polish Institute for International Affairs and the Institute for Research on the Social Problems of Capitalism, in 1984 as *Polityka Stanów Zjednoczonych Ameryki wobec Polski w świetle faktów i dokumentów (1980–1983)*, edited by Hanna Trentowska.

37. Pilna Notatka założenia koncepcja oraz program prac zespołu do spraw kompleksowej koordinacji działań w związku z zastosowanymi wobec polski restrykcjami i tzw. sankcjami przez Panstwa Zachodnie [Urgent note of assumption concept as well as a work program of the group coordinating the matter of complex actions in relation to implementation of Polish restrictions and so-called sanctions by Western Nations], dated September 20, 1983, MSZ, 14/89, W-3, Dep III (1986), AP 223-2-86.

38. Notatka z pobytu w Nowym Jorku w dniach 25 września—1 października 1983 r. [Note from the trip to New York from 25 September to 1 October], dated October 3, 1983, AAN, KC PZPR, V/206, 130–35.

39. Letter from Lech Wałęsa to Lane Kirkland, dated January 28, 1984, AFL-CIO, International Affairs Department Files, Inactive Records, "Committee in Support of Solidarity."

40. Letter from Henryk Jablonski to Pope John Paul II, dated May 2, 1983, attached to the proceedings for the PZPR politburo meeting on May 4, 1983, AAN, KC PZPR, Mikr. 3022, Sygn. 1853, 30–34.

41. Notatka Informacyjna, Kierunki polityki państw NATO w dziedzinie współpracy gospodarczej Wschód-Zachód [Information Note: Political direction of NATO countries in the area of East-West economic cooperation], dated July 6, 1984, MSZ, 59/86, W-7, Dep III (1984), AP 2413-13-84.

42. Notatka Informacyjna [Information Note], dated October 5, 1984, MSZ, 59/86, W-7, Dep III (1984), AP 2413-13-84.

43. "C-R(84)32. Council meeting on 23 May 1984. Item II Study on Poland," dated June 24, 1984, available online (http://www.nato.int/cps/en/natolive/81366.htm).

44. "5206. Italian Delegation. The Amnesty in Poland: Italian Views (Speaking Notes)," dated July 31, 1984, available online (http://www.nato.int/cps/en/natolive/81375.htm). See also "DPA(84)227. Political Affairs Division. Memorandum from the Assistant Secretary General of Political Affairs, F. Dannenbring, to Secretary General, on exchange of views on the amnesty decreed on the 21 July," dated September 5, 1984, available online (http://www.nato.int/cps/en/natolive/81368.htm).

45. Bozo, *Mitterand*, 9.

46. "Record of the meeting Between the Minister of State at the Foreign and Commonwealth Office, Mr. Malcolm Rifkind, and the Polish minister of Foreign Trade, Mr Tadeusz Nestorowicz, at the Ministry of Foreign Trade, 11.30 AM, 5 November 1984," undated, FCO, FOI material released to the author.

47. "Record of the meeting Between the Minister of State at the Foreign and Commonwealth Office, Mr. Malcolm Rifkind, and Deputy Prime Minister Rakowski, at the Council of Ministers Building, 09.00 HRs, 7 November 1984," and "Record of the meeting Between the Minister of State at the Foreign and Commonwealth Office, Mr. Malcolm Rifkind, and Mr. Czyrek, a Secretary of the Central Committee of the Polish United Workers party (PUWP), at 5.00 PM, 5 November 1984," both undated, FCO, FOI material released to the author.

48. "Record of the meeting Between the Minister of State at the Foreign and Commonwealth Office, Mr. Malcolm Rifkind, and Representatives of the Former 'Solidarity' Organization at the Residence of the British Ambassador in Warsaw, 1700 HRS, 4 November 1984," undated, FCO, FOI material released to the author.

49. Briefing Memo, "Visit by the PUS to Bonn: 18–19 November," dated November 16, 1984, and Briefing Memo, "EC Foreign Ministers' Political Cooperation Dinner: Brussels," dated November 20, 1984, both FCO, FOI material released to the author.

50. Węzłowe zadania polityki zagranicznej PRL w 1985 roku [Vital foreign policy tasks for Poland in 1985], dated January 1985, AAN, KC PZPR, V/256, 18–55; quotes from 44 and 19, respectively.

51. Ibid., 39.

52. Ibid., 51.

53. Notatka Informacyjna o wizycie ministra Spraw Zagranicznych RFN Hansa-Dietricha Genschera w Polsce w dniu 6 marca 1985 r [Information Note about the visit by FRG Minister of Foreign Affairs Hans-Dietrich Genscher on 6 March 1985], dated ca. March 7, 1985, AAN, KC PZPR, Mikr. 3083, Sygn. 1914, 471–96.

54. Notatka ze spotkań delegacji polskiej przebywającej w Moskwie w dniach 12 i 13 marca br. na uroczystościach pogrezebowych K. Czernenki, [Note on the Polish delegation's meetings in Moscow on 12 and 13 March during the funeral for K. Chernenko], dated March 1985, AAN, KC PZPR, Mikr. 3084, Sygn 1915, 80–85.

55. The Battle of Monte Cassino was an Allied victory against the Germans, which allowed for the final assault on Rome. Fighting with the British, Polish troops under the command of Lieutenant General Władysław Anders played an important role in the final victory.

56. For information on these brief meetings, see Notatka ze spotkań delegacji polskiej przebywającej w Moskwie w dniach 12 i 13 marca br. na uroczystościach pogrezebowych K. Czernenki.

57. Notatka Informacyjna: Zapis z rozmowy Prezesa Rady Ministrów, gen. armii W. Jaruzelskiego z Federalnym Ministrem Gospodarki RFN, Przewodniczącym FDP, M. Bangemannem w dniu 22 marca 1985 r [Information Note: Transcript of the conversation between the chairman of the Council of Ministers, Gen. Wojciech Jaruzelski, and the FRG federal minister of economics, leader of the FDP, M. Bangemann on 22 March 1985], dated April 1, 1985, AAN, KC PZPR, Mikr. 3086, Sygn. 1917, 146–153.

58. Briefing Memo, "Visit of the Secretary of State to Poland, 11–13 April 1985: Bilateral Relations Financial/Economic Points to Make," dated March 1985, FCO, FOI materials released to the author.

59. Pilna Notatka o wizycie ministra spraw zagranicznych Wielkeij Brytanii, Geoffrey'a Howe w Polsce (11–13 kwetnia 1985 r.) [Urgent Note about the visit of the minister of foreign affairs of Great Britain, Geoffrey Howe, to Poland (11–13 April 1985)], dated April 17, 1985, AAN, KC PZPR, Mikr. 3088, Sygn 1920, 334–74.

60. In July, Fiat signed a $50 million deal to modernize its plant in Poland. The Fiat 126 is the classic "Polski Fiat" or "Małuch" that still can be seen on Poland's streets, and it maintains a cultural cache similar to the East German Trabant. See Christopher Bobinski, "Fiat Signs $50m Deal to Modernise Car Plant in Poland," *Financial Times* (July 12, 1985), A5.

61. Zapis z rozmowy Prezesa Rady Ministrów gen. W. Jaruzelskiego z Premierem Włoch B. Craxim w dniu 28 maja 1985 [Transcript from the conversation of the chairman of the Council of Ministers Gen. W. Jaruzelski with the Prime Minister of Italy B. Craxi on 28 May 1985], dated June 4, 1985, AAN, KC PZPR, V/266, 329–39.

62. Notatka Informacyjna o wizycie oficjalnej w Polsce ministra spraw zagranicznych Japonii, Shintaro Abe, obdytej w dniach 10–11 czerwca 1985 r., [Information Note on the official visit to Poland of the Japanese minister of foreign affairs, Shintaro Abe, on 10–11 June 1985], dated June 18, 1985, AAN, KC PZPR, V/267, 198–218.

63. For the quoted after-report, see Sprawozdania z pobyt delegacji PRL pod przewodnict-wem Prezesa Rady Ministrów, Tow. W. Jaruzelskiego na 40-tej jubileuszowej Sesji Zgromadzenia Ogólnego ONZ w Nowym Jorkku (24–28 września 1985 r.) [Report from the Polish delegation under the leadership of the chairman of the Council of Ministers, W. Jaruzelski, to the 40th Anniversary of the Openning Session of the U.N. in New York (24–28 September 1985)], dated October 2, 1985, AAN, KC PZPR, V/278, 85–123; quote from 87. For information on Jaruzelski's preparations and expectations including a full set of briefing papers, see MSZ, 2/89, W-6, Dep III (1985), AP 22-6-85. For one interview transcript, see "Excerpts from Jaruzelski Interview," *New York Times* (Sept. 29, 1985), A16.

64. Bernard Gwertzman, "U.S., Protesting Arrests, Bars Meeting with Pole," *New York Times* (Sept. 8, 1985), A8.

65. Unsigned Letter from Robert McFarlane to David Rockefeller with attached talking points for meeting, c. September 4, 1985, RRPL, Dobriansky Files, Box 3, Poland Memoranda 1984–1985 [September 1–23, 1985].

66. Memo from William Dietel to David Rockefeller, "September 25 Luncheon Meeting with General Wojciech Jaruzelski," dated October 2, 1985, RRPL, Dobriansky Files, Box 3, Poland Memoranda 1984–1985 [September 1–23, 1985]. For a discussion of Brzeziński's role, see Vaughan, *Zbigniew Brzeziński*, 531–32.

67. Judith Miller, "Mitterand Meets with Jaruzelski," *New York Times* (Dec. 4, 1985), A1.

68. Notatka z rozmowy Przewodniczącego Rady Państwa PRL tow. gen. armii Wojciecha Jaruzelskiego z Prezedentem Francji Francois Mitterand. Paryż, 1985.12.04 [Note from the conversation of the chairman of the Council of Ministers of the PRL, com. Gen. Wojciech Jaruzelski, with the president of France, Francois Mitterand. Paris, 1985.12.04], dated December 9, 1985, AAN, KC PZPR, V/286, 251–62; quoted at 259.

69. Christoph Bobinski, "New Chapter Opens in Poland's Debt Saga," *Financial Times* (July 17, 1985), A2.

70. Briefing Memo, "Visit of the Secretary of State to Poland, 11–13 April 1985: Bilateral Relations Financial/Economic Essential Facts," dated April 1, 1985, FCO, FOI materials released to the author.

71. David Buchan, "West Signs Rescheduling Accord with Poles," *Financial Times* (Nov. 11, 1985), A2.

72. Bilans polityki zagranicznej PRL w 1985 r. [Balance Sheet for foreign policy in 1985], ca. December 31, 1985, AAN, KC PZPR, V/294, 32–53; quote from 40.

73. Ibid., 42.

74. Węzłowe Zadania Polityki Zagranicznej PRL w 1986 r [Vital PRL Foreign Policy Tasks in 1986], dated January 13, 1986, AAN, KC PZPR, V/294, 9–31; quote from 10, 11, and 27.

75. Rakowski, *Dzienniki polityczne 1984–1986*, 131.

76. Notatka Informacyjna o spotkaniu przywódców partii i państw-stron Układu Warszawskiego w Warszawie (26.04.1985 r.) [Information Note about the meeting of party and national leaders of the Warsaw Pact in Warsaw (26.4.1985)], dated April 29, 1985, AAN, KC PZPR, V/264, 11–20; quote from 12.

77. Rakowski, *Dzienniki polityczne 1984–1986*, 258.

78. Notatka informacyjna z oficjalnej wizyty przyjaźni w ZSRR Zastępcy Członka Biuro Politycznego KC PZPR, Ministra Spraw Zagranicznych PRL, Marian Orzechowskiego (Moskwa 5–6 grudnia 1985 r) [Information Note from the official friendly visit to the USSR of Assistant Member of the Politburo of the PZPR Central Committee, minister of foreign relations of the PRL, Marian Orzechowski (Moscow 5–6 December 1985)], dated December 9, 1985, AAN, KC PZPR, V/286, 263–72; quote from 272.

79. Svetlana Savranskaya, "The Logic of 1989," in Savranskaya, Blanton, and Zubok, *Masterpieces of History*, 6.

80. "Speech by Mikhail Gorbachev to Ministry of Foreign Affairs, May 28, 1986," ibid., 224–25.

81. "Memorandum from Mikhail Gorbachev to the CC CPSU Politburo on Topic Questions regarding Collaboration with Socialist Countries, June 26, 1986," ibid., 230–33.

82. On the roots of Gorbachev's reformist instincts, see Zubok, *Failed Empire*.

83. Marie-Pierre Rey, "Gorbachev's New Thinking and Europe, 1985–1989," in Bozo, Rey, Ludlow, and Nuti, *Europe and the End of the Cold War*, 24.

84. English, *Russia and the Idea of the West*.

85. *Bulletin of the European Communities* 18, no. 6 (1985): 88.

86. *Bulletin of the European Communities* 18, no. 10 (1985): 85.

87. *Bulletin of the European Communities* 19, no. 5 (1986): 72.

88. Maslen, "The European Community's Relations," 338–40.

89. Attachment to a letter from Mikhail Gorbachev to Wojciech Jaruzelski, dated September 12, 1985, AAN, KC PZPR, XlA/1412, 15–18; quote from 18. Translated from the Russian by Bora Kim.

90. Notatka Informacyjna dot. narady Doradczego Komitetu Politycznego państw-stron Układu Warszawskiego w Sofii (22–23 października br.) [Information Note regarding a meeting of the Political Consultative Committee of the Warsaw Pact in Sofia (22–23 October of this year)], dated October 24, 1985, AAN, KC PZPR, V/281, 264–73.

91. Chernyaev, *My Six Years with Gorbachev*, 62.

92. Prognoza rozwoju sytuacji międzynarodowej w 1986 r. [Prognosis for the development of the internaitonal situation in 1986], dated January 1986, AAN, KC PZPR, V/294, 54–71; quote from 71.

93. See Notatka Informacyjna dot. stosunków między ZSRR a USA (na podstawie konsultacji grupy uczestników kursu kadry kierowniczej MSZ z dyrektorem Departamentu d/s USA MID A Bessmertnych oraz wykładu dla uczesników kursu z-cy dyrektora Departamentu d/s USA) [Information Note re relations between the U.S. and USSR (following consultations between cadres from the MSZ directorship with the director of the U.S. Department A. Bessmertnii as well as lectures from the director of the U.S. department)], dated April 24, 1985, MSZ, 2/89, W-7,

Dep III (1985), AP 2413-5-85; Chargé d'Affaires Ambasady ZSRR tow. W. Swirin przekazał w KC PZPR następującą o cenę rezultatów Spotkania Helsińskiego ministrów spraw zagranicznych i informację o treści rozmowy E. Szewardnadze z sekretarzem Stanu USA G. Shultzem [USSR chargé d'affairs W. Swirin passed to the Central Committee of the PZPR information about the results of the Helsinki meeting of ministers of foreign affairs and information about conversations between E. Shevardnadze and the Secretary of State G. Shultz], dated August 8, 1985, MSZ, 2/89, W-7, Dep III (1985), AP 2413-5-85 and AAN, KC PZPR, XlA/1420, 293-301; Notatka Informacyjna dot. narady Doradczego Komitetu Politycznego państw-stron Układu Warszawskiego w Sofii (22–23 października br); Notatka na temat stanu stosunków między ZSRR a USA w okresie prezydentury R. Reagana [Note about the state of relations between the USSR and the U.S. during the presidency of R. Reagan], dated November 14, 1985, MSZ, 42/92, W-3, Dep III (1988), Og 22-2-85/88; and Notatka Ambasador ZSRR w Polsce—Tow. A. Aksjonow przekazał członkowi BP, Sekretarzowi KC PZPR—Tow. Józefowi Czyrkowi następującą informację [Note passed by the USSR Ambassador in Poland, com. A. Aksjonov, to Politburo member, and secretary of the PZPR Central Committee, Józef Czyrek], dated November 18, 1985, AAN, KC PZPR, XlA/1420, 306–307. Many of these briefings focused on early arms-control negotiations.

94. Notatka Informacyjna o spotkaniu generalnych i pierwszych sekretarzy partii oraz ministrów spraw zagranicznych państwu UW w Pradze 21 Listopada 1985 r. [Information Note about the meeting of general and first secretaries as well as ministers of foreign affairs from the WP nations in Prague, 21 November 1985], dated November 23, 1985, AAN, KC PZPR, V/285, 7–14; quotes from 11 and 14.

95. Ważniejsze problemy sytuacji gospodarczej w 1985 roku (stan bieżący i wnioski) [Important problems in the economic situation in 1985 (recent conditions and conclusions)], dated October 23, 1985, AAN, KC PZPR, V/281, 200–207.

96. Handel zagraniczny [Foreign Trade], attached to Ważniejsze problemy sytuacji gospodarczej w 1985 roku (stan bieżący i wnioski), dated October 23, 1985, AAN, KC PZPR, V/281, 213–214.

97. Sytuacja piężno-rynkowo [Money-market situation], attached to Ważniejsze problemy sytuacji gospodarczej w 1985 roku (stan bieżący i wnioski), dated October 23, 1985, AAN, KC PZPR, V/281, 208–12; quoted at 209–11.

98. Paczkowki, *Spring*, 484.

99. Stokes, *Walls Came Tumbling Down*, 101.

100. Author's interview with Cameron Munter, June 11, 2004. Munter was a consular officer and then an economics officer at the U.S. embassy in Warsaw from June 1986 to July 1988.

101. Węźłowe zadania polityki zagranicznej PRL w 1986 r. [Vital PRL foreign policy tasks for 1986], dated January 1986, AAN, KC PZPR, V/294.

102. Informacja o wspólnych przedsięwzięciach z udziałem kapitału obcego w krajach socjalistycznych [Information about cooperative ventures utilizing foreign capital in socialist countries], dated November 14, 1985, AAN, KC PZPR, V/292, 91–96.

103. Wydział Ekonomiczny opinia dot.: projektu ustawy o spółkach z udziałem kapitału zagranicznego [Economic Department: opinion about the legislation project for companies utilizing international capital], dated December 30, 1985, AAN, KC PZPR, V/292, 109–11.

104. Uzasadnienie [Justification], dated c. January 1986, AAN, KC PZPR, V/292, 112–118; quote from 112.

105. Paczkowski, *Spring*, 486.

106. Notatka w sprawie Społeczno Rada Konsultaczjnej przy Radzie Państwa z 16 października 1986 r [Note regarding the matter of the Social Consultative Council of the People's Government 16 October 1986], in Dudek and Friszke, *Polska 1986–1989*, 21, as quoted in Antoni Dudek, *Reglamentowana rewolucja*, 76–77.

107. Paczkowski, *Spring*, 486.

108. Author's interview with John Davis, April 27, 2007.

109. Notatka [Note], dated c. November 5, 1985, AAN, KC PZPR, XIA/1420, 323–325; quote from 324. Sujka was apparently an informant to the SB. The same file appears in IPN BU 0248/115, 111–13.

110. Pilna Notatka [Urgent Note], dated December 5, 1985, MSZ, 2/89, W-6, Dep III (1985), AP 220-1-85.

111. For the genesis of the idea, see Action Memorandum from Rozanne Ridgeway to the Secretary, "Dealing with Poland," dated January 23, 1986, RRPL, Dobriansky Files, Box 5, Poland Memoranda 1986–1987 (10); Memorandum for John Poindexter from Paula Dobriansky, "U.S. Emissary to Poland," dated February 4, 1986; and Memorandum for John Poindexter from Paula Dobriansky, "U.S. Emissary to Poland" with attachments, dated February 21, 1986, RRPL, Dobriansky Files, Box 5, Poland Memoranda 1986–1987 (9). Author's interview with Davis, April 27, 2007.

112. Handwritten note from Peter Rodman on Memorandum for John Poindexter from Paula Dobriansky, "Your Meeting with Ambassador Stoessel," dated March 31, 1986, RRPL, Dobriansky Files, Box 5, Poland Memoranda 1986–1987 (9). After Stoessel's visit, the administration took the further step of supporting Dante Fascell's invitation to the politburo member and Sejm delegate Józef Czyrek to visit Washington, but it later decided to make clear that Czyrek would not be received by any members of the administration because of Bujak's arrest and a rise in anti-Americanism. See Action Memorandum to the Secretary from Rozanne Ridgway, "Warning the Poles about Anti-Americanism Next Steps," dated July 1, 1986, RRPL, Dobriansky Files, Box 5, Poland Memoranda 1986–1987 (7).

113. Notatka z rozmów podczas pobytu w USA [Note re conversations during the stay in the U.S.], dated July 28, 1986, MSZ, 14/89, W-3, Dep III (1986), AP 220-1-86. Davis has referred to Stoessel's trip as "a nostalgic trip." Stoessel "talked to everybody," but there were "no major changes. . . . Nothing immediately came of it." Author's interview with Davis, April 27, 2007.

114. Information Memorandum from Richard Solomon to the Secretary, "Poland: Next Steps," dated June 3, 1986, RRPL, Dobriansky Files, Box 5, Poland Memoranda 1986–1987 (7).

115. A significant number of activists had also been arrested in the weeks prior to the party congress, an attempt to limit opposition statements and activities during the event and during Gorbachev's visit. For an in-depth review of human rights violations after the 1984 amnesty, see the Committee in Support of Solidarity's Report, *Human Rights Violations in the Polish People's Republic (January 1984–January 1985)*.

116. Michael Kaufmann, "Jaruzelski Offers Hope of Amnesty for Political Foes," *New York Times* (June 30, 1986), A1.

117. Jackson Diehl, "Jaruzelski Says Amnesty to Be Sharply Limited: No Plans to Upgrade Ties to U.S., Church," *Washington Post* (July 5, 1986), A18.

118. The United States showed particular interest in Bujak's case shortly after his arrest. See Notatka Informacyjna z rozmowy z chargé d'affaires a.i. USA D. Swartz'em w dniu 6 czerwca br. [Information Note from the conversation with U.S. chargé d'affaires a.i., D. Swartz on 6 June], dated June 8, 1986, MSZ, 14/89, W-3, Dep III (1986), AP 22-1-86/A.

119. Diehl, "Poland Releases Solidarity Activist Lis," *Washington Post* (Aug. 1, 1986), A17. As Paczkowski notes in *Spring*, "The formation of the Consultative Council . . . would have been impossible without the release of political prisoners" (486).

120. Quoted in Paczkowski, "Playground of the Superpowers," 388. For the original document, see Notatka z rozmowy z radcą Ambasady USA w Warszawie Davidem Schwartzem [Note from conversation with U.S. embassy counselor in Warsaw David Swartz], dated July 10, 1986, AAN, KC PZPR, XIA/1422, 292–293, and ISPPAN, KM, M/15/9.

121. Cable from UKEmbassy Warsaw to FCO, "Poland: Demarche by the Twelve," dated July 31, 1986, FCO, FOI release to the author.

122. Information Note from Barder to the East European Department FCO, "Demarche by the Twelve," dated July 31, 1986, FCO, FOI release to the author.

123. Cable from UKembassy Warsaw to FCO, "Demarche by the Twelve," dated July 30, 1986, FCO, FOI release to the author.

124. Information Note from Barder.

125. Notatka w sprawie implikacji naszej sytuacji wewnętrznej dla stosunków Polski z państwami Europy Zachodniej [Note concerning the implications of our internal situation for Polish relations with the nations of Western Europe], dated August 6, 1986, AAN, KC PZPR, V/314, 88; also quoted in Paczkowski, "Playground of the Superpowers," 389.

126. Cable from Amembassy Warsaw to Secstate, "A Message from Jaruzelski," dated August 5, 1986, RRPL, Dobriansky Files, Box 5, Poland Memoranda 1986–1987 (5).

127. Propozycje w sprawie rozszerzenia zakresu stosowania ustawy z dnia 17 lipca 1986 r. o szczególnym postępowaniu wobec sprawców niektórych przestępstw [Proposition concerning expanding the law from 17 July 1986 about procedures against criminals], published in Dudek and Friszke, *Polska 1986–1989*, 13–19; quote from 14.

128. Ibid., 14–15.

129. Diehl, "Poland Declares Amnesty, Political Prisoners to Be Released," *Washington Post* (Sept. 12, 1986), A1; and Christoph Bobinski, "Warsaw Decides to Free Remaining Prisoners," *Financial Times* (Sept. 12, 1986), A2.

130. For example, see Dudek, *Reglamentowana rewolucja*, 73–79; and Andrzej Garlicki, *Karuzela*, 5, 24–32.

131. Paczkowski, "From Amnesty to Amnesty."

132. As quoted in Holzer and Leski, *Solidarność w podziemiu*, 115.

133. In his work Paczkowski focuses on the July 9 meeting with Swartz as the catalyst for change. In effect Paczkowski argues that the hope of gaining new credits from the United States was enough to push the PZPR to release the remaining political prisoners. See Paczkowski, "Playground of the Superpowers," 388. Paczkowski's argument is generally accepted in the Polish historiography.

134. Notatka z rozmowy z Radca-Ministrem Ambassdy USA p. Swarz'em [Note from the conversation with Minister-counsellor of the U.S. embassy Mr. Swartz], dated July 28, 1986, AAN, KC PZPR, XIA/1422, 280–282. This note was sent to all politburo members.

135. Notatka z rozmowy z dyrektorem Departamentu Europy Wschodniej Departamentu Stanu USA Martinem A. Wenickiem w dniu 18 sierpnia br. [Note from a conversation with the director of the East European Department of the Department of State, Martin A. Wenick, on 18 August], dated August 18, 1986, MSZ, 14/89, W-3, Dep III (1986), AP 220-1-86.

136. Prognoza rozwoju sytuacji międzynarodowej w 1986 r, 71.

137. Ibid. This paragraph directly proceeded the large quote from the previous paragraph.

138. Author's interview with Tim Simmins, July 9, 2004.

## Chapter 5

1. Whitehead, *Life in Leadership*, 163–65. I have heard numerous versions of this story from American diplomats. It is one that ranks high in the lore of U.S.-Polish relations.

2. As quoted in David Ottoway, "U.S. Hails Announcement of Poland's Amnesty Plan," *Washington Post* (Sept. 13, 1986), A19.

3. Pilna Notatka w sprawie reakcji amerykańskich na decyzję rządu polskiego o zwolnieniu wszystkich osób skazanych oraz aresztowanych za przestępstwa przeciwko państwo i porządkowi publicznemu [Urgent Note regarding the American reaction to the Polish government's decision about freeing all convicted and arrested people for offenses against the nation and the public order], dated October 1, 1986, MSZ, 14/89, W-3, Dep III (1986), AP 22-1-86/A.

4. Congressman Dante Fascell told Ludwiczak in mid-August that he would speak with Shultz about arranging a meeting with Orzechowski in New York, apparently peaking Polish hopes (Notatka dotyczącą ewentualnego spotkania Ministra Spraw Zagranicznych M. Orzechowskiego z Sekretarzem Stanu USA G. Shultzem podczas 41 Sesji Zgromadzenia Ogólnego ONZ w N. Jorku [Note regarding the eventual meeting of Minister of Foreign Relations M. Orzechowski with Secretary of State G. Shultz during the 41st openings session of the U.N.], dated c. August 1986, MSZ, 14/89, W-3, Dep III [1986], AP 22-8-86). The Poles went as far as writing talking points for the possible meeting (Tezy do rozmowy Towarzysza Ministra M. Orzechowskiego z Sekretarzem Stanu USA, G. Shultz'em w czasie pobytu w Nowym Jorku na 41-szej Sesji ZO NZ [Theses for Comrade Minister M. Orzechowski's conversation with U.S. Secretary of State G. Shultz during the trip to New York for the 41st Session of the U.N.], dated September 16, 1986, MSZ, 14/89, W-3, Dep III (1986), AP 22-8-86). The meeting does not appear to have taken place. The Polish record for Orzechowski's visit to New York does not include any mention of a meeting (Notatka o udziała delegacji polskiej w pracach 41 sesji Zgromadzenia Ogólnego NZ w okresie 16 września—3 października 1986 r [Note about the activities of the Polish delegation during the 41st Opening Session of the U.N. from 16 September to 3 October], dated October 8, 1986, AAN, KC PZPR, V/319, 260–270), and the *New York Times* reported that no meetings were planned ("U.S. Considers Lifting Sanctions on Warsaw," [Sept. 27, 1986], A1). During this U.N. session Shultz negotiated intensely with Soviet foreign minister Shevardnadze to dispel the Danilov Affair and made arrangements for the Reykjavik Summit.

5. Pilna Notatka w sprawie reakcji amerykańskich.

6. The letter appears in Polish files in MSZ, 14/89, W-3, Dep III (1986), AP 22-1-86/A.

7. As quoted in "U.S. Considers Lifting Sanctions on Warsaw," A1. See also David Ottaway, "U.S. Weighs Lifting Sanctions against Poland," *Washington Post* (Sept. 27, 1986), A24.

8. Polish American Congress Resolution, dated June 27, 1986, RRPL, Dobriansky Files, Box 5, Poland Memoranda 1986–1987 (6).

9. As quoted in George Moffet III, "Administration urged to lift remaining sanctions on Poland," *Christian Science Monitor* (Oct. 1, 1986): 5. For the PAC's position, see also, Jan Nowak, "Poland and US Sanctions: A Time for Reappraisal," *Christian Science Monitor* (Sept. 16, 1986), 14.

10. As quoted in Marjorie Hyer, "Glemp Ends Seven-Day Visit," *Washington Post* (Sept. 16, 1985), A30.

11. Letter from Archbishop Krol to President Reagan with attachment, dated October 9, 1986, RRPL, Dobriansky Files, Box 5, Poland Memorandum 1986–1987 (4).

12. Letter from Lech Wałęsa to President Reagan, dated September 22, 1986, RRPL, Dobriansky Files, Box 5, Poland Memoranda 1986–1987 (4).

13. Antoni Dudek argues that this move may have been an attempt to signal to the government that Solidarność was serious about negotiating. See his *Reglamentowana rewolucja*, 77. The appeal was published in *Tygodnik Powszechny* on October 10 and then in *Tygodnik Mazowsze* (October 22, 1986), 1–2; available at KARTA.

14. Memorandum for John Poindexter from Paula Dobriansky, "Invitation to Professor Adam Schaff of Poland," dated September 25, 1986; and Memorandum for VADM John Poindexter from Nicholas Platt, "Responding to General Jaruzelski's Offer," dated September 24, 1986, both in RRPL, Dobriansky Files, Box 5, Poland Memoranda 1986–1987 (5).

15. "U.S. Considers Lifting Sanctions on Warsaw," A1.

16. Memorandum for VADM John Poindexter from Nicholas Platt, "Engaging the Polish Government in Dialogue," dated October 6, 1986, RRPL, Dobriansky Files, Box 5, Poland Memoranda 1986–1987 (5).

17. Ibid.

18. Memorandum for John Poindexter from Paula Dobriansky, "US Strategy toward Poland," dated October 20, 1986, RRPL, Dobriansky Files, Box 5, Poland Memoranda 1986–1987 (5).

19. Memorandum for the President from John Poindexter [signed by Al Keel], "U.S. Strategy toward Poland," dated October 27, 1986, RRPL, Dobriansky Files, Box 5, Poland Memoranda 1986–1987 (5).

20. Author's interview with Tom Simons, July 7, 2007. Tom Simons served as deputy assistant secretary of state from mid-1986 until June 1989.

21. Shultz, *Turmoil and Triumph*, 873.

22. Author's e-mail correspondence with Simons, May 22, 2007.

23. Whitehead, *Life in Leadership*, 147, 155–59.

24. Author's interview with John Whitehead, New York, November 20, 2007.

25. Author's interview with George Schultz, Stanford, California, January 18, 2008.

26. Shultz, *Turmoil and Triumph*, 694.

27. Author's interview with Whitehead.

28. Author's interview with Simons.

29. Author's interview with Whitehead.

30. Author's interview with Dan Fried, October 6, 2006. Dan Fried was the desk officer for Poland from 1987 to 1989.

31. Notatka w uzupełnieniu do informacji przekazywanych przez tow. Ludwiczaka, pragnę wstępnie poinformować o wnioskach z moich [Ryszard Frelek] spotkań w Waszyngtonie a przede wszystkim z przedstawicielami Departmentu Stanu oraz Kongresu [Note with the endorsement of information from com. Ludwiczak, informing about conclusions from my (Richard Frelek) meeting in Washington and above all with leaders in the Department of State as well as Congress], ca. October 29, 1986, AAN, KC PZPR, XIA/1422, 300–302; quote from 300. Frelek was a professor at Warsaw University, then the head of the Central Committee Foreign Department in the 1970s, and rose to be Poland's ambassador to the U.N. from 1980–1981. In 1986 he worked

in New York for the Institute for East-West Security Studies. He traveled to Washington mainly to research the upcoming Reykjavik Summit, but he talked with State Department officials and members of Congress about U.S.-Polish relations as well.

32. Notatka z rozmowy członka Biura Politycznego, sekretarza KC PZPR Józefa Czyrka z chargé d'Affaires Stanów Zjednoczonych Johnem Davisem w dniu 30 bm [Note from Politburo member and PZPR Central Committee secretary Józef Czyrek's conversation with United States chargé d'affaires John Davis on the 30th of this month], dated October 30, 1986, ISPPAN, KM, M/15/19. For information on the CSCE meeting at Vienna and changing Soviet bloc attitudes toward human rights, see Snyder, *Human Rights Activism*, 174–216.

33. The meeting with Schaff ultimately did not materialize mainly because it became redundant after contacts during the Vienna CSCE. Also, the Beirut newspaper article that broke open the Iran hostage and then the Iran-Contra scandal was published just as the U.S. delegation was returning from Vienna, and "it just swallowed everything U.S.-Soviet up for the next three months." U.S.-Polish reengagement stayed on track, but the NSC was distracted from the issue. Author's e-mail correspondence with Tom Simons, June 7, 2012.

34. Notatka Informacyjna ze spotkania z Asystentem Sekretarza Stanu USA d/s Europy i Kanady Rozanne Ridgway, w dniu 6 listopada br., w Wiedniu [Information Note from a meeting with Assistant Secretary of State for Europe and Canada Rozanne Ridgway on 6 November in Vienna], dated November 11, 1986, AAN, KC PZPR, V/322, 147–57; quote from 148–50. Quotes are from this document. Other interesting documents on the meeting include Instrukcja do rozmów z R. Ridgway, Asystent Sekretarz Stanu USA, w dniu 6 listopad 1986 r. w Wiedniu [Instructions for the conversation with R. Ridgway, U.S. Assistant Secretary of State, on November 6 in Vienna], dated October 31, 1986; Untitled [Handwritten question and qnswer note about the meeting between Kinast and Ridgway] dated ca. November 1986; Untitled [List re Kinast-Ridgway meeting], dated ca. November 1986; Untitled, [Handwritten notes re Kinast-Ridgway Mtg, 6.xi.1986 in Vienna], dated November 6, 1986; and Odpowiedź na ew. pytanie w sprawie rozmów polsko-amerykańskich [Answers to eventual questions about Polish-American conversations], dated November 10, 1986; all located in MSZ, 14/89, W-3, Dep III (1986), AP 22-9-86. For American records, see "Talkers on Poland [Used by Dep Sec Ridgway in meeting with Kinast]," dated November 6, 1986, RRPL, Dobriansky Files, Box 5, Poland Memoranda 1986–1987 (1).

35. Notatka Informacyjna ze spotkania z Asystentem Sekretarza Stanu USA d/s Europy i Kanady Rozanne Ridgway, 152–53.

36. Ibid., 148. Material within single quotation marks is directly from Ridgway and is not a paraphrase. These quotes are confirmed in the handwritten notes of the meeting, referenced in footnote 34.

37. Media coverage focused almost exclusively on Shultz's meetings with Shevardnadze to discuss arms-control options following the Reykjavik summit.

38. It is interesting to note the different perceptions about this meeting. In Polish records, the Vienna meeting was seen as a turning point. The politburo was included on any information notes that dealt with the Vienna meeting, as well as on developments in line with the "work plan." In interviews with Davis and Simons, however, both had trouble recalling details from the session. Simons even considered the meeting a distraction from ongoing negotiations with the Soviets. The American viewpoint is most likely a factor of low expectations. Nothing Kinast said struck the Americans as particularly new. Davis's and Simons's comments may also reflect their

discomfort to talk about events that remain classified in American records. From the historical perspective, however, this meeting does appear to be a noteworthy point of change.

39. Notatka Informacyjna z rozmowy dniu 21 listopada br. z chargé d'affaires a.i. USA J.R. Davis'em [Information Note on a converszation on November 21 with U.S. chargé d'affaires a.i., J. R. Davis], dated November 23, 1986, MSZ, 14/89, W-3, Dep III (1986), AP 22-9-86. This information note was sent to all members of the PZPR politburo.

40. Cable from SecState to Emembassy Warsaw, "U.S.-Polish Dialogue: November 25 Discussion with Polish Charge," dated December 2, 1986, NSA, End of the Cold War Collection, FOIA 20040096DOS038.

41. Notatka Informacyjna dot. pobytu w Warszawie Thomasa W. Simons'a, Zastępcy Asystenta Stanu USA d/s Europejskich [Information note about the visit to Warsaw of Thomas W. Simons, Deputy Assistant Secretary of State for Europe], dated December 10, 1986, MSZ, 14/89, W-3, Dep III (1986), AP 220-9-86.

42. Cable from Amembassy Warsaw to SecState, "Meeting between DAS Simons and Polish Vice Minister Kinast," dated December 4, 1986, NSA, End of the Cold War Collection, FOIA 20040096DOS038. The OPZZ was founded in 1984 as a government-sponsored trade union.

43. Cable from Amembassy Warsaw to SecState, "Deputy Assistant Secretary Simons' Meeting with PZPR Politburo Member Józef Czyrek," dated December 5, 1986, NSA, End of the Cold War Collection, FOIA 20040096DOS038.

44. Cable from Amembassy Warsaw to SecState, "DAS Simons' Courtesy call on Polish Foreign Minister Orzechowski," December 9, 1986, NSA, End of the Cold War Collection, FOIA 20040096DOS038.

45. The exact timing of Simon's trip to Belgrade remains unclear. In an early interview he remembered going to Belgrade after Warsaw (author's interview with Simons, July 7, 2000). More recently he recalled traveling to Belgrade right after the CSCE meeting in Vienna (e-mail correspondence with Simons, June 14, 2012).

46. Interview with Simons, July 7, 2000. Simons refers to this as the "key memo." The memo has not yet been declassified. While in Warsaw, Simons met with Solidarność representatives, although no records of this facet of his trip have been declassified. Wałęsa did not make the trip down from Gdańsk, but Simons most likely met with Geremek, Onyszkiewicz, Mazowiecki, and Wielowieyski at the residence, with perhaps Michnik and Bujak involved. These Solidarność advisers would have reiterated the opposition's public calls for lifting sanctions.

47. Memorandum for Frank Carlucci from Paula Dobriansky, "Poland," dated February 10, 1987, RRPL, Dobriansky Files, Box 5, Poland Memoranda 1986–1987 (2).

48. Cable from SecState to Amembassy Warsaw, "Official-Informal 2," dated January 7, 1987, NSA, End of the Cold War Collection, FOIA 20040096DOS038.

49. Memorandum from Adrian Karatnycky to Lane Kirkland, "Deputy Secretary Whitehead's Mission to Poland," dated January 23, 1987, AFL-CIO, International Affairs Department Files, Inactive Records, "Poland—AK." The AFL-CIO remained steadfast in support of sanctions until the end. Only on February 16, 1987, two days before the final decision was announced, did the trade unionists drop their support for sanctions. Even then the decision was made "in deference to Solidarność." See "AFL-CIO Executive Council Statement on Poland, February 16, 1987, Bal Harbour, Fla." in GMMA, Minutes of Meetings of the Executive Council 1987, vol. 32. Apparently, when Simons ran into Kirkland at a private function in New York a few days before the final decision, Kirkland was "mad as hell" (author's e-mail correspondence with Simons). As Simons'

recalls, "Steve Forbes in their office in New York had . . . an exhibit of Fabergé eggs and I met Lane Kirkland just before we did the deed in February 1987. He was angry, he was angry at me, he was angry at everyone. They were still objecting at that point. . . . They were dug in until the last minute, and for honorable reasons. We didn't moralize these things" (author's interview with Simons).

50. Cable from Amembassy Warsaw to SecState, "Deputy Secretary Whitehead's Meeting with Polish Foreign Minister Orzechowski, Thursday, January 29, 1987," NSA, End of the Cold War Collection, FOIA 20040096DOS038. See also Tezy do Rozmów z J. Whitehead'em, Zastępcą Sekretarza Stanu USA [Theses for Conversaton with J. Whithead, U.S. Deputy Secretary of State], dated January 26, 1987, MSZ, 35/90, W-5, Dep III (1987), AP 220-2-87.

51. Cable from Amembassy Warsaw to Secstate, "Deputy Secretary Whitehead's Meeting with Prime Minister Messner, Friday, January 30, 1987," dated January 31, 1987, NSA, End of the Cold War Collection, FOIA 20040096DOS038.

52. Briefing Memo, "Statement to the North Atlantic Council, Brussels, Belgium," dated February 6, 1987, NSA, End of the Cold War Collection, FOIA 20040096DOS038.

53. Author's interview with Simons.

54. Whitehead, *Life in Leadership*, 170. Simons confirmed this in my interview with him.

55. The American cable for this conversation has not been declassified. The quotes are taken from the extensive Polish record of the meeting, which reads like a stenographic account: Notatka Informacyjna przesyłam zapis rozmowy przewodniczącego Rady Państwa Tow. Wojciech Jaruzelskiego z Zastępstą Sekretarza Stanu USA Johnem C. Whiteheadem, w dniu 31 Stycznia 1987 roku [Information Note including a transcript of the chair of the National Council com. Wojciech Jaruzelski's conversation with U.S. Deputy Secretary of State John C. Whitehead on 31 January 1987], dated February 17, 1987, MSZ, 35/90, W-5, Dep III (1987), AP 220-2-87. (A slightly different second copy is available in ISPPAN, KM, M/16/3.)

56. Ibid.

57. Ibid. Whitehead refers to this part of the conversation in his memoirs as well (*Life in Leadership*, 170–71); however, the two accounts do not agree on precisely what Jaruzelski said. Only the tenor of the conversation is the same. It is clear from other factual errors in the autobiography that Whitehead was not working from specific documents, but rather his memory. I have chosen to quote from the Polish record, rather than Whitehead's memoirs.

58. In addition to Wałęsa, Michnik, Kuroń, Geremek, Onyszkiewicz, Wielowieyski, Mazowiecki, Klemens Szaniawski, and Witold Trzeciakowski were invited to the dinner.

59. Cable from Secstate to Amembassy Sofia, "Deputy Secretary Whitehead's Dinner Meeting with Lech Wałęsa, Friday, January 30, 1987," dated February 11, 1987, NSA, End of the Cold War Collection, FOIA 20040096DOS038.

60. Cable from Amembassy Warsaw to SecState, "Text of Solidarity Aide-Memoir Presented by Lech Wałęsa to Deputy Secretary Whitehead," dated January 30, 1987, NSA, End of the Cold War Collection, FOIA 20040096DOS038.

61. "Statement to the North Atlantic Council, Brussels, Belgium."

62. Author's interview with Simons.

63. Memorandum for Frank Carlucci from Paula Dobriansky, "Poland," dated February 13, 1987, RRPL, Dobriansky Files, Box 5, Poland Memoranda 1986–1987 (2). See also, Memorandum for Frank Carlucci from Paula Dobriansky, "Poland: Talking Points," RRPL, Dobriansky Files, Box 5, Poland Memoranda 1986–1987 (1).

64. Cable from SecState to All NATO capitals, "Presidential Message on the Lifting of U.S. Economic Sanctions Against Poland," dated February 14, 1987, NSA, End of the Cold War Collection, FOIA 20040096DOS038.

65. "Statement on Lifting of Economic Sanctions against Poland, February 19, 1987," *PPUS* (1987). For details, see also Memo from Frank Carlucci, "Ceremony Lifting Economic Sanctions," dated February 19, 1987, RRPL, Dobriansky Files, Box 5, Poland Memoranda 1986–1987 (1).

66. For the buildup to this meeting and an analysis of it, see Friszke, "Tymczasowa Komisja Koordynacyjna," 159–66; quote from 166.

67. Author's interview with Konstanty Gebert, August 3, 2006. Gebert was an editor and a publisher of independent papers, including *KOS-a*. Only a few members of the leadership, therefore, knew details about money and material coming from the West. This separation gave added protection to the political leaders. It also increased security for operational activists; it was easy to track Wałęsa or Geremek, but lower-level officials were harder to follow.

68. This summary of Solidarność's weakening position is taken from Dudek, *Reglamentowana rewolucja*, 57–73; quote from 68.

69. Diehl, "Poland Declares Amnesty," A1.

70. Statement of Incurred Costs due to the Seizure of a Consignment on 29.xi.1986, undated, AFL-CIO, International Affairs Department Files, Inactive Records, "Poland—AK."

71. Christoph Bobinski, "Polish Underground Press Suffers Fines and Confiscations," *Financial Times* (Dec. 24, 1986), A2.

72. Author's interview with Simons, July 7, 2000.

73. Author's interview with Cameron Munter, May 5, 2006.

74. Ibid. From the limited number of interviews I conducted, it remains unclear just how many staff members were involved in this kind of activity, or when this kind of work began. Embassy staff may well have been engaged in these types of activities from 1982 onward. From the interview, it is clear that other staff members were given similar information-gathering assignments. However, no other people interviewed have offered up these kinds of specifics.

75. Interview with Davis, November 23, 1999.

76. Author's interview with Marilyn Wyatt, July 8, 2004. Contacts with women in the opposition were at least as important as with the men. When the men were in and out of jail, women ran the daily operations of writing, editing, and distributing underground literature. See Penn, *Solidarity's Secret*.

77. Author's interview with Hill.

78. Hill used this term in his interview and relayed a story of hiring someone to plant some roses in his garden. It turned out the person he hired was a former Solidarność member, the first opposition member Hill met.

79. Author's interview with Munter.

80. Ibid. With the security services actively seizing opposition cars in the second half of 1986, it is logical that they would turn to sympathetic diplomats and foreigners to undertake these kinds of activities. Munter's account is included here not as a definitive accounting of all the embassy's activities, but rather as an example of the kind of coordinated operational activities that the embassy was involved in. Munter's SB file at the IPN does not mention his clandestine paper runs (IPN BU 01211/9), so he was apparently quite good at his work.

81. The one congressional delegation to travel to Warsaw (from August 6–8, 1985) was led by Democratic Congressman Neal Smith. Three Democratic and four Republican congressmen from

the House Budget Committee met with ministerial-level government officials, but they did not meet with any of the party leadership. The trip's main purpose was to review embassy procedures as part of a study to revise funding requests by the State Department. See Notatka Informacyjna dotycząca pobytu grupy członków Reprezentantów Kongresu USA [Information note regarding the visit of a group of U.S. congressmen], dated August 10, 1985, MSZ, 2/89, W-6, Dep III (1985), AP 220-5-85. Democratic congressman David Bonior from Michigan planned to visit Poland in May 1984, but there are no records in the MSZ to confirm his visit. See MSZ, 59/86, W-6, (1984), AP 220-1-84.

82. For Solarz's first visit, see MSZ, 14/89, W-3, Dep III (1986), AP 220-10-86; for his second visit, see MSZ, 35/90, W-5, Dep III (1987), AP 220-13-87; on the Specter, Nunn, and Warner visits, see MSZ, 35/90, W-5, Dep III (1987), AP 220-8-87; on Fascell's visit, see MSZ, 35/90, W-6, Dep III (1987), AP 54-10-87; on Kennedy's visit, see MSZ, 35/90, W-5, Dep III (1987), AP 220-6-87; and for the Rostenkowski visit, see MSZ, 35/90, W-4, Dep III (1987), AP 23-5-87. New York Mayor Ed Koch also visited in January (MSZ, 35/90, W-5, Dep III [1987], AP 220-4-87), and Eunice Kennedy Shriver visited in March 1987 as part of a Special Olympics delegation (MSZ, 35/90, W-5, Dep III [1987], AP 53-2-87).

83. Letter from Zbigniew Brzeziński to John and Helen Davis, dated May 26, 1987, LOC, Brzeziński Papers, II: Box 122, 1987 Foreign Travel, May 12–22 Hungary and Poland (1 of 5).

84. Notes, "Trip to Poland, May 16–22, 1987," undated, LOC, Brzeziński Papers, II: Box 122, 1987 Foreign Travel, May 12–22 Hungary and Poland (3 of 5). For reporting on the visit, see *Tygodnik Mazowsze* (May 27, 1987), 1, 4; available at KARTA, Archiwum Opozycji.

85. Author's interview with Davis, November 23, 1999.

86. Ibid.

87. Memorandum, "Condensed Version of NATO Talking Points," undated, NSA, End of the Cold War Collection, FOIA 20040096DOS038.

88. Michael Kaufman, "Kennedy Sees Officials in Poland and Honors Opposition Leaders," *New York Times* (May 23, 1987), A2.

89. Author's interview with Geremek. The interview was conducted in English.

90. Whitehead, *Life in Leadership*, 166.

91. "Deputy Secretary Whitehead's Dinner Meeting with Lech Wałęsa."

92. Ibid.

93. Clymer, *Edward M. Kennedy*, 413.

94. Kaufman, "Kennedy Sees Officials in Poland and Honors Opposition Officials," A2.

95. "Jane Fonda i Tom Hayden Dla 'TM'" [Jane Fonda and Tom Hayden for TM] *Tygodnik Mazowsze* (March 4, 1987), 1, available at KARTA, Archiwum Opozycji.

96. For elected American officials like Solarz, Fascell, and Kennedy, these meetings also had obvious political advantages. It brought their names into the press, with important photo opportunities with a Noble Laureate. For Solarz, who came from a heavily Polish district in Brooklyn, his trip was a way to gain political points.

97. Briefing Memorandum, "Visit of Mr. Rifkind to Poland, 3–7 November 1984: Polish Internal Situation," dated October 29, 1984, FCO, FOI materials released to the author.

98. For Kennedy and Brzeziński, see *Tygodnik Mazowsze* (May 4, 1987), 1; for Whitehead, see *Tygodnik Mazowsze* (February 4, 1987), 1, 2; for Fonda and Hayden, see *Tygodnik Mazowsze* (March 4, 1987), 1; all available in KARTA, Archiwum Opozycji.

99. For the original see, "Spotkanie z Johnem Whiteheadem" [Meeting with John Whitehead], *Tygodnik Mazowsze* (February 4, 1987), quotes from 1 and 4; available in KARTA, Archiwum

Opozycji. Onyszkiewicz's published the article under his pseudonym, Janusz Białołęcki. For the American embassy's translation, see Cable from Amembassy Warsaw to SecState, "Underground Weekly Details Deputy Secretary's Meeting with Solidarity Leaders," dated February 17, 1987, NSA, End of the Cold War Collection, FOIA 20040096DOS038. Prior to Bush's 1987 visit, independent journalists made a similar argument, writing: "The intensity of contacts by the vice president with Solidarność activists proves the acceptance of Solidarność as an important political power"; quoted from "Po wyzycie George'a Bush: Aktywna Polityka" [After George Bush's Visit: Active Policy], *Tygodnik Mazowsze* (September 30, 1987), 1, available at KARTA, Archiwum Opozycji.

100. Report, "A Synthesis of the Internal Situation and the West's Activity," dated August 28, 1987, published in Machcewicz, "Poland 1986–1989." 100.

101. Paczkowski, *Spring*, 488.

102. This quote is often cited by American officials; however, I have never been able to find the original source. For an example of Davis quoting it, see Paczkowski, *Polska 1986–1989*, 238. Jaruzelski lived in the same neighborhood as the U.S. ambassador.

103. "Poland's Renewal and U.S. Options," iii, x, vii.

104. J.H. Res 263, 100th Cong., 1st sess., *Congressional Record* 133 (April 30, 1987): H2998.

105. Extension of Remarks, 100th Cong., 1st Sess., *Congressional Record* 133 (May 4, 1987): E1703.

106. Senate Committee on Appropriations, *Supplemental Appropriations Bill 1987*, 46.

107. For a sample of criticism, see *Congressional Record* 133 (June 2, 1987): S7420.

108. For the original aid to Poland act, see *Omnibus Trade and Competitiveness Act*; Kennedy (and Others) Amendment no. 580, 100th Cong., 1st Sess., *Congressional Record* 133 (July 15, 1987): S10087. The information about Helms's involvement comes from a memorandum from Adrian Karatnycky to Tom Melia, "Second (and third) million dollars for Solidarność," dated July 16, 1987, AFL-CIO, International Affairs Department Files, Inactive Records, "Poland—AK." According to another memo from Tom Melia to Eugenia Kemble, "NSZZ Solidarność on Capitol Hill— recapitulation," dated May 28, 1987, "the goals of these right-wingers [including Helms] seem to be (a) to compel the State Department to be involved in a highly visible manner in providing some material assistance to Solidarity, mainly in order to embarrass Shultz & Whitehead, whom they believe are insufficiently anti-Communist."

The Act did not survive in its original form, but all its provisions were funded. The science-and-technology agreement and allocations of surplus agricultural commodities were included in the Omnibus Trade and Competitiveness Act of 1988. The money for Solidarność was placed into section 530 of the Foreign Relations Authorization Act for Fiscal Year 1988. The time extension for funds for the Church Agricultural Fund—$1,500,000 worth of Polish currency freed for humanitarian projects, and $500,000 worth of Polish currency appropriated to the Institute of Jewish Culture and History at Jagiellonian University in Kraków—were all part of section 613 of the International Security and Development Act of 1987.

109. Guidelines Concerning Financial Aid from Abroad for NSZZ "Solidarność" signed by the TKK, dated October 4, 1986, AFL-CIO, International Affairs Department Files, Inactive Records, "Poland—AK."

110. Letter published in Senate Committee on Appropriations, *Commerce, Justice, State, the Judiciary, and Related Appropriations, FY88, Part 1*, 729–30. Milewski also sent a letter to Kemp outlining the Coordinating Office's $1,360,000 budget needs for 1988: Additional Statements;

U.S. Assistance to NSZZ Solidarność, 100th Cong., 1st Sess., *Congressional Record* 133 (Oct. 23, 1987): S15068.

111. Memorandum from Melia to Kemble, "NSZZ Solidarność on Capitol Hill—recapitulation."

112. Letter from Lech Wałęsa to Lane Kirkland, dated August 11, 1987, AFL-CIO, International Affairs Department Files, Inactive Records, "Poland—AK."

113. House Committee on Appropriations, *Departments of Commerce, Justice, and State, the Judiciary, and Related Appropriations for 1989, Part 5*, 714.

114. See NED President Carl Gershman's comments in House Committee on Appropriations, *Department of Commerce, Justice, and State, the Judiciary, and Related Agency Appropriations FY91, Part 1*, 1000.

115. For a public discussion of these funds, see House Committee on Appropriations, *Departments of Commerce, Justice, and State, the Judiciary and Related Agency Appropriations for 1987, Part 5*, 498–99. The numbers presented here are taken from the NED's Annual Report for 1986, located in loose Polish American Congress (PAC) files. For a full accounting of congressional money sent to Poland, see the appendix.

116. For a public account, see Senate Committee on Appropriations, *Commerce, Justice, State, the Judiciary, and Related Agencies Appropriations, FY88, Part 1*, 733. The numbers presented here are taken from the NED's Annual Report for 1987, located in loose PAC files. For a full account, see the appendix.

117. Stricter reporting oversight was implemented following the growing pains associated with creating a new institution, congressional attempts to slash funding for NED in 1985, and then intense congressional oversight after controversies over the use of funds to influence elections in France. Capitol Hill was also concerned about NED's board, which oversaw the way grants were dispersed and who were prominent members of the four core grantee organizations (AFL-CIO's FTUI, U.S. Chamber of Commerce's Center for International Private Enterprise, National Democratic Institute for International Affairs, and the National Republican Institute for International Affairs), creating the appearance of nepotism. For a full discussion of congressional concerns about management, see House Committee on Foreign Affairs, *Oversight of the National Endowment for Democracy*.

118. The information about specific programs that follows is mainly culled from PAC files, which contained the most complete set of NED records I was able to locate.

119. Letter from Al Mazewski to Carl Gershman, dated January 2, 1986, PAC, Books 4, "NED Grant #86-181-E-047-50 Polish Video Film." The money was sent through a bank account in Paris held by Coordination Pologne, and administered in Paris by Father Eugeniusz Plater. According to reports, more than 60 percent of the sums were used to purchase medicine. Regarding the need for humanitarian aid after the 1986 amnesty, see Letter from Jan Nowak to Carl Gershman, dated January 9, 1987, PAC, Books 4, "NED Grant #86-181-E-047-25."

120. Letter from J. Boniecki (POLCUL) to Myra Lenard re Report on the Distribution of the Grant, dated July 25, 1987, PAC, Books 4, "Grant # 87-181-E-047-17.1 POLCUL." According to the grant report, a family of five could live on $500 for about six months, which was sent by "selected and fully trusted people traveling to Poland." The judges for the awards were a who's who of the émigré community and included the POLCUL president and editor of *Kultura*, Jerzy Giedroyc; Solidarity activist Mirosław Chojecki; poet and Harvard professor Stanisław Baranczak; Jan Nowak-Jezioranski; the head of ANEKS publishing, Eugeniusz Smolar; and J. Swiecicki.

121. On CSS, see chapter 3. On the Information Center for Polish Affairs, see Final Program Report (1 April 1987–31 March 1988) from Jan Radomski to Freedom House, dated April 14, 1988, PAC, NED 89/90, "Uncensored Poland News Bulletin 89–29." On the Helsinki Watch see: Report of Activities of the Polish Helsinki Committee Between January 1, 1986 and April 30, 1987, undated, PAC, Books 4, "Grant #87-181-E-047-17.1 Helsinki Watch—Poland."

122. These publishers in Western Europe had long been supported by a CIA-funded book program run from the 1950s onward by George Minden. He purchased many of their publications for redistribution to countries behind the Iron Curtain, providing free books to travelers from the bloc. See Mattews, "The West's Secret Marshall Plan"; and Reich, *Hot Books in the Cold War*. Minden's reports on regular trips to Western Europe to meet with key émigré individuals in the 1980s are available in the George Minden Collection at the Hoover Institution Archive and provide an amazing analysis of the internal dynamics within émigré circles, particularly tensions between Poles who emigrated after the Second World War and those who emigrated after the 1968 and 1980 crises.

123. This estimate of two-thirds comes following conversations with Idesbald Goddeeris, a scholar at the University of Leuven in Belgium, who hosted a conference on the West European unions' support to Solidarność and completed extensive research on the topic himself. It was confirmed by conversations with Kryystyna Ruchniewicza at a conference in Wrocław in November 2011.

124. The NSZZ Solidarność Budget for Aid from Abroad in 1987, attached to Letter from Lane Kirkland to Lech Wałęsa, dated August 6, 1987, AFL-CIO, International Affairs Department Files, Inactive Records, "Poland—AK." For the operating budget for 1988, which took into account $1 million in additional funds allocated by Congress, Solidarność changed priorities, more than doubling allocations for equipment and increasing funds for the Brussels office, while decreasing funds for humanitarian uses. It is not clear how these percentages were actually implemented. The budgets are a wish list, allocating $1 million dollars in 1987, when funding levels were probably closer to half that amount. Therefore, the percentages are provided to give a general sense of priorities until more definitive records are located or become available.

125. For information on the beginnings of the foundation, Fundusz Wydawnictw Niezależnych (FWN), see Paweł Sowiński, "Siła wolnego słowa—Nowa, Krąg, CDN (1982–1989)," in Friszke, *Solidarność Podziemna*, 662–63. Other information on IDEE's activities is based on my interview with Irena Lasota, June 20, 2007.

126. "Project Coleslaw" received about $100,000 a year from 1986 to 1989. Presumably this money came out of the NED funds provided to FTUI for Solidarność. Memorandum from Adrian Karatnycky to Tom Kahn, "Eastern Europe and the USSR," dated November 28, 1989, AFL-CIO, International Affairs Department, Inactive Records, "Adrian Chron 1989." For further information on the project, see Puddington, "Surviving the Underground." As the Polish opposition and NED have always maintained, no American funds were allocated for equipment designed to be used for violent purposes. All the support was "non-lethal."

127. Author's interview with Jan Piotr Lasota, June 17, 2008.

128. The information about OKN is compiled from three annual reports from 1986, 1987, and 1988. See the files located in PAC, Books 4, "Grant # 86-181-E-047-25.0 OKNO" and "Grant #87-181-E-047-17.1 OKNO," as well as PAC, NED 89/90, "OKNO 1988."

129. Agnieszka Holland later became one of Poland's most famous directors, and she has collaborated with Andrzej Wajda and Krzysztof Kieślowski. She emigrated to France just before

martial law was imposed. Her better-known films include *Kobieta Samotna* (A Lonely Woman), *Europa, Europa*, and *Angry Harvest*.

130. The information in this paragraph is culled from various reports from Agnieszka Holland in PAC, Books 4, "NED Grant #86-181-E-047-50 Polish Video Film." For a fuller list of titles smuggled into Poland and more detailed information on the activities of ZWID, see the report by the PZPR's Governing Body for Propaganda and Agitation: Nagrania Video i Magnetowidowe oraz Telewizja Satelitarna w Działalności Propagandowej Przeciwnika Politycznego [Video and Cassette Tape Recordings as well as Satelite Television in the the Political Opposition's Propaganda Activities], dated May 1986, Hoover Institution Archive, Słuzba Bezpieczeństwa, Box 6, 6:13.

131. The most famous example of critical pieces in the underground press was an article in the independent monthly *KOSa* (by Konstanty Gebert) that condemned the American invasion of Granada (author's interview with Gebert). This was not, however, the only example. Even columnists in mainstream publications like *Tygodnik Mazowsze* regularly commented on the political situation in Chile, drawing parallels between their own situation and that of free trade unionists under Pinochet, both tacitly and directly criticizing American support for the military government. American policy toward Central and Latin America was a common target of criticism.

132. For the classic account of the widespread nature of opposition life in Poland, see Garton Ash's essay "Uses of Adversity" in his *Uses of Adversity*, 105–99; quotes from 113 and 116. The essay was written in June 1985. See also Michael Kaufman's chapter, "Underground Civilization," in his *Mad Dreams*.

133. Letter from J.P. Lasota to Myra Lenard dated February 15, 1987, PAC, Books 4, "Grant # 86-181-E-047-25.0 OKNO."

134. Irena Lasota kept extensive records of whom she sent money, the final destination organization, and the code word that would be printed in the independent press to confirm receipt.

135. Author's interview with Mirosław Chojecki, December 7, 2007.

136. George Minden conversation with Jan Piotr Lasota, recorded in "European Trip Report 1985: December," undated, Hoover, George Minden Collection, Box 2.

137. Paweł Sowinski, "*Ex occidente luxus*: The Poles as Trading Tourists, 1956–1970," unpublished paper.

138. Author's interview with Chojecki, author's interview with Jan Piotr Lasota, and author's interview with Irena Lasota. Rather than sending in large sums of money at any one time, this network relied on a large number of couriers making frequent trips. This was not the method used by the Coordinating Office Abroad, who often preferred to send large shipments of printing materials and other goods at once.

139. Author's interview with Andrzej Paczkowski, December 12, 2007.

140. Author's interview with Chojecki and author's interview with Helena Łuczywo, December 5, 2007.

141. Author's interview with Jane Curry, November 30, 2006.

142. The Statistical Annual of the Main Statistical Office from 1956–1989, as cited in Sowinski, "*Ex occidente luxus*," 2.

143. Letter from Agnieszka Holland to Ms. Lenard, dated January 27, 1987, PAC, Books 4, "NED Grant #86-181-E-047-50 Polish Video Film."

144. Letter from J.P. Lasota to Myra Lenard, dated February 15, 1987.

145. Gebert confirmed this procedure (author's interview with Gebert). It should also be noted that while the funder and the final grantees did eventually come to an understanding regarding

methods of properly reporting how American money was being spent, the issue of providing accounting for dissident activities was a significant source of tension. Agnieszka Holland best summed up this frustration in a letter to Myra Lenard (see note 143): "First of all I have to clear the situation to you: I have no qualifications to be an accountant or bookkeeper and so far the situation does not give me that opportunity to account for monies spent. I am a film director, lucky enough to be quite busy. . . . I had agreed to represent VIDEO in Poland because: I knew people directing that movement, I trusted them, and wanted to help them. . . . I am only a middleman: I accept money from Brussels and pass it on to Poland through authorized individuals by a prearranged password. Those people, in most cases, inform me whether they are taking the money to Poland or will do the buying here. . . . Truly speaking I, also, was not aware of the necessity of keeping books. Had I known that I would never have agreed to be in charge of the program and in the near future I will find someone to take my place, someone less busy and better oriented."

146. Final Narrative Report from Myra Lenard to NED, dated July 29, 1987, PAC, Books 4, "NED Grant #86-181-E-047-25."

147. "Prepared Statement of Carl Gershman," in Senate Committee on Foreign Relations, *Foreign Relations Authorization Act: Hearings*, 395–96.

148. NED Trip Report, Polish Video, OKNO, and POLCUL. Agnieszka Holland and Piotr Lasota, Paris, dated October 20, 1986, PAC, Books 3, "NED Grant #86-181-E-047-25."

149. *Polska 5 lat po Sierpniu*, 186.

150. Szkoła Główna Planowania i Statystyki, *Poland International Economic Report 1990/91*, 199, 205.

151. Informacja o zagranicznych dostawach humanitarnych wlLatach 1982—I kwartał 1987 [Information about foreign aid from 1982 to the first quarter of 1987], dated July 31, 1987, MSZ, 35/90, W-6, Dep III (1987), AP 39-4-87.

152. PACCF Relief for Poland Report, November 1, 1985 to June 30, 1986, dated June 27, 1986, and PACCF Relief for Poland, July 1 to October 31, 1986, dated November 21, 1986, both in PAC, Books 9, "PACCF Registration as a Private Voluntary Organization with AID." These levels of aid in 1986 also reflect onetime initiatives by American charitable organizations to respond to the Chernobyl disaster.

153. Speech by Bishop Czesław Domin in New York, dated June 27, 1986, CRS, EURMENA, XVII-C, Box 4, Poland Correspondence 1970–1986, "Charity Commission of the Polish Episcopate '86."

154. Excerpts from thank-you letters received, attached to PACCF Relief for Poland Report, November 1, 1985 to June 30, 1986.

155. Excerpts from thank-you letters received, attached to Relief for Poland Report, November 1, 1986 to May 31, 1987, dated June 12, 1987, PAC, Books 9, "PACCF Registration as a Private Voluntary Organization with AID."

156. Thank You Letter from Father Edward Dajczak, dated June 9, 1986, CRS, EURMENA, XVII-C, Box 114, General Correspondence 1987–1995, "Poland: General Correspondence 1985–1986." The original is in English.

157. Unsigned Thank You Letter from Warsaw, dated September 26, 1986, Hoover, Assistance Committee for the Democratic Opposition in Poland, Box 3. The Assistance Committee for the Democratic Opposition in Poland was a small, presumably grassroots organization that sent care packages with hard-to-get items (coffee, toothpaste, cooking oil, etc.) to recently released

prisoners and their families. Box 3 in this collection is an amazing collection of thank-you notes from many of the recipients.

158. Thank You Letter from Marek Łukarz, dated September 3, 1986, Hoover, Assistance Committee for the Democratic Opposition in Poland, Box 3.

159. Thank You Letter from Bogdan Guść, dated October 11, 1986, Hoover, Assistance Committee for the Democratic Opposition in Poland, Box 3.

160. Thank You Letter from Polish Seminarian, dated September 24, 1987, CRS, EUR-MENA XVII-C, Box 114, General Correspondence 1987–1995, "Poland: General Correspondence 1985–1986." Numerous cards with opłatki can be found in Hoover, Assistance Committee for the Democratic Opposition in Poland, Box 3.

161. Confidential Memorandum, "Draft Decision Memo on Options for Humanitarian Assistance to Poland," dated May 12, 1982, NSA, Soviet Flashpoints, Box 27, April–June 1982.

162. For the Polish record on these meetings see Tezy do Rozmów tow. J. Czyrka z Sekretarzem Stanu USA—G. Shultzem [Theses for com. J. Czyrek's conversation with U.S. Secretary of State G. Shultz] (dated February 26, 1987); Tezy do Rozmowy z Sekretarzem Handlu USA Malcolm Baldridge w dniu 10 marca 1987 r., godz. 9.30 w gmachu Departmentu Handlu [Theses for conversation with U.S. Secretary of Commerce Malcolm Baldridge on 10 March 1987, at 9:30 a.m. in the Commerce Department] (dated March 9, 1987); Tezy do Rozmowy z Sekretarzem Skarbu USA James'em A. Baker'em III w dniu 10 marca 1987 roku [Theses for conversation with U.S. Secretary of the Treasury James A. Baker on 10 March 1987] (dated March 5, 1987), all located in MSZ, 35/90, W-5, Dep III (1987), AP 220-7-87.

163. Briefing Memorandum from Charles Thomas to the Acting Secretary, "Your Meeting with Polish Party Leader Józef Czyrek on March 10 at 11:30 a.m.," dated March 6, 1987, NSA, End of the Cold War Collection, FOIA 20040290DOS141. For other American records on Czyrek's visit, see Cable from Secstate to Amembassy Warsaw, "Secretary's Meeting with Polish Politburo Member Czyrek," dated March 12, 1987; Cable from Secstate to Amembassy Warsaw, "GOP Suggestions for Bilateral Consultations," dated March 27, 1987; Briefing Memorandum from Rozanne Ridgway to the Secretary, "Your meeting with Polish Politburo Member Józef Czyrek on March 10 at 3:30 PM," dated March 9, 1987; Cable from Secstate to Amembassy Warsaw, "Deputy Secretary's Meeting with Polish Leader Czyrek," dated March 12, 1987; Cable from Secstate to Amembassy Warsaw, "Roundtable Discussion on Polish Issues," dated March 13, 1987; Memorandum for the Record, "Poland: Whitehead Luncheon for Czyrek March 10," dated March 10, 1987; Information Memorandum from Rozanne Ridgway to the Acting Secretary, "Poland: Czyrek Foreshadows Prisoner Releases to Vice President," dated March 4, 1987; and Cable from USDOC to Amembassy Warsaw, "Czyrek Delegation's Meeting with Commerce Secretary Baldridge," dated March 14, 1987; all in NSA, End of the Cold War Collection, FOIA 20040290DOS141.

164. For Polish records on these trips, see MSZ, 35/90, W-6, Dep III (1987), AP 54-1-87, as well as, Notatka Informacyjna z rozmowy z chargé d'affaires a.i. USA J. Davis'em [Information Note from a conversation with U.S. chargé d'affaires a.i. J. Davis], dated February 19, 1987, MSZ, 35/90, W-4, Dep III (1987), AP 23-7-87.

165. "Washington Talk: Briefing," *Washington Post* (Sept. 8, 1987), A20.

166. For Polish records on the meeting held May 26–30, 1987, see MSZ, 35/90, W-6, Dep III (1987), AP 43-3-87.

167. Susanne Lotarski, "Eastern Europe's Economic Plans May Be Dimmed by Harsh Winter," *Business America* (Mar. 30, 1987).

168. See the final chapter of Machciewicz, *"Monachijska menażeria,"* which includes a broader discussion of the PZPR's evolving views on RFE broadcasts in the second half of the 1980s.

169. Pilna Notatka z rozmowy z Dell Pendergrast'em zastępca Dyrektora Biura d/s Europy Agencji Informacyjnej Stanów Zjednoczonych [Urgent Note from a conversation with Dell Pendergrast, assistant director of the European Bureau of the United States Information Agency], dated June 16, 1987, MSZ, 35/90, W-6, Dep III (1987), AP 50-3-87.

170. Pilna Notatka dotycząca propozycji odbycia konsultacji z przedstawicielami Agenci Informacyjnej Stanów Zjednoczonych (USIA) [Urgent Note regarding the proposition to begin consultations with leaders from the United States Information Agency], dated August 29, 1987, MSZ, 35/90, W-6, Dep III (1987), AP 50-3-87. Polish enthusiasm for new agreements continued through the end of the year with government agencies coordinating activities to make a proposal to expand cultural, educational, and scientific exchanges between the two countries. See Notatka: w dniu 21 września br. w DPI odbyło się spotkanie z udziałem przedstawicieli DWKN, Dep III, i DPT poświęcone przygotowaniom do rozmów z USA w sprawie normalizacji współpracy w zakresie informacji, nauki, kultury i wymiany stypendialnej [Note: on 21 September in the DPI there was a meeting to dicuss the matter of normalizing cooperation in information policies, scientific, culture, and educational stipends], dated September 23, 1987, MSZ, 35/90, W-6, Dep III (1987), AP 50-3-87.

171. Pilna Notatka [Urgent Note], dated April 8, 1987, MSZ, 35/90, W-4, Dep III (1987), AP 22-4-87.

172. "Washington Talk: Briefing," *Washington Post* (Aug. 19, 1987), A20. The precise genesis of Bush's visit remains unclear. When he met with Czyrek in March, Bush mentioned his opinion that Reagan should schedule a visit to Warsaw, but he did not mention his own aspirations. According to Simons, the decision to take the trip was made in June or July (author's interview with Simons). The first mention of the trip in opened MSZ files appears in August in a memo about meetings with the vice president's advance team on August 24–26, 1987 (Notatka Informacyjna o przebiegu rozmów przygotowawczych do wizyty wice-prezydenta USA George'a Busha w Polsce [Inforamation Note about the preparatory talks for the visit of Vice President Bush to Poland], dated August 27, 1987, MSZ, 35/90, W-5, Dep III [1987], AP 220-15-87). According to published accounts, Brzeziński brokered the deal for the Bush visit (David Hoffman, "Chanting Polish Crowds Provide Bush with Footage for '88 Campaign," *Washington Post* [Oct. 4, 1987], A18).

173. The two-hats analogy is taken from David Hoffman, "Bush in Iowa Promotes Foreign Policy Credentials," *Washington Post* (Sept. 24, 1987), A17.

174. Author's interview with Simons.

175. For Bush's recollections, see Bush and Scowcroft, *A World Transformed*, 117.

176. "Chanting Polish Crowds Provide Bush With Footage for '88 Campaign." According to this article, the shared drive and the hidden microphone were planned and executed by Bush's campaign advisers. Also, as the article pointed out, "The scene . . . is regarded by Bush campaign strategists as a masterpiece of political theater for a candidate who is often regarded as bland and uninspiring." This kind of grand gesture was much more consistent with Wałęsa's and Solidarność's sense of symbolism, images, and gestures. It remains unclear who provided the original impetus for the idea. According to Davis, these details were handled by the White House, not the embassy (author's interview with Davis, November 23, 1999).

177. For examples of press coverage emphasizing political theater over substance, see A. M. Rosenthal, "The Truths of Poland," *New York Times* (Sept. 29, 1987), A35; Christoph Bobinski, "Bush Visit Does Little to Improve Polish Ties," *Financial Times* (Sept. 30, 1987), A2; and "The World in Poland," *New York Times* (Oct. 4, 1987), D2.

178. As quoted in Vaughan, *Zbigniew Brzeziński*, 533.

179. The Paris Club agreement was signed on December 16, 1987 (available online, www
.clubdeparis.org/sections/pays/pologne).

180. Notatka Informacyjna o oficjalnej wizycie wiceprezydenta Stanów Zjednoczonych
Ameryki G. Bush'a w Polsce [Information Note about the official visit of the Vice President of the
United States, G. Bush, to Poland], dated ca. September 29, 1987, AAN, KC PZPR, V/365, 168. The
quote marks signal that this is a direct quote from Bush; otherwise the material is a paraphrase
of what he said.

181. Ibid., 172.

182. Ibid., 190.

183. For a further discussion of this point, see chapter 6.

184. United States–Polish Relation [in English], dated November 13, 1987, MSZ, 35/90, W-4,
Dep III (1987), AP 22-1-87.

185. For information on the affair involving I. Goreczen, see MSZ, 42/92, W-9, Dep III (1988),
AP 35-5-88.

186. Notatka o dotychczasowych doświadczeniach modelu wizyt zachodnich polityków w
Polsce [Note about future model for visits by Western politicians to Poland], dated October 27,
1987, AAN, KC PZPR, VII/85, 374–382.

187. Notatka Informacyjna o oficjalnej wizycie zastępcy sekretarza stanu Stanów Zjednoczonych Ameryki J.C. Whitehead [Information Note about the official visit of the deputy secretary
of state of the United States, J. C. Whitehead], dated Feburary 8, 1988, MSZ, 42/92, W-6, Dep III
(1988), AP 220-4-88.

## Chapter 6

1. Cable from Amembassy Warsaw to SecState, "High Politics at Warsaw's Fourth of July Reception," dated July 5, 1989, NSA, End of the Cold War, Poland 1989 Cables. A Polish translation
of the cable quoted above, and many of the other cables cited below, can be found in Domber, *Ku
zwycięstwu "Solidarności,"* 307–11.

2. Information Note Wyciąg Tez i Opinii Raportu Banku Swiatowego "Polska: Reforma,
Dostowanie i Wzrost," [Excerpt of the Theses and Opinions of the World Bank Report, "Poland:
Reforms, Adaptation, and Growth"], dated September 9, 1987, AAN, KC PZPR, V/365.

3. Memorandum of Conversation, "Zapis stenograficzny rozmowy Ericha Honeckera z
Wojciechiem Jaruzelskim 16 wrzesnia 1987 r. (fragmenty)" [Stenographic record of a conversa-
tion between Eric Honecker and Wojchiech Jaruzelsi, November 16, 1987], in Dudek and Friszke,
*Polska 1986–1989*, 48

4. Report, "A Synthesis of the Internal Situation and the West's Activity," dated August 28,
1987, in Machciewicz, "Poland, 1986–1989," 98 and 99.

5. Notes, "Trip to Poland, May 16–22, 1987," undated, LOC, Zbigniew Brzeziński Papers,
Box II: 122, 1987 Foreign Travel, May 12–22 Hungary and Poland (3 of 5).

6. Letter from Brzeziński to Jerzy Giedroyc, dated February 8, 1988, LOC, Zbigniew Brzeziński
Papers, Box II: 202, Giedroyc, Jerzy 1986–1988.

7. Information in this paragraph is based on reporting by John Tagliabue for the *New York
Times*. In particular, see "Polish Workers Strike and Win a Raise" (Apr. 26, 1988), A3; "Steel Strike
Widens Polish Labor Unrest" (Apr. 27, 1988), A3; "Steel Strikes Spreading in Poland; Talks with

Official Unions Fail" (Apr. 30, 1988), A1; and "Thousands at Gdańsk Shipyard Join Polish Strike" (May 3, 1988), A1.

8. John Tagliabue, "Security Forces Crush a Walkout at Mill in Poland," *New York Times* (May 6, 1988), A1.

9. John Tagliabue, "Young and Wary Strikers Take Solace from Wałęsa," *New York Times* (May 7, 1988), A1.

10. John Tagliabue, "Gdańsk Workers Reject Polish Offer to End Strike," *New York Times* (May 10, 1988), A10; and "Gdańsk Workers End Nine-day Strike: Key Demand Unmet," *New York Times* (May 11, 1988), A1.

11. Paczkowski, *Spring*, 490

12. Philip Shenon, "U.S. Says Polish Crackdown Jeopardizes Help," *New York Times* (May 8, 1988), A13. Whitehead and Simons also delivered private appeals to Kinast in Washington. See, Notatka Informacyjna z rozmowy z ambasadorem USA w Warszawie J. Davis'em w dniu 12 Lipca br. [Information Note for a conversation with U.S. Ambassador in Warsaw J. Davis on July 12], dated July 13, 1988, MSZ, 42/92, W-6, Dep III (1988), AP 220-21-88. According to Simons, "the press guidance . . . was restraint because we recognized that both sides were in trouble. Solidarity was in trouble from radicalizing young workers. The regime was in trouble if it didn't deal with Solidarity. And we told the regime, I think we told both sides, that really they ought to try to keep a lid on this thing" (author's interview with Tom Simons, July 7, 2000).

13. Letter from Jerzy Milewski to Lane Kirkland, dated June 6, 1988, AFL-CIO, International Affairs Department, Inactive Records, "FTUI." According to Milewski's computations, payments to workers would cost about $117,000. Given the size of these transfers ($500,000 in total) and the language used to describe them, these funds most likely came out of the $1 million allocated by the Congress for 1988, rather than the yearly NED grant.

14. Author's interviews with Cameron Munter, June 11, 2004, and Marilyn Wyatt, July 8, 2004.

15. Dudek, *Reglamentowa rewolucja*, 138-39.

16. Ibid., 141-42.

17. Ibid., 142-47.

18. Ibid., 147. On July 21, Ciosek mentioned to Andrzej Stelmachowski the possibility of creating a Christian political party that could obtain a 40 percent mandate in the Senat as well as appoint Wałęsa as the speaker.

19. Ibid., 148.

20. Wstępna informacja o wizycie Sekretarza Generalnego KC KPZR M.S. Gorbaczowa w Polsce 11-16 lipca 1988 r. [Rough information about the visit of CPSU Central Committee Secretary General M. S. Gorbachev to Poland 11-16 July 1988], dated July 25, 1988, AAN, KC PZPR, V/418, 314-35; quote from 332.

21. Tezy dot. wyników wizyty M. Gorbaczowa w Polsce na spotkanie Tow.Min. T. Olechowskiego z G. Shultzem [Theses regarding effects of M. Gorbachev's visit to Poland on Com. Min. T. Olechowski's visit with G. Shultz], dated August 1988, MSZ, 42/92, W-6, Dep III (1988), AP 220-21-88.

22. See comments by Ciosek, in Paczkowski, *Polska 1986-1989*, 33-34.

23. Olechowski replaced Marian Orzechowski as foreign minister on June 17, 1988. Pilna Notatka w sprawie oficjalnej wizyty ministra Spraw Zagranicznych w Stanach Zjednoczonych Ameryki, 25-29 bm. [Urgent Note regarding the official visit of the minister of foreign affairs to the United States of America, 25-29 of this month], dated July 6, 1988, MSZ, 42/92, W-6, Dep III

(1988), AP 220-21-88. For Washington's take on internal developments, see Notatka Informacyjna z rozmowy z ambasadorem USA w Warszawie J. Davis'em w dniu 12 Lipca br. [Information Note from conversation with U.S. ambassador in Warsaw J. Davis on 12 July], dated July 13, 1988, MSZ, 42/92, W-6, Dep III (1988), AP 220-21-88.

24. Notatka Informacyjna o wizycie ministra Spraw Zagranicznych w Stanach Zjednoczonych Ameryki (25-29 lipca 1988 r) [Information Note about the visit of the minister of foreign affairs to the United States of America 25-29 July 1988), dated August 1, 1988, MSZ, 42/92, W-6, Dep III (1988), AP 220-21-88.

25. For reporting on these strikes, see John Tagliabue's articles in the *New York Times*: "Thousands Strike Major Coal Mine in Poland," (Aug. 17, 1988), A5; "Second Coal Mine Struck in Poland," (Aug. 18, 1988), A3; "Five More Coal Mines Join Strike," (Aug. 21. 1988), A1; "Gdańsk Shipyards to Join Strikers," (Aug. 22, 1988), A1; and "Poland Declares Emergency Rules to Quell Strikes," *New York Times* (Aug. 23, 1988), A1.

26. Dudek, *Reglamentowana rewolucja*, 166. The term "exceptional state" is basically a euphemism for imposing martial law.

27. Dubiński, *Magdalenka: transakcja epoki*, 4.

28. Dudek, *Reglamentowana rewolucja*, 172.

29. Ibid.

30. Geremek, as quoted in Flora Lewis, "Poland's Tired Dreams," *New York Times* (Sept. 4, 1988), D4.

31. Author's interview with John Davis, November 23, 1999.

32. Author's interview with Simons.

33. Letter from John Whitehead to Tadeusz Olechowski, dated August 25, 1988, RRPL, WHORM Subject Files, C0126 (Poland).

34. "Teleprinter Message from the Political and Organizational Committee of the CC PZPR to Members and Associate Members of the Politburo and CC Secretaries, on 'The Question of Talks with the Opposition,'" dated September 2, 1988, in the documents briefing book prepared for the conference, "Poland 1986-1989: The End of the System," in Miedzeszyn-Warsaw, Poland, October 20-24, 1999.

35. "Spotakanie Robocze w Magdalence, 16 września 1988 r., godz. 15.15-19.00" [Working Meeting in Magdalenka, 16 September, 3:15-7:00 P.M.], in Dubiński, *Magdalenka*, 19; emphasis added.

36. Ibid., 20.

37. Jackson Diehl, "Solidarity Agrees to Join 'Round Table'; Warsaw Gives Banned Union No Assurances on Legalization," *Washington Post* (Sept. 17, 1988), A15.

38. Author's interview with Janusz Onyszkiewicz, July 8, 2010. Onyszkiewicz's wife, Joanna, is British. The two were in the United States from September 3 to September 26, 1988, travelling to New York, Washington, Chicago, and Cleveland (where he had relatives). See also, "Rough Schedule of Janusz Onyszkiewicz," undated, RRPL, WHORM Subject Files, C0126 (Poland).

39. Onyszkiewicz's testimony is recorded in Commission on Security and Cooperation in Europe, *Implementation of the Helsinki Accords*, 20, 21, 18, and 16. He testified with Jan Nowak-Jezioranski and Father Eugene Koch.

40. Zbigniew Messner was removed as premier on September 19, and Rakowski was given the job of forming a new government on September 27. This move was widely seen as an attempt to shore up the reformist base in the Sejm. See Garlicki, *Karuzela*, chapter 6.

41. Notatka Informacyjna dot. wizyty w Polsce zastępcy Sekretarza Stanu USA Johna White-head (12–14 października 1988 r.) [Information Note regarding U.S. Deputy Secretary of State John Whitehead's visit to Poland (12–14 October 1988)], dated October 15, 1988, MSZ, 42/92, W-6, Dep III (1988), AP 220–25–88; quote from 7.

42. Ibid., 4.

43. Ibid., 9.

44. Ibid., 9–10.

45. Pilna Notatka z wizyty oficjalnej w Polsce premiera Wielkiej Britanii Margaret Thatcher (2–4 listopada 1988 r.) [Urgent Note from the British Prime Minister Margaret Thatcher's official visit to Poland (2–4 November 1988), dated November 6, 1988, AAN, KC PZPR, V/437, 212–244; quote from 241.

46. Wałęsa, *The Struggle and the Triumph*.

47. Author's interview with Davis, November 23, 1999. For some of the transcript of the debate see Wałęsa, *The Struggle and the Triumph*, 169–71.

48. Friszke, *Polska*, 448.

49. Dudek, *Reglamentowa rewolucja*, 224–25. Dudek does an excellent job explaining all of these maneuvers by Jaruzelski, the details of which are too numerous to include. A record of these conversations is available in Perszkowski, *Tajne dokumenty*.

50. As part of his argument for beginning negotiations, Jaruzelski emphasized international economic considerations: "Without an agreement with the opposition . . . we cannot count on economic support from the West"; quoted from Dudek, *Reglamentowana rewolucja*, 231.

51. "Minutes No. 107 from a meeting of the Politburo after the Conclusion of the discussion on January 17, 1989," dated January 17, 1989, part of the "Poland 1986–1989" briefing book. A Polish version is available in Perzkowski, *Tajne dokumenty*.

52. Paczkowski, *Spring*, 495.

53. Bush and Scowcroft, *A World Transformed*, 37.

54. Author's interview with Davis, November 23, 1999.

55. As Davis admits in the interview, the embassy was not immediately aware of Jaruzelski's role in calling for the vote of confidence to push for legalizing Solidarność. They only learned about it later through rumors. In contrast to these retrospective admonitions, the original cable reporting on the event (which was signed by DCM Daryl Johnson, meaning Davis was out of Warsaw), did not take a very positive view of Jaruzelski's role. For that report, see Cable from Amembassy Warsaw to SecState, "PZPR Plenum Clears way for Round Table, Possible Eventual Relegalization of Solidarity," dated January 18, 1989, NSA, End of the Cold War, Poland 1989 Cables.

56. Cable from SecState to Amembassy Warsaw, "Official-Informal 009," dated January 18, 1989, NSA, End of the Cold War, Poland 1989 Cables.

57. "Spotkanie Robocze w Magdalence, 27 stycznia 1989 r., godz. 11.30–22.15" [Working Meeting in Magdalenka, 27 January 1989, 11:30 A.M. to 10:15 P.M.], in Dubiński, *Magdalenka*, 38–58.

58. For a discussion of this final interruption, see Garlicki, *Karuzela*, 301–3. The actual Round Table Agreements were signed by the heads of the three main working groups.

59. Since the creation of the People's Republic of Poland, the Communist government included a number of "coalition" parties as existed in other Socialist bloc countries. The coalition included the ZSL (Zjednoczonne Stronnictwo Ludowe or United People's Party), SD (Stronnisctwo Demokratyczne or Democratic Party), PAX (Christian Social Association), UchS (Unia

Chześcijańska-Społeczna or Christian-Social Union), and PZKS (Polski Zwiśzek Katolicko-Społeczny or Polish Catholic-Social Union). As the lead party, the PZPR dominated all decision making, giving no real power to the satellite parties.

60. Paczkowski, *Spring*, 500.

61. For an extremely detailed account of how the negotiators arrived at this political compromise, see chapter 5 in Castle, *Triggering Communism's Collapse*. For a basic overview of political agreements, see Amembassy Warsaw to SecState, "Outline of the Round Table's Political Agreement," dated April 24, 1989, NSA, End of the Cold War, Poland 1989 Cables.

62. Cable from Amembassy Warsaw to SecState, "Round Table Agreement to be Signed," dated April 5, 1989, NSA, End of the Cold War, Poland 1989 Cables.

63. Hutchings, *American Diplomacy*, 9.

64. Other diplomats at the embassy in 1989 included agricultural officer John Harrison, defense attaché Colonel Glen Bailey, as well as Steve Dubrow and Alice LeMaistre in the public affairs office.

65. Hutchings, *American Diplomacy*, 6.

66. Ibid., 27.

67. For one account of Gorbachev's New York visit and announcement, see Dobbs, *Down with Big Brother*, 215–16.

68. Bush and Scowcroft, *A World Transformed*, 13.

69. Ibid., 4.

70. For Bush and Scowcroft, see ibid., 4–15. For Baker, see his *The Politics of Diplomacy*, 69–70.

71. Bush and Scowcroft, *A World Transformed*, 12.

72. Ibid., 17.

73. Ibid., 37.

74. National Security Review 4, "Comprehensive Review of U.S.-Eastern European Relations," dated February 15, 1989, GBPL, National Security Reviews, available online at http://bushlibrary.tamu.edu/research/nsr.php.

75. Stokes, *Walls Came Tumbling Down*, 108.

76. For a full exploration of the opposition's own ideas about the transformation it was pursuing, see Domber, "Ending the Cold War, Unintentionally."

77. Bush and Scowcroft, *A World Transformed*, 38, 48.

78. Author's interview with Simons.

79. Hutchings, *American Diplomacy*, 37.

80. Author's interview with Simons.

81. Bush and Scowcroft, *A World Transformed*, 26.

82. For the fullest treatment of these conversations, see Talbott and Beschloss, *At the Highest Levels*, 13–17, 19–20; quote from 19.

83. Thomas Friedman, "Baker, Outlining World View, Assesses Plan for Soviet Bloc," *New York Times* (Mar. 28, 1989), A1.

84. Beschloss and Talbott, *Highest Levels*, 45–46.

85. Sally Jacobsen, "U.S.-Soviet Talks on Eastern Europe Would Be Inappropriate," AP (Apr. 1, 1989). According to Hutchings, the controversy was overblown, as the Kissinger proposal was "never on the agenda, nor ever given serious consideration by any senior administration official." See his *American Diplomacy*, 36.

86. Hutchings, *American Diplomacy*, 37–38.

87. Bush and Scowcroft, *A World Transformed*, 49.

88. Cable from Amembassy Warsaw to SecState, "When the Round Table Ends: The U.S. Response," dated March 7, 1989, NSA, End of the Cold War, Poland 1989 Cables.

89. For the text of the speech, see Remarks to Citizens in Hamtramck, Michigan," dated April 17, 1989, *PPUS* (1989).

90. On the final moves to legalize Solidarność, see Cable from Amembassy to SecState, "Solidarity, Legal Again," dated April 17, 1989, NSA, End of the Cold War, Poland 1989 Cables.

91. For the cable on the Ridgway-Kinast meeting, see Cable from SecState to Amembassy Warsaw, "Demarche to Polish Ambassador on President's Speech on Poland," dated April 17, 1989, NSA, End of the Cold War, Poland 1989 Cables. For the Polish report on the conversation, see "Waszyngton, 17 kwetnia 1989 r. Ambasada Jan Kinast do dyrektor Departamentu III MSZ o swojej rozmowie z Rozanne Ridgway, asystentem sekretarza stanu ds. Europy i Kanady," [Washington, 17 April 1989, Ambassador Kinast to the Director of Department III, MSZ, about his conversation with Rozanne Ridgway, assistant secretary of state for Europe and Canada] in Szlajfer, ed., *Ku wielkiej zmianie*, 112–14. It is interesting to note that the initiatives announced in Hamtramck were in line with the possibilities outlined by Whitehead the preceding October, but more reserved than some of the actions previously offered. This comparison between policy at the end of the Reagan administration and the start of the Bush term provides further evidence for the common criticism that the national security reviews did little to spark new ideas. For Baker's reference to the reviews as "status quo plus," see *Politics of Diplomacy*, 68.

92. These steps were codified as National Security Directive 9, "Actions to Respond to Polish Roundtable Agreement," signed by the president on May 8, 1989, GBPL, National Security Directives, available online: http://bushlibrary.tamu.edu/research/nsd.php.

93. Bush and Scowcroft, *A World Transformed*, 48, 51.

94. Author's interview with Davis, November 23, 1999.

95. Author's interview with Simons.

96. Pilna Notatka dot. implikacji wyboru G. Busha na prezydenta USA [Urgent Note regarding the implications of George Bush's election as U.S. president], dated November 15, 1989, ISPPAN, KM, M/17/25.

97. Zapis z rozmowy przedwodniczącego Rady Państwa gen. W. Jaruzelskiego z D. Rockefellerem w dniu 2 marca 1989 roku [Transcripts from the chairman of the National Council W. Jaruzelski's conversation with D. Rockefeller on 2 March 1989], dated March 8, 1989, MSZ, 2/94, W-8, Dep III (1989), AP 220-4-89.

98. Sugestie do Rozmowy Ministra Olechowskiego z Sekretary of State James A. Baker [Suggestions for Minister Olechowski's conversation with Secretary of State James A. Baker], dated March 1989, MSZ, 2/94, W-7, Dep III (1989), AP 22-6-89.

99. Cable from SecState to Amembassy Warsaw, "Party Secretary Czyrek's call on the Deputy Secretary, May 16, 1989," dated May 17, 1989, NSA, End of the Cold War, Poland 1989 Cables.

100. "Warszawa, 20 kwetnia 1989 r. Notatka informacyjna ministra spraw zagranicznych o wystąpieniu prezydenta Georga Busha w Hamtramck" [Warsaw, 20 April 1989, Information note for the minister of foreign affairs about President George Bush's Speech in Hamtramck], in *Ku wielkiej zmianie*, 120.

101. "Address to the Nation about Christmas and the Situation in Poland, December 23, 1981," *PPUS* (1981). The possibility of a large-scale economic carrot had been pursued by H. Allen Holmes and Francis Meehan through early 1982 (see chapter 2) and was only officially rejected as

a policy option in an NSPG meeting on April 8, 1983. RRPL, Executive Secretariat NSPG, Box 1, NSPG 0061 8 April 1983 [Poland].

102. "Historyczny Porownonia," [Comparative History] *Tygodnik Mazowsze* (March 13, 1982), 4; available at KARTA, Archiwum Opozycji.

103. "Porozumienie a Gospodarka" [Understanding and the Economy], *Tygodnik Mazowsze* (June 30, 1982), 2; available at KARTA, Archiwum Opozycji.

104. "Rozmowa Prezydenta Reagana z Przedstawicielem 'S'" [President Reagan's Conversation with a Official from 'S'], *Tygodnik Mazowsze* (October 24, 1985), 1; available at KARTA, Archiwum Opozycji.

105. "Po wyzycie George'a Bush: Aktywna Polityka" [After George Bush's Visit: Active Policy], *Tygodnik Mazowsze* (September 30, 1987), 1; available at KARTA, Archiwum Opozycji.

106. Author's interview with Onyszkiewicz.

107. Plan Solidarności gospodarczej z Polską [A Solidarnosc economic plan for Poland], dated December 4, 1988, Hoover, Zdisław Najder Files, Box 6, Facts and Views.

108. Amembassy Warsaw to SecState, "Wałęsa Emphasizes the Need for an Appropriate Western Response," dated April 28, 1989, NSA, End of the Cold War, Poland 1989 Cables.

109. SecState to Amembassy Warsaw, "Department Meeting with Solidarity Adviser Jacek Kuroń," dated June 3, 1989, NSA, End of the Cold War, Poland 1989 Cables.

110. Letter from Seweryn Blumsztajn to Carl Gershman, dated April 1, 1989, PAC, NED 89/90, "Video 89-52 Grant Agreements and Amendments."

111. Letter from Seweryn Blumsztajn to Carl Gershman, dated June 9, 1989, PAC, NED, 89/90, "Video 89-52 Grant Agreements and Amendments."

112. The grant is included in the Annual Report for 1989, available at the NED Headquarters library. See also the appendix.

113. Cable from SecState to Amembassy Warsaw, "Acting Secretary Eagleburger's Meeting with Solidarity Leader Geremek," dated May 23, 1989, NSA, End of the Cold War, Poland 1989 Cables.

114. Puddington, "Surviving the Underground." Presumably this money came from NED funds already allocated to PAC and the AFL-CIO. I did not come across any records in either AFL-CIO or PAC files dealing with this transfer of money or programs to raise it. Geremek's decision to accept the cash showed Solidarność's changing calculations regarding charges of foreign influence. Funding a quick election was clearly more important than maintaining perceived distance from the U.S. government.

115. Cable from Amembassy Warsaw to SecState, "Tall Tales about U.S. Marshall Plan," dated June 20, 1989, NSA, End of the Cold War, Poland 1989 Cables.

116. For explanations of PZPR priorities for economic support, see "Waszyngton, 22 lutego 1989 r. Ambasador Jan Kinast do podsekretarza stanu w MSZ o swoich rozmowach z członkami Rady ds. Stosunków Zagranicznych [Washington 22 February 1989 Ambassador Kinast to Secretary of State MSZ about his conversation with members of the Foreign Affairs Committee]," in *Ku wielkiej zmianie*, 68; and "Warszawa, 27 czerwca 1989 r. Podsekretarz stanu w MSZ do ambasadora Jana Kinasta w sprawie korzyście gospodarczo-finansowych z wizyty prezydenta Georgea Busha w Polsce, [Warsaw 27 June 1989 Undersecretary of State MSZ to Ambasador Kinast regarding economic-financial developments with the visit of President Bush to Poland]," ibid., 157–59.

117. "Waszyngton, 17 maja 1989 r., Józef Czyrek do prewodnicącego Rady Państwa Wojciecha Jaruzelskiego o swojej rozmowie z zastępcą sekretarza stanu Lawrencem Eagleburgerem

[Washington, 17 May 1989, Czyrek to Jaruzelski about his conversation with Assistant Secretary of State Lawrence Eagleburger], ibid., 127.

118. Cable from Amembassy Warsaw to SecState, "Geremek Explains the Next Steps," dated April 7, 1989, NSA, End of the Cold War, Poland 1989 Cables.

119. Cable from Amembassy Warsaw to SecState, "Election '89—Election Prospects," dated May 5, 1989, NSA, End of the Cold War, Poland 1989 Cables.

120. Cable from Amembassy Warsaw to SecState, "Campaign '89—Solidarity Spokesman as a Parliamentary Candidate," dated April 28, 1989, NSA, End of the Cold War, Poland 1989 Cables.

121. Cable from Amembassy Warsaw to SecState, "Campaign '89—Ostroleka," dated May 12, 1989, NSA, End of the Cold War, Poland 1989 Cables.

122. "Campaign '89—Solidarity Spokesman as a Parliamentary Candidate." This statement is particularly interesting in light of Geremek's later acceptance of $100,000 from the AFL-CIO and PAC. If the Citizen's Committee stuck to its original budget, this would mean that Americans funded 40 percent of the campaign.

123. Cable from Amembassy Warsaw to SecState, "Campaign '89—Kickoff in Kraków with Brass Bands, Soundtrucks and Political Infighting," dated May 15, 1989, NSA, End of the Cold War, Poland 1989 Cables.

124. "Campaign '89—Ostroleka."

125. On Wałęsa's desire to stay out of politics, see Cable from Amembassy Warsaw to SecState, "Wałęsa to try to Remain 'Above Politics,'" dated April 14, 1989, NSA, End of the Cold War, Poland 1989 Cables. For an account of one of Wałęsa's campaign speeches, see Cable from Amembassy Warsaw to SecState, "Campaign '89—Wałęsa leads Rural Solidarity Rally in Racławice," dated May 19, 1989, NSA, End of the Cold War, Poland 1989 Cables. On posing for campaign posters, see Paczkowski, *Spring*, 504.

126. Krysztof Bobinski, "Poland's Free Vote," *Financial Times* (Apr. 23. 1989), A26.

127. Cable from Amembassy Warsaw to Secstate, "Wałęsa Reiterates a Need for Appropriate Western Response," dated April 28, 1989, NSA, End of the Cold War, Poland 1989 Cables.

128. "Department Meeting with Solidarity Advisor Jacek Kuroń."

129. Jackson Diehl, "Poles Skeptical of Both Sides in Elections," *Washington Post* (May 28, 1989), A29.

130. See for example, Henry Kamm, "In Pro-Solidarity City Poland's Coming Vote Is Stirring Little Excitement," *New York Times* (June 1, 1989), A3; and Krzysztof Bobinski, "Why Solidarity Fears a Landslide at the Polls," *Financial Times* (June 3, 1989), A2.

131. Garton Ash, *Magic Lantern*, 25–26.

132. Cable from Amembassy Warsaw to SecState, "Election '89—The Year of Solidarity," dated April 19, 1989, NSA, End of the Cold War, Poland 1989 Cables.

133. Notes, "Trip to Poland, May 25–30," undated, LOC, Zbigniew Brzeziński Papers, Box II: 126, Foreign Travel May 25–30, Poland (2 of 4).

134. Cable from Amembassy Warsaw to SecState, "Election '89—Growing Confidence and Sharpening Antagonisms in Płock," dated May 19, 1989, NSA, End of the Cold War, Poland 1989 Cables.

135. Cable from Amembassy Warsaw to SecState, "Election '89: Solidarity's Coming Victory; Big or Too Big?" dated June 2, 1989, NSA, End of the Cold War, Poland 1989 Cables.

136. Davis's reporting is also important as it relates to the historiography of 1989. In *American Diplomacy* (59), Hutchings claims that "no one inside Poland or out had expected such a landslide," a common misperception in American and Polish accounts. Davis's April 19 and June 2 cables

patently refute that claim, which is used to defend the United States' lack of foresight and their weak response. It remains possible that American diplomats neglected the analysis of their own representative in Warsaw in favor of the bleaker picture they were receiving from Solidarność visitors to Washington, which better fit conventional wisdom. If so, this reinforces criticisms of the Bush administration that bureaucratic struggles restricted creative and unconventional thinking.

137. Cable from Amembassy Warsaw to SecState, "The National List—Looking Defeat in the Face," dated May 24, 1989, NSA, End of the Cold War, Poland 1989 Cables. It should be noted that Solidarność activists shared the embassy's concerns and in the final days of the campaign, Wałęsa personally tried to convince people to vote for some of the names on the National List.

138. "Election '89: Solidarity's Coming Victory; Big or Too Big?"

139. Cable from Amembassy Warsaw to SecState, "Election '89: First Solidarity Press Conference," dated June 6, 1989, NSA, End of the Cold War, Poland 1989 Cables.

140. Cable from Amembassy Warsaw to SecState, "Election '89—Solidarity's Victory Raises Questions," dated June 6, 1989, NSA, End of the Cold War, Poland 1989 Cables.

141. Ibid.

142. Letter from President George Bush to General Wojciech Jaruzelski (in English), dated May 2, 1989, MSZ 2/94, W-9, Dep III (1989), AP 220-9-89.

143. Cable from Amembassy Warsaw to SecState, "Presidential Trip to Poland and Hungary," dated May 4, 1989, NSA, End of the Cold War, Poland 1989 Cables.

144. Unofficial translation of a letter from General Jaruzelski to President Bush (in English), dated May 11, 1989, MSZ, 2/94, W-9, Dep III (1989), AP 220-9-89.

145. Pilna Notatka w sprawie oficjalnej wizyty w Polsce prezydenta Stanów Zjednoczonych Ameryki, George'a H. Busha [Urgent Note regarding U.S. President George H. Bush's official visit to Poland], dated May 19, 1989, MSZ, 2/94, W-9, Dep III (1989), AP 220-9-89.

146. House Committee on Foreign Affairs, *Consideration of Miscellaneous Bills and Resolutions*, 172. H.R. 2550 was eventually included in Public Law 101–179, "Support for East European Democracy," passed November 28, 1989.

147. Cable from Amembassy Warsaw to SecState, "Possible New Election for a Contested National List," dated June 7, 1989, NSA, End of the Cold War, Poland 1989 Cables. Davis suggests this idea came from a casual conversation he had with Czyrek on June 5. Davis also asks that RFE and VOA broadcasts "avoid heaping scorn on this admittedly contrived expedient."

148. Cable for Amembassy Warsaw to SecState, "Round Table Coordination Committee Meets to Endorse National List Compromise," dated June 9, 1989, NSA, End of the Cold War, Poland 1989 Cables.

149. Author's interview with Davis, November 23, 1999.

150. Cable from Amembassy Warsaw to SecState, "Election's Second Round only a Partial Solution to the National List Problem," dated June 13, 1989, NSA, End of the Cold War, Poland 1989 Cables.

151. Cable from Amembassy Warsaw to SecState, "Peasant Party Loosening its Bonds with PZPR," dated June 15, 1989, NSA, End of the Cold War, Poland 1989 Cables.

152. Cable from Amembassy Warsaw to SecState, "Election Results Pressure Party to Split Sooner than Anticipated," dated June 20, 1989, NSA, End of the Cold War, Poland 1989 Cables.

153. Cable from Amembassy Warsaw to SecState, "How to Elect Jaruzelski without Voting for Him and Will He Run," dated June 23, 1989, NSA, End of the Cold War, Poland 1989 Cables.

154. Ibid.

155. Cable from Amembassy Warsaw to SecState, "Crisis Develops over Election of Polish President," dated June 30, 1989, NSA, End of the Cold War, Poland 1989 Cables.

156. Cable from Amembassy Warsaw to SecState, "Politburo Member warns that U.S. has been Dragged into War of Election of Jaruzelski as President," dated June 16, 1989, NSA, End of the Cold War, Poland 1989 Cables.

157. Cable from Amembassy Warsaw to SecState, "Poland's Political Crisis, Wałęsa's Views," dated July 1, 1989, NSA, End of the Cold War, Poland 1989 Cables.

158. Cable from Amembassy Warsaw to SecState, "Politcal Crisis Intensifies," dated July 3, 1989, NSA, End of the Cold War, Poland 1989 Cables.

159. Cable from Amembassy Warsaw to SecState, "Michnik Proposes a Solidarity Government, Prints the Proposal in the Newspaper," dated July 3, 1989, NSA, End of the Cold War, Poland 1989 Cables.

160. "How to Elect Jaruzelski without Voting for Him and Will He Run."

161. Maureen Dowd, "Bush in Warsaw on Delicate Mission to Push Changes," *New York Times* (July 10, 1989), A1.

162. Maureen Dowd, "For Bush, a Polish Welcome without Fervor," *New York Times* (July 11, 1989), A1.

163. "Schedule of the President and Mrs. Bush to Warsaw, Poland," and "Schedule of the President and Mrs. Bush for Gdańsk, Poland," both dated June 28, 1989, NSA, End of the Cold War, FOIA 20040077DOS030.

164. Dowd, "For Bush, a Polish Welcome without Fervor."

165. Explanations of all of these initiatives are included in declassified briefing materials, ca. July 1989, NSA, End of the Cold War, FOIA 20040077DOS030.

166. Telephone conversation between President Bush and Helmut Kohl, dated June 23, 1989, GBPL, Memcons/Telcons), available online at http://bushlibrary.tamu.edu/research/memcons_ telcons.php. Bush expressed similar sentiments to Jaques Delors, the European Committees Commission President. See Memorandum of conversation between Delors and Bush, dated June 14, 1989, GBPL, Memcons/Telcons, available online.

167. Memo from James A. Baker to the President, "Your Visit to Europe, July 9–18, 1989," dated June 30, 1989, NSA, End of the Cold War, FOIA 20040077DOS030.

168. Memo from James A. Baker to the President, "Your Visit to Poland, July 10–11, 1989," dated June 30, 1989, NSA, End of the Cold War, FOIA 20040077DOS030.

169. Author's interview with John Davis, Washington, D.C., November 23, 1999.

170. Memorandum of Conversation between President Bush and General Jaruzelski, dated July 10, 1989, GBPL, Memcon/Telcons, available online.

171. Bush seems to have particularly latched onto labor's request for three-to-five year maternity leaves for female workers. Memorandum of Conversation between President Bush and Prime Minister Rakowski, dated July 10, 1989, GBPL, Telcons/Memcons, available online.

172. Memorandum of Conversation between President Bush and President Mitterrand, dated July 13, 1989, GBPL, Telcons/Memcons, available online.

173. Bush and Scowcroft, *A World Transformed*, 117.

174. Notatka Informacyjna dot. wizyty oficjalnej prezydenta Stanów Zjednoczonych Ameryki George H. Bush (9–11 lipca 1989 r.) [Information Note regarding the official visit of the President of the United States of America, George H. Bush (9–11 July 1989)], dated July 18, 1989, MSZ, 2/94, W-9, Dep III (1989), AP 220-9-89.

175. Telephone Conversation between Bush and Thatcher, dated June 11, 1989, GBPL, Telcons/Memcons, available online.

176. Notatka Informacyjna dot. wizyty oficjalnej prezydenta.

177. Notatka Informacyjna o naradzie Doradczego Komitetu Politycznego państw-stron Układu Warzawskiego [Information Note of a meeting of the Political Consultative Committee of the Warsaw Pact], dated July 10, 1989, AAN, KC PZPR, V/490, 41–53; quote from 46. Also in ISPPAN, KM, M/18/9.

178. Dudek, *Reglamentowana rewolucja*, 354.

179. Rakowski, *Dzienniki polityczne 1987–1990*, 475.

180. Cable from Amembassy Warsaw to SecState, "Jaruzelski to Face the Nation and then Run for President," dated July 17, 1989, NSA, End of the Cold War, Poland 1989 Cables.

181. Cable from Amembassy Warsaw to SecState, "Jaruzelski meets with the Solidarity Caucus and now Will (#)," dated July 18, 1989, NSA, End of the Cold War, Poland 1989 Cables.

182. Cable from Amembassy Warsaw to SecState, "Solidarity Describes how it Engineered the Election, Debates Whether to Form a Government," dated July 24, 1989, NSA, End of the Cold War, Poland 1989 cables.

183. Hutchings, *American Diplomacy*, 69.

184. There is an increasing consensus among scholars of the Bush administration stressing his focus on stability and continuity during this revolutionary period. See, for example, Engel, "A Better World . . . but Don't Get Carried Away"; Engel, *The Fall of the Berlin Wall,* 132–69; and Sarotte, *1989*.

185. Cable from USMission NATO to SecState, "Presentation by DAS Simons at April 13 NAC on Poland," dated April 14, 1989, NSA, End of the Cold War, Poland 1989 Cables.

186. Cable from USmission NATO to SecState, "NAC Discussion of Responses to Poland," dated April 14, 1989, NSA, End of the Cold War, Poland 1989 Cables.

187. For examples of this reporting, see Cable from Amembassy Rome to SecState, "Western Response to Polish Reforms—Continued Consultations," dated June 1, 1989; Cable from Amembassy Bonn to SecState, "Western Response to Polish Reforms—Consultations with the FRG," dated June 2, 1989; Cable from Amembassy Vienna to SecState, "Western Response to Polish Reforms—Austria," dated June 5, 1989; and Cable from Amembassy Tokyo to SecState, "Western Response to Polish Reforms—Continued Consultations Japan," dated June 5, 1989; all in NSA, End of the Cold War, Poland 1989 cables.

188. "Declaration on East-West Relations," dated July 15, 1989, available via the University of Toronto G-8 Information Center website: http://www.g8.utoronto.ca/summit/1989paris/east .html.

189. Hutchings, *American Diplomacy*, 63. For the meeting at which Deputy Assistant Secretary Curtis Kamman (who replaced Simons in June) explained the results of the G7 summit to Kinast, see Cable from SecState to Amembassy Warsaw, "Briefing the Polish Ambassador on Results of the Paris Summit," dated July 25, 1989, NSA, End of the Cold War, Poland 1989 Cables.

190. Cable from Amembassy Brussels to SecState, "EC Food Aid Program for Poland," dated August 10, 1989, NSA, End of the Cold War, Poland 1989 Cables.

191. Cable from Amembassy Brussels to SecState, "EC-Poland Trade and Cooperation Agreement Signed," dated August 8, 1989, NSA, End of the Cold War, Poland 1989 Cables.

192. Cable from Amembassy Warsaw to SecState, "Kuroń Argues for a Solidarity Government," dated July 25, 1989, NSA, End of the Cold War, Poland 1989 Cables.

193. "Solidarity Describes how it Engineered the Election, Debates Whether to Form Government."

194. Cable from Amembassy Warsaw to SecState, "Solidarity Declines a Role in the Grand Coalition," dated July 27, 1989, NSA, End of the Cold War, Poland 1989 Cables.

195. Cable from Amembassy Warsaw to SecState, "Interior Minister Kiszczak proposed as Prime Minister," dated August 1, 1989, NSA, End of the Cold War, Poland 1989 Cables.

196. Cable from Amembassy Warsaw to SecState, "Sejm Elects Kiszczak Prime Minister despite Defectors," dated August 2, 1989, End of the Cold War, Poland 1989 Cables.

197. Paczkowski, *Spring*, 508.

198. Cable from Amembassy Warsaw to SecState, "Strike Update August 3 and 4," dated August 4, 1989 and Cable from Amembassy Warsaw to SecState, "Strike Synopsis August 7," dated August 8, 1989; both in NSA, End of the Cold War, Poland 1989 Cables.

199. Dudek, *Reglamentowana rewolucja*, 376–77. On these developments, see also Skórzyński, *Rewolucja Okrągłego Stołu*, 376–83.

200. Cable from Amembassy Warsaw to SecState, "Conversation with General Kiszczak," dated August 11, 1989, NSA, End of the Cold War, Poland 1989 Cables.

201. Paczkowski, *Spring*, 508.

202. Dudek, *Reglamentowana rewolucja*, 352.

203. Ibid., 384.

204. Cable from Amembassy Moscow to SecState, "If Solidarity takes Charge, What will the Soviets Do?" dated August 16, 1989, NSA, End of the Cold War, Poland 1989 Cables. This cable, however, did not address the issue of how this move would affect Gorbachev's position in Moscow. Davis was actually most worried about a change in power in the Kremlin. As he recalls, "There was always the question of whether Gorbachev would be overthrown by the military or overruled by the military. In my mind, maybe I was dwelling on it too much. For me I always wondered what the Soviet military would think of giving up the jewel of the satellites, undermining their access to East Germany and so on. They didn't react at all, the way it worked out. They reacted much later, but were in no position to do anything anyway" (author's interview with Davis, November 23, 1999.)

205. Paczkowski, *Spring*, 509. See also, Dudek, *Reglamentowana rewolucja*, 398.

206. Paczkowski, *Spring*, 509.

207. Cable from SecState to Amembassy Warsaw, "Message to Ambassador Davis and Staff from the President," dated August 26, 1989, NSA, End of the Cold War, Poland 1989 Cables.

208. Cable from SecState to Amembassy Warsaw, "Ambassador's Instructions," dated August 24, 1989, NSA, End of the Cold War, Poland 1989 Cables.

209. "Election '89—The Year of Solidarity."

210. Castle's analysis in *Triggering Communism's Collapse* focuses on these constantly changing political dynamics. For her conclusions see the final chapter, "Changing Power," 217–30.

211. For a more in depth analysis of this issue, see Domber, "Skepticism and Stability."

212. Bush and Scowcroft, *A World Transformed*, 117.

213. Baker, *Politics of Diplomacy*, 45. The comparison being made is to the administration's policy of direct discussions with Moscow based on "discreet, measured reciprocity."

214. Gates, *From the Shadows*, 471. Gates was deputy director of the CIA until mid-March 1989 and then deputy assistant to the president for national security affairs.

215. Zelikow, "U.S. Strategic Planning in 2001–2002," 96 and 97.

216. Hutchings, *American Diplomacy*, 8.

217. Beschloss and Talbott, *Highest Level*, 87.

218. Hutchings, *American Diplomacy*, 54.

219. Bush and Scowcroft, *A World Transformed*, 115.

220. The decision to support Jaruzelski as president was in line with many Solidarność leaders' thinking, including Wałęsa's. The United States did not force this decision on the opposition.

221. Bush and Scowcroft, *A World Transformed*, 135.

222. Ibid., 130.

## Conclusion

1. The epigraph comes from Bernstein and Politi, *His Holiness*, 263.

2. Author's interview with George Shultz, Stanford, California, February 19, 2008.

3. Notatka Informacyjna o Spotkaniu przywódców partii i państw-stron Układu Warszawskiego w Warszawie (26.04.1985 r) [Information Note about the meeting of party and national leaders of the Warsaw Pact in Warsaw (26.4.1985)], dated April 29, 1985, AAN, KC PZPR, V/264, 11–20; quote from 12.

4. Author's e-mail correspondence with John Davis, May 18, 2012.

5. Gaddis, *Cold War*.

6. Memorandum of meeting, "U.S. Response to Polish Crisis," dated December 22, 1981, NSA, Soviet Flashpoints, Box 26, December 1–22, 1981.

7. Whitehead, *Life in Leadership*, 166.

8. Cable from Secstate to Amembassy Sofia, "Deputy Secretary Whitehead's Dinner Meeting with Lech Wałęsa, Friday, January 30, 1987," dated February 11, 1987, NSA, End of the Cold War Collection, FOIA 20040096DOS038.

9. Author's interview with Tom Simons, July 7, 2000.

10. Notes, "Trip to Poland, May 16–22, 1987," undated, LOC, Zbigniew Brzeziński Papers, Box II: 122, 1987 Foreign Travel, May 12–22 Hungary and Poland (3 of 5).

11. Reagan, *The Reagan Diaries*, 476.

12. Paczkowski, *Polska 1986–1989*, 238.

13. For an overview of church-state relations see, Dudek and Gryz, *Komuniści I Kościół*.

14. For a full discussion of soft power, see Nye, *Soft Power*. For a fuller discussion of this phenomena in Poland, see also Domber, "Humanitarian Aid, Soft Power."

15. Author's interview with Konstanty Gebert, August 3, 2006.

16. Author's interview with Eugeniusz Smolar, December 4, 2007. Smolar also made clear that they did not receive very much money, explaining, "The majority of money that went to Poland went to Solidarity."

17. See Goddeeris, *Solidarity with Solidarity*.

18. Cable from Amembassy Warsaw to SecState, "Election '89—The Year of Solidarity," dated April 19, 1989, NSA, End of the Cold War, Poland 1989 Cables.

19. Letter from Jerzy Milewski to Lane Kirkland, dated June 6, 1988, AFL-CIO, International Affairs Department, Inactive Records, "FTUI." These installments would have come from the special one million-dollar allocation from Congress.

20. Tagliabue, "Wałęsa Takes to Coal Country to Press for an End to Strikes," *New York Times* (Sept. 3, 1988), A1.

21. Tagliabue, "Appeal by Wałęsa Fails to Resolve All Polish Strikes," *New York Times* (Sept. 2, 1988), A1.

22. Jackson Diehl, "Gdańsk Strikes End, But Others Continue: Polish Union Split Over Government Talks," *Washington Post* (Sept. 2, 1988), A23. For a transcript of those discussions, see Tabako, *Strajk '88*, 295–328.

23. William Echikson, "Who'll Pay the Price If Wałęsa's Risk Doesn't Pay Off?" *Christian Science Monitor* (Sept. 6, 1988), 7.

24. Kenney, *Carnival of Revolution*, 234.

25. Tagliabue, "Workers Heed Wałęsa and Agree to End Last of Strikes," *New York Times* (Sept. 4, 1988), A1.

26. Tagliabue, "Wałęsa Takes to Coal Country," A1. These concerns also appear in the transcript of Wałęsa's meeting with the strike committee; see, for example, Tabako, *Strajk '88*, 314–15.

27. This finding revises existing literature on international influences on democratic breakthrough. In their work on democratic transitions, O'Donnell, Schmitter, and Whitehead argue that it is "fruitless to search for some international factors or context which can reliably compel authoritarian rulers to experiment with liberalization, much less which can predictably cause their regimes to collapse" (*Transitions from Authoritarian Rule*, 18). More recent studies on democratization that do take into account international influences are "concerned with consolidation rather than transition [and] often neglect broader external incentives, constraints, examples and transmission mechanisms" (Magen, "Evaluating External Influence on Democratic Development: Transition"). New scholarship, however, has shown that international dynamics can have important effects on democratic transformations when the correlation of domestic forces for and against a democratic breakthrough is equivalent (Stoner and McFaul, *Transitions to Democracy*).

28. Briefing Memoranda, "Fact Sheet: Poland: Opposition Overview," ca. May 1987, LOC, Zbigniew Brzeziński Papers, Box II: 122, 1987 Foreign Travel, May 12–22 Hungary and Poland (1 of 5). The memo specifically mentions WiP, Fighting Solidarity, and the KPN.

29. For a full explanation of WiP's origins and policies, see Kenney, *Carnival of Revolution*, esp. 59–90; quote from 59.

30. For a full exploration of Orange Alternative, its tactics, and its influence, see ibid., 157–91; quote from 160.

31. Paczkowski, *Spring*, 403–4.

32. On Fighting Solidarity and the security services reactions to them, see Kamiński, Sawicki, and Waligóra, *Solidarność Walcząca w dokumentach*.

33. For a full explanation of the structure and how it evolved, see Leszek Olejnik, "Podziemne stuktury NSZZ 'Solidarność' w regionie Ziemnia Łódzka w latach 1981–1989," in Friszke, *Solidarność Podziemna*, 353–73.

34. Ost, *Politics of Anti-politics*, 163.

35. Briefing Memorandum, "Poland: Political Setting," ca. May 1987, LOC, Zbigniew Brzeziński Papers, Box II: 122, 1987 Foreign Travel, May 12–22 Hungary and Poland (1 of 5).

36. Olejnik, "Podziemne struktury w regionie Ziemia Łódzka," 392–95.

37. Szporer, *Solidarity*, 128–46; quote from 142. On Walentynowicz's founding role in Solidarność, see Penn, *Solidarity's Secret*, 29–65.

38. For the best discussion of the tensions within Solidarność, see Ost, *Politics of Anti-politics*. I am paraphrasing his argument about the union's ultimate shift toward a neocorporatist approach. Neocorporatism or societal corporatism "obtains where the privileged status of certain

key interest groups is forced on the state from below, by independent social institutions, and is established de jure (i.e., legally and institutionally)" (115).

39. For an excellent overview of this group, see Skórzyński, *Rewolucja Okrągłego Stołu*, 315-17.

40. Author's interview with Onyszkiewicz in Warsaw, July 8, 2010.

41. Cable from Amembassy Warsaw to SecState, "Election '89: Solidarity's Victory Raises Questions," NSA, End of the Cold War, Poland Cables 1989.

42. In retrospect and with a little more historical distance, the fragility of the political coalition Wałęsa orchestrated in 1989 appears even more pronounced. The Obywatelski Klub Parlamentarny or Citizen's Parliamentary Club, which included all the Solidarność parliamentarians elected to office in June 1989, only remained solvent until May 1990, when it split into a more conservative, nationalist group, led by Lech Kaczyński, and a group affiliated with the intellectual left, headed by Bronisław Geremek. This right-left split was also seen in the special presidential election called in 1990 in which Wałęsa ran against Mazowiecki. Wałęsa won that election and replaced Jaruzelski as president in December 1990. For an excellent study on the breakup of the Solidarność movement, see Ost, *Defeat of Solidarity*.

43. On Solidarność's social-democratic political philosophy, see Falk, *Dilemmas of Dissidence*. On its moderate program for reform, see Staniszkis, *Poland's Self-Limiting Revolution*; and Domber, "Ending the Cold War, Unintentionally."

44. The Smolars and Irena Lasota all left Poland after short prison sentences for their involvement in the 1968 events. Jan Piotr Lasota was married to the daughter of Leszek Kołakowski, a key figure in the development of the social-democratic opposition with close ties to Kuroń and Michnik. Giedroyc and his circles had close ties to the same group, although a different relationship with the opposition than younger activists working in the West. Author's interview with Eugeniusz Smolar, Warsaw, December 4, 2007.

45. For an example of this support, see the periodical *Pomost*, available in the Indiana University Library collections. In the second half of the 1980s, Carl Gershman at NED came under significant political pressured to provide money to Fighting Solidarity, although it did not significantly change NED's funding priorities.

46. All of the intra-opposition rivalries and conflicts explained were transferred to those working in the West to support their causes. Much of the tension between individuals can also be linked to personality clashes. These divisions and sensitivities were plainly evident during the conference titled "The World towards the Solidarity Movement, 1980-1989," held in Wrocław, October 21-23, 2010. Jerzy Milewski remains a particular focus of ire for his position as the head of the Coordinating Office. See Goddeeris, "Lobbying Allies?" Irena Lasota is also a controversial figure, partially because of her central role in providing Western support.

47. Author's interview with Chojecki, Warsaw, December 2007.

48. Author's interview with Helena Łuczywo, Warsaw, December 5, 2007. The salary was about 6,000 zloty.

49. Ibid.

50. Author's interview with Onyszkiewciz.

51. Garton Ash, *Magic Lantern*, 42.

# BIBLIOGRAPHY

## Primary Source Collections

Records of the Polish United Workers' Party; Archiwum Akt Nowych, Warsaw, Poland

Records of the American Department (Dept. III); Archive of the Polish Ministry
of Foreign Affairs, Warsaw, Poland

Samizdat and Underground Publications; Achiwum Opozycji, KARTA Foundation,
Warsaw, Poland

Miedzyszyn Collection; Institute of Political Studies PAN, Warsaw, Poland

Public Opinion Research; Center for Public Opinion Research, Warsaw, Poland

Security Services Files; Institute of National Remembrance, Warsaw, Poland

Various Poland-related Collections; Hoover Institution Library and Archives,
Palo Alto, California

End of the Cold War and Soviet Flashpoints—Polish Crisis Collections; National Security
Archive, Washington, D.C.

Unprocessed International Affairs Department and Office of the President Files; used by special
permission of the Secretary Treasurer, AFL-CIO

Executive Council Minutes and Press Release Files; George Meany Memorial Archives,
Silver Spring, Maryland

Files of the NSC, White House, and the President; Ronald Reagan Presidential Library,
Simi Valley, California

Office Files; Committee in Support of Solidarity, Washington, D.C.

National Endowment for Democracy Collection; Polish American Congress, Washington, D.C.

Library Collection; National Endowment for Democracy Headquarters, Washington, D.C.

Administrative Records; Catholic Relief Services Archives, Baltimore, Maryland

Zbigniew Brzeziński Papers; Library of Congress, Washington, D.C.

## Interviews

Juliusz Biały, July 12, 2004, Warsaw, Poland

Krysztof Bobinski, May 13, 2004, Warsaw, Poland

Zbigniew Bujak, July 12, 2004, Warsaw, Poland

Mirosław Chojecki, December 7, 2007, Warsaw, Poland

Jane Curry, November 30, 2006, San Jose, California

John Davis, November 23, 1999, Washington, D.C.

John Davis, October 5, 2000, Washington, D.C.

John Davis, April 27, 2007, phone interview from his home in Charlottesville, Virginia

Dan Fried, October 6, 2006, Washington, D.C.

Konstanty Gebert, August 6, 2006, Warsaw, Poland

Bronisław Geremek, July 26, 2006, Warsaw, Poland

Christopher Hill, May 12, 2004, Warsaw, Poland

Adrian Karatnycky, November 21, 2007, New York

Zbigniew Karcz, July 8, 2004, Warsaw, Poland

Eugenia Kemble, January 18, 2008, telephone interview

Lee Kjelleran, November 21, 2007, New York

Irena Lasota, June 19, 2007, Washington, D.C.

Jan Piotr Lasota, June 17, 2008, Paris, France

Janusz Lewandowski, January 1, 2004, Warsaw, Poland

Helena Łuczywo, December 5, 2007, Warsaw, Poland

Zdisław Ludwiczak, June 10, 2010, Warsaw, Poland

Cameron Munter, June 11, 2004, Warsaw, Poland

Janusz Onyszkiewicz, July 8, 2010, Warsaw, Poland

Andrzej Paczkowski, December 12, 2007, Warsaw, Poland

Stanisław Pawliszewski, July 1 and July 7, 2004, Warsaw, Poland

George Shultz, January 18, 2008, Stanford, California

Tim Simmins, July 9, 2004, Warsaw, Poland

Tom Simons, July 7, 2000, Washington, D.C.

Eugeniusz Smolar, December 4, 2007, Warsaw, Poland

Barbara Torunczyk, December 12, 2007, Warsaw, Poland

John Whitehead, November 20, 2007, New York

Marilyn Wyatt, July 8, 2004, Warsaw, Poland


## Secondary Sources

Arbel, David, and Ran Edilist. *Western Intelligence and the Collapse of the Soviet Union, 1980–1990: Ten Years That Did Not Shake the World*. London: Frank Cass, 2003.

Baker, James A., III, with Thomas M. DeFrank. *The Politics of Diplomacy: Revolution, War, and Peace, 1989–1992*. New York: G. P. Putnam's Sons, 1995.

Balcerowicz, Leszek. *Socialism, Capitalism, Transformation*. Budapest: Central European Press, 1995.

Bernhard, Michael H. *The Origins of Democratization in Poland: Workers, Intellectuals, and Oppositional Politics, 1976–1980*. New York: Columbia University Press, 1993.

Bernstein, Carl, and Marcus Politi. *His Holiness: John Paul II and the Hidden History of Our Time*. New York: Doubleday, 1996.

Beschloss, Michael R., and Strobe Talbott. *At the Highest Levels: The Inside Story of the End of the Cold War*. Boston: Little, Brown, 1993.

Beissinger, Mark R. *Nationalist Mobilization and the Collapse of the Soviet State*. Cambridge: Cambridge University Press, 2004.

Bies, Robert J., and Thomas M. Tripp. "Beyond Distrust: 'Getting Even' and the Need for Revenge." In *Trust in Organizations: Frontiers of Theory and Research*, edited by Roderick M. Kramer and Tom R. Tyler, 246–60. Thousand Oaks, Calif.: Sage Publications, 1996.

Blinken, Anthony J. *Ally vs. Ally: America, Europe, and the Siberian Pipeline*. New York: Praeger, 1987.

Bonetti, Shane. "Distinguishing Characteristics of Degrees of Success and Failure in Economic Sanctions Episodes." *Applied Economics* 30 (1998): 805–13.

Bozo, Frédéric. *Mitterand, the End of the Cold War, and German Unification*. Translated by Susan Emanuel. New York: Berghahn Books, 2009.

Bozo, Frédéric, Marie-Pierre Rey, N. Piers Ludlow, and Leopoldo Nuti, eds. *Europe and the End of the Cold War: A Reappraisal*. London: Routledge, 2008.

Brown, Archie. *The Gorbachev Factor*. New York: Oxford University Press, 1997.

Brzeziński, Zbigniew. "The Cold War and Its Aftermath." *Foreign Affairs* 71, no. 4 (1992): 31–49.

——. *The Grand Failure: The Birth and Death of Communism in the Twentieth Century*. New York: Collier Books, 1990.

——. "The Great Transformation." *National Interest* 33 (Fall 1993): 3–13.

——. "New World Order? An Interview with Zbigniew Brzeziński." *SAIS Review* 11, no. 2 (1991): 1–8

——. *Power and Principle: Memoirs of the National Security Adviser, 1977–1981*, rev. ed. New York: Farrar, Straus and Giroux, 1985.

Bush, George. *All the Best, George Bush: My Life in Letters and Other Writings*. New York: Scribner, 1999.

Bush, George, and Brent Scowcroft. *A World Transformed*. New York: Alfred A. Knopf, 1998.

Byrne, Malcolm, Paweł Machciewicz, and Christian F. Ostermann, eds. *Poland 1980–1982: Internal Crisis, International Dimensions; A Compendium of Declassified Documents and Chronology of Events*. Washington: National Security Archive, 1997.

Cannon, Lou. *President Reagan: The Role of a Lifetime*. New York: Public Affairs, 2000.

Castle, Marjorie. *Triggering Communism's Collapse: Perceptions and Power in Poland's Transition*. Lanham, Md.: Rowman and Littlefield, 2003.

Castle, Marjorie, and Ray Taras. *Democracy in Poland*. 2nd ed. Boulder, Colo.: Westview Press, 2002.

Chernyaev, Anatoli. *My Six Years with Gorbachev*. Translated by Robert D. English and Elizabeth Tucker. University Park: Pennsylvania State University Press, 2000.

Clymer, Adam. *Edward M. Kennedy: A Biography*. New York: William Morrow, 1999.

Cohn, Elizabeth. "Idealpolitik in U.S. Foreign Policy: The Reagan Administration and the U.S. Promotion of Democracy." Ph.D. diss., American University, 1995.

Curry, Jane Leftwich, and Lubja Fajfer, eds. *Poland's Permanent Revolution: People vs. Elites, 1956 to the Present*. Washington: American University Press, 1996.

Davies, Norman. *God's Playground: A History of Poland*. Vol. 2. Oxford: Clarendon Press, 1985.

Davis, Helen C. *Amerykanka w Warszawie* [An American in Warsaw]. Warsaw: Społeczny Instytut Wydawniczy Znak, 2001.

Davis, John R. "Developments in Poland, Prospects for the Future." In *Poland in a World in Change: Constitutions, Presidents, and Politics*, edited by Kenneth W. Thompson. Charlottesville, Va.: The Miller Center and University Press of America, 1991.

——. "Postwar Relations: The Long Climb from Yalta and Potsdam to Gdańsk and the Round Table." *Polish Review* 54, no. 2 (2009): 195–228.

——. "Some Reflections on 1989 in Poland." *Polish Review* 44, no. 4 (1999): 389–93.

Dobbs, Michael. *Down with Big Brother: The Fall of the Soviet Empire*. New York: Alfred A. Knopf, 1997.

Dobson, Alan P. *U.S. Economic Statecraft for Survival, 1933–1991: Of Economic Sanctions, Embargoes, and Economic Warfare*. New York: Routledge, 2002.

Domber, Gregory F. "Ending the Cold War, Unintentionally." In *Visions of the End of the Cold War in Europe, 1945–1990*, edited by Frédéric Bozo, Marie-Pierre Rey, N. Piers Ludlow, and Leopoldo Nuti. New York: Berghahn Books, 2012.

———. "Humanitarian Aid, Soft Power, and American Influences on the End of the Cold War in Poland." In *Routledge Handbook on the End of the Cold War*, edited by Craig Daigle and Artemy Kalinovsky. London: Routledge, 2013.

———. "Power Politics, Human Rights, and Trans-Atlantic Relations." In *European and Transatlantic Strategies to Overcome the East-West Division of Europe*, edited by Odd Arne Westad and Poul Villaume. Copenhagen: Copenhagen University Press, 2009.

———. "The Rise and Fall of the Brezhnev Doctrine in Soviet Foreign Policy." *Journal of Cold War Studies*, 7, no. 3 (2005): 186–88.

———. "Rumblings in Eastern Europe: Western Pressure on Poland's Moves toward Democratic Transformation." In *Europe and the End of the Cold War: A Reappraisal*, edited by Frédéric Bozo, Marie-Pierre Rey, N. Piers Ludlow, and Leopldo Nuti. London: Routledge, 2008.

———. "Skepticism and Stability: Reevaluating U.S. Policy toward Poland's Democratic Transformation in 1989." *Journal of Cold War Studies* 13, no. 3 (2011): 52–82.

———, ed. *Ku zwycięstwu "Solidarności." Korespondencja Ambasady USA w Warszawie z Departmentem Stanu styczeń-wrzesień 1989* [Solidarity's coming victory: Correspondence from the American Embassy in Warsaw to the Department of State, January-September 1989]. Warsaw: Institute Studiów Politycznych, 2006.

Dubiński, Krzysztof. *Magdalenka. Transakcja epoki* [Magdalenka. Transaction of the epoch]. Warsaw: Wydawnictwo Sylwa, 1990.

Dudek, Antoni. *Reglamentowana rewolucja. Rozkład dyktatury komunistycznej w Polsce 1988–1990* [Rationing revolution: the disintegration of the Communist dictatorship in Poland, 1988–1990]. Kraków: Arcana Historii, 2004.

Dudek, Antoni, and Andrzej Friszke, eds. *Polska 1986–1989. Koniec systemu* [Poland, 1986–1989: The end of the system]. Vol. 3. Warsaw: Wydawnictwo Trio and Instytut Studiów Politycznych Polskiej Akademii Nauk, 2002.

Dudek, Antoni, and Ryszard Gryz. *Komuniści i Kościół w Polsce (1945–1989)* [Communists and the Church in Poland (1945–1989)]. Kraków: Wydawnictwo ZNAK, 2003.

Edwards, Lee, ed. *The Collapse of Communism*. Stanford: Hoover Institution Press, 1999.

Ehrman, John. *The Eighties: America in the Age of Reagan*. New Haven: Yale University Press, 2005.

Elster, John, ed. *The Round Table Talks and the Breakdown of Communism*. Chicago: University of Chicago Press, 1996.

Engel, Jeffrey A. "A Better World . . . But Don't Get Carried Away: The Foreign Policy of George H. W. Bush Twenty Years On." *Diplomatic History* 34, no. 1 (2010): 25–46.

———, ed. *The Fall of the Berlin Wall: The Revolutionary Legacy of 1989*. New York: Oxford University Press, 2009.

English, Robert. *Russia and the Idea of the West: Gorbachev, Intellectuals, and the End of the Cold War*. New York: Columbia University Press, 2000.

Evangelista, Matthew. "Norms, Heresthetics, and the End of the Cold War." *Journal of Cold War Studies* 3, no. 1 (2001): 5–35.

Falk, Barbara. *The Dilemmas of Dissidence in East-Central Europe*. Budapest: Central European University Press, 2003.

FitzGerald, Frances. *Way Out There in the Blue: Reagan, Star Wars, and the End of the Cold War*. New York: Simon and Schuster, 2000.

Fischer, Beth A. *The Reagan Reversal: Foreign Policy and the End of the Cold War*. Columbia: University of Missouri Press, 1997.

———. "The United States and the Transformation of the Cold War." In *The Last Decade of the Cold War*, edited by Olav Njølstad, 226–40. London: Frank Cass, 2004.

Fiszman, Joseph. *Revolution and Tradition in People's Poland: Education and Socialization*. Princeton: Princeton University Press, 1972.

*Foreign Affairs Chronology, 1978–1989*. New York: Foreign Affairs, 1990.

Friszke, Andrzej. "The Polish Political Scene." *East European Politics and Societies* 4, no. 2 (1990): 305–41.

———. *Polska. Losy państwa i narodu 1939–1989* [Poland: The fate of the people and the nation, 1939–1989]. Warsaw: Wydawnictwo ISKRY, 2003.

———, ed. *Solidarność Podziemna 1981–1989* [Solidarity Underground, 1981–1989]. Warsaw: Instytut Studiów Politycznych PAN, 2006.

Gaddis, John Lewis. *The Cold War: A New History*. New York: Penguin, 2005.

———. *Russia, the Soviet Union, and the United States: An Interpretive History*. 2nd ed. New York: McGraw-Hill, 1990.

Garlicki, Andrzej. *Karuzela* [Carousel]. Warsaw: Czytelnik, 2003.

Garthoff, Raymond. *Detente and Confrontation: American-Soviet Relations from Nixon to Reagan*. Rev. ed. Washington: Brookings Institution, 1994.

———. *The Great Transition: American-Soviet Relations and the End of the Cold War*. Washington: Brookings Institution, 1994.

Garton Ash, Timothy. *The Magic Lantern: The Revolution of '89 Witnessed in Warsaw, Budapest, Berlin, and Prague*. New York: Vintage Books, 1993.

———. *The Uses of Adversity: Essays on the Fate of Central Europe*. New York: Vintage Books, 1990.

Gates, Robert M. *From the Shadows: The Ultimate Insider's Story of Five Presidents and How They Won the Cold War*. New York: Simon and Schuster, 1996.

Gati, Charles. *The Bloc That Failed: Soviet-East European Relations in Transition*. Bloomington: Indiana University Press, 1990.

Goddeeris, Idesbald. "Lobbying Allies? The NSZZ Solidarność Coordinating Office Abroad, 1982–1989." *Journal of Cold War Studies* 13, no. 3 (2011): 83–125.

———, ed. *Solidarity with Solidarity: West European Trade Unions and the Polish Crisis, 1980–1982*. Lanham, Md.: Lexington Books, 2010.

Gorbachev, Mikhail S. *Memoirs*. New York: Doubleday, 1996.

———. *Perestroika: New Thinking for Our Country and the World*. Updated ed. Translated by APN Publishers. New York: Harper and Row, 1988.

———. *Perestroika and American-Soviet Relations*. Madison, Conn.: Sphinx Publishers, 1990.

Grabowska, Alina. *PRL atakuje Radio "Wolna Europa"* [The PRL attacks Radio Free Europe]. Wrocław: Towarzystwo Przyjaciół Ossolineum, 2002.

Haig, Alexander M., Jr. *Caveat: Realism, Reagan, and Foreign Policy*. New York: Macmillan, 1984.

Hardt, John P., Francis T. Miko, and Victoria L. Engel. "Polish Crisis." *Congressional Research Service Report*, January 9, 1982.

Holzer, Jerzy, and Krzysztof Leski. *Solidarność w podziemu* [Solidarity underground]. Lodz: Wydawnictwo Łódskie, 1990.

*Human Rights Violations in the Polish People's Republic (January 1984–January 1985)*. Washington: Committee in Support of Solidarity's Report, 1985.

Hutchings, Robert L. "American Diplomacy and the End of the Cold War." *Polish Review* 44, no. 4 (1999): 394–96.

———. *American Diplomacy and the End of the Cold War: An Insider's Account of U.S. Policy in Europe, 1989–1992.* Washington: Woodrow Wilson Center Press, 1997.

Iwaszkiewicz, Agnieszka, ed. *Archiwum Opozycji* [Opposition Archive]. Vol. 1. Warsaw: Ośrodek Karta, 2006.

Jaruzelski, Wojciech. "Commentary." *Cold War International History Project Bulletin*, no. 11 (1998): 32–39.

———. *Stan wojenny. Dlaczego . . .* [Martial law. Why . . .]. Warsaw: BGW, 1992.

Kaminski, Bartlomiej. *The Collapse of State Socialism: The Case of Poland.* Princeton: Princeton University Press, 1991.

Kamiński, Łukasz, Wojciech Sawicki, and Gzegorz Waligóra, eds. *Solidarność Walcząca w dokumentach* [Fighting Solidarity in documents]. Vol. 1 of *Oczach SB* [In the eyes of the security services]. Warsaw: Instytut Pamięci Narodowej, 2007.

Kaufman, Michael T. *Mad Dreams, Saving Graces.* New York: Random House, 1989.

———. *Soros: The Life and Times of a Messianic Billionaire.* New York: Alfred A. Knopf, 2002.

Kenney, Padraic. *A Carnival of Revolution: Central Europe 1989.* Princeton: Princeton University Press, 2002.

———. "Framing Political Opportunities and Civic Mobilization in the Eastern European Revolutions: A Case Study of Poland's Freedom and Peace Movement." *Mobilization* 6, no. 2 (2001): 193–210.

———. "What Is the History of 1989? New Scholarship from East-Central Europe." *East European Politics and Societies* 13, no. 2 (1999): 419–31.

Kenney, Padraic, and Gerd-Rainer Horn, eds. *Transnational Moments of Change: Europe 1945, 1968, 1989.* Lanham, Md.: Rowman and Littlefield, 2004.

Koralewicz, Jadwiga, Ireneusz Bialecki, and Margaret Watson, eds. *Crisis and Transition: Polish Society in the 1980s.* New York: St. Martin's Press, 1987.

Korbonski, Andrzej. "East Central Europe on the Eve of the Changeover: the Case of Poland." *Communist and Post-Communist Studies* 32, no. 2 (1999): 139–53.

Kostrzewa, Robert, ed. *Between East and West: Writings from "Kultura."* New York: Hill and Wang, 1990.

Kotkin, Stephen, and Jan Gross. *Uncivil Society: 1989 and the Implosion of the Communist Establishment.* New York: Modern Library, 2009.

Kraljic, Matthew A., ed. *The Breakup of Communism: The Soviet Union and Eastern Europe.* New York: H. W. Wilson, 1993.

Kramer, Mark. "The Anoshkin Notebook on the Polish Crisis, December 1981." *Cold War International History Project Bulletin*, no. 11 (1998): 17–31.

———. "Beyond the Brezhnev Doctrine: A New Era in Soviet-East European Relations." *International Security* 14, no. 3 (1989): 25–67.

———. "The Collapse of East European Communism and the Repercussions in the Soviet Union (Part 1)." *Journal of Cold War Studies* 5, no. 4 (2003): 178–256.

———. "The Collapse of East European Communism and the Repercussions in the Soviet Union (Part 2)." *Journal of Cold War Studies* 6, no. 4 (2003): 3–64.

———. "The Collapse of East European Communism and the Repercussions in the Soviet Union (Part 3)." *Journal of Cold War Studies* 7, no. 1 (2005): 3–96.

――. "Jaruzelski, the Soviet Union, and the Imposition of Martial Law in Poland: New Light on the Mystery of December 1981." *Cold War International History Project Bulletin*, no. 11 (1998): 5-14.

――. "The Kukliński Files and the Polish Crisis, 1980-1981: An Analysis of the Newly Released CIA Documents on Ryszard Kukliński." Working Paper No. 59. Washington, Cold War International History Project, 2009.

――. "Soviet Deliberations during the Polish Crisis, 1980-1981." Special Working Paper No. 1. Washington, Cold War International History Project, 1997.

――. "The Warsaw Pact and the Polish Crisis of 1980-81: Honecker's Call for Military Intervention." *Cold War International History Project Bulletin*, no. 5 (1995): 124.

Kreihs, Gabriela. *Dobro ukryte w archiwach. Akcja doborczynna Kościoła katolickiego w czasie kryzysu gospodarczego i politcznego w Polsce lat 1981-1990* [Hidden good in the archives. Charitable actions of the Catholic Church during the political and economic crisis in Poland, 1981-1990]. Cieszyń, Poland: Czieszyńska Drukarnia Wydawnicza, 2004.

Kubina, Michael, and Manfred Wilke, eds. *"Hart und kompromisslos": Die SED contra Polen 1980/81: Geheimakten der SED-Führung über die Unterdrückung der polnischen Demokratiebewegung.* Berlin: Akademie Verlag, 1995.

Levesque, Jacques. *The Enigma of 1989: The USSR and the Liberation of Eastern Europe.* Translated by Keith Martin. Berkeley: University of California Press, 1997.

Łopiński, Maciej, Marcin Moskit, and Maruisz Wilk. *Konspira: Solidarity Underground.* Translated by Jane Cave. Berkeley: University of California Press, 1990.

Loth, Wilfried. "Moscow, Prague, and Warsaw: Overcoming the Brezhnev Doctrine." *Cold War History* 1, no. 2 (2001): 103-18.

Lundberg, Kirsten. *The CIA and the Fall of the Soviet Empire: The Politics of "Getting It Right."* Cambridge, Mass.: Kennedy School of Government, Harvard University, 1994.

MacEachin, Douglas J. *U.S. Intelligence and the Confrontation in Poland, 1980-1981.* University Park: Pennsylvania State University Press, 2002.

――. *U.S. Intelligence and the Polish Crisis, 1980-1981.* Washington: Center for the Study of Intelligence, 2000.

Machciewicz, Paweł. *"Monachijska menażeria." Walka z Radiem Wolna Europa 1950-1989* [Munich menagerie. The battle with Radio Free Europe, 1950-1989]. Warsaw: Instytut Pamięci Narodowej i Instytut Studiów Politycznych, 2007.

――. "Poland, 1986-1989: From 'Cooptation' to 'Negotiated Revolution'; New Documents." *Cold War International History Project Bulletin*, no. 12/13 (2001): 93-128.

――, ed. *Polska 1986-1989. Koniec systemu* [Poland, 1986-1989. The end of the system]. Vol. 1. Warsaw: Wydawnictwo Trio and Instytut Studiów Politycznych Polskiej Akademii Nauk, 2002.

Magen, Amichai, "Evaluating External Influence on Democratic Development: Transition." Paper presented at the conference "Evaluating International Influences on Democratic Development." Center on Democracy, Development, and the Rule of Law, Stanford University, October 25-26, 2007

Mann, James. *The Rebellion of Ronald Reagan: A History of the End of the Cold War.* New York: Penguin, 2009.

Marantz, Paul. "Poland and East-West Relations." *Canadian Slavonic Papers* 25, no. 3 (September 1983): 411-24.

Maslen, John. "The European Community's Relations with the State-Trading Countries of Eastern Europe, 1984–1986." In *Yearbook of European Law*. Oxford: Clarendon Press, 1987.

Mastny, Wojciech. "The Soviet Non-invasion of Poland in 1980–1981 and the End of the Cold War." Working Paper No. 23. Washington, Cold War International History Project, 1998.

Mathews, John P. C. "The West's Secret Marshall Plan for the Mind." *International Journal of Intelligence and Counterintelligence* 16, no. 3 (2003): 409–27.

Matlock, Jack F., Jr. *Autopsy on an Empire: The American Ambassador's Account of the Collapse of the Soviet Union*. New York: Random House, 1995.

———. *Reagan and Gorbachev: How the Cold War Ended*. New York: Random House, 2004.

Maynard, Christopher Alan. "From the Shadow of Reagan: George Bush and the End of the Cold War." Ph.D. diss, Louisiana State University, 2001.

McFaul, Michael, and Francis Fukuyama, "Should Democracy Be Promoted or Demoted?" *Washington Quarterly* (Winter 2007–8): 23–45.

"Memorandum Regarding the Meeting between Comrade Leonid Ilyish Brezhnev, Eric Honecker, and Gusav Husák in the Kremlin, 16 May 1981." *Cold War International History Project Bulletin*, no. 11 (1998): 125–31.

Meyer, Michael. *The Year That Changed the World: The Untold Story behind the Fall of the Berlin Wall*. New York: Scribner, 2009.

Michnik, Adam. *Letters from Prison and Other Essays*. Translated by Maya Latynski. Berkeley: University of California Press, 1987.

Miko, Francis T., Stuart D. Goldman, and Victoria L. Engel. "Martial Law in Poland." *Congressional Research Service Report*, January 6, 1982.

Millard, Frances. "The Shaping of the Polish Party System, 1989–1993." *East European Politics and Societies* 8, no. 3 (1994): 467–94.

Miller, James E., ed. *Foreign Relations of the United States, 1964–1968*, vol. 17 *Eastern Europe*. Washington, D.C.: Government Printing Office, 1996.

Modzelewski, Wojciech. *Pacyfizm w Polsce* [Pacifism in Poland]. Warsaw: Instytut Studiów Politicznych Polskiej Akadamii Nauk, 1996.

"More Documents on the Polish Crisis, 1980–1981." *Cold War International History Project Bulletin*, 11 (1998): 110–33.

Nawojczyk, Maria. "Economic Reform as Ideology in Poland during the 1980s." *History of European Ideas* 19, nos. 1–3 (1994): 317–23.

Nelson, Michael. *War of the Black Heavens: The Battles of Western Broadcasting in the Cold War*. Syracuse, N.Y.: Syracuse University Press, 1997.

Njølstad, Olav, ed. *The Last Decade of the Cold War: From Conflict Escalation to Conflict Transformation*. New York: Frank Cass, 2004.

Nye, Joseph S., Jr. *Soft Power: The Means to Success in World Politics*. New York: Public Affairs, 2004.

Oberdorfer, Don. *The Turn from the Cold War to a New Era: The United States and the Soviet Union, 1983–1991*. Baltimore: Johns Hopkins University Press, 1998.

O'Donnell, Guillermo, Philippe C. Schmitter, and Laurence Whitehead, eds. *Transitions from Authoritarian Rule: Tentative Conclusions about Uncertain Democracies*. Baltimore: Johns Hopkins University Press, 1986.

Ost, David. *The Defeat of Solidarity: Anger and Politics in Postcommunist Europe*. Ithaca: Cornell University Press, 2005.

————. *The Politics of Anti-politics: Opposition and Reform in Poland since 1968*. Philadelphia: Temple University Press, 1990.

Ostermann, Christian. *Uprising in East Germany, 1953: The Cold War, the German Question, and the First Major Upheaval behind the Iron Curtain*. Budapest: Central European University Press, 2001.

Ouimet, Matthew J. *The Rise and Fall of the Brezhnev Doctrine in Soviet Foreign Policy*. Chapel Hill: University of North Carolina Press, 2001.

Paczkowski, Andrzej. "From Amnesty to Amnesty: The Authorities and the Opposition in Poland, 1976–1986." Paper presented at the conference "From Helsinki to Gorbachev, 1975–1985: The Globalization of the Bipolar Confrontation." Artimino, Italy, April 27–29, 2006.

————. "Playground of the Superpowers, Poland 1980–1989: A View from Inside." In *The Last Decade of the Cold War: From Conflict Escalation to Conflict Transformation*, edited by Olav Njølstad. New York: Frank Cass, 2004.

————. *The Spring Will Be Ours: Poland and the Poles from Occupation to Freedom*. Translated by Jane Cave. University Park: Pennsylvania State University Press, 2003.

————. *Strajki, bunty, maifestacje jako 'polska droga' przez socjalism* [Strikes, happenings, manifestations as a Polish way through socialism]. Poznań: Poznańskie Towarzystwo Przyjaciół Nauk, 2003.

————, ed. *Polska 1986–1989, Koniec systemu* [Poland, 1986–1989, The end of the system]. Vol. 2. Warsaw: Wydawnictwo Trio and Instytut Studiów Politycznych Polskiej Akademii Nauk, 2002.

Paczkowski, Andrzej, and Malcolm Byrne, eds. *From Solidarity to Martial Law: The Polish Crisis of 1980–1981; A Documentary History*. Budapest: Central European University Press, 2006.

Paczkowski, Andrzej, and Andrzej Werblan. "'On the Decision to Introduce Martial Law in Poland in 1981': Two Historians Report to the Commission on Constitutional Oversight of the Sejm of the Republic of Poland." Working Paper No. 21. Washington, Cold War International History Project, 1997

Penn, Shana. *Solidarity's Secret: The Women Who Defeated Communism in Poland*. Ann Arbor: University of Michigan Press, 2005.

Perszkowski, Stanisław [Andrzej Paczkowski], ed. *Tajne dokumenty biuro politycznego i sekretariatu KC PZPR. Ostani rok władzy 1988–1989* [Secret documents from the PZPR central committee politburo and secretariat. The authorities' last year]. London: ANEKS, 1994.

Petersen, Roger D. *Resistance and Rebellion*. Cambridge: Cambridge University Press, 2004.

Pienknos, Donald E. *For Your Freedom through Ours: Polish-American Efforts on Poland's Behalf, 1863–1991*. New York: Columbia University Press/Eastern European Monographs, 1991.

Pipes, Richard. *Vixi: Memoirs of a Non-belonger*. New Haven: Yale University Press, 2004.

Pleshakov, Constantine. *There Is No Freedom without Bread! 1989 and the Civil War That Brought Down Communism*. New York: Farrar, Straus and Giroux, 2009.

"Poland's Renewal and U.S. Options: A Policy Reconnaissance." Report prepared for the Subcommittee on Europe and the Middle East of the Committee of Foreign Affairs, House of Representatives, by the Congressional Research Service, Library of Congress. 100th Cong. 1st Sess., 1987.

Polish Helsinki Watch Committee. *1984 Violations of Human Rights in Poland*. London: Libra Books, 1985.

————. *Poland under Martial Law*. Washington: U.S. Helsinki Watch Committee, 1983.

*Polska 5 lat po Sierpniu* [Poland Five Years after August]. London: ANEKS, 1986.

Poznanski, Kazimierz. *Poland's Protracted Transition: Institutional Change and Economic Growth, 1970–1994*. Cambridge: Cambridge University Press, 1996.

Puddington, Arch. *Broadcasting Freedom: The Cold War Triumph of Radio Free Europe and Radio Liberty*. Lexington: University Press of Kentucky, 2000.

———. *Lane Kirkland: Champion of American Labor*. Hoboken, N.J.: John Wiley, 2004.

———."Surviving the Underground: How American Unions Helped Solidarity Win." *American Educator* (Summer 2005), accessed March 3, 2014. http://www.aft.org/newspubs/periodicals/ae/summer2005/puddington.cfm.

Rachwald, Arthur R. *In Search of Poland: The Superpowers' Response to Solidarity, 1980–1989*. Stanford, Calif.: Hoover Institution Press, 1990.

Raina, Peter. *Arcybiskup Dąbrowski—rozmowy Waykańskie* [Archbishop Dąbrowski: Vatican conversations]. Warsaw: Instytut Wydawnicy Pax, 2001.

———. *Kosciół w PRL. Kosciół Katolicki a państwo w swietle dokumentów, 1945–1989* [The Church in the PRL. The Catholic Church and the nation in the light of documents, 1945-1989]. Poznań: W Drodze, 1994.

———. *Wizyty apostoliskie Jana Pawla II w Polsce. Rozmowy przygotowawcze Watykan-PRL-Episcopat* [The apostolic visits by John Paul II to Poland. Preparatory conversations Vatican-PRL-Episcopate]. Warsaw: Wydawnictwo "Książka Polska," 1997.

Rakowski, Mieczysław. *Dzienniki polityczne 1981–1983* [Political diaries, 1981–1983]. Warsaw: Wydawnictwo ISKRY, 2004.

———. *Dzienniki polityczne 1984–1986* [Political diaries, 1984–1986]. Warsaw: Wydawnictwo ISKRY, 2005.

———. *Dzienniki polityczne 1987–1990* [Political diaries, 1987–1990]. Warsaw: Wydawnictwo ISKRY, 2005.

Ramet, Sabrina P., and Christine Ingebritsen, eds. *Coming in from the Cold War: Changes in U.S.-European Interactions since 1980*. Lanham, Md.: Rowman and Littlefield, 2002.

Raymond, Walter, Jr. "Poland: The Road to 1989." *Polish Review* 44, no. 4 (1999): 397–400.

Reagan, Ronald. *An American Life*. New York: Pocket Books, 1990.

———. *The Reagan Diaries*. Edited by Douglas Brinkley. New York: HarperCollins, 2007.

Reich, Alfred A. *Hot Books in the Cold War: The CIA-Funded Secret Western Book Distribution Program behind the Iron Curtain*. Budapest: Central European University Press, 2013.

Rensenbrink, John. *Poland Challenges a Divided World*. Baton Rouge: Louisiana State University Press, 1988.

Rose, Amanda. "Extraordinary Politics in the Polish Transition." *Communist and Post-Communist Studies* 32, no. 2 (1999): 195–210.

Sachs, Jeffrey. *Poland's Jump to the Market Economy*. Cambridge: MIT Press, 1993.

Sanford, George, ed. *The Solidarity Congress, 1981: The Great Debate*. New York: St. Martin's Press, 1990.

Sarotte, Mary Elise. *1989: The Struggle to Create Post–Cold War Europe*. Princeton: Princeton University Press, 2009.

Savranskaya, Svetlana, Thomas Blanton, and Vladislav Zubok, eds. *Masterpieces of History: The Peaceful End of the Cold War in Europe*. Budapest: Central European University Press, 2010.

Schaff, Adam. *Notatki Kłopotnika* [Notes of a troublemaker]. Warsaw: Polska Oficyna Wydawnicza BGW, 1995

Schrecker, Ellen, ed. *Cold War Triumphalism: The Misuse of History after the Fall of Communism.* New York: New Press, 2004.

Schweizer, Peter. *Reagan's War: The Epic Story of his Forty-Year Struggle and Final Triumph over Communism.* New York: Doubleday, 2002.

————. *Victory: The Reagan Administration's Secret Strategy that Hastened the Collapse of the Soviet Union.* New York: Atlantic Monthly Press, 1994.

————, ed. *The Fall of the Berlin Wall: Reassessing the Causes and Consequences of the End of the Cold War.* Stanford, Calif.: Hoover Institution Press, 2000.

Sebestyen, Victor. *Revolution 1989: The Fall of the Soviet Empire.* New York: Pantheon, 2009.

Shevis, James M. "The AFL-CIO and Poland's Security." *World Affairs* 144, no. 1 (1981): 31–35.

Shultz, George. *Toil and Triumph.* New York: Charles Scribner's Sons, 1993.

Simons, Thomas W., Jr. "American Policy and the Polish Road to 1989." *Polish Review* 44, no. 4 (1999): 401–5.

Siwek, Sławomir. *Fundacja rolnicza. Jak władze PRL zablokowały wsparcie przez Kosciół polskich rolników; fakty, dokumenty-negocjacje w latach 1981–1987* [The agricultural foundation. How the PRL authorities blocked support from the church for Polish farmers; facts, documents, negotiations in the years 1981–1987]. Warsaw: Air Link, 2001.

Sjursen, Helene. *The United States, Western Europe, and the Polish Crisis.* Hampshire, U.K.: Palgrave Macmillan, 2003.

Skinner, Kiron K., Annelise Anderson, and Martin Anderson, eds. *Reagan in His Own Hand: The Writings of Ronald Reagan That Reveal His Revolutionary Vision for America.* New York: Simon and Schuster, 2001.

Skórzyński, Jan. *Rewolucja Okrągłego Stołu* [Round Table Revolution]. Kraków: Wydawnictwo Znak, 2009.

————. *Ugoda i rewolucja. Wladza i opozycja 1985–1989* [Agreement and revolution. The authorities and the opposition, 1985–1989]. Warsaw: Presspublica, 1995.

————, ed. *Opozycja w PRL. Słownik biograficzny, 1956–1989* [The opposition in the PRL. A biographical dictionary, 1956–1989]. Warsaw: Ośrodek KARTA, 2000.

Slay, Ben. *The Polish Economy: Crisis, Reform, and Transformation.* Princeton: Princeton University Press, 1994.

Snyder, Sarah B. *Human Rights Activism and the End of the Cold War.* Cambridge: Cambridge University Press, 2011.

Snyder, Timothy. *The Reconstruction of Nations: Poland, Ukraine, Lithuania, Belarus, 1569–1999.* New Haven: Yale University Press, 2003.

Spasowski, Rumoald. *A Liberation of One.* San Diego: Harcourt Brace Jovanovich, 1986.

Staniszkis, Jadwiga. *Poland's Self-Limiting Revolution.* Edited by Jan T. Gross. Princeton: Princeton University Press, 1984.

"Stenographic Minutes of the Meeting of Leading Representatives of the Warsaw Pact Countries in Moscow, 5 December 1980." *Cold War International History Project Bulletin,* no. 11 (1998): 110–20.

Stokes, Gale. *The Walls Came Tumbling Down: Collapse and Rebirth in Eastern Europe.* 2nd ed. New York: Oxford University Press, 2012.

Stoner, Kathryn, and Michael McFaul, eds. *Transitions to Democracy: A Comparative Perspective.* Baltimore: Johns Hopkins University Press, 2013.

Summy, Ralph, and Michael E. Salla, eds. *Why the Cold War Ended: A Range of Interpretations.* Westport, Conn.: Greenwood Press, 1995.

Suri, Jeremy. "Explaining the End of the Cold War: A New Historical Consensus?" *Journal of Cold War Studies* 4, no. 4 (2002): 60–92.

Szkoła Główna Planowanie i Statystyki. *Poland: International Economic Report, 1990/1991.* Warsaw: Central School of Planning and Statistics, 1991.

Szlajfer, Henryk, ed. *Ku wielkiej zmianie. Korespondencja między Ambasadą PRL w Waszyngtonie a Ministerstwem Spraw Zagranicznych styczeń-październik 1989* [The coming big change. Correspondence between the Polish Embassy in Washington and the Ministry of Foreign Affairs, January-October 1989]. Warsaw: Instytut Studiów Politychnych PAN, 2008.

Szporer, Michael. *Solidarity: The Great Workers Strike of 1980.* Lanham, Md.: Lexington Books, 2012.

Tabako, Tomasz. *Strajk '88* [Strike '88]. Warsaw: NOWA, 1992.

*Tajne dokumenty. Państwo-Kościół 1980–1989* [Secret documents. Church-State, 1980–1989]. London: ANEKS, 1993.

Thomas, Daniel. *The Helsinki Effect: International Norms, Human Rights, and the Demise of Communism.* Princeton: Princeton University Press, 2001.

Tighe, Carl. "Adam Michnik: A Life in Opposition." *Journal of European Studies* 27, pt. 3, no. 107 (1997): 323–66.

Tischler, Janos. "The Hungarian Party Leadership and the Polish Crisis of 1980–1981." *Cold War International History Project Bulletin*, no. 11 (1998): 78–87.

"Transcript of the Meeting between Comrade L. I. Brezhnev and Comrade E. Honecker at the Crimea on 3 August 1981." *Cold War International History Project Bulletin*, no. 11 (1998): 131–33.

Trentowska, Hanna, ed. *Polityka Stanów Zjednoczonych Ameryki wobec Polski w świetle faktów i dokumentów (1980–1983)* [United States policies against Poland in light of facts and documents, 1980–1983]. Bydgoszcz: Zakłady Graficzne RSW, 1984.

Tuma, Oldrich. "The Czechoslovak Communist Regime and the Polish Crisis, 1980–1981." *Cold War International History Project Bulletin*, no. 11 (1998): 60–65.

Tyler, Tom R., and Roderick M. Kramer. "Whither Trust." In *Trust in Organizations: Frontiers of Theory and Research*, edited by Roderick M. Kramer and Tom R. Tyler, 1–15. Thousand Oaks, Calif.: Sage Publications, 1996.

Ulam, Adam B. *The Communists: The Story of Power and Lost Illusions, 1948–1991.* New York: Charles Scribner's Sons, 1992.

Urban, George R. *Radio Free Europe and the Pursuit of Democracy: My War within the Cold War.* New Haven: Yale University Press, 1997.

U.S. Congress. Commission on Security and Cooperation in Europe. *Implementation of the Helsinki Accords: The Current Situation in Poland.* 101 Cong., 2nd sess., 1988. Washington, D.C.: Government Printing Office, 1988.

U.S. Congress. House. Committee on Appropriations. *Departments of Commerce, Justice, and State, the Judiciary and Related Agency Appropriations for 1987, part 5.* 99th Cong., 2nd sess., 1986. Washington, D.C.: Government Printing Office, 1986.

———. *Departments of Commerce, Justice, and State, the Judiciary, and Related Appropriations for 1989, part 5.* 100th Cong., 2nd sess., 1988. Washington, D.C.: Government Printing Office, 1988.

———. *Department of Commerce, Justice, and State, the Judiciary, and Related Agency Appropriations FY91, Part 1.* 101 Cong., 2nd sess., 1990. Washington, D.C.: Government Printing Office, 1990.

U.S. Congress. House. Committee on the Budget. *The United States and Poland.* 97th Cong., 2nd sess., 1982. Washington, D.C.: Government Printing Office, 1982.

U.S. Congress. House. Committee on Foreign Affairs. *Consideration of Miscellaneous Bills and Resolutions.* Vol. 1. 101 Cong., 1st sess., 1989. Washington, D.C.: Government Printing Office, 1989.

U.S. Congress. House. Committee on Foreign Affairs. Subcommittee on International Operations. *Authorizing Appropriations for Fiscal Years 1984–1985 for the Department of State, the U.S. Information Agency, the Board for International Broadcasting, the Inter-American Foundation, the Asia Foundation, to Establish the National Endowment for Democracy.* 98th Congress, 1st sess., 1984. Washington, D.C.: Government Printing Office, 1984.

———. *Oversight of the National Endowment for Democracy.* 99th Cong., 2nd sess., 1986. Washington, D.C.: Government Printing Office, 1986.

U.S. Congress. Senate. Appropriations Committee. *Commerce, Justice, State, the Judiciary, and Related Appropriations, FY88, Part 1.* 100th Cong., 1st sess., 1987. Washington, D.C.: Government Printing Office, 1987.

———. *Polish Debt Crisis.* 97th Cong., 2nd sess., February–April 1982. Washington, D.C.: Government Printing Office, 1982.

———. *Supplemental Appropriations Bill 1987.* 100th Cong., 1st sess., 1987. Washington, D.C.: Government Printing Office, 1987.

U.S. Congress. Senate. Foreign Relations Committee. *Agricultural Activities in Poland.* 98th Cong., 2nd sess., 1984. Washington, D.C.: Government Printing Office, 1984.

———. *BIB Supplemental Authorization Act, Fiscal Year 1983.* 97th Cong., 1st sess., 1982. Washington, D.C.: Government Printing Office, 1982.

———. *Foreign Relations Authorization Act: Hearings.* 100th Cong., 1st sess. 1987. Washington, D.C.: Government Printing Office, 1987.

Vaughan, Patrick G. "Beyond Benign Neglect: Zbigniew Brzeziński and the Polish Crisis of 1980." *Polish Review* 44, no. 1 (1999): 3–28.

———. *Zbigniew Brzeziński.* Warsaw: Swiat Książki, 2010.

Wałęsa, Lech. *A Way of Hope.* New York: H. Holt, 1987.

———. *Struggle and the Triumph.* Translated by Franklin Phillip. New York: Arcade Publishers, 1992.

Wallander, Celeste A. "Western Policy and the Demise of the Soviet Union." *Journal of Cold War Studies* 5, no. 4 (2003): 137–77.

Wandycz, Piotr S. "The Polish Road to 1989: The Role of American Foreign Policy, Introduction." *Polish Review* 44, no. 4 (1999): 387–88.

———. *The United States and Poland.* Cambridge: Harvard University Press, 1980.

Wedel, Janine. *The Private Poland: An Anthropologist's Look at Everyday Life.* New York: Facts on File Publications, 1986.

Weiser, Benjamin. *A Secret Life: The Polish Officer, His Covert Mission, and the Price He Paid to Save his Country.* New York: Public Affairs, 2004.

*Wejdą nie wejdą. Polska 1980–1982. Konferencie w Jachrance* [Will they invade, or won't they. Poland, 1980–1982. Conference in Jachranka]. London: ANEKS, 1999.

Wernik, Andrzej. *The Polish Economy in the Eighties: From Destabilization to Destabilization.* London: London School of Economics, 1993.

Whitehead, John C. *A Life in Leadership: From D Day to Ground Zero.* New York: Basic Books, 2005

Wohlforth, William C., ed. *Cold War Endgame: Oral History, Analysis, Debates.* University Park: Pennsylvania State University Press, 2003.

Woldman, Joel M. "The National Endowment for Democracy." *Congressional Research Service Brief*, September 3, 1985.

Woodward, Bob. *Veil: The Secret Wars of the CIA, 1981–1987*. New York: Simon and Schuster, 2005.

Zelikow, Phillip. "U.S. Strategic Planning in 2001–2002." In *In Uncertain Times: American Foreign Policy after the Berlin Wall and 9/11*, edited by Melvyn Leffler and Jeffrey Legro. Ithaca: Cornell University Press, 2011.

Zubek, Voytek. "The Rise and Fall of Poland's Best and Brightest." *Soviet Studies* 44, no. 4 (1992): 579–608.

Zubok, Vladislav. *Failed Empire: The Soviet Union in the Cold War from Stalin to Gorbachev*. Chapel Hill: University of North Carolina Press, 2008.

Zuzowski, Robert. *Political Dissent and Opposition in Poland: The Workers' Defense Committee "KOR."* Westport, Conn.: Praeger, 1992.

# INDEX

Hungary, 1, 13, 15, 102, 153; economic coordination with Poland, 42, 76; 1956 revolution
in, 42, 76, 224, 251, 256; reforms in 1988–
1989, 223–24, 228, 245–46, 249, 280–81
Husák, Gustav, 15, 76, 137
Hutchings, Robert, 222

Ikle, Fred, 56–57
Independent culture, 193
Independent Culture Committee, 117
Independent (niezależny) publishing, 66, 111,
190–91
Independent Poland Agency (IPA), 190, 195
Independent Publishers Foundation, 191
Independent Union of Students (NZS), 13, 276
Information Centre for Polish Affairs, 189–90
Institute for Democracy in Eastern Europe
(IDEE), 5, 190–91, 193, 268
Interim Coordinating Commission (TKK), 93,
123, 126, 155, 178–79, 272, 275, 278; founding
of, 68; and Solidarność Coordinating Of-
fice, 72; calls for strikes, 89, 91; meetings of
103, 135, 187
Intermediate Nuclear Forces (INF) negotia-
tions, 17, 31, 35, 51
International Communications Agency (ICA),
58
International Confederation of Free Trade
Unions (ICFTU), 69, 190
International Freedom to Publish Commit-
tee, 117
International Harvester, 31
International Labor Organization, 141
International Monetary Fund (IMF), 5, 31;
Poland's membership in, 32, 100, 107,
126–27, 128, 142, 144, 147, 168, 171–72; and
programs in Poland, 157, 186, 200, 204, 205,
210, 212, 226, 232, 246
International Rescue Committee, 188
Iran-Contra scandal, 170
Italian Confederation of Workers Trade
Union, 74

Jabłoński, Henryk, 141, 144
Jagielski, Mieczysław, 19–20

Jaruzelski, Wojciech, 6, 9, 23; relations with
Brezhnev, 14–15, 42, 75–76; as a reformer,
23; on martial law, 25–26, 37, 44, 175;
on U.S. sanctions, 45–46, 78–79, 86, 91,
175–76; trip to Moscow (1982), 75–76; trip
to Budapest (1982), 76; November 1982
meeting with Glemp, 91–92; on release
of Wałęsa, 92; on propaganda, 94; and
1983 papal visit, 102, 104; relations with
Andropov, 102; on bilateral relations
with United States, 106, 150–51, 174–76;
on releasing prisoners, 131; meeting with
Genscher, 144; meeting with Kohl, 144;
at fortieth opening session of United Nations, 145–46; trip to Paris (1985), 146–47;
relations with Gorbachev, 150, 257–58;
meeting with Whitehead (1987), 165, 174–
76; on Coca-Cola, 175; on salons at U.S.
ambassador's residence, 186; meeting with
Bush (1987), 203–4; on Polish presidency,
207, 221, 242–45; and threat to resign,
219; meeting with Bush (1989), 242–43; on
Solidarność-led government, 248
Jarzębski, Stefan, 201
Jaworski, Seweryn, 130; trial, 93, 95, 123–26;
rearrest, 135; break with Wałęsa, 275–76
John M. Olin Foundation, 113
John Paul II (pope), 17, 28, 61, 127; papal visit
(1983), 91–92, 99–100, 102–4, 133, 256; view
of sanctions, 121, 167, 263; papal visit (1987),
261
Johnson, Daryl, 221–22, 239
Johnson, Lyndon, 52, 84
Johnston, Philip, 63
July Manifesto coal mine, 212–13, 271–72
Jurczyk, Marian, 18, 130, 275, 276; trial, 93, 95,
123–26

Kaczyński, Jarosław, 247
Kaczyński, Lech, 247
Kádár, János, 15, 42, 76, 137, 223–24
Kahn, Tom, 57, 72, 113, 117
Kania, Stanisław, 14, 23
Karatnycky, Adrian, 113, 174, 191
Karpiński, Jakub, 71, 191

Kassman, Charles, 69

Kasten, Robert, 56

KCEP. *See* Charitable Commission of the Polish Episcopate

Kemp, Jack, 186

Kennedy, Edward, 182, 183, 186–87, 201, 262; and Robert F. Kennedy Human Rights Award, 184, 262

Kinast, Jan, 78, 91, 96, 127, 172; and agrément for Scanlan, 128–29; and Vienna CSCE meeting, 170–72; nomination as ambassador, 203;

Kirkland, Lane, 57, 109, 115, 119, 231; on Solidarność movement, 69, 70; communication with Milewski, 73, 122, 210–11; on sanctions, 121, 174; communications with Wałęsa, 141, 187–88

Kirkpatrick, Jeanne, 49, 55, 106

Kissinger, Henry, 50; back channel to Gorbachev, 225–26

Kiszczak, Czesław, 74, 89, 125, 128, 210, 213, 215, 219, 239, 249; on release of Wałęsa, 92, 131; August 1988 meeting with Wałęsa, 213, 270–72; election as prime minister, 247; August 1989 meeting with Davis, 247–48

Kocjan, Stanisław, 276

Kohl, Helmut, 144, 241

Koivitso, Mauno, 145

Kołakowski, Leszek, 71, 191

Korean Airlines flight (KAL) 007, 106, 128

Korosik, Andrzej: PNG crisis, 79

Kozakiewicz, Mikołaj, 238

Krąg publishers, 66, 191

Krol, Cardinal John, 18, 61; meeting with Reagan, 104, 119, 167

Krystosik, Ryszard, 170

Kukliński, Ryszard, 19–20, 22, 23, 29, 44

Kulikov, Victor, 14, 19, 29

*Kultura,* 66, 190

Kuroń, Jacek, 89, 130, 210, 272; trial of, 90, 95, 123–26; and 10th anniversary of KOR, 134; rearrest, 135; contacts with U.S. embassy, 182–84, 279; visit to Washington, 230; election predictions, 234; support for Solidarność-led government, 246–47

Kvitsinskii, Yuli, 51

Kwaśniewski, Aleksander, 207

Labuda, Barbara, 67

Laghi, Pio, 18

Laos, 42

Lasota, Irena, 27, 71, 112, 114, 117, 193, 196, 278; smuggling operations, 73–74, 113, 190–91, 195

Lasota, Jan Piotr, 191, 193, 278; smuggling operations, 194

League for Industrial Democracy, 72

Lebanon, 53, 83

Lebenbaum, Józef, 193

Lenard, Myra, 196

Lenin Shipyards (Gdańsk), 32, 69, 165, 210, 212–13, 218, 240, 270

Lenin Steelworks (Nowa Huta), 209–10, 212–13

Levin, Carl, 186

Lipinski, Bill, 166

Lipski, Jan Józef, 90

Lis, Bogdan, 12, 41, 67–68, 72, 107, 155, 178, 272; release from prison (1984), 126–27, 130–31, 134; rearrest, 135; release (1986), 156; contacts with U.S. embassy, 180, 182–84

Lityński, Jan, 130; trial of, 90, 95, 123–26

London Club, 54, 98, 138

Long, Clarence, 106, 175

LOT Polish Airlines, 32, 80, 104, 106, 122, 123, 130, 142

Ludwiczak, Zdisław, 79, 105, 127; and agrément for Scanlan, 128–29

Luns, Joseph, 36

Lutheran World Relief, 62

Lyng, Richard, 119

Łojek, Jerzy, 111

Łuczywo, Helena, 278–79

Macharski, Cardinal Franciszek, 181

Madej, Zbigniew, 22, 44, 300 (n. 160)

Magdalenka meetings, 9, 215, 217–18, 220, 238, 250, 270–72

Malinowski, Roman, 248

Marie Składowska-Curie Foundation, 123, 200

Marshall Plan for Poland, 50–52, 86, 216, 251; opposition views on, 229–32

Martial law, 2; preparations for, 15–16; East bloc pressure to declare, 15–16, 19; declaration of, 4, 8, 11, 19, 41–42; U.S. intelligence on and statements about, 20–24, 44; Western banks' view of, 21–22, 44, 54; initial U.S. response to, 11, 24–25, 27–29; suspension of, 92–93, 132; repeal of, 105, 132

Massey Ferguson, 138

Mazewski, Al, 121, 166, 174;

Mazowiecki, Tadeusz, 1, 3, 93, 143, 178, 215, 272; contacts with U.S. embassy, 182–84, 279; election as prime minister, 249, 252

McDonald's restaurant chain, 97

McFarlane, Robert, 119, 146

Meehan, Francis, 28, 50–52, 63, 88; meeting with Czyrek, 79–80; stepping down as ambassador, 95, 255; meeting with Olszowski, 96

Messner, Zbigniew, 174

Michnik, Adam, 109, 130, 134, 155, 178, 207; trial, 90, 95, 123–26; rearrest, 135; release (1986), 156; contacts with U.S. embassy, 182–84; on Bush visit (1987), 203; election predictions, 234; "Your President, Our Prime Minister," 239, 246–47

Mierzewski, Piotr, 126–27, 130

Mikulski, Barbara, 2, 186

Milewski, Jerzy, 72–73, 98, 112, 118, 179, 187, 190, 193; communication with Lane Kirkland, 73, 122, 210, 270, 272; meeting with Reagan, 229

Miller, Leszek, 219

Miłosz, Czesław, 71

Miodowicz, Alfred, 211, 220; debate with Wałęsa, 218–19

Mitterand, François, 36, 38, 83, 146–47, 231, 259

Modzielewski, Karol, 130; trial, 93, 95, 123–26

Mongolia, 42

Morawiecki, Kornel, 274, 276, 279

Morcinek coal mine, 212–13

Most favored nation (MFN) trading status, 32; suspended with Poland, 90–91, 141; reinstatement of, 100, 104, 155, 157, 166, 170, 177–78

Moynihan, Daniel Patrick, 56–57

Mulkerin, Father Terence J., 61–65

Munter, Cameron: information-gathering activities, 180–81; operational support to Solidarność, 181–82

Murkowski, Frank, 166

Mutual and Balanced Force Reduction (MBFR) talks, 31, 35

Myer, Fred: PNG crisis, 135

Naimski, Piotr, 71, 113

Najder, Zdzisław, 111–12

Nance, John, 31

National Commission Working Group (GR KK), 275–76

National Democratic Institute for International Affairs, 116

National Endowment for Democracy (NED), 5, 8, 89, 117–18, 165, 187–88, 188–97, 263, 267; creation of, 114–16, 269; grants for Poland in 1984, 116–17; grants for Poland in 1985, 117; grants for Poland in 1986, 188; grants for Poland in 1987, 188; humanitarian support to political prisoners, 188; support to publishers in the West, 189–90; support to opposition activists in Poland, 190–92; distribution and smuggling network, 193–97; independence of network, 193, 196–97, 267–69; record keeping, 193, 195–96, 268–69, 347–48 (n. 145); support to *Gazeta Wyborcza*, 230–31; effects on opposition activities, 269–72; empowering moderates within the opposition, 272, 278–80; funds granted for work inside Poland, 283–88

National List. *See* Poland: elections

National Security Council (NSC), 5, 11, 21, 86; December 8, 1981, meeting, 24; discussions of Polish sanctions, 30–31, 46; discussions of Soviet sanctions, 31–32, 48; relations with Western Europe, 40, 48; discussions of Polish debt, 54–55, 58, 259; meetings on Siberian pipeline sanctions, 82; and lifting Polish sanctions, 122, 167–68, 177–78; murder of Popiełuszko, 128; and Bush policy review process, 222–26; debate on rewarding liberalizing states, 224–26. *See also* National Security Decision Directives; National Security Review

National Security Decision Directives (NSDD): NSDD 45, 60–61; NSDD 54, 84–85; NSDD 66, 83; NSDD 75, 85–86; NSDD 77, 115

National Security Review (NSR), 4, 223–26

National Republican Institute for International Affairs, 116

Neoconservatives. *See* Pragmatists vs. ideological Cold Warriors

Nitze, Paul, 51

Nixon, Richard, 50, 84

Nondifferentiation. *See* Differentiation

North Atlantic Council (NAC), 31; and decisions during Polish crisis, 35–36; and response to martial law, 37; January 1981 meeting, 40–41, 80; and rescheduling Polish debt, 98, 101; response to liberalization in Poland and Hungary, 245

North Atlantic Treaty Organization (NATO), 4, 5, 8, 11–12, 27, 142, 148

Nowak-Jezioranski, Jan, 98, 111, 166, 174, 230

NOWa publishers, 66, 71, 117

NSZZ Solidarność, 1; formation of, 12–13; organization of, 13; national congress (1981), 18, 275; declared illegal, 90; creation of Temporary Council (TR), 178; legalization of, 215, 216, 218, 219–20, 227; factions within, 274–77

Nuclear Freeze Movement, 53

Nunn, Sam, 182

Nyers, Resző, 223

Obey, David, 57–58

OKN. *See* Education, Culture, Science

Olechowski, Tadeusz, 156, 214, 228; trip to Washington (1988), 212

Olszowski, Stefan, 97, 144

Onyszkiewicz, Janusz, 93, 143, 210, 229–30, 232, 272; on salons at U.S. ambassador's residence, 109, 185; contacts with U.S. embassy, 182–84, 277; on contacts with Western diplomats, 185; visit to United States (1988), 216; on threats to the Round

Table, 276–77; on importance of Western support, 279

OPZZ. *See* All-Poland Trade Union

Orange Alternative, 273–74, 278

Orszulik, Father Aloyszy, 119–20, 211

Ortblad, Dennis, 154

Orzechowski, Marian, 148–49, 151, 166; meeting with Simons, 173; meeting with Whitehead, 174

Overseas Private Investment Corporation (OPIC), 212, 217, 227, 232, 237, 241

Paczkowski, Andrzej, 195

Palestinian Liberation Organization, 53

Palka, Grzegorz, 130; trial of, 93, 123–26

Palmer, Mark, 101

Papandreou, Andreas G., 143

Paris Club, 54, 80, 98–99, 105, 106–7, 141–42, 143, 168, 171–72, 210; agreements to reschedule debt, 147, 200, 203–4, 217, 226, 232, 241, 245–46

Pastusiak, Longin, 155, 160

Patriotic Movement of National Rebirth (PRON), 75, 153

Pawliszewski, Stanisław, 78

Percy, Charles, 56

Perle, Richard, 25, 77

Pertini, Alessandro, 144–45, 155–56

Pinior, Józef, 126

Pinochet, Augusto, 45

Pipes, Richard, 21, 23, 46, 49, 77, 98

Podhoretz, Norman, 59

Poland: agricultural aid, 22, 24, 28, 32–34, 43, 46, 53, 63, 177, 217 (*see also* Credit Commodity Corporation); fishing rights in U.S. waters, 31, 34, 43, 50, 80, 97, 100, 104–5, 106–7, 122, 130, 142, 263; poultry industry, 24, 43, 63; scientific-technical exchanges, 168, 170–71, 172, 201, 203, 217, 241 (*see also* Marie Składowska-Curie Foundation)
—economy: condition of, 16–17, 62, 133, 136–40, 152, 174, 206, 208; first stage reforms, 75, 136–37; reorientation to the East (1982–1983), 76–77, 137, 140, 254, 259; opposition critiques of, 139; second stage

reforms, 152–54, 160, 209, 257; links to domestic stability, 208–9

—elections (June 1989), 1, 207, 221, 232–37, 250, 270, 277; of national list, 221, 233, 235–37, 238, 270, 277; Jaruzelski for president, 236–37, 238–40, 242–43

—foreign investment in: unavailability, 100, 137–38, 259–60; need for, 137–39, 141, 144, 147, 154, 157; and link to 1986 amnesty, 158–60, 161–63, 259–60; after 1986 amnesty, 166, 177–78, 200, 205, 212, 217, 231–32, 251; EEC aid in 1989, 245–46. *See also* Export-Import Bank; Overseas Private Investment Corporation

—international debt: to the West, 3, 16, 53–54, 231–32, 259–60; in default of, 31, 32, 55, 57–58, 98, 259; rescheduling, 41, 54–55, 80, 98–101, 105, 106–7, 138, 147, 241, 245–46. *See also* London Club; Paris Club

—security services (SB), 94–95, 132, 179, 210–11, 266; use of financial punishments, 179

—strikes and protests, 9; in 1956, 12, 265; in 1970, 12, 265; in 1968, 278; in 1976, 12, 265; during the Polish Crisis, 12–13, 18, 26–27; after martial law, 27, 41–42; in May 1982, 68–69; in August 1982, 89–90; in November 1982, 91; in May 1983, 103; in May 1984, 125; spring and summer 1988, 209–11, 212–13, 250, 277; in August 1989, 247, 270–72, 277

POLCUL, 189

Polish American Congress (PAC), 5, 61, 121, 142, 166, 231

Polish American Congress Charitable Foundation (PACCF), 118, 120–21, 189, 194, 197, 231, 265–66

Polish American Enterprise Fund, 241

Polish American Joint Trade Commission, 167

Polish Crisis (1980–1981), 8, 12–19, 251

Polish Helsinki Watch Committee, 93, 114, 190

Polish Institute for Arts and Sciences in America (PIASA), 117, 189–90

Polish Legal Defense Fund, 117, 189

Polish United Worker's Party (PZPR) Central Committee: plenum (1981), 19; plenum (1985), 152–53; plenum (1988–1989), 219–20

Polish United Worker's Party (PZPR) politburo, 6; attempts to strengthen party, 74–75; on Solidarność's waning popularity, 90, 178–79, 185; decision to declare NSZZ Solidarność illegal, 90; decision to suspend martial law, 92–93, 256, 258; propaganda against U.S. sanctions, 94, 141; on trial of KOR and Solidarność members and 1984 amnesty, 124–25; engagement with Western Europe, 144–48, 156, 259; on 1986 amnesty, 156–58, 163, 259–60; on opening talks with Wałęsa, 213, 214, 280; and legalization of NSZZ Solidarność, 219; fractures within 219–20

Polish United Worker's Party (PZPR) Tenth Party Congress (1986), 150, 154, 160, 257

Polish Workers Aid Fund (PWAF), 69, 112–13, 117

Political prisoners, 4, 41–42, 90, 99–100, 162; December 1982 limited amnesty, 93, 133, 255; July 1983 limited amnesty, 105, 133, 256; U.S. sanctions exchanged for, 8, 88, 123–24, 126, 130, 256; July 1984 limited amnesty, 124–26, 133; September 1986 complete amnesty, 4, 134, 154–59, 259–60

Popiełuszko, Father Jerzy: murder of, 128; visits to grave of, 143, 145, 184, 202–3

Poszgay, Imre, 223

Potsdam Agreements, 175

Poznań Trade Fair, 32, 167, 171–72, 266

Pragmatists vs. ideological Cold Warriors, 8, 21, 48–49, 49–50; on Siberian pipeline, 81–82; on East-West trade, 84–85; on Soviet policy, 85–86; on sanctions against Poland, 168–69

Presidential Directive, 21, 52

Pressler, Larry, 56

Project Democracy, 115–16

Project HOPE, 5, 61, 64–65, 118, 120–21, 265–66

Propaganda, 8, 49, 58–59, 86, 175; PZPR propaganda against NSZZ Solidarność, 19, 122; "Let Poland be Poland" program, 59, 262; and U.S. international broadcasting, 59–61,

Walentynowicz, Anna, 276
Wałęsa, Lech, 1, 12, 18, 23, 41, 178; speech to
U.S. Congress, 2; contacts with AFL-CIO,
69–70, 141, 187–88; 1982 meeting with
Ciosek, 90; release from prison, 91–92,
98, 132, 255; meeting with pope (1983),
102, 103–4; on RFE, 112; and Nobel Peace
Prize, 214, 261–62; on lifting sanctions, 122,
167, 176–77, 263; meeting with Whitehead, 165, 176–77, 263; contacts with
U.S. embassy, 182–84; on direct support
from U.S. Congress, 187–88, 263; meeting
with Bush (1987), 202–3; meeting with
Kiszczak (August 1988), 213, 270–71; debate
with Miodowicz, 218–19; meeting with
Mitterand, 231; election predictions, 234;
meeting with Bush (1989), 240, 242, 243;
on grand coalition government, 247; as
hero to the West, 262; efforts to end 1988
strikes, 271–72, 277–78; challenges to
leadership of, 275–77; Western political
support to, 279–80
Walters, Vernon, 18
Warner, John, 182
Warsaw Pact, 5, 50–53; and Polish Crisis, 14–15,
18, 19; political coordination, 94, 103, 148,
150–51, 210–11, 224, 243, 257; and reforms in
Poland, 248–49
Wattenberg, Ben, 60
Weinberger, Caspar, 11, 40, 48–49, 55, 77, 82,
83, 99, 126, 264
Weinstein, Allen, 58–59
Welles, Orson, 59
Wenick, Martin, 160–61, 170–72, 174
West German Trade Union Confederation, 74
West Germany. See Federal Republic of
Germany

Whitehead, John, 9, 146, 169–70, 200; on
Solidarność, 170; visit to Poland (1987), 165,
174–77, 183–84, 204, 279; visit to Poland
(Feb. 1988), 165, 205; on spring 1988 strikes,
210, 212, 214; visit to Poland (Oct. 1988),
216–18; on Wałęsa, 262
Whittlesey, Faith, 121
Wick, Charles, 59–60, 212
Wiejacz, Jozef, 20, 51, 95, 107
Wielowiejski, Andrzej, 211, 240, 272; contacts
with U.S. embassy, 182–84, 277
Wilgis, Herbert E., 20, 78, 95–96
Włocławek PVC plant, 138, 145
Workers' Defense Committee (KOR), 71, 93,
261, 272–80 passim
World Bank, 144, 186, 200, 206, 208, 217, 226,
241
Wozniak, Mariusz: PNG crisis, 79
Woźniak, Marian, 43, 76
Wujec, Henryk, 109, 233, 272; trial of, 90, 95,
123–26; contacts with U.S. embassy, 180,
277
Wujek mines, 42
Wyatt, Marilyn, 181
Wyszyński, Cardinal Stefan, 14

Young, Ken, 69
Yugoslavia, 76, 153

Zablocki, Clement, 104, 120
Zagladin, Vadim, 248
Zelikow, Philip, 250
Zerolis, John: PNG crisis, 79
*Zeszyty Historyczny,* 190
*Zeszyty Literackie,* 117, 190
Zhivkov, Todor, 137
ZWID. See Video Association